READING ELIZABETH BISHOP

Edinburgh Companions to Literature and the Humanities

Published

The Edinburgh Companion to Virginia Woolf and the Arts
Edited by Maggie Humm

The Edinburgh Companion to Twentieth-Century Literatures in English
Edited by Brian McHale and Randall Stevenson

A Historical Companion to Postcolonial Literatures in English
Edited by David Johnson and Prem Poddar

A Historical Companion to Postcolonial Literatures – Continental Europe and its Empires
Edited by Prem Poddar, Rajeev Patke and Lars Jensen

The Edinburgh Companion to Twentieth-Century British and American War Literature
Edited by Adam Piette and Mark Rowlinson

The Edinburgh Companion to Shakespeare and the Arts
Edited by Mark Thornton Burnett, Adrian Streete and Ramona Wray

The Edinburgh Companion to Samuel Beckett and the Arts
Edited by S. E. Gontarski

The Edinburgh Companion to the Bible and the Arts
Edited by Stephen Prickett

The Edinburgh Companion to Modern Jewish Fiction
Edited by David Brauner and Axel Stähler

The Edinburgh Companion to Critical Theory
Edited by Stuart Sim

The Edinburgh Companion to the Critical Medical Humanities
Edited by Anne Whitehead, Angela Woods, Sarah Atkinson, Jane Macnaughton and Jennifer Richards

The Edinburgh Companion to Nineteenth-Century American Letters and Letter-Writing
Edited by Celeste-Marie Bernier, Judie Newman and Matthew Pethers

The Edinburgh Companion to T. S. Eliot and the Arts
Edited by Frances Dickey and John D. Morgenstern

The Edinburgh Companion to Children's Literature
Edited by Clémentine Beauvais and Maria Nikolajeva

The Edinburgh Companion to Atlantic Literary Studies
Edited by Leslie Eckel and Clare Elliott

The Edinburgh Companion to the First World War and the Arts
Edited by Ann-Marie Einhaus and Katherine Isobel Baxter

The Edinburgh Companion to Fin de Siècle Literature, Culture and the Arts
Edited by Josephine M. Guy

The Edinburgh Companion to Animal Studies
Edited by Lynn Turner, Undine Sellbach and Ron Broglio

The Edinburgh Companion to Contemporary Narrative Theories
Edited by Zara Dinnen and Robyn Warhol

The Edinburgh Companion to Anthony Trollope
Edited by Frederik Van Dam, David Skilton and Ortwin Graef

The Edinburgh Companion to the Short Story in English
Edited by Paul Delaney and Adrian Hunter

The Edinburgh Companion to the Postcolonial Middle East
Edited by Anna Ball and Karim Matar

The Edinburgh Companion to Ezra Pound and the Arts
Edited by Roxana Preda

The Edinburgh Companion to Elizabeth Bishop
Edited by Jonathan Ellis

Forthcoming

The Edinburgh Companion to Literature and Music
Edited by Delia da Sousa Correa

The Edinburgh Companion to Charles Dickens and the Arts
Edited by Juliet John and Claire Wood

The Edinburgh Companion to Gothic and the Arts
Edited by David Punter

The Edinburgh Companion to Virginia Woolf and Contemporary Global Literature
Edited by Jeanne Dubino and Paulina Pajak

The Edinburgh History of Reading, Volume 1: Early and Modern Readers
Edited by Mary Hammond and Jonathan Rose

The Edinburgh History of Reading, Volume 2: Common and Subversive Readers
Edited by Mary Hammond and Jonathan Rose

https://edinburghuniversitypress.com/series/ecl

READING ELIZABETH BISHOP

AN EDINBURGH COMPANION

EDITED BY JONATHAN ELLIS

EDINBURGH
University Press

Edinburgh University Press is one of the leading university presses in the UK. We publish academic books and journals in our selected subject areas across the humanities and social sciences, combining cutting-edge scholarship with high editorial and production values to produce academic works of lasting importance. For more information visit our website: edinburghuniversitypress.com

Edinburgh University Press Ltd
The Tun – Holyrood Road, 12(2f) Jackson's Entry, Edinburgh EH8 8PJ

First published by hardback by Edinburgh University Press 2019

Typeset in 10/12 Adobe Sabon by
IDSUK (DataConnection) Ltd, and
printed and bound by CPI Group (UK) Ltd,
Croydon, CR0 4YY

A CIP record for this book is available from the British Library

ISBN 978 1 4744 2133 1 (hardback)
ISBN 978 1 3995 0526 0 (paperback)
ISBN 978 1 4744 2134 8 (webready PDF)
ISBN 978 1 4744 2135 5 (epub)

CONTENTS

ACKNOWLEDGEMENTS

THIS BOOK GREW OUT of an international conference to mark the fiftieth anniversary of Elizabeth Bishop's third collection of poetry, *Questions of Travel*. The first day of that conference took place exactly one month after my dad's death, just ten days after his funeral on what would have been his sixty-eighth birthday, coincidentally the same age as Bishop when she died in 1979. My wife and son, Ana María and Pablo, kept me afloat those days, and it is to them and my brother, Matthew Ellis, that this book is dedicated. Close friends became closer that year too, especially Joe Bray, Maddy Callaghan, Bridget Ellis, Sam Ellis, James Healy Dufosse-Belton, Mel Healy Dufosse-Belton, Hamish Mathison, Amber Regis and Angela Wright.

The conference was generously supported by sponsorship from the School of English and the Elizabeth Bishop Society. Thank you to my then Head of School, Susan Fitzmaurice, and Elizabeth Bishop Society President Thomas Travisano. The conference organising committee – Sophie Baldock, Anna Barton, Maddy Callaghan, Katherine Ebury, Ruth Hawthorn and Katrina Mayson – made sure only the good ideas got through. More importantly, they stepped in when I needed them. Sophie Maxwell, Mat McCann, Spencer Meeks, Carly Stevenson and Ellie Waters made sure everybody was in the right place with the right things on day one. I doubt many people present will forget the back-to-back wine tasting and poetry reading on day two. Richard Mayson was a gracious and witty host and kindly donated many of his own wines for us to taste. Katrina Mayson explained each wine's connections to Bishop's own travels north and south. The poetry reading that followed was just as fun. Thanks to Paul Batchelor, Frances Leviston, Conor O'Callaghan and Caitríona O'Reilly for agreeing to read their work and doing so memorably.

In addition to academic papers, I also commissioned a poemfilm based on Bishop's poem 'Questions of Travel'. The film was created by Charlotte Hodes and Deryn Rees-Jones and premiered at the Site Gallery (Sheffield) in May 2015 as part of that year's Festival of Arts and Humanities. Amy Ryall greenlit the project on behalf of the University of Sheffield and was an ever-present cheerleader and promoter without whom nothing would have happened. (Every university needs somebody like Amy, but not *our* Amy!) Charlotte and Deryn are astonishingly gifted artists in their respective fields; watching them collaborate at close hand was an unexpected pleasure of commissioning the film.

The conference would not have had a second life as this book without the enthusi-asm of my commissioning editor, Michelle Houston. Project manager Rebecca Mack-enzie made sure I have the cover image I've been dreaming about for years – Bishop and Tobias posing in a sports car. Ersev Ersoy put up with my extension requests with patience and understanding. I don't think any of us could have predicted a strike just as I was about to hand in the typescript.

I hope the contributors of this book are as proud as I am of its numerous insights and sharp new readings. I am certain the future of Bishop scholarship is an excit-ing one. On behalf of everyone whose work is collected and/or cited here, I'd like to extend thanks to Dean Rogers of Vassar College for assisting many of us with archival queries and Victoria Fox at Farrar, Straus and Giroux for help with permissions.

Last but not least, I am grateful to Angus Cleghorn, Deryn Rees-Jones and Ana María Sánchez-Arce, who each read and gave feedback on the introduction at more or less the last minute.

Excerpts from unpublished letters written by Elizabeth Bishop to Ruth Foster. Copyright © 2018 by The Alice H. Methfessel Trust. Printed by permission of Farrar, Straus and Giroux, on behalf of the Elizabeth Bishop Estate.

Contributors

Linda Anderson is the author of *Elizabeth Bishop: Lines of Connection* (2013) and *Autobiography* (2011), and has edited, with Jo Shapcott, *Elizabeth Bishop: Poet of the Periphery* (2002). She has published widely on poetry and on autobiography. She is currently editing a collection of essays with Ahren Warner on the *Contemporary Poetry Archive*. She is Professor of Modern English and American Literature at Newcastle University, and founding director of the Newcastle Centre for the Literary Arts and the Newcastle Poetry Festival.

Sophie Baldock is a Teaching Fellow at Harlaxton College. She recently completed a PhD from the University of Sheffield on the relationship between poetry and letter writing in the work of Elizabeth Bishop, Robert Duncan and Amy Clampitt. She has published articles in *The Author* and *The Archive Journal* on the born-digital correspondence of contemporary writers held in archives at the British Library.

Stephanie Burt is Professor of English at Harvard University and the author of several books of poetry and literary criticism, most recently *Advice from the Lights* (2017). Her essays and articles appear regularly in many publications in the US, the UK and New Zealand.

Marvin Campbell is a Visiting Assistant Professor of African American Literature at Wooster College. He has additional work on Elizabeth Bishop and the role of race in her archive forthcoming and an essay in the *Wallace Stevens Journal* examining Stevens through the lens of contemporary African-American poetry. He is currently at work on a book project that situates these twentieth-century poets – Bishop, Stevens, Lorde – and others within the oceanic matrix of a Global South Atlantic.

Jess Cotton is a graduate student and teaching assistant in the English Department at University College London. She was a visiting assistant in research at Yale in Spring 2017. Her thesis examines the representation of queer childhood in the work of John Ashbery, Elizabeth Bishop, Joe Brainard and James Schuyler. Her writing on poetry has been published or is forthcoming in *Ambit*, *Harper's*, *On Joe Brainard*, *Modernist Cultures*, *Oxford Poetry* and *The White Review*.

Jonathan Ellis is Reader in American Literature at Sheffield University. He is the author of *Art and Memory in the Work of Elizabeth Bishop* (2006), co-editor (with Angus Cleghorn) of *The Cambridge Companion to Elizabeth Bishop* (2014), and editor of

Letter Writing Among Poets: From William Wordsworth to Elizabeth Bishop (2015). His essays and reviews have appeared in *English, Mosaic, PN Review, The Times Literary Supplement* and other journals. He is currently writing a book on letter writing for Oxford University Press.

Laura Helyer holds a PhD in Creative Writing for a novel based on the life of Bishop's mother, Gertrude Bulmer Bishop, and the mother-daughter relationship. Her accompanying critical thesis explored biographical fiction and the archive novel. She is a qualified archivist specialising in literary and performance archives. She works as a tutor and freelance creative practitioner. Her publications include a poetry pamphlet *Paper Cairns* (2010). Forthcoming publications include a project about the oil industry in Scotland and postdoctoral research on poetry, dance and the brain.

Marcel Inhoff is completing a PhD on mid-century American poetry, autobiography and religion at Bonn University in Germany. He has published essays on Derek Walcott, Theodore Roethke, Tracy K. Smith, Robert Lowell, Hunter S. Thompson and Elizabeth Bishop. He is also the author of a book of poetry, *Prosopopeia* (2015).

Sarah Kennedy is a Fellow of Downing College, Cambridge. She has published on a variety of modern and contemporary poetry. Recent work includes a chapter on 'Ash-Wednesday and the Ariel Poems' in the *New Cambridge Companion to T. S. Eliot* (2016) and an essay on Eliot and Stevens in the *Wallace Stevens Journal*. She is currently working on a study of twentieth-century poetry, landscape and literary selfhood. Her first book, *T. S. Eliot and the Dynamic Imagination*, was published in 2018.

Ben Leubner is an Assistant Teaching Professor of Literature at Montana State University, specialising in literature of the twentieth century, especially poetry. His current research and writing projects are focused mainly on James Merrill, Elizabeth Bishop, Derek Walcott and David Foster Wallace. He regularly reviews books for *Religion and the Arts* and *Review 31*.

James McCorkle is a Visiting Assistant Professor of Africana Studies at Hobart and William Smith Colleges, Geneva, New York, where he specialises in diasporic poetry and environmental racism. His books include two collections of poetry, *Evidences* (2003) and *The Subtle Bodies* (2014), and, forthcoming in 2019, *In Time*. He is also the author of *The Still Performance* (1989), an examination of John Ashbery, Elizabeth Bishop, W. S. Merwin, Adrienne Rich and Charles Wright.

Katrina Mayson is a PhD student at the University of Sheffield. Her thesis, provisionally titled *Elizabeth Bishop: The Lives of Objects*, looks at how Bishop treats objects in her writing, supplemented by a consideration of her translations. Her essay on Percy Bysshe Shelley's 'The Mask of Anarchy' was longlisted for the 2015 Notting Hill Editions Essay Prize.

Angelica Nuzzo is Professor of Philosophy at the Graduate Center and Brooklyn College (City University of New York). Her recent books include *Kant and the Unity of Reason* (2005), *Ideal Embodiment: Kant's Theory of Sensibility* (2008), *History, Memory, Justice in Hegel* (2012) and *Approaching Hegel's Logic, Obliquely: Melville, Molière, Beckett* (2018).

Michael O'Neill (1953–2018) was Professor of English at Durham University. He published books, editions, chapters and articles on many aspects of Romantic literature, especially the work of Percy Bysshe Shelley, on Victorian poetry and on an array of British, Irish and American twentieth- and twenty-first-century poets. His research concentrated on questions of literary achievement and of poetic influence, dialogue and legacy. He published three volumes of poetry. His fourth volume, *Return of the Gift*, was published by Arc in 2018.

Vidyan Ravinthiran teaches at the University of Birmingham and is an editor at *Prac Crit*, the online magazine of poetry and poetics, as well as the author of *Elizabeth Bishop's Prosaic* (2015), winner of both the University English Prize and the Warren-Brooks Award for Outstanding Literary Criticism. His first book of poems, *Grun-tu-molani* (2014), was shortlisted for first collection prizes including the Forward, and poems towards his next, *The Million-Petalled Flower of Being Here*, won a Northern Writers' Award. He also writes literary journalism, most recently for *Poetry* (verse) and *The Telegraph* (fiction), and is represented as an author of fiction by the Wylie Agency.

Deryn Rees-Jones is a poet, editor and critic, and teaches at the University of Liverpool where she is Professor of Poetry. Her selected poems, *What It's Like to Be Alive*, was published in 2016. Forthcoming books include *Paula Rego: The Art of Story* and a new volume of poetry titled *Erato*.

Susan Rosenbaum is an Associate Professor of English at the University of Georgia. She is the author of *Professing Sincerity: Modern Lyric Poetry, Commercial Culture, and the Crisis in Reading* (2007) and of a forthcoming book titled *Imaginary Museums: Surrealism, American Poetry, and the Visual Arts, 1920–1970*. With Nell Andrew she co-directs UGA's Interdisciplinary Modernism(s) Workshop, and she is a founder with Suzanne Churchill (Davidson College) and Linda Kinnahan (Duquesne University) of *Digital Mina Loy: Navigating the Avant-Garde* (mina-loy.com).

Heather Treseler is an Associate Professor of English at Worcester State University and a Visiting Research Associate at Brandeis University's Women's Studies Research Center. Her essays and poems have appeared in *Boston Review*, *Harvard Review*, *Missouri Review*, *The Weekly Standard* and *The Iowa Review*, among other journals, and in five books about postwar American poetry. She has received support from the National Endowment for the Humanities and the American Academy of Arts and Sciences.

Rachel Trousdale is an Assistant Professor of English at Framingham State University. She is the author of *Nabokov, Rushdie, and the Transnational Imagination* (2010) and the editor of *Humor in Modern American Poetry* (2017). Her book *The Joking Voice: Humor and Empathy in Twentieth-Century American Poetry* is forthcoming from Oxford University Press. She is also the author of a poetry chapbook, *Antiphonal Fugue for Marx Brothers, Elephant, and Slide Trombone* (2015).

Amy Waite is a Postdoctoral Research Fellow at the University of Roehampton. She previously studied at the University of Oxford. Her current project, a monograph provisionally titled *Our Earthly Trust: Mina Loy, Elizabeth Bishop and the Posthuman*, examines poetic encounters between the human and the non-human in the work of these two twentieth-century poets.

J. T. Welsch is a Lecturer in English and Creative Industries at the University of York. Recent criticism includes essays on John Berryman and Delmore Schwartz, creative writing pedagogy, and aspects of creative labour. He has also published six chapbooks of his own poetry, and co-edited *Wretched Strangers*, an anthology of UK migrant poetry (2018).

Melissa Zeiger is an Associate Professor of English at Dartmouth College. She writes and teaches courses on many subjects, including garden literature, ecocriticism, immigrant writing, Jewish women's writing, feminist criticism and theory, queer poetry, politics of the love lyric, modern poetry, women's poetry, Elizabeth Bishop, the poetry and politics of illness, and cultural memory theory. Her first book, *Beyond Consolation* (1997), was a feminist analysis of elegy. She is currently writing a book on the poetics and politics of garden writing, one chapter of which appeared in 2017 as 'Derek Jarman's Garden Politics' in a special issue of *Humanities Journal* on 'Crisis'.

NOTE ON THE TEXT

UNLESS OTHERWISE INDICATED, poems discussed in this book are from Elizabeth Bishop, *Poems* (London: Chatto & Windus; New York: Farrar, Straus and Giroux, 2011), prose from Elizabeth Bishop, *Prose*, ed. Lloyd Schwartz (London: Chatto & Windus; New York: Farrar, Straus and Giroux, 2011).

Introduction: Incompatible Bishops?

Jonathan Ellis

As we move beyond the centenary of Elizabeth Bishop's birth and approach the half-century anniversary of her death, now seems as good a time as any to offer an overview of Bishop Studies.[1] At the recent 'Elizabeth Bishop in Paris' conference at the Sorbonne during which around thirty Bishop scholars gathered to present work-in-progress, American poet Maureen McLane employed the phrase 'incompatible Bishops' to describe the contemporary state of Bishop Studies. I caught myself circling this phrase in my notebook and repeating it in my head in the days and weeks afterwards. Had the friendliness of individual Bishop critics led me to assume there was a consensus of opinion about her work, a consensus that had begun to break down or had perhaps never even been there in the first place? To what extent are critics on the same page when writing about Bishop? If we conclude with McLane that my Bishop is incompatible with yours, any and every interpretation of Bishop incompatible with the next one, what does this say about Bishop and what does this say about us? That she is a poet we cannot or will not agree on or a poet we have not agreed on yet?

I begin my introduction to this collection of twenty-two new essays on Bishop's writing with these deliberately provocative questions front and centre stage to remind myself how little we know about Bishop and how much there is still to learn. Biographical facts remain to be established, influences accounted for and explored. While many letters and notebook entries have been published, much of the correspondence and other prose can only be read in archives. The status of several recently published poems and prose works is also uncertain. Do they deserve to be published alongside the canonical work that Bishop authorised for publication in her lifetime or should they only appear in separate editions mainly for scholars? We do not as yet have critical editions of the poems or stories, never mind a collected letters. In the last decade, new material has been added to the archives every couple of years. Will this process of accretion continue and, if so, for how long?

The contributors to this book are indebted to the groundwork of at least two generations of scholars whose insights continue to inform our readings of Bishop's work today. Four years after her death, an edition of her *Complete Poems* (1983) was published, followed the year after by the *Collected Prose* (1984). Although neither edition was 'complete' or 'collected', the combined effect of both volumes was to create a small but growing readership for Bishop's writing that may not have existed if publication of either volume had been delayed, as has been the case with Bishop's peers, especially Robert Lowell. Biographical work by Peter Brazeau, Gary Fountain and Brett Millier in the early 1990s established the chronology of Bishop's life in a way that simultaneously amplified and encouraged interest in her writing. George Monteiro's edition of interviews with Bishop in 1996 provided another helpful account of her aesthetic development.

Groundwork included locating primary material and transcribing it for future readers. In many cases, scholars became editors by accident rather than design when stumbling upon caches of letters or poems in the course of their research. Lorrie Goldensohn's *Elizabeth Bishop: The Biography of a Poetry* (1992) is one of many monographs in which the author's own biography becomes part of the story. Colm Tóibín's *On Elizabeth Bishop* (2015) and Megan Marshall's *Elizabeth Bishop: A Miracle for Breakfast* (2017) are more recent examples. Some of these books are more successful than others. I personally found Marshall's mini-memoir distracting, Tóibín's lyrical fusion of Bishop's life with his own utterly compelling. In other cases, editors have become scholars in order to provide contextual material for unpublished writing that would make little sense without it. This is certainly the case with Alice Quinn's *Edgar Allan Poe & the Juke-Box* (2006) in which Quinn constructs a critical history of the poems in the notes to the book. Bishop Studies is lucky to have many gifted editor-scholars, critics who are as adept with a manuscript page as a published poem. Articles, book chapters and monographs in which unpublished material features have led directly to editorial projects to make this material more widely available. Lloyd Schwartz and Sybil Estess's compendium of critical material by and about Bishop, *Elizabeth Bishop and Her Art* (1983), was the first book to reprint extracts from her undergraduate essays, alongside interviews and other literary statements. It was also one of the first books to cite from Bishop's correspondence. Schwartz would later edit this material for the Library of America edition of Bishop's *Poems, Prose, and Letters* (2008) and the centenary edition of Bishop's *Prose* (2011). David Kalstone's *Becoming a Poet: Elizabeth Bishop with Marianne Moore and Robert Lowell* (1989) made an implicit case for a *Selected Letters* (1994) a few years afterwards, the success of which led to the commissioning of the complete correspondence between Bishop and Lowell in *Words in Air* (2008) and the publication of Bishop's correspondence with *The New Yorker* (2011).

I draw attention to these diverse publications, most published in the late 1980s and early 1990s, to demonstrate the extent to which critical evaluation of Bishop directly and indirectly prompted editorial work on her writing, as is the case with important monographs by Thomas Travisano (1988), Bonnie Costello (1991), David Kalstone (1989), Lorrie Goldensohn (1992), Victoria Harrison (1992) and Marilyn May Lombardi (1995), all of which contain previously unpublished poems or extracts from longer prose works. The first generation of Bishop critics, those who published criticism on her work in the last two decades of the twentieth century, nearly all helped locate and edit her writing. In a few cases, as with her close friend Lloyd Schwartz, they actually preserved poems she may otherwise have destroyed. We have more Bishop poems and prose to read because of their careful private archiving of her writing. Perhaps other unpublished material lies waiting to be found?

Contributors to this book attest to the continuing importance of this generation's editing and scholarship through citation and engagement with the drafts and unpublished material they helped find or save, and of course their interpretations of it. In such ways, we can feel the influence of one generation on the next, even as new interpretations add to or revise earlier readings. At times, this influence is acknowledged explicitly through quotation. At others, it can be evidenced in choice of material, methodology or tone. Thomas Travisano's alignment of Bishop with a baroque tradition, for example, implicitly informs Tom Paulin's important essay on Bishop's letters in 1994, an approach that is extended further by Vidyan Ravinthiran's book-length study of what he calls Bishop's prosaic (2015). Bonnie Costello's focus on perspective, scale and temporality contributed to a visual turn in Bishop Studies in the 1990s as evidenced in an exhibition of Bishop's paintings in Key West in 1993 and the publication of *Exchanging Hats: Paintings* in 1996. Costello's book, *Questions of Mastery* (1991), is also a key touchstone for both Peggy Samuels's *Deep Skin: Elizabeth Bishop and Visual Art* (2010) and Linda Anderson's *Elizabeth Bishop: Lines of Connection* (2013). Kalstone's work on how Bishop became a poet, at least in part through her dialogue and friendship with Moore and Lowell, was the first in a series of books that analysed Bishop in relation to other poets. These include Jeredith Merrin's *An Enabling Humility* (1990), Guy Rotella's *Reading and Writing Nature* (1991), Joanne Feit Diehl's *The Psychodynamics of Creativity* (1993) and Kathryn Kent's *American Women's Writing and the Rise of Lesbian Identity* (2003), all of whom paired Bishop with Moore, as well as critics like Margaret Dickie (1997), Kirstin Hotelling Zona (2002), Deryn Rees-Jones (2005), Bethany Hicok (2008) and Catherine Cucinella (2010), who identified other female poets with whom to compare and think about Bishop's legacy. Lorrie Goldensohn's ideas on the female body directly inspired Anne Colwell's *Inscrutable Houses* (1997). Goldensohn was arguably the first Bishop critic to consider Bishop's Brazilian poems on their own terms and to engage with their complex appropriation of Brazilian idioms, stories and voices. The questions she asks of Bishop's writing in relation to the intersection of class, gender and race are explored further in Renée Curry's *White Women Writing White* (2000), Camille Roman's *Elizabeth Bishop's World War II–Cold War View* (2001), George Monteiro's *Elizabeth Bishop in Brazil and After* (2012), and Bethany Hicok's *Elizabeth Bishop's Brazil* (2016), as well as essays by Steven Axelrod (2003) and Barbara Page (2014). Victoria Harrison's book on Bishop and intimacy, including a lengthy treatment of Bishop's writing on childhood, deserves more attention than it has currently received. Her chapter on the genesis of 'In the Village' is, in my opinion, one of the most astute but under-read analyses of the influence of psychoanalysis on Bishop's life and writing. Harrison, unlike many critics, places Nova Scotia at the centre of Bishop's artistic story. Her work has understandably proved an inspiring example for Canadian critics like Sandra Barry and Peter Sanger. Readers looking to know more about Bishop and Great Village ought to begin with Barry's short book, *Elizabeth Bishop: Nova Scotia's 'Home-made' Poet* (2011), and her chapter on Bishop and Nova Scotia in *The Cambridge Companion to Elizabeth Bishop* (2014). Marilyn May Lombardi's *The Body and the Song* (1995) devotes a chapter to translation, preparing the way for Mariana Machova's monograph *Elizabeth Bishop and Translation* (2016). Lombardi's interest in Bishop and surrealism has also piqued scholarship by Mark Ford (1997), Marit J. MacArthur (2008) and Susan Rosenbaum (2014), among others.

As these books on Bishop are cited less frequently or begin to disappear from bibliographies altogether, it is important not just to acknowledge the acuity and insight of these initial analyses of Bishop's work but also to read and revisit them so we can hear and take note of their continuing presence in other critics' words. Some prominent authors have clearly been left out of this survey of the first phase of Bishop Studies (1980–2000), mainly because their contributions have been in article or essay form rather than in a monograph. Early notices and reviews by friends who were also critics or critics who became friends inevitably helped establish the terms by which Bishop's poetry was interpreted during her lifetime and how it is interpreted today as well. The implications of Marianne Moore's 1935 introductory remarks on Bishop's poetry, for example – 'In trying to reveal the clash of elements that we are – the intellectual, the animal; the blunt, the ingenious; the impudent, the imaginative – one dare not be dogmatic' (Schwartz and Estess 175) – continue to resonate in the twenty-first century, particularly among eco-critics and those interested in Bishop's animal poems. Randall Jarrell's attention to her moral attractiveness has been just as influential, his statement that 'all her poems have written underneath, *I have seen it*' (Schwartz and Estess 181) one of the most repeated aphorisms about her work. Robert Lowell's decision to rank her work in 'roughly descending order' (Schwartz and Estess 188) has thankfully not been copied. John Ashbery's comments about 'thingness' in his 1969 review of *The Complete Poems* were decades ahead of their time (Schwartz and Estess 203) and have still to be considered properly, ditto Octavio Paz's thoughts on 'objects that know how to keep silent' (Schwartz and Estess 213). Biographers keep struggling to equal never mind beat James Merrill's description of her 'instinctive, modest, lifelong impersonations of an ordinary woman, someone who during the day did errands, went to the beach, would perhaps jot a phrase or two inside the nightclub matchbox before returning to the dance floor' (Schwartz and Estess 259). I am also fond of Mary McCarthy's memorable confession: 'I envy the mind hiding in her words, like an "I" counting up to hundred waiting to be found' (Schwartz and Estess 267). Helen Vendler's 1977 essay on what she called 'the domestic and the strange' in *Geography III* is one of the best close readings of a single Bishop collection. Adrienne Rich's 1983 essay on Bishop's *Complete Poems* in which Rich connected 'the themes of outsiderhood and marginality in her work, as well as its encodings and obscurities, with a lesbian identity' (125) is equally important for feminist literary criticism, her reflections on white privilege in the 1940s still relevant today: 'The personae we adopt, the degree to which we use lives already ripped off and violated by our own culture, the problem of racist stereotyping in every white head, the issue of the writer's power, right, obligation to speak for others denied a voice, or the writer's duty to shut up at times or at least to make room for those who can speak with more immediate authority – these are crucial questions for our time, and questions that are relevant to much of Bishop's work' (131). I have written elsewhere (2010) of the importance of Anne Stevenson's first book on Bishop, published in 1966, and of the correspondence between Bishop and Stevenson that is reprinted in full in the Library of America edition of Bishop's writing and given its own section in the 2011 *Prose*.

The history of Bishop's early critical reception sketched out here is not without problems. Identifying critics as first or second generation depending on the publication of their first monograph on Bishop implies wrongly that the work of Costello, Goldensohn and others is somehow complete, an impression contradicted by their continuing editorial work and scholarship on Bishop up to and including the present day. Indeed, it is worth noting how frequently critics return to Bishop throughout their career as if never quite able to exhaust their ideas about her. In addition to his editing of Bishop and Lowell's correspondence in *Words in Air* and co-editing a collection of essays on *Elizabeth Bishop in the Twenty-First Century* (2012), Travisano has also published a book on American poets in which Bishop features alongside Lowell, Jarrell and Berryman as part of what he terms a *Mid-Century Quartet* (1999). He is currently completing a critical biography of Bishop for Viking. Costello has also returned to Bishop's work in nearly all of her subsequent critical books, including *Shifting Ground: Reinventing Landscape in Modern American Poetry* (2003), *Planets on Tables: Poetry, Still Life and the Turning World* (2008), and *The Plural of Us: Poetry and Community in Auden and Others* (2017). Goldensohn is another force of nature in Bishop Studies. In articles and book chapters, she continues to make sense of Bishop's writing for new audiences, most recently on how to approach Bishop's letters to her analyst Dr Ruth Foster (2014). Once a Bishop critic, always a Bishop critic.

There seems to be something about the sheer variety of Bishop's work that suits the nuggety nature of the essay where authors are free to focus on a relatively narrow subject. I am thinking here of critics like Helen Vendler, who has continued to publish vital readings of Bishop's work even as she has objected to new editorial projects like *Edgar Allan Poe & the Juke-Box*. Barbara Page's essays on Bishop, many drawing on her extensive knowledge of the archive material at Vassar, always push Bishop Studies in new and surprising directions, whether that be by revisiting Wittgenstein 'as a means to an enquiry into Bishop's way of knowing' (12) or by taking time to look at the Brazilian poems Bishop could not complete as a way to reassessing those she did (with Carmen Oliveira, 117–32). It would be lovely to see Page's Bishop essays collected in one book before long. There are certainly enough to deserve one. The same is equally true of Lloyd Schwartz's essays on Bishop's unfinished and unpublished writing and Susan Rosenbaum's work on Bishop and experimental poetics. Langdon Hammer's 1997 essay on Bishop's correspondence is wonderfully sharp on Bishop's use of 'letterlike' features in her poems and on epistolary writing in general (164). The same is equally true of Siobhan Phillips's 2012 essay on 'Elizabeth Bishop and the Ethics of Correspondence' in which she builds on Hammer's letter-writing model to reflect on 'correspondent two-ness [. . .] a kind of writing that is neither singular nor collective, personal nor political' (343, 344).

I am surprised more critics don't return to Lee Edelman's 1985 essay on 'In the Waiting Room', deservedly collected and reprinted in Marilyn May Lombardi's 1993 collection, *Elizabeth Bishop: The Geography of Gender*. Its cautionary footnote about naïve biographical readings – 'The name of the young girl Elizabeth will be placed within quotation marks throughout the essay so as to guard against the tendency on the part of too many critics to conflate this "Elizabeth" with the author of the poem' (107) – is as relevant now as it was in the mid-1980s. Mark Ford is another poet-critic whose work on Bishop deserves a larger readership. His 1997 essay on 'Early Bishop, Early Ashbery and the French' illuminates at least two distinct periods in American poetry overseas, Bishop's time in Paris (roughly between 1935 and 1937) and Ashbery's much longer stay in France (roughly between 1955 and 1965), not to mention their shared interest in surrealist poetics. His 2003 article 'Elizabeth Bishop at the Water's Edge' is equally astute on Bishop in the 1940s, including her close appreciation of Auden and Baudelaire. Other poet-critics to publish important essays on Bishop include Eavan Boland (1988), Seamus Heaney (1988, 1995), Thom Gunn (1990), Tom Paulin (1990, 1994), Alicia Ostriker (1995), Heather McHugh (1996), James Fenton (1997), Jamie McKendrick (2002), Paul Muldoon (2006, 2015), Angela Leighton (2007), Mark Doty (2010), George Szirtes (2010), Maureen McLane (2012), Frances Leviston (2015) and Simon Armitage (2018).

This list is by no means complete. It necessarily leaves out discussions of Bishop in interviews and online, as well as numerous individual poems in which Bishop is cited directly or indirectly through a poet's choice of form, phrase or tone. What's striking about compiling such lists, however incomplete, is the quality of the poets one encounters *and* the quality of their scholarship on Bishop's work (the two don't always go together). Poets do not just like Bishop; they also like talking to other people about why they like her work. Simon Armitage reflected on Bishop's likeability in a lecture he delivered in 2018 as Oxford Professor of Poetry, recently published in *PN Review* under the title 'Like, Elizabeth Bishop'. 'If there can be such a person as the darling of poetry, that person is currently Elizabeth Bishop,' he argues.

> Bishop's semi-untouchable status *can* be seen as something of a conundrum, because while her poetry subtly captured or even anticipated urgent literary themes of gender politics and sexual orientation, hers is, on occasions, a traditional and an orthodox art. By which I mean she is at times an old-school rhymer and versifier, a romantic, a poet who dabbles in homespun wisdom, and someone who, now and again, will offer some fairly queasy perspectives on 'others' and 'otherness'. She is also, here and there, a poet of simple diction, conservative syntax, conventional line breaks and sequential logic, an approachable and relatable writer whose work can be read straight off the page and 'understood' by almost anyone with a reasonable grasp of the English language. [. . .] For such a highly regarded poet within an essentially academic territory, her work is unusually cooperative. (18)

I am not convinced Bishop is as 'cooperative' as Armitage makes out. Take 'approachable' and 'relatable', for example, adjectives I advise my own students never to use, mainly because of their rather modish meaninglessness. Even if we affect to know what they mean, are approachability and relatability attributes we turn to when reading poetry? Should the act of being with a poem, or any other form of literature for that matter, be such a comfortable, predictable experience? Armitage's prose twists and turns all over the place in this passage, unsure (it seems to me) if this is actually what he wants from poetry and, if so, whether this is what he gets from Bishop. That's not to say his take on Bishop is wrong, merely that I am not sure in the end what he likes and doesn't like about Bishop's writing aside from her love of simile. An essay that promises to be about what it's like to like Elizabeth Bishop becomes an essay about how difficult it is to put that feeling into words. Writing about Bishop, in other words, makes Armitage stumble. He becomes the 'unconfident' speaker he mocks elsewhere in the essay for using 'like' as a conversational filler (20).

Bishop critics often come unstuck like this. They admit to not liking or understanding a poem and quickly move on. The frame they have applied successfully up until this point suddenly becomes redundant. Something doesn't quite fit. Literary critics can't down tools like this too obviously. After all, many of us are paid to make sense of poetry, not to admit we know little more than the next person. I don't think enough has been made of such moments in Bishop Studies, moments when the critic doesn't exactly go missing in action so much as fail to make sense. Not liking or understanding poetry may paradoxically be a sign of liking it more than we admit. This is partly Ben Lerner's argument in *The Hatred of Poetry* (2016) that 'poetry and the hatred of poetry are for me – and maybe for you – inextricable' (10). Why can't critics like and dislike Bishop simultaneously? Why can't each of us have our own 'incompatible Bishop'?

Let me draw your attention to a few examples of this in action. The first is from John Ashbery's 1969 review of *The Complete Poems* in *The New York Times Book Review* in which he admits to being flummoxed by the ending of 'Over 2000 Illustrations and a Complete Concordance'. 'After twenty years', he declares, 'I am unable to exhaust the meaning and mysteries of its concluding line: "And looked and looked our infant sight away," and I suspect that its secret has very much to do with the nature of Miss Bishop's poetry. Looking, or attention, will absorb the object with its meaning' (Schwartz and Estess 204). Ashbery allows for mystery and in doing so permits Bishop's poetry to keep secrets. At the same time, he does not pretend to know what these secrets might be. There is a note of irritation in his phrasing. Thom Gunn sounds a similar note of frustration in comparing Bishop's early poems to boxed-in objects. 'The poems in it were like playthings, fresh-painted, decorative, charming, original, and yet tiny. She specialized, Alice-like, in altering the scale of things' (78). Gunn doesn't especially like this aspect of Bishop's poetry – he calls it 'cozy' and '*twee*', 'its cleverness seemed to be an end in itself' (78) – but it nevertheless intrigues him. And on reading her final book, *Geography III*, something about the trajectory of her long career immediately made sense to him: 'all at once, everything was changed. Its longest three poems were directly concerned with uncontainable, unboxable experience. It was only ten poems long, and yet its achievement was such that it retrospectively altered the emphasis and shape of an entire career. My mistake had been a common one, to look for a poet's best poetry among her typical work' (78–9). Gunn doesn't pursue this line of thought much further. The essay concludes with an extended comparison of Bishop's 'The Armadillo' to Lowell's 'Skunk Hour', well-trodden critical ground even thirty years ago, but both his mistake ('to look for a poet's best poetry' among their 'typical' writing) and implied correction (a poet's best poetry might actually be found in 'untypical' places) demonstrate, like Ashbery's aside, that summarising Bishop might be impossible.

There is undoubtedly a gendered element to these readings as well, an idea (if unvoiced) that women poets ought not to be so clever or mysterious. Bishop consistently resists frames that attempt to push her into one box or other. Maureen McLane understands this better than anyone. In her defiantly unboxable essay/memoir/prose poem 'My Elizabeth Bishop / (My Gertrude Stein)', she has aphoristic fun pairing Bishop and Stein and observing what unfolds when two distinct but perhaps overlapping sensibilities collide. 'Everybody likes Elizabeth Bishop because she is nice. Elizabeth Bishop will not cut off your nuts or bare her vagina. She could though make a rose a rose a rose . . .' (31). McLane is interested in the same question as Armitage. Why do so many poets like (or pretend to like) Elizabeth Bishop? Her first answer is remarkably similar to his, if a lot more pithy ('because she is nice'). Unlike Armitage, however, who keeps Bishop at arm's length, McLane allows Bishop's voice to inhabit hers. The adjective employed here self-consciously echoes lines from 'Crusoe in England' when Crusoe mourns Friday by regretting that he had not been born a woman: 'Friday was nice. / Friday was nice, and we were friends. / If only he had been a woman!' (*Poems* 185). You don't normally call somebody you love 'nice' unless you are hiding something. Unless you are keeping secrets. One such secret is Bishop's own sexual orientation. Another might be her desire, like Crusoe, to 'propagate my kind' (185). A third is surely her love for Brazilian architect Lota de Macedo Soares, who had died while visiting Bishop in New York. 'We were friends' in this context becomes less an evasion of emotion and more an almost unbearable statement of grief. Bishop's 'niceness', in other words, is a mask. We like (I would say love) her poetry precisely because it is not as nice as it first appears. McLane gets this in a way Armitage misses when he interprets her 'homespun wisdom' as transparently earnest and sincere. This is, I think, why she juxtaposes Bishop's supposed niceness with the startling image of her as a man-hating predator or sexual exhibitionist ('Elizabeth Bishop will not cut off your nuts or bare her vagina'). Bishop is neither as nice nor as nasty as either of these statements suggest. Just because she avoids exhibiting the body does not mean the body is not present. Like Stein, whose most famous statement McLane cites here, Bishop could also call 'a rose a rose a rose'. If anything, she took Stein's repeating rose a stage further, as in the wonderful lines from 'Vague Poem (*Vaguely love poem*)': 'Just now, when I saw you naked again, / I thought the same words: rose-rock, rock-rose . . . / Rose, trying, working, to show itself, forming, folding over, / unimaginable connections, unseen, shining edges' (*Poems* 325).

Few critics get to the heart of Bishop's aesthetic as quickly and wittily as McLane. She boils down Bishop's contradictions into single lines and phrases, not least the experience of the poems sometimes escaping us: 'I could not help feel that for all the dwelling on the poems the poems were eluding me. They were eluding and unsettling and sometimes boring they were settling in me they bore in me' (51). Ashbery and Gunn present this as an intellectual problem. If I just keep reading the poem's final line, Ashbery implies, I will eventually understand it. If only I had read *Geography III* first, Gunn states, then I would have known how to read the early poems. McLane doesn't promise mastery of Bishop, knowing (surely we know this already, having read 'One Art'?) that 'Bishop was a master who would not play master' (30). She demonstrates not what Bishop knows or thinks but how a Bishop poem gets under the skin. For this reason, I love her criticism on Bishop more than anybody else I have read.

McLane, like other critics who have written on Bishop in this century, has obviously benefited from the new editions of Bishop's writing that have appeared in the last decade, beginning with Alice Quinn's *Edgar Allan Poe & the Juke-Box* in 2006. The fall-out from this publication was dramatic and immediate, expanding the canon of writings published in Bishop's name and expanding in particular our understanding of Bishop as a love poet. In an essay on 'Bishop's Posthumous Publications' (2014), Lorrie Goldensohn contrasts the Bishop we thought we knew in 1983 when *The Complete Poems* was published with the Bishop we now encounter in various editions of her writings:

> In 1983, when Elizabeth Bishop's *The Complete Poems: 1927–1979* was posthumously issued, the style, shape, and focus of a Bishop poem had appeared to settle. In 2006, Alice Quinn, denying that the canon had been completed in 1983, cracked it open with unfinished drafts and previously uncollected poems for her *Edgar Allan Poe & the Juke-Box*. By 2008, when Lloyd Schwartz and Robert Giroux edited *Elizabeth Bishop: Poems, Prose, and Letters*, the idea of her significant work had swollen to some 900 printed pages. By 2011, Bishop's longtime publisher, Farrar, Straus and Giroux, separated poetry and prose into two immensely plain volumes, their covers shorn of Bishop's own delightful paintings. *Poems* 2011

appears in dark navy; *Prose* 2011 in gold, dressed in a cheap, inelegant paper. The visual style could not be balder. But Farrar, Straus and Giroux's answer to the problem of completing the Bishop canon alongside the irrepressible growth of the unpublished and uncollected work was to stuff a modest twenty-seven additional poems into 'Appendix I: Selected Unpublished Manuscript Poems.' In one improvement over Quinn's *Edgar Allan Poe*, however, *each* of the appended poems comes with a neat facing of manuscript facsimile. I hazard that these will be interim editions. (183)

I agree with all of Goldensohn's reservations here. *Poems* and *Prose* do look cheap alongside *The Complete Poems* and *Collected Prose*, and not just because Bishop's paintings are absent. Other important writing is also missing, not least most of the material that had been published in *Edgar Allan Poe*. Goldensohn is right to regard the addition of twenty-seven additional poems into an appendix as a 'modest' rather than spectacular increase to the number of poems that are now part of the formal body of writing. At the same time, the choice of poems to go in this appendix feels arbitrary, perhaps even rushed. Why these poems and not others? As a 'Publisher's Note' to *Poems* rather tantalisingly informs us, 'the published texts have not exhausted what the archive contains – including manuscript poems and translations as yet unpublished, as well as unpublished drafts of eventually completed and published poems, poems by others, song lyrics (blues, ballads) written down or translated, notebook entries' (xiv). Given this, I cannot, like Goldensohn, see how the 2011 editions can be anything but 'interim'. Who knows how long we will wait for a new volume?

Helen Vendler, Gillian White and others, including myself, have written on the significance of *Edgar Allan Poe* for Bishop criticism. I do not wish to repeat our arguments here. Some critics, most famously Vendler in *The New Republic*, thought the book should never even have been published, suggesting that a more accurate title for the volume was 'Repudiated Poems' (33). In our introduction to *The Cambridge Companion to Elizabeth Bishop* in 2014, Angus Cleghorn and I asked at which point poems still labelled 'unpublished' in *Poems* would come to be seen as 'published' (16). We listed nine poems that received repeated treatment in our book: 'To Be Written in the Mirror in Whitewash', 'It is marvellous to wake up together', 'Edgar Allan Poe & the Juke-Box', 'The Soldier and the Slot-Machine', 'For M.B.S., buried in Nova Scotia', 'Apartment in Leme', 'A Drunkard', 'Breakfast Song' and 'For Grandfather'. Might this list, we asked, 'be the beginning of a critical consensus?' (16). A few years on, the question remains unanswered.

The first book to take account of the new editions – which by 2011 included *Words in Air: The Complete Correspondence between Elizabeth Bishop and Robert Lowell* (2008), edited by Thomas Travisano with Saskia Hamilton, and *Elizabeth Bishop and The New Yorker* (2011), edited by Joelle Biele – was *Elizabeth Bishop in the Twenty-First Century* (2012). This collection of seventeen essays looked as much at the work Bishop didn't complete as at the work she did: 'In the unpublished poems, letters, and essays, as well as in the margins of her greatest published poems, we see the outlines of the public poet who might have been, a poet Bishop was never quite willing to become' (7). Its list of contributors includes names familiar to Bishop scholarship over the years such as Lloyd Schwartz and Barbara Page, as well as new readers of Bishop's work such as Heather Treseler, Peggy Samuels and Gillian White. In addition to chapters on sub-genres of Bishop's writing such as elegies and notebook letter-poems, we find analysis of her relationships with specific authors and artists such as Manuel Bandeira, Alexander Calder and Flannery O'Connor. The collection also ponders the value of variorum editions like *Edgar Allan Poe*. As Christina Pugh asks in the concluding chapter: 'What is the nature, whether aesthetic or otherwise, of the literary world's investment in variorum or facsimile editions? In which particular ways do these editions redramatize, recharacterize, or reinscribe our hallucinated relation to a dead poet? Can lyric poems in manuscript format be co-opted by the thrall of the "unfinished" that is operative in a more experimental poetics?' (274). Pugh answers her own questions by urging readers not to 'let graphic considerations replace or displace voice when we read lyric poetry, or the manuscripts of lyric poets', since to do so runs the risk of ignoring 'poetry itself' (287). If there has been an archival turn in Bishop Studies, it has not been smooth or uncontentious.

I hesitate to speak of a second generation of Bishop scholars as if critics could be neatly divided into one camp or other depending on their age or career status, but perhaps the publication of *Edgar Allan Poe* in 2006 does form a dividing line of sorts between one generation and the next, or at least a body of work that responds to Bishop using different primary material than the critics who began writing about Bishop in the twentieth century and even early 2000s, roughly the time when I began my own PhD on Bishop. Put simply, Bishop critics writing about her work before 2006 could only analyse the notebooks and unpublished material by visiting the archives; after 2006 enough new material was out there not to necessitate such a trip as early and urgently in the research process. If anything, the Elizabeth Bishop publishing juggernaut is gathering pace rather than slowing. Alice Quinn is due to deliver a new edition of Bishop's unpublished material soon, provisionally titled *Elizabeth Bishop's Journals*. Two further editions of correspondence in which Bishop features prominently – *Efforts of Affection: The Complete Correspondence of Elizabeth Bishop and Marianne Moore*, edited by Eleanor Chai and Saskia Hamilton, and *The Dolphin Letters*, also edited by Hamilton – are forthcoming in the next couple of years. Hot on the heels of Tóibín and Marshall's hybrid auto/biographies are at least two new major biographies of Bishop by Thomas Travisano and Langdon Hammer. Angus Cleghorn and I are also currently co-editing *Elizabeth Bishop in Context*. I cannot help but wonder whether these new books will constitute a further dividing line between generations of critics, with a third generation of scholars ready to take over in the 2020s. (Many of their names can be found in the book you are reading.) If so, we might think of a second generation of Bishop critics as those scholars working roughly between the publication of *Edgar Allan Poe* in 2006 and the publication of the *Journals* and new correspondence in 2019 and 2020.

It's difficult to speak of criticism as it is happening, particularly as I also consider myself a member of this generation. Earlier in this introduction, I dated phase one of Bishop Studies to the last two decades of the twentieth century. Perhaps to be more accurate it needs to stretch a little into the early years of the twenty-first century. Dates aside, for me one of the distinguishing elements of the new generation of Bishop critics publishing today has been their ability to place Bishop within a larger historical and political context, an ability at the same time to claim Bishop as a feminist writer without making apologies for her style or tone. Liberated from the pressure to construct a linear narrative of Bishop's artistic development, mainly because earlier critics like

Travisano, Kalstone, Costello and Goldensohn had already done this work so well, they have been able to focus instead on discrete periods of Bishop's career, particular genres, or subject matters she made her own. I have mentioned some of these works already. In the order in which they were published from 2000 onwards, I am thinking here of Renée Curry's book on Bishop and colour that historicises Bishop's racial politics by also analysing the poetry of H.D. and Sylvia Plath; Camille Roman's book on mid-century militarisation, in particular Bishop's response to the Korean War as 'a haunting historical turning point in the country's Cold War narrative' (2); Priscilla Paton's focus on Bishop as a New England author; and Siobhan Phillips's scholarship on the poetics of the everyday, which, like other twenty-first-century accounts of Bishop's work, looks to other poetic traditions within which to situate her writing, in Phillips's case the poetry of Wallace Stevens, Robert Frost and James Merrill. The eco-turn in Bishop Studies began as long ago as Guy Rotella's 1991 book on *Reading and Writing Nature*, pre-dating Jonathan Bate's *The Song of the Earth* (2000) (in which Bishop is granted a small but significant role) by a full decade, and is represented in more recent work by Jeffrey Gray (2005), Robert Boschmann (2009), John Felstiner (2009) and Susan Rosenbaum (2014). I am surprised somebody has not written a book specifically on Bishop's Animals but no doubt this will happen soon. There have been not one but two books on Bishop and religion, Cheryl Walker's *God and Elizabeth Bishop: Meditations on Religion and Poetry* in 2005 and Laurel Snow Corelle's *A Poet's High Argument: Elizabeth Bishop and Christianity* in 2008. There have also been two books on Bishop and visual art, the first by Sarah Riggs on Stevens, Bishop and O'Hara in 2002, the second, just on Bishop, by Peggy Samuels in 2010.

My own book, *Art and Memory in the Work of Elizabeth Bishop* (2006), appeared around the same time as these works and was structured according to the artistic tropes of Bishop's writing rather than the facts of her life. In doing so, I attempted to give up the idea of an ordered life story, or for that matter an ordered critical study. 'One cannot divide the life into neat, sequential periods of discovery and movement forward,' I suggested (15). 'An imaginative life does not proceed from youth to maturity as we sometimes think. On the contrary, it moves accidentally forwards and backwards, stumbles upon breakthroughs and then forgets them, hits form for a time and then takes years to recover it' (15). I have not substantially changed my mind or methodology since then. Looking back, it is striking to see other scholars following a similar formalist or, if you like, new formalist path at the same period. Other books that demonstrate a keen, perhaps even obsessive attention to detail include Kirstin Hotelling Zona's wonderful 2002 study *Marianne Moore, Elizabeth Bishop, and May Swenson: The Feminist Poetics of Self-Restraint* and Linda Anderson's equally sharp *Elizabeth Bishop: Lines of Connection* (2013).

Eleanor Cook's 2016 critical study *Elizabeth Bishop at Work* marks the probable end point of this kind of scholarship. Cook moves methodically poem by poem through each of the four major collections that Bishop published in her lifetime – *North & South*, *A Cold Spring*, *Questions of Travel* and *Geography III* – with brief interludes on different formal elements of her poetry, including language, rhythm and genre. There are even some writing exercises for apprentice poets ('Keep a file for words whose meaning you wrongly thought you knew'; 'Write a short poem mostly in ordinary diction that also includes a word or two that may be hard to define precisely'). Cook has little time for those interested in Bishop's life ('I found

myself frustrated by those who were fascinated by her biography but not her work'),
doesn't think much of Bishop's unpublished material ('these drafts have their own
interest, but they are mostly unfinished'), and dismisses Bishop critics as more or less
universally inadequate ('admirers who talked about her quiet art but didn't demon-
strate it'). As a Bishop scholar interested in Bishop's life, unfinished work and the
readings of others, it is tempting to take issue with each of these statements in turn,
none of which I endorse, but that would no doubt require a further introductory
chapter. Cook's approach, in common with the wider go-slow movement in cook-
ing, travel and life in general, is 'to slow down when reading most poems' (5). What
Cook means by this is not simply to read line by line or poem by poem, though this is
certainly one of the things she does well, but to look, for example, at a poem's place
in a collection or a word's frequency across a body of work. We learn, for example,
that Bishop's use of 'yard-goods' in 'The Map' is the first recorded use of the word in
the English language. You might have guessed that one of Bishop's favourite words in
a poem was 'dream' (the concordance to her work shows thirty-eight examples), but
not that she was similarly fond of 'breath' (twenty-two examples).

In 2014 and 2015 two of my favourite recent books on Bishop were published:
Lyric Shame by Gillian White and *Elizabeth Bishop's Prosaic* by Vidyan Ravinthiran.
I have no doubt both books will continue to be read by Bishop scholars for years to
come. *Lyric Shame* is, as its title suggests, more than just about Bishop, and more
than just about lyric poetry. In her close readings of Bishop, Anne Sexton, Bernadette
Mayer, James Tate and others, White asks us to think about reading twentieth-century
poetry in relation to and partly as a response to discourses that associate lyric poetry
with shame. 'Poems are ashamed', she argues, 'but have no sense of shame' (1). For
White, reading a Bishop poem can 'induce the vertiginous sense that we are both
inside and outside the world of the poem' (84). Bishop's poems, she concludes, 'treat
familiar language as an object of social analysis, rather than striving to make it a con-
duit of voice or expression of personality' (93). Ravinthiran's focus on what he calls
Bishop's 'prosaic' or at times her 'poetics of prose' is equally interested in language's
social dimension. 'Her style', he suggests, 'is interested in other people, and therefore
vulnerable – she cleaves to prose, or something like it, because she believes in the value
of communication, not simply self-expression' (xviii). In different but perhaps comple-
mentary ways, both White and Ravinthiran open up the space of a Bishop poem to
include the language and style of what one might call the anti-lyric, the non-poetic
and the non-verbal. In doing so, they defamiliarise the Bishop we have become famil-
iar with, cracking open the singular voice to reveal a much more social and sociable
writer, but one with contradictions, flaws and rough edges just like everybody else.
Somebody we might charitably characterise as incompatible.

This introduction has necessarily focused on critical accounts of Bishop's writing.
Acknowledgement must also be paid to engagement with Bishop in films, paintings
and other visual media too. Bruno Baretto's 2013 feature film *Reaching for the Moon*,
adapted from Carmen Oliveira's *Floras raras e banalissimas*, received a mixed recep-
tion in North America but was generally well received in Brazil. It certainly increased
Bishop's profile internationally. Barbara Hammer's 2015 documentary of Bishop,
Welcome to This House, which focused on the homes she shared particularly with
other women, is, alongside Adrienne Rich's review of *The Complete Poems*, one of
the subtlest queer readings of Bishop's art and life I have yet encountered. Charlotte

Hodes and Deryn Rees-Jones's poemfilm based on 'Questions of Travel', also released in 2015, highlights an underappreciated musical dimension to Bishop's writing. (I am glad to say Angus Cleghorn is currently editing a new collection, *Elizabeth Bishop and the Music of Literature*, on precisely this subject. The book will include chapters on song, syntax and tone and on specific debts to and references in Bishop's writing to blues, jazz and Brazilian popular music.)

One catches sight of Bishop in other places too. In 2012, contemporary writer Ali Smith embedded a beautiful short close reading of 'One Art' within a novel written in essay form called *Artful*. The book is composed of four more or less equal essays, each of which cites from or otherwise responds to the title of a missing or unfinished lecture by the narrator's lover, who has been dead for a year and a day as the story begins. The third essay, entitled 'On edge', begins with a reproduction of 'One Art', its presence more or less ignored until the following reveal, more than thirty pages later. 'What was left of On Edge', the narrator confides ('On Edge' being the title of the lost lover's now also lost lecture), 'was a poem you typed up and printed up: One Art, by Elizabeth Bishop.'

> You'd written in pencil in the margin next to it, quite legibly for you, *the villanelle form holds all the lost things safe and simultaneously releases them, lets them be lost. NB how the level of loss builds to become a joke – until we get to the crux, the point, the prospect (way beyond, much worse than losing rivers and continents) of 'losing you'*.

> I read the poem. It made me laugh. I liked how the poet dared herself, and how she was lying, making things rhyme. You'd clearly planned to compare a poem by Yeats about a man called Wandering Aengus who goes fishing, catches a beautiful girl on his line, then, when she disappears, vows to keep walking till he can find her and take her hand, with a poem by Stevie Smith called Fairy Song, about someone who goes into the woods, gets lost, meets a 'creature' who tells the speaker to sing a song, that singing a song will make the time pass, and that holding hands with him will make the speaker not be scared any more. (138–9)

Critics rarely write about Bishop's sense of humour. I wish more would do so. 'One Art' doesn't often make people laugh and, if it does, relatively few people write about it. (An exception to the rule is Rachel Trousdale's new collection of essays, *Humor in Modern American Poetry* (2018), in which Hugh Haughton writes eloquently of humour in Moore and Bishop. Trousdale has a chapter on Bishop's comedy of self-revelation in this book.)

Reading the passage from Smith's book, I was reminded of an astonishing essay by Deryn Rees-Jones called 'Writing Elizabeth', in which she also connects Bishop and Yeats via a dream about cooking Seamus Heaney trout. (If you read the footnotes carefully, you'll find a wonderful recipe for trout by an anonymous Irish poet, as well as Bishop's own recipe for chocolate brownies.) Rees-Jones's account of the dream is both funny and very touching. As a vegetarian she cannot take part in the 'Parnassian meal' even if she eventually finds the recipe for trout she is looking for (46). What she learns from the dream 'is the importance of Bishop as a role model [. . .] Not because she is a woman poet, but because she demands of herself the need to look into the self and transform the self and the world in the process of writing' (58). What Smith similarly describes as the process by which poetic form '*holds all the lost things safe and simultaneously releases them, lets them be lost*' (138).

The chapters that follow this introduction necessarily add to, complicate, and in some cases reject the readings of Bishop I have outlined above. They bridge, I think, where Bishop Studies has been since the publication of new material and where it is likely to travel in the next decade. Some of the chapters draw on material not previously available to critics, particularly Bishop's letters to her analyst Dr Ruth Foster that were only deposited at Vassar recently. In most cases, however, contributors are looking at poems, stories and other prose that are well known to readers, if not always well understood. The book is divided into five parts, Identity, Thought, Poetry, Prose, and Other Places, Other People, categories that roughly correspond to the strands and trajectories of previous scholarship on Bishop's writing. At the same time these categories should be considered fuzzy and hopefully easy to ignore. Identity and Thought are, for example, often interchangeable. There are chapters on Bishop's influences and on how Bishop influences others; on how Bishop thinks and what others have made of her thought processes; chapters on Bishop as an avant-garde writer, a literary critic and screenwriter; chapters on Bishop in Florida, Washington and Brazil; chapters on comedy, identity politics and numbers; chapters on empathy, simplicity and time.

Instead of introducing each chapter in turn, I prefer to introduce them together. My Elizabeth Bishop / (Your Elizabeth Bishop). Contradictory, complex, incompatible, but gloriously so.

Note

1. A complete Works Cited for this chapter would be extremely long. Since the majority of works discussed here will already be familiar to most Bishop readers, I have chosen to list only those works that are cited from directly or difficult to locate.

Works Cited

Armitage, Simon, 'Like, Elizabeth Bishop', *PN Review* 44.6 (July–August 2018): 17–24.

Cleghorn, Angus, Bethany Hicok and Thomas Travisano (eds), *Elizabeth Bishop in the Twenty-First Century: Reading the New Editions* (Charlottesville: University of Virginia Press, 2012).

Cook, Eleanor, *Elizabeth Bishop at Work* (Cambridge, MA: Harvard University Press, 2016).

Edelman, Lee, 'The Geography of Gender: Elizabeth Bishop's "In the Waiting Room"', in Marilyn May Lombardi (ed.), *Elizabeth Bishop: The Geography of Gender* (Charlottesville: University Press of Virginia, 1993), pp. 91–107.

Ellis, Jonathan, *Art and Memory in the Work of Elizabeth Bishop* (Aldershot: Ashgate, 2006).

Ellis, Jonathan, 'Between Us: Letters and Poems of Bishop and Stevenson', in Angela Leighton (ed.), *Anne Stevenson* (Liverpool: Liverpool University Press, 2010), pp. 28–54.

Ford, Mark, 'Elizabeth Bishop at the Water's Edge', *Essays in Criticism* 53.3 (2003): 235–61.

Ford, Mark, 'Mont d'Espoir or Mount Despair: Early Bishop, Early Ashbery, and the French', *PN Review* 114 (March–April 1997): 22–8.

Goldensohn, Lorrie, 'Bishop's Posthumous Publications', in Angus Cleghorn and Jonathan Ellis (eds), *The Cambridge Companion to Elizabeth Bishop* (Cambridge: Cambridge University Press, 2014), pp. 183–96.

Gunn, Thom, 'Out of the Box: Elizabeth Bishop', in *Shelf Life: Essays, Memoirs and an Interview* (London: Faber and Faber, 1993), pp. 77–86.

Hammer, Langdon, 'Useless Concentration: Life and Work in Elizabeth Bishop's Letters and Poems', *American Literary History* 9.1 (Spring 1997): 162–80.

Lerner, Ben, *The Hatred of Poetry* (London: Fitzcarraldo, 2016).

McLane, Maureen, *My Poets* (New York: Farrar, Straus and Giroux, 2012).

Page, Barbara, 'Elizabeth Bishop: Stops, Starts, and Dreamy Divigations', in Linda Anderson and Jo Shapcott (eds), *Elizabeth Bishop: Poet of the Periphery* (Newcastle upon Tyne: Dept of English Literary & Linguistic Studies, University of Newcastle, in association with Bloodaxe, 2002), pp. 12–30.

Page, Barbara, and Carmen Oliveira, 'Foreign-Domestic: Elizabeth Bishop at Home/Not at Home in Brazil', in Angus Cleghorn, Bethany Hicok and Thomas Travisano (eds), *Elizabeth Bishop in the Twenty-First Century: Reading the New Editions* (Charlottesville: University of Virginia Press, 2012), pp. 117–32.

Phillips, Siobhan, 'Elizabeth Bishop and the Ethics of Correspondence', *Modernism/modernity* 19.2 (2012): 343–63.

Pugh, Christina, '"A Lovely Finish I Have Seen": Voice and Variorum in *Edgar Allan Poe & the Juke-Box*', in Angus Cleghorn, Bethany Hicok and Thomas Travisano (eds), *Elizabeth Bishop in the Twenty-First Century: Reading the New Editions* (Charlottesville: University of Virginia Press, 2012), pp. 274–88.

Ravinthiran, Vidyan, *Elizabeth Bishop's Prosaic* (Lewisburg: Bucknell University Press, 2015).

Rees-Jones, Deryn, 'Writing Elizabeth', in Linda Anderson and Jo Shapcott (eds), *Elizabeth Bishop: Poet of the Periphery* (Newcastle upon Tyne: Dept of English Literary & Linguistic Studies, University of Newcastle, in association with Bloodaxe, 2002), pp. 42–62.

Rich, Adrienne, 'The Eye of the Outsider: Elizabeth Bishop's *Complete Poems, 1927–1979*', in *Blood, Bread, and Poetry: Selected Prose 1979–1985* (New York: W. W. Norton & Company, 1986), pp. 124–35.

Roman, Camille, *Elizabeth Bishop's World War II–Cold War View* (New York: Palgrave, 2001).

Schwartz, Lloyd, and Sybil P. Estess (eds), *Elizabeth Bishop and Her Art* (Ann Arbor: University of Michigan Press, 1983).

Smith, Ali, *Artful* (London: Penguin, 2012).

Vendler, Helen, 'The Art of Losing', *The New Republic* 3 (April 2006): 33–7.

White, Gillian C., *Lyric Shame: The 'Lyric' Subject of Contemporary American Poetry* (Cambridge, MA: Harvard University Press, 2014).

PART I

IDENTITY

1

Disturbances of the Archive: Repetition and Memory in Elizabeth Bishop's Poetry

Linda Anderson

I

Aᶠᵗᵉʳ ᵗʰᵉ ᵈᵉᵃᵗʰ ᴵᴺ 2009 of Alice Methfessel, Elizabeth Bishop's literary executor and lover, a cache of letters and other materials by Bishop was discovered amongst Methfessel's possessions and saved from destruction, to be subsequently acquired by Vassar College and deposited in Bishop's archive there. Amongst these letters is a group to the doctor and psychoanalyst Ruth Foster, written in 1947, in the course of Bishop's year-long analysis with her, and during a period when Bishop's life and drinking had slipped out of control.[1] Lorrie Goldensohn has recently published an article about the contents of these letters which are spread across some twenty-two pages, and seemingly composed in the course of one intense weekend. Goldensohn appropriately draws our attention to the curiosity of their existence as carbon copies, and the fact that there are no clues as to who copied them or whether they were ever sent. The only thing we can know, writes Goldensohn, mitigating the feelings of intrusiveness we must inevitably feel reading the letters, is that 'the first person to lay them aside safe from destruction was Elizabeth Bishop herself' (2).

Did Bishop write these letters with the intention they should be read – by one other at least? The fact that they were typed, as Bishop typed most of her letters to make them legible for others, coupled with the clear sense of an interlocutor, whose name and presence is frequently invoked, suggests on balance that they *were* sent or maybe rather given to her analyst as part of her treatment and that what we have are therefore the copies she kept for herself. However, whether they were sent or not, the Foster letters, arising as they do from a psychoanalytic setting, inevitably raise some of the same problems as Diane Middlebrook experienced when presented with the tapes made by Anne Sexton's psychoanalyst Dr Orne of their sessions together, problems which, as Jacqueline Rose suggested in her review of Middlebrook's biography, are not solely ethical. For Rose, the danger the tapes posed was that they would be read in terms of an 'ultimate revelation', the unveiling of secrets about a life, rather than as another version in an endlessly narratable sequence (22).[2] Judith Butler has written about this whole problem of giving an account of oneself: 'I can tell the story of my origin and I can even tell it again and again, in several ways [. . .] but of no single one can I say with certainty that it alone is true' (37). We know Bishop objected to the underlying assumptions of a book by Rebecca Paterson entitled *The*

Riddle of Emily Dickinson, on the grounds that it collapsed something as 'singular and manifold' as literary work into a detective story, organised around one single cause or origin which related back to a lesbian relationship (*Prose* 264–5). Her well-documented hostility to confessional poetry, represented particularly by the work of Anne Sexton, seems to have been driven by a similar belief: not that poetry should avoid being autobiographical – how else could one write, as she conceded to Robert Lowell – but that poetry's rationale was not self-revelation, even indeed if that were possible, given the endlessly proliferating nature of 'truth' (*Words in Air* 758). In her careful study of the different drafts of the 'Dear Dr' poems, poems addressed to Dr Foster, and written at the same time as Bishop's analytic sessions with her, Heather Treseler notes how in one particular draft Bishop does not attempt to describe a stable past accessed through memory, but rather a past emanating in plural memories that are analogous to, and as fluid as, 'all the photographs & notes / manufacturing fluences every minute' (100–1). Bishop refers to different forms of representation in relation to memory – 'photographs and notes' – suggesting its status as a retrospective construction, but she also, as Treseler points out, uses the archaic word 'fluences'. Perhaps Bishop had in mind less its Latin root than its use in seventeenth-century poetry, where it can mean a fluency of speech as well as a general sense of flux; it thus seems to combine in one word the effort towards articulation with its continual departure or vanishing.

Of course the Foster letters can and will be read as adding to our sum of knowledge about Bishop's life and particularly her childhood, as providing evidence that it was even more chaotic and painful than we so far knew. At the end of the letters there is even a helpful chronology up to 1944 which Bishop seems to have assembled at the same time as she wrote the letters, trying to get the record straight in her own mind at least. Significantly the two years between 1944 and 1946, the years immediately preceding the therapy, are blank. However, the letters are also writerly accounts, 'manufactured' – to use the term in the 'Dear Dr' poems – and build the sense of a world with the same kind of immersive detail and 'descriptive compulsion' that is key to all Bishop's writing. Of one particularly traumatic incident, Bishop says 'the whole experience might very well eventually be used in writing', and then adds in pen, as if sensing a greater symbiosis between form and content, 'or rather it seems to form a story'. Did Bishop keep these letters, we have to ask, because, as a writer, she thought they were simply too good to throw away? Throughout the letters, Bishop refers to her drinking, and relives a familiar pattern of succumbing, then shameful aftermath. 'If only I didn't feel I were that dreadful thing an "alcoholic",' she writes at one point, and at another, 'Oh why the hell did I have to go & get drunk.' Partly the letters seem to have been written under the influence of drink, alcohol supplying the boldness that allowed her also, as we know, to make intimate late-night phone calls to her friends, to express the needs that, sober, she would otherwise repress. One night in this same period she even rolled up at Marianne Moore's as 'drunk as a skunk' according to Arthur Gold, to a shocked yet kindly response from Moore (Fountain and Brazeau 96). Drinking also allowed Bishop to start affairs. 'Every love affair I've been involved in since college, excepting Robert [Seaver], has begun when I've been drunk,' she confesses in the letters.

Yet if the Foster letters give us some indication of what Bishop's late-night garrulity might be like, they also suggest that any freeing up of repression was not just painfully won but transient, and that Bishop both used and revised her breakthrough moments in her poetry. At one point, explaining that 'all of sudden' she felt better, and that 'something had really occurred', and that she feels 'happy', she later scribbles in the margin, 'I'm afraid this didn't last very well', documenting, one suspects, the mood swing caused by the alternation between drunkenness and sobriety. Yet, the ability to extend beyond moments of inebriated insight or epiphanic vision, into a longer temporal narrative that can also include the falling away from those states, with neither taking precedence over the other, is the hallmark of Bishop's later poetry. In a famous exchange between herself and Robert Lowell in 1957, she resisted with wry mockery the idea that she had preceded or anticipated his own 'breakthrough' in *Life Studies*. Instead she positions herself, as she typically did, on the sidelines: 'But "broken through to where you've always been" – what on earth do you mean by that? I haven't got anywhere at all, I think. Just to those first benches to sit down and rest on, in a side-arbor at the beginning of the maze' (*Words in Air* 247). By grounding her response in realistic detail, Bishop is also enacting a kind of rebuttal to the grandiosity of Lowell's pronouncement. Later, in 1965, in a review of her collection *Questions of Travel*, Robert Lowell had written that 'each poem is inspired by her tone of large, grave tenderness and sorrowing amusement' (*Words in Air* 580). Moved, Bishop wrote back to him: 'Isn't it odd, out of all the nerves & troubles something fairly "serene" does come?' (*Words in Air* 583). Serenity is a word that is regularly applied to Bishop's later poetry, yet it was a quality she had difficulty integrating into her sense of self. One year after her response to Lowell, she is reported by a student as saying: 'Because I write the kind of poetry I do, people seem to assume that I'm a *calm* person. Sometimes they even tell me how *sane* I am. But I'm not a calm person at all [. . .] There are times when I really start to wonder what holds me together – awful times' (Wehr 43). Many of the issues that took Bishop into therapy, she never resolved. Yet what the Foster letters show us – and where their value lies, I think – is less with discovering more about the 'awful times' than with offering us insight into how Bishop was developing trust in herself to write freely, without censorship, and thus begin to create for herself, through writing, connections and continuities.

II

At this point I want to take a little detour in order to address the question of who Dr Ruth Foster was, the psychoanalyst whom Bishop called 'pretty smart' (*One Art* 179) as well as 'good and kind' (206), and whose presence in biographical and critical studies of Bishop is now, because of the letters, likely to loom ever larger.[3] Like others, I have found the lack of publications either about her or by her frustrating, particularly because Bishop, claiming privileged insight on the topic in a letter to Robert Lowell in 1947, refers to the fact that a 'psychoanalyst friend' – presumably Ruth Foster – is writing an article about dreaming and colour, a reference that reoccurs in the 'Dear Dr' poems (*Words in Air* 16). However, it is also possible that this article was always in part an illusion or fabrication on Bishop's part. In the Foster letters themselves, Bishop refers to a painting by Joan Miró, introduced to her by her friend Margaret Miller, which has the phrase 'La couleur de mon rêve' inscribed on the canvas. She then goes on: 'That's what I thought of when I saw your manila envelopes labelled something like that and I do so wish you'd write about it right away.' We'll never know, of course, what might have been discussed between them about the contents of the envelopes, but Bishop's comment here leaves the idea of either a planned or completed article at least in doubt.

The facts I have found out about Dr Foster to add to the record come first of all from an obituary in *The New York Times* in September 1950, where we learn that she died alone at her apartment at the age of fifty-six (one has to assume suddenly, given that she died at home and was still seeing patients, according to Bishop, at the time of her death); that she came from Boston, where she attended Winsor School, later attending Goucher College in Baltimore; that she did her medical training at Johns Hopkins; and that she was survived by her mother and three brothers, who still lived in Boston.[4] From these clues, it has been possible to trace a record of her at Goucher College,[5] including an address, which identified her father as Reginald Foster, a Yale-educated lawyer, himself the son of Dwight Foster, who served as Massachusetts Attorney General. An old Boston family and part of the governing élite, they were clearly wealthy and moved between Boston and a summer residence in Magnolia, Massachusetts.

More interesting in many ways are the records relating to Ruth Foster that are held in the medical archives at Johns Hopkins. Between 1937 and 1939 she wrote several times to Adolf Meyer, the prominent psychiatrist who was professor and psychiatrist-in-chief at Johns Hopkins Hospital from 1910 to 1941, and who established the Henry Phipps Psychiatric Clinic there.[6] He practised and taught a mixture of neurobiological and Freudian psychoanalytic methods, and pioneered the importance of empirical observation and careful case histories. Ruth Foster seems to have come into contact with him when she was working in the neurology laboratory for a month, and she later attributes her interest in psychiatry to him, though she had no direct contact with him in that role. In asking for references, Foster reveals some of her work experience and training. Her medical degree was in fact from the University of Maryland – she graduated in 1931[7] – and afterwards she spent three years at Baltimore City Hospital as Intern in Neurology, before switching to psychiatry and working first at Manhattan State Hospital (Wards Island), and then under Dr Helen Flanders Dunbar at the Presbyterian Hospital, Manhattan. Her mentor at this time, Flanders Dunbar, was a complex character who had studied medieval literature and religion before turning to medicine, and who became famous for establishing the field of psychosomatic medicine. Foster set up her own private practice in 1937.

References to Foster turn up later in relation to the William Alanson White Institute, which had been founded in 1943 in New York when Eric Fromm, Frieda Fromm-Reichmann, Harry Stack Sullivan, David Rioch, Janet Rioch and Clara Thompson seceded from the American Psychoanalytic Association, wanting to modify rigid Freudian clinical practice by adopting a broader and more eclectic approach, where social and interpersonal issues could be given due weight.[8] Foster is also listed as a consulting psychiatrist on the original staff list for the Northside Center, which, established by Kenneth and Mamie Clark in 1946 in Harlem, was an attempt to offer psychiatric care and counselling to socially deprived and predominantly black communities.[9] In a listing in 1949 of applicants to the American Association of Public Health, Ruth Foster also appears, described as 'Neuropsychiatrist and Consulting Psychiatrist, Northside Center for Child Development'.[10] Fully enmeshed in the dynamic relations between neurology, psychiatry, psychoanalysis and a more socially informed care in

the 1930s and 1940s, and allied with some of the most important and radical prac-
titioners of this formative and fraught period in the development of psychiatry and
psychoanalysis in the USA, Foster emerges as an unusually progressive woman, whose
interest in people rather than disease increasingly determined her career path, and who
seems to have been open to new ideas. Megan Marshall has also recently added to this
picture, having been in contact with surviving members of Foster's family, noting that
her pioneering choice of profession, so rare for a woman at this time, came at the cost
of 'estrangement' from her 'proper Bostonian family' (*Elizabeth Bishop* 78). We can
only surmise how this sense of estrangement may have deepened her understanding
of Bishop.

The fact that Bishop appreciated Foster is attested to, of course, by the letters
themselves and the degree of trust she obviously inspired in Bishop. Nevertheless,
Bishop was disappointed that her asthma stubbornly remained a problem despite
Foster's therapeutic intervention. 'I had hoped that going to Dr Foster might help,
but it didn't seem to – at least not yet at any rate,' Bishop wrote in 1948 to Dr Bau-
mann, who had originally suggested visiting Dr Foster (*One Art* 163–4). Eventually
in 1954, having acknowledged to Baumann that Dr Foster had helped her 'more
than anyone in the world', she talks about the analysis as a 'fiasco', having discov-
ered the cause, so she thinks, by reading about 'abandonment neurosis' in a book
by Germaine Guex. 'Although I try not to take such reading "personally"', Bishop
writes disingenuously, 'I think it has showed me exactly where Dr Foster and I went
wrong.'[11] This remark makes an intriguing coda to the analysis, and reinforces the
idea that Bishop was disappointed that she had not been 'cured' either psychologi-
cally or physically, though the word 'fiasco' might suggest a more dramatic ending.
If Guex was thought by Bishop to provide a reason, it might well have been because
for Guex the trauma of abandonment is distinctive and cannot be 'worked through'
easily since it has not been in any way 'accepted and "digested" nor repressed' by the
analysand (Guex xxiv). One thinks of the way this seems to anticipate more recent
work on trauma that has emphasised how trauma can be registered as affect or phys-
ical symptom long before it becomes available to narrative recall (Caruth 4). For
Guex, abandonment was a pathology of the pre-oedipal phase, which was therefore
difficult to treat in classical Freudian terms. The psychoanalytic narrative of gradual
amelioration and change through interpretation and the 'talking cure' might simply,
according to Guex, however insightful the analyst, overlay the patient's trauma and
confirm her sense of abandonment. Is this, one wonders, what Bishop felt at the end
of her treatment?

III

Going back to the letters themselves, I suggest that Bishop arrived at the idea of a
putative article by Dr Foster about dreaming and colour by combining Margaret
Miller's reference to Miró's painting with her own observations or projections. The
same overlap between painting and psychoanalysis also seems to emerge elsewhere.
In 1947 Bishop is reading the newly published study *The History of Impressionism*
by John Rewald, and it seeps into a dream, which takes France as its setting, as well
as the painterly motifs of looking and windows. In this long extract from the letters,
she refers again to this book, drawing on a quotation from it by Degas for her own

insights about memory, and her changed attitude to repetition in her writing. 'Dear Ruth,' she starts:

> One thing, among many others, that I realize this is doing to help my work is mak-
> ing me get over the fear of repetition. I've always envied painters in a way because
> they seemed to be able to use the same material over & over & over again and
> paint almost the same pictures over again without anyone's giving it a thought . . .
> I think that so far I have regarded every single poem as something almost abso-
> lutely new – I know this can't quite be true because people have told me I do have
> a style of my own or a speaking voice of my own or something but I've never been
> able to feel it myself – they all sound quite different to me. One of the remarks of
> Degas in this book on impressionism I've been reading is 'Art doesn't grow wider,
> it recapitulates.' And I have just noticed that I've lost the fear of repeating myself
> to you, in fact I've known I've been doing it and gone right ahead. And I feel that
> in poetry now there is no reason why I should make such an effort to make each
> poem an isolated event, that they all go on into each other or overlap etc. and are
> really all one long poem anyway. Perhaps this is what you meant when you said
> they had been 'tight', no I guess you were probably thinking more of strict form,
> weren't you, or was it the ideas, or what.

Here, the idea of repetition, derived first from thinking about painting, links both poetry and psychoanalysis in Bishop's mind. Her notion is that her development depends not on abandoning repetition but on lessening its hold over her as something she must avoid: psychoanalysis allows her to repeat herself and she begins to conceive of a writing where the boundaries between one work and another can overlap, become more porous, or fluid. In his essay 'Remembering, Repeating and Working-Through', originally published in 1914, and in revised form ten years later, Freud had of course recognised that there was more to remembering than just remembering: repression frequently stood in the way, deflecting memories into compulsive action – what he famously called the compulsion to repeat. 'We have learnt that the patient repeats instead of remembering, and repeats under the conditions of resistance' (151). One of the consequences of this repetition was that the past and present become contempora-neous, a past trauma transforming itself into recurrent behaviour in the present. Freud saw this repetition as being acted out in the transference, the transference itself being both a form of repetition and the transference of a forgotten past to the present. At the end of this essay, his choice of title, so Freud says, obliging him to go further and move into a different temporality, he extols the therapist not to give up in the face of the patient's resistance. Knowledge of the resistance – the analytic work of interpretation – will not be enough to awaken memories, he writes. What the patient also needs is time. 'The doctor has nothing else to do than to wait and let things take their course, a course which cannot be avoided nor always hastened' (155).

Bishop may well have protected her own originality at the beginning of her career as carefully as she declares and describes to Dr Foster. Certainly, Bishop recorded in her late essay about Marianne Moore, 'Efforts of Affection', that she was still registering a 'slight grudge' about the way Moore, always more opportunistic as a poet than Bishop, had used a phrase of hers in a poem, unacknowledged (*Prose* 130). In this question of influence and originality, however, the more important battle for Bishop in relation to

Moore was to fight off, as politely but decisively as she could, Moore's forceful incursions into her own poetry, particularly in relation to her famous attempted rewriting of Bishop's poem 'Roosters'. Bishop berated herself as 'mulish' and 'cranky' in order to lighten the tone of rejection, but the boundary she put down between them in 1940 also marked a turning point for their future interactions (*One Art* 97). Yet if originality for Bishop, at the beginning of her career, was equated by her with avoiding repetition, repetition, according to Freud, is also a form of avoidance, and indeed, in Bishop's construction here, the repetition she fears can only itself take the form of relentless – and repeated – inhibition. As Adam Phillips expresses it, 'the super-ego is reiterative [. . .] it never brings us any news about ourselves'. In the same essay, Phillips suggests as an alternative to single-track and monotonous self-criticism a way of seeing from multiple perspectives, and of exploring alternative selves. 'We judge ourselves before we see ourselves,' he writes (13). What might it mean to reverse the order, and begin instead with seeing?

Everywhere in Bishop's early poetry the themes, motifs and forms of repetition register themselves, even as Bishop strives to separate herself from them and write every poem in terms of a new beginning. Her repeated return to early morning in poems such as 'Love Lies Sleeping', 'A Miracle for Breakfast' and 'Paris, 7 A.M.' seems compulsive at the same time as it is an attempt to start anew and outwit the guilt or melancholia or death that gradually comes to encumber the poems, and to determine their ending. In other poems she directly confronts the themes of obsessional or mechanical action. In one of the drafts of an unpublished poem, 'Edgar Allan Poe & the Juke Box', a poem preoccupied with darkness and a fall that is perhaps both literal and symbolic, she implicates and unites poetry with the 'mechanical' pleasures of alcohol; in another unpublished poem, 'The Soldier and the Slot-Machine', she transfers the soldier's inebriation to the machine itself (*Poems* 285, 287–9). In 'Cirque d'Hiver', a poem which uses the symbolist motif of a mechanical toy as its focus and thus less directly explores the experience of her own habitual drinking, she describes the all too predictable and restricted action of horse and ballerina. At the same time the motion is represented through a verse form that is equally hobbled, as Bonnie Costello has pointed out, thus associating poetry with this same circularity (50). Yet in the desperate face-to-face encounter between horse and poet at the end, a different time is signalled, a 'now' that interposes itself into the repetitive action and opens up a time which is inhabited by a question and by an otherness, which cannot be collapsed into more of the same.

> Facing each other rather desperately –
> his eye is like a star –
> we stare and say, 'Well, we have come this far.' (*Poems* 32)

Bishop explored what it means to experience face-to-face encounters in other poems too, for instance in 'The Man-Moth' and 'The Fish', where any narcissistic mirroring is thwarted by the sense of otherness, a space between which also implies the suspension of teleology or predetermination. Similarly 'this far' may be as far as we have come in the poem 'Cirque d'Hiver' but it is not the same, or not necessarily the same, as an end.

The most interesting poem to explore from this point of view is 'The Prodigal', a poem that had its origins at the same time as Bishop's analysis with Dr Foster, though she did not publish it until 1951, after Dr Foster's death. The poem takes the form of a double sonnet, and throughout Bishop's early poetry the use of forms and patterning, variations and re-enactments, also seems to help pose the question of how we locate ourselves in time. In this particular poem the repeated form seems to reinforce the sense of stasis. The prodigal defies the narrative momentum of the parable he draws his identity from and instead stays where he is. The 'shuddering insights, beyond his control, touching him' of the second stanza, that suggest a return of the repressed, and that interrupt the brutish state described in the first stanza, the alcoholic miasma the prodigal is lost in, are not enough. Still, Bishop tells us, 'it took him a long time / finally to make his mind up to go home' (*Poems* 69). This complex statement hints, like the ending of 'Cirque d'Hiver', at another time, in this case a 'finally', outside the frame of the poem, not yet entered into. However, the intervention of the 'long time', an attenuation of the present, also calls up Freud's time, the time of duration and waiting, the time that for Freud was necessary, before the patient could fully receive the effects of therapeutic intervention, and understand the meaning of their memories as memories.

IV

In 1950, a year she designated 'her worst year yet' – and also the year Dr Foster died – Bishop turned to her notebook, to describe how she felt unhappiness could affect one's sense of time:

> I think when one is extremely unhappy – almost hysterically unhappy, that is – one's time-sense breaks down. All that long stretch in K.W. for example, several years ago – it wasn't just a matter of not being able to accept the present, that present, although it began that way possibly. But the past and the present seemed confused or contradicted each other violently and constantly and the past wouldn't 'lie down'. (I've felt the same thing when I tried to paint – but this was really taught me by getting drunk, when the same thing happens, for perhaps the same reasons, for a few hours.)[12]

If this seems to describe the same depressed temporality that deprives the subject of a narrative for their lives, endlessly repeating painful affects that nevertheless remain inaccessible, the fact that Bishop links it with painting suggests that something creative could also emerge from this confusion of times and tenses. For Freud the compulsion to repeat could become useful, if allowed into a definite field, the playground of the transference, which he also saw, anticipating Winnicott's notion of an intermediate area, as an 'intermediate region between illness and real life' (150). For Luce Irigaray, the feminist theorist and psychoanalyst, writing in 1985, and unhappy with a purely Freudian approach to psychoanalysis, there was an important comparison to be drawn between psychoanalysis and painting, and the way painting can connect repetition and new creation:

> The point about painting is to spatialize perception and make time simultaneous, to quote Klee. This is also the point about dreaming. The analyst should direct his or her attention not only to the repetition of former images and their possible interpretation, but also to the subject's ability to paint, to make time simultaneous, to build bridges, establish perspectives between present-past-future. (155)

While, like Freud, Irigaray emphasises the patience or the time required to work through the repetitions, she also wants to see this as the time and space in which the patient can regain their balance, by building his or her ground or territory. The analyst in effect paints along with the patient, creating a 'framework of simultaneity, a perspective, a depth of field' (155). Two aspects of the process are particularly important, and both are opposed to Freud's emphasis on interpretation, which Irigaray sees as abstract and as cutting into the patient's subjectivity: these are colour and voice. Irigaray wants to summon the patient into a 'vivid sensual universe', where the subtle gradations and grains of the senses, both sight and hearing, experienced in the present, can be employed fully. More than simply being perceived as 'layers of catastrophe', memory can be freed to synthesise with the imagination. The imagination is key and forms 'a seed', around which the past – and the past of the imagination – gathers. 'All this', she writes, however, first 'requires there be a present' (156).

Bishop in the Foster letters gives special attention to one poem in particular, which she links with the analytic process, and attempts to interpret for Dr Foster. This is 'At the Fishhouses'. Though she acknowledges that 'knowledge is historical' was a 'random thought' she wrote down years ago, she also wants now to see its relevance to the process of psychoanalysis. She offers various other symbolic associations. The seal in the poem is connected with Foster herself, and she muses about the double meaning of seal, with a kiss being 'a sort of seal'. This follows on from her report about a drunken doze where she has a dream in which 'everything was very wild & dark & stormy and you were in it feeding me from your breast'. She notes the way there is a 'sort of interchange between kissing & feeding', linking the dream with the seal. In a more casual way, for good measure, she adds in 'the fish is always the symbol of Christ I suppose and burning one's hand a test of innocence'.

However, whatever its character as intermediary, positioned like an analyst within a transitional or intermediate area, the seal bristles with such curiosity and particularity, it is difficult to sacrifice it to Bishop's interpretation here:

> Cold dark deep and absolutely clear,
> element bearable to no mortal,
> to fish and to seals . . . One seal particularly
> I have seen here evening after evening.
> He was curious about me. He was interested in music;
> like me a believer in total immersion,
> so I used to sing him Baptist hymns.
> I also sang 'A Mighty Fortress Is Our God.'
> He stood up in the water and regarded me
> steadily, moving his head a little.
> Then he would disappear, then suddenly emerge
> almost in the same spot, with a sort of shrug
> as if it were against his better judgment.
> Cold dark deep and absolutely clear,
> the clear gray icy water . . . (*Poems* 63)

The seal emerges between the repeated resonant chords of the line – 'cold dark deep and absolutely clear' – with a repetition being used formally to set up a sound, a deep vibration that we return to despite the seal's slightly comic and differently pitched counterpoint. Seamus Heaney has reminded us how important pace is in this poem, with the moment of hesitation, the different register inhabited by the seal, enabling a daring poetic leap (105–6). Much of the power of the poem has indeed to do with its formal means, and an evocative interplay between the human senses and repetition and abstraction. The repetition transfers the description of the water to another realm, a depth beyond human sensation where apparent opposites – dark and clear – can coexist, and the repetitive force of seeing it 'over and over', 'the same sea', is not only submerged in a knowledge of transience, but is itself equated with transience, both 'flowing and flown'.

If Bishop's interpretive forays can perhaps help us to understand the origins of what David Kalstone called in relation to this poem a 'vestigial, implacable female presence behind the scene' (121), and what Robert Lowell flinched at in her use of the word 'breast' (*Words in Air* 7), ultimately Bishop was herself dissatisfied at approaching this important poem in such an explanatory, reductive way. 'Of course I didn't think of any of this when I wrote it – only the connection with you at the end,' she wrote. She also describes herself as ambivalent towards 'psychological reading' that discredits anyone's love of nature as 'just some sort of escape mother substitute', because, though she knows that may have some truth in her case, taking long walks and admiring the scenery was also part of her social and family ethos: 'In my mother's family it was always the thing to take long walks and admire the scenery and my god what would I have done without it.' Then, making a link between her writing and being 'in nature', she goes on:

> I feel compelled to describe & describe & describe – that's all my notebooks or diaries are usually, but it is – well I can't say it clearly just yet. But we all are obviously the children of the earth anyway.

If Bishop found solace in nature, it was partly to do with its continuance, its ordinary cycles. In her poem 'Anaphora', a poem placed significantly at the end of her first collection, *North & South*, and which at first seems to initiate the familiar pattern of descent from the optimism of daybreak, we can maybe detect a change as she attempts to find an answer in the 'assent' of renewal, the diurnal round itself. It is perhaps significant in this respect too that in her early poem 'Large Bad Picture' it is less the overall aesthetic value of the painting that appeals to her than the careful process within it of registering the natural scene. Just as the painters she envied in the earlier quotation from the letters paint the same picture over again, Bishop finds her relation to nature to be one of repeated acts of description. The sentence Bishop quotes from Degas's letter from John Rewald's book about art as recapitulation goes on to say how the artist must 'grow espalier-fashion. You remain there throughout life, arms outspread, mouth open to take in what passes, what is around you, and to live from it' (Rewald 275–6). It is a vivid image that one must assume Bishop also read, and which in some ways corresponds with Bishop's much-quoted and more sophisticated later evocation to Anne Stevenson of the artist's 'self-forgetful, perfectly useless concentration' (*Prose* 414). In this compulsion to describe, linked to her sense of integration into the natural world, we could see Bishop as creating a ground to stand on, preferring synthesis to analysis, and refusing omniscience or a position outside her own process of experiencing or writing. Later, this would become a confident, if slightly provocative, stance about her poetry and the limited uses of theory:

> No matter what theories one may have, I doubt very much that they are in one's mind at the moment of writing a poem or that there is even a physical possibility that they could be. Theories can only be based on interpretations of other poet's [*sic*] poems, or one's own in retrospect, or wishful thinking. (Schwartz and Estess 281)

More informally, to Robert Lowell, she wrote in 1963, 'all this explaining should mostly go without saying', and then, giving vent to her irritation, 'to hell with explainers – that's really why I don't want to teach' (*Words in Air* 465).

Returning to the letters, it is important that Bishop not only offers insights and interpretations to Dr Foster but also embeds them in prolonged descriptions of her journeys, first around New Hampshire and then in Nova Scotia. In a lengthy passage she describes the bus journey she undertook on leaving her Aunt Grace:

> Well, to go on – when I left Aunt Grace's late at night on the bus to come back to N.Y. something funny happened. She had given me a drink of rum before I left & I think I took a sleeping pill. After midnight or so there were very few people on the bus, it was very dark, going through forests mostly. There were two women seated far back behind me and they kept talking all night or so it seemed to me. One voice was a little louder than the other's and had an intonation very much like my Aunt Grace's – much more Nova Scotian than hers is but that same sort of <u>commiserat-ing</u> tone. I was so filled with it by then and had been thinking about it so much all the time I was there that this just seemed like a continuation of the talks I had had with her. The other voice I couldn't hear so well and that was you [. . .] The next night on the bus the same thing happened only by then there were no more Nova Scotian accents to be turned into Aunt Grace and of course I was much wearier so the voices were made of all the creakings in the side of the bus right under my ear [. . .] For two or three weeks after that I could hear Aunt Grace's voice very distinctly talking talking just before I went to sleep, then it stopped gradually – then I came to see you again & yr real voice took up the tale.

The word that seems important here and that is also enacted throughout is 'continuation'. Voices keep going, crossing the boundary between waking and sleeping, and between one person and another. Beginnings and endings are blurred and the experience seems part of a story that has already begun – 'Well, to go on' – and has no definite conclusion ('yr real voice took up the tale'). In the earlier quotation we looked at from the letters, Bishop talked about the importance of seeing poems less as isolated events than as one long poem anyway: 'They all go into each other or overlap,' she wrote. Voice has the capacity to surround us, and yet to pull us towards where it is coming from; to make us think about the particular, and yet to remind us of other voices, even, as Susan Stewart says, the 'first voices' (108). In Bishop's description of her experience here it is the very particularity of regional accent and intonation – a 'sort of commiserating tone' – that holds the memory, even as it becomes one with the vehicle, the bus, that carries her across time and distance.

Voice is, of course, the privileged medium of psychoanalysis, and Bishop's experi-
ence of listening to voices seems inevitably to bring her back to her psychoanalyst.
Irigaray wanted to add the dimension of colour to the psychoanalytic reliance on voice
and she advocated the creative interplay between voice and colour in order to create
some temporal space. Noting the linguistic oddity of this phrase, Irigaray then added:
'This paradoxical expression highlights a major problem in psychoanalysis. And per-
haps in painting too?' (155). In an obscure passage in her notebook, written during her
experience of psychoanalysis, Bishop explored the relationship between the aural and
the visual and how they were not always in step with each other: 'I see a man hammer,
over at Toppinos, (or saw him chopping wood at Lockeport) then hear the sound, see
him, then hear him etc. The eye and the ear compete, trying to draw them together,
to a "photo finish" so to speak.'[13] The photo finish is neither static nor permanent,
but arrives from the effort to draw together different perceptions and energies for a
moment. Building a ground, in Irigaray's terms, is not the same as a structure meant to
last; as a temporal space, it is inhabited by time.

Bishop came back to her experience of those voices she heard on the bus in her
poem 'The Moose', which she worked on over the next thirty years. She used many
of the features of her description to Dr Foster in her wonderful evocation of 'a gentle,
auditory / slow hallucination . . .', the creakings of the bus, the half-heard voices, the
Nova Scotian intonation, inducing memory and the sense of continuation, as even life
and death are placed as syntactic equivalents:

> 'Yes . . .' that peculiar
> affirmative. 'Yes . . .'
> A sharp, indrawn breath,
> half groan, half acceptance,
> that means 'Life's like that.
> We know *it* (also death).' (*Poems* 192)

However, the poem also turns on the sudden jolt of vision, interrupting this dreamy
divagation, with a moose's having entered the road from the 'impenetrable wood'. It
might again be possible to offer the kind of psychoanalytic explanation Bishop did in
relation to her seal in 'At the Fishhouses'. Instead, however, it is perhaps more enlight-
ening to think about the way the moose exists in time – she comes and goes in the
poem – and yet is also described as 'taking her time', as creating a space for herself, a
temporal space, and in this way as not simply cutting across, but becoming in the end
integrated with, folded into, the voices which also reach towards her.

In this chapter I have not attempted a full survey of Bishop's letters to Ruth Foster
and the many revelations they contain but have used them in a more symptomatic
way to explore what they tell us about the development of Bishop's writing at this
important time in her career. The letters suggest how Bishop wrote, and kept writing,
across many different forms – notebooks, letters and multiple drafts of poems – and
as she did so she created a sense of continuity for a life that could seem discontinu-
ous or even broken: 'I feel compelled to describe & describe & describe.' One of the
ways we have come to understand Bishop's career has been in terms of the security
her life in Brazil offered her, and the way it enabled her to look back at her childhood
in Nova Scotia and to use memory as narrative. I want to suggest she had already

begun to create the ground for her later poems at the time she was seeing Dr Foster by modelling a present in the letters that could also bind and gather the traces of her past, without fear of repetition. The Foster letters disturb the archive not only because they introduce new unsettling information into the record but also because they suggest the way the archive is never finished, never complete, always capable of both revision and new meaning. This principle of belatedness – of the future giving meaning to the past – was of increasing importance to Bishop herself as she drew on her notebooks and letters and drafts written years, if not decades, before, and their insights, latent or as yet unassimilated (including, of course, the rich detail of the Foster letters), to write her most enduring poetry.

Notes

1. Vassar Archive, folder 118.33 (Letters to Ruth Foster, 1947). The listing says there are five letters and Goldensohn says three, but there is agreement that we are talking about twenty-two pages. It is difficult to tell in many ways where one letter ends and the next begins, and the page numbers are not consecutive throughout. I have not attempted to give detailed references.
2. This essay is a review of Diane Wood Middlebrook's *Anne Sexton: A Biography* (London: Virago, 1991).
3. Megan Marshall's new biography, *Elizabeth Bishop: A Miracle for Breakfast*, published in 2017, adds some new facts to my account here, including that Ruth Foster also trained in London, though no further detail is added, and that the cause of her death was pancreatic cancer.
4. See obituary in *The New York Times*, 30 September 1950. Ruth Foster died on 29 September.
5. See *Donnybrook Fair Yearbook*, Goucher College, 1923, <http://cdm16235.contentdm. oclc.org/cdm/compoundobject/collection/p16235coll5/id/12882/rec/1> (last accessed 28 September 2018).
6. See *The Adolf Meyer Collection*, Series 1, Correspondence, folders 1 (1937–8) and 2 (1938–9), Alan Mason Chesney Medical Archives, Johns Hopkins Hospital.
7. Records at the University of Maryland confirm this.
8. See M. R. Green and R. M. Crowley, 'Revolution within Psychoanalysis: A History of the William Alanson White Institute', New York, 1983; twenty-page typescript, available online: <https://opus4.kobv.de/opus4-Fromm/frontdoor/index/index/docId/24944> (last accessed 28 September 2018).
9. See Gerald Markowitz and David Rosner, *Children, Race and Power: Kenneth and Mamie Clark's Northside Center* (New York and London: Routledge, 2000), p. 264, n. 13.
10. See *American Journal of Public Health* 39 (February 1949): 263.
11. Letter to Dr Baumann, 1954, quoted in Siobhan Phillips, *The Poetics of the Everyday* (New York: Columbia University Press, 2010), p. 256, n. 33.
12. This passage from her unpublished notebooks is quoted in Anderson, p. 92.
13. From an unpublished notebook, quoted in Anderson, p. 67.

Works Cited

Anderson, Linda, *Elizabeth Bishop: Lines of Connection* (Edinburgh: Edinburgh University Press, 2013).
Bishop, Elizabeth, *Edgar Allan Poe & the Juke-Box: Uncollected Poems, Drafts, and Fragments*, ed. Alice Quinn (New York: Farrar, Straus and Giroux, 2006).

Bishop, Elizabeth, *One Art: The Selected Letters*, ed. Robert Giroux (London: Chatto & Windus, 1994).

Bishop, Elizabeth, and Robert Lowell, *Words in Air: The Complete Correspondence between Elizabeth Bishop and Robert Lowell*, ed. Thomas Travisano with Saskia Hamilton (London: Faber and Faber, 2008).

Butler, Judith, *Giving an Account of Oneself* (New York: Fordham University Press, 2005).

Caruth, Cathy, 'Trauma and Experience: Introduction', in Cathy Caruth (ed.), *Trauma: Explorations in Memory* (Baltimore and London: Johns Hopkins University Press, 1994), pp. 3–12.

Costello, Bonnie, *Elizabeth Bishop: Questions of Mastery* (Cambridge, MA: Harvard University Press, 1991).

Fountain, Gary, and Peter Brazeau (eds), *Remembering Elizabeth Bishop: An Oral Biography* (Amherst: University of Massachusetts Press, 1994).

Freud, Sigmund, 'Remembering, Repeating and Working-Through', *The Standard Edition of the Complete Psychological Works of Sigmund Freud* (London: Vintage, 2001), vol. 12, pp. 147–56.

Goldensohn, Lorrie, 'Approaching Elizabeth Bishop's Letters to Ruth Foster', *The Yale Review* 103.1 (January 2015): 1–19.

Guex, Germaine, *The Abandonment Neurosis* [1950], trans. Peter D. Douglas (London: Karnac Books, 2015).

Heaney, Seamus, *The Government of the Tongue* (London: Faber and Faber, 1998).

Irigaray, Luce, 'Flesh Colours', in *Sexes and Genealogies*, trans. Gillian C. Gill (New York: Columbia University Press, 1993), pp. 151–65.

Kalstone, David, *Becoming a Poet: Elizabeth Bishop with Marianne Moore and Robert Lowell* (New York: Farrar, Straus and Giroux, 1989).

Marshall, Megan, *Elizabeth Bishop: A Miracle for Breakfast* (New York: Houghton Mifflin Harcourt, 2017).

Phillips, Adam, 'Against Self-Criticism', *London Review of Books*, 5 March 2015, pp. 13–16.

Rewald, John, *The History of Impressionism* (New York: Museum of Modern Art, 1946).

Rose, Jacqueline, '"Faking It Up with the Truth": Anne Sexton', in *On Not Being Able to Sleep: Psychoanalysis and the Modern World* (London: Chatto & Windus, 2003), pp. 17–24.

Schwartz, Lloyd, and Sybil P. Estess (eds), *Elizabeth Bishop and Her Art* (Ann Arbor: University of Michigan Press, 1983).

Stewart, Susan, *Poetry and the Fate of the Senses* (Chicago: University of Chicago Press, 2002).

Treseler, Heather, 'Dreaming in Colour: Bishop's Notebook Letter-Poems', in Angus Cleghorn, Bethany Hicok and Thomas Travisano (eds), *Elizabeth Bishop in the Twenty-First Century: Reading the New Editions* (Charlottesville: University of Virginia Press, 2012), pp. 88–103.

Wehr, Wesley, 'Elizabeth Bishop: Conversations and Class Notes', in George Monteiro (ed.), *Conversations with Elizabeth Bishop* (Jackson: University Press of Mississippi, 1996), pp. 38–46.

2

'Manuelzinho', Brazil and Identity Politics

Vidyan Ravinthiran

[*Brazil. A friend of the writer is speaking.*][1]

THE EPIGRAPH TO 'MANUELZINHO' has a lot of work to do. It states where the poem is set, and that it's a dramatic monologue; 'is speaking' emphasises the form, suggesting Bishop's talent for capturing in her verse the minutest spoken inflections, and the intimacy that adjoins. But who really is speaking? A 'friend of the writer' is rather vague, and a half-truth, for Bishop's letters reveal the voice as that of Lota Soares – who was, of course, far more than a 'friend'. Bethany Hicok puts it beautifully: 'when the Brazilian aristocrat Lota de Macedo Soares offered her a home in Brazil, Bishop opened herself up to a person and a place in a way that she had never done before' (1). The person and the place were intertwined: Bishop's relationship with Lota is relevant to the controversial politics of this poem, its portrait of the snobbery of the upper-middle-class Brazilian landowner towards her farmer-tenant. For when we love someone (as Bishop loved Soares), especially someone from another background, we enter into their prejudices, and their vulnerabilities, often more deeply than we would wish. And then there's the question of to what extent we may enter into, and responsibly evaluate, the culture which gave them life, and which is their gift to us.

In a letter of 19 October 1967 to U. T. and Joseph Summers, Bishop confirms Lota as the speaker of the poem, in defending the poem against its critics:

> I wonder who the reviewer was who misunderstood 'Manuelzinho' so – but then I've been accused of that kind of thing a lot, particularly in the social-conscious days – 'Cootchie,' etc., were found 'condescending,' or I lived in a world (I was obviously VERY RICH) where people had Servants, imagine, and so on. Actually, Brazilians like 'Manuelzinho' very much. I've had several English-reading friends tell me, 'My God (or Our Lady), it's *exactly* like that.' And that's why Lota is supposed to be saying it . . . (*One Art* 479)

The poem has, writes Barbara Page, 'drawn the fire of some American and Brazilian readers for what they see as insensitivity to Manuelzinho's painful social and economic condition'; she cites Charles Tomlinson's review of *Questions of Travel*, in which he remarks that 'the better off have always preferred their poor processed by style'; also Frank Bidart, who identifies within the poem a 'whiff of noblesse oblige' (131). Bishop's letter on the subject is remarkable in its close resemblance to the poem it discusses, and would clear the air about. When she says that her Brazilian 'friends' aren't offended, that they like the poem – 'Friends of Lota's upper-class social set, that is,' comments Page – Bishop defensively invokes the same relationship, of writer to 'friend', mentioned in the epigraph to 'Manuelzinho'.

In the poem, the voice of the 'friend' is acknowledged as separating the 'writer' from the views expressed in the poem. In the letter, to have Brazilian friends is to know something true about Brazil, and (Bishop insists) to have one's views of it validated, in a way poetry reviewers can't appreciate. Her epistolary prose grows rushed, hectic, defensive. It doesn't quite achieve the airiness, the aloofness from such supposedly petty complaints, for which it aims; there remains something anxious in how she combines criticism of this poem about a poor Brazilian tenant-gardener with the response to her previous verse about African Americans. Indeed, Bishop's rhetoric is familiar, for those given to coat-trailing remarks often evoke, to deflect the objections of the 'social-conscious', a conveniently citable friend of the relevant gender, nationality, race or sexual orientation, who happens to find their joke amusing.

Bishop likes the word 'exactly', which may style a verse-perception as an experience to be shared. In 'A Cold Spring', for instance, she writes that fireflies rise 'exactly like the bubbles in champagne', and there is the feeling, as always with her similes of this kind, of both an aesthetic judgement and a joyous pointing-out (*Poems* 56). Fireflies are important to 'Manuelzinho', too, for there is, as we'll see, a crucial moment in that poem where an observation about fireflies *cannot* be shared. Yet, to stick with the word 'exactly': the problem with Bishop's defence of the poem in terms of its documentary precision – the truth of it, attested to by her Brazilian friends – is that 'Manuelzinho' is not a straightforwardly descriptive poem. It's a dramatic monologue in which not just one but two sensibilities are analysed; thronged with nuancing possible ironies, it has, so to speak, a picture of both a poor farmer and a rich Brazilian landowner inside it. Whose side the poem is on is unclear, and its chosen form reveals a scepticism as to the feasibility of moral position-taking.

In saying this, I diverge from Hicok's finely informed reading of this poem in her book *Elizabeth Bishop's Brazil* – which I remain indebted to. There she writes that

> In Bishop's poem, Manuelzinho is as much a part of the landscape as are the house, the mountains, the fog, as he appears in rain and 'twined in wisps of fog'. There is no indication that Bishop is making a judgment about this class arrangement that makes possible their life on the mountain; the poem is effective, not for its critical judgment, but in its faithful rendering of this particular relationship. (28)

Bishop is well known as a careful describer – of nature, cities, other people. But in this chapter I hope to argue, with the help of Hicok and others who know more about Brazil than I do, that 'Manuelzinho' is not simply a valuably exact record of Brazilian class-relations. As I see it, when the description of Manuelzinho and his family becomes elemental and mysterious, this is in fact Bishop's way of insisting on a charged distance between him and the speaker which might yet be crossed, and which parallels that between the non-Brazilian 'writer' and her 'friend'. That's to say, the sympathetic interval between Bishop and Lota is as relevant to 'Manuelzinho' as that which exists between the speaker and the man who lives on what she considers her land. Rather than seeing the poem as refraining from 'critical judgement', I think it engages at various points with the problem of making judgements about others – who may be of our culture, or another – in a style which challenges, rather than confirms, the assumptions of our own 'social-conscious' times. 'Manuelzinho' does this in a gradual, unresolved, moment-to-moment way – through, that is, its poetic *form* – which means it also challenges the existing division in literary criticism between political analysis and close reading.

These complexities emit an incoherence in Bishop's letter. Take that strange hinge: 'And that's why Lota is supposed to be saying it.' 'And that's why' builds a creaking bridge between the comments of Brazilian readers and the poem's status as a dramatic monologue with a Brazilian speaker. 'Lota is supposed to be saying it' describes a tonally various poem of shifting perspective as if it were a single statement – that offensive joke, perhaps, which Bishop appears to be apologising for. Returning to the epigraph – '*Brazil. A friend of the writer is speaking*' – it's possible to read it as a pre-emptive apology, the writer's insurance against the accusation of being, as Bishop has it in her letter, 'condescending'. But it also announces quite clearly that what's important is, perhaps, less what the friend 'says' than the way in which she 'speaks'. She 'is speaking', but not to the writer mentioned; she seems to be speaking to Manuelzinho, a silent auditor, but in fact this remains one half of a fantasized (blocked, impossible-seeming) conversation which is yet to take place. In the dramatic monologue, says Robert Langbaum, there is always a 'tension between sympathy and moral judgment' (85). So Bishop's attempt to remove her poem from the realm of ethics is disingenuous, for such is the element this modern verse form, keyed to a relativistic morality, lives and breathes. Her letter is a response to an accusation; her poem is one in which the speaker accuses Manuelzinho, and also a poem whose form accuses that speaker herself.

There's also a parallel to be drawn between Bishop's letter, with its rapid inadequate conflation of separate injustices, and the beginning of the poem:

> Half squatter, half tenant (no rent) –
> a sort of inheritance; white,
> in your thirties now, and supposed
> to supply me with vegetables,
> but you don't; or you won't; or you can't
> get the idea through your brain –
> the world's worst gardener since Cain.

The first two lines speed through the relevant details of land possession, wealth and race in a manner reminiscent of Bishop's letter. The speaker signals her awareness of the hard, determining realities of Manuelzinho's existence, with the haste of someone impatiently trying to unknot the problem – or push these facts to one side. Hicok gives the set-up at the house in Samambaia: 'For all intents and purposes, Macedo Soares was the paternalistic Brazilian landowner, the *patroa* (*patrão* is the male version of the term).' She quotes the historian Thomas Skidmore, who explains this hierarchy as a residue of colonialism, and specifies how 'the culture inculcates a sense of intimacy along with a sense of distance, thus allowing the elite to dominate society with little fear of challenge'. This faltering and ever-renewed intimacy, unclear where kindness fades into obligation, gives 'Manuelzinho' its distinct flavour. The poem concerns (Hicok draws on Bishop's letters, and the account of Mary Morse)

> Manuelzinho Alves's family whose 'little hut' had been on the land before Lota developed it, one of the many 'poor people in little houses around who would take animals and vegetables to the fair to sell,' according to Morse. But Manuelzinho was a favourite. As Morse noted, 'Lota liked him as a person, so she let him stay on a piece of land right near her house. He didn't work for Lota. He worked for himself, and he was just on a piece of her land, hoping he wouldn't be put off.' As a squatter, he and his family had a tenuous hold on the land they occupied, and Bishop captures this precarious existence in poems about them, including 'Manuelzinho,' 'Squatter's Children,' and the unpublished drafts of 'Gypsophilia.'[2]

The undecidability of Lota and Manuelzinho's relationship is crucial from the start. It bespeaks a power-dynamic occluded by a condescending favouritism that maintains, it doesn't undermine, the status quo. But it's also this undecidability, infuriating to the speaker of the poem, which the 'writer', that is, Bishop, takes as her subject. It allows the question to be posed of what one person – a Brazilian – morally owes to another.

In separating the 'writer' from the 'friend' who monologues, I follow the language of the epigraph, and differ from Hicok's characterisation of the speaker as 'a sort of fusion of poet and *patroa*' (27). In a poem concerned with socio-cultural differences which may become impermeable, such a 'fusion' is not to be taken for granted. We see this when we begin to conceive of the poem as an attempt to think through the problem, and as evincing from line to line alternative impulses. Returning to the start, I'd observe, for instance, how the word 'supposed' is curiously underlined, not only by the speech-sound captured by the verse, but also by the enjambment. The question here is whether the speaker of the poem is also in control of its form. Does the emphasis placed on the word 'supposed' by the speaker's irritation correspond to what is communicated to the reader by the attention-drawing line break? We could say the same of the line 'but you don't; or you won't; or you can't', whose lineation summarises neatly two commonplace attitudes towards the poor. Do they have little because they're lazy, because they 'don't' or 'won't' act to improve their lot, or because the structure of society actually means that they 'can't' improve their condition? The sentence continues, altering the value of 'can't', but the previous reading persists, held in suspension by the line break. So it could be that Bishop's line breaks are designed to ironise her speaker, as is standard in dramatic monologues of the type Langbaum describes. The speaker may 'suppose' Manuelzinho to have any number of duties towards her, but the poem isn't as sure; there is again a parallel with Bishop's letter: 'And that's why Lota is *supposed* to be saying it.' The letter anxiously reinhabits the language of the poem; it's a sharer in its anxieties about the possibility, and appropriateness, of hitherto unimagined, or only partially imagined, relationships.

At this point it's worth considering that 'Manuelzinho' is a poem which has become more, not less, controversial with time. Bishop was not an impoverished Brazilian tenant-farmer, and for this reason, one school of thought would have it that she could not possibly write an adequate poem on this subject. The landowner is presumably speaking to Manuelzinho in the Portuguese he would understand (if he could hear her, and respond) but the poem is in English, even though the 'writer' mentioned in the epigraph never identifies herself as, also, a translator; there are, indeed, no foreign words in the poem, a contrast with others Bishop wrote about Brazil. All of this connects with Cary Nelson and Stephen Watt's description of 'Manuelzinho' as an instance of a 'major poet writing in what would now be a politically unacceptable way. The poem violates so many contemporary taboos that it is almost unthinkable from a late twentieth century perspective' (172). Through analysis of the verse, I'm trying to show that the poem isn't collusive with oppression, but critical of it. Yet even this reading must press back against the perspective Nelson and Watt outline, in that I continue to view the depiction of the speaker's snobbery as artistically worthwhile, and meaningfully expressive of both quite specifically Brazilian failures of communication, and more abstractly human ones – which should be acknowledged and understood, rather than exiled from artistic representation.

If Bishop is using poetic form not to confirm the speaker's judgement of Manuelzinho, but to judge, and find wanting, the speaker herself, then this would itself appear to trouble contemporary attitudes, for it means that a relatively privileged US poet is daring to critique Brazilian society. Hicok observes that Bishop, 'like Lota [. . .] felt that the poor in Brazil really didn't know how to look after their children', and the speaker of 'Manuelzinho' is particularly aggrieved by the behaviour of his offspring, who hide 'behind bushes / as if I were out to shoot them! / – Impossible to make friends, / though each will grab at once / for an orange or a piece of candy'. The *patroa* laments the rapaciousness of the ill-bred poor, who reject her friendship. In 'Squatter's Children', however, Hicok suggests that Bishop is able to feel her way into their condition:

> These children are, in a sense, homeless, a condition that was deeply resonant with Bishop's own experience and one she explored even as she herself was finding a real home for the first time in her life. 'Squatter's Children' seems to tap into some deep seam of Bishop's own childhood experience and demonstrates her real compassion for the disenfranchised children of Brazil. (31)

Is it only through shared experience that one can truly understand another person? This goes right to the heart of today's social politics, and our assumption that if the more privileged person claims to feel, in the moment, what the less privileged does, then this must be a self-serving gesture, an arrogant seizure of a grievance-authority not rightly theirs. (The irony is that, in literature, this position may harm rather than help, since if the burden of representation is placed entirely upon the disenfranchised, this nullifies their intellectual freedom. The white middle-class man gets to write poems; the rest of us provide photographs of ourselves, in postures of empowerment.) Yet, as Jonathan Ellis tells us, Bishop set for her Harvard students an exam question on Shelley's 'Defence of Poetry', where he says 'The great secret of morals is love; or a going out of our own nature, and an identification of ourselves with the beautiful which exists in thought, action, or person, not our own' (119). She felt that such a movement outside the confines of one's own experience was possible, if arduous. This isn't an outmoded, sentimental, culturally unspecific universalism – it is, instead, that her verse is as sceptical as Shelley's of the very concept of secure individual identity.

'Manuelzinho' is therefore a poem which does not coincide with but challenges twenty-first-century identity politics. Bishop lived a long time in Brazil, and she loved, deeply, a Brazilian woman; this poem is written, she claims, in that woman's voice – a voice which, by the monologue's end, rounds on its own clamped spite and would do better:

> You helpless, foolish man,
> I love you all I can,
> I think. Or do I?
> I take off my hat, unpainted
> and figurative, to you.
> Again I promise to try.

'I promise to try' is at a double remove from actual doing and social transformation. The speaker has already tried and failed, and is unsure of her feelings towards Manuelzinho; she is, however, at least periodically sure – the ending of the poem, with its strong image and rhyme, has that certainty – of her moral duty towards him.

The 'hat' is a reference to Manuelzinho's own straw hat, whose crown and brim he paints (aggravatingly inexplicably, in the speaker's eyes) and which appears to be the same 'holey hat' which earlier in the poem flies off his head, as in a cartoon, when she yells at him. Headwear is meaningful in this poem, for Manuelzinho's father, when he dies, is described as 'a superior old man / with a black plush hat'; the man himself also wears a burlap bag over his head for protection, as his children wear blue sugar bags.[3] These various hats or pseudo-hats depict practices which emerge from bare utility (the sugar bags) and become markers of identity. The speaker of the poem feels excluded by their arbitrariness. In the uncollected poem 'Exchanging Hats', Bishop imagines that playful activity as a liberation from constricting views of gender and sexuality:

> Unfunny uncles who insist
> in trying on a lady's hat,
> – oh, even if the joke falls flat,
> we share your slight transvestite twist
>
> in spite of our embarrassment.
> Costume and custom are complex.[4]

This poem contains a view of identity as fluid and happily up for grabs. Today, this perspective coexists alongside a notion of rooted authenticity which, as David Bromwich has recently observed, sits oddly, in its 'blood-and-soil' intimations, with the values of the left (60). This is the story about ourselves he classifies as 'culturalism', identifying an unexamined contradiction between liberal thought and the identity politics it has fused with: 'the thesis that there is a universal human need to belong to a culture – to belong, that is, to a self-conscious group with a known history, a group that by preserving and transmitting its customs, memories and common practices confers the primary pigment of individual identity on the persons it comprehends' (41).

Championing the 'moral imagination', which allows for the possibility of understanding others in a more than tokenistic way, Bromwich is sceptical of a politics that would unquestioningly affirm the authenticity, rather than examine the cultural engineering, of the boundaries drawn between person and person by alternative upbringings. Touching on the quotation from Shelley which Bishop set as an essay question, he observes that

> One remarkable thing about this definition is its refusal to confine the object of identification to a person; we may equally sympathize with an action or a thought: an extension and decomposition of the idea of sympathy that seems consistent with Shelley's most original poetry. But notice that on his view – which Shelley derived from Wordsworth's early poems and the Preface to *Lyrical Ballads* – the more unlikely or remote the path of sympathy, the surer the proof of moral imagination. Thus, to sympathize with someone like myself is commendable, perhaps, but it shows nothing much. It is a plausible extension of the future-regarding aspect of ordinary egotism [. . .] But to feel with the mother who has lost her idiot boy, or, as in *Frankenstein*, with a monstrous creature who must learn humanity from people even as he finds that people turn away in horror and disgust – these are truer tests of a 'going out of our nature'. (12)

We should question a supposed open-mindedness incapable of moving decisively beyond disguised self-admiration; incapable of more than a condescending appreciation – this isn't a paradox – of the intricacies of other cultures, which it claims to love for their historical particularity, but in a way which becomes touristic and commercial all too readily, and which encompasses no re-evaluation of itself. The speaker of 'Manuelzinho' is intolerant of the farmer she has power over, but by the end of the poem she is forced to the point of calling her own beliefs into question – she isn't self-satisfied. Her experience of defensive hostility, and her recognition of this feeling, is important, for it places within the poem a genuinely self-questioning perspective. Bishop's experience of life outside of the US; her travels, which do bespeak an abiding homelessness, a deeply suffered lack, but also a more than surface affection for alternative societies, which that absence of the culturalist bond makes possible; all of this makes her a savvy observer of power-relations, and a resister of hierarchical assumptions. An abiding sense of herself as out of place, ill at ease, existing slightly to one side of things, separated from the people around her – this is a self-consciousness which Bishop transforms in her poetry into a critical stance. But it also places her at a remove, though we may try to deny it, from the assumptions of our day. Bishop steps outside of Anglo-American culture and expresses admiration for other places; her eye isn't domineering, it acknowledges, in 'Brazil, January 1, 1502', for example, the realities of colonialism, and how she herself is implicated. But her verse also places cultures we are afraid to criticise, to claim to speak authoritatively about, under scrutiny; 'Manuelzinho' is one such poem. It records in its very form and texture the unachieved and continual work of the moral imagination.

Returning to Manuelzinho and his hat with this in mind, we might see the speaker's frustration as a real, if prickly, engagement with the complexities of 'costume and custom'. The poem captures that shudder of tangible alienation which may accompany an encounter with someone different, and which some would hastily deny rather than conscientiously analyse:

> You paint – heaven knows why –
> the outside of the crown
> and brim of your straw hat.

Perhaps to reflect the sun?
Or perhaps when you were small,
your mother said: 'Manuelzinho,
one thing: be sure you always
paint your straw hat.'
One was gold for a while,
but the gold wore off, like plate.
One was bright green. Unkindly,
I called you Klorophyll Kid.
My visitors thought it was funny.
I apologize here and now.

The speaker is a snob, but a self-recognising one, whose feigned curiosity (a rhetoric
of mocking bafflement) turns gradually genuine. Her attempts at explaining Manuel-
zinho's behaviour take place within a conversation we're still having, in the twenty-
first century, across cultures and about them. (The remark attributed to his mother
recalls another poem from *Questions of Travel*, 'Manners': 'My grandfather said to
me / as we sat on the wagon seat, / 'Be sure to remember to always / speak to everyone
you meet'; *Poems* 119.) To repeat: we might ask whether an ostentatious cherishing
of artefacts from another heritage, or a different class – Manuelzinho's hat removed,
say, from its living context and framed on a wall for bohemian approval – would
truly be morally preferable to the conflict revealed here within the speaker. The gold
hat would seem to be his way of giving himself a real, kingly 'crown' – or a halo.
The syntax, delayed by the interjection 'heaven knows why' and the line break, sug-
gests (briefly, again) that he really *paints*, is creative like one of the primitive painters
Bishop loved, and whose tender and vulnerable art she evokes and immortalises in
her essay about Gregorio Valdes. (Manuelzinho's bonkers gardening – 'You edge /
the beds of silver cabbages / with red carnations, and lettuces / mix with alyssum'
– expresses another creative departure from common sense, as well as a disturbing
mixture of one plant with another that travesties the social and psychological parti-
tion between *patroa* and squatter.)

    One wonders, again, if we're seeing contradictions in the mentality of the speaker,
or Bishop's use of the dramatic monologue as a form of social critique through con-
sistent irony. Certainly the speaker experiences conflicting impulses, and is aware
of their alternation – she feels one way towards Manuelzinho, then another – but
the reach of her self-doubt and self-criticism is debatable. Bishop's letter reveals her
own uncertainty, a good deal, really, of inexpungible class guilt. If, as I've suggested,
she appears to defend the poem as a single compromised utterance (as one usually
defends a scandalous remark, or joke), then this is the moment in the poem when
that offensive joke appears. The speaker disparages Manuelzinho in his green hat
as if he were a poorly dressed cowboy; intriguingly, unlike Bishop in her letter, she
doesn't think that her 'visitors' (who correspond to those Brazilian 'friends') finding
it funny lets her off the hook. Rather, their amusement confirms her unkindness –
she insulted Manuelzinho simply to amuse – and she insists: 'I apologize here and
now.' As this spoken apology is given its place in the poem, and is fixed in writing,
it gains the appearance of a genuine commitment. Yet she also acknowledges only a
few lines later that her impulse to make things right comes and goes; it doesn't last,

and develop into political action. So 'here and now' is less decisive than it seems, and more acknowledging of the speaker's self-consciously inconsistent generosity.

Thomas Travisano reads the poem at least partly as a criticism of the Brazilian gentry, and the inequalities they oversee:

> Bishop observes a poor man with empathy and humour, but she also implicitly presents her observations of leading characteristics of the Brazilian gentry: their paternalism, their puzzlement at the curious ways of their tenants, and, yes, their condescension. Condescension is the implicit but central issue of the poem. Sympathetic but trapped in an outmoded feudal relationship, Manuelzinho's boss is often distrustful. She expresses affection colored by anger – dutiful protectiveness, even admiration, blend with frustration, vexation, and incomprehension, since by necessity Manuelzinho lives a life whose values are totally different from hers [. . .] The narrator consciously brings out the differences. Her own comfortable superiority receives at least as much irony as her tenant's odd ways. Bishop's vantage point makes it clear that Manuelzinho's curious antics are forced upon him as he attempts to maintain his autonomy under compromising circumstances. (146–7)

Travisano's reading is valuable in its insistence on the dramatic monologue; also in its feeling for tone, and how an array of vexed emotions are encompassed. But I think 'implicitly' does rather too much work here, in fixing and ascribing the perhaps undecided motivations of the poem as a larger entity, aligned with Bishop herself; where does this hygienically separate 'vantage point' materialise, which makes clear a politics scandalised readers have never been able to confirm? I've tried to suggest that this perspective emerges in the very form and idioms of the poem at particular points – we sense it, as the line breaks interact with, or deconstruct, the speaker's authority – but it's no more reliably available than the speaker's periodical kindliness towards Manuelzinho.

To return to an earlier point in the poem, lines Travisano quotes to illustrate his argument; and where the relationship is already fraying, and ajar:

> I watch you through the rain,
> trotting, light, on bare feet,
> up the steep paths you have made –
> or your father and grandfather made –
> all over my property,
> with your head and back inside
> a sodden burlap bag,
> and feel I can't endure it
> another minute; then,
> indoors, beside the stove,
> keep on reading a book.

'Manuelzinho' is a firmly if unobtrusively structured poem, and the speaker's surveillance of her tenant here will, as we'll see, be matched by an equal scrutiny later on. What is it she feels, briefly, she can't 'endure'? There are the visible evidences of his poverty: the bare feet in the rain, the sodden burlap bag. A long sentence evokes a complex experience: what she sees, and as a result feels, but then fails to remedy. An awareness of her own contrasting comfort, and privilege, and also of her complicity in Manuelzinho's degradation. But don't we also sense, in the third, fourth and fifth lines, those conflicting impulses? 'Up the steep paths you have made all over my property' would be straightforwardly accusing. The interjection – 'or your father and grandfather made' – intimates a moment of self-criticism, an awareness that perhaps this really is Manuelzinho's land, and that persisting inequities should be righted. 'All over *my* property' is, then, a recovery on the part of the spiteful person within the speaker. The characterisation of Manuelzinho as 'light' on his feet – the idea, here, that he isn't really suffering, perhaps even the self-pitying suggestion that she, the speaker, is the one pained beyond endurance – is part of her attempt to convince herself. (She no doubt feels she's being charitable, by continuing to 'endure' his presence on her land.) Bishop's is an extraordinarily accurate and technically accomplished evocation of the bristling postures the aggrieved self manages, or stage-manages, in its refusal to come to terms with the other. These attitudes manifest from line to line in a manner true to psychological impulsiveness and caprice. What this shows is that to fully appreciate Bishop as a poet of cultural critique, close reading must come together with historical analysis; we must reject a false distinction between the formal brilliance of this poem and its political content. Instrumental readings of texts in terms of race, class and gender often operate in a totally different realm to that of stylistic analysis, but in this case it's only through reading closely that we understand this poem's inclusion of discomfiting material.

'The other' is an overused term which flattens out many kinds of difference. What I'd stress here is how the controversy around Bishop's poem responds to its courageous acknowledgement of awkwardnesses which those of us on the left self-protectively obscure. The poem insists we spend a good amount of time in the head of a haughty Brazilian landowner – refusing, for instance, the media criterion of 'relatability' by which literature, like other art forms, is increasingly judged. As a result, 'Manuelzinho' has much to say about how distortions of power and class affect relationships more generally, and in Brazil, at the time of writing. Elizabeth Neely is the first scholar to observe the 'backdrop of peasant uprisings in the Northeast in the mid-1950s and the resulting political and legal fights for peasant land possession'; the poem may express the *patroa*'s 'deep-rooted fear of losing her grip on her own property based on the territorial gains squatters and peasants achieved in other locations [. . .] Francisco Julião, a young lawyer and deputy from the Brazilian Socialist Party, was instrumental in creating peasant leagues which provided rights and new power to squatters and peasants in rural Brasil. These organizations alarmed the aristocratic landowning class.'[5]

So the speaker of the poem may be a little afraid of Manuelzinho. We don't see in the poem any threatening behaviour on his part, but this doesn't mean the speaker doesn't feel threatened; self-interest may infiltrate her longing for resolution. Bishop also glosses the phenomenon of phone 'tapping', endemic in the *favelas*. This word refers not, as it's now used, to surveillance activities, but to the hijacking of existing connections:

> You steal my telephone wires,
> or someone does. You starve
> your horse and yourself

and your dogs and family.
Among endless variety,
you eat boiled cabbage stalks.

The accusation dwindles into aimless frustration: the thief could be anyone. It's that moment, common to tirades, when the speaker's pressed to acknowledge that the target of their ire may not be to blame; still, there must be somebody to lash out at, so one's own injury is acknowledged. At this revealing moment, the objectivity of her account is called into question. She recovers her footing – her sense of herself – through the angry iteration of 'you'; 'Manuelzinho' is a poem whose interplay of personal pronouns generates a deeply sophisticated analysis of Brazilian class-relations. 'You starve' alliterates with 'you steal'; the speaker tries to make sense of the situation, as if she were building a watertight case against Manuelzinho. (Those 'boiled cabbage 'stalks' will arrive to clinch the argument.) Yet, once again, Bishop's line breaks cultivate ambiguity. The visual pause on 'starve' initially suggests an intransitive verb – Manuelzinho is himself at risk of starvation; as the sentence continues, the speaker insists he's responsible for his own situation. This is precisely the move made by those furious at the poor simply for being poor, who seek to resolve this feeling, which could mature into an awareness of injustice, and a commitment to change, by, instead, blaming the victim for their condition.

The imagery of telephone wires is also important because this is a poem about communication, which Bishop once described to Randall Jarrell as 'an undependable but sometimes marvelous thing' (*One Art* 312). Wires occur throughout Bishop's published and unpublished writing, as in 'Electrical Storm', which also appears in *Questions of Travel* and gives to Bishop's relationship with Soares an outline both tender and touching:

We got up to find the wiring fused,
no lights, a smell of saltpetre,
and the telephone dead. (*Poems* 98)

The lovers are cut off, and will not communicate – perhaps even with each other. Here is that undependability essential to communication (which is always an achievement, always endangered), which also concerns Bishop in 'Manuelzinho', as that poem deftly tracks the speaker's anxious to-and-fro movement with relation to her tenant. Ultimately she would like to communicate with him, but within the time frame of the poem she fails to. There is also, as Bishop's letter demonstrates, the possibility of a failure of communication between poem and reader – the reviews show this – expressive of a cultural moment we share. The poem continues to provoke; we might consider here that genuine communication *must* be undependable. It must risk misunderstanding, blockage, delay. These phenomena are included in Bishop's poem, but, we might ask, how rawly? Is 'Manuelzinho' a controlled masterpiece in which the poet analyses the interaction of Brazilian snobbery with an impending social conscience, using the form of the dramatic monologue to maintain a distancing irony; or is it a poem in which Bishop's own feelings are revealed, and the speaker's emotional inconsistencies are so believable because they aren't simulated, but turbulently experienced? The scandal of the poem has to do with the distance between the 'writer' and the 'friend' who is speaking – a distance which might seem to break down, given its spoken intimacy, how Bishop so thoroughly inhabits the monologue, which is given life by verse-features, habits of noticing and description, that we associate with her work more generally. It's at this point, where we witness Bishop judging one type of Brazilian for judging another type of Brazilian, that we might see 'Manuelzinho' as pinpointing a doubt, a flimsy place, in our understanding of other cultures; how the Anglo-American imagination has sought reinforcement through a self-regarding approval of the strangeness and colour of other people living in other ways, rather than genuinely considering, following such encounters, if we or they should live differently.

This is part of Bishop's long-standing investigation as to where nature intersects with culture; if we see her verse as miming the tangents of perception, feeling and thought, we should understand it not as a vehicle for delivering pre-fabricated conclusions, but as a way of continually revisiting, and thinking about, politics. Hicok's reading sees Manuelzinho as merged with his surroundings, so he becomes part of nature and not a separate person; as I've mentioned, I see the ethereal imagery in this section of the poem as outlining, rather, a space of possible unrealised communication. Here the speaker contemplates not just the man but his whole family:

> Twined in wisps of fog,
> I see you all up there
> along with Formoso, the donkey,
> who brays like a pump gone dry,
> then suddenly stops.
> – All just standing, staring
> off into fog and space.
> Or coming down at night,
> in silence, except for hoofs,
> in dim moonlight, the horse
> or Formoso stumbling after.
> Between us float a few
> big, soft, pale-blue,
> sluggish fireflies,
> the jellyfish of the air . . .

The phrase 'I see you all up there' suggests both a real and an imagined landscape, present to the mind's eye more than the literal eye; the fogginess and dimness also intimate murky imaginings, instead of a clarity of recall. 'I see you all up there' may be read in different ways; in a curmudgeonly, monitory voice, for instance – the speaker, aware of those peasant rebellions, warns Manuelzinho that she can see what he and his family are up to. Once again, this is to isolate a line of verse which traces a particular tonal arc – to lift it out of a longer sentence more descriptive than confrontational. Bishop uses the dramatic monologue to explore how one emotion may hide, or slide into, another, more self-doubting or more hostile or more virtuous; also, how the generosity we manage towards other people may contain within it suppressed, or admirably transformed, vectors of ill feeling. She refuses to separate her politics from an understanding of how human beings truly operate, in tandem with inequalities hard to acknowledge – and if we, today, find her poem tough to align with our proprieties, we should experience this as a challenge rather than a reason to declare her old-hat and unenlightened. That is to say, twenty-first-century readers are pressed by this poem (as its speaker is, by the presence of Manuelzinho) to examine their own lives, rather than defensively condemn what's different.

There are indeed devices in this passage which we remember from Bishop's other poems (and which move her speaker dangerously close, for the 'social-conscious' reader embarrassed by this poem, to the writer herself). One is the use of the word 'suddenly'. Bishop is remarkable as a poet for how she takes this hackneyed word, which really belongs in lesser fiction and poems which too reliably aspire to epiphany, and nuances it. In 'At the Fishhouses', 'In the Waiting Room' and 'The Moose', it characterises encounters (with a seal, her aunt's cry, the moose itself) troubling of the speaker's identity, which is confirmed as relational – just as here, in 'Manuelzinho'. Also characteristic is the manner in which Bishop combines super-accurate description with a dream dimension. The impulse to specify – the rhyme, for example, on 'few' and 'pale-blue' – becomes, paradoxically, how she leads us beyond the empirically available, the literally verifiable; in this case, the present cultural impasse. Presenting an imagined landscape in high definition is how the speaker tries to picture her relationship with Manuelzinho; how she apologises, perhaps, for her inability to make contact.

Unlike her friend and influencer Robert Lowell, Bishop uses ellipses sparingly, weightily. So while the dots here might, say, cleverly resemble the fireflies floating through the air, their function as a grammar of moral implication is more important. The device arrives to insist on the mysteriousness, the unpredictability, of relationships; it's another brushstroke comprising a landscape particularly Brazilian – both exotic (is this really the speaker addressing Manuelzinho, or Bishop writing for the US reader?) and wearily known already. I mentioned earlier the firefly simile in 'A Cold Spring'. In that poem, dedicated to Bishop's friend Jane Dewey, and set on her property, the observation about fireflies initiates a moment of shared understanding. In this poem, the speaker's remarkable observation will never reach her auditor; in a real and disturbing sense, this isn't a poem written *to* Manuelzinho. The speaker talks to him, or the idea of him, but in a language of unshareable exquisiteness; the description carries her not towards but away from him, for really she is identifying and seeking to analyse a threatening situation. It's not the shape and size but the movement of the fireflies which makes them like jellyfish (or slugs), turning the foggy air to water itself, awkward to wade, to swim-walk, through, given the resistance; and of course jellyfish can be poisonous, so you wouldn't want to enter that water. We see how disturbing it is to the speaker of the poem to even think about crossing the distance which separates her from Manuelzinho and his family.

That the atmosphere created by these lines has a deeper significance is confirmed by the many details shared with 'Gypsophilia', Bishop's unpublished third poem about Manuelzinho and his family. It begins with more light-effects and spooky animal noises:

> I like the few sad noises
> left over in this smokey sunset.
> That idiot dog! – He barks in *oblique* barks,
> chop-chopping at the mountains with a hatchet.

> (*Poems, Prose, and Letters* 245)

As in 'Manuelzinho', Bishop is concerned with the 'air' itself, transformed not only by the dying of the day but also by an alien presence – mysterious, threatening (notice, also, the reappearance of the farmer's hat):

> Up here the air is thinner:
> it's daylight still. And then the blue
> deteriorates all at once. We're in
> some dark sub-stratum of dew.
> *Dinner.*
> A child's voice rises, harsh and thin.
>
> Manuelzinho's family: Jovelina,
> Nelson, Nina
> Jovelina bears   bends
> a load of dead branches
> her hair hangs down under her husband's old felt hat
> a figure like a young witch's –
> at a half-trot (246)

As in 'Manuelzinho', 'blue' provides a structuring rhyme, but here the commitment to further rhymes paralyses. 'Deteriorates' is a strange word – is Bishop thinking of a *relationship* deteriorating? – chosen for the paradox it presents, of a process happening 'all at once'. The visual situation resembles that of 'Manuelzinho'; as the collective pronoun placing the speaker (and Lota?) inside the scene – 'We're in' – is rejected by the 'child's voice' rising, 'harsh and thin', the same disconnection is expressed between Bishop and the tenant-farmer's family. Manuelzinho's wife 'bears' – perhaps she will have more children – and 'bends' menially under 'a load of dead branches'. It's a compelling image, but the verse splinters. Once again, a hat of Manuelzinho's provides an enlivening instance of his idiosyncrasy, but the casting of his wife as a 'young witch' doesn't know how whimsical or ominous it wants to be. The opacities which the other poem gives voice to in layered verse lead, here, to poetic breakdown. Bishop isn't writing a dramatic monologue, and so cannot approach the encounter through a mediating persona. This failed poem provides a fuller sense of what 'Manuelzinho' achieves – the social and political obstructions it depicts, discovers and analyses from an implicated perspective, whose lived reality is confirmed by Bishop's harassed response to its reviewers. Its double-minded structure sympathetically critiques Brazil, human psychology more generally, and, given the mutations in our politics of identity, has become a provocation to which the truly 'social-conscious' twenty-first-century reader must respond.

Notes

1. All quotations from 'Manuelzinho' are taken from the centenary edition of Bishop's *Poems* (New York: Farrar, Straus and Giroux, 2011). The poem runs from page 94 to page 97.
2. I draw for this block quotation and the material above it from pages 17 and 26 of *Elizabeth Bishop's Brazil*. The Skidmore quotation is from *Brazil: Five Centuries of Change*, p. xiii.

3. I owe much of what I make of hats in Bishop to my undergraduate students of 2015–16, who drew this out in a seminar discussion.
4. *Poems* 230. A discussion of headwear and cultural beliefs in Bishop would also include 'Over 2,000 Illustrations and a Complete Concordance', in which the Arab guide, Khadour, stands amused in his 'smart burnoose' while the speaker of the poem struggles with the religious aura hanging around an ancient grave (58).
5. I quote here from a paper Neely delivered at an ALA conference in 2014, and which she kindly shared with me. I'm very grateful to her, and also Neil Besner, for enriching my argument with a good deal of information about Brazil and the references to its socio-politics secreted within 'Manuelzinho'. I must also thank Maria Lúcia Milléo Martins and Regina Przybycien for responding to my queries, and note that the argument advanced here with the help of Neely's paper is not one which all these scholars of Bishop and Brazil accept.

Works Cited

Bishop, Elizabeth, *One Art: The Selected Letters*, ed. Robert Giroux (London: Chatto & Windus, 1994).

Bishop, Elizabeth, *Poems, Prose, and Letters*, ed. Robert Giroux and Lloyd Schwartz (New York: Library of America, 2008).

Bromwich, David, *Moral Imagination: Essays* (Princeton and Oxford: Princeton University Press, 2014).

Ellis, Jonathan, *Art and Memory in the Work of Elizabeth Bishop* (Aldershot: Ashgate, 2006).

Hicok, Bethany, *Elizabeth Bishop's Brazil* (Charlottesville: University of Virginia Press, 2016).

Langbaum, Robert, *The Poetry of Experience: The Dramatic Monologue in Modern Literary Tradition* (New York: W. W. Norton & Company, 1957).

Nelson, Cary, and Stephen Watt, *Office Hours: Activism and Change in the Academy* (New York: Routledge, 2004).

Page, Barbara, 'Home, Wherever That May Be: Poems and Prose of Brazil', in Angus Cleghorn and Jonathan Ellis (eds), *The Cambridge Companion to Elizabeth Bishop* (Cambridge: Cambridge University Press, 2014), pp. 124–40.

Skidmore, Thomas, *Brazil: Five Centuries of Change* (New York: Oxford University Press, 1999).

Travisano, Thomas, *Elizabeth Bishop: Her Artistic Development* (Charlottesville: University Press of Virginia, 1988).

3

ELIZABETH BISHOP'S IMMERSION IN 'THE RIVERMAN'

Melissa Zeiger

IN THIS CHAPTER I shall consider Elizabeth Bishop's poem 'The Riverman' as a work in which travel, both literal and figurative – in particular Bishop's Brazilian relocation – prompts her to articulate a new poetics that at once distinguishes her from her former poetic self and allows her to create new forms of relation to powerful predecessors and interlocutors. I will argue that Bishop's move to Brazil means a new relation to poetry, one based in a new sense of her poetic powers and at the same time a willingness to explore new poetic modes. Her recent arrival at the time of writing this poem gives her access to a new experimental energy, new sources of imagery, and the liminal position from which so much of her best poetry proceeds, what she describes in the late poem 'Santarém' as the desire 'to stay awhile / in that conflux of two great rivers'.[1]

Through a shamanic figure, the riverman of the title, Bishop is radically reimagining herself and her poetry as 'other', in an aesthetic of magical realism, wondering what strange poetic worlds and reincarnations are habitable. At the same time, she positions herself within a known literary world that will sustain her even as she sustains and transforms it. In her never-published essay 'Writing poetry is an unnatural act . . .' she refers to her favourite poets as being like 'best friends' (*Prose* 328), their relations characterised by both bonding and separation.

Bishop's riverman is assisted in his shamanic training by Luandinha, a river spirit named by Charles Wagley in his book *Amazon Town* (225), one of the main sources for the poem. In order to achieve power as a great practitioner of magic, he needs various aids to study, among them

> a virgin mirror
> no one's ever looked at,
> that's never looked back at anyone,
> to flash up the spirit's eyes
> and help me to recognize them. (*Poems* 105)

Like the riverman, Bishop needs a new way to look past herself, the mirror not reflecting her or the visible world, but providing entry into another realm (a realm of others) not governed by human or physical laws (as in her beloved *Alice Through the Looking Glass*, and in almost all of the numerous mirrors throughout her poems). The poem recalls Bishop's earlier poetic developments and transformations, but also conceives of a poetics not solely determined by and emanating from her own experience.[2]

Although 'The Riverman' has not always received sustained critical attention, the poem was highly salient in Bishop's contemporary exchanges with Robert Lowell, particularly because of his astute recognition of its importance in her development and her incipient acclimatisation to Brazil. This exchange draws attention to, among other things, the relation of this poem to Bishop's revision of an English tradition of mermaid poetry. The poetic exchange with Lowell points to what is for Bishop the crucial literal and figurative ability to breathe and to the threat of suffocation. Both of these concerns are related for her to questions of poetic freedom and constraint. They mark 'The Riverman' as a poem of ambitious poetic reconceptualisation in which questions of gender and poetic persona are implicated.

For 'The Riverman' is an answer not only to Lowell, but to a history of mermaid poems, and, by extension, the history of literature, that set of resources and obstacles for the female poet. Luandinha, the poem's regal serpent-woman and river goddess, is not the mer-person in this world; she is the underwater host, the mistress of ceremonies, and the teacher. In their otherworldly and potent song – for instance, the star-propelling 'sea-maid's song' of *A Midsummer Night's Dream* – mermaids connote poetry, but they also present figures of seductive malice and narcissistic self-absorption. Even more to the point for 'The Riverman', their speciality is drowning the men who hear their song, while Luandinha does the opposite, allowing men to breathe underwater. Bishop's poem echoes the imagery of the mermaid tradition – perhaps most the green and gold and the moonlit mer-realm of Matthew Arnold's 'The Forsaken Merman', to which Lowell will compare 'The Riverman' (Lombardi 40). Earlier, in 'Pleasure Seas' (1939), Bishop has imagined the waves 'Pistachio green and Mermaid Milk' (*Poems* 279). (She may have been remembering Marianne Moore's approval of the phrase 'the mermaid's pap', by Christopher Smart; see Kalstone 80.) The poem returns as well to many images of sea-life from her earlier poems, particularly 'At the Fishhouses', connecting seal with dolphin, cold water with warm, rocky breasts with suckling river, 'total immersion' with underwater travel (*Poems* 62).

Bishop seems strongly to have cathected this poem, which she alternated between claiming and disowning. She reported that her Brazilian lover Lota disliked the poem, finding it anti-modernist – 'primitive' – in ways that conflicted with Lota's own aspirations for Brazil. Nonetheless, for reasons Bishop never explains, the poem is important to her. While telling Lowell that he need not pretend to like the poem, that she doesn't like it herself, she confesses that she 'couldn't seem to get rid of it'. Although this reaction is the opposite of the one she describes in 'The Fish' – '[a]nd I let the fish go' (*Poems* 43) – both aquatic explorers, the fish and the riverman, exert a hold over the poet that reaches beyond rational consciousness. David Kalstone points out that 'The Fish' 'taps and identifies nonhuman sources of human energies' (87); 'The Riverman' makes this process of derivation explicitly magical. As Eleanor Cook writes,

'The Riverman' is the charm poem par excellence, all the more because the subject itself is charm or enchantment. All the signs are there: moonlit night, magic mirror, compulsion, bodily change, tokens: 'I don't eat fish any more,' 'I look yellow, my wife says,' 'Every moonlit night / I'm to go back again.' (158)

It is a poem of what Thomas Greene calls magic 'fiat' (133), the poet's wish tendered as edict, though no guarantee can be given of its success. Thomas Campion's 'The

Charm', for instance, begins with the spellbinding formula 'Thrice toss these oaken ashes in the air, / Thrice sit thou mute in this enchanted chair' but ends with defeat ('In vain are all the charms I can devise: / She hath an art to break them with her eyes') (Campion 102).

In 'The Riverman', Bishop's masculine protagonist leaves the upper air to travel underwater and learn magic from the river spirits, thereby becoming the amphibious 'riverman' of the title. He is summoned by a dolphin-man, who takes him to the river, where suddenly a door opens in the river, 'groaning a little, with water / bulging above the lintel'; a party is going on, with liquor and cigars, and finally the river goddess, 'a tall, beautiful serpent / in elegant white satin, / with her big eyes green and gold / like the lights on the river steamers – / yes, Luandinha, none other' (*Poems* 104). She enchants or hypnotises him, and he travels underwater with her and her entourage, seeking the river's curative powers. The riverman's underwater travel is marked by freedom and companionship; with speed, ease, pleasure, union with the natural elements. With a group of allies, he pursues his magical goals: 'travelling fast as a wish, / with my magic cloak of fish / swerving as I swerve' (*Poems* 106).

The riverman's account offers a powerful but ambiguous model: he may be insane, and hallucinating these wonderful encounters. He may be an alcoholic, angrily rejecting the alternatives to liquor offered by his wife. Or he may be ill: if he has deluded himself about his ability to thrive underwater, his clammy skin and yellowing complexion may show that rather than achieving a new plane of existence, he is really dying. All of these possibilities echo fears Bishop probably harboured about herself, given her life history and the lives of so many poets of her generation. All potentially disabling for her poetic project, they also represent challenges to be overcome by artistic discipline.

Though she had familiarised herself with Amazonian lore, Bishop had written the poem, unusually for her poems of travel, before ever seeing the Amazon. Victoria Harrison recounts that Bishop told several friends 'that she was drafting a much better Amazon poem. Its inauthenticity bothered her' (157). But later, she is delighted to discover how 'accurate' she had been in 'The Riverman' (Millier 306) about the difference of river dolphins from salt-water ones. Nevertheless, she once again writes about its authenticity in another, different mood: 'When I finally got to the Amazon [in February and March 1960] I found I hadn't been too accurate at all, thank goodness' (Lombardi 41).

Bishop had taken the story of the riverman from the book she excerpts for her epigraph, Charles Wagley's ethnographic study of the small Brazilian village of Ita, *Amazon Town*. As Travisano points out, she uses this book as raw material – for names and rituals – but rejects its ethnographic condescension (Travisano 158). Wagley's epigraph from Arnold J. Toynbee quotes the historian as 'guessing' that his age 'will be remembered [. . .] for its having been the first age since the dawn of civilization [. . .] in which people dared to think it practicable to make the benefits of civilization available for the whole human race' (Wagley vi). The implicit assumptions in Toynbee's sentence belong to an earlier and now discredited way of understanding 'First World' interventions, but his views do not entirely differ from those of the Brazilian elite Lota belonged to, and whose wish to modernise Brazil sometimes expressed itself as anti-primitivism.

Although Wagley quotes Toynbee with apparent approval (the sentence is Wagley's epigraph, after all), his own understanding of Brazil's situation is more complex. He does not view the process of 'enlightenment' as unambiguously benign, warning against 'the danger that Ita will lose its rich cultural traditions in exchange for second-rate participation in modern and industrial society' (Wagley 287). To some degree his record may be part of a wish to counter that loss, at the very least by recording what may disappear. The most useful chapter of *Amazon Town* for Bishop's purposes is called 'From Magic to Science'. Even while Wagley advocates a programme of scientific and cultural improvement initiated by United States intervention, he sympathises with the magical practices he describes, clearly in some way affected by their enchantment (Wagley 215–56). His rich detail, so useful to Bishop, suggests involvement.

One of the magical properties – the crucial property, in fact – that the riverman enjoys under the water is the ability to breathe. He doesn't drown or feel suffocated. He can live in an otherwise fatal medium, a metaphor for the ways Bishop can achieve poetic articulation in contexts – literary, social, psychological – that might otherwise suffocate her. And the river breathes, with purifying agency:

> The river breathes in salt
> and breathes it out again,
> and all is sweetness there
> in the deep, enchanted silt. (*Poems* 106)

Finally, air and water appear in a perfect, breathable fusion: '[t]he smoke rose like mist / through the water, and our breaths / didn't make any bubbles' (*Poems* 104). What might have been fatal becomes a source of life and magic, a storehouse of riches, literal and figurative ('health and money'): 'everything must be there / in that magic mud' (*Poems* 106).

The terror associated with loss of breath permeates Bishop's poetry; we are never far from being reminded in her work that breath is the margin between life and death. In the 'dreamy divagations' of 'The Moose' (*Poems* 192), 'A sharp, indrawn breath / [. . .] / [. . .] means "Life's like that. / We know *it* (also death)."' When the gills of 'The Fish' are 'breathing in / the terrible oxygen', the oxygen holds terror for the fish because it is a source of death instead of life outside the water (Lombardi 38). His breathing mechanism holds terror for Bishop too, 'the frightening gills, fresh and crisp with blood, that can cut so badly' (*Poems* 43). In 'Breakfast Song', she dreads death because she will be in a 'cold, filthy place', without her lover,

> without the easy breath
> and nightlong, limblong warmth
> I've grown accustomed to. (*Poems* 327)

And in *A Cold Spring*'s unhappy love poem 'O Breath', each line is broken by a gap in the text, spaces for breathing when speech is absent but also representing an alienation from the lover. An enigmatic energy manifests itself in these: under the 'loved and celebrated breast' (celebrated throughout poetry, that is, as well as by the speaker) is 'something moving but invisibly, / and with what clamor why restrained / I cannot fathom even a ripple' (*Poems* 77). The 'something' points to the vulnerability of any breathing body.

In a happier fantasy, one that has echoes in 'The Riverman', Bishop writes a letter about a memory from Florida of catching and then dreaming about a beautiful fish, 'metallic' and 'rose color', who in the dream led her to a gathering of other fish:

> He led the way through the water, glancing around at me every now and then with his big eyes to see if I was following. I was swimming easily with scarcely any motion. In his mouth he carried a new, galvanized bucket [. . .] He was taking them a bucket of air [. . .] I looked in – enough water had got in to make the bucket of air a bucket of large bubbles. (Millier 117)

Admittedly, the friendship with the fish has an equivocal quality, since though he is leading her to 'some sort of celebration' (Millier 117), she is on record as a fisher-woman rather than an ideal guest at a fish party. (Unlike the riverman, she has given no indication of giving up eating fish.) But the fish leads her – protectively? – like the Dolphin in 'The Riverman', and welcomes her with the 'big eyes' of Luandinha.

In 'O Breath', a chapter of Marilyn May Lombardi's *The Body and the Song: Elizabeth Bishop's Poetics*, she connects the recurrent images of air and water in Bishop's poetry to the poet's lifelong debilitating asthma, showing that in her poetry and in her life Bishop is always seeking oxygen, metaphorically as well as actually (Lombardi 15–43). Breath seems to be a metaphor for the ways Bishop can find self-expression amid constrictions that might otherwise suffocate her. Breath stands for life, and often in Bishop's poems it appears as the longed-for object, the marker not only of life but of being at ease, or, more exactly, at home in life.

Poetry, breath and poetic friendship frequently intersect in Bishop's work. Breath has a long history as a metaphor for poetry, the 'inspiration' provided by something or someone of another world, access to the 'air' that is another word for 'song'. Sometimes her literary friends and mentors could provide this access. Though Joanne Feit Diehl sees Bishop's relationship with Marianne Moore as primarily competitive – a Kleinian, ambivalent mother-child dyad with envy as the uppermost motive of the relationship (Diehl 10–49) – Bishop's airy metaphors suggest otherwise. In her memoir of the older poet, 'Efforts of Affection', for example, she describes Marianne Moore's 'atmosphere' as 'a diving bell from a different world, let down through the crass atmosphere of the twentieth century', after which descent she always felt stronger, more independent, 'happier: uplifted, even inspired, determined to be good, to work harder, not to worry about what other people thought'. 'To change the image from air to water', she continues,

> somehow, under all the subaqueous pressure at 260 Cumberland Street – admonitions, reserves, principles, simple stoicism – Marianne rose triumphant, or rather her voice did, in a lively, unceasing jet of shining bubbles. I had 'taken' chemistry at preparatory school; I could also imagine that in this water, or heavy water glass, I saw forming the elaborate, logical structures that became her poems. (*Prose* 127–8)

Bishop notably does not change the image from air to water, though she says she will: in both metaphors it is possible to breathe while submerged, and throughout her poetry, and definitely in 'The Riverman', that ability will be associated with nourishment, with poetry, with companionship, and even with salvation. Certainly,

Bishop needed to distance herself from the literary, and sometimes social, imperiousness of Marianne Moore (and of Moore's mother while the mother was still alive). But Moore's company made poetry possible: she gave Bishop an air she could breathe. That air was a literary atmosphere: a breath of Moore's energy, her famous 'gusto' of friendship. It was inspiration in all its senses. In 'A Cold Spring', the fireflies rise 'exactly like the bubbles in champagne' in this poem to her friend, 'Jane Dewey, Maryland' (*Poems* 55). As Jonathan Ellis points out, 'friendships, and poems about them, are protective (albeit fairly provisional) bubbles throughout Bishop's writing.'[3]

In her decades-long friendship with Robert Lowell, too, the access to air was a key topic. Bishop's preoccupation with breath is reflected, as Lombardi shows, in a 1948 letter from Bishop to Lowell about her depression: 'I've got it bad and I think I'll just send you a note before I go out & eat some mackerel. [. . .] I've been indulging myself in a nightmare of finding a gasping mermaid under one of these exposed docks. You know, trying to tear the mussels off the piles for something to eat, – horrors' (Lombardi 36). When she expressed her fear, in a 1960 letter, that he might think 'The Riverman' 'silly', he wrote back in a way that showed his brilliantly insightful sympathy with her: Lowell called this poem 'the best fairy story in verse I know', adding that 'it brings back an old dream of yours, you said you felt you were a mermaid scraping barnacles off a wharf-pile. That was Maine, not Brazil' (Lombardi 40). By reminding her that she was exploring a new world, and by referring to that dream of twelve years earlier, Lowell acknowledges the psychic profundity of the poem and its reach both to her personal and literary past and to the future in which she could achieve new freedoms. Five years later, when the volume was published, he described it again, as 'a sort of forsaken Merman, and a very powerful initiation poem that somehow echoes your own arrival in Santos' (*Words in Air* 464).

Lowell would base a poem on her mermaid dream in 1961, the year after reading 'The Riverman', recalling a day that they had spent together in Stonington, Maine, over a decade earlier, in 1948. In it he describes a seaside with

> dozens of bleak
> white frame houses stuck
> like oyster shells
> on a hill of rock (*Life Studies and For the Union Dead* 7)

The poem, 'Water', treats from his perspective his and Bishop's relationship, permeated (pleasurably) but not defined (threateningly) by erotics until that Stonington visit. As a manic phase precipitated, he became uncomfortably affectionate, a fact he later acknowledged and apologised for (Fountain and Brazeau 161). Periodically, still, though knowing that she was a lesbian, he would continue to entertain fantasies of their marrying. The poem illustrates what he seems to have seen or at least wished to see as a mutual failure of passionate feeling:

> We wished our two souls
> might return like gulls
> to the rock. In the end,
> the water was too cold for us. (*Life Studies and For the Union Dead* 8)

Perhaps, having mentioned 'The Forsaken Merman' apropos of 'The Riverman', he is thinking of Arnold's merman mourning his lost earthling, and recommending 'the cold strange eyes of a little mermaiden'.[4] He may also be remembering the mermaids in 'Prufrock', with its own echoes of 'Dover Beach', one of Lowell's favourites, both poems, arguably, of failed sexuality.

Lowell's poem features Bishop's mermaid 'nightmare':

> One night you dreamed
> you were a mermaid clinging to a wharf-pile,
> and trying to pull
> off the barnacles with your hands. (*Life Studies and For the Union Dead* 8)

Clearly, Lowell understood 'The Riverman' as a momentous event in Bishop's poetic life, and his generous praise reassured her. Any neglect of the poem in criticism is corrected by a recognition of how important the poem was in their exchanges, and how acute Lowell's perception of it was. At the same time, however, he was distorting her experience in minor but important ways. Bishop had, after all, described 'finding' a starving and gasping mermaid, not being one, and described it as a waking fantasy – 'I've been indulging myself in a nightmare' – a conscious act of imagining. He also gives her something less satisfying than mussels to scrape: barnacles. (In real life, we recall, she is off to eat mackerel.) In 'The Riverman' she summons up a potentially entirely nourishing world. In the magical landscape of the Amazon basin, 'the moon shines and the river / lies across the earth / and sucks it like a child' (*Poems* 107), in what may be the only image of an actually nurturing breast in all of Bishop's poetry. Gasping for air, scraping at old encrustations – earlier ways of writing? – isn't quite enough for Bishop, and the water is not too cold for her. In associating the mermaid fantasy with 'The Riverman', Lowell acknowledges the importance for Bishop of exploring poetic alien realms, but not her ability to survive and be nourished by them. His own persona in 'Water' cannot do anything: he sees himself here as staying within the frame of houses 'stuck to the rock'.

Bishop may, years later, be remembering this line in her elegy for Lowell, when she addresses him in its final stanza: 'You left North Haven, anchored in its rock, afloat in mystic blue' (*Poems* 211). Here both appositives ambiguously refer to the town or to Lowell. The town can comfortably be both anchored and afloat, but not Lowell, who seems still to be stuck to the rock of all those years earlier, though perhaps also in another, mystical dimension evoked by D. H. Lawrence's poem 'The Mystic Blue'. (Lowell's own poem describing his institutionalisation, 'Waking in the Blue', is an echo here as well.)

With a glance at the disturbances of Lowell's sexual life, she ruefully remembers his description of learning to kiss in adolescence at this beach town: '[f]un – it always seemed to leave you at a loss' (*Poems* 210). Set in Maine, like 'Water', on the same sea, the poem grieves over the loss of Lowell but also his loss to himself: 'Sad friend, you cannot change.' Throughout the conversation Bishop and Lowell conducted through poems addressed to one another, we find great mutual admiration and succour, but also a need on Bishop's part to distance herself from Lowell's attitudes toward the world, toward poetry and especially toward women. Bishop's relation to Lowell and to her poetic future may have involved a review of her own gender position and the politics of gender. Certainly that politics receives clear-eyed treatment in *Questions of Travel*, as in the threat of rape in 'Brazil, January 1, 1502' (*Poems* 90). 'In the Waiting Room' (*Poems* 179), too, in the next volume, evinces its own horror at the way women are acculturated – and diminished and imprisoned – across cultures. In her own life as a writer, she would occasionally protest at the difference between the reception of male and female poets.

Bishop seems also to need to achieve a perspective from the other side – of the initiation ritual, from under the water, in a masculine persona. Her preoccupation with her body's troubles, and conceivably with its pleasures, would provide incentives to escape as well as explore the body. Unlike the Forsaken Merman to whom Lowell refers, the riverman longs to go into the dangerous other element, and it opens for him like a speakeasy, opacity becoming transparent, a lintel appearing in the water. The river is a source that draws energy from the world and infuses it into men, attenuating their human connection; our narrator is neither 'man' nor 'river', but the composite 'riverman'. Like the protagonist of 'The Man-Moth', another moonlight-dweller and composite poet-figure, he travels at high speeds and avoids humans.

Unlike a mermaid, the riverman is not a muse figure but an avatar of the artist, of Bishop herself. He is, moreover, a man who leaves his wife behind with only slight regret – female humans repel him. This misogyny suggests a measure of ironic distance for Bishop from the riverman – identification, after all, comprises desire and projection, but does not have to preclude self-consciousness. The careless abandonment of the riverman's wife – and the suggestion of infidelity – may also have contributed to Lota's dislike of the poem.

From slightly outside of that identification, the poem performs a critique of the way women are banally constructed and positioned on land, as opposed to under the river. They offer unpleasant teas instead of a special, mind-altering drink; they snore rather than speak magical language; they look in mirrors to shore up their worldly attractiveness rather than using them to seek union with the spirits. The houses they tend look like bits of laundry – and the riverman leaves his clothing on shore when he goes under the river. As a lesbian, Bishop might find the image of traditional, heterosexual femininity 'fascinating' but 'slightly repellent', as she says of '[what] the words "little girl" should mean' in her story 'Gwendolyn' (*Prose* 54). She is rejecting not women but what female socialisation implies. That the riverman identifies with both Luandinha and the dolphin-man seems important. At the underwater party, he recounts, 'Luandinha, none other – / entered and greeted me' (*Poems* 104). Did she enter *him* as well as the underwater space? The ambiguity recalls that of 'In the Waiting Room': a cry came from 'inside' (*Poems* 179).

The legends Wagley discusses in *Amazon Town*, moreover, represent gender and sex very fluidly. The pagé, or shaman, can be man or woman, and Wagley reports at length on some female pagés. Bishop, then, has specifically chosen to represent her speaker as masculine, a choice reminiscent of other lesbian writers such as Willa Cather, whose male alter egos afforded her options for expressing desire and power beyond her moment's conventions. And the riverman's relationship with the Dolphin potentially bears as much eroticism as that with the seductive Luandinha. When the riverman hears the Dolphin's call, he sweats, tears off his clothing, and goes to the river sacramentally naked, for ritual purposes, but also as though to meet a lover. 'I thought once of my wife, but I knew what I was doing' (*Poems* 103).

In Wagley's account, the dolphin-man, or boto, is 'a creature of high magical potency' (238) – and of high sexual potency as well, so much so that husbands are always on the jealous lookout for them (241). On the whole, magic in Ita, as Wagley describes it, produces more dread and sense of danger than it does the benign productivity the riverman praises, and pagés spend most of their time attending to or trying to prevent illnesses. They make medicines like the wife's 'stinking teas' out of roots, herbs and leaves (244). Bishop leaves out most of this lore about omnipresent illness, though she touches on it lightly, mentioning 'elixirs' and 'health' at two points in the poem and describing the riverman's looks as changed in ways that make his wife think he is sick. An arresting feature of the boto in Wagley's account is that his sexuality is not only irresistible to women but potentially fatal. Women who have sex with the boto 'become thin and yellow, and may even die if the relations are not interrupted' (239). The riverman's wife says that he looks yellow, and his 'hands and feet are cold'. Is the riverman becoming ill because he is in love with the boto? If so, the poem maintains that connection as a secret, or a partial secret. The riverman's art requires secrecy and privacy, as Bishop's art did in relation to her own sexuality. She may have been drawn to him in part because he was an outsider too. Travisano explains that '[t]he riverman's stealthy yet taunting posture, which brands him as society's enemy and friend, is historically in keeping with Wagley's observation that the pagés of the Amazon are officially banned by a society that continues to consult them on the sly' (161).

Mark Harris, in an essay on rivers as sites for transformative reflection, briefly discusses the poem in light of its use of a river as a liminal space, 'an "alternative epistemology" of the liquid imagination' (29). Perhaps the poem's alternative epistemology comprehends other liminal spaces or states of being, a fluid in-between-ness of gender and sexuality that can open new creative possibilities. Susan McCabe sees the poem's liminality as the source of its imaginative energy: '[b]eing able to give up one place for another, to stand within a threshold, is part of Bishop's strength; her riverman shares this ability to inhabit imagined places, places of otherness' (174). Bishop's late poem 'Exchanging Hats' suggests the value of changing places: 'The headgear of the other sex / inspires us to experiment' (*Poems* 230), with 'headgear' suggesting not only millinery but consciousness, what goes on inside the head. To revert to her characteristic image of the mirror, Bishop needs a new way of looking, a virgin mirror, and one that won't present her to herself as a woman smiling placatingly or absorbed in the world of ordinariness.

'The Riverman', for all Bishop's doubts about it, marked a resurgence of poetic productiveness for her. Conceivably, the doubt and the productiveness were related, as they often are when one is embarking on something new. In July 1959, she wrote to her friend and doctor Anny Baumann from Rio de Janeiro about the poem's sale:

> *The New Yorker* just cabled me that they were buying a long, *long* (nice for me) poem. [. . .] I don't know when they'll be using it yet, but you may be interested because it's about the Amazon. I've never seen the Amazon, but never mind! I've been doing a whole group of poems again at last, thank heavens. This Amazon one is the one I like the least, so I thought I'd send it off first – the others are better, I think, or hope, and all together should make enough for a new book sometime next year. (*One Art* 373)

And to Pearl Kazin, in September of that year, she wrote:

> Thank you for your kind remark about 'The Riverman,' and I trust something much better will pass through your hands soon. I've really got a lot going, after two years, but worry too much, I think – maybe one worries poetry right out of existence, finally, and stops. (*One Art* 376)

Sometimes Bishop seems to feel that any poetry she writes must be won from a world of resistance. In this poem that she couldn't 'get rid of', however, the struggle is worthwhile, with rewards beyond the pain of striving. Her 'fiat' has worked. As the riverman she can ask, 'Why shouldn't I be ambitious?'

Notes

1. I am grateful to my editor, Jonathan Ellis, for helpful suggestions throughout, and to Jonathan Crewe, Stacy Hubbard, Beth Newman, Peter Swaab and Julie Vandivere for valuable readings, discussions and feedback.
2. Compared with other poems in the *Questions of Travel* volume, 'The Riverman' has received little attention until recently, perhaps because it does not register as a typical Bishop poem. Even George Monteiro's otherwise detailed account of Bishop's experience in Brazil and its influence on her, *Elizabeth Bishop in Brazil and After: A Poetic Career Transformed*, mentions it only briefly (3, 15), though it might seem to offer the perfect context for his study. Important readings by Lorrie Goldensohn, Marilyn May Lombardi and Thomas Travisano do treat the poem at length, however (Goldensohn 210; Lombardi 39–43; Travisano 158–61), as a poem of rededication, of searching, of a call on creative powers. Goldensohn sees 'belief and identification' with the poem's magic premise, rather than 'a patronizing acting out, conducted from an unfeeling distance' (218), though that sense of Bishop's identification has been questioned in later criticism. More recently, for example, post-colonial and other political readings have refocused the poems, assessing Bishop's attitudes in relation to her Brazilian context, generally as those of political and racial naïveté at best, of appropriation at worst. See especially Bethany Hicok and David R. Jarraway (Hicok 125–30; Jarraway 175–9).
3. As Ellis observed to me via personal correspondence, a great number of her poems are 'dedicated to close friends/lovers. Of her four main collections, *North & South* is the only collection of poems not to be dedicated to a friend or lover. *A Cold Spring* is dedicated to Dr Anny Baumann, *Questions of Travel* to Lota de Macedo Soares, *Geography III* to Alice Methfessel.' (Author's note: I am grateful to Ellis for other important suggestions about friendship in Bishop's work.)
4. When Bishop in 'Crusoe in England' later has her castaway remember his island's deceptive snail-shells ('at a distance, / you'd swear that they were beds of irises'), she may be thinking of a line in 'Water' in which Lowell writes that the rock they sat on seems, in retrospect, 'the color of iris, rotting and turning purpler'. In reality, though, 'it was only / the usual gray rock / turning the usual green / when drenched by the sea'.

Works Cited

Bishop, Elizabeth, *One Art: The Selected Letters*, ed. Robert Giroux (London: Chatto & Windus, 1994).

Bishop, Elizabeth, and Robert Lowell, *Words in Air: The Complete Correspondence between Elizabeth Bishop and Robert Lowell*, ed. Thomas Travisano with Saskia Hamilton (New York: Farrar, Straus and Giroux, 2008).

Campion, Thomas, *The Works of Dr. Thomas Campion* (London: Chiswick Press, 1889).

Cleghorn, Angus, Bethany Hicok and Thomas Travisano (eds), *Elizabeth Bishop in the Twenty-First Century: Reading the New Editions* (Charlottesville: University of Virginia Press, 2012).

Cook, Eleanor, *Elizabeth Bishop at Work* (Cambridge, MA: Harvard University Press, 2016).

Diehl, Joanne Feit, *Elizabeth Bishop and Marianne Moore: The Psychodynamics of Creativity* (Princeton: Princeton University Press, 1993).

Fountain, Gary, and Peter Brazeau (eds), *Remembering Elizabeth Bishop: An Oral Biography* (Amherst: University of Massachusetts Press, 1994).

Goldensohn, Lorrie, *Elizabeth Bishop: The Biography of a Poetry* (New York: Columbia University Press, 1992).

Greene, Thomas M., *Poetry, Signs, and Magic* (Newark: University of Delaware Press, 2005).

Harris, Mark, 'From the River: Making Local Histories of the Imagination', in Mark Harris and Nigel Rapport (eds), *Reflections on Imagination: Human Capacity and Ethnographic Method* (Dorchester: Dorset Press, 2015), pp. 23–40.

Harrison, Victoria, *Elizabeth Bishop's Poetics of Intimacy* (Cambridge: Cambridge University Press, 1993).

Hicok, Bethany, *Elizabeth Bishop's Brazil* (Charlottesville: University of Virginia Press, 2016).

Jarraway, David R., *Going the Distance: Dissident Subjectivity in Modernist American Literature* (Baton Rouge: Louisiana State University Press, 2003).

Kalstone, David, *Becoming a Poet: Elizabeth Bishop with Marianne Moore and Robert Lowell* (New York: Farrar, Straus and Giroux, 1989).

Lombardi, Marilyn May, *The Body and the Song: Elizabeth Bishop's Poetics* (Carbondale: Southern Illinois University Press, 1995).

Lowell, Robert, *The Letters of Robert Lowell*, ed. Saskia Hamilton (New York: Farrar, Straus and Giroux, 2005).

Lowell, Robert, *Life Studies and For the Union Dead* (New York: Farrar, Straus and Giroux, 2007).

McCabe, Susan, *Elizabeth Bishop: Her Poetics of Loss* (University Park: Pennsylvania State University Press, 1994).

Millier, Brett C., *Elizabeth Bishop: Life and the Memory of It* (Berkeley: University of California Press, 1993).

Monteiro, George, *Elizabeth Bishop in Brazil and After: A Poetic Career Transformed* (Jefferson, NC: McFarland, 2012).

Travisano, Thomas J., *Elizabeth Bishop: Her Artistic Development* (Charlottesville: University Press of Virginia, 1988).

Wagley, Charles, *Amazon Town: A Study of Man in the Tropics* (New York: Knopf, 1964).

4

'THE COLOR OF THE WORLD ALL TOGETHER': ELIZABETH BISHOP'S DIFFRACTION PATTERNS

Amy Waite

I

IN ELIZABETH BISHOP'S AUTOBIOGRAPHICAL story 'In the Village', which describes her early childhood days living in Nova Scotia, young Bishop is kindly gifted a five-cent piece by the poor village dressmaker. This small silver coin becomes a source of immediate fascination for the child:

> It is very tiny, very shiny. King George's beard is like a little silver flame. Because they look like herring – or maybe salmon – scales, five-cent pieces are called 'fish-scales'. One heard of people's rings being found inside fish, or their long-lost jackknives. What if one could scrape a salmon and find a little picture of King George on every scale?
>
> I put my five-cent piece in my mouth for greater safety on the way home, and swallow it. Months later, as far as I know, it is still in me, transmuting all its precious metal into my growing teeth and hair. (*Prose* 67)

On the one hand, the coin provides young Bishop with a template of the sovereign human subject. The outline of King George's profile presents a human ideal: the very pinnacle of what it is to be an authoritative, autonomous subject. However, the coin also looks like a non-human particle, an iridescent fish scale. This widely accepted similarity causes young Bishop to muse upon the various ways in which human life is oddly entangled with other forms of life and materiality: both animals and objects. She engages in a which-came-first/chicken-or-egg type of thought experiment, collapsing traditional nature/culture binaries (remembering tales where a number of knick-knacks have been found within the bellies of fish). She develops the thought experiment further, imagining a complex layering of man, coin and fish – a mosaic of peeled salmon scales, each organically printed with the image of King George. As though testing this hybridity hypothesis, young Bishop – much like the 'man-moth' who gulps down that one tear (*Poems* 17) – swallows her five-cent piece. The effect is remarkable. From within, it infects her growing body with a precious silvery, metallic substance: she grows a scaly sheen. Her profile is no longer singularly human, a mere replica of King George's stable, sovereign image. Rather, it is posthuman: plural, strong and iridescent.

This chapter examines Bishop's fascination with material entanglements, and the curious posthuman figures that emerge in her work. It argues that Bishop's poems encourage strange encounters between the human and the non-human, opening up ontological borders and celebrating the various processes of merger and radical intra-relation that continuously constitute and reconstitute our world. Reading Bishop alongside contemporary posthuman theory, I consciously break with critical traditions that label Bishop as a belated modernist, a mild postmodernist, or as vacillating somewhere in between. Instead, I present Bishop as a poet preoccupied with what Karen Barad terms 'diffraction patterns' and 'interference effects': tropes of iridescence (manifest, in the poems, as fish scales, soap bubbles or pools of gasoline) that both point to and embolden lively posthuman activity.

For a while now, the critical word du jour around Bishop has been 'displacement'. In the early 1990s, moving away from early critical emphasis on Bishop's modernist 'modesty' (her immaculate use of form; patient and over-attentive descriptions of external objects; strategies of self-restraint),[1] a sudden flurry of full-length studies sought to resituate her as a postmodern poet with a prevailing interest in the displacements, pluralities, discontinuities and complex interconnections of subjectivity.[2] In many of these studies, two biographical anecdotes about Bishop are repeated: the fact that Bishop had read Newton's *Optiks* (Bishop discloses this in the series of interview letters to Anne Stevenson), and the time Bishop worked in an optical shop during the war surrounded by prisms, binoculars and telescopes (few mention that Bishop, although initially attracted to the idea, actually loathed working in the shop and only lasted five days there, finding the work tedious, repetitive and an 'eye-strain'). As a result, the Newtonian principles of reflection and refraction have become widely accepted metaphors for Bishop's poetic practice. In *Questions of Mastery*, Bonnie Costello describes Bishop's poetics as something of a physics experiment: 'the self is projected into the world and, conversely, the mutable world enters the domain of the self. Bishop sees at the threshold, along a pane of glass' (60). Here, both 'self' and the 'world' are figured as rays of light that splinter and refract as they cross into different mediums. Thomas Travisano, in his essay on biography in *The Cambridge Companion to Elizabeth Bishop*, similarly argues that Bishop's 'art of displacement' is 'one of her most pervasive and persistent artistic strategies' (34).

This line of criticism reaches something of a zenith in 2010, with the publication of Peggy Samuels's brilliant *Deep Skin: Elizabeth Bishop and Visual Art*. Placing Bishop in conversation with the visual arts, Samuels develops an intricate four-way metaphor that imagines verse, painting, skin and the interface between nature and the mind as

> two-dimensional surfaces capable of opening out three-dimensionally into each other through complex relations of absorption, reflection, modulation and resistance. The interior of the self and a deep outer world pass through to one another via a 'skinless' boundary more like a sea surface than the boundary of the human body. ('Verse' 306)

Samuels refines a critical language that successfully articulates the nuances of an open, fluctuating subjectivity and offers a series of close readings that emphasise the materiality of verse, and its function as the site of encounter. As suggested by the chapter titles – 'Infiltration and Suspension', 'Modulation', 'Immersible Nets, Lines, Fabrics, and Entanglements' – Samuels foregrounds Bishop's strategies of displacement: exploring the nature of reflective and refractive activity across porous surfaces and mobile membranes (*Deep Skin* vii). In describing this activity, the study repeats (and is driven by) the prefix 'inter': interaction, intermingling, interpenetrating, interfaces, intermittent, interstices, interpermeate. The effect of this is twofold. Yes, it draws attention to Bishop's preoccupations with connectivity and relationality. However, in so doing, it also exposes the two major ontological presumptions of refraction: (1) that there is a pre-existing distinction between object and subject, self and exteriority; and (2) that cause naturally precedes effect. For all its emphasis on material entanglements, Samuels's argument nevertheless protects and celebrates a world governed by the tenets of individualism.

Indeed, we might apply further pressure to Samuels's four-way metaphor by examining Bishop's 'Poem', a work that draws explicit connections between verse, painting, skin and the interface between nature and mind. The speaker studies a small picture of a Nova Scotia landscape, a 'minor family relic' of little monetary or aesthetic significance (*Poems* 196). Immediately, the lexical focus is on the miniature, the negligible. This 'little' painting has accrued many 'looks' from different owners, with varying degrees of attention and interest, over its seventy years of existence. It acts as an interface between the past and the present: connecting the minds of family members across generations, and inviting different memories – of the local scene depicted, of Canadian landscapes generally, of ancestry, of cold springs (and, therefore, of old poems) – to surface from hidden depths and intermingle. The vitality surrounding the initial creation of the sketch – it is said to have been finished quickly, 'in one breath' – initially seems to be replicated in the painting's extended afterlife, colours, textures and shapes all intensifying in the whorl of different experiences and images that filter across the painting's surface. The cows may be 'tiny' but they are 'confidently cows' (shored up by the knowledge and memories of cows that each viewer brings with them); the colours of the iris are 'fresh-squiggled from the tube' and the air 'is fresh and cold'.

For the speaker, initially unable to identify the specific scene depicted, the painting first conjures only general memories of a Canadian landscape: 'It must be Nova Scotia; only there / does one see gabled houses / painted that awful shade of brown.' The deictic 'there', lent emphasis through enjambment, imbues the painted houses with any number of remembered hues from across the peninsula (intensifying the 'awful shade' to something collective/plural). However, at the same time, it has the effect of detaching the speaker from the scene. If the painting is, indeed, 'a mobile membrane that allows materials from the world to cross into the self' (Samuels, *Deep Skin*, 3) and vice versa, then it is a highly selective, semi-permeable membrane: the viewer exerts stringent control over which parts of the self and the world interact. Hence the oddly cold disclaimers that emerge as the poem develops: 'Those particular geese and cows / are naturally before my time' and, later on, 'it's still loved, / or its memory is (it must have changed a lot)'. We get two explicit disavowals of responsibility – the first, for a past iteration of that particular scene, and the second, for the current iteration. The speaker might be happy to let her memories of Miss Gillespie's house and specific shades of brown merge with the painting, but she refuses to become fully entangled in its complex historialities. Accountability only extends to her particular version of the scene.

This kind of selectivity seems highly problematic. It fosters apathy, whilst simultaneously masking it beneath claims of connection. It celebrates difference, whilst also neutralising it via deceptive displacement practices. It is this strange and unsettling series of dichotomies that we find in the final sequence of the poem:

> I never knew him. We both knew this place,
> apparently, this literal small backwater,
> looked at it long enough to memorize it,
> our years apart. How strange. And it's still loved,
> or its memory is (it must have changed a lot).
> Our visions coincided – 'visions' is
> too serious a word – our looks, two looks:
> art 'copying from life' and life itself,
> life and the memory of it so compressed
> they've turned into each other. Which is which?
> Life and the memory of it cramped,
> dim, on a piece of Bristol board,
> dim, but how live, how touching in detail
> – the little that we get for free,
> the little of our earthly trust. Not much.
> about the size of our abidance
> along with theirs: the munching cows,
> the iris, crisp and shivering, the water
> still standing from spring freshets,
> the yet-to-be-dismantled elms, the geese. (*Poems* 197)

The phrase 'our looks, two looks' successively downgrades the speaker's initial statement of active, ambitious and communal enterprise – 'Our visions coincided' – to basic shared viewing and then, finally, distinct and separate viewing. It exhibits a real wariness of full entanglement, and an odd flattening out of difference: 'compressed', 'cramped', 'dim'. Displacement practices are reflective and refractive – 'art "copying from life"', life and memory turning into each other – so that it becomes difficult, in the midst of this optical gamut, to tell 'which is which?'. The word 'abidance' (noticeably archaic, connoting conformity and compliance) disrupts the final fragile image of democracy: cows, iris, water and elms all standing together. It cancels difference whilst simultaneously enforcing the nature/culture distinction between 'ours' and 'theirs'. The speaker can now *thrice*-assert their sense of diminished responsibility: 'the little that we get for free / the little of our earthly trust. Not much.' Any sense of vitality – of ongoing activity and participation – is paused, that 'one breath' of initial creation hanging in suspended animation (hence the final cluster of oddly 'frozen' present participles: 'munching', 'shivering', 'still standing').

In his ambitiously titled book *Can Poetry Save the Earth? A Field Guide to Nature Poems*, John Felstiner argues that this type of suspended animation – 'the way poems hold things still for a moment' (357) – awakens a mindfulness in each reader that might eventually inspire a collective will to act judiciously. He sees the diminished responsibility encapsulated in Bishop's phrase 'the little that we get for free / the little of our earthly trust' as a positive precaution; the landscape in 'Poem' offers about 'as much life as we can bear. Art gives us what, being mortal, we can take' (235). Anything more would be dangerous, even destructive – well beyond our individual, human capacity.

This, however, seems to hugely underestimate both art and human capacity – divorcing them from the external energies and expansive environments of life. As Felstiner sees it, poetry *can* save the earth: by encouraging us to retreat even further from everything exterior to man and 'lighten our footprint in a world where all of nature matters vitally' (xiii). And yet, it is this very hesitance to embrace full entanglement – and the responsibilities that come with it – that endangers the earth in the first place.

So we find art cannot offer salvation, glimpses of the bigger picture, when its moments of vital interaction are reclaimed as ones of refractive self-recognition or reproduction. The human subject is too prone to individualism, even (or especially) as it attempts to escape that very condition. Robert Pinsky, in his work *Democracy, Culture and the Voice of Poetry*, identifies this paradox as the greatest source of anxiety in contemporary culture:

> We are simultaneously afraid of constraints making us so much like one another that we will lose something vital in our human nature, and also in fear of becoming so fluently different, so much divided into alien and brutally competitive fragments, gangs, or fabricate nationalisms, that we cannot survive. (6)

As citizens of democracy, we escape solitude by overcoming the differences that would separate and distinguish us. At the same time, this equality often only returns man to himself and his own solitude by removing the principle of difference. Thus, the nightmare of undifferentiation is simultaneously the nightmare of individualism – a contradiction enacted through Bishop's 'Poem'.

Pinsky goes on to argue that Alexis de Tocqueville, in his classic tome on democracy, made a prophetic claim about the direction of poetry in a democratic culture. Tocqueville insisted that 'in the end democracy diverts imagination from all that is external to man and fixes it on man alone' – a refractive process if ever there was one (Pinsky 13). Here, the poet becomes a representative figure of the anxiety-ridden democratic citizen, forced to narcissistically address his own existence and participate exclusively in acts of self-recognition. Whitman is the obvious example. 'Song of Myself' exists as a celebration both of the individual and of the democratic collective (18). The poem struggles to negotiate these two poles, shifting erratically between local moments of lyric intensity and bloated catalogues of human diversity. We get a 'canal boy', a 'connoisseur', a young wife, a squaw, a prostitute, a president (19). In order to maintain the sovereignty of the individual amid such variety, Whitman counts each figure as a potential aspect of the self: 'And these tend inward to me, and I tend outward to them / And such as it is to be of these more or less I am' (19). Self is imaged identically in every direction: a perfect plural that, under the weight of democratic anxieties, is effectively a non-plural. It is this kind of tenuous, faux collective that Bishop warns against in 'Poem'.

II

If refraction, governed by too many ontological presumptions, is incapable of successfully describing true connective activity (in life, and in art), then we need to find a new metaphor: one that doesn't differentiate/separate, but still maintains – and is defined by – difference. And this is where Bishop's poetic practice and the language of critical posthumanism converge. In 2007's *When Species Meet*, Donna J. Haraway – focusing specifically on man's interaction with biological life-forms, the 'myriad of entangled coshaping species of the earth' – describes posthuman subjects as 'meaning-making figures that gather up those who respond to them into unpredictable kinds of "we"' (5). Haraway believes that, rather than a condition we must move towards, the posthuman is something we have always been and already are. 'To be one is always to become with many' (2): heterogeneity and hybridity are natural occurrences (she celebrates the fact that the human genome is only found in about ten per cent of cells in the human body; 'the other 90 percent of the cells are filled with genomes of bacteria, fungi, protists, and such' (1)). Furthermore, Haraway argues that to 'become with' is to 'become worldly', integrated within a vast fabric of being (1). This suggests a monistic world, composed of fluid connections. Haraway searches for a new optical metaphor that sufficiently expresses this ontological inseparability, and in the 1992 essay 'The Promises of Monsters' she settles on diffraction: 'Diffraction does not produce "the same" displaced, as reflection and refraction do. Diffraction is a mapping of interference, not of replication, reflection or reproduction. A diffraction pattern does not map where differences appear, but rather maps where the effects of difference appear' (300).

It is Karen Barad's reading of Haraway, through a quantum understanding of diffraction, that feels most pertinent to Bishop's work. Barad begins with the classical definition of diffraction – 'the ways waves combine when they overlap and the apparent bending and spreading out of waves' (74) when they encounter interference by an obstruction – and points to the many opportunities we have in daily life to observe this phenomenon:

> the swirl of colours on a soap bubble or a thin film of oil on a puddle is also an example of a diffraction or interference phenomenon. The iridescence of peacock feathers, or the wings of certain dragonflies, moths and butterflies – the way the hue of these colours changes with the changing viewing position of the observer – is also a diffraction effect. From the perspective of classical physics, diffraction patterns are simply the result of differences in (the relative phase and amplitudes of) overlapping waves. (80)

Barad updates this definition, by focusing it through the lens of quantum physics and – most particularly – the experimental work of Niels Bohr. She refers to Bohr's two-slit diffraction experiment: an apparatus that induces different forms of interference, to determine whether light acts as particles (as first deduced by Newton) or as waves. The experiment showed that changes in the apparatus would actually change the nature of the observed phenomena – under certain conditions light acted as particles, whilst under other conditions it would act as waves. This suggests that 'edges or boundaries are not determinate either ontologically or visually' (Barad 156). In recognition of such ontological inseparability, Barad introduces the term 'intra-action' (139). She argues that distinct entities do not precede, but rather emerge through, their intra-action – and that they are only distinct in relation to their entanglement with each other (they don't exist as individual elements).

If environments and bodies are 'intra-actively co-constituted' (Barad 170), matter possesses inexhaustible vitality, dynamism and generative capabilities. The physical phenomenon of diffraction then – rainbow swirls, flashes of iridescence, sudden and vibrant shifts in hue – 'makes manifest the extraordinary liveliness of the world' (Barad 91). Which is perhaps why we find it so often in Bishop's poetry. In fact, I would go so far as to modify Thomas Travisano's original displacement statement to: Bishop's 'art of diffraction' is one of her most 'pervasive and persistent artistic strategies' – her fascination for optics, and subsequent reading habits, moving well beyond the classical Newtonian conceptions of reflection and refraction. In an interview with poet Elizabeth Spires for *The Paris Review*, Bishop – discussing her affinity for, and appreciation of, the art of Joseph Cornell – reveals her delight at an unexpected shared interest between herself and Cornell: 'When I looked at his show in New York two years ago I nearly fainted, because one of my favourite books is a book he liked and used. It's a little book by an English Scientist who wrote for children about soap bubbles' (120–1). This book, *Soap Bubbles: Their Colours and the Forces Which Mould Them* by C. V. Boys, a physics primer aimed at early learners, is full of simple experiments that demonstrate, amongst a variety of other phenomena, the mesmerising, beautiful and disorienting effects of diffraction. One chapter examines the make-up of oil, and the highly coloured films that appear on its surface when it is spilled; another describes the interference that produces iridescence across soap-bubbles, detailing how soap bubbles move from transparency to colour, why these colours increase in brilliancy and what causes sudden shifts in hue. Boys is meticulous in describing the colourful choreography of soap bubbles, but ends his tract by acknowledging and celebrating the endless fecundity of diffraction: 'the variety of patterns and movements is so great that it is impossible to describe all that may be seen. I would only urge anyone who has taken an interest to set up the very simple apparatus required [. . .] there will be abundant reward' (164).

For Bishop, there was little need to set up experiments. For the better part of fifteen years, she lived within an apparatus (the 'extremely modern' house she shared with her partner Lota de Macedo Soares) and an environment (the wild, unpredictable Brazilian countryside) that induced interference at every turn, generating any number of kaleidoscopic diffraction patterns. In February 1952, Bishop described the house in a letter to Marianne Moore:

> I have been staying mostly at my friend Lota's country house in Petrópolis, about 40 miles from Rio, and it is a sort of dream-combination of plant & animal life. I really can't believe it at all. Not only are there highly impractical mountains all around with clouds floating in & out of one's bedroom, but waterfalls, orchids, all the Key West flowers I know & Northern apples and pears as well. (*One Art* 234)

The house was under construction for several years (Lota was a prominent architect in Brazil) and Bishop would frequently write to her friends about the joys of living in an unfinished house: open to the elements, local creatures, and frequent atmospheric changes. Thousands of moths, mice and 'large black crabs like patent leather' would scuttle inside, attracted to the light from the burning oil lamps (*One Art* 238). Pregnant clouds would pass through the rooms as Bishop was writing, immersing her in a thick fog and leaving traces of moisture in the air and on the furniture. And when she and Lota headed to bed each evening, they would find themselves surrounded by 'dogs, moths, mice, bloodsucking bats, etc'. Bishop admitted that she enjoyed this intimate menagerie so much that she kept thinking she had 'died and gone to heaven' (*One Art* 249).

'Song for the Rainy Season', the poem Bishop wrote about the Brazil house, captures something of this intimacy, depicting relationships and connections that might be categorised as radical 'intra-actions' rather than interactions.

> Hidden, oh hidden
> In the high fog
> The house we live in,
> Beneath the magnetic rock,
> rain-, rainbow-ridden,
> where blood-black
> bromelias, lichens,
> owls, and the lint
> of the waterfalls cling,
> familiar, unbidden
> [. . .]
> House, open house
> to the white dew
> and the milk-white sunrise
> kind to the eyes,
> to membership
> of silver fish, mouse,
> bookworms,
> big moths; with a wall
> for the mildew's
> ignorant map (*Poems* 99–100)

The narrow stanzas, together with excess hyphenation, evoke the 'closeness' of the house and its inhabitants, forcing words, textures and creatures to jostle together at close quarters, dissolving boundaries. Critics traditionally home in on the 'rainbow' aspect of the house, holding up refraction processes, and the resultant spectrum of colours, as loaded signifiers of diversity, inclusivity and freedom. However, this reading overlooks the fact that the house is 'rainbow-ridden' – more than one rainbow converges on it, the morpheme 'rain' (coming before the full compound 'rainbow') suggesting something of a doubling, or supernumerary effect. And the rare phenomenon of supernumerary rainbows is actually caused by light interference: the result of diffraction rather than refraction processes.

And then there is the 'lint' from the waterfalls that clings everywhere. As moisture builds up, a thin film begins to form across the surface of things – so much so that an entire wall becomes covered with the 'mildew's / ignorant map'. This, in turn, causes the objects within the house to become 'darkened and tarnished'. The thin film of moisture, and then mildew, interferes with light activity: first darkening objects, before developing the iridescent sheen that one finds on old tarnished coins or cutlery. Bishop describes this process in greater detail in 'Apartment in Leme', another poem written about one of Bishop and Lota's Brazilian homesteads. Once again, we get the play of light and moisture:

Pale rods of light, the morning's implements,
lie in among them tarnishing already,
just like our knives and forks.

Because we live at your open mouth, oh Sea,
with your cold breath blowing warm, your warm breath blowing cold,
like in the fairy tale.

Not only do you tarnish our knives and forks
– regularly the silver coffee-pot goes into
dark, rainbow-edged eclipse; (*Edgar Allan Poe* 134)

Interference often induces an 'eclipse' effect – either a darkening, or a thinning into transparency – whilst also producing iridescence. Think about the way soap bubbles swirl from transparency into colour (and back again), depending on the play of light and changing perspective of the viewer. So often we find these 'soap bubble' moments in Bishop's poems: bricks becoming 'half-transparent' (*Edgar Allan Poe* 160), houses and towers turning the 'colour of air' (*Edgar Allan Poe* 27), black places containing 'illuminated scene[s]' (*Poems* 23), and blurred redbuds 'almost more / like movement than any placeable colour' (*Poems* 55). In her Brazil letters, Bishop alludes to the enormous 'pale blue iridescent' butterflies that would arrive in the grounds during summer: 'they are drifting along all over the place, sometimes in clusters of four or five, and when they come close or come *in*, they are semi-transparent' (*One Art* 255).

Yes, in 'Song for the Rainy Season', iridescence makes manifest 'the extraordinary liveliness of the world' – highlighting the intra-actions that bring fish, mice, moths and 'bookworms' (whom we might assume to be Lota and Bishop, hybridised) under one roof in brilliant heterogeneous 'membership'. This posthuman phenomenon, in all its spectral glory, is 'kind to the eyes' indeed. However, being both a measure and an effect of ontological inseparability, iridescence also points towards its own disappearance (via sudden shifts into darkness or transparency). Nothing, not even iridescence, can remain a constant in a world that is forever being remade. In 'Song for the Rainy Season', this becomes apparent in the final stanza which details the end of the rainy season. Creatures will move on, waterfalls will shrivel, and the proliferation of rainbows will eventually fade. But this isn't the end. As Barad points out, we must have faith, 'since each intra-action matters, since the possibilities for what the world may become call out in the pause that precedes each breath before a moment comes into being and the world is remade again' (255).

Bishop frequently tests this faith, pushing iridescence to its breaking point. In 'At the Fishhouses', the old man scrapes 'creamy iridescent coats of mail' from fish with a knife, leaving only a few semi-sparkly 'sequins' behind (*Poems* 63). In 'Cape Breton', iridescence has faded to 'dull, dead, deep peacock colours' (*Poems* 65). In 'Going to the Bakery', tin hides have the iridescence of 'dying, flaccid toy balloons' (*Poems* 173). And, at the close of 'Under the Window: Ouro Prêto', we find iridescence lying in a ditch:

The seven ages of man are talkative
and soiled and thirsty.
                    Oil has seeped into,
the margins of the ditch of standing water

and flashes or looks upward brokenly,
like bits of mirror – no, more blue than that:
like tatters of the *Morpho* butterfly. (*Poems* 176)

The rainbow sheen of the pool of oil is likened to those blue, iridescent butterflies that drift through the Brazilian countryside – although their tilt into transparency has, in this poem, become a full-on descent into tatters. The body of the poem charts the snatches of conversations heard, and little scenes witnessed, from Bishop's window in the city (she bought a property in Ouro Preto in 1965). The window overlooks a public fountain, which has been visited by every creature imaginable – donkeys, dogs, 'bottle-green swallows', old men, women with babies, tourists – for several centuries, water drawing everything and everyone together in exuberant (if rather dirty and dilapidated) intra-activity. There is a lot about this activity that is bleak: the obvious poverty, the 'dirty hands' that women are forced to feed their babies via, the gossipy allusions to decapitations and rising prices. However, we get the sense – as we do at the end of 'The Bight' – that, despite everything, 'all the untidy activity continues, / awful but cheerful' (*Poems* 59). The world will continue to be remade, with only minor changes and adjustments.

The poem posits three ways one might respond to this ongoing situation via the description of the old statue that once housed the fountain: 'the water used to run out of the mouths / of three green soapstone faces. (One face laughed / and one face cried; the middle one just looked. // Patched up with plaster, they're in the museum)' (*Poems* 175). Most readers of Bishop would agree that, of the three, the final option – i.e. simple, detached observation – is the one that our poet would pick time and again. However, the poem suggests that all three responses are somewhat antiquated (those statues now patched up in a museum somewhere). Remaking the world has to matter, in both senses of the word. Participating in intra-activity, in the becoming of the world, is deeply entangled but should also be deeply and actively ethical. We can remain satisfied with 'awful but cheerful' tatters of rainbow, allowing intra-activity to simply continue, or we can try and advance iridescence to its most brilliant and luminous state.

III

This is what we find in 'The Fish'. The speaker, out on a fishing trip, catches a 'tremendous' fish, her hook and line becoming entangled in his mouth. She proceeds to study the fish intently, holding him half out of the water for close inspection:

He didn't fight.
He hadn't fought at all.
He hung there a grunting weight,
battered and venerable
and homely. Here and there
his brown skin hung in strips
like ancient wallpaper,
and its pattern of darker brown
was like wallpaper:

shapes like full-blown roses
stained and lost through age.
He was speckled with barnacles,
fine rosettes of lime,
and infested
with tiny white sea-lice,
and underneath two or three
rags of green weed hung down. (*Poems* 43)

The fish is the epitome of material entanglement: not only has the speaker's fishing line become caught up in his mouth, but various different life-forms – sea lice, barnacles – have become enmeshed within his body over the years. The speaker, much like young Bishop in 'In the Village', imagines the history of these entanglements to be packed, layered, within his flesh. His scales may not reveal a 'little picture of King George', but his skin – hanging in strips – does expose 'shapes' that have formed over a lifetime of intra-activity.

The question is, how should this particular intra-action – between the catcher and the caught – play out? The speaker can imagine the 'coarse white flesh / packed in like feathers', the pattern of bones, entrails and swim bladder inside, because man's intra-action with fish is typically invasive and destructive. The speaker only has to look (and she does, keenly) at the fish's mouth to see evidence of this activity: multiple hooks, pieces of fish line and wire have embedded themselves in his skin over the years. We might again call this history of intra-activity 'awful but cheerful'. Awful, because the fish has suffered multiple lacerations and body-altering wounds. Cheerful, because – thus far – the fish has always managed to escape capture. The speaker notes how the broken hooks and lines resemble ribboned 'medals', borne proudly by a seasoned war veteran. Nevertheless, something has changed. The fish isn't fighting at all in the speaker's hands. The history of abuse seems to have finally defeated him, and he just hangs there: battered, bruised and venerable, his gills taking in the 'terrible oxygen' that could finally kill him.

The speaker's curiosity seems to get the better of her at first, as she pulls the fish in closer – despite his obvious discomfort above water:

I looked into his eyes
which were far larger than mine
but shallower, and yellowed,
the irises backed and packed
with tarnished tinfoil
seen through the lenses
of old scratched isinglass.
They shifted a little, but not
To return my stare.
– It was more like the tipping
of an object toward the light. (*Poems* 43–4)

Yet again, we get one of Bishop's soap bubble moments. As the speaker looks into the eyes of the fish, she is confronted with a tarnished surface – teetering between blackness, transparency and potential colour. The allusion to isinglass (a substance man obtains from the dried swim bladders of fish, mainly used for filtering alcohol) marks one possible intra-active pathway: the speaker can pull the fish onboard, wait for him to suffocate, and use his body/flesh/organs for any number of purposes. Or she can drop him back into the water. This is the wavering 'pause that precedes each breath before a moment comes into being' (Barad 255) – it is the 'tipping' of the soap bubble towards light, and its next phase. The speaker stares and stares, intensifying the intra-active connection, before a decision is made. And she lets the fish go, sur-rounded by a luminous pool of oil that has spilt and is filling up the boat. This is iridescence at its most brilliant. Diffraction at its most dizzying. In a multicoloured, supernumerary moment of 'rainbow, rainbow, rainbow', the world is remade into something quite different. Something better.

If the speaker had, like the third of those fountain faces, 'just looked' at the fish – continuing her intense observation – she would have killed it by default: keeping him out of the water, and sending more of that terrible oxygen into his gills. Instead, the speaker and fish experience a moment of shared 'victory'. By fighting to modify a history of 'awful but cheerful' intra-action, the speaker is as much a warrior as the embattled fish. Furthermore, by reading the poem in this particular manner, I might also share in this victory. Through my intra-action with the text, I've interpreted 'let the fish go' as a moment of physical release (back into the water) rather than one of euphemistic eutha-nasia (ending the fish's suffering by killing him). In other words, the reader becomes caught up in the material and ethical entanglements depicted. Worlding is as much the reader's responsibility as it is the fish's, the speaker's and the poet's. In the ever-changing manifold of intra-activity, 'responsibility is not ours alone. And yet our responsibility is greater than it would be if it were ours alone' (Barad 394).

Bishop's poetry very rarely, if ever, leaves us contemplating 'the little that we get for free'. On the contrary, it frequently instils a sense of the sheer enormity of our task: the extraordinary breadth and depth of our combined responsibilities, and the work we must put in to meet them. Sometimes, this realisation is overwhelming (think of the speaker's horror in 'In the Waiting Room', when her realisation spins the turning world – another of Bishop's revolving soap bubbles – into a 'cold, blue-black' phase (*Poems* 180)). Sometimes, it is a quietly joyful interruption like the end of 'The Moose', when the 'awful but cheerful' nattering of the world-weary bus passengers is altered by the sudden appearance of the moose, shifting their journey into a new gasoline-fuelled 'gear' (*Poems* 193). And sometimes it comes as a stark warning. We might return, once again, to 'Poem', where the speaker's resistance to full entanglement only highlights the fragility of the 'yet-to-be-dismantled elms' (*Poems* 197). But it is always a call to action or, more precisely, conscious intra-action. In a world that is constantly changing *through* and *with* us, there is little room for complacency.

Nowhere is this more apparent than in 'Pleasure Seas' (a much-overlooked poem, composed in 1939 and sold to *Harper's Bazaar* but never printed). Peggy Samuels sees the subject of this poem – at every stage – as 'refraction': a narra-tive of displaced trajectories through and across different mediums. However, I would argue that this is Bishop's most intensely diffractive poem. Interference pro-duces multiple forms of iridescence (we get allusions to soap bubbles, oil and fish scales in a single poem) that overlap and cross-pollinate, reconfiguring the world at a dizzying – even dangerous – rate. The first section of the poem describes a 'perfectly flat' pane of water in a walled-off swimming pool, through which bathers are 'dipping themselves in and out' (*Poems* 279). Once again, we might imagine the surface of the water – here already compared to the surface of a painting, via the 'Seurat' allusion and paintbrush connotations – as a semi-permeable membrane. Like the speaker in 'Poem', these bathers refuse to fully immerse themselves in the depths available: theirs is a selective, highly controlled *inter*action. The swimming pool is governed by an ontology of individualism/cause and effect. The passing clouds reflect 'amoeba-motions' on to the surface of the water; changes in the sky's colour result in a subsequent change in the shade of the water. Within these walls, the 'little that we get for free' is protected, policed and bordered off. Accountability is easily measured and limited.

Out in the open water, things are very different. Colours, currents, tides collide: unconstrained and effervescent. The first diffraction pattern emerges quite unexpectedly, disrupting the cause-effect duality that has governed the first section of the poem:

> But out among the keys
> Where the water goes its own way, the shallow pleasure seas
> Drift this way and that mingling currents and tides
> In most of the colors that swarm around the sides
> Of soap-bubbles, poisonous and fabulous. (*Poems* 279)

The moving waters gleam like the unpredictable eddies around the side of a soap bubble. This colourful holiday scene – witnessed by a man in an aeroplane above – seems capable of supporting a huge variety of life (entangled with weeds, fish, bell-buoys) and proliferating pleasure. So enticing is this prospect that a couple of the more courageous bathers from the tightly controlled swimming pool dare to strike off from its edge and enter the swarming currents – hoping it will provide the same delightful freedoms and excess as a 'well-ventilated ball-room'. Of course, there is no such safety here. Diffraction patterns multiply, pushing iridescence into glittering darkness – 'A Grief floats off / Spreading out thin like oil' – and total confusion: Love sets out 'determinedly in a straight line', only to shatter, suffer refraction and come back in 'shoals of distraction' (or shoals of diffraction). In this whirling frenzy of intra-activity, emotion – much like it does in 'The Map' – 'too far exceeds its cause' (5). We wonder: is it wiser to remain contentedly removed from these mingling currents and tides – 'Happy the people in the swimming pool and on the yacht / Happy the man in that airplane, likely as not' – or risk diffraction? The answer, it seems, is that we have no choice. As the ominous pool of oil on the water's surface predicts, those who attempt to fly above the tumult will inevitably end up crash-landing in its midst. Better to participate consciously in the colourful chaos, taking responsibility for our ongoing part in it, than futilely battling to deny its existence (something Bishop, writing 'Pleasure Seas' in 1939, was all too aware of).

'So *that* is the color of the world all together,' the speaker exclaims at the spectral array in 'On the Amazon' (another poem where supernumerary rainbows emerge: 'under a rainbow, too – / the rainbow has taken shape' (*Edgar Allan Poe* 124)). Iridescence marks a veritable hive of intra-activity, and all that seems to be required is 'water / and a little sun / and a gentle acquiescent world' (124). But the world isn't always acquiescent, and it certainly isn't always gentle. Intra-activity too often involves slipping into a dark, rainbow-edged eclipse – from which one is never quite sure one can recover. We just have to trust that darkness, transparency and iridescence are all part of the worlding process, where things can split into multiple rainbows just as quickly, and just as intensely, as they can descend into oily obscurity. Diffraction is, indeed, both poisonous and fabulous. But Bishop's posthuman poetry encourages us: to approach entanglement with as much curiosity and gumption as the scaly child in 'In the Village', to fight for our place in a world that is constantly being remade, and to acknowledge the full, dazzling spectrum of 'our earthly trust'. Perhaps *this* is how poetry might just, someday, save the earth.

Notes

1. See C. K. Doreski, *Elizabeth Bishop: The Restraints of Language* (Oxford: Oxford University Press, 1993).
2. Thomas Travisano, *Elizabeth Bishop: Her Artistic Development* (Charlottesville: University Press of Virginia, 1988) and *Midcentury Quartet: Bishop, Lowell, Jarrell, Berryman and the Making of a Postmodern Aesthetic* (Charlottesville: University Press of Virginia, 1999); Victoria Harrison, *Elizabeth Bishop's Poetics of Intimacy* (Cambridge: Cambridge University Press, 1993); Susan McCabe, 'Writing Loss', *American Imago* 30.1 (Spring 1993); Marilyn May Lombardi, *Elizabeth Bishop: The Geography of Gender* (Charlottesville: University Press of Virginia, 1993); Kim Fortuny, *Elizabeth Bishop: The Art of Travel* (Boulder: University Press of Colorado, 2003).

Works Cited

Barad, Karen, *Meeting the Universe Halfway: Quantum Physics and the Entanglement of Matter and Meaning* (Durham, NC, and London: Duke University Press, 2007).

Bishop, Elizabeth, *Edgar Allan Poe & the Juke-Box: Uncollected Poems, Drafts, and Fragments*, ed. Alice Quinn (Manchester: Carcanet, 2006).

Bishop, Elizabeth, *One Art: Letters*, ed. Robert Giroux (New York: Farrar, Straus and Giroux, 1994).

Boys, C. V., *Soap Bubbles: Their Colours and the Forces Which Mould Them* (London: Macmillan, 1920).

Cleghorn, Angus, and Jonathan Ellis (eds), *The Cambridge Companion to Elizabeth Bishop* (Cambridge: Cambridge University Press, 2014).

Costello, Bonnie, *Elizabeth Bishop: Questions of Mastery* (Cambridge, MA: Harvard University Press, 1993).

Felstiner, John, *Can Poetry Save the Earth? A Field Guide to Nature Poems* (New Haven: Yale University Press, 2009).

Haraway, Donna J., 'The Promises of Monsters: A Regenerative Politics for Inappropriate/d Others', *Cultural Studies* (New York: Routledge, 1992), pp. 295–337.

Haraway, Donna J., *When Species Meet* (Minneapolis: University of Minnesota Press, 2008).

Pinsky, Robert, *Democracy, Culture and the Voice of Poetry* (Princeton: Princeton University Press, 2009).

Samuels, Peggy, *Deep Skin: Elizabeth Bishop and Visual Art* (Ithaca: Cornell University Press, 2010).

Samuels, Peggy, 'Verse as Deep Surface: Elizabeth Bishop's New Poetics, 1938–39', *Twentieth-Century Literature* 52.3 (Fall 2006): 306–29.

Spires, Elizabeth, 'The Art of Poetry, XXVII: Elizabeth Bishop', in George Monteiro (ed.), *Conversations with Elizabeth Bishop* (Jackson: University of Mississippi Press, 1996), pp. 114–32.

Travisano, Thomas, 'Bishop and Biography', in Angus Cleghorn and Jonathan Ellis (eds), *The Cambridge Companion to Elizabeth Bishop* (Cambridge: Cambridge University Press, 2014), pp. 21–34.

Whitman, Walt, 'Song of Myself', in *The Portable Walt Whitman*, ed. Michael Warner (London: Penguin, 2003), pp. 3–67.

PART II

THOUGHT

5

'I take off my hat': Elizabeth Bishop's Comedy of Self-Revelation

Rachel Trousdale

Elizabeth Bishop's laughter in her poems often appears to be at someone else's expense. But it generally gives way to self-critique. Humour in Bishop's work combines empathy with judgement: her speakers' failures of sympathy are to be both rejected and felt as our own, as her poems make laughter the unstable, temporary ground for intersubjective empathy and self-revelation.

This simultaneous heightening of sympathy and critique is possible because Bishop rejects Henri Bergson's model of humour, in which the self/other dichotomy is the basis for laughter. Bergson – adapting a model of humour that goes back to Aristotle, but which is most succinctly summarised by Thomas Hobbes's description of laughter as the 'sudden glory' we feel when we recognise that we are better than someone else (Hobbes 124) – believes that laughter stems from a feeling of superiority over the objects of our laughter. While Bishop shares Bergson's interest in superiority-based humour, she also suggests another form of laughter, occurring when that sense of superiority is replaced with empathy. In joking asides, absurd fantasies and mocking descriptions throughout her work, Bishop repeatedly implies that subjective experience can briefly be continuous between observer and observed, and that laughter marks the infrequent moments when we recognise that continuity.

Bishop's humorous attempts to share the experience of others echo Edith Stein's conception of empathy as 'the basis of intersubjective experience' – a conception which emphasises not just knowledge of the other's state of mind but an ability to perceive ourselves through their eyes (Stein 60). Bishop suggests that empathy may allow us to see ourselves as others see us, providing a basis for self-knowledge and self-scrutiny. At the same time, however, one of the important problems with empathy is that it is difficult to know that our empathic imaginings are correct.[1] Bishop's moments of transcendent humour are therefore partial, rendered suspect by the very self-awareness that enables them: the act of speculating about another's interiority, she suggests, carries with it a presumption of failure which it is the moral burden of the poem to acknowledge. Instead of simply inviting us to laugh at the object of her mockery, then, the target of Bishop's humour is frequently unstable, as both the poem's apparent object of ridicule and its speaker become the subjects of critique. In her combination of sympathy and self-criticism, Bishop models the true complexity of the relationship between humour and empathy, acknowledging laughter's multidirectionality and its power both to unite and to alienate.

Bishop suggests that communion, when it happens, derives from the consciousness of all participants – whether poets, gardeners, madmen or dogs. In 'Exchanging Hats', the 'flat' joke of an 'unfunny uncle' leads to speculation about a shared experience of life after death. The 'joking voice' Bishop adopts in 'One Art' shows how pain and joy, joker and audience, lover and beloved, are not just simultaneous but mutually constitutive. For Bishop, humour arises from the tension between sympathy and distance, marking the moment of revelation and the inevitability of that moment's passing.

Some of Bishop's best readers have noted the centrality of humour to her work. Jeredith Merrin shows how closely related Bishop's humour and playfulness are to her interest in 'transmogrification and changeability', reading Bishop's 'whimsy' as causally connected both to her 'delight in the possibilities of change' and to her sexuality (Merrin 154). Merrin's discussion of Bishop's 'gaiety' – the conjunction of her humour and her sexuality – helpfully situates Bishop in the critical discourse of queer boundary-crossing. Bonnie Costello takes Bishop as her first example in an essay on humour in twentieth-century American poetry, suggesting that Bishop 'asks us to consider the similarities of comic and aesthetic form, and perhaps more specifically, jokes and poetry' ('Tragicomic Mode' 461). Susan Rosenbaum notes her productive use of puns. Herbert Marks briefly but perceptively discusses the sly humour in 'North Haven', Bishop's elegy for Robert Lowell, finding a teasing mockery which is 'only partly malicious' in the list of flowers at the poem's end (203–4). These critics recognise humour's structural importance to Bishop's work; most others mention her humour and her serious use of comic devices only in passing, occasionally complaining that they render her poems flip or sarcastic. Some appear to believe that levity is irresponsible, indicating a refusal to think attentively about her subject.[2] But if Bishop's brief autobiographical gestures – her rare references to her mother, her reminiscences of childhood – tell us what has happened to her, her humour tells us who it happened to. Bishop's laughter is frequently tied to intimacy, when a speaker reveals her concerns by pretending to conceal them. For Bishop, laughter, even mocking laughter, turns out to be a test of sympathy.

In a 1964 letter to Anne Stevenson, Bishop cites humour as an important shared quality among her friends and lovers:

> I have been very lucky in having had, most of my life, some witty friends, – and I mean real wit, quickness, wild fancies, remarks that make one cry with laughing. (I seem to notice a tendency in literary people at present to think that any unkind or heavily ironical criticism is 'wit,' and any old 'ambiguity' is now considered 'wit,' too, but that's not what I mean.) The aunt I liked best was a very funny woman: most of my close friends have been funny people; Lota de Macedo Soares is funny [. . .] Marianne [Moore] was very funny – [E. E.] Cummings, too, of course. Perhaps I need such people to cheer me up. (*Poems, Prose, and Letters* 858)

Bishop's suggestion that her witty friends 'cheer her up' seems characteristically to downplay the depth and complexity of the humour she appreciates. The humour Bishop loves, 'real wit, quickness, wild fancies, remarks that make one cry with laughing', is incisive and creative, and it is deeply connected to the basis of her friendships. Like surprise, which Barbara Comins identifies as linked in Bishop's work to the creative impulse, humour is a manifestation of her friends' originality, intelligence and insight, and – as it appears in the descriptions of odd people or places in her letters – of her own.[3]

The interplay Bishop sees between humour and friendship is worked out in 'Manuelzinho'. The poem treats humour alternately as an obstacle to intersubjectivity and a means to achieve it: friendship becomes another term for the balance between laughing at and laughing with, tendentious and empathic humour. Since, as Bishop acknowledged, the speaker of the poem is based on Lota, this exploration of friendship – whether between 'writer' and 'friend' or between 'friend' and 'tenant' – is highly charged in its alternation between superiority-based and intersubjective laughter. For Bishop, these two kinds of humour cannot be separated; instead, laughter's multivalent expressions of the loving and the mean-spirited help us recognise the complexity of other people's interiorities behind their often laughable exteriors.

Bishop's humour in 'Manuelzinho' initially appears almost entirely tendentious. The speaker makes fun of her subject ('I called you Klorophyll Kid. / My visitors thought it was funny' (*Poems* 97)) and then recognises that she has been unkind ('I apologize here and now'). But the poem undercuts this mockery in favour of more ambivalent humour, in which laughter at another person's expense is transformed into laughter at the incongruity between the interior and exterior self.

The speaker of 'Manuelzinho' is self-aware, noting her own failures of sympathy ('I watch you through the rain, / [. . .] / and feel I can't endure it / another minute; then, / indoors, beside the stove, / keep on reading a book' (*Poems* 94)). By identifying her as a 'friend of the writer', the headnote of the poem marks the narrative voice as an individual apart from the poet, albeit one toward whom Bishop feels affection. This device identifies the poem from the start as, on the one hand, dealing with questions of friendship and affection, and, on the other, addressing the difficulty of accurately representing another person's mind and voice. While Brett Millier argues that the speaker's condescension is consistent with views expressed in Bishop's letters (Millier 272), her self-criticism combined with her distance from 'the writer' suggests that the poem's affectionate mockery extends beyond the landlord/tenant relationship to the more intimate relationships between friends and lovers. We are asked to join the speaker in her laughter and to recognise how that laughter is morally compromised, because the poem's humour holds several incommensurable judgements in view simultaneously – not least of which is our conflicted judgement of the speaker's capacity to achieve the understanding she claims to try for.

The speaker's gaze constantly bounces off its object. Manuelzinho is always partly obscured: by the 'sodden burlap bag' (*Poems* 94) he wears in the rain; by the 'white thread' like 'blueprints' with which his wife reinforces his pants (97). His final inscrutability comes from an extra layer of protection:

> You paint – heaven knows why –
> the outside of the crown
> and brim of your straw hat.
> Perhaps to reflect the sun?
> Or perhaps when you were small,
> your mother said, 'Manuelzinho,
> one thing: be sure you always

paint your straw hat.'
One was gold for a while,
but the gold wore off, like plate. (97)

The speaker is baffled by Manuelzinho's paint – her 'heaven knows why' implies that any mortal onlooker would be. Her first speculation concentrates on surfaces: the paint reflects the sun, protecting his head from the glare as it protects him from her assessments. Her second suggestion, that he paints his hat out of obedience to his mother, rejects physical motives entirely, instead speculating about Manuelzinho's history and emotions. The description of the gold paint peeling 'like plate', however, suggests how the poem's contradictory interiors and exteriors – Manuelzinho's behaviour and motives; the speaker's past jokes and her present repentance – still allow some possibility that we can peel away protective layers to view the core.

Manuelzinho's unknowability provides an occasion for self-knowledge: the speaker recognises that her humour is 'unkind'. Her apology, though, is suspect. Remembering calling him 'Klorophyll Kid' for the amusement of her 'visitors' foregrounds the poem's evasiveness about its audience. While addressed to Manuelzinho, its composition in English and status as published text indicate that the true audience remains Bishop's literate, anglophone readership. The closing of the poem acknowledges that self-awareness is unstable and that her attempts at sympathy will continue to fail:

You helpless, foolish man,
I love you all I can,
I think. Or do I?
I take off my hat, unpainted
and figurative, to you.
Again I promise to try. (97)

The final question – 'Or do I?' – shifts the direction of the speaker's gaze, as she recognises that she is unable to be certain in her judgements about her own motives. The poem turns out to be an account of the difficulty of understanding anyone, friend, lover, even oneself: the speaker's unpainted, figurative hat habitually shades her, too, from observation. To take off one's hat and 'to try' turn out to be the same action, an inadequate but essential gesture of respect and vulnerability. When the speaker recognises the presence of her own protective 'hat', she acknowledges that the problem is not Manuelzinho but the broader human problem of real communication. The poem's comic narrative of failed comprehension makes this promise an almost redemptive moment of self-revelation – brief, partial and doomed to fail, but more honest for that. Instead of joining in the visitors' laughter, we retain the 'friendship' identified in the headnote, both with the speaker and with Manuelzinho himself, so that our own laughter comes from the very insight that mockery denies.

This insight is characteristic of Bishop's humour – and of her serious discussions of laughter. Her best-known reference to humour, in which such insight is framed as one of the fundamental purposes of laughter, is not itself very funny. It comes in the final stanza of 'One Art':

– Even losing you (the joking voice, a gesture
I love) I shan't have lied. It's evident
the art of losing's not too hard to master
though it may look like (*Write it*!) like disaster. (*Poems* 198)

While the poem's losses appear to escalate from trivial (lost keys) to cataclysmic (a lost continent), culminating in the loss of the lover, many of the losses named in the poem imply other, sometimes deeper losses before or after them. The lost keys prefigure the lost house and may necessitate a trivial version of the 'hour badly spent' looking for them; the loss of 'my mother's watch' suggests that the mother herself is already gone.

The poem's narrative of escalation is not to be taken literally, however. The lost continent and the keys have not vanished in the same way. 'One Art' treats the word 'loss' punningly. 'Losing' covers temporary misplacements, permanent ones, frustrating uses of time, displacement from a former home, the death of a loved one, and the end of a love affair. Bishop occupies a deliberately naïve position in 'One Art', pretending that the fact that we can use the word 'lose' to refer to minor inconvenience or to 'disaster' suggests that the different losses are comparable. The notion that losing your keys prepares you for the loss of your lover is, if not funny, a laughable false equivalency.

At the climax of her catalogue, Bishop indirectly identifies the comic nature of her device. In the parenthesis, she lists two attributes of her lost lover: '(the joking voice, a gesture / I love)'. This is the only time the speaker admits that she actually feels love: unlike the 'lovely' cities and the 'loved' houses, this statement identifies the lover. As in 'Manuelzinho' and the letter to Anne Stevenson, joking is inextricably linked to love in this phrase. The beloved's 'joking voice' is one of the poem's primary losses and marks its turn from semi-comical listing to overt grief. While the speaker's confession is to love of a 'gesture', this aside about the 'joking voice' brings her closer than anywhere else to a bald admission that the reason these losses are serious is that they are predicated upon real love for a real person.

The aside occurs as the poem switches into present tense. Joking marks the moment of crisis, which both comically and seriously turns the apparently disparate losses into a narrative. The climactic joke isolates the instant in which loss is so disastrous as to form an 'evident' pattern: the moment of absurd resolution is also the moment of long perspective, in which the accruing meaning of different losses in the poem (as constructed by the poet) and in life (as constructed by chance or fate) becomes comically and tragically clear.

'Manuelzinho' uses humour to show different subjectivities simultaneously; 'One Art' uses it to fuse an individual's experiences over time into a meaningful pattern. The similarity of these two undertakings – the way that Bishop's humour consistently brings incommensurable subjectivities into dialogue – becomes clear when we read both of them next to 'Pink Dog', which contemplates the perils faced by a hairless dog surviving on the streets of Rio. Unlike the speaker of 'Manuelzinho', however, the speaker of 'Pink Dog' is for the most part not callous in her humour (although she reports callous jokes by others). Instead, she discerns a surprisingly human interior in the dog's naked body, and suggests ways that the dog may avoid the very real threat of being killed for her homeless, hairless state.

This sympathy sets her apart from other onlookers, and derives both from her understanding of the others' fears and from her attention to the dog's features:

> Of course they're mortally afraid of rabies.
> You are not mad; you have a case of scabies
> but look intelligent. Where are your babies? (*Poems* 212)

The dog is not only unthreatening but visibly, intelligently maternal, not to puppies but to 'babies'. Her condition is distressing in part because it makes her more closely resemble a (white) person; her pink nakedness reminds Bishop and other implied onlookers of their own. Their identification with her, however, does not increase most onlookers' ability to empathise with her. On the contrary, it renders her more threatening, as it makes them fear that they will catch whatever is wrong with her: rabies and scabies are both communicable to humans. But her illness is superficial, a skin disease rather than one of the brain. As in 'Manuelzinho', then, the poem shows the gap between interior and exterior, locating the cause for fear entirely on the surface of the dog's body, in both its aesthetic and its medical attributes. Identifying with the dog's grotesque figure is no more dangerous than an itchy skin disorder – potentially uncomfortable, but totally unlike mind-altering, fatal rabies.

In this case, however, the difference between interior and exterior is resolved as the speaker reads traces of the dog's mind and relationships in her naked body. The poem suggests that motherhood is inherently both a physical state and an emotional one: the dog's 'hanging teats' show that she is a 'nursing mother' (212), a role in which the physical (birth; the act of nursing) and the emotional (maternal love) become inextricable. The dog's position as object of sympathy turns out to come not simply from the vulnerability of nakedness, but from the fact that, as an 'intelligent' creature, she has an inner life which a similarly intelligent onlooker can intuit.

Unlike Manuelzinho, whose ridiculous hat both demonstrates and obscures his idiosyncratic interiority, the dog's problem is that she is entirely unmasked. The speaker chattily suggests, 'Now look, the practical, the sensible // solution is to wear a *fantasía*', diminishing a death threat to a question of fashionable self-presentation. Axelrod takes the idea of a masked dog as a sign that 'being is figurative all the way through' ('Heterotropic Desire' 76), but the dog's body is distinctly physically present in the poem. Catherine Cucinella reads the dog as a figure for the 'abjected female body' (73), but the poem also makes the dog a specific individual who 'look[s] intelligent' – her mind is central to the poem. As with Manuelzinho, this individual can be understood to represent a social class – beggars, abjected femininity, outcasts – but the poem also directs us toward her individual qualities, whether admirable (intelligence) or not (scabies). Much of the poem's humour, in fact, is based in the dog's simultaneously allegorical and individual status: the poem playfully moves back and forth between personal and social levels, refusing to let on just how seriously it takes either its sympathy with the dog or its larger social critique.

Bishop's comic device here is striking among humorous treatments of suffering for its emphasis on the limits of the solution it provides. This fantasy of invisibility ('no one will ever see a // dog in *máscara* this time of year') is only 'practical' until Ash Wednesday, at which point the dog will need to find a new survival strategy. The temporary nature of Carnival is, however, part of what makes the strategy, and Carnival itself, work. Where the comic instability built into 'Manuelzinho' acknowledges that the speaker will inevitably turn away from sympathy, in 'Pink Dog', Carnival's temporality is central to its ecstatic possibilities. While 'they' may say that 'Carnival's degenerating',

> Carnival is always wonderful!
> A depilated dog would not look well.
> Dress up! Dress up and dance at Carnival! (*Poems* 213)

Carnival's emphasis on appearances, on dancing, on celebration, means that Carnival 'is always wonderful!'; it is impossible to spoil, its gaiety not just unaffected but driven by the cruelty of the city. Unlike the dog, or the human body, Carnival does not and cannot decay, both because it is a celebration of forces which ostensibly lead to decay (chaos, sexuality, upheaval) and because of its strictly bounded irruption. Carnival is a perfect example of Freud's notion of the joke as a release from reason: its power comes from its simultaneous acknowledgement and flouting of social rules. While Carnival cannot provide a long-term solution to the dog's problems, or to the broader problems of Rio's poor, its atmosphere of shared play encourages mutual recognition among its participants. It is not sufficient to say, as Bakhtin does, that Carnival masks liberate their wearers; for Bishop, the act of wearing a mask entails an invitation to look beneath it, an acknowledgement that there is an interiority to protect and suffering to overcome. Like the 'joking voice' of 'One Art', the self-disguise of the *fantasía* is transparent; more startlingly, the injunction to 'Dress up and dance' suggests the possibility of a deeper mutual understanding based on common 'gestures'. Locating this solution within the framework of Carnival renders it both explicitly temporary ('Ash Wednesday'll come') and eternally recurrent ('Carnival is always wonderful!'), a continuing cycle of revelation and occlusion. The speaker's conflation of 'the practical, the sensible' and the preposterous echoes the Carnival season itself, emphasising the abiding power of its temporary transformations.

'Pink Dog', in other words, does exactly what 'Manuelzinho' does not: it allows its speaker substantive insight into the interiority of another. This insight is made possible because of its limitations, both temporal and practical: the dog is far more alien than Manuelzinho, whose difference from his observer is not of species but merely of class, making other differences more baffling to the speaker. The dog both has value in her own right and provides an exercise in the sympathy we should extend to others. In each poem, Bishop's comical description of clothing – Manuelzinho's hat, the dog's *fantasía* – also describes the speaker's attempt at piecing together the other's subjectivity.

The key to Bishop's humour in both of these poems is in recognising the incongruity between the absurd surface and the subjectivity it covers. Whether or not a speaker succeeds at empathising with her subject depends, to a large degree, on whether she is willing to recognise that subject's 'intelligence': whether, in other words, she gives the individual she describes credit for conscious self-presentation, and for sharing the wit that distinguishes her friends.

'One Art' examines the extent to which humour can break down the boundaries between consciousnesses or conceptual categories; 'Manuelzinho' imagines humour as a means to promote intersubjectivity and self-scrutiny; 'Pink Dog' emphasises the temporary and epiphanic nature of these boundary-crossing revelations. These poems play with the incongruities not just of their subjects but of humour itself, bringing empathic humour's capacity for redemption into dialogue with potentially deadly mockery. Bishop suggests that these apparently contradictory modes can be brought together to form an empathic imagination which retains a self-protective sense of its own individuality and a sceptical distance from its own undertakings.

The connection Bishop draws between self-protection – especially protective clothing – and comic revelation leads her to reconsider the balance between self-effacement and comic revelation within stereotyped gender performances in 'Exchanging Hats', a poem in which a niece's observation of her aunt and uncle's joking cross-dressing gives way to speculation about life after death. As in 'Manuelzinho' (which was published the same year, 1956), funny hats suggest a point of potentially productive conflict: they deflect the observer's gaze while revealing the wearer's interiority. (Bishop may have been aware of Samuel Beckett's hat-related existential comedy in *Waiting for Godot*, which had its first American production in the same year.) Once again, the full comic insight of the poem comes from seeing an apparent disjunction alongside a deeper continuity. In 'Exchanging Hats', however, the initial examination of one-on-one intersubjectivity, the possibility that we may be able to guess what another individual is thinking, extends to encompass the possibility of understanding broader groups like members of the older generation, people of the opposite sex, and maybe even the dead. 'Pink Dog' only implies that the experience of empathy between two individuals (the speaker and the dog) may help us to understand other people beyond that intersubjective dyad, but 'Exchanging Hats' explicitly examines the idea that empathy with idiosyncratic individuals can also illuminate common human experiences – including the paradoxically universal experience of being a unique individual.

'Exchanging Hats' is in tightly rhymed iambic tetrameter quatrains, a form frequently used for light verse. The poem opens with a failed joke:

> Unfunny uncles who insist
> in trying on a lady's hat,
> – oh, even if the joke falls flat,
> we share your slight transvestite twist
>
> in spite of our embarrassment. (*Poems* 230)

The 'unfunny uncles' are notable not for their humourlessness but for their failed *attempts* at humour. Once again, humour marks an uneasy coexistence of sympathy and mockery, this time of an older generation's experiments with gender. Costello argues that the humour of the poem is 'sinister', because it 'exposes "a slight transvestite twist" in us all, which we suppress' (*Questions of Mastery* 83). Axelrod agrees, pointing out that the phrase 'unfunny uncles' 'plays on the cliché of the "funny uncle," the family member who cracks jokes and/or is somehow outside of gender norms. But these particular uncles are "unfunny," implying both that their joke does not amuse and that their ostensible gender peculiarity is really not unusual' ('Bishop, History, and Politics' 46).

The niece is embarrassed not so much by cross-dressing itself as by the revelation that the uncles want to do it. The 'transvestite twist' is pleasurable more because of the speaker's embarrassment than despite it; she experiences both superiority-based humour at the uncles' expense and a Freudian release from repression in the acknowledgement that she and the uncles share transgressive desires. To put it more broadly, the fact that the joke is a cliché also makes it a revelation: transgressive desire is so common as to have a familiar vocabulary and a permitted form of expression. The joke's very banality – its formulaic dependence on gender norms and consequent failure to transgress – also situates those desires within a larger continuity of experience, in which caricatured gender performance turns out to provide meaningful insight into how individuals recognise their commonality with others.

The revelation of shared desire prompts Bishop to be merciless with the uncles' and aunts' experiments with gender – the uncles in a lady's hat are 'unfunny'; the aunts emit not laughs but an 'exhibitionistic screech'. The problem with the 'unfunny uncles' is not their transgression (which 'we', the niece, many nieces, the next generation, and the readers, share); rather, it is their transgression's insufficiency. The joke with a lady's hat is too formulaic, too stagey – too explicitly 'exhibitionistic' – to constitute a significant venture into an unfamiliar gendered subjectivity. It grants the uncles no access to a lady's experience. Manuelzinho's painted hat offers immediate insight into his peculiarity because it really is eccentric: he is not following a script, and as a result the flaking gold paint on his hat is deeply moving. The exchange of hats the aunts and uncles engage in, by contrast, conforms to familiar patterns of gender performance and mild subversion, rendering the joke 'flat' in its familiarity. The poem suggests that we should aspire to more substantive transgressions, productive of comic, world-changing intersubjectivity.

The uncles' dependence on cliché suggests why they are plural. The address to 'unfunny uncles' implies a generalisation from a case (a single 'unfunny uncle' standing in for a whole generation), but that generalisation removes the possibility of individual understanding: we can imagine what the uncle is thinking only insofar as he is representative of a broader group. Similarly, wearing a lady's hat may give us some insight into the physical constraints of women's clothing, but it does not give us a sense of what distinguishes one lady's experience from another's. The uncles' form of humour is essentially generic, and the 'unfunny uncles' and 'anandrous aunts' are themselves subject to ridicule to the same degree that they are plural. These comic descriptions are no more productive of intersubjective insight than the literal, physical exchange of hats is, because, like their hats, the roles of 'uncle' and 'aunt' are formulaic markers of gender and of identity. The plural uncles are part of a prescribed spectrum of possible behaviours, and generate humour according to the familiar formula of mild incongruity rather than through individuating 'wild fancies'.

The inadequacy of the uncles' experiments is all the more striking because 'Exchanging Hats' is one of the few poems in which Bishop overtly examines the mutability and constructedness of gender and sexuality. That experiment interests feminist critics like Kathleen Brogan (who reads 'Exchanging Hats' as uncovering 'the fictive nature of an unambiguous, unitary sexual identity' (69)), and Bishop's deployment of hats as markers of gender seems almost designed for discussion as an example of Butlerian gender performativity. As Judith Butler argues, the performance of gender turns out also to be part of the production of the subjective self, the 'speaking "I"' (7–15). The poem examines the limits within which our bodies determine our identities: the more meaningfully we exchange hats, the more possible it is to take on attributes ascribed to another gender and thus treat sexual identity as fluid.

The stakes of this experimentation turn out to be life and death, and as Bishop concludes, the poem's consideration of the uncle and aunt's viewpoints from within their hats becomes far more sympathetic. At the end of the poem, the speaker addresses the uncle to ask, 'tell us, can't you, are there any / stars inside your black fedora?' and wonders what 'slow changes' the aunt sees under the 'vast, shady, turned-down brim' of her final hat. Here, mockery gives way to sympathy as the uncles and aunts become singular. The uncle remains 'unfunny', and his comic repertoire is still limited to hats, but he gains the possibility of 'stars' (echoing Manuelzinho's peeling gold). He and the aunt thus become speculative models for the experience of eternity. The possibility of transcending one's gender is linked to the attempt to transcend mortality, and death is rewritten as a transformation akin to but far more serious than the exchange of hats.

At the same time, the switch to the singular raises the possibility of communion, as the 'exemplary' aunt is now the subject of an intimate first-person address. But by becoming individuals to whom the niece can speak, the aunt and uncle, isolated within their hats, paradoxically become mediums through whom the niece can experience the universe. By shifting from the plural to the singular, the poem both specifies its subjects (this aunt, this uncle) and broadens its ambition to a deliberately ambiguous consideration of death, loneliness and the infinite.

The speaking voice remains plural. But unlike the plural uncles, 'we' feel complex emotions throughout. Costello argues that Bishop and other twentieth-century poets use the first-person plural to '"make toward" [. . .] a union, a group, even a community' ('Lyric Poetry' 194). When Bishop writes that 'we' share the uncle's 'twist', she suggests both literal cousins embarrassed by their elders and a shared metaphorical cousinship among readers seeking to understand one another. But the 'we' may extend still further: 'our' imaginative leap as we attempt to understand the aunt's 'exemplary' experience establishes, as the opening stanzas cannot, our own place in the continuous experience of occupying varied roles. We will eventually be figures in the older generation, the exemplary aunts to the next, and we, too, will some day find out what lies inside the final hat. This insight is sparked by the initial failed joke, which springs from the common experience of uncommonness and signals the absurdity of realising that our individuating idiosyncrasies actually make us part of a group. The poem's discontinuities – the aunts and uncles' failure to communicate in life, their silence in death – are also continuities, as 'we' first make a leap of imagination into another's consciousness and then take on the other's role.

Far from depending on superiority or failed communication, the final humour of the poem is a form of communication more successful than that between the uncles and 'us'; it brings 'us' our best guess at the incommunicable experience of death. While, as Costello notes, this guess is not an excessively hopeful one – 'She is not sure that there are any stars under the uncle's black fedora or that the aunt has seen any genuine changes, however slow, within the unlagging tides of sexual and social fashion' (*Questions of Mastery* 85) – 'Exchanging Hats' is a sustained and boundary-crossing exploration of the extension of sympathy by an observer to the individual she observes. Where class in 'Manuelzinho' presents the speaker with an insuperable barrier for sympathy, death in 'Exchanging Hats' (like species in 'Pink Dog') apparently does not; even if the phrase 'can't you' emphasises the impossibility that the dead will answer, the request to 'tell us' – a pronoun suggesting mutuality among speaker, poet and readers – goes further than Bishop usually dares toward suggesting that the object of laughter or sympathy can respond in kind.

A third poem written in 1956, 'The Wit', also follows this progression from individual to group to stars. The sonnet opens with a line spoken by 'you', which is at once reported speech and an intimate address to a single person: '"Wait. Let me think a minute," you said' (*Poems* 229). During that minute, 'we', the listeners within the poem, see 'Eve and Newton', 'Moses with the Law', 'Socrates' and 'many more from Greece / all coming hurrying up to now', as the wit summons the dead to her aid. The speaker's 'brilliant pun' then scatters the 'flustered [. . .] helpers',

> and through the conversational spaces, after,
> we caught, – back, back, far, far, –
> the glinting birthday of a fractious star. (229)

The poem does not report the pun itself. Rather, it focuses on the listeners' shared experience of watching wit at work. The process of composing the pun gives wit and audience alike access to a genealogy reaching back through science and philosophy to Eve, and then beyond the mythical origins of humanity to the scientific origins of the solar system. The pun gives us a glimpse not just into the interiority of the wit, who summons all these forces to her aid, but into the interiority of the star itself, which, having a birthday and being 'fractious', turns out to be surprisingly human. Fusing religion and science, Eve and Newton, the pun takes us across vast distances, but what we find across a huge expanse of space and time turns out to be reassuringly, comically familiar.

In these poems, humour is a marker of the precise point at which conflicting pressures meet. The connection humour provides between different viewpoints must, Bishop suggests, be unstable, because it depends on a kind of extreme awareness possible only in the moment of crisis: at the loss of a lover, at Carnival, at death. Wit is a prerequisite for friendship not simply to 'cheer me up' but because it enables an otherwise impossible transgression of the boundaries between selves. But because humour takes place in moments of crisis and transformation, its cheering effects, like the insights it grants, are temporary, with the result that Bishop – and, she suggests, the rest of us – will only rarely be able to combine the opposed modes of sympathetic and mocking humour. In more ordinary moments, we will continue to alternate between the superiority-based and the empathic view of others.

Bishop rejects the idea that the cognitive dissonance between superiority-based and empathy-producing humour is too great to allow us to engage in both simultaneously. Her poems clearly demonstrate humour's multiplicity, its resistance to reduction to a single theory, its multivalent social, psychological, interpersonal and artistic functions. If we are seeking a unified field theory of humour, Bishop may provide it, not by providing a fundamental account of the nature of laughter but by emphasising that even the most reductive comic impulse contains the potential – often unrealised – for complex interpersonal insight.

Notes

1. See for example Matravers.
2. See for example Parker (127).
3. James Merrill, in a memorial essay, emphasises Bishop's playfulness in everyday life: 'Thus the later glimpses of her playing was it poker? with Neruda in a Mexican hotel, or ping-pong with Octavio Paz in Cambridge, or getting Robert Duncan high on grass – "for the first time!" – in San Francisco, or teaching Frank Bidart the wildflowers in Maine. Why talk *letters* with one's gifted colleagues? They too would want, surely, to put aside work in favor of a new baby to examine, a dinner to shop for and cook, sambas, vignettes: Here's what I heard this afternoon (or saw twenty years ago) – imagine! Poetry was a life both shaped by and distinct from the lived one' (259).

Works Cited

Axelrod, Stephen Gould, 'Bishop, History, and Politics', in Angus Cleghorn and Jonathan Ellis (eds), *The Cambridge Companion to Elizabeth Bishop* (Cambridge: Cambridge University Press, 2014), pp. 35–48.

Axelrod, Stephen Gould, 'Heterotropic Desire in Elizabeth Bishop's "Pink Dog"', *The Arizona Quarterly* 60.3 (2004): 61–81.

Bergson, Henri, 'Laughter', trans. Cloudesley Brereton and Fred Rothwell, in Wylie Sypher (ed.), *Comedy* (Baltimore: Johns Hopkins University Press, 1956), pp. 61–192.

Bishop, Elizabeth, *Poems, Prose, and Letters*, ed. Robert Giroux and Lloyd Schwartz (New York: Library of America, 2008).

Brogan, Kathleen, 'Lyric Voice and Sexual Difference in Elizabeth Bishop', in Suzanne W. Jones (ed.), *Writing the Woman Artist: Essays on Poetics, Politics, and Portraiture* (Philadelphia: University of Pennsylvania Press, 1991), pp. 60–78.

Butler, Judith, *Bodies that Matter: On the Discursive Limits of 'Sex'* (New York: Routledge, 1993).

Comins, Barbara, '"Shuddering Insights": Bishop and Surprise', in Laura Jehn Menides and Angela G. Dorenkamp (eds), *'In Worcester, Massachusetts': Essays on Elizabeth Bishop* (New York: Peter Lang, 1999), pp. 177–86.

Costello, Bonnie, *Elizabeth Bishop: Questions of Mastery* (Cambridge, MA: Harvard University Press, 1991).

Costello, Bonnie, 'Lyric Poetry and the First-Person Plural: "How Unlikely"', in Stephen Burt and Nick Halpern (eds), *Something Understood: Essays and Poetry for Helen Vendler* (Charlottesville: University of Virginia Press, 2009), pp. 193–206.

Costello, Bonnie, 'Tragicomic Mode in Modern American Poetry: "Awful but Cheerful"', in Erik Martiny (ed.), *A Companion to Poetic Genre* (New York: Wiley-Blackwell, 2011), pp. 459–77.

Cucinella, Catherine, '"Dress up! Dress up and Dance at Carnival!": The Body in Elizabeth Bishop's "Pink Dog"', *Rocky Mountain Review of Language and Literature* 56.1 (2002): 73–83.

Freud, Sigmund, *The Joke and Its Relation to the Unconscious*, trans. Joyce Crick (New York: Penguin, 2002).

Hobbes, Thomas, *Leviathan*, ed. C. B. MacPherson (New York: Penguin, 1985).

Marks, Herbert, 'Elizabeth Bishop's Art of Memory', *Literary Imagination: The Review of the Association of Literary Scholars and Critics* 7.2 (2005): 197–223.

Matravers, Derek, 'Empathy as a Route to Knowledge', in Amy Coplan and Peter Goldie (eds), *Empathy: Philosophical and Psychological Perspectives* (New York: Oxford University Press, 2011), pp. 19–30.

Merrill, James, 'Elizabeth Bishop, 1911–1979', in Lloyd Schwartz and Sybil P. Estess (eds), *Elizabeth Bishop and Her Art* (Ann Arbor: University of Michigan Press, 1983), pp. 259–62.

Merrin, Jeredith, 'Elizabeth Bishop: Gaiety, Gayness, and Change', in Marilyn May Lombardi (ed.), *Elizabeth Bishop: The Geography of Gender* (Charlottesville: University Press of Virginia, 1993), pp. 153–72.

Millier, Brett C., *Elizabeth Bishop: Life and the Memory of It* (Berkeley: University of California Press, 1993).

Parker, Robert Dale, *The Unbeliever: The Poetry of Elizabeth Bishop* (Chicago: University of Illinois Press, 1988).

Rosenbaum, Susan, 'Elizabeth Bishop and the Miniature Museum', *Journal of Modern Literature* 28.2 (2005): 61–99.

Stein, Edith, *On the Problem of Empathy*, trans. W. Stein (Washington: ICS Publications, 1989).

6

'THIS HEAPED-UP AUTOBIOGRAPHY': THE ROLE OF RELIGION IN ELIZABETH BISHOP'S POETRY

Marcel Inhoff

IN THIS CHAPTER I will highlight the marked influence of Charles Baudelaire and of religious thought on Elizabeth Bishop's writing of personal poetry. Bishop was well versed in religious traditions and some of her ideas and aspects of her poetry fall in line with religious philosophies contemporary with (or postdating) her work, such as those of Emmanuel Levinas. Bishop did not immediately embrace personal poetry, rather in the course of her career moved from covert to overt life writing, a shift in which both Baudelaire and religious tradition were instrumental. I will conclude with 'The Bight', the poem most frequently discussed in connection with Baudelaire's impact on Bishop, and will show how it functions in Bishop's oeuvre as a first attempt to switch from a private to a public mode.

In a 1960s lecture Elizabeth Bishop never published, she refers to her 'three "favorite" poets – not the best poets whom we all admire, but favorite in the sense of one's "best friends," etc. [who] are Herbert, Hopkins, and Baudelaire' (*Prose* 328). Bishop scholars have stressed the importance of Herbert and Hopkins for her poetry, but Baudelaire, whose portrait adorned the wall of Bishop's studio in Brazil (Millier 263), has not enjoyed the same level of scholarly attention.[1] Most explorations that do exist trace his influence on Bishop as a foil to discuss her growth and development as a poet.[2]

Another aspect of Bishop seldom attended to is her relationship to religion, despite her numerous allusions to religious writers and thinkers. In the same 1960s lecture, for example, two sentences before Bishop enumerates her three 'best friends', she mentions Simone Weil's collection of essays *Waiting for God*. Such explicit nods to religious tradition are glossed over since Bishop herself lacked a personal religious faith. I maintain that the workings of both Baudelaire and religious tradition in Bishop's poetry need to be explored in greater depth.

I do not mean to dismiss the fine scholarship that addresses Bishop's life writing and poetic development. Examining the roles of Baudelaire and religion in Bishop's work enhances our understanding of Bishop's strategies of masking and unmasking, and of the way Bishop used and structured observations of nature, cities and other people. Religious tradition provided a toolkit for her to do all this, and Baudelaire's poetry provided an example. For one thing, closer examination of Baudelaire, and attention to Baudelaire scholarship, can go a long way towards putting an end to the common assumption of an unbridgeable divide between Bishop, the poet celebrated for her observations, and Baudelaire, the symbolist.[3] Baudelaire's heightened sense of aesthetics feeds, contrary to assumptions, *not* primarily on an overactive imagination.

It relies instead on observations (Kadi 92): Baudelaire's 'analogies [. . .] remain specifi-
cally of *this* world' (Leakey 211). One needs to take account of such critical insights
into Baudelaire's poetry, especially given Bishop's in-depth knowledge and profound
understanding of it. Her responsiveness to Baudelaire's poetry also bore upon her own
writing, and there are many evocations of unusual details[4] and allusions to his lesser-
known poems.[5]

Bishop employed 'masks' (Leviston 437), but critics have not yet pointed out that
Baudelaire might have been an influence in her development of masking techniques.
In fact, Baudelaire's life writing involved a form of self-masking, which is so typical
of his poetry that this technique can be singled out as 'prototypically Baudelairean'
(Burt 85). Baudelaire's self-masking through mirrors (Burt 96) relates to his 'marked
preference for [. . .] impersonal writing' (Burt 85), and to his toying with perspectives
and representation. All these one finds in Bishop as well.[6] The two poets also share
a similar sense of religion as a textual influence rather than a question of faith or the
lack thereof. Even so, there are complications in Bishop's relationship to Baudelaire,
unsurprising given his views on women and queer sexuality, and indeed it is the con-
flict as well as the similarities with the French poet that inform Bishop's poetry. 'The
Bight', published in Bishop's second collection *A Cold Spring*, is frequently regarded as
a poem wherein she airs her disagreements with Baudelaire. I will return to it towards
the end of this chapter to highlight the way her use of Baudelaire helped her examine
the conflicts between private and public life writing.

Bishop's manner of engaging with conflicts between private and public was some-
thing she developed over time, and Baudelaire was not Bishop's only example of how
to do it. Hers was a continuous process, one long attempt at figuring out a literary
problem and finding different solutions for it: writing the lines 'you are an *I*, / you are
an *Elizabeth*' (*Poems* 180) was not the result of a sudden change, but the culmina-
tion of a process of discovering a way to write a narrative of self that is not openly
'confessional'. A host of letters and interviews demonstrate Bishop's unease with the
confessional mode of writing. This does not represent a general resistance to personal
writing. Bishop found her own approaches to it through her reading and understand-
ing of a very specific religious tradition. From letters, remarks and textual evidence, we
know that she read spiritual autobiographies by St Augustine, St Teresa of Avila and
St Ignatius of Loyola, as well as the religious poetry of Herbert and Hopkins. There
are many points of comparison between Bishop's work and that of Hopkins and
Herbert and her debt to these two poets has been explored in many excellent studies.
I am focusing on Avila and Loyola instead, in addition to Baudelaire, none of whom
has been accorded the same courtesy, with the aforementioned exceptions.

Bishop's embrace of Baudelaire dates back to her time spent in Paris in the mid-
1930s when she immersed herself in French literature. These years left an indelible
mark on her. During that period she learned French, and 'began translating French
poetry [. . .] as a way of disciplining her own verse' (Millier 89). The French poet who
most enduringly influenced her was Baudelaire. 'A Miracle at Breakfast', for example,
which invokes the Eucharist, bears Baudelaire's imprint: he himself often refers to the
Eucharist and many of his poems provide commentary on or criticism of the Catholic
sacrament. More specifically, in the prose poem 'Les Foules', Baudelaire connects the
'bain des multitudes' with the idea of 'universelle communion' (Pines 201), and the
three wine poems ('L'Âme du Vin', 'Le Vin des Chiffoniers' and 'Le Vin de l'Assassin')

contain discussions of the Eucharist along with a table, grains or crumbs and a reference to the sun (Pines 207), all three of which reappear in Bishop's poem. Most convincing, however, is the connection between Baudelaire's frequent uses of the transformative power of the poet's gaze (Pines 204) and the Eucharist, given that Bishop's poem features a concern with gazes, perspectives and (failed) transformations.

Another poem marked by Baudelaire's influence is 'Quai d'Orléans', one of Bishop's metropolitan poems from *North & South*. Critics who discuss it, tempted by its final lines, turn their attention mostly to its knotty reflections on memory and consciousness. These readings are valid and accurate, but I want to stress something else. This poem does not describe one isolated event; instead, it begins with continuity: 'Each barge on the river tows / A mighty wake' (*Poems* 29). Ellis, one of the few critics to note this, observes that Bishop's poem involves 'the natural cycles of rivers and tides' (Ellis 72). Crucially, the metaphors of the poem connect these cycles with the realms of habitual culture (the regular stream of boats down the Seine). An example of this mélange is the description of 'throngs of small leaves, real leaves' which 'disappear [. . .] down the sea's / dissolving halls' (*Poems* 29). In this image, we have our first strong connection in Bishop's poetry to 'Correspondances', the famous poem by Baudelaire to which 'The Bight' alludes. Here is the opening quatrain of that poem:

> La Nature est un temple où de vivants piliers
> Laissent parfois sortir de confuses paroles;
> L'homme y passe à travers des forêts de symboles
> Qui l'observent avec des regards familiers. (Baudelaire 55)[7]

The link from this quatrain to the small observation in Bishop's poem may not be immediately obvious, despite the main similarity of a natural aspect (the widening of the sea) that is described in terms of an edifice (halls of a house). A parallel observation by Frances Leviston regarding an unpublished Bishop poem makes the link more obvious: in her essay on 'The Bight', she mentions this same opening quatrain of 'Correspondances' in connection to a draft of the unpublished poem 'Current Dreams'. Bishop, she argues, '[a]ppropriat[ed] Baudelaire's symbols and syntax' to write a text involving 'the sea' and its 'shifting sidewalks' (Leviston 450). For Leviston, the 'shifting sidewalks' are a clear link to Baudelaire's text; 'the sea's / dissolving halls' (*Poems* 29) are clearly a parallel construction, bearing out my initial claim regarding Bishop's phrase in 'Quai d'Orléans' and 'Correspondances'.

A second early Bishop poem, 'Seascape', alludes to 'Correspondances' and its famous first stanza. 'Seascape' seemingly has no speaker, but the use of determiners like 'this' suggests a quiet presence, and the initial description of the landscape very carefully uses perspective. Bishop creates the appearance of chaos by allowing her readers to 'observe the scene from multiple perspectives' (Mehta 72). The poem was 'initially inspired by a tapestry based on a Raphael cartoon of the miraculous draught of fishes, which she saw in the Vatican in November 1937' (Ford 246). There are two miraculous catches of fish in the Bible, John 21: 1–14 and Luke 5: 1–11, and the Raphael painting depicts the latter. Jesus calls his first disciples and closes with his words to Peter, 'Fear not; from henceforth thou shalt catch men' (King James Version). This connects the poem to others like 'Roosters' and 'The Fish'. 'Seascape' does not flaunt its religious inspiration, but it makes repeated reference to religion and introduces a lighthouse that embodies the ills of institutional religion that Bishop abhorred. The connection to Baudelaire can be discerned, as in 'Quai d'Orléans', in a seemingly innocuous phrase. Bishop describes, halfway through her examination of florid nature, the 'suggestively Gothic arches of the mangrove roots' (*Poems* 41). In Baudelaire's poem, nature is a temple, and in Bishop's poem, nature shapes itself in accordance with sacred architecture.

Baudelaire's poem invokes Swedenborgian principles, but this should not lead to any assumptions about Baudelaire's religious leanings. In fact, discussions of Baudelaire's religiousness often prompt opposing answers, with strong convictions on both sides. One might, for example, read Baudelaire as an aesthete who was deeply knowledgeable in biblical matters and references, and who used the rhetoric of suffering offered by Catholicism.[8] His queer relationship to religion is best shown in the rejection by T. S. Eliot in the 1930s. To Eliot at that point, in contrast to the Eliot of the 'Preludes', Baudelaire's faith is merely 'rudimentary' (Mackinnon 37). Eliot's reservations are 'institutional and orthodox', Baudelaire's more personal use of Christian influences and tenets not fitting the newly minted Anglican poet's understanding of what it is to be religious. An example of Baudelaire's use of religious sources is the image of nature as a temple with living pillars, reproduced by Bishop in 'Seascape', which inverts a phrase in Chateaubriand's *Génie du Christianisme*, where the author suggests that 'Gothic architects constructed their first "temples" in imitation of the [. . .] forest' (Leakey 201). There is no reason to assume Bishop had an opinion either way on the convoluted question of the shape of Baudelaire's faith, poetic or personal, but the basic context of Baudelaire's poem clearly follows Christian tradition. The humorous passage suggesting that bird droppings on leaves are reminiscent of illuminations, the 'cartoon' by Raphael, the reference to Luke, all of these are Christian references, used in a joking or, if we follow Costello, ironic way. The poem's first half moves 'towards a religious claim' (Ravinthiran 20) as the description ends with the insistent phrase 'it does look like heaven'. Vidyan Ravinthiran explains that this phrase 'approaches [. . .] the brink of logical argument' (20), its musicality prefiguring the personified lighthouse.

A critical assessment of Baudelaire can be discerned in the poem's second half. Baudelaire's theology is fundamentally concerned with redemption and the impossibility thereof. If we assume, as we should, that Bishop was a careful and attentive reader of Baudelaire, she presumably reached the same conclusion. It explains the second half of the poem as it turns from complex description to Baudelairean personification when a local lighthouse joins the conversation. The theology pointed forward in this section of the poem reflects the harsh theology of institutional religion, which Bishop so abhorred. Bishop, as Ravinthiran notes, subtly shifts the prose rhythms of the poem to a more regular beat. This shift to regular metre works like a reference to the structures (and strictures) of religious speech, which include 'stylized and restricted intonational contour' (Keane 52) and aim to be recited rather than spoken. The poem's 'generous prose-rhythm' (Ravinthiran 22) gives it a flexibility which undermines and simultaneously comments on the rigidity of religious speech.

Bishop famously had a bone to pick with institutionalised religion. In a much-cited letter to Anne Stevenson, she writes: 'I dislike the didacticism, not to say condescension, of the practicing Christians I know. [. . .] But I am interested in *religions*' (*Prose* 415). While 'Seascape' criticises the oppressive structures of religions, it also, on a more indirect level, criticises Baudelaire, whose most famous poem it almost directly references. Bishop toys with nature, theology, Baudelaire and her thinking about all three, as well as on the nature of religious language itself. Ravinthiran suggests a connection between the lighthouse's 'remember[ing] something / strongly worded to say on the subject' (*Poems* 41) and George Herbert's final two words in 'Prayer (I)', 'something understood' (Ravinthiran 23). Religious oratory, 'something [. . .] to say', is implicitly contrasted with 'something understood', but the source for this second impulse is also religious, showing that Bishop infused the poem not with blanket criticism of religion, but with her own understanding. 'Quai d'Orléans' and 'Seascape' are not major poems for Bishop, but they show us how certain topics are connected by her. 'Seascape' in particular shows the scope – and limit – of Baudelaire's influence.

The neglect of Bishop's religious influences is in part due to what I believe to be a selective reading of letters and other sources. For example, while an important study has been written about the famous 'Darwin letter', and there are several articles on Darwin's influence on Bishop more generally, other texts mentioned in her letters receive less attention. In an intriguing letter to Marianne Moore, Bishop discusses her interest in autobiography and states: 'I am reading St. Augustine's *Confessions*, Amiel's *Journals*, and Wordsworth's *Prelude*, and this headed-up auto-biography is having extreme results, maybe fortunate' (*One Art* 45). In the so-called Darwin letter itself, she also explains: 'I enjoy reading, say, St. Teresa, very much, and Kierkegaard (whom I read in vast quantities long ago, before he became fashionable), Simone Weil, etc.' (*Prose* 415). Foremost among the non-autobiographical readings in religious tradition is Ignatius of Loyola[9] whom Bishop read 'in the early 1930's, well before [he] became popular among literary critics, and [she] used [the *Spiritual Exercises*] as a poetic resource many times' (Walker 19). Walker doesn't go into details here, but an example of Bishop using the *Spiritual Exercises* as a poetic resource can be found in her attention to detail and memory. Scholars do not make a habit of mentioning instances of this, but Costello does, in a small remark, connect Bishop's use of synaesthesia to a passage from Ignatius's book. Bishop also kept St Teresa's *Way of Perfection* 'with her at all times' (Walker 19) and upon reading Augustine's *City of God*, a heavily theological text, exclaimed 'It is one of the most exciting things I've ever read!' (Walker 21). These thinkers, poets and priests focused on matters of expressing and hiding the self, working and struggling with form. While all of these writers are very dependent on their faith, concerns with form are paramount, even for texts as seemingly formless as Henri Amiel's *Journaux Intimes*.

Among the most widely discussed (and least controversial) aspects of Bishop's poetry are her powers of observation. Critics throughout the past decades have highlighted how much Bishop values the act of observation and attention: 'for Bishop, observation is a moral act' (Travisano 126). And yet, for all the observation that takes place, explicitly named observers are rare.[10] Bishop has perfected a technique of hiding her voice in the folds of her poetry, to the extent that Gillian White argues that her method constitutes a radical experiment. This technique of obscuring and hiding, where not influenced by Baudelaire, can be traced back to Teresa of Avila. St Teresa was a teacher[11] at a time when doing so as a woman could mean finding oneself tortured and jailed. In the sixteenth century, St Paul's invective against women teaching was taken very seriously. Alison Weber points out how St Teresa employed a wide range of techniques in order to write both as a woman and as 'a manly soul' (Weber 17). Bishop's autobiographical writing specifically makes use of this older tradition that exists alongside of – and commenting on – the male writing of the self. Ultimately, the appreciation and use of texts like St Ignatius's and St Teresa's is not something that *requires* faith, which is why Bishop's faith (or lack thereof) is beside the point here. The *Spiritual Exercises*, despite their title, are really rooted in the process of *writing*, their purpose being the invention of a language (Barthes 44), a language for how to speak about imagination and memory, how to integrate past and present. Bishop's productive but not faith-based use of Ignatius and Teresa bears out this analysis: clearly, there is an application of the ideas of firmly religious writers to not particularly religious texts. There appears to be a stigma in looking at the influence of theological texts on literature when the influenced text is not primarily (or at all) religious. Bishop's use of Ignatius, Teresa, Augustine, Amiel and others is evidence of the problems with such an approach.

In 'The Bight', the third poem in Bishop's 1955 collection *A Cold Spring*, much of what I have discussed comes together, but before I take a look at the poem I want to draw attention to the way it is placed in the book. The two poems preceding it comment upon and contextualise the poem within a certain tradition, something that was first noticed by Alfred Corn. Corn notes how, in the collection's first poem, 'A Cold Spring', the landscape is ambiguously described, either in terms of ownership or as if it takes on attributes of the human body (Corn 159). The dedication to Jane Dewey also reminds us of how, in Bishop's landscapes, 'the land becomes for the poet an image of her own desire' (Paton 170), and not primarily sexual desire. Bishop thus configures her landscapes in a way that makes them especially expressive of interiority. Now if we look at what exactly makes up this identity, we find allusions to Christian tradition. As we learned from White, Bishop trained herself to choose more complex religious allusions that are not immediately obvious, rather than draw from the stock of conventional tropes. Corn points to the fact that in a poem dealing with the seasons, she refers to vegetation that is strongly associated with religion, in particular the dogwood, 'beams from which (according to legend) were used to make the cross' (Corn 160). If we are prepared to read the poem in this enhanced context, we notice even more. When Bishop writes that the cardinal (the bird) 'cracked a whip and the sleeper awoke' (*Poems* 55), we could associate this with the 'seasonal hymn ['Sleepers, Awake'], an injunction to the daughters of Jerusalem to go and meet the heavenly bridegroom' (Corn 160), only that this time it 'is subverted against the patriarchal pattern' (ibid.).

In the second poem of the sequence, 'Over 2,000 Illustrations and a Complete Concordance', the allusions and sources are more obvious and direct, but the primary role religion plays in the poem is through absence. This, too, has an echo in St Teresa, where we have a dialectic between cataphatic spirituality[12] and apophatic spirituality. Theologies of the *deus absconditus* belong in the latter category. It is a spirituality that stresses the unknowability of God, the absence: '[a]pophatic spirituality [. . .] stresses "imageless-ness" and "wordless-ness"' (Mujica 741). This returns us to the poem, since, as David Kalstone argues, the 'infant sight' at the end of the poem 'keeps its Latin root, "speechless"' (Kalstone 27). After a poem like 'A Cold Spring', with its 'animal birth' (Corn 165), the second poem in the collection ends with a nativity scene.

Viewed in this order, it is fitting that with the third poem, we arrive at 'The Bight', a poem in which 'Bishop turns to her own birthday' (ibid.).

In her excellent essay on 'The Bight', Frances Leviston explains in detail the possible biographical significance of the poem, which, subtitled 'on my birthday', invites such scrutiny. 'The Bight' is the only poem that mentions Baudelaire by name so critics have taken the opportunity to use it as a way to discuss his influence. Nearly unanimously, when they comment on Baudelaire at all, they read the lines 'One can smell it turning to gas; if one were Baudelaire / one could probably hear it turning to marimba music' (*Poems* 59) as evidence of Bishop's breaking with Baudelaire's influence. Leviston, by contrast, notes that the poem, closely examined, displays 'the persistence of [Bishop's] sympathies with Baudelaire' (Leviston 454). She uses three poems, 'Bénédiction', 'Danse Macabre' and 'Correspondances', to make her case.

In 'The Bight' Bishop makes the connection to Baudelaire explicit for the first time, a turn which Leviston relates to Bishop's life. It is Bishop's first attempt to break through what Costello calls 'masks' (cited in Leviston 437). There is a more apposite term, however, which Ann Fisher-Wirth uses in her discussion of William Carlos Williams: 'private autobiography', a genre which Fisher-Wirth defines as 'the poet's act of self-centering and self-recollecting' (12). This use of 'private' rather than 'secret' or 'hidden' allows us to read Bishop's progress in light of broader cultural debates on the issue of private vs public. 'The Bight' turns out to be a poem where Bishop very tentatively turns the private to public through the use of the subtitle, as Leviston demonstrates persuasively. This switch from private to public and its reverse are intimately connected to the emergence of confessional poetry, as Deborah Nelson shows in her study on the invention of privacy as a Constitutional value in the United States. Baudelaire may not appear to be a good partner in this, but Bishop, a careful reader of the French poet, zeroes in on poems that help her express this subtle turn without having to be explicit about it.

For my purposes here, the most important Baudelaire poem that Bishop alludes to in 'The Bight' is 'La Musique'. Eleanor Cook notes (117) that the two lines invoking Baudelaire are probably a reference to that poem's first verse, 'La musique souvent me prend comme une mer!' (Baudelaire 118).[13] Humorously, Bishop inverts Baudelaire's melodramatic statement. A possible reading of 'La Musique' could see it 'as the emergence of self-conscious subjectivity out of the looming antagonism between storm and calm' (Miner 162). My suggested reading of 'The Bight' as a move from private to very tentatively public autobiography could also be described as an 'emergence of subjectivity'. 'La Musique' charts a voyage gone wrong, ending with the speaker looking into a mirror of despair during times of calm.[14] Though there are no mirrors in this Bishop poem (the water is explicitly described as 'sheer'), in *North & South*, many of the Baudelairean poems revolve around mirrors, a method that is particularly noticeable in 'Love Lies Sleeping' and 'The Fish'. If in 'The Bight' Bishop slowly moves towards a near-public version of life writing, previously she had employed devices like the mirror to achieve a more private effect. Being a close reader of Baudelaire can only have been of help in this endeavour since his writing, which 'appear[s] to eschew the autobiographical' (Burt 106), is instead a process of 'persistent self-masking' (Burt 85), a game with self-expression and the audience. If we read Bishop's poetry as moving from covert to overt personal expression, then a familiarity with the Baudelairean modes of self-masking would have helped her create similar strategies. Baudelairean influence emerges not as one of impersonality, but as one of *feigned* impersonality. The way 'Love Lies Sleeping' engages debates on self and reality and the way 'Quai d'Orléans' challenges memory are examples of that. It is not surprising that, as Ellis has highlighted, Bishop, who made such heavy use of the mirror metaphor in her first collection, would end up apparently abandoning that device later, as she no longer had need for indirect speech. Contra Ellis, I would, however, suggest that Bishop never completely declines the use of the device, preferring to pivot towards encounters.

A dry run of such encounters can be found in the early poems 'The Fish' and 'The Man-Moth'. 'The Fish', with its opaque eyes, and 'The Man-Moth', with his dark eyes, both offer confrontations that help shape the speakers of Bishop's poems. Bishop's method, which culminates in 'In the Waiting Room', a poem full of encounters with a variety of others, can be described in terms of the philosophy of Emmanuel Levinas. Granted, Bishop's poems precede Levinas's philosophy, and cannot be read as referring to it. Even so, Levinas's work offers a good tool to understand how Bishop's poetry of life writing works. What interests me most is his conception of alterity. For Levinas, subjectivity develops in a relationship of selves and others. 'The *I* is inconceivable without the *Thou*' (Purcell 136), but for Levinas, the relationship is asymmetrical. For Levinas, the Other is absolutely opaque. This is how we, according to the Jewish philosopher, develop a sense of self, of ethics and responsibility. While Levinas specifically excludes animals from his philosophy, Bishop leans heavily on encounters with the animal world as ways to shape her speakers and display them to her readers in their imperfection. This difference from Levinas does not presuppose a secular tradition. On the contrary, this focus has a long tradition in Christian thought. Ignatius, for example, insists that meditation on animals turns them into 'tools and guides' that can help to 'enrich [. . .] spiritual understanding' (Randall 69). Nevertheless, Levinas's theology helps us elucidate in which way Bishop turns her Baudelairean source on its head at the end of 'The Man-Moth'. The final stanza of the poem, a clear allusion to the end of Baudelaire's 'Tristesse de la Lune', inverts the final gesture of Baudelaire's poet, who catches or steals a tear and keeps it hidden for himself. Bishop's poem, by contrast, ends with the tear being handed over. Baudelaire's poem focuses on poetic creation, whereas Bishop's focus is on the encounter between speaker and the Man-Moth. It offers a moment of vulnerability. This same vulnerability is, in Levinas's ethics, a precondition to honestly encountering another human being (Alford 133, 145). This is a central element in Levinas's thinking, and it is similarly a preoccupation of Bishop's, much as the freeing of the eponymous animal at the end of 'The Fish' is also a moment of personal recognition, of community, a covenant struck with the world.[15]

Yet, as the later poem 'The Bight' shows, a poem full of 'feelings of aimlessness [. . .] not to mention the obvious loneliness' (Ellis 97), this covenant is an uneasy accord. Bishop declines the union of the *symboliste* aesthetic (Pickard 184). At the same time, she does not reject the underlying aesthetic elements. Much depends, though, on how we read the reference to 'Correspondances'. If we emphasise the unity aspect of Baudelaire's poem as Barbara Johnson does (193), we would see Bishop's reference as dismissive, since Bishop's poem is fairly distanced from concepts of 'metaphysical unity'. If, on the other hand, we follow Leakey, we adopt a reading of the 'correspondences' as a form of synaesthesia. This enables us to connect Baudelaire's approach to senses and the self with Bishop's since there is a relation in Bishop's work between ideas of synaesthesia, religion and autobiographical writing. Costello alludes to this when she mentions that Bishop copied into her notebook a passage from St Ignatius's *Spiritual Exercises* that invokes 'the senses, synesthetically merged' (114), but she does not then examine what further role Ignatius may have played in Bishop's work.

Bishop's use of Baudelaire in 'The Bight' is most evident in her use of allegory. In many ways, the poem is an allegory of the act of poetry writing. In a letter to Robert Lowell, Bishop describes much of the scene in 'The Bight', with the added observation that it 'reminds [her] a little of [her] desk' (*Words in Air* 23).[16] Pickard has noted Bishop's complicated relationship to allegories. In a short essay on Baudelaire, Hans Robert Jauß offers a reading of the modern allegory of Baudelaire as negotiating a new terrain of interiority. Where medieval allegories served to illuminate interiority and, at the same time, the unity of the outside world with the inside world, Baudelaire's addresses their modern disruption (Jauß 181). Given how closely tied Bishop's 'The Bight' is to its Baudelairean influence, Bishop is offering a middle path between Baudelaire and the older tradition. Her use of allegory, then, does not ask to be deciphered, which critics enumerated by Pickard seek to do, nor dismissed, as Pickard himself does, but to be recognised *as allegory*, with all the attendant cultural, religious and literary expectations and traditions. At the same time as the poem is very clearly interested in providing either a form of life writing or a commentary on it, Bishop was aware that Baudelaire's poetry was often concerned with trying to reconnect the broken modern world through writing. Nature does not become beautiful unless the poet looks at it. Modern allegory is particularly insistent on this[17] and Bishop's poem is overtly and overwhelmingly asking us to read it allegorically, thus making us aware of her place within this tradition. And while Romantic poetry has many examples of wanderers, it is surely Baudelaire, whose walks as doomed attempts to make it all cohere are a staple in his poetry, who provided an example to Bishop.

Similarly, it appears clear that Bishop's generic elusiveness owes much to the example of St Teresa. Women writing within the frameworks of autobiography, especially in spiritual autobiographies, often make the writing itself explicit, switching between genres, moving the self as an immersive presence behind the self as a visible creation. This explains the way St Teresa's work, like that of Sor Juana and other female religious writers, pivoted towards hagiography as a way to pre-empt criticism rather than towards the autobiographical structure of contemporaneous male writers. Teresa's autobiography switches persistently in and out of different genres (Slade 9). Similarly, Bishop very carefully calibrated her public image, of which her letters are part, as well as her poems, which sometimes took decades to find the right shape. In one of her most famous poems, the late 'One Art', we can find the same calibrated hagiographical style of the much earlier tradition. Indeed, the poem's concentric circles of loss, 'losing further, losing faster', including houses and continents, gain some complexity when we consider its structure to include a clever use of the different dwelling places in St Teresa's *Interior Castle*.

Both 'One Art' and Teresa's *Interior Castle* offer a progression at the end of which we find a reckoning with love. Teresa's book is a mystic progression of the soul towards love, and while it is divine love, Teresa draws on the writings and allusions of erotic spirituality. Its most important antecedent is Augustine's triad of faculties that make up love (Slade 86). For Augustine, memory leads to self-knowledge and understanding, and 'when the soul is thus known to itself, the faculty of will binds all three together in love' (ibid.). Teresa's progression begins with small acts of using memory to gain self-knowledge, but swiftly moves to a reminder that worldly things need to be discarded for spiritual things. Memory's role in this is central: it is the most important faculty to reach understanding (Slade 100) and until the soul reaches a point of transformation, the interplay between memory and understanding is the essential mechanism. The second important mechanism involves the way Teresa's book very skilfully navigates the genre of erotic spirituality which was particularly hazardous for women. Texts of this nature, it was said, 'should not be allowed to circulate [. . .] especially among women' (Weber 119). So Teresa (not entirely successfully) tried to mask her intentions with rhetorical tricks.

We find both of those central mechanisms, in a changed but recognisable form, in Bishop's poem. The progression in 'One Art' is not of the mystic kind: it leads the reader from losing minor worldly things to larger worldly things and finally a sense of home and, ultimately, love. The central kind of loss that we keep encountering involves memory. Some of it is a direct loss of memory, of 'places, and names'. Some of it is a loss of things that are remembered but no longer accessible, from a watch to whole continents. From all these elements, as with Teresa, we piece together an understanding of self. The second mechanism, the rhetorical devices to hide an emotional or risqué core, can also be found in Bishop's poem. 'One Art' is a poem of mourning. Ever since Augustine, female mourning was assumed to be full of 'hysteria' (Levy 85). Accordingly, Bishop had to deal with the expectations of male readers and adapted her literary devices accordingly. We know she was successful because Richard Howard, at the time editor of *The New Yorker*, wrote to her approvingly that the poem had 'just the right amount of distance' (Marshall 274).

Thus, Bishop's poem functions in many ways like a dark, inverted mirror of Teresa's progression. Bishop's way of dealing with sources often involves such an inversion, from the uncovered tear in 'The Man-Moth' to the music in 'The Bight'. Beside the mechanisms described above, there are additional details. The upsetting period in Bishop's life that produced 'One Art' also resulted in drinking. The inversion of this in *The Interior Castle* is a comparison of 'the soul in rapture to a drunkard' (Weber 105). Another inversion is Bishop's ironic claim of mastery, whereas a claim of incompetence is central to *The Interior Castle*. There are too many such details for the symmetries to be entirely accidental. However, the relationship of the two texts is not that of a simple positive/negative image where one offers positive spiritual gains towards love gained and the other negative worldly losses towards love lost. Instead, Bishop uses Teresa's book as an intertext to transport a sense of (erotically charged) hope that runs like a powerline underneath her sad poem of loss and anxiety. The prayerful intertext is itself a mirror to the current of the poem, but in an indirect form, an end result of decades of poetic development that started with the Baudelairean mirrors in *North & South*.

In 'The Bight', Bishop steps away from the encounters and mirrors that dominate much of the earlier poetry. Instead, she uses her influences to do something new, just in time for her first almost explicitly personal poem: she discusses time (and life) in terms of space and nature. Regularly, she comes up with new ways to use literary tradition – this is surely one of the reasons why her work still challenges readers. Bishop had to reach and carefully choose each of the texts that she ultimately relied on. I would like to come back to Travisano's assertion that for Bishop observation was a moral act. Bishop's poetry, viewed through a Levinasian lens, is moral in the way it deals with others. Ultimately, I think her most important task, which she achieved with care, kindness and accuracy, was giving an account of herself that represented her exactly right: as a reader, a writer and a person adrift in the world, without self-pity or cruelty towards others. It amounted to 'an untidy activity' (*Poems* 59), full of stops and starts.

Notes

1. Most references to Baudelaire in studies of Bishop are dismissive of his influence. An exception is Jonathan Ellis's *Art and Memory in the Work of Elizabeth Bishop*. There are no monographs dedicated to Baudelaire's influence, but there are two essays: Ernesto Toste's 'Baudelairean Echoes in Elizabeth Bishop' from 2003 and Frances Leviston's essay on 'The Bight' from 2015.
2. Marilyn May Lombardi's assertion that in Bishop's second collection, *A Cold Spring*, she 'leaves behind Baudelaire [. . .] and immerses herself in life' (96) is representative of this scholarly opinion.
3. Jamie McKendrick's puzzled question 'why is Bishop conscripting the French symbolist for a poem which describes a stretch of Floridan coastline?' (124) is representative of this assumption.
4. Eleanor Cook notes, for example, Bishop's attention to a 'surprising word' in Baudelaire's poem 'Le Balcon' (Cook 50).
5. The most striking instance of this is Bishop's close evocation of 'Tristesse de la lune' in the final stanza of 'The Man-Moth' (see Toste 158 and Anderson 71).
6. Another one can be seen in Burt's evocation of the dandy sleeping in front of the mirror and early poems like 'Love Lies Sleeping', which, additionally, could be argued to both refer to and invert Baudelairean antecedents like 'Rêve Parisien' and 'Paysage'.
7. 'The pillars of Nature's temple are alive / and sometimes yield perplexing messages; / forests of symbols between us and the shrine / remark our passage with accustomed eyes' (Baudelaire and Howard 15).
8. M. H. Abrams is quite clear on the 'extraordinary appeal' that the 'theological premise of fallen man and a fallen nature' had on Baudelaire due to his personal 'ambivalence toward life' as well as other factors (Abrams 123).
9. Ignatius's influence has most famously been stated by Louis Martz's book *The Poetry of Meditation*. However, current scholarship holds that Martz's claims about Ignatius's influence have to be revised (Pooley 166).
10. There are exceptions, obviously, Crusoe being one of them.
11. The question of whether Teresa, in contrast to other famous religious women of her time, could indeed be considered a teacher is easily resolved by looking at the historical record: in her time, Teresa was seen as a woman who 'taught others', to quote Papal Nuncio Felipe Sega (Weber 18).
12. That which purports to find 'God in created things and uses images to stimulate spiritual experience' (Mujica 741).
13. 'Music often takes me like a sea' (Baudelaire and Howard 71).
14. 'D'autres fois, calme plat, grand miroir / De mon désespoir.' Incidentally, the previous storm in the poem, 'la tempête et ses convulsions', could be the 'last bad storm' mentioned by Bishop in 'The Bight'. In Howard's translation: 'a raging storm / on the great deep / my cradle, and dead calm the looking-glass / of my despair' (71).

15. The 'rainbow, rainbow, rainbow' could be read as referring to the covenant God made with humanity after the Flood. The poem's possible allusion to Mallarmé's 'Azur' and Baudelaire's 'L'Aube spirituelle' can be seen as further evidence of a religious symbolism rather than plain observation.

16. Alfred Corn's essay, which first appeared in a magazine in 1985, was the first to read the scene as an allegory for writing, without the added benefit of the letters, the publication of which postdates Corn's essay.

17. See Madsen 129, 133, *et passim*.

Works Cited

Abrams, M. H., 'Coleridge, Baudelaire and Modernist Poetics', in Wolfgang Iser (ed.), *Immanente Ästhetik, Ästhetische Reflexion: Lyrik als Paradigma der Moderne* (Munich: Fink, 1966), pp. 113–38.

Alford, Fred C., *Levinas, the Frankfurt School and Psychoanalysis* (New York: Continuum, 2003).

Anderson, Linda R., *Elizabeth Bishop: Lines of Connection* (Edinburgh: Edinburgh University Press, 2013).

Barthes, Roland, *Sade, Fourier, Loyola* (Paris: Éditions du Seuil, 1980).

Baudelaire, Charles, *Les Fleurs du Mal*, ed. John E. Jackson (Paris: Librairie Générale Française, 1999).

Baudelaire, Charles, and Richard Howard, *Les Fleurs du Mal: The Complete Text of The Flowers of Evil* (Boston: D. R. Godine, 1982).

Bishop, Elizabeth, *One Art: Letters*, ed. Robert Giroux (New York: Farrar, Straus and Giroux, 1994).

Bishop, Elizabeth, and Robert Lowell, *Words in Air: The Complete Correspondence between Elizabeth Bishop and Robert Lowell*, ed. Thomas Travisano with Saskia Hamilton (New York: Farrar, Straus and Giroux, 2008).

Burt, E. S., *Regard for the Other: Autothanatography in Rousseau, De Quincey, Baudelaire, and Wilde* (New York: Fordham University Press, 2009).

Cook, Eleanor, *Elizabeth Bishop at Work* (Cambridge, MA, and London: Harvard University Press, 2016).

Corn, Alfred, *The Metamorphoses of Metaphor: Essays in Poetry and Fiction* (New York: Viking, 1987).

Costello, Bonnie, *Elizabeth Bishop: Questions of Mastery* (Cambridge, MA: Harvard University Press, 1991).

Ellis, Jonathan, *Art and Memory in the Work of Elizabeth Bishop* (Aldershot: Ashgate, 2006).

Fisher-Wirth, Ann W., *William Carlos Williams and Autobiography: The Woods of His Own Nature* (University Park: Pennsylvania State University Press, 1989).

Ford, Mark, 'Elizabeth Bishop at the Water's Edge', *Essays in Criticism* 53.3 (2003): 235–61.

Jauß, Hans Robert, *Studien zum Epochenwandel der ästhetischen Moderne* (Frankfurt: Suhrkamp, 1989).

Johnson, Barbara, *Persons and Things* (Cambridge, MA: Harvard University Press, 2008).

Kadi, Simone, *Proust et Baudelaire: Influences et Affinités Électives* (Paris: La Pensée Universelle, 1975).

Kalstone, David, *Five Temperaments: Elizabeth Bishop, Robert Lowell, James Merrill, Adrienne Rich, John Ashbery* (New York: Oxford University Press, 1977).

Keane, Webb, 'Religious Language', *Annual Review of Anthropology* 26.1 (1997): 47–71.

Leakey, F. W., *Baudelaire and Nature* (Manchester: Manchester University Press, 1969).

Leviston, Frances, 'Mothers and Marimbas in "The Bight": Bishop's Danse Macabre', *Twentieth-Century Literature* 61.4 (2015): 436–59.

Levy, Allison, 'Augustine's Concessions and Other Failures: Mourning and Masculinity in Fifteenth-Century Tuscany', in Jennifer C. Vaught and Lynne Dickson Bruckner (eds), *Grief and Gender, 700–1700* (New York: Palgrave Macmillan, 2003), pp. 81–94.

Lombardi, Marilyn May, *The Body and the Song: Elizabeth Bishop's Poetics* (Carbondale: Southern Illinois University Press, 1995).

McCabe, Susan, *Elizabeth Bishop: Her Poetics of Loss* (University Park: Pennsylvania State University Press, 1994).

McKendrick, Jamie, 'Bishop's Birds', in Linda R. Anderson and Jo Shapcott (eds), *Elizabeth Bishop: Poet of the Periphery* (Newcastle upon Tyne: Dept of English Literary & Linguistic Studies, University of Newcastle, in association with Bloodaxe, 2002), pp. 123–42.

Mackinnon, Lachlan, *Eliot, Auden, Lowell: Aspects of the Baudelairean Inheritance* (London: Macmillan, 1983).

Madsen, Deborah L., *Allegory in America: From Puritanism to Postmodernism* (Basingstoke: Macmillan, 1996).

Marshall, Megan, *Elizabeth Bishop: A Miracle for Breakfast* (New York: Houghton Mifflin Harcourt, 2017).

Mehta, Diane, 'Elizabeth Bishop: An Active Displacement in Perspective', *Harvard Review* 16 (1999): 72–4.

Merrim, Stephanie, *Early Modern Women's Writing and Sor Juana Inés de la Cruz* (Nashville: Vanderbilt University Press, 1999).

Millier, Brett C., *Elizabeth Bishop: Life and the Memory of It* (Berkeley: University of California Press, 1993).

Miner, Margaret, 'Music and Theatre', in Rosemary Lloyd (ed.), *The Cambridge Companion to Baudelaire* (Cambridge: Cambridge University Press, 2005), pp. 145–63.

Mujica, Barbara, 'Beyond Image: The Apophatic-Kataphatic Dialectic in Teresa de Avila', *Hispania* 84.4 (2001): 741–8.

Nelson, Deborah, *Pursuing Privacy in Cold War America* (New York: Columbia University Press, 2002).

Paton, Priscilla, *Abandoned New England: Landscape in the Works of Homer, Frost, Hopper, Wyeth, and Bishop* (Hanover: University Press of New England, 2003).

Pickard, Zachariah, *Elizabeth Bishop's Poetics of Description* (Montreal: McGill-Queen's University Press, 2009).

Pines, Sarah, *Pariser Schnappschüsse: Sehen und Blindheit bei Baudelaire* (Paderborn: Wilhelm Fink, 2014).

Pooley, Roger, 'Introduction', in Rebecca Lemon, Emma Mason, Jonathan Roberts and Christopher Rowland (eds), *The Blackwell Companion to the Bible in English Literature* (Chichester: Wiley-Blackwell, 2009), pp. 155–69.

Purcell, Michael, *Levinas and Theology* (Cambridge: Cambridge University Press, 2006).

Randall, Catharine, *The Wisdom of Animals: Creatureliness in Early Modern French Spirituality* (Notre Dame: University of Notre Dame Press, 2014).

Ravinthiran, Vidyan, *Elizabeth Bishop's Prosaic* (Lewisburg: Bucknell University Press, 2015).

Slade, Carole, *St. Teresa of Avila: Author of a Heroic Life* (Berkeley: University of California Press, 1995).

Toste, Ernesto Suárez, 'Loin des Yeux du Soleil: Baudelairean Echoes in Elizabeth Bishop', in Ignacius M. Palacios Martinez (ed.), *Fifty Years of English Studies in Spain (1952–2002): A Commemorative Volume* (Santiago: Universidad de Santiago de Compostela Publicacións, 2003), pp. 155–60.

Travisano, Thomas J., *Midcentury Quartet: Bishop, Lowell, Jarrell, Berryman, and the Making of a Postmodern Aesthetic* (Charlottesville: University Press of Virginia, 1999).

Vendler, Helen, *The Breaking of Style: Hopkins, Heaney, Graham* (Cambridge, MA: Harvard University Press, 1995).

Walker, Cheryl, *God and Elizabeth Bishop: Meditations on Religion and Poetry* (New York: Palgrave Macmillan, 2005).

Weber, Alison, *Teresa of Avila and the Rhetoric of Femininity* (Princeton: Princeton University Press, 1990).

White, Gillian C., *Lyric Shame: The 'Lyric' Subject of Contemporary American Poetry* (Cambridge, MA: Harvard University Press, 2014).

7

ELIZABETH BISHOP: LIFE CHANGE AND POETIC TRANSFORMATION

Angelica Nuzzo

I

'SHOULD WE HAVE STAYED at home and thought of here?' is one of Elizabeth Bishop's most direct questions of travel – a counterfactual question that immediately complicates its apparent simplicity by giving rise to a proliferation of other questions, by creating the wave of a back-and-forth pull from 'here' to 'home' and back 'here' again. In fact, 'we' have not stayed at home; and where is home, anyway? Indeed, 'Where should we be today?' had we not come here. As it turns out, where we presently are – the 'here' with way too many waterfalls or rather not-yet-waterfalls – is (or will soon be) 'home'. That initial question reflects the traveller's contradictory predicament as she eagerly looks for change but is clearly uncomfortable in it as she doubts, retrospectively, the decision to leave 'home' but then, immediately retracting that doubt because drawn to the appealing novelty of her surroundings, retorts to herself: 'But surely it would have been a pity / not to have seen the trees along this road'. And this is just the first in a string of other 'not to have[s]' which would have been a pity not to have experienced ('not to have had to stop for gas and heard' the sound of wooden clogs, 'heard the other, less primitive music of the fat brown bird / who sings above the gasoline pump'; *Poems* 91–2) – experiences that now tie the traveller to the present place, the 'world inverted' of Brazil, possibly Samambaia ('Insomnia', *Poems* 68).

'A bottle of perfume has leaked and made awful brown stains. Oh, marvelous scent, from somewhere else! It doesn't smell like that here; but there, somewhere, it does, still,' observes the narrative voice of the prose poem 'In the Village'.[1] And reviewing with admiration the bundle of postcards lying on the floor, she notices:

> Postcards come from another world, the world of the grandparents who send things, the world of sad brown perfume, and morning. (The gray postcards of the village for sale in the village store are so unilluminating that they scarcely count. After all, one steps outside and immediately sees the same thing: the village, where we live, full size, and in color. (*Prose* 65)

The postcard is a hopeful, liberating sign coming from somewhere else that triggers the work of the imagination away from the well-known reality under the child's eyes. The postcard from far away is more compelling than the familiarity of home when we are at home (this dynamic is already at work in 'Florida', where the postcard, however, becomes self-referential: Florida, 'the poorest / post-card of itself'; *Poems* 34). Home, however, remains an unknown, opaque, unreflected presence despite its being full size, in colour; despite its being 'the village, where we live'. Displacement is a contradictory predicament. It is only by being somewhere else that the memory of 'home' can be brought back – and it is in memory (not in direct acquaintance) that knowledge begins. Memory, knowledge and their poetic appropriation occupy Bishop throughout a long biographical and poetic itinerary. Through this itinerary her Nova Scotian childhood is now made poetically alive, much more alive than a black-and-white postcard could ever be (Harrison 21–2, 107–40; Barry). Viewed from the distance of Brazil, the childhood memories of 'In the Village' end up illuminating the only true 'home' she has had after childhood up to the beginning of the 1960s: Samambaia. Brazil is now 'home', Nova Scotia is 'elsewhere' (*Poems* 117). But Nova Scotia was home once, and Brazil was a travel destination among many possible ones, a far-away, indeterminate somewhere else (from which 'letters' were sent with those postage stamps with 'very inferior' glue that always come undone; 'Arrival at Santos', *Poems* 88).

This fluid criss-crossing is the trajectory of change. The *need* for change; the unavoidable *necessity* of change; the fear and discomfort but also the longing for change. Change is central in Bishop's life and poetic work. Change is a contradictory predicament; it implicates time and place, memory and history and geography; it is the movement from 'elsewhere' to 'home' and then on to somewhere else again. It expresses the mutability that ties together inextricably the settings of life and its internal landscapes. It is the difficult process that constitutes the poet's identity but also constantly undoes it, only to reconstitute it yet again. Ultimately, this is the process of life itself. But how can this mutability be understood or described? How can change even be detected when we are right in the middle of it, when change is the elusive dimension of our present experience? In fact, for Bishop, this is the question of how the mutability that animates her life and experience can be translated poetically – how change can happen and make sense in and through the medium of the poetic word – and perhaps only in this way. For, otherwise, change can easily destroy or indeed 'kill us' (*Edgar Allan Poe* 178). Now this, in turn, leads to the real question: how does poetry make change happen? This, I submit, is Bishop's central question – or, most properly, it is her most precious answer.

In this chapter, I shall follow the escalating unfolding of these three questions. They connect the issue of describing change in its happening, or the question raised by the (generic) traveller or observer, to its poetic appropriation and imaginative transformation. This is Bishop's question as a keenly observing poet-traveller soon to become settler. These questions finally lead to the miracle of the 'poetic transformation' produced by her lyric poetry. As Marianne Moore writes to her early on in their acquaintance, commenting on the 'insidiousness of creativeness' which she sees proper to Bishop's 'things': in a poet the 'ingeniously contrived' feeling is not enough; 'a thing should make one feel after reading it, that one's life has been altered or added to.'[2] This latter, I submit, touches the most genuine core of Bishop's work. I shall use Bishop's own interrogation in the collection *Questions of Travel* as my starting point and further pursue the issue both backwards, by briefly selecting examples from the earlier *North & South* and *A Cold Spring*, and forwards, in *Geography III* and in Bishop's late uncollected poems. It is here that the transformative power of her art becomes most remarkable. Indeed, 'there is always something transformative' about Bishop's poetry (whereby the transformative value is contrasted to the 'spectacular'; Heaney 332). The lyric imagination changes the world and makes things happen. As Seamus Heaney has argued (with regard to 'At the Fishhouses'), Bishop's 'poetic imagination' engages in the process whereby 'a world is brought into being' (Heaney 187). The transformation produced by the poem is 'creation' in the most proper sense. Jeredith Merrin has also drawn attention to the playfulness and 'gayness' of Bishop's insistence on transformation and even 'metamorphosis' (of self, places, cultures), to her attraction to 'the way, in poetry, things can change into other unexpected things', underscoring how 'changeability holds a uniquely preeminent place in Bishop's poetics' (Merrin 160, 161).

The problem of the poet-traveller can also be described in the following way. It seems that change cannot be grasped from the standpoint of immanence – distance is required, a perspective must be gained, a point of standstill obtained from which to observe. But then what is being described from a distance is not really change – not *our* change. Change has to be lived; it has to directly happen to us; it cannot be fixed in a still description (indeed, it cannot be enclosed in a postcard). In fact, what changes is not simply the setting or the landscape of life. Change cuts deeper. It is life itself that is always immanently and forever transformed. The way out of this seeming contradiction is *to make change happen*. This is the miracle produced by Bishop's poems: they change the world in which they happen. Or, as Marianne Moore puts it, they alter our life; they add meaning to it. Ultimately, they make life bearable. ' – Yesterday brought to today so lightly! / (A yesterday I find almost impossible to lift.)' ('Five Flights Up', *Poems* 203). Only poetry can lift that unbearably heavy 'yesterday' to the possible slight opening of a future tomorrow.

II

Our constellation of questions brings to light the distance that separates the 'tourist' of 'Arrival at Santos' from the 'sandpiper' that appears at the end of *Questions of Travel*. The book develops between these two poles. Bishop is both the traveller and the sandpiper. Her experience changes as her life changes, moving from one incarnation to the other. The voice of the 'tourist' first disembarking in Brazil is a voice of continuity that takes up the end of the previous collection, *A Cold Spring* (the poem now appears reprinted with only one slight variation). While the disappointing insufficiency of the tourist's perspective had already been explored in 'Over 2,000 Illustrations and a Complete Concordance', the tourist arriving at Santos is a tourist who is soon to become a settler, who, as it turns out, is in Brazil to stay and to find a home. The tourist observes everything at a distance; for her everything is new and different. Everything *must* be new and different (hence the surprise that Brazil, too, has a flag: 'I somehow never thought of there *being* a flag'; 'Arrival at Santos', *Poems* 87). The tourist registers the differences but does not really *feel* them, is not touched by them. The landscape unfolds in front of her in a neat but fractured series of stills (postcard-like, as it were): 'Here is a coast; here is a harbor; / here, after a meager diet of horizon, is some scenery'. For her the landscape has changed but life has not – or not yet. She invests the new country with the load of all her 'immodest demands': she wants no less than 'a different world, / and a better life, and complete comprehension / of both at last, and immediately' (*Poems* 87). She sees the new world as being there to answer her – and to answer immediately and completely. Immodest demands indeed. But we all know this well: the more intently we seek change, the less chance we have that change will really happen to us. And besides, the tourist is not ready for it. Difference must be there for her to observe and prick her curiosity but must only selectively touch her: 'The customs officials will speak English, we hope, / and leave us our bourbon and cigarettes' (*Poems* 88).

A similar mixture of novelty and familiarity characterises the perspective of the Christian colonisers in 'Brazil, January 1, 1502', the second poem of *Questions of Travel*. As it turns out, the tourist and the coloniser have something in common. To this extent, the poet's voice is not entirely distanced from that of the colonisers – although it seeks to draw that distance. Bishop is clearly searching for the right position or perspective. The tourist is too close to the coloniser.[3] In the latter case, however, the balance is tilted toward continuity and sameness only to disclose in the end the destructiveness of historical change. Those 'hard as nails' Christians 'came and found it all, / not unfamiliar' – the double negation effectively capturing their expectations and consequent actions. There may not be immediate identity in the details ('no lovers' walks, no bowers, / no cherries to be picked, no lute music') but there is nonetheless a 'correspondence'. The new land corresponds to – and indeed in their mind fulfils – 'an old dream of wealth and luxury / already out of style when they left home' (*Poems* 90). By correcting the historical caducity of the coloniser's dream, geographical displacement fulfils it in an act of male imperialistic power. The coloniser erases difference as he immediately – and violently – appropriates it. And this is the ground for the forced continuity of the coloniser's history that, stretching back centuries, resists change and is ultimately unable to understand and really feel the new country. A similar violence, the violence of human action on the natural and animal world, emerges in 'The Armadillo' (*Poems* 101–2). Violence is the expression of such a resistance to change and difference – the violence of appropriation and sameness. In the end, this process brings to light a dangerous imbalance. While the coloniser's world is the same, only vaster, the life of the colonised is dramatically changed, indeed destroyed. In its conclusion, the poem's perspective suddenly shifts and voices the different, in fact incommensurable, female experience. What remains are the cries of those 'maddening little women who kept calling, / calling to each other [. . .] / and retreating, always retreating, behind it' (*Poems* 90), women's cries desperately merging – and disappearing – into birds' cries.

III

The coloniser neither properly travels – he exports his dreams of power to a far-away land and imposes them on it, the distance notwithstanding – nor, most importantly, has any question to raise. Different is the case of the 'we' through which Bishop expresses her in-between state in 'Questions of Travel': no longer a visiting tourist but rather someone who is contemplating the possibility of a new home. Compared with the fragmented landscape that greets the tourist upon her arrival at Santos, the images that open the third poem of the collection have already begun to sink into the poet's consciousness, and capture the uneasiness of a shifting and changing internal landscape. We are indeed moving 'to the interior' ('Arrival at Santos', *Poems* 88). There is a discomfort in which the external landscape meets the internal turmoil. 'There are

too many waterfalls here; the crowded streams / hurry too rapidly down to the sea[.]'
It is the discomfort caused by the different rhythm and the increased acceleration with
which everything happens 'here'. The time of consciousness cannot keep pace with
the time of nature – the latter overpowers the former and renders comprehension dif-
ficult (first and foremost the comprehension of place). Indeed, ages go way too 'quick'
here. Knowledge can hardly keep up (it tries to anticipate the waterfalls from 'those
streaks, those mile-long, shiny, tearstains'; although they 'aren't waterfalls yet' they
will probably very soon be). And yet the strange landscape and the displaced poetic
voice meet in their restless predicament: those streams and clouds 'keep travelling,
travelling' just as the poet is travelling (*Poems* 91). The alien ever-changing character
of the Brazilian natural landscape and the failure of knowledge to adequately grasp it
can be contrasted with the indifferent and detached sameness of the Nova Scotian sea
of 'At the Fishhouses' ('I have seen it over and over, the same sea, the same, / slightly,
indifferently swinging above the stones'; *Poems* 63). The sea is here, directly, itself an
image of knowledge – of imagined knowledge: 'It is like what we imagine knowledge
to be'. At the end of the poem 'our knowledge' has managed to perfectly sink with the
ocean's knowledge and ever-flowing rhythm – human historicity keeping pace with the
eternal flow of the currents.

At this point, a pause takes place to allow a question to be asked – the question
that indirectly discloses the work of the imagination or of poetic abstraction as the
only force that may be capable of offering a possible answer, of connecting 'here' to
'home' to here-as-home (to the 'home' of the past, in memory and recollection, and
to the home-to-be that Brazil/Samambaia will soon become for the poet). The pause
that allows the poet to gain a distance from the acceleration of innumerable water-
falls and the breathless unfolding of Brazilian ages is a self-injunction that brings
her back to the different world of 'home'. 'Think of the long trip home.' Pause and
think. And then the question comes: 'Should we have stayed at home and thought
of here? / Where should we be today?' (*Poems* 91). But since we *are* here, a moral
question must be (rhetorically) raised – the question that undermines from the outset
the very narrative of travel (or rather the self-justification of travel) that is laid out in
the two central stanzas: 'Is it right to be watching strangers in a play / in this strang-
est of theatres?' The spectator's standpoint, untouched by the changing places and
events she observes, must be abandoned. The question remains a valid one, but it is
now clear that the answer cannot be pursued by the traveller's detached spectatorial
stance. It is then to the poetic 'imagination' that Bishop turns in order to address her
question. '*Is it lack of imagination that makes us come / to imagined places, not just
stay at home?*' (*Poems* 92). If it is, then that imaginative lack should be corrected by
the imagination itself. But the '*here*' ('*or there . . .*') that triggers the question is not
just an imagined place, and it is also not a dreamed place ('Oh, must we dream our
dreams / and have them, too?'; *Poems* 91), just as it is not the place forced to fulfil
the imperialistic 'dream of wealth' of the Christian colonisers. Rather, it is the urg-
ing reality of the place where we presently are that both refutes the value of Pascal's
attitude of '*just sitting quietly in one's room*' (*Poems* 92) and requires the expansive
workings of the poetic imagination, the transformative gesture of poetic abstrac-
tion. In fact, we *are* here; we have *not* sat quietly in our room; we cannot go back
('Think of the long trip home'); but we can no longer maintain the tourist's or the
spectator's (or the coloniser's) standpoint. What then is to be done? The act of lyric

transfiguration through the imagination is the channel that allows the poet to pause and ask, for the first time, the question of travel – the question that neither the tourist nor the conqueror could even begin to articulate. The poetic imagination captures change at the intersection of what the body feels and what the mind understands and remembers. From this point on, 'Squatter's Children', 'Manuelzinho' and 'The Riverman' are all poems that embrace Brazil from an insider's perspective. Even 'The Burglar of Babylon', in which the poet was really and explicitly a detached observer (one of those 'Rich people in apartments' who 'Watched through binoculars / As long as the daylight lasted'; *Poems* 113), imaginatively inhabits the unfolding of Micuçu's desperate escape by endorsing his fugitive standpoint. My more general claim here intends to challenge the usual connotation of Bishop's poetry as a poetry of 'distance' and distanced observation. Such generic connotation does not capture the progression taking place in *Questions of Travel*.

IV

In 'Song for the Rainy Season' we find a significant shift. No longer a tourist or a detached spectator, Bishop has now settled in her new Brazilian home. The strange waterfalls of 'Questions of Travel' have become the familiar landscape in which 'the house we live in' is nested, protectively enveloped and 'hidden' by the surrounding nature (*Poems* 99). A point of harmony and balance has been reached in which consciousness seems to have caught up to those too-quickly-moving Brazilian ages: 'In a dim age / of water / the brook sings loud / from a rib cage / of giant fern' (*Poems* 99). The natural details of the landscape, previously seen as too expansive, disconcertingly out of scale, utterly ungraspable, are now a friendly presence that contribute to creating a comforting and secluded sense of home. The 'vapor' from the brook 'effortlessly' embraces both 'house and rock, in a private cloud' (*Poems* 99). The 'house we live in' is at the same time 'hidden' and 'open' to the natural world.

But then, suddenly, an intimation or anticipation binds together seamlessly the contradiction of change. The happy balance that joins house, water and rock cannot last. Change is inscribed in the natural world with an even stronger necessity than harmony is. This explains the *carpe diem*-like exclamation 'rejoice! For a later / era will differ' (*Poems* 100). Consciousness now anticipates the unfolding of natural eras (instead of being left behind by their sweeping rhythm) and is disquieted by what it anticipates. The parenthetical invocation surges, and captures the very essence of life-change: '(O difference that kills, / or intimidates, much / of all our small shadowy / life!)' (*Poems* 100). Change implies and requires 'difference' – and difference 'kills'. The natural landscape '[w]ithout water' is (or rather will be) utterly transformed: 'the great rock will stare / unmagnetized, bare, / no longer wearing / rainbows or rain,' the waterfalls will shrivel, 'the owls will move on' (*Poems* 100). But more broadly and disquietingly, although perhaps less significantly in the general order of things, it is life itself that changes; it is 'our small shadowy life' that is swept away, intimidated and even destroyed.

Importantly, however, this changed landscape is a poetic creation. It is the way in which poetic abstraction transforms the reality it inhabits. The poetic word does not register the change that happens (it is no longer the detached observer's word); rather, it makes change happen. What lies under the poet's eyes is the flourishing harmony of the rainy season. But the poetic imagination runs ahead of the landscape it inhabits – and profoundly transforms it. Change happens in the poetically transfigured landscape, not in the real one. And yet it is the poetic transformation that deeply affects us and produces the lasting feeling that concludes the poem. The poetic word changes our world and thereby does justice to it. To this extent, I would push Heaney's claim with regard to Bishop's poetry – 'One has a sense of justice being done to the facts of a situation even as the situation is being re-imagined into poetry' (Heaney 332) – even further: justice is being done to the facts precisely by the act of poetically reimagining them. The transformative vision of the poet replaces (and is indeed more effective and more powerful than) the masculine violence of colonisation, appropriation and detached spectatorship. This fulfils, paradigmatically, what Heaney considers the highest value of lyrical poetry, its 'governing power', as it were (Heaney 190). This way of living change in seamless poetic anticipation, which is ultimately Bishop's peculiar way of making things happen lyrically, comes close to the one articulated in the unpublished poem 'It is marvellous to wake up together . . .'. This poem begins by registering a sudden atmospheric change, the sudden inception of a rain storm, which is described through the feeling it evokes in the couple awakened ('together') by the rain pounding on the roof. In its conclusion, however, the poem opens up the disquieting possibility of a suddenly transformed world: 'The world might change to something quite different, / As the air changes or the lightning comes without our blinking, / Change as our kisses are changing without our thinking' (*Poems* 283). Sudden change might shake our world. There is no way we can control it as change happens like lightning, faster than our blinking, 'without our thinking'. And yet, the act of poetic abstraction has the answer here: poetry can change our world and our feeling in an even more powerful way. In this respect, poetry teaches us a way of letting go, of abandoning ourselves to the rhythm of life that is closer to the immediate rhythm of nature (the storm, the act of awakening or kissing) than to the controlled activity of thinking.

In the 1976 unpublished poem tentatively titled – with a Wordsworthian echo (I'm thinking here of both 'Lines Composed a Few Miles above Tintern Abbey' and 'Yarrow Revisited')[4] – 'Florida Revisited', the difference that shatters and kills by producing sweeping change reappears even more dramatically but also in a painfully unresolved way. The Florida of the earlier poems is now 'revisited' – literally, in the wake of Bishop's new trip to the state, and then, again, revisited in memory. And what remains at the end of the poem is the desolation and void left by change. 'Change is what hurts worst; change alone can kill. / Change kills us, finally – not these earthly things. / Finally one hates all the immutability, / Finally one hates the Florida one knows, / the Florida one knew' (*Edgar Allan Poe* 178). A point of no escape seems to have been reached here; a finality as hard and irrevocable as death. Change does not belong to the same register to which all the painful vicissitudes of life seem to belong: difference and change kill us, not 'these earthly things'. But immutability and the frozen images of memory kill us just as well.

This tension, which dramatically paralyses the choice between change and immutability, a tension that in 'Florida Revisited' is painfully unresolved both existentially and poetically, finds instead a brilliant and quietly sad composure in Bishop's tribute to the memory of her friend Robert Lowell, in the 1978 'North Haven'. Recalling the place that has been the stage of many shared summers, the poem begins: 'The islands haven't shifted since last summer / even if I like to pretend they have'. Obviously the islands don't change their position, yet for the poet they do, 'drifting, in a dreamy sort of way'. And it is this kind of poetic transformation that Bishop wants to convey to her dead friend – a geographical and poetical shift that affectively overrides all factual truth. For the reality of poetry is more powerful and has more lasting affecting value than 'true' reality has. This offers an interesting reversal if compared with the opening of the earlier 'The Shampoo' in which poetic memory holds on to a still, unchanged reality refuted by the ongoing change of the surrounding world (although the spreading lichens, 'still explosions on the rocks', constantly grow, 'within our memories they have not changed'; *Poems* 82). While in the earlier work the poetic word is charged with the task of fixing the value of a changing image, in 'North Haven' it does something much more ambitious. The poetic imagination changes the world: it shifts unmovable islands. But Bishop's thought here is subtler. In fact, properly, nature is neither mutable nor immutable. Rather, 'Nature repeats herself, or almost does: / *repeat, repeat, repeat; revise, revise, revise*' ('North Haven', *Poems* 210). Repetition and revision – the movement of change that does not change or only imperceptibly changes what it touches – are the link between the cyclic renewal of the natural world and the tormented creativity of the poetic act. And this link, in turn, allows Bishop to summon the memory of her friend, which is a poetic memory. The same flowers return, the 'Goldfinches are back', or rather 'others like them' (*Poems* 210) – natural repetition is substitution; the species remains the same, individuals die and are replaced. But not so with Bishop's friend: 'you've left / for good. You can't derange, or re-arrange, / your poems again. (But the Sparrows can their song.)' In the case of the poet, the individual cannot be replaced; death has a finality that nature does not have. 'The words won't change again. Sad friend, you cannot change' (*Poems* 211). And yet what remains, in the end, is a different poetic word, the living word of Bishop's last address to Lowell.

V

But if change hinges on difference, as Bishop directly remarks in 'Florida Revisited' and as the first poems of *Questions of Travel* clearly suggest (it hinges on the tourist's act of noticing differences and on the coloniser's violent act of erasing and appropriating them), then the question emerges: how is difference detected in the first place? And how can difference be brought to consciousness? As is often the case, Bishop shows us that this issue is much more difficult and interesting than we ever thought it could be. And this brings us to the sandpiper.

The sandpiper faces a problem that is the opposite of the problem that confronts the tourist or the spectator – the tourist who so intently desires change and notices differences everywhere yet is unable to really participate in the life of the new places she visits. The sandpiper lives immersed in the rhythm of the rising and retreating tides but he can't tell you whether at the present moment the tide is 'higher or lower' ('Sandpiper', *Poems* 129). He can't tell you because he is so totally immersed in it that he can't *see* the difference. He directly *lives* the difference. He knows how the tidal rhythm *feels* – and that's also all he needs to know. Whether the tide is actually higher or lower is immaterial; what matters is the changing flow. His life *is* this rhythm; he does not properly 'observe' it. The 'big white horse' of 'Twelfth Morning; or What You Will' shares the same predicament. Don't ask him, 'Are you supposed / to be inside the fence or out? He's still / asleep' – but then, 'Even awake, he probably / remains in doubt' (*Poems* 108). Bishop had already explored this predicament in the early poem 'The Gentleman of Shalott' – the divided creature who is 'in doubt / as to which side's in or out / of the mirror' and is even uncertain 'Which eye's his eye?' (*Poems* 11).[5] The sandpiper knows that constant change is unavoidable. This does not make it less frightening or ominous. He accepts it, however, as an integral part of life. 'The roaring alongside he takes for granted, / and that every so often the world is bound to shake.' The sandpiper's world, his attitude toward life, is the lesson Bishop takes from him – an existential as well as a poetic lesson. This world – roaring and shaking every so often, a world 'minute and vast and clear' made of millions of sandy particulars moved backwards and forwards by the Atlantic tides – is not the world described by a detached observer. It is not the fixed world framed in neat postcards or lusciously embroidered tapestries (the world of 'Arrival at Santos' and 'Brazil, January 1, 1502'). It is rather the background in which the sandpiper's life is always already inscribed (it is therefore taken 'for granted'); it is the horizon that is never really seen because it constitutes, somehow, the condition of all his anxious running and obsessive searching about, of his focus on the millions of grains of sand that, in a wonderful confusion of foreground and background, self and world, he hardly distinguishes from his own toes.

Just like the sandpiper, the poet neither just 'sees' differences and change nor attempts to detachedly 'understand' them (and master them in knowledge). Just like the sandpiper, she immediately *lives* and intimately *feels* change. Herein we have reached Bishop's final answer to the question of travel. Ultimately, the answer points to the practice of the same belief in 'total immersion' that the poet shared with the curious Baptist seal of 'At the Fishhouses' (*Poems* 63). This belief has led her all the way to Brazil, to the journey to its – and her own – 'interior', to the exploration of 'home' and 'elsewhere'. Ultimately, this is also what Bishop explicitly acknowledges as the moment – or indeed the miracle – of art's creativity, the 'self-forgetful, perfectly useless concentration' that she discusses in the famous letter to Anne Stevenson of January 1964 in connection with the work of the young Darwin. At issue is the mysterious point in which Darwin's 'endless heroic *observations*' yield to the feeling of estrangement characterising his scientific undertaking, to the feeling of his 'sinking or sliding giddily off into the unknown' (*Poems, Prose, and Letters* 861). While 'observation' is famously crucial to Bishop's art ('Lack of observation', she remarks in the same letter, 'seems to me one of the cardinal sins'), observation is not enough. What is needed beyond observation 'is a living in reality that works both ways, the non-intellectual sources of wisdom and sympathy' (860). This is indeed the direction taken by Darwin's work, by the lived immersion proper both to the Baptist seal and to the poet-sandpiper. Triggered by precise – indeed 'heroic' – observation, the poetic word allows for that integral immersion in reality that feels almost like an 'escape' (861) and is, instead, the creation of a different order. The poetic transfiguration of factual observation eliminates the distance separating the self from the object, the distance that is the very condition of observing. But it eliminates, at the same time, the steady point of reference represented by the observing 'self', a point of reference always taken for granted (and the other condition of observation) even though a merely 'assisting presence rather than an overbearing pressure', as Heaney notices (184). Now, in the creative moment, that humble 'assisting presence' of the self disappears. Hence the 'self-forgetfulness' and the feeling of vertigo that arises, a feeling 'of sinking or sliding' into the 'unknown' close to the one experienced in the poem 'In the Waiting Room' (yet such as to produce giddiness instead of anxiety). Moreover, the loss or suspension of the self that Bishop addresses in relation to Darwin is the moment of 'concentration' in which the poetic 'self' gathers just before springing into the creative act – into the 'unknown'. Self-forgetfulness is, more properly and paradoxically, the concentration leading to the expansion of the self according to the same natural-poetic rhythm with which the sandpiper's tides alternate from higher to lower (without the bird distinguishing them as one or the other) or 'our knowledge' being historical matches the ever-flowing rhythm of the sea ('At the Fishhouses', *Poems* 64). When the reader is brought into the picture, the concentration-expansion that constitutes the selfless poetic act displays a reflective character: it is 'a focus where our power to concentrate is concentrated back on ourselves' (Heaney 190). There is no utility, no calculation, no means-end relation in this gesture, which remains accordingly 'perfectly useless' indeed. For this is ultimately the nature of the creative act (or the nature of 'inspiration', as Heaney suggests (180)).

VI

In the conclusion of 'Sunday, 4 A.M.', the poem that immediately precedes 'The Sandpiper' in *Questions of Travel*, Bishop brings to light the transformative power of poetry within the world – the transforming force of the bird-poet. Here the situation is apparently opposite to that in 'The Sandpiper': 'The world seldom changes,' she posits. But in fact it is exactly the same attitude of taking for granted the changing rhythm of life – its roaring waves, the alternating high and low tides – as that of the sandpiper. In a journal entry on time and change written on board the *SS Bowplate* en route to Brazil, Bishop expressed a similar conciliation of opposites: 'When I read something like "The question about time is how change is related to the changeless" – & look around – it doesn't seem so hard or so far off. The nearer clouds seem to be moving quite rapidly; those in back of them are motionless – Watching the ship's wake we seem to be going fast, but watching the sky or the horizon, we are just living here with the engines pulsing, forever' (cited in Millier 239). Indeed, although 'the world seldom changes', it is still 'bound to shake' every so often. Accordingly, we might as well take this for granted. But at this point Bishop adds an important thought. This world, which integrates difference and change, this world lived from within in its mutable yet at the same time changeless or merely repetitive rhythm – the rhythm of nature, the rhythm of small repeated everyday occurrences – is still an incomplete world, a suspended world waiting for something to happen: something small and minimal and yet utterly momentous and true. This is the miracle that her poetry makes happen: a miracle that does not belong to the world but is brought to it by the poetic word so as to complete it. The bird-poet changes the world. 'The world seldom changes, / but the wet foot dangles / until a bird arranges / two notes at right angles' (*Poems* 128). Indeed, the poet not only *sees* the world at right angles – like Keaton in the homonymous draft: 'I was made at right angles to the world / and I see it so. I can only see it so' (*Poems* 303). The bird-poet '*arranges*' (my emphasis) the world according to her unique vision and brings it into existence according to that shape. With this turn we have approached the poetic of *Geography III* and of some extraordinary later poems.

Now, by way of conclusion, I want to briefly hint at two moments of this later vision and compare them with Bishop's stance in her earlier work.

In her last published collection, Bishop pushes the transfiguring power of the poetic act deeper in the direction of stoic acceptance already hinted at in the sand-piper's attitude of 'taking for granted' the occasional yet unavoidable upheavals of life. The poetic word is now endowed with a power of creative reconciliation of opposites that despite their remaining hard opposites in reality do allow life to go on in their poetic 're-arrangement' and, truly, sublimation. The poet-sandpiper's accep-tance of life change – his taking it for granted as he lives entirely immersed in it – has its counterpart, in the human world, in the Nova Scotian stoic 'yes' that resounds in 'The Moose'. The indrawn Nova Scotian 'yes' sums up for Bishop a whole phi-losophy of life: '"Yes" . . . that peculiar / affirmative. "Yes . . ." / A sharp, indrawn breath, / half groan, half acceptance, / that means "Life's like that. / We know *it* (also death)"' (*Poems* 192). In 'Five Flights Up' we are again in the animal world. Set in contrast with the human emotional landscape, the bird and the neighbour's barking dog seem to possess the highest form of wisdom – a poetic wisdom, as it were. They do not even need to raise questions since they know that all their 'Questions – if that is what they are' are 'answered directly, simply' by the inception of the day itself. The dog 'and the bird know everything is answered, / all taken care of, / no need to ask again' (*Poems* 203). The questions of life, which all questions of travel ultimately turn out to be, have now found a definitive answer. The answer that overrides the question, the answer that properly dissolves all questions and all acts of questioning (and 'inquiring'), is the power of the poetic imagination. Taken up by the transfigur-ing rhythm of the poem, the natural repetition of the cycle of night and daybreak becomes the only saving force that allows the unbearable 'yesterday' to be lifted and carried over to a new day. It is only parenthetically in the conclusion of the poem that Bishop comes to own the weight of that yesterday, thereby putting herself next to the 'unknown bird' and the 'little black dog' whose questions are always already answered by the day – 'no need to ask again'. For, in the end, the poem has done for her what the day does for those creatures. The poem *is* the answer, because it is the poem – and it alone – that can lift that impossibly heavy 'yesterday', bringing it to today: ' – Yesterday brought to today so lightly! / (A yesterday I find almost impos-sible to lift.)' (*Poems* 203).[6]

In order to measure the distance Bishop has gone in her poetic trajectory, one needs only compare the late position of 'Five Flights Up' to the tormented, proliferative and unresolved existential questioning of the early 'Faustina, or Rock Roses'. Herein 'The acuteness of the question / forks instantly and starts / a snake-tongue flickering; / blurs further, blunts, softens, / separates, falls, our problems / becoming helplessly / prolif-erative' (*Poems* 72). There is no answer here. The question of life and death caught in an exhaustingly escalating rhythm only generates more dramatic questions by splitting in a disjunctive unresolved conundrum. Utter helplessness is the result. The poetic word can only run after that helplessness, echoing its open-ended lack of resolution.

In 'The Weed' from *North & South*, Bishop captures with an intriguing image a recurring idea of life change. Properly, at stake here is life after – or rather in – death (in a dreamed-of death state), the growth, first timid then increasingly self-affirming, of a weed 'through the heart' of the dreaming-dead voice of the poem. Through the flourishing weed, the heart becomes 'rooted', and this is the beginning of its changing state: to be sure, not the act of going back to life (the beating of the heart) but a much more radical transformation. 'The rooted heart began to change / (not beat) and then it split apart / and from it broke a flood of water.' What begins to take shape here is the first of many divided creatures that populate Bishop's poetry, from the Gentleman of Shalott to the 'creature divided' of the late 'Sonnet'. The division is not so much a crisis as rather the ambiguous (and at times ironic) point of departure of unresolved new possibilities. Another recurring image, that of flowing water, lends further poignancy to what is happening to the dead heart now animated – and split – by the growing weed. 'Two rivers glanced off from the sides, / one to the right, one to the left, / two rushing, half-clear streams' that almost sweep away the weed. The poem's conclusion restates the division of the self as the predicament that life will never overcome: 'I grow' is the weed's answer to the surprised heart, 'but to divide your heart again' (*Poems* 23).

In the late poem 'Santarém' the image of two rivers – this time converging instead of diverging – captures a different thought and produces a different poetic resolution. Dialectic and its contradictory duplicity are explicitly invoked. It is clear to Bishop that while the contradiction – which is ultimately the contradiction of travel and of life itself – cannot be solved in reality, it can be poetically overcome. And this act of overcoming is the poem itself. While in 'The Weed' change is apprehended through the filter of a dream framed as a post-mortem fiction, in 'Santarém' the distancing filter is memory: 'Of course I may be remembering it all wrong / after, after – how many years?' The contradiction is there from the outset. The traveller desires to stop travelling: 'That golden evening I really wanted to go no farther'. And the desire coalesces in the place she has reached, the 'conflux of two great rivers, Tapajòs, Amazon' – or, rather, in the 'idea of the place'. That idea takes a bit to settle in the cultural references it conjures. 'Two rivers. Hadn't two rivers sprung / from the Garden of Eden? No, that was four / and they'd diverged. Here only two / and coming together.' 'Literary interpretations' surface at this point, but they are brushed off although they are nonetheless importantly voiced: 'Even if one were tempted / to literary interpretation / such as: life/death, right/wrong, male/female / – such notions would have resolved, dissolved, straight off / in that watery, dazzling dialectic' (*Poems* 207). The desire to stop, to pause the flow of life, is mirrored by but also projected on to the confluence of the two great rivers as the convergence of two opposite forces. Change happens here, and the traveller who stops travelling finally embraces it in all its oppositions ('life/death, right/wrong, male/female'). It is this act of embracing the opposition (not the will to resolve them) which allows the poet to find the point of standstill from which alone the poem can flow. And the poem flows indeed just like the two rivers in the point of their convergence. Importantly – and accurately – the 'dialectic' for Bishop belongs not to the binary fixity of the literary oppositions but to their resolution (Merrin invokes here the trope of 'thirdness' which does not do justice, in my view, to what happens here (Merrin 167–8)). And the resolution – or rather the dissolution – belongs to the 'watery, dazzling dialectic' of the rivers, which is the dialectic of the poetic imagination. Flowing to the end of the poem, the poetic imagination ultimately accomplishes the reconciliation that allows the poet to move on: 'Then – my ship's whistle blew. I couldn't stay' (*Poems* 208). As she leaves, she leaves richer, carrying with her the fascinating mystery of the wasps' nest gift of the local pharmacist, incomprehensible (and indeed 'ugly') to anyone else but her.

Notes

1. See Ravinthiran, in particular chapters 1 and 5.
2. Letter of 7 March 1937 (Moore 384).
3. Goldensohn 199–202.
4. I am grateful to Jonathan Ellis for bringing this reference to my attention.
5. See, for a different reading, Goldensohn (105, 109, 112).
6. The poem 'One Art' accomplishes the same transfiguration of existential despair (and indeed 'disaster') into a bearable experience, explicitly adding the (self) injunction '*Write it!*' (*Poems* 198).

Works Cited

Barry, Sandra, 'In the Village: Bishop and Nova Scotia', in Angus Cleghorn and Jonathan Ellis (eds), *The Cambridge Companion to Elizabeth Bishop* (Cambridge: Cambridge University Press, 2014), pp. 97–110.

Bishop, Elizabeth, *Edgar Allan Poe & the Juke-Box: Uncollected Poems, Drafts, and Fragments*, ed. Alice Quinn (New York: Farrar, Straus and Giroux, 2006).

Bishop, Elizabeth, *Poems, Prose, and Letters*, ed. Robert Giroux and Lloyd Schwartz (New York: Library of America, 2008).

Goldensohn, Lorrie, *Elizabeth Bishop: The Biography of a Poetry* (New York: Columbia University Press, 1992).

Harrison, Victoria, *Elizabeth Bishop's Poetics of Intimacy* (Cambridge: Cambridge University Press, 1993).

Heaney, Seamus, *Finders Keepers: Selected Prose 1971–2001* (London: Faber and Faber, 2002).

Merrin, Jeredith, 'Gaiety, Gayness, and Change', in Marilyn May Lombardi (ed.), *Elizabeth Bishop: The Geography of Gender* (Charlottesville: University Press of Virginia, 1993), pp. 153–72.

Millier, Brett C., *Elizabeth Bishop: Life and the Memory of It* (Berkeley: University of California Press, 1993).

Moore, Marianne, *The Selected Letters of Marianne Moore*, ed. Bonnie Costello, Celeste Goodridge and Cristanne Miller (New York: Knopf, 1997).

Ravinthiran, Vidyan, *Elizabeth Bishop's Prosaic* (Lewisburg: Bucknell University Press, 2015).

8

'Swerving as I swerve': Elizabeth Bishop's Fugitive Empathy

Sarah Kennedy

Elizabeth Bishop has long been fixed in the collective imagination by Robert Lowell's description of her as the 'famous eye'.[1] She is often imaged as a writer whose scrutinising gaze travels with an Empedoclean directness and lucidity across the shadow-play of its distant surroundings. For Adrienne Rich, Bishop's was 'the eye of the outsider' (15), while David Kalstone describes Bishop's early poetry as marked by an unsettling combination 'of observation and alienation', suggesting a lone 'monitory eye' as the appropriate image for her poetry of the 1930s ('Bishop and Moore' 112). A reflective entry in Bishop's notebook for 1934–5 describing a visionary response to a rain-strewn window pane contains a series of startling images of ocular enclosure and isolation:

> I tried to look out, but could not. Instead I realised I could look into the drops, like so many crystal balls, each one traces of a relative or friend: several weeping faces slid away from mine; water plants and fish floated within other drops, watery jewels, leaves and insects magnified, and strangest of all, horrible enough to make me step quickly away was one large drop containing a lonely, magnified human eye, wrapped in its own tear. (Kalstone, *Becoming a Poet* 14)

In this passage, as Linda Anderson has observed, Bishop's acuteness of vision attains an almost hallucinatory clairvoyance (38). The corollary of this inward clear-sightedness is a separation from and blindness toward everything external to the scope of vision. The focal acuity of Bishop's perception is at times in danger of becoming a centripetal force, narrowing the poet's vision to the point of its terrible concentration: 'I tried to look out, but could not.'

Bishop's piercing power of observation appears at first to create a strict delinea-tion between the poet and the distant, non-human world she describes. It involves a self-conceptualisation as spectator rather than participant, as jealous of its observant loneliness as her Man-Moth, slyly preserving one stinging tear, his 'only possession' (*Poems* 17). Helen Vendler describes Bishop as a poet of 'radical solitude' (826), while Bishop herself once asked of her friend Wesley Wehr, 'Can one ever have enough defences?'(Fountain and Brazeau 327). Her most characteristic imaginative metaphors involve the delicate tonal abstractions of maps, and the glacial striations of icebergs adrift in the dark cold of endless seas. Where Bishop's poetry does approach an imme-diacy of affect, the emotion is displaced, mapped on to other, more safely phenomenal territories of experience. Thomas Travisano has rightly characterised Bishop's 'art of displacement' as 'one of her most pervasive and persistent artistic strategies' (34). How is it, then, that in her Brazilian poems Bishop is sometimes able to clutch at what Eric Ormsby calls 'the quick slippery density of a living thing' (92)?[2] And on what terms was Bishop able to develop a poetics in which 'the self is projected into the world and, conversely, the mutable world enters the domain of the self' (Costello 60) with such disarming propinquity?

I argue that the development and refinement of Bishop's concept of poetic consciousness can be construed as a swerve, such as that traced in the motions of man and fish in one of Bishop's Brazilian poems, 'The Riverman' (1965, from *Questions of Travel*). To 'swerve' is to deviate, to transgress and to stray. The motion encompasses the strategic (deliberate deviation) and the responsive (deflection). For a poet forever at odds with the personal and the self-revelatory, the swerve enables a fugitive form of empathy, related both to Maurice Merleau-Ponty's image of the *chiasm*, the criss-crossing interplay between flesh and world, and to the *clinamen* of Lucretius. This fundamental feature of Bishop's late poetics can be discerned in the formal and semantic structures of her work as well as in the imaginative contours of her poetic development which are my focus here. Animated by the figure of the swerve – and by the possibilities of transposed knowledge it offers – this chapter excavates some of the complex, interrelated structures of empathy and indirection in Bishop's later poetry, and considers the productive tensions between them. It focuses its analysis on three prose poems Bishop composed during her time in Brazil, collected under the title 'Rainy Season; Sub-Tropics' (1967), that have been subject to scant critical attention. The chapter undertakes a close reading of the missed connections, glancing blows and altered trajectories of the denizens of the Rainy Season poems, exploring concepts of subjectivity, transitivity and intra-species empathy in the poems' phenomenological framing.

Bishop was a migratory poet – not always voluntarily so – exposed to multiple latitudes, landscapes and contexts. She spent her early childhood in Nova Scotia, Canada; in later childhood she was displaced, moving around within Massachusetts. She lived as an adult in New York, in Key West, Florida, and in Washington DC for a time, and settled in Brazil for nearly twenty years. Her travels gave Bishop an acute awareness of the gradations of *here* and *there*, and of the contingency and porosity of the self. The writerly self formed by the austerity of pale northern landscapes found her emotional contours subtly but decisively altered by the plenitude of the tropical south. Peggy Samuels writes of how in the late 1930s Bishop was beginning to develop her theories of poetic consciousness, grounded in an awareness of nature's 'gradations or modulations as it touched itself, crisscrossing different materials and registers' (315). Samuels relates this to the fascination in Bishop's work of the period with superficies: panes of glass, thresholds of understanding, the reflective surfaces of mirror and water all serve to delimit the extremities of the poet's responsiveness (and, indeed, continued to haunt Bishop throughout her life – as in the valedictory poem 'Sonnet' (1979), fixated on 'the bubble / in the spirit-level' and 'the narrow bevel / of the empty mirror' (*Poems* 214)). In the late 1950s and 1960s, during the Brazilian phase of her poetic development, Bishop's conceptualisation of poetic consciousness began to press these imaginative and emotional peripheries from both sides. This new-found intersubjective responsiveness and sensuous amplitude is what we might accurately call empathy.

David Kalstone writes of Bishop's time in Brazil as creatively enabling (*Becoming a Poet* 152), but the poet was nevertheless worried about the potentially exploitative nature of her creative relationship with her adopted country. In an interview published in the winter of 1966, Bishop was careful to emphasise the prosaic, self-deprecatory dimension of her Brazilian experiences, positioning herself in a culturally ambivalent expatriate space:

> Living in the way I have happened to live here, knowing Brazilians, has made a great difference. [. . .] Most New York intellectuals' ideas about "underdeveloped countries" are partly mistaken, and living among people of a completely different culture has changed a lot of my old stereotyped ideas. (Monteiro 19)

Bishop's poem of disembarkation in Brazil, 'Arrival at Santos', turns a similarly self-suspecting scrutiny on the traveller's 'immodest demands for a different world, / and a better life, and complete comprehension' (*Poems* 87). It is, as Kevin McNeilly writes, a repudiation of 'the tourist's mode of knowing' (89), with its pursuit of novelty, its encroachments and appropriations.

It may have been because of her anxieties of creative response that Brazil was rendered such a fertile environment for Bishop's poetry. From the very beginning of her immersion in the cloud-wrapped environment of waterfalls and mist, magnetic rocks and ferns, Bishop was ruminating on the limits of her imaginative and sensory involvement in this new milieu. Her poem 'The Riverman', written early in 1960, is self-consciously exotic in its shamanistic subject matter and jarring ethnographic pretensions (the poem's epigraph refers the reader to anthropologist Charles Wagley's 1953 *Amazon Town: A Study of Man in the Tropics* for further details). Yet the poem is also deeply concerned with the ways in which imaginative construction and sensory immersion can extend consciousness beyond the bounds of its confining medium. Informed by Amazonian folk legends of therianthropy (human to animal transformation), 'The Riverman' is spoken in the voice of a prospective *sacaca*, an Amazonian shaman whose healing magic derives from the river. The poem starts a movement from the defined thresholds of the domestic into a hyperreal fluvial world where the life-giving silt in the river's depths sustains the amphibious abundance of crayfish and turtles, crocodiles, worms and fish. Enticed by the salt breath of the river's sweetness, the riverman seeks to effect a profound self-transformation, becoming an embodiment of the river's quintessence.

The cultural anthropologist Candace Slater notes that the *sacaca* are unique amongst spiritual practitioners within the *Encantados* belief system for their ability to undertake shamanic journeys not just in spirit, but in body, assuming the physical shape of a dolphin, fish or anaconda (112). She quotes an Amazonian healer: 'The sacaca's flesh is the same as his spirit' (122). The poem is reflexive in its concerns: the would-be shaman ruminates on his ambition and the dislocation from human society necessary to achieve this; he occupies an uneasy and unstable position between two worlds and cultures in much the same way Bishop must have felt she did, as a recent settler in Brazil. The poem charts the gradual interpenetration of mind and environment as the riverman is initiated into the underwater world of the dolphin-spirit. This otherworld, through the looking-glass of the water's surface, is full of slippages and elisions in identity. The dolphin is 'a man like myself' and the river goddess a tall and comely serpent in 'white satin'. Mirrors are not mere looking-glasses to support the vanity of children, but serve as agents of supernatural recognition, flashing 'up the spirits' eyes'. The heterotopic possibilities the poem offers are compromised by its dependence on the use of an indigenous mythology by an interloping poet. The poem's seductiveness similarly depends on complicit readerly desire for 'the river's long, long veins' and its 'pure elixirs' (*Poems* 103–6). Yet 'The Riverman' manages to stop short of exploitation. The tourist's destructive desire for experience is inverted into a parable of self-abrogation, anchored by visceral involvement with the river in all its brackish glory.

'The Riverman' provides a prototype of the swerving intersubjective mode that characterises Bishop's late work, from *Questions of Travel* to *Geography III*. Although the riverman bears the marks of his entry into the river-world – the 'fine mud' cakes his scalp and the smell of the river lodges in his hair (*Poems* 104) – the poem refrains from depicting a complete metamorphosis in favour of the more tentative image of the riverman swimming in synchrony with an encompassing school of fish:

> When the moon burns white
> and the river makes that sound
> [. . .]
> I'll be there below,
> as the turtle rattle hisses
> and the coral gives a sign,
> travelling fast as a wish,
> with my magic cloak of fish
> swerving as I swerve,
> following the veins,
> the river's long, long veins,
> to find the pure elixirs. (*Poems* 106)

For the Roman poet Lucretius, the spontaneous swerving of atoms was the under-lying motion of the phenomenal universe, and the foundation of his philosophy. *De rerum natura* envisions atoms as bodies falling through space, propelled by their own weight, but subject to minuscule, unanticipated alterations of trajectory:

> Unless inclined to swerve, all things would fall
> Right through the deep abyss like drops of rain. (*The Nature of Things* 42)

The swerve (or *clinamen*) is a liberating figure of the indeterminacy of the world of things, and forms the basis for Lucretius's concept of free will.[3] The random swerve, the chance deflection, breaks the chain of predetermination in the lives of all creatures. It makes possible the process of emergence: the spontaneous order arising from the microcosmic interactions of multiple separate entities. The swerve is thus the means by which the organic, self-organising universe can generate an infinity of new and unpredictable patterns. Its affinities with theories of cognitive linguistics and meaning generation are clear. Lucretius's swerving atoms provide the counter-image to Bishop's nightmare vision of raindrops as 'watery jewels', made sinister by their isolation. The awful possibility of the abyss is never far away in either formulation, but the unexpected turn with its creative potential is an imaginative structure shared by Lucretius's cosmology and Bishop's poetic consciousness.

The phrase 'swerving as I swerve' encapsulates the dynamic synchrony between shamanic healer and his living cloak of fish. It is no accident that the poem where Bishop most explicitly portrays the synchronous interplay of human and animal draws on magical imagery. Theorists of affect have long understood the relation of synchrony to magical forms of mimesis (Gibbs 189). Synchrony's transposal of form is 'a fundamental communicational principle running through all levels of behaviour' (Condon 37), linking 'human and animal bodies [. . .] to other rhythmic processes in the natural world' (Gibbs 187). The rhythmic dimension of this pulse – its turn-taking pattern of call and response – extends its valency from somatic to linguistic processes, so that the motions of man and fish trace, in their turn, the tangled trajectories of Bishop's negotiations between self and world, and between speaking and thinking.

As an alteration of or deviation from a pre-existing trajectory, the swerve is a continuing motion, simultaneously extending backwards and forwards in time. In its responsive modality – as a form of deflection – it carries the consequences of the past forwards into the future. Yet deflection also implies avoidance (or at least its attempt), and may therefore also be considered as a strategy for self-protection. In discussing Bishop's bleakly autobiographical 1965 poem 'First Death in Nova Scotia', David Kalstone comments that the child's emotional attention is '*deflected*' from moments of potential trauma by the radiance of arrayed objects (*Becoming a Poet* 220). Helen Vendler similarly finds the poem's trajectory, structured around a series of bewildered deflections, to be 'a picture of the mind at work'. She goes on: 'It will not change, in its essentials, throughout Bishop's poetry. The frightened child makes up three helpless fictions, trying to unite items of the scene into a gestalt' (Vendler 835). 'First Death in Nova Scotia' is bereft of the sinuous energy of the earlier 'The Riverman', and its rhythm of motion is chaotic: ricocheting and rebarbative. But the poem provides an insight into Bishop's ongoing use of the dynamic of swerving as a means of thinking and feeling through lived experience. In the Amazonian poem, the swerve makes a virtue of deflection. The traumatised child's instinct to recoil is transposed into the quicksilver patterns of darting fish. This associative dynamic is strikingly prefigured in 'In the Village' (1953), also written in Brazil. The concluding passage provides a first-person childhood recollection in which the child – en route to send a package to her incarcerated mother – stops on a bridge and stares down at the space where 'everything except the river holds its breath':

> All the little trout that have been too smart to get caught – for how long now? – are there, rushing in flank movements, foolish assaults and retreats, against and away from the old sunken fender of Malcolm McNeil's Ford. (*Prose* 77)

The particular configuration of the riverman's swerve, with all the joyful plangency and momentum of the river, has a Joycean antecedent in the looping opening lines of *Finnegans Wake*, 'riverrun, past Eve and Adam's, from swerve of shore to bend of bay' (3: lines 1–2). Both contexts convey a sense of inexorable motion and position the swerve transverse of, yet somehow deeply entwined with, the structures of psychological genealogy embedded in the text. But the distinct doubled nature of Bishop's image – 'swerving as I swerve' – implies an exquisite series of attunements within the fluid interplay of man and schooling fish absent in the earlier work. Its intricate dynamics function as the underlying physical logic of Bishop's poetic relations with the world: a fascination both cautious and caught up. This logic is developed and articulated further in the Rainy Season poems.

Bishop composed the three prose poems collected under the title 'Rainy Season; Sub-Tropics' (*Poems* 163–5) in January 1967, during a lull in the turbulent breakdown of her relationship with Lota de Macedo Soares and with Brazil (Millier 386). They were first published in *The Kenyon Review* in the November of the same year.[4] They consist of three extended prose poems, narratives voiced in turn by a Giant Toad, a Strayed Crab and a Giant Snail. These creatures are sympathetic grotesques, or (as Brett Millier perceptively describes them) three of nature's 'radical misfits' (387). Despite being situated in their natural sub-tropical habitat – localised to the rocky ledges, lichen-dappled escarpments, and mist-covered pool beneath a waterfall – the Toad, Crab and Snail are all, in one sense or another, out of place. This is foregrounded at the beginning of the first two poems:

> I am too big. Too big by far. Pity me. (*Poems* 163)

> This is not my home. [. . .] I wasn't meant for this. (*Poems* 163–4)

And forms a refrain in the third:

> I am too big. I feel it. Pity me. (*Poems* 165)

All three poems are obsessively preoccupied with the dynamics of self and other. All three purport to record the perceptional experience and subjective awareness of a non-human subject. Each poem combines minute self-examination with an externalising self-consciousness that projects itself on to an imagined community of observers. The Giant Snail, the poems' prototype of thwarted but instinctive empathy, observes the dislocating effect of its own gigantism, filtered through a feeling in common with the Giant Toad and expressed in the patterning of syllabic inflations:

> That toad was too big, too, like me. His eyes beseeched my love. Our proportions horrify our neighbours. (*Poems* 165)

Each of the three poems tracks an uneven outward progress, beginning with self-description and moving into a narrative of travel and not-quite-realised encounter, as the animals attempt to resituate themselves within the landscape. Along the way, their musings encompass other relations, removed in time and contained by memory and imagination: the Giant Toad recounts his cruel mistreatment by the children who set lit cigarettes in his mouth; the Strayed Crab recalls with proprietary interest the 'many small gray fish' he catches up and eats from his pool; and the Giant Snail imagines a congeries of Snail Gods streaming down the cliff-face in the steaming wake of the waterfall. These are all, strikingly, meditations on misshapen encounters. They are meaningful not as moments of engagement or parity, but as cautionary instances, entailing (respectively) violation, exploitation and a failure of nerve.

Given the evident self-revelatory richness of these poems, it is surprising that they have received relatively scant critical attention (although Zhou Xiaojing gives a helpful extended reading of the poems as 'dialogic' investigations of subjectivity). Helen Vendler observes that these 'revealing [. . .] monologues' reflect acutely on Bishop's self and art (825). As an instance of this, Vendler points to the snail's confession:

> I give the impression of mysterious ease, but it is only with the greatest effort of my will that I can rise above the smallest stones and sticks. (*Poems* 164)

This is, Vendler implies (825, 829), an expression of the poet's striving to achieve 'naturalness of tone'. Vendler draws a parallel between 'Bishop's socially unacceptable beasts' and 'Baudelaire's albatross, powerful in the air but ludicrous on deck' (827). We might recall that Baudelaire's albatross is, expressly, a proleptic simile for the Poet. Bishop's fugitive presence seems on occasion to speak directly within these poems, such as when the Strayed Crab says:

> I admire compression, lightness, and agility, all rare in this loose world. (*Poems* 164)

Yet in focusing on these apparent instances of authorial ventriloquism, we may overlook some of the most striking features of the Rainy Season poems, located in the specific imaginative formulations of the poems' therianthropy.

Bishop wrote a number of animal poems: some celebrated, some less so. Her poems about animals combine the emotional desire for communion beyond the human with the aesthetic demand for precision, and initiate a dynamic tension between the inherently subjective character of experience and the tendency to universalise experience as a means of self-recognition. For the poet, animal selfhood provides a particularly acute iteration of the problem of other minds because, in addition to being ontologically subjective and therefore unverifiable, the experience of animal consciousness occurs outside of human language. This compounds the problem of representation and creates multiple aesthetic and ethical pitfalls (appropriation, universalisation, solipsistic self-dramatisation, to name a few).

Bishop's recourse to the prose-poem form – uncommon in her oeuvre – at once signals her ambition and her caution in attempting the dialogic and the hybrid in an animal/human context. In his recent analysis of the Rainy Season poems' formal qualities, Vidyan Ravinthiran invokes Clive Scott's description of the prose poem as

> a site of poetic and prosodic transformation, where one kind of verse structure is converted into another, or where prose acts as an embedding medium in which prosodic structures are free to imagine and constantly reimagine themselves. (Scott 119)

Ravinthiran goes on to describe 'Rainy Season; Sub-Tropics' as providing 'a comparable experience of generic transformation and reflexive reimagining' (158). The protean ambitions of the form are counterbalanced by the modesty of Bishop's zoological choices (Ravinthiran argues persuasively for the prose poem's association with democracy (173)).

Crucially, in the Rainy Season poems the poetic consciousness engages in repeated acts of imaginative self-transposal, speaking – insofar as is possible – from within an animal-shaped space, and describing a world mediated by (imagined) animal sensory experiences and projections. The subject-position depiction of non-human minds distinguishes these poems from Bishop's other treatments of animals: it differs from the anthropomorphic humour of the curious seal in 'At the Fishhouses' ('interested in music; like me a believer in total immersion') and from the alienated contemplation of 'The Fish' (whose eyes 'shifted a little, but not / to return my stare'). It may be going too far to suggest that the Rainy Season poems depict Bishop's animal equivalent of the 'I, Elizabeth' moment of revelation in 'In the Waiting Room' (1976), but they come close. Their concern is not, as in 'At the Fishhouses', with the extension of a human consciousness into the elemental reaches of the non-human, but with feeling out – as best they might – the contours of toad, crab and snail from the inside. This provides a rationale for Bishop's choice of animals: the toad's amphibious skin and the exoskeletons of crab and snail provide distinctively non-human models of phenomenological experience.

On the principle that an encounter with an alien consciousness is itself alienating, we might say that human encounters with the reflective otherness of animals have the potential to defamiliarise us from ourselves, and to create scope for a reconceptualisation or adjustment of identity. Suzanne Keen defines empathy (presumably between humans or fictional human characters) as 'a vicarious, spontaneous sharing of affect, [which] can be provoked by witnessing another's emotional state, by hearing about another's condition, or even by reading' (4). Jay Griffiths goes further, describing the empathy unleashed through imaginative identification with animals as an almost physical force, 'exact, sensitive and enraged'. Kristin Hotelling Zona has observed that Bishop's poetry is preoccupied with 'probing the complex and often discomforting nature of self as it is shaped through interaction with the world' (49). This is especially – almost painfully – true of Bishop's giant sub-tropical creatures, feeling out their imaginative limits and sensual self-boundaries in relation to the perceived world of the external. Empathy and its lack or displacement are explored both within and through these poems. An empathy of imagination is the medium through which the creatures interact and react to each other, but it is also the primary metatextual concern of the poem-cycle as a whole. In allowing the reader or listener an immediacy of imaginative entry into the nervous system and somatic awareness of her sub-tropical creatures, Bishop generates a physically rooted structure of empathy that extends beyond the colloquial sense of the term (as a loose synonym for sympathy) to embrace affective and cognitive insight. Susan Lanzoni (a historian of sciences of the mind) describes empathy, as it was understood at the turn of the twentieth century, as a theory of aesthetics that characterised the 'participatory and kinaesthetic engagement' of the spectator with objects of art as 'an imagined bodily immersion in the shapes, forms, and lines of objects and the natural world' (34). This historical understanding provides an interpretive context for the Rainy Season poems' emphasis on movement and trajectory. Lanzoni sees 'images of felt or bodily movement', in their elision of action and imagination, as being particularly significant in engendering an empathic response (39). The literary scholar Richard Harter Fogle defines *poetic* empathy in related terms, as the 'presence of motor, kinaesthetic, or organic imagery so powerful in effect as to evoke kindred impulses in the reader' (149).

Lorrie Goldensohn writes that the consciousness evident in Bishop's work 'feels like a sympathy without skin extending deeply and unnervingly everywhere' (56). The observation is acute, but leaves us to imagine Bishop's sympathy (or, in my terms, empathy) as an undifferentiated mass of nerves and tissue rather than as the finely differentiated, swerving vectors I am arguing it is best conceptualised as. Movement through space is, as Elżbieta Wójcik-Leese suggests, one of the most basic forms of interaction between human consciousness and the physical environment (6). Utilising the vocabulary of cognitive poetics, she terms the 'path image schema' a 'recurrent pre-conceptual pattern', which 'orders our knowledge of motion' and experience of travel (7). Invoking Bishop's celebrated poetic aspiration to 'portray, not a thought, but a mind thinking' (as she found it described by M. W. Croll), Wójcik-Leese characterises Bishop's poetics 'as the motion of the observing mind' (7). Hence the early elision of purpose and vision in 'The Colder the Air' (1936), where 'The target-center in her eye / is equally her aim and will' (*Poems* 8). Hence, too, the linkage in Bishop's oft-quoted 1964 letter to Anne Stevenson (the 'Darwin Letter') between 'unexpected moments of empathy' and 'peripheral vision':

> glimpses of the always-more-successful surrealism of everyday life, unexpected moments of empathy (is it?), catch a peripheral vision of whatever it is one can never really see full-face but that seems enormously important. (*Poems, Prose, and Letters* 861)

The progress of the mind as a body in motion is played out in the Rainy Season poems' precise sensory imagery. The Giant Toad finds himself limned by droplets of mist that accumulate on his skin, describing his contours and defining the boundaries of his physical being:

> The mist is gathering on my skin in drops. The drops run down my back, run from the corners of my downturned mouth, run down my sides and drip beneath my belly. Perhaps the droplets on my mottled hide are pretty, like dewdrops, silver on a moldering leaf? They chill me through and through. I feel my colors changing now, my pigments gradually shudder and shift over. (*Poems* 163)

What begins as an immediate sensory response to cutaneous stimuli quickly modulates into an imagined visual perception – an envisioning – of the toad's self as viewed from outside. This is followed by a counter-movement ('They chill me through and through') simultaneously returning the sensory perception to the core of the body whilst revealing the fragility and permeability of that core. The semantic repetition gestures towards the further body of the reader, whose physicality ghosts the passage. The effect of the toad's hyper-responsiveness to its environment is a synaesthesia of vision and touch: 'I *feel* my colors changing'. The toad's earlier statement eliding these senses ('My eyes bulge and hurt. [. . .] They see too much') is extended here to encompass the whole of its physical being. The toad feels its pigments 'shudder and shift'. Vendler has pointed to an echo of Bishop's earlier poem 'The Prodigal',[5] in which

> he felt the bats' uncertain staggering flight,
> his shuddering insights, beyond his control,
> touching him. (*Poems* 69)

In both instances, the poem's perception draws on an unstable compound of internally and externally sited phenomena. In 'The Prodigal', the hazy magical thinking (or pathetic fallacy) characteristic of the desperate inebriate obscures the extent of the poem's radical intersubjectivity. Yet the prodigal and the Giant Toad are fellow sufferers. Like the alcoholic, the toad is subject to physical compulsion ('I live, I breathe, by swallowing'). He must ingest the air, even where this might prove fatal, as in the episode with the cigarettes ('We could not help but smoke them, to the end. I thought it was the death of me').[6] The prodigal and the toad alike suffer the pervading agonies of a world brought 'too close'. They recall the agonised, dissolving consciousness of Rilke's second 'Elegy' (1912): 'But we, when moved by deep feeling, evaporate; we / breathe ourselves out and away' (Rilke 11). These figures test the limits of proprioception – the physiological feedback mechanism by which the body senses the relative position of, and relations between, its parts and sustains an awareness of itself. Because proprioception relies on external factors like gravity to map the body to itself, it is also, necessarily, a modulating sense. It is the body's knowledge of its orientation and coordination in space: a somatic negotiation between inner and outer worlds.

The reversibility of the Giant Toad's flesh – its simultaneous sense of touching and being tangible – is an instance of Maurice Merleau-Ponty's concept of *chiasm*, the criss-cross intertwining of flesh and world. Merleau-Ponty used the figure of the *chiasm* (crossing-over) as a means of exploring the gaps and slippages between subjective experience and objective existence. He argued that moments of embodied subjectivity are located at the cross-points in the oscillating convergences and divergences of world and individual, where the body knows itself as simultaneous subject and object:

> between my body looked at and my body looking, my body touched and my body touching, there is overlapping or encroachment, so that we may say that the things pass into us, as well as we into the things (Merleau-Ponty 132)

For Merleau-Ponty, such moments are transformative, allowing for self-understanding and empathy for others. For Bishop's toad, the subjective and objective experiences of self which subtend upon one another produce a panicked dissonance in identity, experienced as a physical pain at the world's penetration. The toad's traumatic experience of its loss of control results in its imaginative reversal of the flow of sensory influence. In response to its recollection of violation by its juvenile torturers, the toad ceases to absorb the colours of the dewdrops. It no longer meditates on the feel of the impressions left by the rough lichens on its feet, nor revels in the sensual pleasure of swallowing 'mouthfuls of cold mist'. Instead, the toad's final statement is a rumination on its own ability to suffuse the surrounding air with 'the almost unused poison' it carries: 'If I will it, the poison could break through, blue-black, and dangerous to all. Blue-black fumes would rise upon the air.' 'Beware, you frivolous crab,' the toad says. This moment expands the poems' frame, admitting the simultaneous presence of other creatures and initiating the relational dynamics between them. Significantly, the Toad's poisonous compound colouration reappears later in 'In the Waiting Room', when the child Elizabeth experiences

the sensation of falling off
the round, turning world
into cold, blue-black space. (*Poems* 180)

This disorienting moment enacts the vertiginous drop of the Lucretian fall through the abyss, until countered by an intervening swerve. The child's spontaneous 'sidelong glance' – with its compound visual and spatial resonance – shifts the poem's plane of attention from a vertical to a horizontal axis, thereby arresting her fall.

Bishop once wrote to May Swenson that her primary struggle in poetry was 'a problem of placement' (*One Art* 360). Although she was talking about the placement of words or images, Eric Ormsby has observed that 'it applies to her placement of the things in her poems as well' (93). A preoccupation with relative placement, with angles and trajectories, is a recurrent feature of Bishop's poetry, as Lorrie Goldensohn has suggested (113). We might think of Buster Keaton, who despite being 'made at right angles to the world' must 'turn always to the leeward' (*Poems* 301–2); and of 'The Monument', where 'the angles alternate' (*Poems* 25). Bishop's work is full of oblique angles: the tilt, the skew, the incline; her poetry looks at the world aslant.

Placement and the related precision of boundaries are major concerns for the Strayed Crab, whose muscular armature presents a hard contrast to the toad's moist and vulnerable skin: 'I am the color of wine, of *tinta*. The inside of my powerful right claw is saffron-yellow. See, I see it now; I wave it like a flag.' For the crab, there is no imaginative distinction between the other he commands to 'see' and his own vision. His somatic consciousness inheres in his rigid surfaces ('my shell is tough and tight') and angular orientations ('I believe in the oblique'). Accustomed to precedence over the 'small gray fish' that he can see right through ('Only their large eyes are opaque'), he finds his immediate surroundings an intolerable challenge ('This place is too hard,' he says. 'How did I get so far from water?'). The crab's narrative is a pattern of reverberation and rebuff. His hard, pointed feet echo off the rocks: 'on this strange, smooth surface I am making too much noise.'

Unlike the riverman and the fish, or even the heavy but amphibious toad, the crab cannot weave and undulate. It is trapped within a rebarbative dynamic precluding any generosity of interaction. Faced with the 'stifling' prospect of the 'big soft monster, like a yellow cloud' that pats the crab's back (presumably the giant toad, although the toad strangely doesn't refer to the gesture), the crab brandishes its claw. Positioned transverse to a world whose overtures it is unable to accept, the crab deflects what might have been an instance of contact into a glancing blow. The crab's contemptuous response to its environment exemplifies deflection and indirection as ethical and imaginative failures, as well as physiological necessities for an animal that can only move sideways. Ironically, for a creature that admires 'agility', the crab's lack of imaginative or empathetic agility produces persistent misapprehension and self-delusion. The creature exemplifies the psychology of infinite regress, T. S. Eliot's 'backward half-look / Over the shoulder, towards the primitive terror' (196).

The crab mistakes the toad's general indifference for hostile attention:

There, I have frightened it away. It's sitting down, pretending nothing's happened. I'll skirt it. It's still pretending not to see me. Out of my way, O monster. [. . .] I want nothing to do with you, either, sulking toad. (*Poems* 164)

This shadow-play is entirely of the crab's own devising. The poem does allow the crab one near-instance of empathetic connection, as its circumventions place it athwart the snail:

> Cheer up, O grievous snail. I tap your shell, encouragingly, not that you will ever know about it. (*Poems* 164)

The snail feels the crab's touch ('What's that tapping on my shell?') but its 'blind, white bull's head' cannot catch sight of the crab, and the moment comes to nothing. This missed connection is deliberately engineered as such by the crab: less a moment of intra-species empathy than a form of self-consolatory obliquity (it is significant, I think, that the crab taps the snail's shell – the only feature these two animals have in common). The crab's jarring designation of the snail as 'grievous' invokes the word's original, literal description of something that presses heavily (it is related to 'gravid'). The syntactic indeterminacy admits the possibility that the crab is referring to the snail's physiological burden (rather than the crab's response to its presence). However, setting the word against the crab's earlier description of the toad as 'stifling' suggests that the crab remains confined within tight phenomenal boundaries, its 'indirect approach' predicated on an immediate retreat into the safety of solipsism.

The Giant Snail alone figures the chiastic possibilities of displacement and deviation as routes to meaningful understanding. As might be expected, the snail's soft body ('like a pallid, decomposing leaf') is vulnerable to despoliation by the abrasive world. 'Covered with sharp gravel' and in fear of the 'rough spears of grass', the snail's mantra is 'Don't touch [. . .] Draw back. Withdrawal is always best.' And yet, despite its unwieldiness and susceptibility, the snail is responsive to the beseechings of its surroundings. There is a tension between the snail's physiological limitations and its imaginative capabilities that mirrors Merleau-Ponty's entwined yet divided body:

> Although I move ghostlike and my floating edges barely graze the ground, I am heavy, heavy, heavy. (*Poems* 164)

The snail's heaviness, its billowing looseness and deliquescence, are the necessary conditions for its imaginative communion with its environment. The snail's self-perception is based on an acceptance of its protean formlessness:

> My sides move in rhythmic waves, just off the ground, from front to back, the wake of a ship, wax-white water, or a slowly melting floe.
> [. . .]
> The sides of my mouth are now my hands. They press the earth and suck it hard. (*Poems* 165)

This is a creature able both to celebrate its own quintessence and to move with empathetic grace into other spheres of experience. A free-flowing amalgam of 'the body sensed and the body sentient' (Merleau-Ponty 138), the snail is able to think, feelingly, through its hybrid, compounding senses: hands that are also mouth, body that is also foot, the snail's perceptual mediations slip between sensory categories. Even the physiological mechanism of the snail's movement – its micro-undulations – enacts a swerve in miniature form. The snail's final aspiration, to rest in the 'steady pulsing' of the waterfall that will 'vibrate' through its shell and body, suggests the oscillant perfection of its self/other configuration: 'I shall be like a sleeping ear.'

The sleeping ear vibrating to the shared pulse of the world: Bishop's closing image resists empathetic comprehension in any conventional sense. It cannot be made to fit within Martha Nussbaum's definition of empathy as the 'imaginative reconstruction' of others' experience (301) – for what snail has ever imagined itself a human ear? Bishop's empathy for nature's 'radical misfits' (Millier 387), fugitive and failed as it so often is, is an imaginative self-transposal that yearns toward the posthuman. The revelatory power of the Rainy Season poems lies in their indirectness, their light touch, and their willingness to remain unconsummated. As unsettling and strange as the silt-sallowed transmutations of her riverman, Bishop's imaginative convergences resist conscription by any project to build civic virtue through the consumption of literary counter-experience. The dynamic *clinamen* of Bishop's late poetry enables expression of the poet's radical intersubjectivity even as it protects the poet from self-revelation. In the words of the Strayed Crab, 'I believe in the oblique, the indirect approach, and I keep my feelings to myself' (*Poems* 164). Bishop's swerve is a rejection of the antinomy between self and world. A complex and fluid form of propinquity, it grants to the poet and her readers the flexibility to be near and not near, of yet not of, and identified yet disguised.

Notes

1. Lowell used the phrase in introducing Bishop at a poetry reading at the Guggenheim Museum on 6 May 1969.
2. Ormsby uses this phrase of Hopkins, in contradistinction to Bishop, in his review of *Poems, Prose, and Letters*, but the phrase is suggestive of something submerged but present in Bishop's work too.
3. I am using the figure of the swerve in its Lucretian incarnation as an intervening shift, as distinct from the Deleuzian formulation of *clinamen* as an innate (pre-existing) characteristic.
4. 'Rainy Season; Sub-Tropics', *The Kenyon Review* 29.5 (November 1967): 665–70.
5. The incident underlying the poem occurred in 1946 (Monteiro 143). The poem underwent many iterations before being published in *The New Yorker* in 1951.
6. These lines echo and invert Bishop's biblical allusion at the conclusion of 'Roosters': 'The sun climbs in, / following "to see the end," / faithful as enemy, or friend' (*Poems* 40).

Works Cited

Anderson, Linda, *Elizabeth Bishop: Lines of Connection* (Edinburgh: Edinburgh University Press, 2013).
Bishop, Elizabeth, *One Art: Letters*, ed. Robert Giroux (New York: Farrar, Straus and Giroux, 1994).
Bishop, Elizabeth, *Poems, Prose, and Letters*, ed. Robert Giroux and Lloyd Schwartz (New York: Library of America, 2008).
Carus, Titus Lucretius, *The Nature of Things*, trans. A. E. Stallings (London: Penguin, 2007).
Condon, William, 'Communication and Empathy', in Joseph Lichtenberg et al. (eds), *Empathy* (Hillsdale: Analytic Press, 1984), pp. 35–58.

Costello, Bonnie, *Elizabeth Bishop: Questions of Mastery* (Cambridge, MA: Harvard University Press, 1991).

Eliot, T. S., *The Poems of T. S. Eliot, Volume I: Collected and Uncollected Poems*, ed. Christopher Ricks and Jim McCue (London: Faber and Faber, 2015).

Fogle, Richard Harter, *The Imagery of Keats and Shelley: A Comparative Study* (Chapel Hill: University of North Carolina Press, 1949).

Foucault, Michel, 'Of Other Spaces, Heterotopias', *Architecture, Mouvement, Continuité* 5 (October 1984): 46–9.

Fountain, Gary, and Peter Brazeau (eds), *Remembering Elizabeth Bishop: An Oral Biography* (Amherst: University of Massachusetts Press, 1994).

Gibbs, Anna, 'After Affect: Sympathy, Synchrony, and Mimetic Communication', in Melissa Gregg and Gregory J. Seigworth (eds), *The Affect Theory Reader* (Durham, NC: Duke University Press, 2010), pp. 186–205.

Goldensohn, Lorrie, *Elizabeth Bishop: The Biography of a Poetry* (New York: Columbia University Press, 1993).

Griffiths, Jay, 'Forests of the Mind', *Aeon* (12 October 2012), <https://aeon.co/essays/how-the-jaguar-shamans-took-the-arrows-from-my-mind> (last accessed 8 October 2018).

Joyce, James, *Finnegans Wake* (London: Faber and Faber; New York, Viking Press, 1939).

Kalstone, David, *Becoming a Poet: Elizabeth Bishop with Marianne Moore and Robert Lowell* (New York: Farrar, Straus and Giroux, 1989).

Kalstone, David, 'Elizabeth Bishop and Marianne Moore', in Diane Wood Middlebrook and Marilyn Yalom (eds), *Coming to Light: American Women Poets in the Twentieth Century* (Ann Arbor: University of Michigan Press, 1985), pp. 105–22.

Keen, Suzanne, *Empathy and the Novel* (New York: Oxford University Press, 2007).

Lanzoni, Susan, 'Empathy Aesthetics: Experimenting between Psychology and Poetry', in Meghan Marie Hammond and Sue J. Kim (eds), *Rethinking Empathy through Literature* (New York: Routledge, 2014), pp. 34–46.

McNeilly, Kevin, 'Toward a Poetics of Dislocation: Elizabeth Bishop and P. K. Page Writing "Brazil"', *Studies in Canadian Literature/Études en littérature canadienne* 23.2 (1998): 85–107.

Merleau-Ponty, Maurice, *The Visible and the Invisible*, ed. Claude Lefort (Evanston: Northwestern University Press, 1968).

Millier, Brett C., *Elizabeth Bishop: Life and the Memory of It* (Berkeley: University of California Press, 1993).

Monteiro, George (ed.), *Conversations with Elizabeth Bishop* (Jackson: University Press of Mississippi, 1996).

Nussbaum, Martha, *Upheavals of Thought: The Intelligence of the Emotions* (Cambridge: Cambridge University Press, 2001).

Ormsby, Eric L., *Fine Incisions: Essays on Poetry and Place* (Erin: Porcupine's Quill, 2011).

Ravinthiran, Vidyan, *Elizabeth Bishop's Prosaic* (Lewisburg: Bucknell University Press, 2015).

Rich, Adrienne, 'The Eye of the Outsider: The Poetry of Elizabeth Bishop', *Boston Review* 8.2 (April 1983): 15–17.

Rilke, Rainer Maria, *Duino Elegies and The Sonnets to Orpheus*, trans. Stephen Mitchell (New York: Vintage International, 2009).

Samuels, Peggy, 'Verse as Deep Surface: Elizabeth Bishop's New Poetics, 1938–39', *Twentieth-Century Literature* 52.3 (2006): 306–29.

Scott, Clive, *Vers Libre: The Emergence of Free Verse in France, 1884–1914* (Oxford: Clarendon Press, 1990).

Slater, Candace, *Dance of the Dolphin: Transformation and Disenchantment in the Amazonian Imagination* (Chicago: University of Chicago Press, 1994).

Travisano, Thomas, 'Bishop and Biography', in Angus Cleghorn and Jonathan Ellis (eds), *The Cambridge Companion to Elizabeth Bishop* (Cambridge: Cambridge University Press, 2014), pp. 21–34.

Vendler, Helen, 'The Poems of Elizabeth Bishop', *Critical Inquiry* 13.4 (1987): 825–38.

Wójcik-Leese, Elżbieta, *Cognitive Poetic Readings in Elizabeth Bishop: Portrait of a Mind Thinking* (Berlin: De Gruyter Mouton, 2016).

Xiaojing, Zhou, '"The Oblique, the Indirect Approach": Elizabeth Bishop's "Rainy Season; Sub-Tropics"', *Chicago Review* 40.4 (1994): 75–92.

Zona, Kristin Hotelling, 'Bishop: Race, Class, and Gender', in Angus Cleghorn and Jonathan Ellis (eds), *The Cambridge Companion to Elizabeth Bishop* (Cambridge: Cambridge University Press, 2014), pp. 49–61.

9

REPETITION AND POETIC PROCESS:
BISHOP'S NAGGING THOUGHTS

Deryn Rees-Jones

I

ELIZABETH BISHOP BEGAN WORK on her poem 'Questions of Travel' in January 1956, having by that time been resident in Brazil for five years (see early draft of the poem below). *North & South*, her first collection, published ten years previously, had recently been republished alongside her second book *A Cold Spring* in 1955 and won the Pulitzer Prize. If, at the age of forty-five, the now solidly realised idea of staying permanently in Brazil offered a new domestic security to sit alongside her increasing profile as a poet in the US, it also set up a dynamic between 'home' and 'elsewhere'

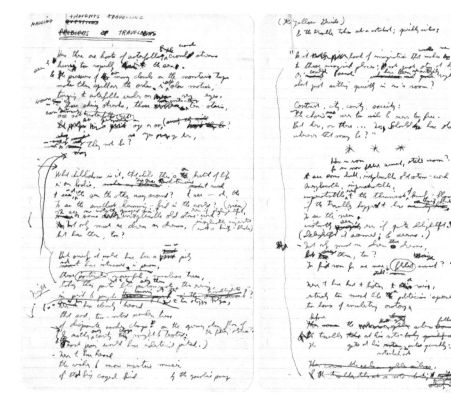

which complicated ideas of the foreign and the familiar, past and present. In analysing the drafts of the 'Questions of Travel' poem – which gave its title to her third collection – I look at the use of repetition of the sounds that are clustered in Bishop's writing around the word 'home', as well as her use of repeated patterns of words, and homophones, to offer insights into the deeper shifts in her writing that were becoming a central characteristic of her style, and which might be seen to underpin and indeed run in parallel to the drafting process as a whole. For Bishop, the 'nagging thoughts travelling' (one of her draft titles) that the poem reaches for in its creation might be seen as an attempt to connect trauma and memory within her poetics.

As such the poem is central to her writing, its interrogation of empiricism versus imagination, its engagement with temporal and geographical 'here' and 'thereness' working in complex counterpoint to an understanding of a relationship between memory and loss. As I approach the 'Questions of Travel' poem I do so through the lens of psychoanalysis, as much as a theoretical tool as a way of exploring the impact Bishop's own brief engagements with psychoanalysis as an analysand might have had on her own thinking about the heterochronic nature of temporality, and her ability to establish 'the links between the here and now and there and then' (Perelberg 189). In her brief and in some ways unsatisfactory analysis Bishop nevertheless found the artistic method for transforming the process of remembering (which also included, we learn in her 1947 letters to her analyst, sexual and violent abuse from her uncle) into a poetics. In her book *The Poetics of the Everyday*, Siobhan Phillips describes the way creative repetition through aesthetic form might be seen in terms of an overcoming of 'the constrictive recurrence' of a past history, which 'with the poem's healing use of formal patterns [. . .] combats the compulsions of deathly repetitions' (Phillips 15). I take a slightly different route here, seeing the psychoanalytic process as a part of Bishop's developing aesthetic. The rhythms and repetitions of Bishop's developing body of work are examined instead as a negotiation of nagging emotional impasse but also as a signalling of artistic movement and creation (rather than re-creation) towards what feminist philosopher Rosi Braidotti might term a cartography of becoming.[1]

II

As many commentators have remarked, the death of Elizabeth Bishop's father, William, when she was eight months old, and the subsequent distress of her mother Gertrude (who according to her admissions notes had attempted both murder and suicide before eventual incarceration in a psychiatric hospital when Bishop was five), were to leave an irradicable mark on her work.[2] In her seminal book on Bishop's poetics, Susan McCabe places these losses at the heart of Bishop's poetic vision of uncertainty and indeterminacy in which the self and 'a sense of temporal perception (the two "so compressed, / they've turned into each other")' are offered up 'for inquiry' (194). In turn I would like to suggest, in my speculative unpicking of Bishop's creative processes, that the two distinctive parental losses which occurred at very different points in Bishop's linguistic and psychic development underpin her writing thematically as well as stylistically, creating a highly textured rendering of loss that is embedded both structurally and thematically within the two sections of *Questions of Travel*, 'Brazil' and 'Elsewhere', and which is ultimately transformed.

Gertrude Bulmer Bishop died in hospital in 1934 at the age of fifty-four when Bishop was twenty-three; subsequent to her leaving the family home, there is no record of her being in touch with her daughter ever again. As Diana Fuss points out, in a convincing and nuanced reading of Bishop's autobiographical prose poem 'In the Village' (1953), Bishop's problem as she charts the disturbances of those early years is 'not how to hold on to her mother but how to lose her'. For Fuss it is this sense of the mother who is both here and not here that 'provokes Elizabeth's real anxiety, and prohibits true mourning'. Given this context, it is difficult also not to imagine that the open-ended nature of Bishop's mother's absence might very well also have reignited the feelings of the earlier loss of her father, when Bishop was so young that she had no way of putting those thoughts or feelings into language. As the narrative of 'In the Village' unfolds, Fuss argues that Bishop 'depicts maternal presence as not nurturing but annihilating':

> Here it is the *mother's* grief that makes the *child* disappear. Gertrude's scream eclipses Elizabeth, cancels her; Elizabeth 'vanishes,' as if it were the child and not the mother who had never existed. At the sound of the maternal scream, Bishop herself vanishes into the third person, reclaiming her first person voice only when her mother recedes from narrative view. ('How to Lose Things')

Christopher Bollas's concept of the 'unthought known' seems especially useful in understanding the complexities of Bishop's processes here. In *The Shadow of the Object* Bollas describes how he sees the formation of the psyche in prelinguistic object relations: 'the experience of the object', he writes, 'precedes the knowing of it' (39). A preverbal early trauma becomes preserved in the infant's subsequent moods, and interplay with otherness. It is then in the transformative space of creativity that 'the artist both remembers for us and provides us with experience of ego memories of transformation' (28–9). Bishop's anxieties about her mother being in some way both alive and dead repeat and transform, and, temporarily at least, resolve in language, through the poetic process, the anxiety induced by not remembering. That the two experiences of paternal death and maternal loss, so close to each other and yet so different, might lie palimpsestically across each other – so that even as that knowledge of early death was itself precariously understood, it was also impossible to consign to the past – surely adds something difficult to that moment of artistic transformation, which we can recognise in the repetitions and somehow unresolved pulsings of the poem, both in its process of composition and in its finished state.

As we can see from the fragment of the draft reproduced at the start of this chapter, 'Nagging Thoughts Travelling' was only one of several unpromising titles Bishop deliberated using as a title in the successive drafts of 'Questions of Travel'. Its importance as a title poem signals Bishop's wider attempts in *Questions of Travel* as a whole to locate, explore, hold and transform the inevitable tensions that underlie these nagging but not easily identified thoughts. Indeed, the apparent revisions and hesitations that recur in Bishop's work to suggest the mind in action – what Barbara Page has referred to as Bishop's enactment in her writing of the 'failures of a mind to sustain its own rhetoric or narrative' – might also, as Page suggests, be seen as stylistic attempts to 'embody acts of knowing; knowledge of feeling, or even knowledge as feeling' (13) in a way which signals a complex and uncanny recognition of kinds of trauma which cannot quite be recognised in language.

My suggestion is then that the 'nagging' repetitions to which Bishop is to some extent subsequently alert in the poems mark the moment of the psychic movement 'between' feeling, knowing and 'not-knowing' the difference between death and loss. Further, and keeping both Page and Bollas in mind, I want to show that these embodiments of 'knowledge as feeling' become worked through in various ways: as a series of repetitions of sounds, specifically the sound 'o' in various guises alongside apostrophic exclamation; in the uncanny doubling-up of the same words, separated by a comma; and in homophonic repetitions. In this respect the poems in which these repetitions appear offer a framework to shift, and at some level distinguish between, such kinds of knowledge. In this complex matrix of understanding that runs across differing frameworks of language acquisition, memory and aesthetics, these uncanny repetitions might also now be read as a series of sonic gestures *towards knowing*. To this end it is worth remembering that 'In the Village' is built around awareness of noises and silences; importantly, the sound of the maternal scream that begins the narrative is juxtaposed throughout with the sound of the blacksmith's clang. It is the sound of 'the made thing' of art, for which the noise of the hammer on the anvil stands, which is able in the final section to hold within it the elemental, the mundane and peripheral, as well as the acute pain of the scream.

Bishop's moving advocacy of art's relationship to the eternal and elemental is not resolved in 'In the Village', but ends with her questioning, by juxtaposition, art's capacity to contain in its beauty the transitory ordinariness of human life:

> It is the elements speaking: earth, air, fire, water.
>   All those other things – clothes, crumbling postcards, broken china; things damaged and lost, sickened or destroyed; even the frail almost-lost scream – are they too frail for us to hear their voices long, too mortal?
>   Nate!
>   Oh, beautiful sound, strike again! (*Prose* 78)

Alongside the sound of the striking anvil of art is the human voice. As well as emulating the vocative O! 'Oh' is a sound literally full of breath and life, responsive in its invocation to both an internal sound and an external other. Such apostrophic cries, as Jonathan Culler has argued, 'remov[e] the opposition between presence and absence from empirical time and locat[e] it in a discursive time' (149). Placed in the context of Bishop's own poetic attempts to move between temporal and geographic structures, Culler's general comments seem especially pertinent to our understanding of Bishop when he writes:

> The temporal movement from A to B, internalized by apostrophe, becomes a reversible alternation between A and B; a play of presence and absence governed not by time but by poetic power. (149–50)

And as Linda Anderson shrewdly remarks, '[u]sing sound as a medium means that the "clang" of Nate's anvil – like the scream that quickly vanishes leaving only an afterimage, a reverberation – encapsulates both the trauma and its transformation' (116).

Thus the 'oh' cries in the poems, which privilege poetry's ability to hold together presence and absence, are for Bishop also a movement towards discovering the quality of the 'not-known' which emerges as a recurrent pulse that offers connection to, and signals estrangement from, an experience. Not only do the 'oh' cries recur variously at key moments in poems, but their sound becomes part of a textual grain of open 'o' vowels in 'Questions of Travel' which echo and resound as a way of containing and repeating feeling.[3] 'In the Village' had been originally placed in the *Questions of Travel* volume at the start of 'Elsewhere', the second of the two framing sections 'Brazil' and 'Elsewhere'; it is hard not to think of its disappearance in all subsequent reproductions of the volume as a kind of acting-out of Bishop's anxieties, its status as prose poem, or prose even, perhaps marking it out as anomalous, but like Bishop's mother in the narrative appearing and then disappearing from sight.

I want now to turn specifically to two poems which sit in counterpoint across the two sections of *Questions of Travel*, the title poem 'Questions of Travel' (1956), placed in the 'Brazil' section, and the poem 'Filling Station' (1955), which appears in the 'Elsewhere' section and which allows Bishop to step back in chronological time as well as to relocate back to the US geographically. Looking at the poems in the order in which they were written, rather than in the order in which they are presented in the volume, offers particular insight into Bishop's creative process as the strikes of sounds, the nags, and repeats, see her returning again and again to clusters of sounds which connect poems written during this transitional period in her life. 'Oh, but it is dirty!' begins 'Filling Station'. The unspoken absence of the mother (has she died, has she left?) and the ensuing domestic dirtiness 'oil-soaked, oil-permeated' is inflammatory in its emotional potential. As a sister poem to 'Questions of Travel' (which itself references 'a grease-stained filling-station floor'), 'Filling Station' feels much more wrought; its six six-lined stanzas are tidily gathered together; its setting resonates with emptiness (we can't fail to think that it is its emptiness which is in need of 'filling'). This absence is visually signalled by empty circles, the holes in the wickerwork, the crocheted doilies, the shape of the O in the lined-up susurrating oil cans which spell out in silent series ESSO-SO-SO. And yet with all its melancholic, Hopper-like bleakness, and the potential for irony in the final line of the poem, 'Somebody loves us all', it is hard also not to hear the word 'sew' in so, or to connect the absent female who has left behind the crocheted mats as a presence who somehow (as the poem is so carefully knotted together) also holds things together. That stream of 'sos' which looks forward so much to a future (all consequential and linked, not unlike the and-and-and of free-associative thought) suggests ongoingness and purpose, however limited. The 'Oh' of exclamation which also begins the poem foreshadows the final repetition of the 'o' sound in the lined-up, iconic cans of Esso petrol whereby the 'so – so – so' of the cans transforms so memorably and magically from the SoS signal of disaster into the so of 'Somebody who loves us all'. I find it hard, too, not to hear the being of 'esse' in Esso. It's worth noting also the relationship established between the words 'pitch' and 'match' in the two poems, which associate across their rhyme. Again the sound-shift between the words 'pitch' in 'Filling Station and 'pity' in 'Questions of Travel' draws between the two poems an association of fire and feeling.

But perhaps the most important conversation that is going on between the two poems – and not of course unconnected from those fiery feelings of association – is the link between the exclamatory 'Oh' in 'Questions of Travel' and the rich elusive lines which follow it: 'Oh, must we dream our dreams / and have them, too?' To dream and to have our dreams is to be located uncomfortably between fantasy and reality, and as such the line speaks of the trauma of a reality that cannot easily be borne. I think here of the extraordinary and painful anecdote of the burning boy in Freud's *Interpretation of Dreams*, which Cathy Caruth places at the centre of her writing on trauma. It is possible, of course, that Bishop was also familiar with the passage in which Freud describes a scene in which a father sits in vigil beside his dead son's body before his funeral. Exhausted, he falls asleep, and the candles surrounding the corpse accidentally set the child on fire. During this reality the father dreams that the living child has come to him, calling to him to come to his aid, with the haunting cry, 'Father, can't you see I'm burning?' While the dream, Caruth writes,

> seems to show the reality of the burning outside, it in fact hides [. . .] the reality of the child's death. The dream thus transforms death into life and does this, paradoxically, with the very words that refer to the reality of the burning. It is in order to fulfill the wish to see the child alive, in other words, that the knowledge of his child's burning is turned into a dream. If the father dreams rather than wakes up, it is because he cannot face the knowledge of the child's death while he is awake. (95)

The image of the burning child recurs in Bishop's work: not only in 'In the Village' when the child narrator hallucinates that something (perhaps her mother?) 'is in the room; red flames are burning the wallpaper beside the bed' (*Prose* 74). Another early poem, 'Casabianca' repeats the poet Felicia Hemans' line 'And love's the burning boy' in another kind of nagging repetition; and the late, unfinished draft 'A Drunkard' (c. 1971) recalls the 1914 Salem fire which a mother and child witness from a distant window. In this poem we might also see (with its reiterations and spaces that emerge as it drunkenly fails to be written, remaining always as a draft) that the fire is once again imagined in the room, 'my white enammelled crib was red / and my hands holding to its rods – / the brass knobs holding specks of fire' (*Poems* 317). Might fire, as in Freud's story, signal as well as hide the reality of death?

III

'Questions of Travel' is unusual in Bishop's oeuvre for its irregularity of line, its raggedy, we might even say littoral edges signalling its impulse to move both away from and towards the left-hand spine of the poem. What strikes me in particular, though, are the repetitions of a cluster of words at the start of the poem which read 'here, waterfalls, streams, sea, clouds, mountaintops' only to become repeated and reordered by the pattern 'waterfalls, tearstains, waterfalls, here, streams, clouds, mountains'. The repetition in this first stanza of the word 'travelling', sitting as it is so that the word transforms from its continuous past ('keep travelling') to a travelling in the present tense ('keep travelling, travelling'), is a repetition which responds to the subsequent lines – 'calling, / calling', 'and retreating, always retreating' – moving away from its self and returning. The poem's musical impulse towards repetition is both a desire to travel and also a continuing attempt to 'get itself started'. Like the nagging thought there is a return without resolution, and the poem's repetitions are tightly bound to its continual shifting for reassurance of tone at the same time as fixing the experience of reading and looking in the present. Such repetitions we associate more with Gertrude Stein, whose first name Bishop would have no doubt been especially alert to given its recall of her own mother's name. Bishop was, of course, acutely aware of Stein's writing, and writes about her in her extraordinary undergraduate essay 'Time's Andromedas', where she wrestles with Stein's time-position theory. Notably, Bishop concludes the essay by asking: 'Is it possible that there may be a sort of *experience-time*, or the time pattern in which realities reach us, quite different from the hour after hour, day after day kind?' (*Poems, Prose, and Letters* 659).

If there is a tension being set up in 'Questions of Travel' between movement and the stasis of home, between a spatio-temporal experience of the 'here and thereness', past and present, which otherwise structures the entire *Questions of Travel* volume, we see how Bishop's repetition of sounds in the poem also becomes intimately connected to a refusal of temporal and geographic categories. In the atemporal geography of our consciousness we can, of course, be both here and there, and as we see here in my marked-up version of the poem which emphasises the repetition, the irregularity of the poem's form appears to be determined by not only aural but visual repetition as it effortlessly trips forward, gathering associations of sound, rhyme and sense:

> Think of the long trip **home**.
> Should we have stayed at **home** and thought of **here**?
> Where should we be **today**?
> Is it right to be watching **strangers** in a **play**
> in this **strangest** of **theatres**?
> What childishness is it **that** while there's a breath of life
> in our bodies, we are **determined** to rush
> to see the sun the other way **around**?
> The tiniest green **hummingbird** in the **world**?
> To stare at some inexplicable old stonework,
> inexplicable and impenetrable,
> at any **view**,
> instantly seen and **always, always** delightful?
> Oh, must we **dream our dreams**
> and **have** them, **too**?
> And **have** we **room**
> for one more folded sunset, still quite **warm**?

The word 'home' sits above 'home' in the first and second lines of the second stanza; 'always' is repeated in line twelve in a way which mimics the earlier 'travelling, travelling', and the stanza is held together in the echoed rhymes at the ends of lines of 'home', 'dreams', 'room' and 'warm'. What is most remarkable in the poem, if we start to focus increasingly on the sounds of the words, is the almost over-determined way in which we see how words, in the connective of sound, transform into other words and things in a stream of free-associative generation. Thus the word 'home' spawns the 'hum' of the 'hummingbird' (known of course for its intricate and intense movements in the service of staying still); the word 'dream' spawns half-rhymes 'room' and 'warm'. The apparently simple question 'must we dream our dreams / and have them, too?' sits right at the centre of the poem and exhibits not only the connective 'and' which keeps thought in a state of movement, but also the repetition of words which sound and look the same but which are being used in grammatically different ways. So we see 'dream' as verb and 'dream' as noun; 'have' as transitive verb meaning to experience or 'have' meaning to own.

The careful musical structures that Bishop is setting up are to some extent part of her genius of ear which allows her to bind ideas within poetic structures – in part through free association, and in part by her careful accentuation and ordering of sounds which accrue in the drafting process. Like dream images, it is impossible to trace the associations they might have held for Bishop; in the poem they come to account for a kind of travel, a thinking which moves her between objects which all have things in common – the clog, the church, the birdcage. They are receptacles of space, are all made of wood, and all also relate to sound. In their different ways the knocking of the clogs, the church and the birdcage might all be seen to hold language or song. Clogs are a kind of shoe but they are also stoppages (we might think of the saboteurs), perhaps not too unrelated to the nag. Perhaps, like the endless prohibition 'not' which occurs a metronomic five times in the third stanza, their repetitive intensity also clogs up our thinking. The associated homophones which occur as aural repetitions (would and wood) also point towards a 'hereness' of the material tangible world and a 'thereness' of the future conditional tense as Bishop's train of thought sees her attempting to make connections (to ponder 'Blurr'dly and inconclusively, / on what connection can exist for centuries') between disparate things.

What I'd like to venture is that the nagging pulse of the third stanza, the repeated 'nots' which sit verbally as prohibition (to not imagining and perhaps not remembering), also homophonically (potentially even like associative knots in wood) signal the way in which Bishop is negotiating ideas of seeing and testing out experience. Repetition of identical words, her use of homophones, ask uncannily how we know and don't know a thing as itself. And as all those repetitions create a structure, a church, a cage, perhaps, a holding maternal body even, so too do they create a space for knowing what sits between three distinct modes: the sound of speech like rain, the 'sudden golden silence', and the written word of the traveller with his or her notebook in a room, who is both here and there in the creative space between the page and the imagination.

As early as 1933 we find Bishop writing to Donald Stanford of her own writing processes:

> I become very intent upon what I *must* say, the series of ideas being built up in my head, and 'I tend to exaggerate in my own mind' the ease with which the series piles up, and forget the reader will not have my excitement to carry him over the awkward spots which seem simple and even necessary to me at the time. (*One Art* 13)

The fragments of apparently scattered but nevertheless coalescing experience are, of course, both the dream material and method of poetry. As Bishop's work develops, pushing further an aestheticisation of elements of the free-associative technique, that series of pile-ups becomes, as we will see, profoundly connected with the search for a deepening understanding and embedding into her poetic structures of time and memory. The 'awkward spot' sits as the space between one thought and another, its silent linkage offering a way in to the unconscious of its maker. As a phrase it also recalls Wordsworth's 'spots of time'. Wordsworth's compression of the geographic and temporal becomes embodied within Bishop's more modern idea of the 'awkward spot'. Bishop did not read Wordsworth until 1936; in July 1951, he was very much on her mind, as she described herself in a letter to Lowell as 'a minor female Wordsworth' (*Poems, Prose, and Letters* 773). T. S. Eliot was also in her thoughts. In juxtaposition to this kind of preverbal remembering and knowing, I want finally to highlight here the importance of two key intertextual references in 'Questions of Travel' which enact a different kind of remembering and not-remembering, showing how these rich overlayings of psychic activity mark a pivotal point in Bishop's work.

If in the first draft of 'Questions of Travel' the title looks more like a neatly balanced visual equation for the troubled thoughts the poem suggests, and of which it is symptomatic, by the next draft the problems of titling are again revealing as we see the introduction of the phrase 'Another Country' as title (see copy of later draft below). In his discussion of this phrase, George Monteiro has pointed out how it sends us back to Eliot's famous use of Marlowe's *The Jew of Malta* as epigraph to his 1915 dramatic monologue 'Portrait of the Lady': 'It was in another country and besides the wench is dead.' The phrase 'another country', unlike the other potential titles for the poem, remains embedded in the poem, marking an important transition in its developing thinking. 'In another country', writes Bishop, 'the clogs would all be tested. / Each pair there would have identical pitch.' The poem at this point seems to celebrate difference rather than the man-made or uniform; it celebrates individuality and difference rather in the way that 'wood' sounds like 'would' but isn't the same. The underpinning, conscious or not, which sees Bishop incorporating Eliot's mysterious and somehow unmoored voice in 'Portrait of a Lady' is the first of two intertextual allusions which crucially underwrite the composition of the

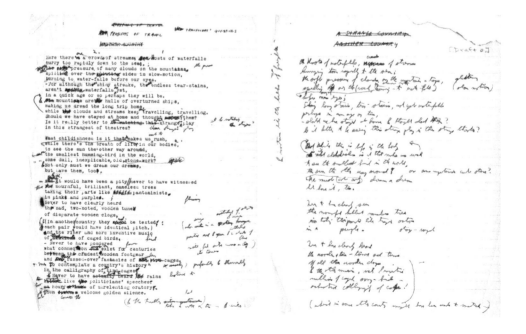

poem, incorporating a kind of poetic remembering. Towards the end of 'Portrait of a Lady' the male speaker reflects on his encounters with an older woman.

> And I must borrow every changing shape
> To find expression . . . dance, dance
> Like a dancing bear,
> Cry like a parrot, chatter like an ape. (Eliot 13)

The poem imagines that the older woman will die, leaving the writer sitting alone, pen in hand: 'Doubtful, for quite a while / Not knowing what to feel or if I understand.' 'Not knowing what to feel or if I understand' seems extraordinarily resonant here, as does the poem's explicit engagement with the failure of language to adequately hold meaning. The body, the movement of the dance, the non-linguistic sounds of animals, the repetitions of identical words which run across commas, all feel central components of a process, and an aesthetic, in which Bishop is staging an encounter with unknowable death.

As Bishop draws on Eliot in 'Questions of Travel', moving across and through feelings about maternal absence, her mind seems also to be in direct conversation with several key passages from Book 11 of Wordsworth's *The Prelude* (1805) as he explores his idea of 'spots of time', those moments of experience that form around the trauma that has occurred at (or in relation to) certain places. Two sections stand out in their relevance. The first is the initial memory Wordsworth draws on of being a six-year-old child and coming to the place of a hanging:

> I led my Horse, and, stumbling on, at length
> Came to a bottom, where in former times
> A Murderer had been hung in iron chains.
> The Gibbet-mast was mouldered down, the bones
> And iron case were gone; but on the turf,
> Hard by, soon after that fell deed was wrought,
> Some unknown hand had carved the Murderer's name. (566)

Like her intertextual use of the Eliot, the poem evokes a death, but this time it is the death of a murderer whose name has been etched into the landscape. The second, slightly later memory is of again encountering something man-made in the natural landscape. Here Bishop's description in 'Questions of Travel' of staring at 'some inexplicable old stonework, inexplicable and impenetrable' conjures a hybrid memory both of the hanging site and also of the second passage where Wordsworth sits remembering his father's death:

> And the bleak music from that old stone wall,
> The noise of wood and water, and the mist
> That on the line of each of those two roads
> Advanced in such indisputable shapes;
> All these were kindred spectacles and sounds
> To which I oft repaired, and thence would drink,
> As at a fountain. (568)

These passages work as an intertextual signalling of the memory that the wall might open up while also indicating an inability to reach beyond the not-known or interpretable in the poem. For as much as we too encounter the music of the old stone wall, so, too, are we halted by a kind of emotional impasse it represents. Bishop perhaps has this passage in mind a second time in the poem 'Manners', which appears in the first edition of *Questions of Travel* in 1965, directly after 'In the Village'. The poem carries the dedication 'for a Child of 1918' and in it a grandfather and child give a lift to a young boy, particularly relevantly here, called Willy. Bishop's poem, with its evocation of a passing historical moment shared by old man and young boy, is less traumatic than Wordsworth's, but seems importantly placed in its position as the poem that follows 'In the Village'. In the absence of 'In the Village' in later editions of *Questions of Travel*, the subtle evocation of the Wordsworth passage in 'Manners' in some small way also performs, through loose association, its psychic work for her.

In her essay 'Dimensions for a Novel', which begins by addressing Eliot's essay 'Tradition and the Individual Talent', Bishop transposes the model of art as 'simultaneous order' to the sequence of events in a novel. 'All the past forms,' she writes, 'to use a musical expression, a frame of reference for the future, and the two combine to define and expand each other.' She continues, quoting a passage from Eliot for a second time, to confirm her point:

> for order to persist after the supervention of novelty, the *whole* existing order must be, if ever so slightly, altered; and so the relations, proportion, values . . . toward the whole are readjusted; and this is conformity between the old and the new. (*Poems, Prose, and Letters* 673)

Certainly if Eliot's 'Portrait of a Lady' allowed Bishop to access difficult feelings about her lost mother, Wordsworth, himself so much engaged in an exploration of paternal loss, becomes a poet who for Bishop, by 'Crusoe in England', stands for access to that which has been forgotten and can only be partially recalled. As we have seen, free association – and to some degree also repetition – offers a kinetic model that also allows Bishop to 'travel' so that looking, and the way we look, is given a provisionality and timelessness on the one hand, whilst also being situated in and alongside a more chronological historical temporality. Bishop's references to the two poems also allow a movement back in time, so that old and new sit in internal juxtaposition, and alteration, repeated and transformed, and in a way that is deeply embedded in the poem.

IV

'Not remembering' Freud sees as a kind of 'forgetting' which 'is limited in the main to losing track of connections, misremembering the sequence of events, recalling memories in isolation' (*Beyond the Pleasure Principle* 35). As we have seen, the building-up of images through association in 'Questions of Travel' creates a method for identifying what is not known. The urge for Bishop is to find an aesthetic – and most importantly a vital – stage for this remembering. Deciding to use *Questions of Travel* as the title of her third collection highlights Bishop's awareness of the importance of both the psychic and the aesthetic work the poem was doing for her.

Writing to Ruth Foster, with whom Bishop was in analysis during the winter of 1946–47, Bishop reflects on her own ambivalence about repetition:

> One thing, among the many others, that I realize this is doing to help my work is making me get over the fear of repetition [. . .] I've lost the fear of repeating myself to you. [. . .] And I feel that in poetry now there is no reason why I should make such an effort to make each poem an isolated event, that they go on into each other or overlap, etc, and are really one long poem anyway.[4]

Bishop draws attention to two important things here. First, the sense that one might approach a memory or feeling in repeated ways and contexts as a way of speaking it out loud and knowing it not only as words but as affect, and also in terms of the inter-connectedness of experiences. Secondly, that poems might, in different ways, work through ideas and memories offering us alternate understandings of them.

'Questions of Travel' sees Bishop in an act of working through her own becoming which we see in marvellous fruition in the 'oh' sound in the much later poem 'In the Waiting Room' (1976), where the expression of the 'oh' of pain heard and also somehow simultaneously voiced by the young Elizabeth leads to the ability by the end of the poem for its speaker to announce 'I am an Elizabeth'. In the repetition of these 'oh' sounds, Bishop clusters together a set of poems written as part of a developing sequence of thinking, a working through about the relationship between lively and deathly feelings, between absence of the mother and also her own presence as a maker of poems.

Finally, I would like to venture here that such vitality depends upon Bishop's ability to move towards a rethinking of subjectivity in what Braidotti calls nomadic post-human time, 'a complex and non-linear system, internally fractured and multiplied over several time-sequences' in which 'affect and memory become essential elements' (*The Posthuman* 167). Braidotti's conceptualising of posthuman time allows us to see Bishop escaping from what Braidotti calls the 'chronological linearity and the logo-centric gravitational force' of autobiography. 'Memories', writes Braidotti, 'need the imagination to empower the actualization of virtual possibilities in the subject.' She continues:

> Memory works in terms of nomadic transpositions, that is to say as creative and highly generative inter-connections which mix and match, mingle and multiply the possibilities of expansion and relations among different units or entities. (167)

Overcoming the nagging thought, and foregrounding such transpositions within an aesthetic, we see Bishop moving towards a conception of a self whereby 'memory in the posthuman nomadic mode is the active reinvention of a self that is joyfully discontinuous, as opposed to being mournfully consistent'; it is the movement from individual sounds and homophones that remind us of, and return us to, a non-verbal, affective way of knowing. Bishop's use of repetitions, exclamations, homophones and what I see as free-associatively driven connectives does not offer a coherent but fixed narrative of the self, or even a 'cure' in their writing of the effects of those early traumas. The repetitions in Bishop's work are not contained by form, but what is not-known is discovered, in the process of writing. In setting up poem against poem

Bishop's 'dazzling dialectic' means that repetitions dramatise, but also actively resist, a potentially regressive or neurotic model of repetition-compulsion. Instead we see Bishop's work slowly move over a period of ten years to bring into the present an emerging self who, by *Geography III*, is not just a visitor to Elizabeth but 'an' Elizabeth who can claim her self in the moment of her cry.

Notes

1. See *Nomadic Subjects: Embodiment and Sexual Difference in Contemporary Feminist Theory*.
2. See Diana Fuss, 'How to Lose Things: Elizabeth Bishop's Child Mourning'.
3. The shift between 'oh' and 'o' occurs again significantly in 'Song for the Rainy Season', in a move from an 'oh' at the start of the poem that subsequently becomes an 'O', invoking a 'Difference that kills, / or intimidates, much / of all our small shadowy life!' (*Poems, Prose, and Letters* 81–3).
4. See Linda Anderson's chapter in this book for a full account of Bishop's correspondence to and relationship with Dr Ruth Foster.

Works Cited

Anderson, Linda, *Elizabeth Bishop: Lines of Connection* (Edinburgh: Edinburgh University Press, 2015).

Bishop, Elizabeth, *One Art: The Selected Letters*, ed. Robert Giroux (London: Chatto & Windus, 1994).

Bishop, Elizabeth, *Poems, Prose, and Letters*, ed. Robert Giroux and Lloyd Schwartz (New York: Library of America, 2008).

Bollas, Christopher, *The Shadow of the Object: Psychoanalysis of the Unthought Known* (London: Free Association Books, 1987).

Braidotti, Rosi, *Nomadic Subjects: Embodiment and Sexual Difference in Contemporary Feminist Theory* (New York: Columbia University Press, 2011).

Braidotti, Rosi, *The Posthuman* (Cambridge: Polity Press, 2013).

Caruth, Cathy, *Unclaimed Experience: Trauma, Narrative, and History* (Baltimore: Johns Hopkins University Press, 1996).

Culler, Jonathan, *The Pursuit of Signs: Semiotics, Literature, Deconstruction* (Ithaca: Cornell University Press, 1981).

Eliot, T. S., *The Poems of T. S. Eliot, Volume I: Collected and Uncollected Poems*, ed. Christopher Ricks and Jim McCue (London: Faber and Faber, 2015).

Freud, S., *Beyond the Pleasure Principle* (London: Penguin, 2003).

Freud, S., *The Interpretation of Dreams* (Oxford: Oxford University Press, 2008).

Fuss, Diana, 'How to Lose Things: Elizabeth Bishop's Child Mourning', <http://post45.research.yale.edu/2013/09/how-to-lose-things-elizabeth-bishops-child-mourning/> (last accessed 8 October 2018).

Goldensohn, Lorrie, 'Approaching Elizabeth Bishop's Letters to Ruth Foster', *The Yale Review* 103.1 (January 2015): 1–19.

Harrison, Victoria, *Elizabeth Bishop's Poetics of Intimacy* (Cambridge: Cambridge University Press, 1993).

McCabe, Susan, *Elizabeth Bishop: Her Poetics of Loss* (Philadelphia: Penn State University Press, 1994).

Monteiro, George, *Elizabeth Bishop in Brazil and After: A Poetic Career Transformed* (Jefferson, NC: McFarland, 2012).

Page, Barbara, 'Elizabeth Bishop: Stops, Starts and Dreamy Divagations', in Linda Anderson and Jo Shapcott (eds), *Elizabeth Bishop: Poet of the Periphery* (Newcastle upon Tyne: Dept of English Literary & Linguistic Studies, University of Newcastle, in association with Bloodaxe, 2002), pp. 12–30.

Perelberg, Rosine Jozef, *Murdered Father, Dead Father: Revisiting the Oedipus Complex* (London: Routledge, 2015).

Phillips, Siobhan, *The Poetics of the Everyday: Creative Repetition in Modern American Verse* (New York: Columbia University Press, 2010).

Wordsworth, William, *A Critical Edition of the Major Works*, ed. Stephen Gill (Oxford and New York: Oxford University Press, 1984).

Part III

Poetry

10

'SOLID CUTENESS': ELIZABETH BISHOP'S ART OF SIMPLICITY

Jess Cotton

IN A REVIEW OF BISHOP'S *The Complete Poems* in 1969, John Ashbery remarks that 'at last we have someone who knows and is not didactic. Few contemporary poets can claim both virtues' (*Selected Prose* 120). To know and yet not to know too much, or rather, to know and yet not reveal how much one knows; to parade a certain un-knowingness, a performance of naïveté, had, as Ashbery saw, something particularly contemporary about it. It showed him how he might navigate the current impasse within the American poetic tradition, and find space within it. More specifically, Bishop showed Ashbery that the establishment could not 'be all that bad' if it could accept Bishop's subtly subversive forms within its heavily circumscribed field, one whose outlines had been sharply defined by New Criticism, a practice that Bishop herself saw as making poetry 'more and more pretentious and deadly', as she writes in a 1960 essay for John Ciardi's *Mid-Century American Poets* (Millier 218). One way in which Bishop counters this pretension and deadliness is by cultivating a lightness in her poetry that at once dramatises the difficulty of taking a female poet seriously and rhetorically moves the tradition to a place where she might begin to be taken at her word.

Bishop knows, from her own reading of modernist texts, that it is in reclaiming childishness and sentimentality – that which is denigrated in modernist aesthetics, most notably by Wyndham Lewis – that she might find a way forward within a tradition that has historically been gendered male. This childishness is a salient presence in Bishop's early writing, evident in the first essays and short stories she published in her high school literary magazine, *The Blue Pencil*, and in her 'Poems from Youth', in which she demonstrates a knowingness that goes far beyond her youthful years, and which sits uncomfortably with the idea of Bishop as a slow-moving, slow-developing poet.[1] Maybe, as she suggests in her early essays and criticism, this slowness is not the female poet's own, but rather the disjunct that she must necessarily work through between her contemporary reality and the poetic language available to her that is not yet quite commensurate with it (*Edgar Allan Poe* 183). In a 1960 letter to Robert Lowell, Bishop recalls writing a story at Vassar that was much admired by a teacher whom she describes as struggling to be 'both ladylike and modern' (*Words in Air* 447). Bishop associates the feminine element in poetry with 'niceness', with a capitulating to the reader that ensures that he or she is 'not going to mis-place them socially' (*Words in Air* 333), and she recognises that she has to subvert this 'niceness' within an ostensibly traditional form if she is to demonstrate how a childish or feminine viewpoint might, in fact, offer, as Alison M. Jaggar argues, 'a less partial and distorted and there-fore more reliable view' (168).

In subscribing to the childish, Bishop brings us back to the simplicity of surfaces, to make us look again at the particular, showing us how there is something in the detail that exceeds visual knowledge, that allows us to see *through* the image; to trouble the existent boundaries between inside and outside. The detail is what the child notices because it has not yet become fully accustomed to an acculturated way of seeing, and its sincere act of looking undercuts the sophisticated or the pseudo-sophisticated, taking us back to what Bishop calls, in 'Over 2,000 Illustrations and a Complete Concordance', 'our infant sight' (*Poems* 58). This infant sight, which fails, or rather chooses not, to distinguish between primary and secondary texts, between imagina-tion and reality, allows for various realities to be kept in play at once. In not cutting off any of its possible stories, or in subverting affective to epistemological responses, the poem bears constant rereading because it continually shifts the grounds on which we read. Bishop presents us with an image of a text whose value lies precisely on its shimmering surface; she 'stops courageously at the surface', as Nietzsche writes in *The Gay Science*, advocating what he calls an art of 'cheerfulness', which is 'a second dangerous innocence [. . .] more childlike and yet a hundred times subtler than one has ever been before', because it draws us back to that which we thought we knew so well to show us what we don't quite know, that which might be infinitely ambiguous, or which can only be held in contradiction (37–8).

In 'A Flight of Fancy', a short story written for *The Blue Pencil* in 1929, Bishop suggests that the poet must learn not to be taken 'entirely seriously' nor to be 'too much at home' in her work, for it is in maintaining an 'exquisitely light and buoyant' position in the text (*Poems, Prose, and Letters* 508–10) that one is able to disrupt the stability of these forms and create 'marvellous progeny' that underwrite that which has gone before (Wylie 33). The short story, which is composed as an oblique com-mentary on three temporally and generically disparate texts, Elinor Wylie's *Vene-tian Glass Nephew*, Coleridge's 'Something Childish, but Very Natural', and George Meredith's *Diana of the Crossways*, is typical of Bishop's early writing in that it slips playfully between fiction and criticism, between primary and secondary texts, sub-verting the distinctiveness of those categories and raising questions about how we read, and distinguish between, forms of literature. The short story, which is told in an airborne conversation between two 'literary' men, debating the place of sentiment in literature, might be read as a repost to Lewis's short story 'Buy Me an Air-Ball, Please!' (1926), in which he laments a culture in which adults have become childish and in which 'real children also play at being "children"' (182–4). For Bishop, this childishness, which Lewis rightly saw as altering the relationship between back-ground and foreground, illuminates the importance of emotion in establishing cer-tain kinds of knowledge and allows for an art form which, in its concern for the small, the particular and the overlooked, is invested in what she calls in a 1958 letter 'That strange kind of modesty that I think one feels in almost [everything] contem-porary one really likes' (*Words in Air* 250).

The two literary men who narrate 'A Flight of Fancy' are introduced at the begin-ning of the story by an anonymous 'hostess', and their less-than-ideal responses to the cultural work that sentiment performs in poetry are mediated by her knowing tone. The story centres on their failure to come up with a language that is adequate to their situation, and it is in this failure, in the space that is created between their responses, that Bishop, whom we might think of as slipping between the roles of the first gentleman and the hostess, imagines an alternative literary terrain in which ideas emerge like 'gleaming blue bubble[s]' and 'luminous fire-balloons' – iridescent images that reoccur throughout Bishop's work – that allow us to rise above our immediate present and gain perspective on that which has become habitual. Bishop establishes a complicated relationship to sentiment in this early publication. On the one hand, she seeks to distance herself from its 'ladylike' properties – its excessive emotion that is heard in the second gentleman's 'voluptuous, sad note', and in his tendency to simply reproduce that which has gone before, that tone 'all sentimental people use for all quotations' (my italics). On the other hand, she accepts that she must continue to work through sentimental affects if she is to generate and legitimise questions of female identity in her work.

The idea of Bishop as an invisible hostess, *performing* hospitality in the text, is important for it suggests how certain poetic spaces might be opened up and made possible when one is not fully 'at home' in the text, when the division between inside and outside becomes less readily definable. Note, for example, the effect that this 'curious' airborne state has on time: 'I had never seen', the first gentleman remarks, 'the twilight part of evening last so long'. In this dialogic poetic flight, Bishop shifts conventional spatial and temporal coordinates, creating a slantwise direction in the text that allows her to trouble the relationship between sentimentality and femininity without diminishing their importance, revealing, by extension, how a side-eye glance is necessary to discern the tone of her own work. It is this slantwise affective direction that allows for what she calls a 'constant re-adjustment' within the tradition, an adjustment that returns us to the object of contemplation, the book in the gentleman's hands (*Poems* 12):

> My mind was afloat and lost as a leaf in a stream, with this companion and his thin voice and equivocal talk. But the book in his fingers looked fairly solid. (*Poems, Prose, and Letters* 511)

The book in question, *Diana of the Crossways*, a nineteenth-century novel written by a man on the 'woman question', is an unlikely choice on which to mount a defence of the sentimental in modern literature. It is 'hardly as lovely as poetry', as the narrator concedes, but it reveals the difference between that which is 'humorous in reality' and that which is *performed* as humorous. This crucial distinction is indicated in the text by the hostess's interruption, which at once playfully posits and surreptitiously negates the gentlemen's speech, with the effect that it precludes any aesthetic judgement.

When Bishop thinks about how she might create a performative or faux-naïf register in her own work as a means of navigating her modernist legacy – how she might become a *marvellous progeny* of modernist poetics – she thinks, in particular, about W. H. Auden, a poet whose 'childlike vividness of imagination' F. R. Leavis famously judged as demonstrating 'the disabilities of the childish' which he found 'peculiarly ominous because of the attendant sophistication there was, manifest in the writer's uncertainty as to the degree of seriousness he intended' (167). Bishop, in her precocious sophistication, was certain that she would need to adopt a 'childish' manner if she was to trouble the value of this 'serious' sensibility upheld in literary studies. In a 1934 essay,

'Mechanics of Pretence: Remarks on W. H. Auden', Bishop identifies this childishness as the principle through which Auden is able to bring about an alternative poetic language, one that is characterised by a subversive lightness that reveals a new 'emotional experience' previously kept from – or hidden within – the tradition. This new affective horizon is, she suggests, dangerous because of its capacity to unsettle the existent order of things and must consequently be brought into view in the subtlest of manners. Such readjustment takes time, she cautions, and a pretence, which ostensibly upholds the tradition, must initially be created in order that such a horizon be eventually illuminated within it. This performance is not merely preliminary, however, she suggests, but is important in itself, for it 'raise[s] the imagination to a higher pitch':

> Much can be done by means of pretence. Children pretend to speak a foreign language or inscribe its imitation alphabet in their school books, and inspired by the same motives, grow up to become linguists, grammarians, and travellers [. . .] In his earliest stages the poet is the verbal actor. One of the causes of poetry must be, we suppose, the feeling that the contemporary language is not equivalent to the contemporary fact; there is something out of proportion between them [. . .] To connect this disproportion a pretence is at first necessary [. . .] The play becomes a play on a stage dissolving to leave the ground underneath. (*Edgar Allan Poe* 183–4)

Bishop associates the prodigal poet's position within the tradition with this original act of pretence, with the child's imitative form of learning, which, as she writes, is the grounds on which it both maintains a position within the existent order of things and imagines that order otherwise so that its reality eventually emerges at the point where this performance unravels.

This mechanics of pretence is evident in the earliest poems that Bishop wrote, which are frequently voiced by a feminine or childlike speaker, who is at one remove from the world that he or she inhabits and consequently must perform a lightness or naïveté in the text as a means of invisibly moving through its formal contours. In the poem 'I Introduce Penelope Gwin', which has been tentatively dated to the late 1920s by Alice Quinn, and which Bishop most likely wrote at Walnut Hill School, the speaker tells us that Penelope, the archetypal storyteller of this tale of lightness, is a 'friend' of hers, 'through thick and thin'. Perennially moving through the world, she proves infinitely elusive, and her companionable elusion is that which permits the speaker to also travel through these 'foreign parts' with a lightness that allows her to elude the fixity of home. Underwriting domesticities, she belongs only to '*le beau monde*', which Bishop associates with a new poetic space in which the speaker might begin to introduce herself (*Edgar Allan Poe* 3–4). This ambiguous, *formless* friendship suggests that Bishop, like Penelope, is at a remove from the world of her poem, and that the poet must become the hostess of her tale before she might eventually create a language in which she is perfectly at home.

Storytelling – or the performance of hospitality in the text – is the means by which Bishop is able to overcome the 'depression' that she associates with 'family life' and imagine things otherwise. As Walter Benjamin notes, storytelling allows for 'the most extraordinary things, marvellous things' to be 'related with the greatest accuracy', without forcing 'the psychological connection of the events' on the reader (89). Bishop's Penelope is able to continue 'Pursuing culture and the arts' with this poetic licence, and it is at the point where this storytelling and friendship meet that Bishop is able to envisage a new tradition, one that has the advantage of being 'formless', and it is in this formlessness that a '"slantwise" position' is created 'in the social fabric', one that allows new 'virtualities to come to light', which is to say, alternative means of becoming female in the text (Foucault 138). As Bishop writes in her early poem 'Pleasure Seas' (1939), it is the possibility of this new formless becoming that keeps one 'skip[ing] / Over the tinsel surface' and our 'eyes on / The bright horizon' where new relations begin to take shape (*Poems* 279). Again, Bishop returns to an image of 'A blue balloon' in the poem, the only possession that Penelope is said to carry with her (along with a pot plant, perhaps a nod to Keats's 'pot of basil'), an iridescent object that, in her contemplation, draws her outside of herself into an ecstatic attentiveness where pleasure becomes the focus of all relations.

The faux-naïf tone of the poem is established principally through its simple or 'bad' rhyme which, as Simon Jarvis notes, 'rings out its refutation of the dead metaphysics which would bore us into believing that all categories [. . .] refer to real and really separable fields' (19). Bad rhyme allows Bishop to bring that which is traditionally kept in separate spheres into play. If, as Jarvis suggests, good rhyming is 'serious' and 'masculine' – 'rhyme which does *work*' (my italics) – in employing 'bad' rhyme, Bishop establishes a subversive feminine virtuosity within the text, one whose surface impropriety undercuts the tradition in which she moves. A faux naïveté is also evident in the overtly childish drawings that illustrate the only manuscript copy of the poem that survives. The comically simple yet subtly subversive illustrations, which include a Russian Aunt-Eater, depicted as a toy monkey on a puppy's back, and Penelope herself as a child with a watercolour set, suggest that Bishop saw that in playing off this childishness against the *beau mode* sophistication of her protagonist, she might trouble, so as to illuminate, certain aesthetic categories and bring about a contemporary poetic language that is aligned with her feminine realities. This new poetic language works both with and against the 'honeyed words' – the cuteness – that is ushered from Miss Ellis's 'frank and honest eyes' – both with and against the convenient 'disguise' that she (presumed to be based on Bishop's schoolteacher) uses to navigate her at once 'ladylike' and 'modern' position.

A rhythmical playfulness or lightness in poetics has historically been bound up with a political contestation of the literary establishment. But in Bishop's work, this lightness is always coupled with an upholding of literary *manners*, a quality that she frequently esteems in those she meets. When Bishop thinks of what 'good', 'tactful' manners look like in person and on the page, she is reminded, as she writes in a 1938 letter, of 'the *tone* of George Herbert: "Take the gentle path"', a line from his poem 'Discipline' (*One Art* 68). To have literary manners is, for Bishop, to cultivate a mechanics of pretence, which allows for various kinds of literary meaning to play off one another. Such lightness is evident in Bishop's poem 'Manners', which is exemplary in its combination of 'bad' rhyme, faux naïveté and its mapping of this lightness of tone on to a historically specific moment in childhood, which links it to the later poem 'In the Waiting Room'. The poem is voiced by a child who knows her manners and who also knows the cultural work that she must perform to uphold them. The poem's simple rhyme echoes such mannered behaviour and draws out the absurdity of such social practices which, like the hard-to-voice three-beat line, feel incongruous to the child's own sense of propriety. The faux naïveté that is voiced by the knowing child has the effect of placing the reality of that social discourse in quotations, just as the child does to her grandfather's speech, with the effect of upholding the form of that discourse whilst suggesting that the reality of it, like the crows that cross the child's path, might be read aslant.

Mapping the literary against the personal and the cultural, Lionel Trilling argues that it is almost impossible to define *manners*. It is, he writes, 'the whole evanescent context of its explicit statements. It is that part of a culture which is made up of half-uttered or unutterable expressions of value' (11–12). In the poem, Bishop plays on the asynchronous and anachronistic nature of this cultural performance to suggest how its values might be adjusted and how childhood might consequently be otherwise experienced. To talk of manners is to talk of tone, which Sianne Ngai defines as 'a speaker's "attitude to [her] listener"' (*Ugly Feelings* 41). Tone has an affective dimension; it is the manner in which certain things are spoken, and this manner demonstrates how the speaker's intent is inseparable from the listener's reading of it. We cannot listen to the child speaker of the poem without being aware of the tone, gesture and rhythm that she is taught to emulate and by which she enters into a cultural field. By combining and varying poetic forms of meaning, Bishop draws out the affective dimensions of the child's tone so that what we hear is the disjuncture between the sing-song rhythm of the child's mannered speech and the sincerity of her own voice which breaks through towards the centre of the poem. In the faux naïveté of the speaker's tone, we catch a glimpse of how a single system of manners conceals a complex variety of other manners that lie behind it and which are discernible in the small details and actions that Bishop's poems draw out, like the anxious sound of the crow's voice with which the child identifies.

To be childlike, as Robin Bernstein notes, 'was not to forget one's name or one's manners' (6). Both attributes of the child, which are linked to past practices, become straitjackets in Bishop's work that the child must wrestle against by cultivating a faux naïveté in the text which allows her to surreptitiously usher in another kind of meaning within an ostensibly mannered poetics. This is seen most clearly in 'In the Waiting Room', the last poem Bishop wrote that directly relates to her childhood experience, in which the fear of a forward development is linked to the imposition of a name upon the childhood self and, with it, the suffocating feeling of objecthood it induces. To be in waiting and to spatialise that temporal delay is to be in a state of uncertainty which, as Kathryn Bond Stockton notes, is 'tremendously tricky as a conception' for it demands that we chart unfamiliar territory; it places the child in a position where she lies outside, and is therefore unprotected from, what she approaches (4). The child in Bishop's poem is tasked with keeping the adult's, her aunt's, appointment, which is to say, with keeping time, waiting until the appropriate moment to make herself present. She is there in good manners, but in that uncertain space a temporal shift occurs that leads to a moment of recognition that Bishop conceives of as a falling into gender, a fall that is disorientating because it depends on an identification with other bodies, on a similarity that compromises her particularity. The child's sense of integrity implodes as she is forced to contemplate the gaze of the other and herself at a remove, which, like the foreign bodies she studies intently on the page, suddenly becomes unfamiliar to her.

In Bishop's poem, the trickiness of this suspended state is prompted at the place at which race, gender and sexuality meet on the pages of a 1918 copy of the *National Geographic*, which the child peruses whilst she waits.[2] In the poem, a knowledge of racialised bodies exposes the construction of childhood innocence, which is revealed not as essential but as historically located and deeply imbricated with the construction of whiteness. For it is at the touchpoint between 'black' and 'naked' that Bishop's own historically contingent sense of self is revealed to her. As this innocence slips from the already knowing child, the waiting room, as a spatialisation of her interior, implodes, shifts and becomes cavernous as the child maps this knowledge on to it. To survive this vertiginous fall into knowledge and the strangeness of the bodies around her, she clings to the surface of things, to a mannered way of being, reading the magazine 'straight through', being 'too shy to stop'. By glueing her eyes intently to the magazine's cover, the child cultivates a surface knowledge, a contingent facticity that enables her to keep at bay the intense solipsism that threatens and which makes her aware that she is both a (white) subject and a (female) object among other objects, 'an *Elizabeth*' and 'one of *them*'. In sticking to the surface of things, the child is able to forestall hearing the prescriptive pain that is uttered in the next room. Here surface knowledge is what attunes us to the child's 'sidelong glance', to a way of seeing that at once destabilises historical periodisation and remains firmly within its parameters (*Poems* 159).[3]

In 'Manners', the child's poetic journey draws her into the future, and she is left struggling to voice such cultural performance over the automobiles that overtake her as the poem moves towards a contingent modernity. In this struggle between the child's own bodily response and the past cultural principles that she is charged with upholding, Bishop suggests that such mannerisms are neither historically stable nor internally coherent and that any poetic tone must adjust accordingly to new conceptions of reality. In upholding these mannerisms, Bishop is able to reveal the advantages of marrying a conventional form with a faux-naïf tone for it allows her to establish a new affective bearing and orientation within an ostensibly traditional conception of reality. Being attuned to manners moreover demands that the reader listen more intently to the tone of the work, to how something is said rather than what is said, and in so doing, it shifts the way we read, moving us from an epistemological to an affective engagement with the text, making us look again at the poem's surface for what its details might reveal about the story that is being told. Bishop likens the surface of poetry to the surface of water, and it is at this refractive surface that we acquire the kind of attentiveness that allows us to distinguish between different linguistic registers.[4] Faux naïveté, like Trilling's notion of the indefinable subject of manners and like Paul de Man's concept of irony, troubles definitional language and traditional reading practices. It blurs generic distinctions and it makes it hard to say anything definite about what is being said, or indeed about its speaker (de Man 165). It shifts the focus of interest in the poem from the speaker or the work in itself to our ability to affectively decode what we are presented with; to see how aesthetic tone coincides with collective mood.

In 'Over 2,000 Illustrations and a Complete Concordance', a poem that is less ostensibly playful and light than those we have looked at thus far, we are nevertheless invited to move out of the 'serious, engravable' image towards a 'watery prismatic' surface which refracts our knowledge of it. Against the abstract image of the poem's opening, which is notable for its absence of detail, and the fragments of text and image that follow, Bishop presents us with 'a page alone or a page made up' – the lack of distinction is crucial because it suggests a more fluid understanding of the boundaries between reality and imagination, primary and secondary texts, transforming an either/or position into that which is 'only connected by "and" and "and"' (*Poems* 58). In

bringing our attention to the particular, to the detail, and hence to the feminine ele-
ment in the text, the lines of the poem begin to jostle and move apart, creating space
within the poem for other possibilities to emerge on its imaginative horizon. The 'page
alone', childish in its form, is 'arranged in cattycorned rectangles / or circles', and it
is this childish form that enables the speaker of the poem to resolve the 'initial letter'
– the process of naming – into a 'watery prismatic white-and-blue' image in which
knowledge becomes less readily graspable, creating a break within the circuit of recog-
nition where other forms of naming and other means of identification begin to emerge.
This refractive image takes the weight off the heavy reading of the poem's opening and
allows us to focus on how we move through the particulars of the scene. We move
'painfully', as Bishop points out, but this pain is not to be avoided for it brings us to
that which 'ignites', to the burning bush that doesn't burn itself up, but which allows
for new kinds of knowledge to emerge within the text (*Poems* 57–8).

This image of attentive involvement scatters the text's knowledge, transforming the
epistemological certainties with which the poem opens into a 'spreading fingerprint',
to a knowledge that is tactile, contingent and subject to change. Moving out of that
which is 'vast and obvious' to that which is uncharted within the diagrammatic text, a
slantwise perspective comes into view:

> Collegians marched in lines,
> crisscrossing the great square with black, like ants.

In the simplicity of its childlike analogy, the image calls to mind Bishop's early ekphras-
tic poem 'Large Bad Picture', with its 'scribbled [. . .] fine black birds' that hang in '*n*'s'
(*Poems* 13). But here, Bishop combines a childish or 'primitive' aesthetic with a sophis-
ticated viewpoint so that we are moved into a position where we must contemplate
these two different registers simultaneously. This slantwise perspective is enabled in
the second stanza, leading to a transition from historical to affective knowledge, by the
sidelong glances of the Arab guide who, unlike the historian's abstract forms of knowl-
edge, directs us with *lightness*. The guide's subversive glance draws our attention to the
blind spots in the text, revealing how the dead text might again be illuminated when
we 'make eyes' within it. It is from this slantwise position that we are able to finally
see the historical scene again, renewed, with 'infant sight'.

This subversive sidelong glance, like Penelope Gwin's, who, we are told, 'mostly
look[s] the other way', brings an ambivalence within the text and, more specifically,
within the realm of the sacred. It is often assumed that Bishop is merely drawing atten-
tion here to how the space of the sacred has been left void and how, by extension,
poetry might fill that gap.[5] But, I think, she is doing more than that: she shows us how
the sacred might be brought into alignment with the imaginary and, more specifically,
with the feminine. This new identification with the sacred allows for a new intimacy
in the text and, more specifically, with the object of the poem, the ambiguous book
in question, so that we are able to feel its weight in our hands, a weight that seems
to counteract the weight of the past and its historical sources. In the at once overly
familiar and yet strangely impenetrable final scene of the nativity, which, Bishop sug-
gests, cannot be decoded in empirical terms, we are invited to look again – to look
simply – at the wonder of that which is kept from the history books: that 'dark ajar'
and the 'unbreathing flame' which, we are told, is 'colorless', which is to say the object

contemplated without our prior perception of it. If, as Wittgenstein writes, 'Roughly speaking: objects are colourless' (31), then it is this absence of colour that allows us to return to a more ambiguous poetic language, one that brings us to the blank slate of possibility that comes into view in the poem's final line: 'and looked and looked our infant sight away'.

This final line, which meditates on a childlike way of seeing and, by extension, on the value of childishness in art, is a line that left its mark on Ashbery, who has returned to it year after year, still 'ravished and unsatisfied', a line that in its ecstatic attentiveness brings us back to the body, to an erotic way of looking which, as he writes, is 'both our torment and our salvation' (*Selected Prose* 122–3). Like Bishop's at once tantalisingly simple and impenetrable final line, Ashbery's comment refracts interpretation; it works both ways in the sense that in order to cut through the image, to penetrate that which is ultimately impenetrable, we will necessarily experience pain, but this pain is necessary because it is the precondition of the possibility of pleasure that is imagined in the affective relation posited in the final line. It creates, as Barthes argues, the most radical position in the text because it indicates a disturbance in adjustment, a disturbance that signals the presence of an alternative model of identification, one whose becoming is conceived in ecstatic time (25). Bishop's 'infant sight' permits a 'constant re-adjustment' within the text, allowing for new models of identification to arise that are predicated on an emotional kind of knowledge. The child's sight, its stories, might consequently be thought, as Bishop writes in the poem 'Objects & Apparitions', as 'the opposite of History', as that which puts 'the laws / of identity through hoops' (*Poems* 201).

Bishop shows how the childish touches upon the meaning of the feminine and it is at the meeting point between these two signs that one's accumulations lend themselves to the other. Both signs are invested in the surface, in a resistance to knowing too much and an understanding of the value of performance in art. This association of femininity and childishness becomes particularly apparent in Bishop's short stories 'In the Village' and 'Gwendolyn', written in the early 1950s, which are narrated by an ambiguously gendered precocious child who must work against the prescriptive forms of femininity that are available to her. In her understanding of how gender is constructed she renders the child's position – its purported unknowingness – faux naïf and we consequently see how she must work to produce innocence in the text, creating a pretence of childhood that demonstrates at once the danger of knowing too much too soon and the impossibility of innocence as a position in the text.[6] In these stories, Bishop consolidates her thinking about the relationship between subordinate positions and 'minor' aesthetic judgements, demonstrating how an alignment with the child's point of view might give us access to what José Esteban Muñoz refers to as the 'anticipatory illumination of art' (3). But Bishop also knows that to adhere to an aesthetics of childishness is also to risk fetishising powerlessness or 'cuteness', and in her work from the late 1950s and early 1960s she contemplates how she might allow for a childish or feminine perspective in the poem without turning it into 'solid cuteness', as she writes in a 1960 letter (*Words in Air* 319).

Whilst Bishop frets over her lightness, comparing it to the lofty *seriousness* of her contemporaries, she recognises that this faux naïveté is indispensable in her art for it ensures that she doesn't 'miss any detail' (*Words in Air* 18). 'Solid cuteness' is, therefore, not simply a failing on Bishop's part to inhabit a more respectable form that is, as she writes of Lowell's work, 'significant, illustrative, American', but a way of at once continuing and destabilising that tradition (*Words in Air* 247). 'Cuteness', as Ngai writes, 'generates ever more cuteness' by drawing out 'small-sized adjectives and diminutive ejaculations' from 'those who would perceive it in others': it draws us back to the small-scale and to intimate connection; but it also risks tipping over into the sentimental (*Our Aesthetic Categories* 60). In the poem 'Questions of Travel' (1965), Bishop considers, in discursive poetic form, the fine line between sentimentality and a childish aesthetic that validates what we see – what we *imagine* we know – rather than that which is certified. In the poem's half-answered, recurrent questions ('surely it would have been a pity'), Bishop suggests that this sentimental position is at least as valid as empirical modes of reading for it directs us to that which in being 'inexplicable and impenetrable' returns us to the details of the scene, to a place where we 'pondered, / blurr'dly and inconclusively' (*Poems* 91–2).

Bishop was conscious that in performing childishness in the text she was being in 'bad' taste, tainting poetry with that which is in excess, bringing the impure within the space of representation. If cuteness allows for inconclusive thinking in the text, 'cute' is also the condition that Bishop suggests her child protagonist Gwendolyn suffers from; it is that which leads her to an untimely death, because she becomes, rather than inhabits, her performance, so that 'the role [of girlhood] grew and grew until finally it had grown far beyond the slight but convincing talents she had for acting it' (*Prose* 55). Bishop's task is to allow for bad taste in poetry, which she sees as making the difference in art, without allowing it to overcome the 'lovely finish' of her poems (*Edgar Allan Poe* 11). The cuteness that she seeks is, therefore, not the commodity aesthetics that Gwendolyn incarnates in her all-American girlhood, but rather the 'genuine primitive' quality that she is always drawn towards in art (*One Art* 619). Bishop distinguishes this 'genuine primitive' art from the primitivism that has been incorporated within the history of modernism, for its virtue lies not in appropriation, but rather in demonstrating something, as she writes in 'Gregorio Valdes, 1879–1939':

> But surely anything that is impossible for others to achieve by effort, that is dangerous to imitate, and yet, like natural virtue, must be both admired and imitated, always remains mysterious. (*Prose* 31)

Bishop is not interested in a modernist-mediated primitivism, but in the kind of naïveté in art that she observes in her uncle's painting, and with the work of Valdes: an aesthetic simplicity that does not cling too closely to mimesis, but rather draws out the detail in the work, allowing for alterity within the pictorial plane, thus keeping alive the possibility of an alternative reality in which difference is not erased. The 'primitive painter', as Bishop writes, 'loves detail and lingers over it and emphasises it at the expense of the picture as a whole' (*Prose* 107). What this detail allows for, Bishop suggests, is an art form that does not erase the historical conditions in which the art is produced and which, as Bishop suggests of the work of Jimmy O'Shea, an aspirant writer with whom she corresponded in her role as a creative writing teacher, is an illumination within the art that makes his 'simple tales' appear like 'paper lanterns' (*Prose* 108). This primitive aesthetics not only justifies Bishop's lightness, it also enables the reader to overcome a contemplative distance so that we might look outward from within the contemplated object of the poem and experience an ecstatic attentiveness that allows us to create a world that is momentarily small and manageable and to get a handle on the kind of 'generalities' which Bishop so feared, as she writes in 1961, she – and, by extension, we – could not presently '*stop* making' (*Words in Air* 372).

The primitive artefact has historically been posed as more 'immediate' and more 'magical' than the ordinary art object, and it is this magic, or aura, which distinguishes a commodified cuteness from an illuminating childishness. What Bishop seeks in her work is a form that preserves a 'luminous spread' of knowledge without domesticating it or resolving it into a formula. Primitive modernism negotiates, as Anne Anlin Cheng writes, a complex relationship between subjecthood and objecthood: in both its assimilative form and its antidote, there is a 'predicament of embodiment' and a 'crisis of visuality' that can only be worked through by reinstating the feminised detail and by foregrounding the failure of sexual difference in modernist aesthetics (115). In 'The Prodigal', a poem that Bishop began the same few weeks as 'Over 2,000 Illustrations and a Complete Concordance', she suggests both where this primal longing for connection comes from and the difficulty of achieving this luminous 'infant sight'. 'The Prodigal' is unusual amongst Bishop's body of work in that it dispenses with a 'lovely finish' and it invites us to plough through the uncertain terrain that the prodigal poet must journey through whilst it awaits a new poetic language to coincide with its illuminated horizon.

'The Prodigal' reads as an abject other to the illumination of 'Over 2,000 Illustrations and a Complete Concordance' and the lightness that carries Bishop through her early work. It is a poem that accounts for the weight of the past, for the difficulty of moving to a position where we can gain an aerial perspective on the scene of representation, as it moves through 'the dark ajar' that the precocious poet knows she must endure if she is to arrive at a place that is not steeped in tradition or generalities, and which shows us the kind of awful cheerfulness, or the childish horror, that permits such alterity to emerge within the text. Though well received by *The New Yorker* when she sent them a finished draft of the poem in January 1951, 'The Prodigal' does, as Bishop notes, seem a little 'too grim' for their clean pages and amongst Bishop's own polished artefacts in its admittance of filth and shame into the space of the lyric. In situating the lyric at this boundary space that gives rise to abjection, Bishop suggests that it is at the point of 'uncontrollable relationality' that the question of identity arises, and that it is in the affective resonance of this question that we might get a glimpse of how the sacred operates in the modern world (Sedgwick 37).

'The Prodigal', which is voiced by a male speaker, reveals the limits of the feminine poet's constant performance, reminding us, as Judith Butler writes, that 'the body is the blindspot of speech, that which acts in excess of what is said, but which also acts in and through what is said' (11). The prodigal's ability to manage its bodily form depends on keeping an ecstatic object of contemplation in sight, on the 'pacing aureole' of a lantern that guides its path through the dark (*Poems* 69). This object of contemplation ensures that the relationship between inside and outside remains blurred, inconclusive, and thus permits new forms of relation to emerge in that intimate, affective sphere of knowing. In 'The Dolors of Colombine', a poem written the same year as 'The Prodigal' and 'Over 2,000 Illustrations and a Complete Concordance', Ashbery too considers the pain of feminine performance, which he, as another prodigal poet, must also embrace, acknowledging that it is precisely in identifying with the feminine that he is able to slip in and out of identities, to slide beneath surfaces and keep them moving, and yet it is this feminine performance that makes him an 'anachronic subject', at one remove from himself, a poet who is 'split twice over, doubly perverse' (Barthes 14). This double perversity allows the poet to become infinitely evasive, and has the advantage of creating space within the tradition, but it also means that the prodigal never entirely escapes their performance.

The proof, Bishop claims in her essay on Auden, that this pretence works is in 'the mounting, uncalculated waves of influence' that the poet goes on to experience (*Edgar Allan Poe* 185). Ashbery, like Bishop, and like Auden, whose influence has definitively mounted and been finely calculated, belongs to a lineage of prodigal poets who grow in and out of the tradition, subtly adjusting its terms from within. They demonstrate that that which is traditionally acknowledged as mutually exclusive in modernist aesthetics – the feminine and the abstract, the childish and the serious – might be realigned, and in their realignment used to critique the forms of masculinity enshrined in modern culture, demonstrating the ever more zany contemporary template of artistic production *as* feminine performance. These prodigal poets know the value of the child's sight and the potential of childishness to disrupt the relationship between aesthetic categories; they keep our eyes fixed on the constantly shifting horizon where the real and the imagined are recalibrated and where change comes about. They know that they must perform an identity before they are able to fully inhabit that role, and they know the risk they run in getting caught up in that performance. But they also know that this new ground that is made possible by performance is what poetry depends on; that, as Bishop famously remarked, 'if, after I read a poem the world looks like that poem for 24 hours or so I'm sure it's a good one' (*Words in Air* 403). For Ashbery, Bishop's 'Over 2,000 Illustrations and a Complete Concordance' was that poem.

Bishop's prodigal poem has continued to make and remake the world as Ashbery sees it, and in the poems that he bestows on us year after year he shows us the potential of that illumination to 'create a hunger for itself', to make addicts of us all, as it overwrites that which we previously took to be given, renewing our capacity to perceive, and to be surprised by what we see, which, as Bishop knows, is the condition of art. Ashbery has returned to Bishop's work repeatedly over his long career, creating a dialogue that positions her work as a template against which the contemporary poet might position her or his own, and in the process displaces the primacy of modernist writers that Bishop felt the need to work so hard to position herself against. In so doing, he validates the aesthetic merit of this feminine performance within the poetic tradition.[7] As Chris Kraus writes, the performative text *is* feminine; it is a 'text that is both live and lived' (23), which is one reason why Bishop's pretence might have proved so successful and why her influence seems to be felt more fully than any of her more 'serious' or 'illustrative' contemporaries. If Bishop's work is playful around structures of knowledge, it is so to demonstrate how women and children are always at the mercy of simplifications and how their subordinated positions might, after all, make them the most reliable witnesses in and readers of the text, the speaker par excellence, who is always, even in her performance, emotionally sincere, and this sincerity is that which creates a field of affect around the poem that ensures that we are never entirely finished with being shown new things about it, with lingering on its constantly shifting surfaces.

Queer lineages sit uncomfortably with the idea of 'continuity', and, as Ashbery and Bishop know so well, that which continues what has gone before must be subject to change if it is to ensure that our identities remain unfixed and the complex relationship between art and gender continues to create space for new forms of intimacy and new kinds of knowing. This model of continuity-as-change is evident in Ashbery's late poem 'The Burden of the Park' (into which we are surely invited to read 'The Burden of the Past'), a poem in which he deliberates on Bishop's much-quoted line from the end of 'The Bight', 'awful but cheerful', historicising it in the context of pre- and post-Stonewall cruising:

> Once, on Mannahatta's bleak shore,
> I trolled for spunkfish, but caught naught, nothing save
> a rubber plunger or two. It was awful
> at that time. Now everything is cheerful.
> I wonder, does it make a difference? (*Wakefulness* 20)

In a poem that argues for the need to continue to create difference out of the same, out of that which has gone before, Ashbery suggests that this light-hearted defiance of convention is what we still need to keep in sight, even after we have long passed 'Land's End' and arrived at this 'falling-off place', where the need for performance seems to be over. What we need to ensure, he suggests, is that pleasure is still doing its work in the text, and that in its *jouissance* and its transgression, in its double perversions and constant readjustments, it continues to preserve the dangerous, mysterious and inimitable knowledge that is our 'infant sight'.

Notes

1. For the relationship between Bishop's precocity and slowness see Thomas Travisano, 'Emerging Genius: Elizabeth Bishop and *The Blue Pencil*, 1927–1930'.
2. Much has been made of the inaccuracy of the date of the *National Geographic* issue cited in the poem. For more, see Lee Edelman, 'The Geography of Gender: Elizabeth Bishop's "In the Waiting Room"', *Contemporary Literature* 26.2 (Summer 1985): 179–96, and Corinne E. Blackmer, 'Ethnoporn, Lesbian Childhood, and Native Maternal Culture: Reading *National Geographic* with Elizabeth Bishop', *GLQ: A Journal of Lesbian and Gay Studies* 4.1 (1998): 17–58.
3. Lota de Macedo Soares's comment on 'In the Waiting Room' might be useful here in thinking through its periodisation and facticity: 'Like a sail in the wind but attached by some facts, one National Geographic, Worcester Mass, like nails to the mast' (cited in Marshall, *Elizabeth Bishop: A Miracle for Breakfast*, p. 210).
4. For a more detailed reading of Bishop's 'glassy water' surfaces, see Samuels, *Deep Skin: Elizabeth Bishop and Visual Art*, pp. 37–9.
5. Bonnie Costello notes that Bishop leaves it open as to whether these sacred places are to be considered 'historical or theological' in *Elizabeth Bishop: Questions of Mastery* (Cambridge, MA: Harvard University Press, 1993), p. 133.
6. For more on the precocious child's position in the text see Daniela Caselli, '"Tendency to Precocity" and "Childish Uncertainties" of a "Virago at Fourteen": Djuna Barnes's "The Diary of a Dangerous Child"', *The Yearbook of English Studies* 32 (2002): 186–204.
7. See also Mark Ford, 'Mont d'Espoir or Mount Despair: Early Bishop, Early Ashbery, and the French', *PN Review* 114 (March–April 1997): 22–8.

Works Cited

Ashbery, John, *Collected Poems 1956–1987*, ed. Mark Ford (Manchester: Carcanet, 2010).

Ashbery, John, *Selected Prose* (Manchester: Carcanet, 2004).

Ashbery, John, *Wakefulness* (New York: Farrar, Straus and Giroux, 1998).

Barthes, Roland, *The Pleasure of the Text*, trans. Richard Miller (New York: Hill and Wang, 1975).

Benjamin, Walter, *Illuminations*, ed. Hannah Arendt (London: Random House, 1999).

Bernstein, Robin, *Racial Innocence: Performing American Childhood from Slavery to Civil Rights* (New York: New York University Press, 2011).

Bishop, Elizabeth, *Edgar Allan Poe & the Juke-Box: Uncollected Poems, Drafts, and Fragments*, ed. Alice Quinn (New York: Farrar, Straus and Giroux, 2006).

Bishop, Elizabeth, *Elizabeth Bishop and The New Yorker: The Complete Correspondence*, ed. Joelle Biele (New York: Farrar, Straus and Giroux, 2011).

Bishop, Elizabeth, *One Art: Letters*, ed. Robert Giroux (New York: Farrar, Straus and Giroux, 1994).

Bishop, Elizabeth, *Poems, Prose, and Letters*, ed. Robert Giroux and Lloyd Schwartz (New York: Library of America, 2008).

Bishop, Elizabeth, and Robert Lowell, *Words in Air: The Complete Correspondence between Elizabeth Bishop and Robert Lowell*, ed. Thomas Travisano with Saskia Hamilton (New York: Farrar, Straus and Giroux, 2008).

Bond Stockton, Kathryn, *The Queer Child, or Growing Sideways in the Twentieth Century* (Durham, NC: Duke University Press, 2009).

Butler, Judith, *Excitable Speech: A Politics of Performance* (New York and London: Routledge, 1997).

Cheng, Anne Anlin, 'Skins, Tattoos, and Susceptibility', *Representations* 108.1 (Fall 2009): 98–119.

De Man, Paul, *Aesthetic Ideology*, ed. Andrzej Warminski (Minneapolis and London: University of Minnesota Press, 1996).

Foucault, Michel, *Essential Works of Foucault 1954–1984, Vol. 1: Ethics*, ed. Paul Rabinow (London: Penguin, 2000).

Jaggar, Alison M., 'Love and Knowledge: Emotion in Feminist Epistemology', *Inquiry: An Interdisciplinary Journal of Philosophy* 32.2 (1989): 151–76.

Jarvis, Simon, 'Why Rhyme Pleases', *Thinking Verse* 1 (2011): 17–43.

Kraus, Chris, 'Continuity', in Christine Wertheim (ed.), *Feminaissance* (Los Angeles: Les Figues Press, 2010).

Leavis, F. R., *New Bearings in English Poetry* (London: Faber and Faber, 2011).

Lewis, Wyndham, *The Art of Being Ruled* (London: Chatto & Windus, 1926).

Marshall, Megan, *Elizabeth Bishop: A Miracle for Breakfast* (New York: Houghton Mifflin Harcourt, 2017).

Millier, Brett C., *Elizabeth Bishop: Life and the Memory of It* (Berkeley: University of California Press, 1993).

Muñoz, José Esteban, *Cruising Utopia: The Then and There of Queer Futurity* (New York and London: New York University Press, 2009).

Ngai, Sianne, *Our Aesthetic Categories* (Cambridge, MA, and London: Harvard University Press, 2012).

Ngai, Sianne, *Ugly Feelings* (Cambridge, MA, and London: Harvard University Press, 2007).

Nietzsche, Friedrich, *The Gay Science*, trans. Walter Kaufmann (New York: Vintage, 1974).

Samuels, Peggy, *Deep Skin: Elizabeth Bishop and Visual Art* (Ithaca: Cornell University Press, 2010).

Sedgwick, Eve Kosofsky, *Touching Feeling: Affect, Pedagogy, Performativity* (Durham, NC: Duke University Press, 2003).

Travisano, Thomas, 'Emerging Genius: Elizabeth Bishop and *The Blue Pencil*, 1927–1930', *The Gettysburg Review* 5.1 (Winter 1992): 32–47.

Trilling, Lionel, 'Manners, Morals and the Novel', *The Kenyon Review* 10.1 (Winter 1948): 11–27.

Wittgenstein, Ludwig, *Tractatus Logico-Philosophicus* (New York: Cosimo, 2007).

Wylie, Elinor, *The Venetian Glass Nephew* (Chicago: Academy Chicago Publishers, 1984).

11

ELIZABETH BISHOP AND 'A BAD CASE OF THE *THREES*'

Katrina Mayson

I'VE LONG FOUND ELIZABETH Bishop's line 'Poe said poetry was *exact*' (*Poems* 285) intriguing, particularly the additional emphasis that Bishop gives the word '*exact*', which leaves me with the impression that she was trying to settle an ongoing debate or discussion. The line is taken from Bishop's unpublished poem 'Edgar Allan Poe & the Juke-Box', a poem that explores the mechanisation of pleasure against a background beat of music and poetry. What is it about Bishop's assertion of Poe's formulation of poetry that is so intriguing? Or does that sense of intrigue distract the reader from a larger question, that of whether Bishop is directly quoting Poe's formulation or trying to codify poetic principles of her own? In the notes to the poem (*Edgar Allan Poe* 271–5), Alice Quinn quotes extensively from Bishop's notebooks. These excerpts are conversational in tone, adding weight to the idea that the line is not a direct quotation from Poe, more a summation of Bishop's engagement with his critical writings. Angus Cleghorn, writing in *Elizabeth Bishop in the Twenty-First Century*, quotes the same line and comments that the poem 'is a corrective to Poe's poetics' (79–80), going on to weave this idea through a discussion of Bishop's evolving mechanics of metre, marked by her aptitude for precision.

To be exact or to exercise precision is a notable feature of Bishop's poetry, much commented on by readers and critics alike. Her meticulousness is not limited to the quality of observation she is famed for; Bishop was also a poet who wrote tight, sinuous poetry with a finely attuned ear and eye to poetic form.[1] This is not to suggest that Bishop's poetry is formulaic; on the contrary, her poetry is often considered ambiguous, a characteristic that facilitates a multiplicity of readings and allows individual readers to formulate and find their own response within her poetry. Nor does Bishop make it easy for critics who would like to find the theory behind her poetry; she left many tantalising hints in her letters, notebooks and unfinished essays, but no single work summarises her philosophy of composition. There are tensions inherent in the statements she did leave us with, such as her often quoted remark that the qualities she most admires in poetry are '*Accuracy, Spontaneity, Mystery*' (*Prose* 328). 'Accuracy' dovetails neatly with 'exact', but the qualities of spontaneity and mystery complicate the equation. How is the poet meant to combine the three qualities to create the necessary tension for poetry to soar beyond the prosaic?

I want to explore here how Bishop interweaves the ability to be exact with the impression, real or intuited, of also being ambiguous. Music – as suggested by the juke-box – is an important component of this, but what I was originally struck by was how often the number three appears in Bishop's poetry. I then started to think about the rhythm and movement that three facilitates in her poetry. Numbers are important to Bishop; the number three appears in her poetry in a myriad of guises. Poems such as 'Roosters', 'Objects & Apparitions' and 'Pink Dog' explore and exploit the rhythm and musicality of the triplet form. Then there are the three objects Manuelzinho leaves arranged at the speaker's feet, suggesting the influence of concepts such as the Holy Trinity. Bishop often uses the rhetorical trope of three in statements such as 'My three "favorite" poets – not the best poets, whom we all admire, but favorite in the sense of one's "best friend," etc. are Herbert, Hopkins, and Baudelaire' (*Prose* 328). Her poem 'One Art' details the loss of three houses,

> I lost my mother's watch. And look! my last, or
> next-to-last, of three loved houses went. (*Poems* 198)

Notice the detail in the specific placement of the houses; it is not the penultimate house but the next-to-last house. So Bishop scores (musically and manually) the sense of three with 'next-to-last' and then confirms it with 'three' houses. In Bishop's work numbers are usually accompanied by a sense of scale, and it is the manipulation of scale that hints at how she complicates the attribute of being exact so that she can also seem to be spontaneous. It is easier to track this in some of her earlier poems, such as 'The Monument', where we are told that

> The monument is one-third set against
> a sea; two-thirds against a sky. (*Poems* 25)

There is another three here; the monument is set in thirds. This is the scale of a poet used to working with a visual eye, transcribed into the written word. The sense of scale works in conjunction with the speaking voices of the poem who view the monument in the present, consider its past and speculate about what it may mean for the future. The poem ends with the present imperative to 'Watch it closely' (27). In this aspect, 'The Monument' almost reads like a draft of 'In the Waiting Room', where Bishop expertly employs scale and perspective alongside past, present and future to subvert the linear nature of time in lines such as

> I – we – were falling, falling,
> our eyes glued to the cover
> of the *National Geographic*,
> February, 1918.
>
> I said to myself: three days
> and you'll be seven years old. (180)

Here is another three: the three that stands between Bishop and her seventh birthday. Just as with the thirds in 'The Monument', these are small particulars of poetic composition, and I am wary of the pitfalls of excessive emphasis on small details against the background of Bishop's wider body of work. Are these instances merely coincidental? Both 'The Monument' and 'In the Waiting Room' are important poems. In both cases, Bishop uses numbers against scale to manipulate perspective; this points towards one of the most important attributes of the threes that Bishop employs in her writing. Scholars and readers frequently identify with the quality of reticence in Bishop's poetry, often referring to it as the 'other' or 'third' space where the reader can find or suggest meaning between what is written and what is read. Yet surely this same tripartite structure can be used to create a safe space in which dangerous emotions or thoughts can be safely spoken, something akin to what Gillian White in *Lyric Shame* terms Bishop's 'quiet talking [. . .] unsurprising revolt' (96). This creation of a safe space is exactly what the rhythm of the threes establishes in 'In the Waiting Room'. In line 46, the speaking '*me*' is split into 'I', 'we' and 'our' (*Poems* 180, lines 50, 51), a split held together by a precise moment in time, the instant of being when three days hold off the threshold of being seven years old. The split echoes again in the created first person of the 'you are an *I*' of '*I*', the child-self becoming both '*Elizabeth*' and '*them*' (lines 60–2).

I said earlier that numbers are important to Bishop and in this context I want to pause to look at 'Roosters' and explore what it reveals, particularly regarding Bishop's choice of rhyme scheme. The publication of the poem in 1941 was significant for Bishop, principally because it proved pivotal in affirming her poetic independence from Marianne Moore. The two poets disagreed fundamentally over the objectives of the poem. In a letter to Moore, Bishop took issue with a number of her criticisms and decisively defended her choice of end rhyme (*aaa* or *aba*) in 'Roosters', asserting that it enabled a 'very important "violence" of tone – which I feel to be helped by what *you* must feel to be just a bad case of the *Threes*' (*One Art* 96). Steely yet light-hearted, Bishop insists on the repetitive violence of her rhyme, her shorthand reference to the '*Threes*' alluding to the ability of rhythm and rhyme to deliberately complicate the metrical stress of the poem. It is interesting to note that in the same exchange over 'Roosters', Moore praises Bishop for what she calls her 'Pope-ian sagacity' (*Selected Letters of Moore* 403), enviably consummated in some of her rhyme scheme. One of the many axioms in Pope's 'Essay on Criticism' is his comment that 'True ease from writing comes from art, not chance', and Moore, masterful critic and appreciator, is immediately alert to Bishop's poetic art.

Bishop's formulation of the violence of tone in 'Roosters' signals the impact of the spoken word on her poetry. By this I don't just mean the impact of hearing a poem read aloud, rather than absorbed textually, although this is important. I mean also the mental wiring that forms during language acquisition and then underlies usage, reflecting not only on the poet's cultural context but also on their appreciation and assimilation of past masters. Note that in Bishop's case, her influences were not limited to the English language, but also include French, Spanish, Portuguese, Greek and Latin. In the background of the disagreement around 'Roosters' is Bishop's interest in French poets, namely Mallarmé, Rimbaud, Laforgue and Baudelaire. Whilst considering the impact of Mallarmé on Bishop, I came across J. H. Prynne's essay 'Mental Ears and Poetic Work', in which he discusses Mallarmé amongst others. This is not the place to consider further Prynne's fascinating ideas on a phonological analysis of poetic form, but his comment that 'the poet works with mental ears' (128) resonated strongly with my perception of Bishop's working practice. Think of her deep disquiet over Lowell's translation of Rimbaud, Baudelaire and Racine, where despite being worried that she sounds like 'the teacher of French 2A' (*Words in Air* 356) she writes a detailed letter questioning the tone and accuracy of Lowell's work. Prynne notes that it is not only poets but also readers who, using 'mental ears', will hear 'in older sounds the then new sounds of making and marking a track into forward space: a future in the past' (133).

Consider this in the context of Bishop's unfinished essay on Gerard Manley Hopkins, written while still a student at Vassar. It contains both careful scansion of his lines and appreciation of the form and function of sprung rhythm.[2] Bishop writes that whilst Hopkins's poetic devices may destroy the rhythmic framework of the poem, they 'do break down the margins of poetry, blur the edges with a kind of vibration and keep the atmosphere fresh and astir. The lines cannot sag for an instant; [. . .] A single short stanza can be as full of, aflame with, motion as one of Van Gogh's cedar trees' (*Prose* 474). I think this is one of Bishop's most extraordinary and vital reactions to poetry. That poetry should not 'sag' becomes a vital consideration for her, reflected in her image of poetry as language in flight, and echoing her earlier appreciation of mystery and spontaneity. On rereading these lines, I realised that to my ear, the real force of the prose is held by the combination of prepositions and punctuation, the cedar trees being 'full of, aflame with, motion'. Foregrounding this idea is the figure of Gertrude Stein and her visceral reaction to words, and her influence on Bishop. Bishop didn't wholly agree with Stein, but in 'Time's Andromedas', an early essay about Stein's manipulation of time, Bishop recognises the strength of Stein's auditory perception. Bishop writes that 'there is in her novel a complete lack of any sensation whatever except the sound of the words, and there is in her wordiness itself a feeling of conversation, of talking the thing' (*Poems, Prose, and Letters* 658). To my ear, 'talking the thing' resonates strongly with Bishop's own use of words in her appreciation of Hopkins, and in the emphasis they place on the continuous present. These are conjunctions that have physical, almost kinetic force, and Bishop later uses this force in her own poetry, specifically in 'Over 2,000 Illustrations and a Complete Concordance', where repetition of 'and' echoes through the last stanza to carry the poem towards a sense of conclusion, a conclusion that remains paradoxically unresolved. As Eleanor Cook notes in her essay 'Grammar and the King James Bible',[3] Bishop not only opens the last stanza with 'Everything only connected by "and" and "and"', she also closes the poem with three "ands":

> and, lulled within, a family with pets,
> – and looked and looked our infant sight away. (*Poems* 58)

This extraordinary last line has as many different readings as it has readers; my point here is only to note that the reader is primed to be alert to the force of preposition which connects and collides different parts of speech held within its framework, a poetic version of her perception of Stein 'talking the thing'.

There is so much to think about and appreciate in these lines that it is almost a hindrance to focus on one particular aspect. Nonetheless, it is important to stress that the force created is not a matter of chance, but also a deliberate and consummate use of poetic sensibility. Setting foot scansion momentarily aside, note how the rhythmic balance of lines such as 'Everything only connected by "and" and "and"' is achieved by the deliberate offsetting of two tri-syllabic words (everything, connected) against the monosyllabic (by, and, and, and). Note how 'only', visually a polysyllabic word, is rendered – at least to my ear – virtually monosyllabic by the rhythmic pattern of the line, where the weight of the line comes at the end. Punctuation reinforces this: the line is end stopped; the speech marks frame 'and'. I've deliberately not scanned the line because I want to remain attentive to the idea that pattern is not always exclusively metrical, and return to the sense that rhythm, rather than metre, is what can take all aspects of the poem's stream of sound into account. Writing about other poets, Bishop's comments can seem almost idiosyncratic, such as when she writes to Moore that despite her admiration for Wallace Stevens's *Owl Clover*, she dislikes 'the way he occasionally seems to make blank verse *moo*' (*One Art* 48). The flow of sound is crucial to Bishop's poetry, and here I am thinking not only of the influence of Mallarmé but also of Hopkins. Recall Hopkins writing to Bridges that one should not only read with the eyes but 'take breath and read it with the ears' (79). Reading Bishop out loud helps the reader notice – but not necessarily resolve – deliberate interruptions to rhythm, such as the moment in 'Arrival at Santos' where

> Her home, when she is at home, is in Glens Fall
>
> s, New York. There, we are settled. (*Poems* 87, 88)

Despite the gap between stanzas, the reader's eye might be tempted to skip over the slip of the 's', assimilating it as an oddity, as opposed to an intentional manipulation of syntax. Reading with ears is also useful to apply to the poem 'O Breath' (77), the fourth in the series titled 'Four Poems'. Here Bishop has deliberately inserted a mid-line space in each line. Assuming that this gap indicates an unwritten caesura or, more simply, an opportunity to 'take breath', and using the other points of punctuation to pause or breathe, the experience of reading the poem out loud becomes oddly constricted by the breath, especially where the line is enjambed, and thus not dissimilar to hearing an asthmatic – which Bishop was – reading.[4]

Bishop seeks to be as precise in her manipulation of sound as she does in her descriptions. She was a musician and played the piano and clavichord, as well as being knowledgeable about music theory and composition. One aspect of Bishop's relationship with music is that invoked by poems such as the early, uncollected 'Sonnet' (*Poems, Prose, and Letters* 186) where the poet longs for music to flow over her fingertips, not only inducing a sense of peace but also enabling a release of the written. Other poems such as 'Roosters' bear the imprint of a specific piece of music. In an interview with Ashley Brown in 1966, Bishop expanded on her difficulties in writing 'Roosters', saying 'I got hopelessly stuck; [. . .] Then one day I was playing a record of Ralph Kirkpatrick performing Scarlatti: the rhythms of the sonata imposed themselves on me and I got the thing started again' (25). Given the link with Kirkpatrick, Bishop was presumably referring to Domenico Scarlatti, and certainly listening to a clip of Scarlatti makes it easy to hear the similarity in rhythm. However, my intention is not to suggest a simplistic transference of emotion or rhythm from music to poetry, but instead to recognise that Bishop's knowledge of music theory and composition would have been part of the development of her own unique poetic form. I think it is significant that Bishop began to learn the clavichord in the 1930s, a period when she also travelled to Europe and was immersed in the study of French poets such as Baudelaire. In a letter to Frani Blough, Bishop quotes Ezra Pound as saying that '"The further poetry departs from music, the more decadent it gets," etc., and I want to learn whatever I can about the period when it hadn't yet departed – which is approximately up to the end of the clavichord days' (*One Art* 31). Like so many of Bishop's comments, this one holds out a number of enticing strands of thought for the critic to explore. In this context I limit myself to commenting that music gives us a mental map for reading accentual verse; that is, in music many different combinations of notes or silence can fill the same period of time. Music, like mathematics, exploits the characteristics of the notation of three; to give but one example, in music a triad is a chord of three notes, whilst in mathematics, the rule of three is a method for finding a fourth quantity given three known proportional quantities.

Numbers, and understanding their proportionality, is important to Bishop. In *The Redress of Poetry*, Seamus Heaney identified her supreme gift as being to 'ingest loss and transmute it'; to do this, 'she would count to a hundred by naming the things of the world, one after another' (165). Numbers help create a structure for Bishop to function within, both psychologically and poetically. Responding to the number three gives us a way into Bishop's fascination with the rhythm of sound and how she captured this in her poetry. In her eponymous short story Bishop recalls playing with the delicate, diabetic Gwendolyn Appletree, whose name she found fascinating. Gwendolyn, says Bishop, had a 'beautiful name. Its dactyl trisyllables could have gone on forever as far as I was concerned' (*Prose* 54). These 'dactyl trisyllables' – I've never been able to read those words without saying them out loud. It's a wonderful moment when Bishop stops the reader in their tracks, focusing attention on the form of a specific sound and pausing to allow it to be enjoyed. The passage continues, describing Gwendolyn's other attributes, but the name now counts as one of the marks on what Heaney described as Bishop's 'scale of memory', as well as being an object in itself, composed of dactyl trisyllables. It is also a counter-intuitive moment because, in general, a polysyllabic word will take less time to say than an equivalent number of monosyllabic words, but defining the components of Gwendolyn's name slows it down. At a meta-level, despite all her travelling, Bishop seems to me to be someone who resists speed, preferring instead to cultivate a stillness. The threes have a part to play in this. There is a sense that running – unlike flight – is not something she enjoys; people or animals who run in her poems do not seem to do well. Think of the scolding that the little black dog in 'Five Flights Up' (*Poems* 203) gets as he runs in the yard, or the flurried actions of the sandpiper, running across the sands 'looking for something, something, something' (129). Running brings no release; the three repetitions of 'something' slow the poem down to focus on the grains of sand and at the same time echo the immensity and impossibility of the sandpiper's search for meaning. In this poem, repetition in triplicate is part of what allows Bishop to manoeuvre between a slowing down and a magnification of the minute.

In situations where the intention is to indicate a third space or something or someone other,[5] the triple is often formulated as one, two and (an)other. This trope of 'otherness' often accompanies a critical discussion of Bishop's sexuality and her willingness – or reluctance – to reveal her lesbian preferences. I am less inclined to consider the 'other' through a gender lens here and instead would like to think about the space created for the reader in ideas of a third space or the other. What, for example, is the meaning of the third rail in 'The Man-Moth', who

> does not dare look out of the window,
> for the third rail, the unbroken draught of poison,
> runs there beside him. (17)

A literal reading would indicate the third rail electrifying the railway, or it can be read as a marker on a scale that indicates an inversion or change in perspective.[6] I borrow from Mark Ford the observation that the Man-Moth owes much to Laforgue, principally his fluidity, and his quietness (14). Typically for Bishop, the third rail is ambiguous, not simple or straightforward; it is also poisonous, running beside the unfortunate Man-Moth, unforgiving in its companionship. The rail also functions as an indicator of another space, a liminal world echoed in the felicitous misprint that inserted the hyphen between 'man' and 'moth'. Textually, 'The Man-Moth' is an early example of how Bishop used punctuation and typography to create the opportunity for the reader to experience the white space on the page as an integral part of reading her poetry, so that the concept of 'another' space inhabited by the reader is evoked not just by the literary but also by the visual and spatial interaction between the page, the poem's frame and the reader.

Questions of how Bishop used the format of the page and the paratext to her poems to frame her work are thrown into relief in any consideration of *Geography III*. Why *III*? The visual nature of the Roman numeral adds a further dimension for the reader to explore, and I hear the echo of another three, that of Marianne Moore saying to Bishop 'you are three-fourths painter always, in whatever you write' (*Selected Letters of Moore* 440). It is pertinent to ask where are, or what did Bishop consider to be, books one and two? Is she referring the reader back to the polarity she established in *Questions of Travel*, 'Brazil' and 'Elsewhere'? Is then the geography of *Geography III* that of Bishop or of the place in which the reader is situated? To my mind, as is the case so often with Bishop, there is no one 'right' reading. 'Santarém' contains a clear warning to critics and readers about literary interpretations, but despite this caveat, engaging with questions of interpretation reveals a play between the hidden and the exposed. This play forms a part of the structure placed round the 'other' space, the space in which it is the reader that searches to find meaning in between the hidden and the exposed. Before moving on to this other space, I would like first to consider Bishop's warning. She writes:

> Even if one were tempted
> to literary interpretations
> such as: life/death, right/wrong, male/female
> – such notions would have resolved, dissolved, straight off
> in that watery, dazzling dialectic. (*Poems* 207)

Note how Bishop's numbers underlie the construction of the thought; the list of interpretations is ordered as a series (a triple) of binary conditions. The internal rhyme in 'resolved, dissolved' – a perfect example of consonance – creates an onomatopoeic moment where the resolution is itself dissolved, left to disperse throughout the ongoing sound rhythms of the poem. However, literary interpretations aren't all bad; there is some attraction in the 'dazzling dialectic', and the earlier line 'I liked the place; I liked the idea of the place' frames the discussion. 'Santarém' is a poem where Bishop enjoys playing with her number scale, the most obvious examples being the numbers two (rivers, binary interpretations), four (rivers) and twelve (nuns). There is a rhythmic, accentuated three in the lines 'so that almost the only sounds / were creaks and *shush, shush, shush*'. Although these are only the most superficial use of numbers in a very carefully constructed poem, they do rouse Poe's exhortation to the critic to 'most by numbers judge a poet's song'. There is a lot of activity – for Bishop, and for the reader – around numbers in poetry. Recall that in music many different combinations of notes, including the pause, can take up the same amount of time. Similarly, although numbers form part of the structure of the poem, they are also elastic. In 'Santarém' one of the clearest examples of this is the effect of the internal rhyme of 'resolved/dissolved' on the imposition of binary opposites. Numbers don't so much offer a complete disclosure as enable the emergence of the other.

This elasticity of one, two and another is, in my reading, part of how Bishop employs what Octavio Paz first crystallised as Bishop's 'Power of Reticence'. Reticence has since become an important part of the Bishop lexicon, used to convey a holding back but also, paradoxically, an invitation in. Writing in 1977, Paz noted that 'we are drowning not in sea but in a swamp of words. We have forgotten that poetry is not in what words say but in what is said between them, that which appears fleetingly in pauses and silences' (213). This is a reaction echoed by many readers, most recently Colm Tóibín, who finds 'something in the space between the words [. . .] which made me sit up and realize that something important was being hidden and something equally important being said' (105). What Tóibín does not say, at least not directly, is that if Bishop is both hiding something and saying something in her poetry, then the reader is the implicit third figure who searches and finds meaning somewhere between the two polarities of the hidden and the said. A reading that finds a gap or space in Bishop's poetics is a familiar one; perhaps more surprising is the idea that alongside the hidden and the said there can also be an inclusion. Using three again as an example, note how the triplet in 'Sestina' (*Poems* 122) draws a tight frame around the form, suggesting a safe space for the words to speak such deep and potentially dangerous emotions. Something similar happens in 'Electrical Storm' (98), where dangerous electrical forces are contained by the domesticity of the final three lines; the empty sheets are warm enough to hold the cat, and the trees are promised regeneration by virtue of being Lent trees.

In the spirit of continuing to take the idea of the threes for a walk, it seems pertinent to explore further the idea of another space in poetry, generated by thinking about numbers. Consider 'Pink Dog' (212), a poem written towards the end of Bishop's working life. It is an example of a poem written in almost perfect triplet form; like 'Roosters' the rhyme promotes a violence of tone. I don't find it an easy poem to respond to, not because of the subject matter, which is a direct assault on the poverty underlying the dazzling beauty of Rio, symbolised by the celebration of Carnival, but because of its sound. I've always thought of it as a disobedient poem, both in the sense of political rebellion and also because, spoken out loud, it jars so strongly as to be almost deafening or obtuse. The poem has many instances of contained danger; the dog herself is disobedient, unabashedly crossing the road, her hairlessness more likely a damning comment on the conditions that have led to canine alopecia, rather than a deliberate breeding choice. In the eighth stanza, a bitter joke is made of the appalling conditions the homeless face; the beggars subvert the attempts of the authorities to clear them off the streets by wearing life jackets and resisting attempts to drown them. These are moments that stand in stark contrast to the blazing sun and the blue sky, to the tourism and wealth that is also such a part of Rio de Janeiro. The triplets strain to contain the menace inherent in the images. The rhyme scheme works against the structure of the triplets. To my ears, the disobedi-ence or threat is mimicked by the acoustic sense of the poem going against the grain, a result of the insistent stress on assonance in the rhyme scheme. This is a popular rhyme form in Portuguese but is less natural in English, and it is partly the cause of the strange moment in the tenth stanza, when the word 'an' is split by a hyphen (or dash, depending on the type) and runs over to the next line. I'm not certain that this split is justified in purely metrical terms, but what it does do is open up some unusual sonorous opportunities. In English, the 'a' is either soft or hard, depending on whether it is 'an' or 'a' or 'ā' then 'n'. The soft 'a' resonates with the Portuguese pronunciation of 'fantasía' and 'máscara'. Or you can read the rhyme in those lines as 'a- / a' (which almost looks like an A minus), but where does that leave the 'n'?

In thinking about how the triplet form encloses 'Pink Dog', and how Bishop manipulates her number scale, it seems to me that one potent aspect of what she is experimenting with is her ability to describe an object so that it moves away from what it is, and suggests something else. Perhaps this is what led Octavio Paz to praise her translation of 'Objects & Apparitions' so highly. The concept of inclusion is always complex in Bishop; 'Objects & Apparitions' is the clearest demonstration of how she prefers her boxes to leak, to offer the possibility of movement in or out. A shadow box has, by necessity, one face made of glass; it allows things to escape as much as it holds others in place. Conversely, the fact that the glass face is transparent enables movement from the other direction, by making it possible for the reader to step into the scene within. Recall the mathematical rule of three, which states that a fourth quantity can be calculated based on three known proportional quantities. With this in mind, note that glass is also reflective, and thus the image of the reader becomes the fourth side of the box. It is an object that carries the echo of childhood memories for Bishop: recall Mr Johnson the post-master in 'In the Village', who 'looks out through the little window in the middle of the bank of glass-fronted boxes, like an animal look-ing out over its manger' (*Prose* 77). The boxes hold Mr Johnson back, just as Bishop also holds back and, sometimes, holds the reader back. Note that the Bulmer family box was number 21 – another multiple of three – and empty. With shadow boxes and holding back in mind, consider briefly the quotation from the Portuguese poet Luís Vaz de Camões at the beginning of *Questions of Travel*. It is the last two lines of the final tercet of a sonnet, and reads:

> . . . *O dar-vos quanto tenho e quanto posso,*
> *Que quanto mais vos pago, mais vos devo.* (*Poems* 83)

My literal translation is as follows: 'The giving to you of what I have and what I can, / the more I give the more I owe.' It is a paradox reminiscent of John Donne with its three aspects of giving, being that as much as possible is given, but the more that is given (or repaid), the more that is owed. One way of reading this dedication is as one of Cornell's shadow boxes: an opaque dedicatory preface that hints at the flux and flow within. Perhaps Bishop decided to leave it in Portuguese because she did not want to flaunt her relationship with Lota Macedo Soares with the wider public. Alternatively, perhaps she felt it meant more to Lota to read it in her native language. Or, moving away from bio-graphical interpretation altogether, perhaps she felt that it was untranslatable. In many respects the 'why' of the decision does not matter. What weighs with the reader is the desire to understand that which is written, and here Bishop is deliberately holding her typical, English-speaking reader back.

If, as in 'Objects & Apparitions', a glass-sided shadow box can hold the viewer at arm's length from its contents, it can also provide a space where things change as they are examined, just as 'memory weaves, unweaves the echoes' (201). The ability to change is a crucial and prized notion in Bishop's poetry. In 'North Haven' (210), Bishop's poem in memoriam of Robert Lowell, one of the unspoken regrets is that whilst her memories can still change, his cannot. The first stanza is written in the present tense and reads like the spoken voice, an impression accentuated by italicisation. The second addresses the shift in perception of the present moment that memory brings to bear. Bishop states:

> The islands haven't shifted since last summer,
> even if I like to pretend they have
> – drifting, in a dreamy sort of way,
> a little north, a little south or sidewise

The past is not absolute; the islands – or memories – can drift three ways, north, south or sidewise; as our memories of the past change, so too does the perception of the present. Nor is the future strictly linear; the poem describes the natural beauty of the island, and then comes an evocation where

> Nature repeats herself, or almost does:
> *repeat, repeat, repeat; revise, revise, revise.*

The rhythm of repetition is emphasised by the symmetry and italicisation of each triad, and yet the reader is alerted to the minor changes each repetition brings. Bishop's decision to uses italics here prompts my curiosity; what is she trying to achieve? Normally, italicisation emphasises precision or quotation (recall the italicised '*exact*' of 'Edgar Allen Poe & the Juke-Box'), and yet in this case precision and repetition seem to be held in a paradoxical arrangement, fashioned by the idea of revision. Nominally, the words are two sets of three exact replicas, and yet the three repetitions suggest a change in state. Furthermore, to revise is not to repeat, at least not exactly. Think of the spoken voice and consider the physical effects of italicisation on reading aloud; the reader would naturally place a different level of stress on each word. Time means that no one moment in the present can be identical to one in the past; inherent in the idea of revision is the concept of alteration. One of the consequences of retelling a memory – as Bishop does in this poem – is to alter it. To remember well is also to be aware of the need to forget, a forgetting that comes about by the revision and retelling of events. The final stanza closes with Bishop's lament for Lowell:

> You can't derange, re-arrange,
> your poems again. (But the Sparrows can their song.)
> The words won't change again. Sad friend, you cannot change.

Here, it is the ability to change that marks the difference between the living and the dead. Bishop's lament holds an echo of her active manipulation of a number scale to create the tension in the lines. Numbers are not as obvious as the threes in the earlier lines, but notice for example how 'derange, re-arrange' is seemingly binary, until the dual meaning of 'derange' is considered. First, even if the reader had no biographical knowledge of Lowell, the poem points towards the moments of insanity he suffered. The internal rhyme encourages the emergence of another layer of meaning; in this case the 're-arrange' balances out the suggestion of insanity with the primary meaning of derange, that is 'To disturb or destroy the arrangement or order of; to throw into confusion; to disarrange' (*OED*). Bishop adds another layer of rhyme by using 'change' in the final line to interrupt any temptation to read derange/re-arrange as a self-enclosed moment. It is an interruption further accentuated by the parenthesis in the intervening line: '(But the Sparrows can their song.)' I am reminded of Pope's warning against employing dull rhymes; it seems to me that 'song' not only holds apart the adjacent rhyme of 're-arrange/change', but also adds another layer to Bishop's lament – that is, her admiration for Lowell's poetic ability, her sadness that his song is silenced.

In *Lyric Shame*, Gillian White not only provides another way of reading Bishop, but also opens up a way to see her as a poet who does engage, albeit quietly, with poetic politics. In the context of considering how Bishop uses numbers to create spaces for dangerous or disobedient emotions, I was struck by her comment that 'Bishop even shared with Language writers the belief that the most useful way to resist high-capitalist modes as they had shaped culture was to reveal and disrupt habits of language to produce interpretive space and to foster critical self-awareness' (96). White's suggestion of a disruption of habits of language is, I think, largely what lies behind the fallen 's' in 'Arrival at Santos', or the split of 'a-n' in 'Pink Dog'. Nonetheless, these moments are unusual in Bishop's poetry, and they are far from being enough to convincingly describe Bishop as avant-garde in the sense that the Language poets were. White's broader characterisation of Bishop as a poet who seeks to achieve the creation of a space for interpretation and criticism through 'rhetoric and discourse, not radical syntax' (96) is more accurate.

My intention has been to take the idea of the threes for a walk through Bishop's poetry. Numbers are one way of creating the impression of being exact, and yet they are also elastic. The best analogy is that of music, where different combinations of notes and pauses can take up the same length of time. Once we look behind Bishop's number line, some of the planks that lie behind her seemingly narrative poems are illuminated, elements like her interest in time, movement and memory. Examining how numbers work, the detail of rhyme and rhythm reinforces the strength of Bishop's poetry as being a poetry of cognition, not simply of biography. In many ways, three is the ideal number to start with, because it is an odd number and as such it is much harder to hold in oppositional balance. This helps the critic follow the reader into the elusive space between what is said and what is not said. When I began to think about the threes, the image I held in my head was of the three objects the gardener leaves in a triangle at the speaker's feet in 'Manuelzinho' (*Poems* 95). The leaving of objects at the feet, the triangle, the vanishing as if into fairy tale, seemed so rich in allusion, ranging from the Holy Trinity and the biblical to attitudes of servitude and colonialism, or the positioning of Brazil as the magical, tropical unknown against the more prosaic North America. Then, as I explored Bishop's use of three in more detail, I came to think of Cornell's shadow boxes, which with their three solid and one glass side seemed to be a better image for what three was pointing towards. Shadow boxes are unreliable boxes;

their glass face leaks interpretation to the eye of the beholder. Cornell's artwork is a space where the invisible becomes visible by the conjunction of seemingly disparate objects. Bishop achieves this alchemy by creating a tension between being exact and yet enabling spontaneity and mystery. The temptation is to try to create a formulation to explain this alchemy or defend a specific reading. In fact, one of the liberating aspects of tracking the threes as I have done here is that there was no specific agenda to either prove or disprove a theory, nor does it seem reasonable to impose one. Numbers are only one aspect of the alchemy in Bishop's poetry, only one part of the tension – to paraphrase Bishop – not of a thought, but of a mind thinking. In this respect we can be grateful if they are also the glass face through which we are allowed a glimpse of the contents of the box.

Notes

1. See, for example, Vidyan Ravinthiran's *Elizabeth Bishop's Prosaic* (2015) or Eleanor Cook's *Elizabeth Bishop at Work* (2016) for extended critical discussion of Bishop's prosody.
2. This same essay, 'Gerard Manley Hopkins: Notes on Timing in His Poetry', contains Bishop's often quoted remark (itself a quotation from M. W. Croll) that the writers of baroque prose intended 'to portray, not a thought, but a mind thinking' (*Prose* 473), a formulation that intrigued Bishop and continues to intrigue her readers.
3. Cook's broader argument is about Bishop's deep knowledge of the King James Bible, including biblical grammar and syntax.
4. For an extensive reading of this poem and the body see the chapter '"O Breath": Asthma and Equivocality' in Marilyn May Lombardi's *The Body and the Song: Elizabeth Bishop's Poetics*.
5. See Judith Merrin's essay 'Gaiety, Gayness and Change' for a discussion of what she terms Bishop's trope of 'thirdness'.
6. See Merrin in 'Gaiety, Gayness and Change'.

Works Cited

Bishop, Elizabeth, *Edgar Allan Poe & the Juke-Box: Uncollected Poems, Drafts, and Fragments*, ed. Alice Quinn (New York: Farrar, Straus and Giroux, 2006).

Bishop, Elizabeth, *One Art: The Selected Letters*, ed. Robert Giroux (London: Chatto & Windus, 1994).

Bishop, Elizabeth, *Poems, Prose, and Letters*, ed. Robert Giroux and Lloyd Schwartz (New York: Library of America, 2008).

Bishop, Elizabeth, and Robert Lowell, *Words in Air: The Complete Correspondence between Elizabeth Bishop and Robert Lowell*, ed. Thomas Travisano with Saskia Hamilton (London: Faber and Faber, 2008).

Brown, Ashley, 'An Interview with Elizabeth Bishop', in George Monteiro (ed.), *Conversations with Elizabeth Bishop* (Jackson: University Press of Mississippi, 1996), pp. 18–29.

Cleghorn, Angus, 'Bishop's "Wiring Fused": "Bone Key" and "Pleasure Seas"', in Angus Cleghorn, Bethany Hicok and Thomas Travisano (eds), *Elizabeth Bishop in the Twenty-First Century* (Charlottesville: University of Virginia Press, 2012), pp. 69–87.

Cook, Eleanor, *Elizabeth Bishop at Work* (Cambridge, MA: Harvard University Press, 2016).

Cook, Eleanor, 'Grammar and the King James Bible: The Case of Elizabeth Bishop', *Literary Imagination* 14.1 (2012): 55–60.

Ford, Mark, 'Early Bishop, Early Ashbery, and the French', in Lionel Kelly (ed.), *Poetry and the Sense of Panic* (Amsterdam: Ropodi, 2000), pp. 9–27.

Heaney, Seamus, *The Redress of Poetry: Oxford Lectures* (London: Faber and Faber, 1995).

Hopkins, Gerard Manley, *The Letters of Gerard Manley Hopkins to Robert Bridges*, ed. Claude Colleer Abbott (London: Oxford University Press, 1955 [1935]).

Lombardi, Marilyn May, *The Body and the Song: Elizabeth Bishop's Poetics* (Carbondale: Southern Illinois Press, 1995).

Merrin, Judith, 'Gaiety, Gayness and Change', in Marilyn May Lombardi (ed.), *Elizabeth Bishop: The Geography of Gender* (Charlottesville: University Press of Virginia, 1993), pp. 153–72.

Monteiro, George (ed.), *Conversations with Elizabeth Bishop* (Jackson: University Press of Mississippi, 1996).

Moore, Marianne, *The Selected Letters of Marianne Moore*, ed. Bonnie Costello, Celeste Goodridge and Cristanne Miller (London: Faber and Faber, 1998).

Paz, Octavio, 'Elizabeth Bishop, or the Power of Reticence', in Lloyd Schwartz and Sybil P. Estess (eds), *Elizabeth Bishop and Her Art* (Michigan: University of Michigan Press, 1983), pp. 211–14.

Pope, Alexander, 'An Essay on Criticism', Poetry Foundation, <https://www.poetryfoundation.org/articles/69379/an-essay-on-criticism> (last accessed 26 November 2018).

Prynne, J. H., 'Mental Ears and Poetic Work', in *Chicago Review* 55.1 (2010): 126–57.

Ravinthiran, Vidyan, *Elizabeth Bishop's Prosaic* (Lewisburg: Bucknell University Press, 2015).

Tóibín, Colm, *On Elizabeth Bishop* (Princeton: Princeton University Press, 2015).

White, Gillian, *Lyric Shame* (Cambridge, MA: Harvard University Press, 2014).

12

THE CASE OF THE FALLING *S*: ELIZABETH BISHOP, VISUAL POETRY AND THE INTERNATIONAL AVANT-GARDE

Susan Rosenbaum

I

THIS CHAPTER READS ELIZABETH Bishop's poem 'Arrival at Santos', with its odd breakage of the letter *s* from the word 'Falls', as an experiment in visual poetry shaped by the work of the international avant-garde. The fallen *s* occurs in a description of a ship passenger, Miss Breen:

> Her home, when she is at home, is in Glens Fall
>
> s, New York. There. We are settled. (*Poems* 87–8)

In these lines, Bishop hasn't enjambed a word or a phrase, but the final letter of the word 'Falls', resulting in an amputated *s*, which appears to have 'fallen' to the next line and stanza. Read on its own, the line – 's, New York. There. We are settled' – is non-sensical. To make the *s* mean semantically, it must be reattached to the preceding word and line. Indeed, the need to stop reading the poem in a linear fashion arises from the visual experience of seeing the *s* on its own as a detached letter followed by a comma: struck by the oddness of this amputated *s* in the context of a poem that is not overtly experimental, the reader must look backwards to the previous word and line to make it mean. The *s* is semantically attached to but visually detached from the word 'Falls', and thus works as both a verbal and a visual sign: it hovers between its linguistic function as a letter of the alphabet and, in its unusual spatial placement, a graphic notation whose function is primarily visual and iconic.

The breaking of a word between consonants was unusual for Bishop, but it was not at all unusual for her avant-garde precursors and peers. Scholars have explored Bishop's engagement with the visual arts as a painter of watercolours, as a lifelong student of modernist painting, sculpture and architecture, and as a writer who derived poetic strategies from the visual arts and wrote many ekphrastic poems. Bishop's debts to the Surrealist avant-garde and to visual experiments such as frottage have been widely acknowledged as important to her 1946 collection *North & South*, and Peggy Samuels, who approaches Bishop's 'conception of the surface of the page of poetry as akin to the surface of a painting' (3), has explored Bishop's engagement with the methods of Klee, Schwitters, Calder and Cornell at mid-century. However, scholars have paid less attention to the importance of the visual design and spatial layout of Bishop's poems in the context of avant-garde experiments with visual poetry. As Willard Bohn argues, visual poems 'are conceived not only as literary works but also as works of art', as much visual as textual compositions (*Modern Visual Poetry* 15). Elisabeth Frost defines visual poetics 'as writing that explores the materiality of word, page, or screen. Combining text with image and/or highlighting the materiality of the medium, visual poetics privileges acts of seeing in acts of reading' (340). The fallen letter *s* offers a glimpse of Bishop's subtle adaptation of avant-garde experiments in visual poetry as she began writing the poetry that would become *Questions of Travel*. More generally, in tracking the slippery *s*, I make the case for the importance of visual poetics to Bishop's poetry, and argue that Bishop is more experimental in this regard than has been recognised.

II

In the autumn of 1951 Bishop boarded a ship scheduled to travel around the continent of South America. She disembarked at the Port of Santos in Brazil in November 1951 and was in Rio de Janeiro, staying with her friends Lota de Macedo Soares and Mary Morse, by the end of the month. Bishop intended to stay only a couple of weeks while she recovered from an illness, but ended up living in Brazil for fifteen years; Lota would become Bishop's lover and partner until her death in 1967. Bishop began writing the poem 'Arrival at Santos' in December 1951, completed it in January 1952, and published it in *The New Yorker* on 21 June 1952. Although it appeared as one of the final poems in her second book, *A Cold Spring* (1955), Bishop republished it as the first poem in *Questions of Travel* (1965), and dated it January 1952, emphasising from a retrospective vantage that it marked a new phase of her life and work.[1]

The year 1952 was also an important one for the poetic avant-garde in Brazil. Augusto de Campos, Haroldo de Campos and Décio Pignatari formed the Noigandres group in São Paulo, and began publishing and theorising 'concrete poetry', in which the visual appearance (typography, size, design and spatial location) of words on the page is as important as their verbal meaning. Concrete poets abandoned conventions of grammar in favour of a 'spatial syntax', using space as a structuring device that allowed words to be combined vertically, horizontally, diagonally and so on: concrete poems invite both reading and looking. For instance, Eugen Gomringer's poem 'Wind' (1954) uses overlapping, intersecting linear arrangements of the letters *w*, *i*, *n*, *d*, to invite the eye to move in different directions, dramatising both the force of the wind and also the verb 'to wind' or bend. Rejecting mimesis, concrete poets approached the poem, in Willard Bohn's words, as 'an object in and of itself rather than an interpreter of external objects or subjective sensations' (*Reading Visual Poetry* 119).

I am not arguing for a relation of influence between 'Arrival at Santos' and concrete poetry, but rather suggest that in 1952 they were floating in the same modernist sea.[2] Bishop remarked in 1970, 'As for concrete poetry, I like only Cummings – a brilliant and good humored poet, one who really had something to say. Concrete poetry that other poets make, I find uninteresting. It has only an initial impact – a word game, at times amusing and witty, but useless and impossible to remember' (Colônia 52). Bishop's dismissal of concrete poems as 'witty' but ultimately superficial word games suggests that her own use of 'Fall // s' is more than a witty visual joke, which is how most critics regard it.[3] Bishop's treatment of Cummings as a brilliant 'concrete poet' with 'something to say' is telling; the Noigandres group also emphasised Cummings as an important precursor, and in this shared if distinct appreciation for Cummings we can track a common lineage.

Bishop knew Cummings from her time in Greenwich Village in the 1940s, and in the 1950s was immersed in his work.[4] In 1950 she voted for Cummings for the Pulitzer Prize, and her review of his *XAIPE* appeared in the *US Quarterly Book Review*. In this review she characterised Cummings' method of visual poetry as that of a 'smart-alec Greenwich Village child saying to his friends: "Look! I've just made up a new game. Let's all write poems. There! I've won!" And in front of the wood and coal man's basement shop, on the wall of the Chinese laundry, along the curbs of the dingy but flourishing park, appear poems and ideograph poems in hyacinth-colored chalks' (*Prose* 261). Although Bishop likens Cummings' visual experiments to a child's game, she also implies their radical effects: his poems become a vibrant part of the environment of shops, laundry and park, and incorporate these locales into their substance in a new way. The shop front, park curbs and laundry wall become the 'page' upon which the poems are chalked, and in using hyacinth – a colour that is also a flower – to describe Cummings' chalk, Bishop suggests that the poems are structured 'naturally' by the urban setting.

Although the term 'concrete poetry' had not been coined when Bishop wrote the 1950 review, her term 'ideograph poem' betrays her knowledge of the history of visual poetry informing Cummings' experiments.[5] Visual poetry has a long history, originating in the shaped poetry of Ancient Greece (and includes the shaped poems of George Herbert, one of Bishop's favourite poets), but by the 1890s, advances in photo-mechanical reproduction permitted new kinds of experiments with the printing, typography and visual layout of the text. These experiments went hand in hand with the avant-garde's interart collaborations, and with challenges to and expansion of understandings of poetry. Important works of visual poetry included Mallarmé's 'Un coup de des/Roll of the Dice' (1896), Apollinaire's *Calligrammes*, Marinetti's futurist poems guided by his concept of 'Words-in-Freedom',[6] Pound's and Fenollosa's ideograms, Mina Loy's feminist *Love Songs* and manifestos, and poetry inspired by Cubism (Blaise Cendrars, Max Jacob, Pierre Reverdy, W. C. Williams), Dada (Kurt Schwitters, Raoul Hausmann), Surrealism (poem-objects of Breton), and Lettrism (Isidore Isou).[7] While extremely various, the visual poems associated with the avant-garde use the innovative spatial layout of words and letters as a means of breaking with conventions of linearity, reference, syntax, punctuation, spelling and poetic voice, and explore the plastic possibilities of print through play with typography, font and graphic design.

Bishop's privileging of Cummings in this history illuminates her own method. As George Monteiro points out, Bishop's amputation of the *s* in Glens Falls 'echoes the use of such disjuncture by E. E. Cummings in several poems in *XAIPE*' (38). Letters are a key element of Dadaist, Futurist and Lettrist visual poems: Marinetti used letters to generate visual and sonic effects, while Schwitters stated that 'the basic material of poetry is not the word but the letter' (Webster 129), a sentiment that was echoed by Isidore Isou in his desire to resist the hegemony of the word. These artists emphasised the materiality of the letter – its visual shape, placement and sound – over its linguistic function. For instance, in Marinetti's 1915 'Après la Marne, Joffre visita le front en auto', the letter *s* pictorially constitutes roads and *m* suggests mountains, while the repetition of the letter *a* onomatopoetically indicates the sounds of an engine, in a 'verbalisation dynamique de la route' (Webster 36–9).

In contrast, while Cummings' visual poems are indebted to Dadaist and Futurist techniques, he does not entirely abandon linear syntax nor the lyric tradition, and his use of the letter relies on both its visual and its verbal dimensions. As Michael Webster argues, Cummings 'manipulates spatial, visual and syntactical elements of language as material, creating physical effects on the page. These effects *iconically* reinforce meaning and emotion' (120). Cummings uses letters as icons – as a sign (a word or graphic symbol) whose form suggests its meaning – in various ways: he often breaks up words into component letters that serve as individual icons, as in an *o* that signifies the moon, or he vertically spaces out the letters in a phrase such as 'leaf falls' to iconically mimic the leaf's fall (Webster 128, 138):

l(a

le
af
fa

ll

s)
one
l

iness (*Complete Poems* 673)

Cummings used letters, as well as punctuation, capitalisation, line breaks and the space of the page, as elements of visual design that require visual as well as verbal reading.

III

At first glance, 'Arrival at Santos' seems much less experimental than Cummings' poems and the visual poems of the avant-garde. Bishop employs a lyric speaker, unfolds an accessible narrative, adheres to conventions of punctuation and grammar, and follows a regular stanzaic pattern and rhyme scheme: the poem consists of ten stanzas of four lines that rhyme abcb, and that lack a regular metre. But the truncated *s* provides a clue that all is not as it seems. If we return to the word 'Fall // s', it's possible that Bishop follows Cummings in allowing the *s* to function as part of a word while also playing with its spatial location and shape to iconically dramatise a fall, the *s* perhaps signifying the water moving over the fall at Glens Falls, or indicating a slight fall as Miss Breen tries to find her footing on the tender ('Fall // s' is followed by 'There. We are settled', suggesting some final movement before a settling occurs).

More generally, Bishop follows Cummings in 'establishing analogies between the visual, spatial [and syntactic] structure of the text and the kinds of physical, emotional movement evoked in the poem' (Webster 121). As the speaker and her elderly fellow passenger Miss Breen descend from their ship into a tender that will take them to port,

Bishop uses enjambment – the suspense generated at the end of the poetic line as the spatial line ends but the grammatical phrase or sentence continues – to enact their perilous descent:

> And gingerly now we climb down the ladder backward,
> myself and a fellow passenger named Miss Breen,
>
> descending into the midst of twenty-six freighters (*Poems* 87)

The continuation of the sentence after the line break following 'backward' works to propel the reader's eye down the page, even as the next line, 'myself and a fellow passenger named Miss Breen', refers the reader 'backward', by qualifying the 'we' of the previous line. In this way the reader's eye moves downwards while referring backwards, just as the narrator and Miss Breen climb down the ladder backwards. The lines here can be regarded as rungs of a textual 'ladder' that the reader navigates, with the commas at the end of the lines marking the slight pause one takes before 'gingerly' finding the next rung down and then landing in the tender. Similarly, the line break coupled with a stanza break before the present participle 'descending' generates a visual space on the page analogous to the spatial gap that must be crossed into the tender, and also to the time that elapses during the descent. In these ways, Bishop uses the spatial placement of lines and carefully chosen line breaks to dramatise the movements in time and space that the poem describes.

Notably the visual structure and syntax of Bishop's poem provide analogies for movements that are unstable, including bumps, falls and slips: the poem begins in a boat suspended in water and records a tender approaching, the passengers' descent into the tender, the movement of the tender towards the port, and the slippage of soap and stamps. Barbara Page points out that the traveller in 'Questions of Travel' 'must suffer the uneasy sensation of motion sickness and its disorientations' (129). The port, which functions to facilitate the movement of cargo elsewhere, embodies this sensation of 'motion sickness': through its bumps and falls the poem destabilises the tourist-speaker's understanding of home and qualifies any notion of arrival.

Peggy Samuels convincingly argues that Calder's mobiles influenced Bishop's depiction of bumpy, unpredictable movement in 'Arrival at Santos'; she suggests that 'the speaker inhabits a Calder-like system, in which disparate elements appear seemingly out of nowhere and knock or move into other elements, sometimes with the humor that commentators mentioned frequently in their characterizations of Calder's work' (184). This affects the spatial design of the poem: 'Calder's work allows for lyric images and verse lines [. . .] to be arranged as events emerging in responsiveness to other events' (186). Although the poem may appear conventional in form, Samuels's work helps us to see that Bishop's spatial design of lines and stanzas is distinctly visual and modernist.[8] More specifically, Samuels suggests a connection between Calder's mobiles and what I have described as Bishop's use of enjambment: 'Like Calder, Bishop links suspense in time (the always being poised in one's own mental motion for the next event that will enter the "scene") with suspense in space (traveling on a trajectory that will "hit" or "be hit")' (184).

The analogy between the physical movements described by the speaker as the boat arrives at Santos and the material nature of the text is emphasised by the poem's deictic style. The speaker's present-tense remarks on features of the landscape that come into view (punctuated by the words 'here', 'there' and other signs of pointing) generate a partial, fragmented picture shaped by the bumps and turns of arrival. One effect of this deictic method is that the speaker's unfolding depiction of the scene is both temporally and spatially analogous to the reading and seeing of the poem that unfolds; as the poem enacts the experience described through lineation, enjambment, punctuation and so on, the reader experiences the bumpy arrival alongside the speaker, as a 'tourist' encountering both poem and port. In a related manner the poem can be read, like many of John Ashbery's poems, as self-reflexively commenting on its own unfolding form and procedures, thinking equally about the landscape of the port and the landscape of the text.

The verbal and visual status of the fallen *s* is central to this experience of reading. If we approach the *s* iconically, as visually mimicking a fall, it contributes to the analogy between the poem's visual design and the external landscape it depicts. But the *s* also disrupts this analogy. By 'falling' upon the letter *s* detached from the word, both the linear movement of reading and the illusion of mimesis are interrupted: the reader stops to consider the letter, and then looks backwards at the previous word and stanza. The need to engage with the materiality of the letter *s* figures literal and figurative blocks to vision: the *s* interrupts the relation between the verbal and the visual, what we read and what we imagine, signs and their referents. Its blockage of linear reading and of realist description of the port enacts a dizzying fall into the tender and surface of the text.

As she does with the earlier enjambments, Bishop provides analogies for these blocks to realist vision through the speaker's and Miss Breen's rocky descent into the tender. Just as the reader 'Fall // s' and looks backwards to make sense of the *s*, so Miss Breen and the speaker, in climbing down the ladder backwards, cannot see what they step into (making possible a literal fall into the tender). The speaker is also figuratively blinded by her 'immodest demands for a different world / and a better life, and complete comprehension / of both at last, and immediately', a blindness signified by her dissatisfaction with the visual scenery of the port, with its 'feeble', 'unassertive' colours, and by the desire that this new place accommodate her 'customs' of English, bourbon and cigarettes. Despite the speaker's resistance to adapting to the new landscape, the fall and the poem's visual design more generally demonstrate that her movements will be altered regardless. As Helen Dennis argues, the tourist-speaker and reader are 'stripped of various cultural assumptions, including the assumption that we are of sufficient significance for the landscape to render up meaning for us' (61).

As the *s* interrupts linear, mimetic reading, a self-referential reading of the text comes into sharper focus, in which the scene and action described can be read as referring not only to the external landscape of the port, but to what takes place literally and visually on the landscape of the page. Echoing Stein's *Tender Buttons*, the 'tender' of Bishop's poem is an agent that loosens words from their referents.[9] The tender refers to a boat used for unloading passengers and cargo from larger ships; it moves the speaker and Miss Breen from the relatively stable 'suspension' of their ship to the port, from the known to the unknown, progressively loosening them from their origins. The poem states, 'The tender is coming, / a strange and ancient craft, flying a strange and brilliant rag. / So that's the flag.' The tender is 'strange', and an agent of estrangement; it forces the speaker to revise her visual perspective and assumptions, the 'rag' upon closer scrutiny turning out to be the 'flag', presumably of Santos or Brazil. The tender is a 'strange and ancient craft', 'craft' referring not only to a boat but to a practised skill such as writing. The descent into the tender precipitates the fall into the surface of the text: as in Stein's text, parts of speech in the poem become slippery. For example, the word 'Fall // s' is both a noun and a verb, and the breakage of the *s* underlines that ambiguity. When the *s* is split from 'fall', the word is made strange and we question its part of speech. One effect of this grammatical ambiguity is to make the reader consider the literal feature of the landscape that gives the town Glens Falls its name. Although the name is a proper noun, Glens Falls refers to the movement and instability of water falling: as the name of Miss Breen's home literally falls apart, proper noun becoming verb, the poem literalises its challenge to stable homes and origins.

In a similar way, the slippage of letters is literalised in the poem. Bishop writes in stanzas 8–10 (bold emphases mine):

> Ports are necessities, like **postage stamps**, or **soap**,
>
> but they seldom seem to care what impression they make,
> or, like this, only attempt, since it does not **matter**,
> the unassertive colors of **soap**, or **postage stamps** —
> wasting away like the former, slipping the way the **latter**
>
> do when we mail the **letters** we wrote on the boat,
> either because the glue here is very inferior
> or because of the heat. (*Poems* 88)

Read literally, 'letters we wrote on the boat' may refer not to epistolary communication but to individual letters of the alphabet inscribed on to the surface of the boat, as in Bishop's description of Cummings' poems written in chalk on the pavement. Just as the slippage of stamps threatens the arrival of mailed letters, so the literal slippage of the *s* off the end of 'Falls' destabilises the arrival and meaning of language. In turn, we can track the repetition of the words 'stamps' and 'soap' visually, as a literal movement or slipping of the words down the page, emphasised by the long em dash that follows their second appearance.[10] The dash ends and extends the poetic line, visually suggesting a slippage or attenuation, and the slippery inability of words to 'stick' to their referents.[11] The glue that would make letters, and meanings, stick is 'very inferior', liquefying 'because of the heat'; the slippage of tenders, ports, colours, soap and stamps are all due to the power of water, and in its aqueous dissolution of the visual landscape as a stable, realist referent, the poem's method connotes watercolour.

In this fluid textual landscape, letters take on the substance of bodies, and human bodies become letter-like.[12] This effect is enhanced by syntactic ambiguity that depends on the spatial arrangement of lines and line breaks, as in the description of the descent into the tender:

> And gingerly now we climb down the ladder backward,
> myself and a fellow passenger named Miss Breen,
>
> descending into the midst of twenty-six freighters
> waiting to be loaded with green coffee beans. (*Poems* 87)

Given the line break between 'freighters' and 'waiting', grammatically it becomes unclear whether the phrase 'waiting to be loaded with green coffee beans' refers to the freighters, or to the speaker and Miss Breen; both are possible antecedents. A spatial syntax is at work here: the poem's spatial layout conflates tourists with coffee beans as cargo to be loaded, commodities to be processed through the port. It is this confusion that leads the boy to hook Miss Breen instead of a box of coffee beans, a confusion visually emphasised by the similarity of the letters in the rhyme (Breen/beans). In positioning the tourists as freight, the visual design of the text subtly undermines the passengers' pretensions.

Rhyme can be read not only sonically but visually, as a literal slippage of letters. On the one hand, we can read the amputated *s* as a product of the abcb rhyme scheme, which necessitates the rhyming of 'tall' with 'fall' (rather than 'falls'). The imposition of rhyme as an external constraint may signify the physical structures that impinge on the passengers' movements, like the hook that catches Miss Breen's skirt. But we can also read rhyme, particularly internal and slant rhyme, in terms of the literal slippage and substitution of letters. For instance, the 'ladder' climbed down backwards into the tender in stanza 5 becomes the 'matter', 'latter' and 'letters' of the final two stanzas. The small slips in letters allow the words to change shape, like the soap and stamps, suggesting the malleability of language in this aqueous environment. In the visual poetry of the avant-garde, the treatment of the letter as a material sign often foregrounds its sound; the hiss of the *s* is embedded in the name of the port – Santos – and recurs throughout the poem, perhaps onomatopoetically alluding to a slip or fall.[13]

Bishop's detachment of the letter *s* from 'Glens Falls' may at first glance register as a small, iconic joke, but as Bishop commented of Cummings, his visual designs 'really had something to say'. I've suggested that her use of this *s* in both its visual and its verbal capacities challenges linear reading, the relation between language and realist vision, and the presumed connection between seeing and knowing: as the fall challenges and confounds the visual and verbal mastery of both the tourist-speaker and the reader, it figures and permits a more significant fall. Bishop's generation of vertigo in the poem – a sensation of falling (from *vertere*, 'to turn') – extends to an epistemological questioning of all stable coordinates and received assumptions. Thus when the speaker asserts at the end of the poem that 'We leave Santos at once; / we are driving to the interior', the reader understands that this pretence of control will quickly dissolve in the face of what's unseen, unknown or ungovernable about the landscape and self.[14] By the end of the poem, both speaker and reader have 'arrived' where Bishop wants them at the opening of *Questions of Travel*, falling.

IV

The falling *s* demonstrates Bishop's interest in visual poetics, and her practice of exploring analogies between visual features of the poem, and the landscape, experience or thing described. Bishop repeated the truncation of a letter just once, in 'Pink Dog', which Brett Millier dates to 1963 (343) and which Bethany Hicok dates to 1962 (115–16), although the poem was not completed until 1979 (Millier 343). Bishop's visual treatment of the letter reveals her commentary on the situation of a 'naked' dog, a nursing mother suffering from scabies and living by her wits in Rio:

> In your condition you would not be able
> even to float, much less to dog-paddle.
> Now look, the practical, the sensible
>
> solution is to wear a *fantasía*.
> Tonight you simply can't afford to be a-
> n eyesore. But no one will ever see a
>
> dog in *máscara* this time of year. (*Poems* 212–13)

Bishop emphasises the splitting of 'an' with a hyphen, in contrast to 'Fall // s', perhaps to indicate that the word has not fallen apart, but has been violently broken apart. As in 'Arrival at Santos', we can read the truncation of the *n* as required by the rhyme: '*fantasía*', 'to be a-', 'ever see a'. In the visibly awkward breakage of 'a- / n', Bishop provides a visual, iconic analogy for 'eyesore'.[15]

The imposition of the rhyme scheme as an inviolable structure may allude to the structure of state-sponsored violence hinted at earlier in the poem, a violence that involved the 'disappearance' of 'beggars [. . .] idiots, paralytics, parasites', all those deemed marginal, weak and powerless in Rio. The breakage of the word 'an' by the rhyme and line break not only dramatises the dog as a visual eyesore, then, but may signify the bodily dismemberment of the dog, should she not conceal herself with a costume. The splitting of 'a- / n' thus visually demonstrates the need for the dog to wear a *fantasía* (Carnival costume), to disguise the visible signs of her bodily suffering and marginality (class, gender, maternity) through socially mandated ritual performances (of costume, dance, gender). This unusual breakage of a word helps to establish an analogy between the letters of the text and the visual appearance of the female dog, inviting a reading of the poem's spatial structure and visual design as of a piece with its treatment of the desperation at once concealed and expressed by the costumes and dances of Carnival.[16] The 'a- / n' provides a crucial crack in the poem's visual 'costume', through which we glimpse the violent treatment that may await the naked dog and the necessity for the dog's disguise, simultaneously.

This theme of gendered costuming invites a look back at 'Arrival at Santos'. The hooking of Miss Breen's skirt is also perhaps a meditation on concealing bodies that do not fit societal norms, specifically the body of Miss Breen, coded as queer yet costumed in the conventional signifier of heterosexual femininity, a skirt. The speaker comments, 'Please, boy, do be more careful with that boat hook! / Watch out! Oh! It has caught Miss Breen's // skirt! There!' (*Poems* 87). The line and stanza break in the phrase 'Miss Breen's // skirt' creates an analogy to the hook that spatially catches, and thus temporally delays, the descent of the skirt, which arrives on the following line, or may create an analogy to the skirt itself, being lifted through space and then descending. The movement of the hook/skirt may be iconically signified by the *s* which ends the word 'Breen's' and begins the word 'skirt': this carry-over of the letter *s* from the end of one line to the next dramatises the movement of the hook/skirt through space, anticipating the *s* that falls off Glens Falls.[17] Between lines, then, the hook catches and presumably lifts Miss Breen's skirt, revealing her body.[18] Although many interpretations of the lifted skirt are possible, reading the visual text (including the spaces between lines) suggests that along with slips between letters and words, words and their referents, reading and seeing, the relations between costumes and the gendered, sexual bodies they clothe and signify are also unsettled and potentially reconfigured by the experience of travel.[19]

The pink dog in Rio de Janeiro during Carnival and the North American female travellers arriving at the Port of Santos are out of place, moving through unknown, unstable and, for the dog, potentially dangerous environments. This is also true for the hen in 'Trouvée', a 1967 poem that foregrounds its visual and material nature through its allusion to the 'objet trouvée' or found object of the Surrealists. The 'trouvée' refers to the body of a hen, 'run over / on West 4th Street', and the speaker reflects on the extraordinary nature of finding a hen in this location:

> She was a white hen
> — red-and-white now, of course.
> How did she get there?
> Where was she going? (*Poems* 172)

André Breton defines the found object in a passage from *Mad Love* (1937) that describes his walk with Alberto Giacometti through the Paris flea markets. Giacometti, in trying to resolve how to make the head of a sculpture, was drawn towards a fencing mask that solved his problem. Although the found object may be mass produced, the manner of its finding, as in Giacometti's case, is singular and subject to chance, unconscious desire and unplanned intution (Hopkins 90–1; Xiaojing 103–4). In that Bishop's trouvée is an 'object' that was once alive, Bishop may also allude to Breton's *Nadja* (1928). Breton 'finds' Nadja in the streets, due to chance and erotic attraction, and describes her 'free genius' (111) as that of one

> who enjoyed being nowhere but in the streets, the only region of valid experience for her, in the street, accessible to interrogation from any human being launched upon some great chimera, or (why not admit it) the one who sometimes fell, since, after all, others had felt authorized to speak to her, has been able [*sic*] to see in her only the most wretched of women, and the least protected. (113)

In contrast to Nadja, the hen of 'Trouvée' did not fall (literally or morally) in the street, but met her death there:

> Her wing feathers spread
> flat, flat in the tar,
> all dirtied, and thin
> as tissue paper. (*Poems* 172)

In likening the wing feathers to tissue paper, the poem considers not only the violent end to the hen, but its own 'paper-y' representation of her. Here the visual design comes to the fore, with line breaks between 'spread / flat' and 'thin / as' dramatising a spreading and thinning of the hen's body through the space of the page and time of reading. Similarly, the repetition of 'flat, flat in the tar' visually enacts an elongation or flattening. As in 'Pink Dog', the use of an em dash in ' — red-and-white now' dramatises a violent breaking of the hen's body, establishing an analogy between visual text and visual body.

The act of violence Bishop considers is not just that of the vehicle that has run over the hen, but the flattening, objectifying violence of verbal and visual representation, an issue addressed in the final two stanzas:

> Just now I went back
> to look again.
> I hadn't dreamed it:
> there is a hen
>
> turned into a quaint
> old country saying
> scribbled in chalk
> (except for the beak). (*Poems* 172)

The verbal violence stems from turning this particular hen's mysterious life and death into a 'quaint / old country saying', into a generalised truism, cliché or dead metaphor. The well-worn saying Bishop probably had in mind is the joke 'Why did the chicken cross the road? To get to the other side', 'other side' referring literally to the other side of the road or figuratively to the other side of life (death). To turn the hen into an example of this joke risks repeating the flattening violence inflicted by the car.

Bishop also emphasises the flattening violence of verbal and visual representation through allusions to the diction and visual designs of an earlier poet of the hen, Geoffrey Chaucer.[20] 'The Nun's Priest's Tale' features a blazon of the rooster Chauntecleer which Bishop admired and typed out in a 1948 letter to Robert Lowell.[21] In Middle English the blazon refers to a shield bearing a heraldic device, and as a literary term it refers to a poem that catalogues a person's, often a woman's or lover's, physical attributes. Cynthia Camp suggests that Bishop had an 'inverted blazon' in mind in 'Trouvée': instead of describing the innate, beautiful features of a glossy rooster that could adorn a heraldic shield, Bishop describes the characteristics of a hen flattened into a papery 'shield' by violence. In this Chaucerian context the lines 'there is a hen / turned into a quaint' allude to the Middle English 'queynte', an adjective that means 'wise, clever, prudent', 'crafty, wily', 'strange, unusual; remarkable, marvelous', or, in its noun form, refers to 'a clever or curious device or ornament', 'with punning on cunte [. . .] a woman's external sex organ', 'sexual intercourse' (*Middle English Dictionary*). Chaucer uses 'queynte' as a pun or euphemism for 'cunt' in 'The Wife of Bath's Prologue' and in 'The Miller's Tale' (Camp). Due to the spatial arrangement of lines and line breaks, if we pause at the end of the line 'turned into a quaint' we can read 'quaint' as a noun; as we read further down the page, we can also read 'quaint' as an adjective qualifying 'old country saying'. The spatial design allows us to encounter the possibility of the noun first, a sense of the word that is difficult to dispel even as noun becomes adjective.

Through a spatially generated syntax, Bishop implies that the hen has been turned into a queynte, a word that carries a history of sexual objectification and misogyny. In choosing this word Bishop emphasises that sexualised violence colours the way the hen is viewed and represented: she is 'turned' into a 'queynte' through a societal gaze that sexually objectifies and punishes women, especially 'wayward' women who have strayed into the urban street, beyond their expected role and sphere. The car has exposed her insides, leaving her body naked and vulnerable. The pink dog is similarly vulnerable to violence due to the visible signs of her gender, maternity, illness and poverty in the highly policed fashionable districts of the city. Dog and hen do not simply allegorise women, as their animal status marginalises them further. While a homeless woman who had been hit by a car would garner official attention, the hen is left in the street to decay, or to be thrown in the trash.

Although the poem draws attention to the object-making violence of the car and of verbal/visual representation, it resists inflicting this representational violence on the hen. Bishop refers to the hen becoming a saying 'scribbled in chalk', as if the hen's flattened and bloodied body has literally been turned into writing on the pavement. The phrase 'scribbled in chalk' echoes Bishop's discussion of E. E. Cummings' 'ideograph' poems, written in hyacinth-coloured chalks on curbs, shop fronts and parks. George Monteiro, who also connects 'Trouvée' to Bishop's quote about Cummings, argues that since Bishop wouldn't keep this found object, the poem can be viewed as an 'inscription of the actual hen's carcass as mapped or outlined by the thinking-feeling poet' (83). With this argument in mind, the parentheses of the last line visually demarcate a space of depth, intimacy or protection, to indicate what has not been flattened into the tar, country saying or poem: the hen's beak. Indeed, the parentheses can be viewed iconically as a vertical beak, ( ).[22] The beak serves as a counter-balance to the queynte, as it's the only part of the body that hasn't been flattened. More pointedly, the beak is what permits the hen's voice, and the dead hen can be regarded as a figure of the wandering female poet, as in a trouvère, a medieval travelling performer of songs and sung stories, suggesting a pun on the title.[23] The poem's visual design, then, serves both to reveal the violence – of the car, language, the patriarchal gaze – that has flattened the hen, and to create a visual space in the text that protects and preserves the beak and the bird's particular voice and experience from such flattening.[24]

The poem offers a feminist twist on the Cummings-esque concrete poem and Surrealist objet trouvée. Although Breton recalls Nadja telling him about the violence inflicted on her by men in the streets, and acknowledges that her poverty has caused her homelessness (142), when Nadja ultimately ends up institutionalised due to mental illness (136), Breton does nothing to help: what has happened to the woman herself is not his concern.[25] Rather, Nadja's importance for him is as a muse and embodiment of Surrealist ideals, who enables him to explore the self-directed question 'Who am I?' (11). In contrast, Bishop's 'Trouvée' begins with what has happened to the hen, the documentary fact (versus the Surrealist 'dream') of the hen's death and transformation into a flat object, so as to raise questions about the unknowable mystery of her life. Bishop omits the 'objet' from the title but maintains the 'trouvée' to resist the forces that have objectified the hen, implying the need to explore the overlooked, everyday violence visited upon animals, women and other marginal figures who transgress their expected roles and places. The poem may also provide a pointed, feminist rejoinder to the violent fragmentation and objectification of the female body in many Surrealist objects.

Elisabeth Frost argues that women were rarely involved in concrete poetry of the 1950s and 1960s (345). However, she singles out Mary Ellen Solt's *Marriage: A Code Poem* (1976) and *Flowers in Concrete* (1966) and May Swenson's *Iconographs* (1970) as feminist experiments indebted to concrete poetry, and to E. E. Cummings' work in particular (346–7). The poems I have discussed here could be considered with this group. But Bishop's interest in visual poetics was long-standing, and her influences extended beyond Cummings.[26] Methodologically, paying attention to Bishop's interest in avant-garde experiment requires that we read her corpus of work differently: we need to approach her poems as visual as well as verbal artefacts. The visual text, including the use of punctuation marks and the spatial design and layout of words, lines and stanzas, should not be considered secondary features of her poems. Problems of reading and seeing figure other kinds of problems in Bishop's poetry and provide a useful entry point into her experimental style and methods.

Notes

1. Bishop made some slight changes in the 1965 edition, including substituting 'bourbon and cigarettes' for the earlier 'Scotch and cigarettes' in line 31 (*Poems* 342).
2. Bishop served as co-editor with Emanuel Brasil of *An Anthology of Twentieth-Century Brazilian Poetry* (1972), reflecting her knowledge of the Brazilian modernist and avant-garde tradition.
3. Most scholars have discussed 'Fall // s' as an example of Bishop's wit and/or have noted the demands of the rhyme scheme. While both elements are important, usually the analysis ends there, while I argue that 'Fall // s' reflects a deeper engagement with visual poetics. For instance, Eleanor Cook describes the enjambment as 'a little fun' and 'mischievous' (144–5), while Gillian White emphasises the poem's 'almost comic insistence on keeping its conventional rhyme scheme' (266).
4. Bishop worked to bring recognition to Cummings in Brazil in the 1950s by encouraging the translation and anthologising of his work. In particular she associated Manuel Bandeira's poetry with that of Cummings; she wrote to Cummings in 1956 about her efforts to have Bandeira translate his work (Monteiro 91).
5. Bohn argues that 'ideographic expression depends on the juxtaposition of pictographic signs, which may combine to form either a single word or a whole sentence'; he adds, 'each image not only translates an abstract concept into concrete terms but serves as a visual metaphor' (*Modern Visual Poetry* 43). In contrast to the letters of the alphabet, an ideograph is not the picture or sign of a sound but a picture of a thing or combination of things (34).
6. While free verse challenged conventions of metre and pursued organisation of the poem by new means, avant-garde visual poetry went further in pursuit of freedom, seeking what Marinetti called 'untrammelled imagination', which he defined as 'the absolute freedom of images or analogies, expressed by means of Words-in-Freedom, unencumbered by syntactical conductors or by punctuation' (124).
7. For good discussions of this history, see Bohn, Frost, Taylor, Webster.
8. Peter Swaab suggests that Bishop's abrupt enjambments in the poem are indebted to Hopkins (personal conversation), and also sees Hopkins's influence in Bishop's notable use of punctuation marks (exclamation marks, brackets, dashes, ellipses and italics). Marilyn May Lombardi argues that Bishop praised Hopkins for his ability to 'catch and preserve the movement of an idea – the point being to crystallize it early enough so that it still has movement' (95). A 'balancing of mobile and crystallized emotion' embodies Bishop's poetic structures and enjambment serves to 'channel the flow of her emotions without arresting their movement' (96).
9. Bishop heard Stein's 10 November 1934 lecture in Avery Hall at Vassar on 'Portraits I Have Written and What I Think of Repetition, Whether It Exists or No', which was published in *Lectures in America* in 1935 ('A Documentary History of Vassar College', <http://chronology.vassar.edu/records/1934/1934-11-10-stein-lecture.html> (last accessed 17 October 2018)).

10. *The New Yorker* asked Bishop to change some punctuation in her original draft. She removed three em dashes: in stanza 7, line 1; at the start of stanza 9, line 4; and at the start of stanza 10, line 2. The em dash at the end of stanza 9, line 3, was initially a comma, but Bishop added an em dash when she was asked to remove one from the beginning of the following line (*Elizabeth Bishop and The New Yorker* 80). Bishop's struggles with *The New Yorker* editors over punctuation (xliv–xlv) take on new meaning in the context of visual poetics.

11. Linda Anderson has emphasised the shared understanding of the line in Paul Klee's and Bishop's work, pointing out that Klee saw the line as an unfolding motion that was temporal and spatial (148), relevant to the process of both drawing and writing: 'That lines can cross into different mediums and practices, forging connections, is part of their fascination' (150). Anderson argues, 'If lines provide a suggestive trope within her writing as well as her painting, they might also be seen, operating at the margins or edges of what is figurable, as suggesting connections and extensions which go beyond the immediate work' (149).

12. In '12 O'Clock News' Bishop uses dramatic juxtapositions of scale to create analogies between textual and literal landscapes, e.g. a typewritten page that when enlarged can be regarded as an airstrip or cemetery (Rosenbaum).

13. Bishop may use the *s* as a mark of slips and surfaces in intentional contrast and relation to the *o* of 'Oh, tourist', 'So', 'Watch out! Oh!' and 'Santos'. An absorption of ideas that unsettle the self, an exclamation of surprise or distress at the lifted skirt, the indrawn breath or the open mouth: collectively these *o*s may signify new openings in a surface, a departure from habits/conventions of depth/interiority made possible by the slippery arrival at the port.

14. Robert Boschmann argues that just as the Port of Santos is the 'skin of Brazil', and soap and stamps are 'made only for contact with surfaces', they 'call forth the kind of slippery thinking and perceptions that can arise when binaries are invoked' (75). Helen Dennis argues that by the final line 'the interior is just the interior, alien and resistant to the tourist's quest' (61). Gillian White points out that the poem's 'deconstruction of voice' (266) 'undermines the expectation that it will function as a revealing self-exploration in which speaking subject and poet are identified' (265).

15. Elizabeth Neely reads the 'a- / n' as 'the most graphic line break eyesore' in Bishop's poems (108). Monteiro writes that Bishop's 'fealty to the word "eyesore" compels her into this concocted eye rhyme, and her fealty is rewarded by the implication that, perhaps, the sore(s) the dog is suffering from may be more apparent than real' (77). Catherine Cucinella argues that in showing 'the need for costume in order to render the abjected female body invisible, it implicitly recognizes that the masquerade renders female sexuality and female desire visible', but in a manner that does not threaten patriarchy (80).

16. Mena Mitrano offers a reading that accounts for the importance of the poem's line breaks; she argues that the pink dog is 'a signifier that keeps the poem (and us) oscillating between two semantic clusters: "woman" and "dog"', with line breaks working to 'create the expectation of an unmasked signifier "woman" in the place of "dog"' (34).

17. Jonathan Ellis argues, regarding the hooking of Miss Breen's skirt: 'In a beautiful symmetry, the poet's rhyme ("beans") also snags on "Miss Breen", removing her skirt a second time, this time through a line and stanza break. Poetic form thus cleverly pulls Miss Breen in two different directions in imitation of the subject of the poem that also drags the tourist in between thoughts of home and the desire to experience foreign places' (115).

18. Colm Tóibín has emphasised that the unsaid and the unspoken, 'what was in between the lines of her poems' (48), contributes to their tone and structure (47–8, 105–6). The visual design and spatial layout of Bishop's poems helps us to read the presence of the unsaid.

19. Brett Millier notes that Bishop 'got from this brief acquaintance [. . .] a vision of an accomplished and successful lesbian life' (239). Henry Abelove reads the lines as 'an almost

burlesque comeuppance for the closety skirt' (82). In a discussion of the poem, Michael Davidson argues that it 'announces the links between exterior and interior, surface reticence and private sexuality, that would dominate her middle years' (172).

20. The allusion to Chaucer emerges when the speaker refers to the hen as a 'poor fowl'. Chaucer frames the 'Parliament of Fowls' as a dream vision, while Bishop's speaker wonders if she has dreamed the dead hen, but looks again and insists on the facticity of her description.

21. In her letter to Robert Lowell of 18 May 1948, Bishop commented that she 'bought a Modern Library Chaucer, the only one I could get – only the Tales' (*Words in Air* 34). Lowell replied in a letter dated 20 May that Chaucer is 'the author who has all the slow, open, common-sense, loving, secure, wise-in-people etc. virtues that we were talking about and that the modern world has little of' (*Words in Air* 35). In a letter dated 30 August 1948, Bishop comments that 'I am reading the "Nonnes Preestes Tale," which I'd never read before, & of course I was much taken with: "His coomb was redder than the fyn coral, / and batailled, as it were a castel wal. His bile was black, & as the jeet it shoon; / like asure were his legges, & his toon: / His nayles whitter thn the lili flour / and like the burned gold was his colour." & "his sustres & his paramours," & "For Goddes love, as take some laxatyf"' (*Words in Air* 55).

22. Rei Tartakovsky argues that Cummings' parentheses can function iconically, but also in 'delimiting, enclosing, encircling' works to 'engender conceptual separation, protection, and intimacy' (221–2).

23. The hen flattened by traffic suggests a demystified or diminished poet/poem, recalling Frost's 'Oven Bird' and Baudelaire's poet-speaker in 'Loss of a Halo', who reports crossing the muddy boulevard 'where death arrives at a gallop from every direction', losing his halo in the 'mire on the macadam road' due to the need for a 'sudden movement' (69).

24. Bishop and her neighbours Wheaton Galentine and Harold Leeds witnessed the dead chicken one evening in July 1967; Bishop wrote the poem that night and shared it with them the following morning. At this time Bishop was in New York and Lota was in Brazil, suffering severe depression (Millier 404; Monteiro 80–1). In a letter to them dated 5 December 1967, Bishop thanks them for helping her after Lota's death, and comments, 'I feel quite sure I wouldn't have survived at all without you. (And I shall dedicate something better than the poor HEN at least, sometime, to you, as one other small footnote of gratitude.)' (*One Art* 483–4). The published poem bears this dedication, and was thus marked by the biographical circumstances prior to and following Lota's death. Megan Marshall notes that Bishop sent the poem to Lota, who found it to be '"adorable," "perfectly balanced," "like a small Calder"' (212). Lota showed it to Decio de Sousa, the analyst who had been seeing both Lota and Bishop in Rio, and reported that 'for him you are the "hen" . . . white, lovely, and crushed by the big city and by the last evenements', which Marshall translates as 'the tumultuous events of the past year' (212). When Lota travelled to see Bishop in New York in September 1967, she brought a copy of the poem with her (Marshall 216).

25. Breton decries sanatoriums and the confinement of irrational forces in culture, and cites his 'general contempt for psychiatry [as] [. . .] reason enough for my not yet having dared investigate what has become of Nadja' (141).

26. For instance, in poems such as 'I felt a Funeral in my Brain' ('And then a Plank in Reason, broke, / And I dropped down, and down – / And hit a World, at every plunge, / And Finished knowing – then – '), Emily Dickinson uses a visual mark (which for convenience has been called a 'dash') to generate syntactic ambiguity and possibility: the dash may function as a full stop, an end to the speaker's knowing, or may signify what happens next, after knowing has stopped. The speaker's dizzying fall, embodied in the final ambiguous dash, allows Dickinson to dissolve the planks upon which conventional knowledge rests. Dickinson's generation of poetic vertigo through the 'dash' is echoed by Bishop with her 'Fall // s' and other elements of visual design.

Works Cited

Abelove, Henry, *Deep Gossip* (London: University of Minnesota Press, 2003).

Anderson, Linda, *Elizabeth Bishop: Lines of Connection* (Edinburgh: Edinburgh University Press, 2013).

Baudelaire, Charles, *The Parisian Prowler: Le Spleen de Paris, Petit Poèmes en Prose*, trans. Edward Kaplan (Athens: University of Georgia Press, 1989).

Bishop, Elizabeth, *Elizabeth Bishop and The New Yorker: The Complete Correspondence*, ed. Joelle Biele (New York: Farrar, Straus and Giroux, 2011).

Bishop, Elizabeth, *One Art: Letters*, ed. Robert Giroux (New York: Farrar, Straus and Giroux, 1994).

Bishop, Elizabeth, 'Review of XAIPE: Seventy-One Poems by E. E. Cummings', *The United States Quarterly Book Review* (June 1950): 160–1; reprinted in *Prose*, p. 261.

Bishop, Elizabeth, and Robert Lowell, *Words in Air: The Complete Correspondence between Elizabeth Bishop and Robert Lowell*, ed. Thomas Travisano with Saskia Hamilton (New York: Farrar, Straus and Giroux, 2008).

Bohn, Willard, *Modern Visual Poetry* (Newark: University of Delaware Press, 2001).

Bohn, Willard, *Reading Visual Poetry* (Madison: Fairleigh Dickinson University Press, 2011).

Boschmann, Robert, *In the Way of Nature: Ecology and Westward Expansion in the Poetry of Anne Bradstreet, Elizabeth Bishop, and Amy Clampitt* (Jefferson, NC: McFarland, 2009).

Breton, Andre, *Mad Love*, trans. Mary Ann Caws (Lincoln: University of Nebraska Press, 1986).

Breton, Andre, *Nadja*, trans. Richard Howard (New York: Grove Press, 1960).

Camp, Cynthia, 'Re: Middle English Question', email to Susan Rosenbaum, 20 September 2015.

Chaucer, Geoffrey, *The Tales of Canterbury*, ed. Robert A. Pratt (Boston: Houghton Mifflin, 1974).

Colônia, Regina, 'Poetry as a Way of Life', in George Monteiro (ed.), *Conversations with Elizabeth Bishop* (Jackson: University Press of Mississippi, 1996), pp. 50–3.

Cook, Eleanor, *Elizabeth Bishop at Work* (Cambridge, MA: Harvard University Press, 2016).

Cucinella, Catherine, '"Dress up! Dress up and Dance at Carnival!" The Body in Elizabeth Bishop's "Pink Dog"', *Rocky Mountain Review of Language and Literature* 56.1 (2002): 73–83.

Cummings, E. E., *Complete Poems, 1904–1962*, ed. George J. Firmage (New York: Liveright, 1991).

Davidson, Michael, *Guys Like Us: Citing Masculinity in Cold War Poetics* (Chicago: University of Chicago Press, 2004).

Dennis, Helen M., 'Questions of Travel: Elizabeth Bishop and the Negative Sublime', in Lionel Kelly (ed.), *Poetry and the Sense of Panic: Critical Essays on Elizabeth Bishop and John Ashbery* (Amsterdam: Rodopi, 2000), pp. 53–64.

Ellis, Jonathan, *Art and Memory in the Work of Elizabeth Bishop* (Aldershot: Ashgate, 2006).

Frost, Elisabeth A., 'Visual Poetics', in Linda A. Kinnahan (ed.), *A History of Twentieth-Century American Women's Poetry* (Cambridge: Cambridge University Press, 2016), pp. 339–58.

Hicok, Bethany, *Elizabeth Bishop's Brazil* (Charlottesville: University of Virginia Press, 2016).

Hopkins, David, *Dada and Surrealism: A Very Short Introduction* (Oxford: Oxford University Press, 2004).

Lombardi, Marilyn May, *The Body and the Song: Elizabeth Bishop's Poetics* (Carbondale: Southern Illinois University Press, 1995).

Marinetti, Filippo Tommaso, *Critical Writings*, ed. Günter Berghaus, trans. Doug Thompson (New York: Farrar, Straus and Giroux, 2006).

Marshall, Megan, *Elizabeth Bishop: A Miracle for Breakfast* (New York: Houghton Mifflin Harcourt, 2017).

Millier, Brett C., *Elizabeth Bishop: Life and the Memory of It* (Berkeley: University of California Press, 1993).

Mitrano, Mena, 'Bishop's "Pink Dog"', *Explicator* 54.1 (Fall 1995): 33–6.

Monteiro, George, *Elizabeth Bishop in Brazil and After: A Poetic Career Transformed* (Jefferson, NC: McFarland, 2012).

Neely, Elizabeth, 'Cadela Carioca: Bishop's "Pink Dog" in its Brasilian Cultural Context', *South Central Review* 31.1 (Spring 2014): 99–113.

Page, Barbara, 'Home, Wherever That May Be: Poems and Prose of Brazil', in Angus Cleghorn and Jonathan Ellis (eds), *The Cambridge Companion to Elizabeth Bishop* (Cambridge: Cambridge University Press, 2014), pp. 124–40.

'Queynte, *n., adj*', *Electronic Middle English Dictionary* (University of Michigan, 2001), <https://quod.lib.umich.edu/m/med/> (last accessed 17 October 2018).

Rosenbaum, Susan, 'Elizabeth Bishop's Theater of War', in Eric Haralson (ed.), *Reading the Middle Generation Anew: Culture, Community, and Form in Twentieth-Century American Poetry* (Iowa City: University of Iowa Press, 2006), pp. 55–82.

Samuels, Peggy, *Deep Skin: Elizabeth Bishop and Visual Art* (Ithaca: Cornell University Press, 2010).

Stein, Gertrude, *Tender Buttons* (Los Angeles: Sun & Moon Press, 1990).

Swaab, Peter, 'Elizabeth Bishop and the Art of Exclamation' (unpublished conference paper), 'Elizabeth Bishop's Questions of Travel: 50 Years After', 25–27 June 2015, Sheffield, UK.

Swaab, Peter, personal conversation with author, at 'Elizabeth Bishop's Questions of Travel: 50 Years After', 25–27 June 2015, Sheffield, UK.

Tartakovsky, Rei, 'E. E. Cummings's Parentheses: Punctuation as Poetic Device', *Style: A Quarterly Journal of Aesthetics, Poetics, Stylistics, and Literary Criticism* 43.2 (Summer 2009): 215–47.

Taylor, Carole Anne, *A Poetics of Seeing: The Implications of Visual Form in Modern Poetry* (New York: Garland Publishing, 1985).

Tóibín, Colm, *On Elizabeth Bishop* (Princeton: Princeton University Press, 2014).

Webster, Michael, *Reading Visual Poetry after Futurism: Marinetti, Apollinaire, Schwitters, Cummings* (New York: Peter Lang, 1995).

White, Gillian, '*Words in Air* and "Space" in Art: Bishop's Midcentury Critique of the United States', in Angus Cleghorn, Bethany Hicok and Thomas Travisano (eds), *Elizabeth Bishop in the Twenty-First Century: Reading the New Editions* (Charlottesville: University of Virginia Press, 2012), pp. 255–73.

Xiaojing, Zhou, 'Bishop's "Trouvée"', *Explicator* 54.2 (Winter 1996): 102–5.

13

'THE MOOSE' AS MOVIE: ELIZABETH BISHOP AS SCREENWRITER

J. T. Welsch

I

OTHERS HAVE COMMENTED EXTENSIVELY on visual aspects of Elizabeth Bishop's writing, focusing on its relationship to visual art, and especially painting: Bonnie Costello's *Elizabeth Bishop: Questions of Mastery* (1991), Jonathan Ellis's *Art and Memory in the Work of Elizabeth Bishop* (2006), Peggy Samuels's *Deep Skin: Elizabeth Bishop and Visual Art* (2010) and other work has followed an essential and fruitful line of inquiry, exploring the influence of specific painters as well as the relationship between Bishop's own painting and her writing practice, offering nuanced considerations of the poet's visual approaches. This chapter extends these approaches by considering the practical influence of film on Bishop's poetry, drawing out various cinematic techniques at work in her narrative poem 'The Moose'. I begin by tracing Bishop's personal interest in film, before proceeding with a more speculative reading of 'The Moose' in relation to film and screenplay form, and concluding with the animal encounter at the end of that poem, which is compared to the wider cinematic trope of such encounters.

Comparisons to visual art often draw on Bishop's own comments regarding the importance of painting for her work. In 1966, for instance, she told an interviewer 'I think I'm more visual than most poets', before citing the art critic Meyer Shapiro, who had suggested 'She writes poems with a painter's eye'. 'I was very flattered,' she continued. 'All my life I've been interested in painting. [. . .] I'd love to be a painter' (Monteiro, *Conversations*, 24). While Bishop never expresses a similar desire to make or write films, any reader of her letters and essays will have been struck by the frequency with which she refers to them. Her tastes in film appear to have been fairly broad, and she seems acutely aware of film's shifting cultural status in the mid-twentieth century, offering informal reviews and analysis of everything from art film festivals to Disney cartoons. A letter to Robert Lowell from 1969 captures this range of interests, while lamenting what she sees as a decline of culture around her in Brazil: 'I used to go to the movies almost every night, just for fun, to see really good things – foreign films, old ones, sometimes advance showings' (*Words in Air* 659). In her memoir essay on Marianne Moore, Bishop recalls, 'Sometimes we went to movies together', noting a distinction between their preferences with an anecdote about someone else taking Moore to see Sergei Eisenstein's *Battleship Potemkin* (1925), adding: 'I never attempted to lure her to any dramatic or "artistic" films' (*Prose* 137).

Although Bishop never relates it to the making of poems, there is some evidence of her having taken an interest in film as a distinct visual medium. In the context of painting, Bonnie Costello elaborates on her regard for Bishop as 'a profoundly visual poet with an eye for the particular and mutable', arguing that her 'sense of the visual particular is deeply complicated by her awareness of the mediation of signs, the abyss of representation in which we are conscious' (12). This interest in mediation and the medium is present in a scene from Bishop's sequence 'The Riverman', where a bedroom shines 'with the light from overhead, / a steady stream of light / like at the cinema' (*Poems* 105). The grammatical double-sense of this likeness – in which the image might be compared to something seen on-screen as well as to the film projector's unreconstructed beam – attests to her sensitivity to film's unique material nature. Similarly, Jonathan Ellis compares the opening sentences of Bishop's story 'In the Village' to the process of developing still photographs. 'There is an ambiguity about recollection', Ellis writes, 'that Bishop evidently thinks comparable to the developing process' (162).

Direct references to film in Bishop's poetry or critical writing are fairly scant, however, and often point to film as a more general phenomenon, in which she felt herself and culture involved, for better or worse. When interviewed by Edward Lucie-Smith for *The Times* in 1964, she joked that 'being in England is rather like going to the movies after you've read the book' (Monteiro, *Conversations*, 13). At times, the connotations are even more negative – complaining that the Americans she was staying with in Paris 'are just like people out of the movies, so it wasn't as pleasant as it should have been' (*One Art* 34), or that Rio's Carnival had lately 'turned into a movie nightmare', with costumes imitating then-popular biblical epics (*Brazil* 88). This self-consciousness about film's cultural status also flickers in the poem 'Invitation to Miss Marianne Moore', where Bishop asks the older poet to '[mount] the sky with natural heroism [. . .] above the malignant movies' (*Poems* 80). And yet, in the essay fragment 'Writing poetry is an unnatural act . . .', she praises the famous last stanza of Auden's 'The Fall of Rome' by saying, 'It's accurate, like something seen in a documentary movie. It is spontaneous, natural sounding [. . .] mysterious' (*Prose* 329).

It is not my intention to suggest a conscious influence for film comparable to that of painting on Bishop's poetry. The idea that 'The Moose' may be read as a kind of screenplay in verse, with an often specific plan for a kind of short film that might play in the reader's mind, is more a way to argue for and emphasise the deep, perhaps entirely unconscious effect all of this film viewing may have had on her poetry. Although Bishop never published any form of scriptwriting in adulthood, Brett Millier's biography notes that one of her first publications, in Walnut Hill high school's *Blue Pencil*, was a play about her grandparents and cousins in Nova Scotia, and that after graduating from Vassar, she initially spent time planning a verse play or opera libretto project (80). In later life, she seems fascinated by her friend Vinícius de Moraes adapting his libretto for the Brazilian film *Black Orpheus* (1959). The following year, she wrote to Lowell: 'I think your Ford grant to study opera is amazing [. . .] I have dreamed of a libretto for years' (*One Art* 383). Again, this shows nothing more nor less than an interest in the process, alongside her attention elsewhere to film's narrative aspects. Other passing references to film in existing Bishop criticism – Costello's comparison of 'The Man-Moth' to the silent films of Charlie Chaplin or Buster Keaton (51), or George Monteiro's sense that the execution in 'The Hanging of the Mouse' echoes James Cagney's final scene in *The Public Enemy* (*Elizabeth Bishop in Brazil and After* 156) – hint at the more sustained work to be done. The analysis here is intended to make room for other distinctly filmic comparisons, helping to situate film alongside visual art in its importance for her writing.

<h1 style="text-align:center">II</h1>

While the influence of film may be read into different poems by Bishop, the famously long gestation of 'The Moose' certainly would have allowed more time for the many drafts and reconfigurations of the poem to absorb, in historical terms, a greater range and depth of cinematic experience. The biographical details underlying the poem begin with a bus journey to Boston from Great Village, Nova Scotia, where Bishop had been visiting family in August 1946: 'a dreadful trip,' she tells Moore, briefly recounting the appearance of a moose in the road, who 'walked away very slowly into the woods, looking at us over her shoulder' (*One Art* 141). From that experience, it would be twenty-six years before she completed 'The Moose' for a reading at Harvard and publication in *The New Yorker* in 1972. Drafts exist throughout the period and the published poem retains some of the language from the letter to Moore, including descriptions of the landscape and the driver's phrase 'curious creatures' ('curious beasts' in the letter). In a letter from 1956 to her aunt Grace Bulmer Bowers, Bishop writes optimistically: 'I've written a long poem about Nova Scotia. It's dedicated to you. When it's published, I'll send you a copy' (*One Art* 334). Another sixteen years later, after the Harvard reading, she admits, 'I had to get the damned poem *written*, first' (*One Art* 568).

Beyond any link between filmic approaches to the moose in the poem, the close relationship between animals and film in Bishop's personal writing connects with the centrality of animals to the wider history of film and film technology. Eadweard Muybridge's photographs of 'Sallie Gardner at a Gallop' (1878) remain emblematic of early cinema experiments, with their use in his zoopraxiscope film projector experiments in the late nineteenth century. The prominent dog and horses in the Lumière brothers' footage of 'Workers Leaving the Lumière Factory at Lyon' (1895) and the Edison company's infamous 'Electrocuting an Elephant' (1903) also help place animals at the heart of the medium's early history. Bishop attests to audiences' persistent fascination with animals on screen in her various references to animal films. In early 1935, not long after graduating from Vassar and moving to New York, she tentatively invites Marianne Moore to see a film: 'I'm wondering if you have seen Martin Johnson's moving picture *Baboons*? It *looks*, from the previews, as if it might have in it a few very nice animals [. . .] I wonder if you would care to go with me one afternoon this week?' If not that, 'I have had my eye on another animal film called, I think, *Sequoia*, but it doesn't sound as promising as *Baboons*' (*One Art* 30). The 1935 film *Baboona* (not *Baboons*) was edited together using footage from Martin and Osa Johnson's pioneering flights over Mount Kilimanjaro and other parts of Africa and was billed at its premiere – the week before Bishop's letter – as an 'aerial safari'. The latter option, *Sequoia*, was a fictional release produced by MGM in 1934, about a young girl who raises a fawn and mountain lion to be friends. Although there is no record of whether Bishop (or Moore) saw either film, the poet's interest in the Johnsons' African exploits is shown both prior to this outing and persisting in the couple's appearance in 'In the Waiting Room' – written in the mid-1970s, but with an issue of *National Geographic* from 'February, 1918', where the Johnsons are shown 'dressed in riding breeches,

/ laced books, and pith helmets' (*Poems* 179). In 'Efforts of Affection', Bishop also remembers watching, with Moore, 'an exceptionally beautiful film, a documentary in color about Africa, with herds of gazelles and giraffes moving across the plains' (*Prose* 130), which probably refers to another of the Johnsons' aerial productions.

The animal films that captured Bishop's and wider audiences' imaginations through-out the first half of the twentieth century often combined location footage with staged studio scenes in order to construct their loose narratives. The primitive rear projection techniques in the wildly popular *King Kong* and *Tarzan* films of the 1930s exemplify these manipulations, exploiting the emotional response to animal imagery that Bishop seems to have shared in her preference for documentaries. As Jonathan Burt writes, 'Animal imagery in film has a peculiar status in that, despite a general awareness of the contrivances of the medium, audiences often respond differently to animals or animal-related practices than they do to other forms of imagery' (10). The result, Burt argues, is a complex response, in which the emotional response to animals both precedes and is conditioned by the medium itself:

> On the one hand, it can be argued that an emotional response to animals is an empa-thetic and hence straightforward natural expression of sentiment toward fellow crea-tures. On the other hand, it can as easily be said that it is film itself that, since its arrival in the mid-1890s, has increasingly influenced the constructions of the animal in the public domain and that the force of the viewer's response to the animal is imbued with the techniques by which film provokes feelings in its audience. (10)

Bishop's self-reflectiveness about the emotional reflexes associated with animal imag-ery is evident in a number of poems – 'The Fish', 'Pink Dog', 'The Armadillo', 'Roost-ers', 'Sandpiper' and, certainly, 'The Moose' – which balance documentary accuracy of their depictions with a characteristic self-consciousness regarding those human-animal identifications and their manipulation in verse. Angus Cleghorn and Jonathan Ellis summarise her approach: 'Like the moose's sudden appearance at the end of the eponymous poem, there is something both "homely" and "otherworldly" about all of Bishop's animal poems' (10). Rather than place a seemingly 'natural expression of sentiment' in opposition to more intellectual responses, Bishop seems to draw upon the initial emotional connections offered by the appearance of non-human animals in order to reflect upon that response's construction, through both narrative and form. In that sense, Bishop's animal poems work to resist easy anthropomorphism or sym-bolism, partly by deconstructing their own imagery. Linda Anderson, discussing the oblique influence of Marianne Moore's 'cinematic' approach, notes that

> the kind of looking involved in early film often depended [. . .] on isolating bodily fragments, gestures and objects, and then, like Moore's poems, reconstituting them – splicing them together – in a different, unfamiliar context. (12)

Anderson continues:

> Moore enabled Bishop to see the potential for poetry of the detailed observation of objects and animals; more broadly, through the use of different perspectives and scales she helped to open up areas of vision that were oblique or peripheral, not dominated by tradition or authority. (14)

In Bishop's animal poems, this defamiliarisation and fragmentation – placing subjects and details of subjects at different focal lengths and in different combinations of 'shots' – is a recurring strategy for achieving the sense of startling ambiguity with which so many of her creatures appear and depart.

III

Colm Tóibín's discussion of 'The Moose' in his recent *On Elizabeth Bishop* (2015) makes the comparison to cinema explicit:

> It gradually becomes clear that, in the same way a camera can move from filming a scene to filming a face to filming the world as seen by the eyes in that face, the poem has moved into the core of a single sensibility. (21)

In a recent podcast discussion of the poem for *The New Yorker*, perhaps inspired by Tóibín's reading, the poet Nick Laird makes a similar suggestion when host Paul Muldoon asks him, 'What is it that makes this such a great poem, would you say?' Laird immediately answers, 'It's very cinematic.'

In what follows, I want to take the analogy of Bishop's filmic proclivities slightly further, to look at particular splicing or editing effects that become prominent throughout 'The Moose'. This includes the microscopic close-ups, for instance, as fog crystals

> form and slide and settle
> in the white hens' feathers,
> in gray glazed cabbages (*Poems* 190)

with sweet peas clinging 'to their wet white string' or bumblebees creeping 'inside the foxgloves (stanzas 8–9), which work towards the sort of defamiliarisation described by Anderson. However, the movement between 'different perspectives and scales', which Anderson and Tóibín both point to (and which Laird compares to zooming in and out on Google Earth), seems even more striking in 'The Moose', and more essential to its narrative construction. In this light, the poem may begin to resemble a miniature screenplay on the page, and in a way that might help us reinterpret certain details. The long opening sentence, for instance, is often misread as introducing the bus's journey or views from the bus itself, moving through the Nova Scotia landscape. It seems obvious, however, from

> the windshield flashing pink,
> pink glancing off of metal,
> brushing the dented flank
> of blue, beat-up enamel

that the initial point of view is not only outside the bus, but watching from a fixed point. In fact, as Laird suggests, 'in cinematic terms', the first four stanzas make use of 'lots of establishing shots' (*New Yorker* podcast). With the scene set, the disembodied perspective in stanza 5 (the 'single sensibility', as Tóibín calls it) is finally attributed to our never-named 'lone traveller' protagonist, who has watched the windshield glare in the distance and eventually the detail of its 'dented flank' as it approaches their stop. This slow montage, establishing the initial setting, is then marked out from the journey that follows by a kind of unmarked voice-over for that traveller figure, saying: 'Goodbye to the elms, / to the farm, to the dog.' (For emphasis, the only other time this direct narrative voice intervenes is in the poem's climactic question, regarding the 'sensation of joy' after the moose encounter.) In formal terms, the non-diegetic farewell also prefigures a contrast with the reported or paraphrased speech of other passengers that accumulates between these voice-over bookends.

As the journey begins, stanzas 8–12 consist entirely of exterior shots, or views from the bus more specifically. Here, the 'splicing' technique identified by Anderson helps to condense the first part of the drive, as the bus makes its way along the bay from Great Village, Nova Scotia, before turning north toward New Brunswick. The close vegetable montage of stanzas 8 and 9 gives way to a series of stops at various villages before the shot of a woman shaking a tablecloth 'after supper' gives way to nightfall. The manipulation of time, bringing us as quickly as possible to the night scene of the poem's second half, dovetails with the subtle 'editing' of passing villages, appearing out of order from their actual locations. (The order along the Trunk 2 road travelling west from Great Village would be Five Houses, Bass River, Upper, Middle, then Lower Economy, then Five Islands.)

Even when the sun is 'gone', from the start of stanza 11, Bishop makes use of the disorienting effect that isolated lights can have on film, where 'a red light swim[ming] through the dark' and 'two rubber boots' are 'illuminated'. Like a good film editor, Bishop uses the new passenger's entrance as the transition to our first interior shots, as the elderly woman enters 'with two market bags' and greets the driver. The brief exchange allows for the abbreviation of another few hours, skipping 100 kilometres north to the New Brunswick woods. It also breaks the perspective and introduces the inside of the bus as a scene of action. Stanza 14 looks outside the bus again, establishing the dark wood's moonlit atmosphere, in order to juxtapose it with the dream state induced among the passengers in the following stanza.

Although such narrative tools are not unique to cinema, once could argue that language in 'The Moose' – its unusual present tense, fragmented grammar and removed perspective – adheres surprisingly closely to screenplay conventions. Without suggesting Bishop had any intention of following such rules, it is possible to read lines like

> She regards us amicably.

> Moonlight as we enter
> the New Brunswick woods

as references to the viewer's plural first-person perspective, in a manner that would also have been employed in the film reviews and film magazines that Bishop read avidly. Other stage directions here are particularly script-like as well: 'The passengers lie back. / Snores. Some long sighs.'

IV

While this sort of screenplay reading could be applied to the rest of the poem, I want to shift the focus in this second half of the chapter to what it means for the climactic moose encounter specifically. The scene structure of the second half of the poem is clear enough: stanzas 15–20 describe the 'dreamy divagation' of night-time conversations within the bus, becoming more and more precise in their reported dialogue. In stanza 21, however, a whirl of memory is triggered (though still without a first-person perspective) in which the voices 'talking the way they talked' blend into those heard in childhood, with disconnected images that are difficult not to picture in the soft focus of film flashbacks. With the layering of fragmented dialogue throughout these stanzas, Bishop seems to have moved beyond her earlier formulation of the link between memory and cinema, in a notebook describing the past as 'a silent film "high and dry" and far away' (Anderson 123).

As the protagonist – whose 'sensibility' continues to structure these transitions – drifts toward sleep, the sound and visuals are rendered all the more ethereal by the sudden interruption halfway through stanza 22, leading to the star turn we will have been awaiting since the title. But even that entrance is mediated by a 'smash cut' out of the flashback, indicated with the line's initial em dash: ' — Suddenly'. First we see the driver, as he '*stops* with a jolt, / [and] *turns* off his lights' (emphasis added), the only place in the 168-line poem where two active verbs begin adjacent lines. Then the following line, for the showstopping visual, shifts abruptly to the first exterior shot in nine stanzas:

> A moose has come out of
> the impenetrable wood
> and stands there, looms, rather,
> in the middle of the road.
> It approaches: it sniffs at
> the bus's hot hood.

This stanza not only includes five verbs – more than any of the other twenty-seven stanzas, most of which get by with one or two – but also includes the single instance of the present perfect in the poem. The moose *has come*. It is already there when the poem cuts, creating a kind of 'jump scare', in horror parlance, then subverted by the slowness with which it *stands, looms, approaches* and *sniffs*. The passengers articulate the typical hysterical relief that tends to follow these jolts, typified by the bus's mansplainer, who 'assures us' (and himself) the creature is 'Perfectly harmless . . .'. All of this works perfectly within the diegetic film logic, as the last five stanzas of the poem alternate neatly between exterior and interior views: we look at the moose (stanza 24), get passengers' reactions (25), watch some more (26), have the driver's comments (26), then pull away (27). Nick Laird and Paul Muldoon's half-serious debate about whether the moose could realistically be smelled within the bus overlooks Bishop's tidy and undeniably film-like structure in this conclusion (*New Yorker* podcast).

Muldoon's sense that 'it's almost as if we've found ourselves outside the bus' also points, I want to argue, to a crucial inconsistency with the famous view of the moose, back in stanza 24:

> Towering, antlerless,
> high as a church

If we were to judge this in empirical terms, the trouble here is perspective. On average, an adult female eastern moose will reach a height of around six feet at the shoulder. The best assumption, based on a Greyhound advertisement from June 1946, announcing the new route Bishop took from Nova Scotia to Boston in August of that year, is that we're talking about a Yellow Coach model 843, which were used by Eastern Canadian Greyhound Lines at the time, and which stand at around nine and a half feet tall. In other words, from the bus itself, you would be looking down at the moose, or at best into its eyes. The image of it 'towering' or appearing anywhere near 'high as a church' can only be a trick angle from *outside* the bus, rather than the perspective of anyone on the bus. In this big moment, Bishop breaks the hitherto 'single sensibility' suggested by Tóibín.

It would be fair enough to accept this bit of poetic licence, which describes, perhaps, how large the moose *seemed*. But I would argue that this forced low angle has everything to do with a much more basic, persistent concern with this iconic encounter: namely, what does it mean? Rather than compete with any number of gendered or psychoanalytic interpretations, or the likely tens of thousands of undergraduate essays on what the moose in Bishop's poem might symbolise, I want to suggest that the artifice of this 'shot' is part of how the poem resists reductive signification. As Tóibín writes:

> It would be easy to say that the moose, since this is a poem, must stand for something – the eternal, say, or the disruptive in nature, or the mystery of things – other than being a mere moose. But it resists the idea that it stands for something. Rather it *is* something. (22)

V

It may help to compare this moose sighting to a tradition of 'beastly encounters', which might be defined as a trope of seemingly profound and often heavily symbolic inter-species moments. In her essay 'My Private Property', the poet Mary Ruefle describes a typical encounter, which she assumes the reader will recognise (while comparing it to her encounter with a museum's shrunken head):

> We stood facing each other the way, when you come upon a deer unexpectedly, you both freeze for a moment, mutually startled, and in that exchange there seems to be but one glance, as if you and the other are sharing the same pair of eyes. (59)

Deer are common in these scenarios, perhaps for their heavy symbolic baggage or perhaps for their wider prevalence and relative height. In the final scene of Krzysztof Zanussi's social satire *Kontrakt* (1980), two partygoers, recovering from a night of revelry with a walk in the woods, suddenly meet a stag, which stares back defiantly as a dissonant chord strikes on the soundtrack and the film abruptly ends. In this case, the point seems to be that the terrifying and irreducible 'wildness' of the creature, of nature red in tooth and claw, cuts across the characters' bourgeois melodramas. In other cases, the epiphany is more specific, as in J. K. Rowling's novel *Harry Potter and the Prisoner of Azkaban* (1999), where the wizard protagonist first encounters his 'patronus' (like a spirit animal) in its stag form:

> It stopped on the bank. Its hooves made no mark on the soft ground as it stared at Harry with its large, silver eyes. Slowly, it bowed its antlered head. (347)

In plot terms, this is the moment when Harry realises his father also had a stag patronus, along with the ability to shape-shift into one.

Beyond the physical confrontation, there is an emphasis in each of these examples on the reciprocated stare, an exchange, as Ruefle puts it, in which 'there seems to be but one glance'. Horses are also popular for such scenes, with their large eyes. In the 2007 film *Michael Clayton*, George Clooney has a cryptic moment in a field with some wild horses, just before his car blows up and they scatter. Section XXVIII of Charles Reznikoff's 'Autobiography: New York' sequence from 1941 includes one of countless poetic versions of the trope, where the speaker addresses a fox who presages Bishop's moose in some ways:

> A fine fellow, trotting easily without a sound
> down the macadam road between the woods
> you heard me,
> turned your pointed head,
> and we took a long look at each other,
> fox and man;
> then, without any hurry, you went into the ferns,
> and left the road to the automobiles and me –
> to the heels and wheels of the citizens. (191)

Within animal studies, Jacques Derrida's naked encounter with his cat, in his late lecture 'The Animal That Therefore I Am', has become emblematic in its emphasis on the 'absolute alterity' by which the animal gaze exposes us to our own, less literal nakedness. Derrida describes this enigmatic but penetrating look, 'the insistent gaze of the animal, a benevolent or pitiless gaze, surprised or cognizant'. As in these examples, there is also the sense of wisdom behind the creature's look, as 'the gaze of a seer, visionary, or extra-lucid blind person' (4).

It is with such cultural expectations, based on our historical relationship with and projections on to non-human animals, that the reader approaches or is approached by Bishop's moose. As with the profound identification in Ruefle's account, the piercing reality of Zanussi's, the oedipal revelation of Rowling's, or the bodily shame affected in Derrida's, these encounters are typically structured in a way that either produces or accepts some sort of figurative meaning, something for the human participant to take away, beyond the creature's reality. In this context, the impulse towards 'symbolic' interpretations of Bishop's moose is unsurprising, as is the more typical reading of the poem's climactic moment as 'an affirmation of life', according to James McCorkle, who has not been alone in suggesting that 'the sight of this moose (or other) revitalizes the self and affirms the mystery in every being' (32).

Crucially, however, there is no such meeting of gazes in 'The Moose'. The word 'look' is repeated three times in the last four stanzas, following the creature's appearance, but merely calls attention to its casual disinterest, as 'she looks the bus over'. The repeated entreaty to 'Look!' also highlights the structural detachment or absence of a specific observer, via whom the reader might have performed that gazing loop. Even in her earlier poem 'The Fish', where we do have a clear speaker-subject *I* (and eye), and where sustained attention to the animal's visual organs sits at the centre of the poem, Bishop pointedly resists the more Romantic formula, noting that those eyes 'shifted a little, but *not* / to return to my stare' (*Poems* 44, emphasis added). In place of the returned stare, Bishop's depiction of the moose as a whole creature, eluding fragmentation, similarly acknowledges and frustrates the traditional form of seemingly profound or symbolic interspecies encounters. In doing so, its more ambiguous presence is manipulated, in Anderson's words, 'through the use of different perspectives and scales', opening up new 'areas of vision [. . .] not dominated by tradition or authority' (14).

The species itself is well chosen for the mixed messages we are eventually offered instead. As noted above, it is worth remembering that the title is actually our first encounter with 'the moose', allowing the twenty-two stanzas before the word or animal's entrance into the body of the poem plenty of time for that signifier's cultural baggage to accrue in the reader's imagination. Like other large game animals, descriptions of moose – and their size in particular – are easily adapted to narrative requirements, especially those of hunters. At the start of his chapter on moose hunting in *The Bowhunter's Handbook*, for instance, the sportsman M. R. James begins his stereotypical fisherman's tale: 'Believe me, at three short yards, a red-eyed rutting moose is an imposing sight' (196). In her 1909 memoir *The New North*, on the other hand, Agnes Deans Cameron seems intent on diminishing her trophy:

> What an ungainly creature he looks as we draw in nearer, all legs and clumsy head, – a regular grasshopper on stilts! He reminds me of nothing so much as those animals we make for the baby by sticking four matches into a sweet biscuit. (347)

These exaggerated accounts are all the more flexible given the unlikeliness that anyone living outside a particular region of North America will have seen a live moose. Their resulting near-mythical status is captured in the recent graphic novel *Moose*, by the Belgian writer-artist Max de Radiguès and published by Nova Scotia-based Conundrum Press in 2015. Here, the bull moose that later helps the protagonist stand up to his bully is first shown standing over the boy where he has stumbled in the snow, before its height is emphasised in a smaller frame that, unusually for the medium, shows a first-person perspective of the towering creature, not unlike Bishop's editing technique. Muldoon falls into a familiar routine in the *New Yorker* podcast as well, asking Nick Laird whether he has ever seen a moose himself, then, when Laird says he hasn't, telling him of time he has spent in Vermont, where 'one might go down at dusk of an evening and more or less park beside one'. Muldoon conjures them as 'quite overwhelming, actually' – so 'huge', in fact, that the poem's length may have been necessary 'to take it all in' (*New Yorker* podcast). As with the hunters' tales, the poem itself implies a similar sense of good fortune in the spotting of the sacred-seeming beast, even for passengers presumably familiar with the area.

When the moose shows up at last, its movements are delineated before any spe-
cific visual detail is given, and most of those actions (with the possible exception of
'looms') are left fairly blank for the reader's imagination: 'It *approaches*; it *sniffs* at /
the bus's hot hood' (emphasis mine). Although the forced low-angle shot that follows,
of the moose 'towering [. . .] high as a church', might nod to expectations for the
transcendent animal encounter, this iconic view is firmly undercut, first by affirming its
'harmless'-ness, then by another voice on the bus, who finds 'It's awful plain'. Again,
the phrase, beyond its colloquial authenticity, may be read as a calculated contradic-
tion in terms, winking at the sublime awe in that banality.

Comparing this confrontation to the over-determined evocations of the trope
described above helps us see again how effectively Bishop's poem resists easy significa-
tion. The further example of an admittedly memorable scene from Stephen Frears's
2006 film *The Queen* sits in stark contrast at the other end of a spectrum of symbol-
ism. When Elizabeth II, played by Helen Mirren, finds herself stranded with a broken-
down Jeep on a hillside at Balmoral, the sudden appearance of a stag interrupts her
moment of tearful solitude and functions pivotally in the film's plot, as she gathers
herself to face the press after Diana's death. The scene has its own dark ambiguity,
especially when the same stag is spotted among the spoils of a hunt, but its clear pur-
pose in the script is emphasised by the cinematographer's self-conscious allusion to
Edwin Landseer's *Monarch of the Glen* (1851) in the heavily processed shot and fairy-
tale scoring. Elizabeth's exclamation 'Oh, you beauty!' is a far cry from 'It's awful
plain'. And yet the poem's rendering of the moose, outside that dialogue, as 'grand,
otherworldly', prompts a similarly overwhelming cry, as the narrative voice from near
the start of the poem bursts back in with its question:

> Why, why do we feel
> (we all feel) this sweet
> sensation of joy?

Rather than place Bishop's moose above or beyond the Romantic tradition of
beastly encounters, which tend to subjugate the animal's reality – first for the human
character's plot needs, then for the human viewer's/reader's sense of visual meaning –
I have hopefully shown some of the ways this scene brackets its contrivance within
the meticulous structure of the poem. Relating the poem to the personal and histori-
cal influence of cinema on Bishop's work simply helps us to draw out the careful
manipulations of the entire naturalistic episode. For admirers of Bishop's deceptive
artfulness elsewhere, this may be an awfully plain conclusion in itself, or a sense of
the poem that might be as readily aroused by the intricate, often inaudible variation
on ballad form she is using. Although I would not be willing to argue that Bishop
had screenplay form in mind for any substantial part of the twenty-five years it took
her to finish 'The Moose', reading it in this way, and against these examples, does
help us to reconsider the strategies by which so many of Bishop's poems acknowl-
edge their textual contingency, as all scripts must. Any script's performance is only
activated in relation to conventions brought to bear upon the text. In this case, an
awareness of the more typical, egocentric animal encounter offers just enough gaps
for us to reflect on those conventions. In lieu of long, meaningful looks, consoling us
with 'nature', the text itself stares back.

Works Cited

Anderson, Linda, *Elizabeth Bishop: Lines of Connection* (Edinburgh: Edinburgh University Press, 2014).

Bishop, Elizabeth, *Brazil* (Life World Library) (New York: Time Incorporated, 1962).

Bishop, Elizabeth, *One Art: The Selected Letters*, ed. Robert Giroux (London: Chatto & Windus, 1994).

Bishop, Elizabeth, and Robert Lowell, *Words in Air: The Complete Correspondence between Elizabeth Bishop and Robert Lowell*, ed. Thomas Travisano with Saskia Hamilton (New York: Farrar, Straus and Giroux, 2008).

Burt, Jonathan, *Animals in Film* (London: Reaktion Books, 2002).

Cameron, Agnes Deans, *The New North: Being Some Account of a Woman's Journey through Canada to the Arctic, 1909* (New York: D. Appleton and Company, 1910).

Cleghorn, Angus, and Jonathan Ellis (eds), *The Cambridge Companion to Elizabeth Bishop* (Cambridge: Cambridge University Press, 2014).

Costello, Bonnie, *Elizabeth Bishop: Questions of Mastery* (Cambridge, MA: Harvard University Press, 1991).

Derrida, Jacques, *The Animal That Therefore I Am* (New York: Fordham University Press, 2008).

Ellis, Jonathan, *Art and Memory in the Work of Elizabeth Bishop* (Aldershot: Ashgate, 2006).

Franklin, Chester M. (dir.), *Sequoia* (USA: MGM, 1934).

Frears, Stephen (dir.), *The Queen* (UK: Pathé Pictures, 2006).

Gilroy, Tony (dir.), *Michael Clayton* (USA: Warner Bros, 2007).

James, M. R., *The Bowhunter's Handbook*, 2nd edn (Iola, WI: Krause Publications, 2004).

Johnson, Martin, and Truman Talley (dirs), *Baboona* (USA: Fox Movietone News, 1935).

Laird, Nick, and Paul Muldoon, 'Nick Laird Reads Elizabeth Bishop', *The New Yorker: Poetry*, podcast, 18 May 2016.

Lumière, Louis (dir.), *La Sortie de l'usine Lumière à Lyon (Workers Leaving the Lumière Factory in Lyon)* (France: Lumière, 1895).

McCorkle, James, *The Still Performance: Writing, Self, and Interconnection in Five Postmodern American Poets* (Charlottesville: University Press of Virginia, 1989).

Millier, Brett C., *Elizabeth Bishop: Life and the Memory of It* (Berkeley: University of California Press, 1993).

Monteiro, George, *Elizabeth Bishop in Brazil and After: A Poetic Career Transformed* (Jefferson, NC: McFarland, 2012).

Monteiro, George (ed.), *Conversations with Elizabeth Bishop* (Jackson: University Press of Mississippi, 1996).

Porter, Edwin S. (or Jacob Blair Smith) (dir.), *Electrocuting an Elephant* (USA: Edison Manufacturing Company, 1903).

Radiguès, Max de, *Moose* (Wolfville: Conundrum Press, 2015).

Reznikoff, Charles, 'Autobiography: New York', *The Poems of Charles Reznikoff, 1918–1975*, ed. Seamus Cooney (Boston: Black Sparrow, 2005), pp. 184–95.

Rowling, J. K., *Harry Potter and the Prisoner of Azkaban* (London: Bloomsbury, 1999).

Ruefle, Mary, *My Private Property* (Seattle: Wave Books, 2016).

Samuels, Peggy, *Deep Skin: Elizabeth Bishop and Visual Art* (Ithaca: Cornell University Press, 2010).

Tóibín, Colm, *On Elizabeth Bishop* (Princeton: Princeton University Press, 2015).

Zanussi, Krzysztof (dir.), *Kontrakt* (Poland: Film Polski, 1980).

PART IV

PROSE

14

Migrating Letters

Sophie Baldock

From the Floridian birds of *North & South* and *A Cold Spring* to the Brazilian, Nova Scotian and New England birds of *Questions of Travel* and *Geography III*, birds are everywhere in Bishop's poetry and prose. For Bishop, writing poetry was itself an attempt to capture a sense of freedom and flight. In her 1934 essay on Gerard Manley Hopkins, 'Notes on Timing', Bishop admired his ability to portray in poems 'not a thought, but a mind thinking', an idea she borrowed from an essay by Morris Croll titled 'The Baroque Style in Prose' (quoted in *Prose* 473). This style of writing, which Bishop argues applies as much to poetry as it does to prose, involves the capacity to 'catch and preserve the movement of an idea' (*Prose* 273) while it is still alive in the mind, like the catching of a wild bird. Similarly, Tom Paulin has applied this concept to Bishop's epistolary style and the way that her letters catch and preserve a moment in time. Paulin suggests that Bishop's letters 'enact her addictive communicativeness, her aim to achieve an illusion of complete immediacy' (221) as if her correspondent is in the room with her. Bishop's letters are themselves objects that 'fly' between and connect correspondents, as in the epistolary-inspired poem 'Invitation to Miss Marianne Moore', where Bishop imagines correspondents like birds greeting one another from across the Brooklyn Bridge. Crucially, writing letters was also a way for Bishop to keep poetic ideas aloft, and her correspondence demonstrates how she collected bits of description that she later used, albeit altered and transformed, in poems.

In this chapter, I look at the connections between the letters that Bishop wrote in the first few years of her residence in Brazil in the 1950s and her Brazil poems, focusing particularly on the long title poem of her collection *Questions of Travel* (1965). I argue, building on previous analyses of Bishop's correspondence, that Bishop borrows from her Brazil letters a sense of immediacy that she then seeks to recreate in her poems. This is what gives Bishop's Brazil poems, like her letters, their sense of in-the-moment spontaneity and vitality, as if the reader is watching 'a mind thinking' (Croll 430) and making observations in real time. My analysis of Bishop's creative method is based on her own early fascination with 'the baroque style' as described by Morris Croll, which she explored in relation to birds in Hopkins's poems in her 1934 essay 'Gerard Manley Hopkins: Notes on Timing in His Poetry', written while she was still an undergraduate at Vassar.

Croll used the term 'baroque' to describe the prose style of several seventeenth-century prose writers, including scientists and philosophers such as Thomas Browne and Blaise Pascal. The hallmarks of this style include 'expressiveness rather than formal beauty' (Croll 428), an apparent lack of revision and a sense of looseness, incompleteness, movement and energy often achieved through the use of metaphor and long, complex sentence structures. What struck Bishop particularly, as she observed in 'Notes on Timing', was the way that Croll's ideas about prose seemed to map perfectly on to the central components of Hopkins's poetry, and his attempts to recreate, in deliberately imperfect and seemingly contorted ways, an impression of the original spark of inspiration behind his poems. Bishop's descriptions of Hopkins's baroque style, and his use of sprung rhythm in poems such as 'The Windhover', often reach for avian metaphors to describe this process. She likens Hopkins's sense of poetic timing to shooting a clay pigeon where the marksman 'must shoot not at it directly but a certain distance in front of it' (*Prose* 472) in order to hit the pigeon. In a similar manner, Bishop writes, 'Hopkins, I believe, has chosen to stop his poems, set them to paper, at the point in their development where they are still incomplete, still close to the first kernel of truth or apprehension that gave rise to them' (*Prose* 472). The aim of Hopkins's poems, as Bishop describes it, is to capture this sense of the feverish excitement of their creation. She explains that the goal is 'to catch and preserve the movement of an idea, the point being to crystallize it early enough so that it still has movement' (*Prose* 473), as if describing the careful preservation of a rare tropical bird for display in a museum cabinet. Similarly, Bishop characterises Hopkins's idiosyncratic scansion and use of 'rove over' lines as lending his poems 'a fluid, detailed surface, made hesitant, lightened, slurred, weighed or feathered', gesturing at the birds that the poems simultaneously describe and try to mimic. These were 'baroque' effects that Bishop strived for in her own poetry, as she explains in a 1933 letter to poet-friend Donald Stanford, written at the same time as she was drafting the essay:

> But the best part, which perfectly describes the sort of poetic convention I should like to make for myself (and which explains, I think, something of Hopkins), is this: 'Their purpose (the writers of Baroque prose) was to portray, not a thought, but a mind thinking . . . They knew that an idea separated from the act of experiencing it is not the idea that was experienced. The ardor of its conception in the mind is a necessary part of its truth.' (*One Art* 12)

Bishop's own poems seek to express a sense of energy, immediacy, looseness and incompleteness. The idea that a poem should represent 'not a thought, but a mind thinking' and preserve a feeling of movement is central to her poetic method.

Bishop's fascination with the baroque style and its imaginative connection to birds did not end with this early essay. Instead, Bishop's thinking about the subject continued to develop throughout her career, particularly in her Brazil poems, where attempts to 'catch and preserve the movement of an idea' (*Prose* 473) in a letter, a journal or a poem take on a new significance. In Brazil, where the baroque is associated with colonisation by Portuguese settlers, and is visible in church architecture, Bishop becomes increasingly aware of troubling associations between attempts to capture and control ideas, people and animals. While Bishop did embark on travels within Brazil during the time she spent living there, to the baroque town of Ouro Preto, and on a trip down the Amazon in 1961, much of the knowledge she acquired came from her extensive and eclectic reading about the country. Her letters to friends describe the letters, journals and travelogues that she was reading, including nineteenth-century accounts by Richard Burton in *Explorations of the Highlands of Brazil* (first published in 1869) and Charles Darwin in his *Diary of the Voyage of H.M.S. Beagle* (1933). Bishop was also rereading

Emily Dickinson's letters and poems in Brazil. Although Dickinson rarely travelled beyond the confines of her father's house, and certainly never to South America, her imaginative travels, and particularly her letter-poem 'A Route of Evanescence', inform Bishop's writing. Bishop reuses and reframes elements from these sources in a way that recalls the 'baroque style'. She gives her poem 'Questions of Travel' a unique sense of time and immediacy by incorporating images and phrases from her own letters, a fleeting and enigmatic allusion to Dickinson's letter-poem, along with sections from Charles Darwin's *Beagle Diary*.

Bishop often incorporated sections of prose and letter-like elements in her poems to lend them a vivid sense of immediacy. Recent analysis has found close and complex connections between Bishop's poetry and letters. Jonathan Ellis and Joelle Biele have shown that Bishop uses her letters as an animated, and partly self-sufficient, form of draft material for her poetry. Ellis writes: 'letters are not so much the rooted floor on which Bishop's published work rests, as the imaginative balloon of images and words itching to be released' (*Art and Memory* 175). In her article on the Brazil letters and poems, Biele argues that Bishop viewed her letters as 'sentient rough drafts' (96) that allowed her to try out her writing voice, and to furnish many of the details of the poems. Biele finds connections between passages in Bishop's letters and 'The Armadillo', which was originally titled 'From a Letter' (95). More recently, Heather Treseler and Siobhan Phillips have drawn on archival material to reframe the significance of the letters in relation to psychoanalytic and ethical or intersubjective models. Treseler argues that Bishop adopts 'letter-like' qualities, such as 'the conceit of privacy', a sense of 'absent presence' and 'reciprocity', in several unpublished poems (88, 93, 102). These include two poems from a series titled 'Dear Dr.' in a Key West notebook Bishop kept in the 1940s in which she uses the frame of the letter as a means of exploring the psychological trauma of the early loss of her mother. Phillips observes that Bishop's poems borrow an ethical commitment to collaboration and two-party exchange from her correspondence, and she highlights the significance of birds in relation to/as correspondents. Her analysis of Bishop's draft poem 'The Swan with Two Necks', based on the letters of Jane and Thomas Carlyle, shows how 'the double bird' of the poem's title acts 'as a symbol of the Carlyles' relationship – and the epistolary dynamics of that relationship in particular' (343). What I think these critics have in common is a desire to see Bishop's letters as continuous with, rather than inferior to, her poetry. They also share a sense that Bishop borrows from her letters, and seeks to recreate in poems the sense of energy, intimacy, collaborative exchange and provisionality that are so evident in the correspondence.

Images and phrases that occur in Bishop's letters written in Brazil and sent to friends in North America, particularly those to Marianne Moore and Kit and Ilse Barker, reoccur and seem to carry over to the Brazil poems. One of the key figures that makes the journey from letter to poem, and also offers a way of conceptualising the physical movement of letters, both between spaces and between genres, is the bird. I will look at two birds in particular that Bishop mentions in letters: her beloved toucan, Uncle Sam, and the hummingbird in 'Questions of Travel'. I argue that, although he is not named in the poem, Sammy the toucan is present in 'Questions of Travel', and descriptions of Sammy sent in Bishop's early Brazil letters offer an insight into the sources behind the poem's questioning of fantasises of travel and ownership. The other bird in the poem, which flies in at the end of stanza 2, is 'the tiniest green hummingbird in the world', and I want to suggest it acts as a double for the physical (and psychological) path that Bishop herself, and her letters, take from South to North.

Bishop's Brazil letters amply demonstrate the way that she collected observations, experiences and images that she later reused in her poetry. She writes to the Barkers in 1953: 'I've been thinking so much about writing you that I've collected a lot of related themes and odds & ends' (*One Art* 258). Letters to the Barkers and others emphasise the strangeness of her new surroundings. Bishop arrived in Brazil in November 1951 and by February 1952 she was living with Lota at Samambaia. The house was still being built, and Bishop's letters from the time are full of news of this project as well as observations and anecdotes about her surreal new life living on the edge of a cliff in a half-built house in a strange new country. Poems such as 'Arrival at Santos' and 'Questions of Travel' take from her letters a particular tone, which sits or perhaps, like the unbuilt house, seems to teeter somewhere on the edge of the genres of letter and travelogue.

Descriptions of Bishop's pet toucan, Sammy, in letters from this period, particularly one to Moore written on 14 February 1952, find their way into 'Questions of Travel', although specificities are erased and replaced with a more general, philosophical tone. Sammy the toucan is not present in 'Questions of Travel', but elements of Bishop's descriptions of him are. In her letter to Moore, Bishop writes:

> The zoo man – I can't believe this yet myself, and we have no common language even – gave me a TOUCAN for my birthday, the other day. He, or she (the toucan), is very tame and mischievous – throws coins around the room – flies off with the toast from my breakfast tray. He is black, to begin with, but with electric-blue eyes, a blue-and-yellow marked beak, blue feet, and red feathers here & there – a bunch under his tail like a sunset when he goes to sleep . . . (*One Art* 236)

The descriptions of Sammy that Bishop provides are like small sketches made in preparation for a larger painting or, in this case, poem. Although, in the journey from letter to poem, Sammy the toucan disappears, he leaves a trail of feathers behind. I think he is at least in part the inspiration for the final image in stanza 2, in which Bishop asks, 'Oh, must we dream our dreams / and have them, too? / And have we room / for one more folded sunset, still quite warm?' (*Poems* 91). Sammy is also present in the sense that comes across in this line, which seems like a twist on the familiar concept of having one's cake and eating it too, that there is something sinful and excessive about dreams that become a reality. In a letter to the Barkers, Bishop describes the gift of the bird as fulfilling 'my lifelong dream' (*One Art* 234). And in another letter to Dr Anny Baumann, she cautions that wish-fulfilment seems so quick and easy in Brazil that it is almost dangerous to make them:

> There are so many mice that I said I wanted to get a cat and the animal dealer who gave me a toucan immediately said, 'Oh – would you like a pair of Siamese? I'm importing 200.' So I guess I shall have them soon – wishes seem to come true here at such a rate one is almost afraid to make them any more. (*One Art* 243–4)

The recurrent images of dreams and references to 'exaggerated' landscapes, in both letters and 'Questions of Travel', paint Brazil as a kind of dream space. Bishop's confusion over the inverted seasons of Brazil, and her sense of its dream-like, upside-down qualities, are reflected in the 'mountains' of stanza 1 that appear as the upside-down 'hulls of capsized ships'. Real and imagined geographies overlap in the poem where shape-shifting clouds appear to 'spill over the sides' of mountains, turning first into 'mile-long-shiny-tearstains', and eventually 'waterfalls' (*Poems* 91).

In this section I want to suggest that the figure of the hummingbird in 'Questions of Travel' encapsulates this deliberate blurring together of real and imagined geographies, as well as the genres of letter and poem. The bird makes a fleeting appearance in the middle of stanza 2 as the speaker asks:

> What childishness is it that while there's a breath of life
> in our bodies, we are determined to rush
> to see the sun the other way around?
> The tiniest green hummingbird in the world? (*Poems* 91)

Although there are many hummingbirds that are native to Brazil, Bishop may be thinking here of the migratory ruby-throated hummingbird, which, like Bishop herself, and like the letters she writes to friends in North America, makes a journey from North to South and back again. The ruby-throated hummingbird is tiny and green, with a flash of red on its neck visible in certain lights, and it makes a thousand-mile yearly migration from as far north as Nova Scotia over the Gulf of Mexico to as far south as Panama. It is a hummingbird Bishop would have seen while growing up in Canada, and which (almost) connects her two 'homes' of Nova Scotia and Brazil. Since Bishop was also writing her autobiographical short story 'In the Village' at this time, the connection is perhaps not just a flight of fancy. She remarks in a letter to the Barkers in October 1952 that it is amazing how travelling to Brazil has prompted her to write 'In the Village', inspired by what she calls 'total recall about Nova Scotia – geography must be more mysterious than we realise even' (*One Art* 249). I think these comments inform the lines in 'Questions of Travel' in which the speaker wonders about the 'childishness' of rushing 'to see the sun the other way around'. They also confuse our sense of the geography of the next line, 'The tiniest green hummingbird in the world?', for it could be located in either Brazil or Nova Scotia. If this hummingbird is a migratory ruby-throat it adds to the irony in the poem of rushing 'to see the sun the other way around', only to see where you originally came from more clearly.

The hummingbird in 'Questions of Travel' also echoes Emily Dickinson, whose poems and letters Bishop was rereading during her early years in Brazil. Bishop's hummingbird recalls Dickinson's poem 'A Route of Evanescence' and Dickinson's own deliberately confused geography, since ruby-throated hummingbirds do not migrate quite as far south as Brazil, nor do they migrate to North Africa as Dickinson has it:

> A Route of Evanescence
> With a revolving Wheel
> A Resonance of Emerald
> A Rush of Cochineal
> And every Blossom on the Bush
> Adjusts it's tumbled Head –
> The Mail from Tunis, probably,
> An easy Morning's Ride. (Johnson II 640)

The hummingbird here is a postal metaphor for the way that letters travel and connect recipients. The poem was originally sent in/as a letter to Dickinson's friend Helen Hunt Jackson in 1879. As Hugh Haughton observes, the poem mingles genres so much that it becomes difficult to see where one ends and the other begins: 'This is an example of a letter that becomes a poem, or a poem sent in and as part of a letter. Which is it? The poem is a riddle, but its status is riddling too. As the inscription records, the tiny missive is a portrait not of a multi-coloured wheeled vehicle but of a tiny mobile bird' (58).

The poem's riddling status does not end there. As Bonnie Costello remarks, Dickinson's poem contains a further puzzle relating to the bird's species and the poem's geography. The glittering green and flash of red point to the hummingbird's status as a ruby-throat, and given this, '[t]he mail in this case could not possibly be from Tunis. The hummer is a New World bird and, as the ruby-throat is Amherst's only visitor, her mail must be from Mexico or Cuba.' In the context of nineteenth-century representations of the hummingbird, Dickinson's fusion of the real and the make-believe is not unique. Costello traces representations of hummingbirds in the work of famous nineteenth-century naturalists including John James Audubon, John Gould and Martin Johnson Heade. The nineteenth century saw a growing fascination with these jewel-like birds, and a desire to collect them: 'At the heyday of New World export 3,000 skins of one species were shipped at a Brazilian port in one month; in 1888, 400,000 skins were auctioned' (Costello). This was matched by a demand for paintings and lithograph prints of tropical birds, which tended to tread a line between fantasy and reality. Despite never having visited South America, John Gould produced a five-volume set of hummingbird lithographs, issued between 1849 and 1861, which sold thousands.

Dickinson's letter-poem, with its nod to the status of these tiny birds as collectible objects, offers clues to the fleeting inclusion of the 'tiniest green hummingbird' in Bishop's poem, and its mediations on questions of travel, freedom and enclosure. Bishop's early residence in Brazil coincided with her developing interest in, and appreciation for, Dickinson's poems and letters. This was sparked by the publication of several new editions of Dickinson's work in the 1950s, particularly Thomas H. Johnson's 1955 edition of *The Poems of Emily Dickinson*, which for the first time made available a complete collection of her poems that replicated her manuscripts as closely as possible. Bishop was rereading Dickinson's poems at the same time as she was drafting or redrafting 'Questions of Travel', as well as attempting drafts of a poem that linked Gerard Manley Hopkins and Dickinson, presenting the two poets as 'self-caged birds' (*Prose* 412).[1] In the year before her voyage to Brazil, Bishop had also written a review of Dickinson's letters to Dr and Mrs Josiah Gilbert, titled 'Love from Emily' and published in 1951 in *The New Republic* (*Prose* 262–3). Although Dickinson's hummingbird is not mentioned in the letters to the Gilberts that Bishop reviewed, it does appear towards the end of the volume of Dickinson's letters that Bishop also owned.[2] Thus, Bishop is very likely to have seen and read 'A Route of Evanescence' in 1951 at the time of writing her review, just prior to her arrival in Brazil. Certainly, the migratory ruby-throated hummingbird, with its yearly transcontinental passage, acts as an image for travelling letters in Dickinson's poem. Given Bishop's figurative travels between Brazil and Nova Scotia during the writing of *Questions of Travel* and 'In the Village', this tiny travelling bird must also have caught her imagination.

The bird-like airborne movement of Dickinson's thoughts is central to Bishop's review of the letters to the Gilberts. Bishop quotes a letter in which Dickinson writes, 'I'd love to be a bird or a bee, that whether hum or sing, still might be near you' (quoted in *Prose* 262). The insect-like hummingbird is perhaps again hovering just out of the frame here. Bishop goes on to say that these sentimental 'embarrassing remarks' are 'rescued in the nick of time by a sentence like, "If it wasn't for broad daylight, and cooking-stoves, and roosters, I'm afraid you would have occasion to smile at my letters often, but so sure as "this mortal" essays immortality, a crow from a neighbouring farmyard dissipates the illusion, and I am here again"' (262). This is reminiscent of Dickinson's remark in another letter that 'A Letter always feels to me like immortality because it is the mind alone without corporeal friend' (Johnson II 460). Here, a crow breaks the spell as everyday elements like the 'cooking-stoves' and 'roosters' intrude on the letter's 'illusion' of 'immortality', drowning out the ethereal hum of the bird/bee. As in Bishop's 'Roosters', crowing cocks are associated with brute reality: 'At four o'clock / in the gun-metal blue dark / we hear the first crow of the first cock' (*Poems* 36). However, as Bishop observes, it is the inclusion of these everyday elements, roosters as well as hummingbirds, and the abrupt change in tone in a single letter from rapturous devotion to self-mocking humour, which rescue Dickinson's letters and elevate them from mere expressions of 'extreme sentimentality' (*Prose* 262).

As Vidyan Ravinthiran has observed, what drew Bishop to Dickinson's letters was their sense of freedom and simultaneous resistance to facile confessionalism, both reminiscent of the baroque prose stylists: 'Bishop finds in Dickinson a poet with a very different relationship to prose; also a resister of the confessional, who reveals herself to the reader in a style closer to the baroque prose writers Bishop admired' (92). Bishop praises the 'terse and epigrammatic qualities' of Dickinson's letters, concluding that 'these letters have structure and strength. It is the sketchiness of the water-spider, tenaciously holding to its upstream position by means of the faintest ripples, while making one aware of the current of death and darkness below' (*Prose* 263). Like hummingbirds, water-spiders must constantly move in order to hold their position. Jonathan Ellis remarks in relation to Bishop's critique of Dickinson's letters: 'The crucial thing in all this is movement. A letter had to be in flight from its author to be seen as art, yet it had to retain a dive and shape characteristic enough to recall its maker' (*Art and Memory* 157). This bird-like movement and ability to move from the autobiographical to the descriptive, and back again, is very like Bishop's own epistolary style.

Although it is clear that Bishop's admiration for Dickinson and her poems grew during her residence in Brazil, an unfinished draft poem titled 'Notes for the E. Dickinson/Hopkins Poem', begun in 1955, demonstrates a lingering ambivalence surrounding Dickinson and her work. The draft links together Dickinson and Hopkins, listing their similar birth and death dates, and compares their lives of solitude and asceticism. It centres on the characterisation of the two poets as 'self-caged birds' (as Bishop explains in a later letter to Anne Stevenson, *Prose* 412), and meditates on forms of writerly enclosure. Bishop depicts the two poets carefully and painstakingly constructing their own cages:

> . . . peeled withies & a village elegance
> They chose, themselves, their cages, one
> . . one – the other – made by hand
> peeled withies, cut along the brook – (Bishop Papers 74.14)

'Peeled withies' refers to a strong, flexible willow stem, used to create structures like baskets or, in this case, birdcages. The phrase recalls Bishop's description of the 'structure and strength' of Dickinson's letters. Yet here the focus is not on freedom, but on the way that the intricately constructed imaginary worlds created by these two poets became a cage that enclosed them.

In this fragmentary draft we see elements and ideas that Bishop explores, in a different but related way, in 'Questions of Travel'. Images of birds, poems and their authors intertwine. Bishop connects feathers with quill pens: 'FEATHERS / barbs, barbules, hooklets vanes / 'structured colours'? quill & shaft'. Later in the draft Bishop notes that the 'metallic, prismatic' feathers of certain birds (including hummingbirds, although she does not specify this) are in fact 'horny outgrowths', and it is not pigments but 'structural peculiarities' which give the feathers their colour. Moreover, references in the draft to 'elaborate, wires & sliding doors / pseudo-gothic (Gothic revival!)' correspond with the 'whittled fantasies of wooden cages' in 'Questions of Travel', and its depiction of fanciful handmade objects as allegories for poems. The sense of ambivalent admiration in the draft tallies with what Bishop later says about Dickinson in a letter to Anne Stevenson: 'I still hate the oh-the-pain-of-it-all poems, but I admire the others, and, mostly, phrases more than whole poems. I particularly admire her having dared to do it all, all alone – a bit like Hopkins in that' (*Prose* 412). Bishop both admired and rejected Dickinson's chosen life of solitude and self-denial. However, as she suggests, certain 'phrases' stayed with her and influenced her poems. Dickinson may be in part the inspiration behind the speaker's regret in the third and fourth stanzas of 'Questions of Travel' when she imagines what 'a pity' it would have been not to have travelled but instead to have stayed 'at home', as Pascal advised, 'sitting quietly in one's room' (*Poems* 92).

In the poem, various sources that Bishop had encountered and read merge and crystallise, including her reading of Charles Darwin's *Beagle Diary*. Darwin's diary is another example of 'a mind thinking'. The spontaneity and energy that Darwin manages to capture in his prose informs the imagery and shifting temporal structure of Bishop's poem. Although several critics have observed Darwin's influence on Bishop's poetry, previous analyses have focused on her reading of the later *Journal of Researches* (first published in 1839).[3] However, Bishop's letters demonstrate that during her early residence in Brazil she was reading the *Beagle Diary*. She wrote to Moore in 1953 that she had 'just finished Darwin's Diary on the *Beagle* – not the Journal, although I guess it's mostly the same – and I thought it was wonderful' (*One Art* 257). Although there are similarities between the two versions, the earlier *Beagle Diary*, first published in 1933, is a direct transcription of Darwin's manuscript diaries that accompanied him on the voyage, portions of which he sent home to his family to read along with letters, and thus it provides a vivid record of his first-hand, immediate impressions.

Darwin's *Beagle Diary* exhibits a number of characteristics that tally with the attributes that Morris Croll identifies in seventeenth-century baroque prose. The development of scientific theory through the gradual and careful accumulation of what Bishop, in her 'Darwin letter', calls 'facts and minute details' (*Prose* 414) mirrors the way that baroque prose often moves from a 'literal to a metaphoric statement' where the reader sees the 'author's mind turning toward a general truth, which emerges complete and abstract' (Croll 435). Croll's description of Thomas Browne's scientific writings is an almost perfect depiction of Darwin's prose in the *Diary*: 'He writes like a philosophical scientist making notes of his observation as it occurs. We see his pen move and stop as he thinks' (448). It seems as if Bishop is also thinking back to this passage in Croll's essay when she writes to Anne Stevenson in her 'Darwin letter':

> But reading Darwin, one admires the beautiful solid case being built up out of his endless heroic *observations*, almost unconscious or automatic – and then comes a sudden forgetful relaxation, a forgetful phrase, and one *feels* the strangeness of his undertaking, sees the lonely young man, his eyes fixed on facts and minute details, sinking or sliding giddily off into the unknown. (*Prose* 414)

Several passages from Darwin's diary correspond to passages in 'Questions of Travel', particularly Darwin's depiction of Brazil as a fantastical space. Following a trip to mountains near Rio de Janeiro in March 1832, Darwin observes, 'Brazilian scenery is nothing more nor less than a view in the Arabian Nights, with the advantage of reality. – The air is deliciously cool & soft; full of enjoyment one fervently desires to live in retirement in this new & grander world' (*Beagle Diary* 43). Bishop's clouds overflowing in 'soft slow-motion' match Darwin's 'deliciously cool & soft' air. Darwin's diary also records the thrill of a hummingbird sighting (73). This is perhaps another source, along with Dickinson's letter-poem, for the 'tiniest green hummingbird' in 'Questions of Travel'. In a 1953 letter to Pearl Kazin, in which Bishop describes a trip to the baroque town Ouro Preto, her language again recalls Darwin's delight in observing Brazilian scenery. She writes: 'This place is *wonderful*, Pearl. I just spend too much time in looking at it and not working enough. I only hope you don't have to get to be forty-two before you feel so at home' (*One Art* 262).

However, despite the casual dismissiveness of her comments, 'just [. . .] looking' at things is a central facet of Bishop's poetics. In 'Questions of Travel' she complicates the implications of spending 'too much time in looking at [things] and not working enough' where careful observation is not a wasteful but a rich and resonant activity. This comment is also similar to the way that Bishop describes the practice of letter writing itself. In a letter to Kit and Ilse Barker, Bishop writes that she loves to write letters because it is 'kind of like working without really doing it' (*One Art* 273). Critics have found this last comment difficult to read as straightforward. Brett Millier and Joelle Biele observe that writing letters *is* a form of working for Bishop, though she might not recognise it, and observations in letters often turn up later in poems after undergoing a kind of artistic distillation process.[4] Looking at things and writing letters were both valuable forms of working for Bishop. They are central to the accumulation of 'facts and minute details' that underpins both Bishop's and Darwin's working methods.

But when does 'just [. . .] looking' turn into a desire for possession? A kind of touristic window-shopping is not enough to satisfy 'the traveller' (*Poems* 92) in Bishop's 'Questions of Travel', who desires not only to 'dream our dreams' but to 'have them too' and take home 'one more folded sunset' as a keepsake from their travels. Further sections of Darwin's diary appear to inform the poem, including the temptation on the part of 'the traveller' (*Beagle Diary* 73; *Poems* 92) – a phrase that both Darwin and Bishop employ as a third-person description of themselves – to treat Brazil as a fantasy, or 'a view in the Arabian Nights' (*Beagle Diary* 43) to use Darwin's words. For example, Darwin observes that the exaggerated scenery is like that of an opera or theatre, writing: 'I do not know what epithet such scenery deserves: beautiful is much too tame; every form, every colour is such a complete exaggeration of what one has ever beheld before. – If it may be so compared, it is like one of the gayest scenes in the Opera House or Theatre' (70). These same thoughts are found in sections of Bishop's poem that use theatrical metaphors and refer to the scenery as 'exaggerated'. In the second stanza Bishop's speaker asks, 'Is it right to be watching strangers in a play / in this strangest of theatres?' and at the beginning of the third stanza adds, 'But surely it would have been a pity / not to have seen the trees along this road, / really exaggerated in their beauty, / not to have seen them gesturing / like noble pantomimists, robed in pink' (*Poems* 91).

Although it seems clear that Bishop picked up observations and phrases from the *Beagle Diary*, there is a subtle difference in tone between the two texts. Where Darwin observes, Bishop questions. There is a hint of self-consciousness in Darwin's phrasing – 'if it may be so compared' – which Bishop elaborates on and extends in her poem. Darwin's tentative unease becomes the question: 'Is it right to be watching strangers in a play?' Bishop's is a stronger questioning of the dangers of viewing a country as a form of spectacle, and beautiful scenery as something that, like the specimens that Darwin collected, can be packed up and taken home in a suitcase. Observation, such as that of the naturalist and/or poet, is something to be admired for its beauty but also questioned for its attempts to possess or capture that beauty. In this context, the 'beautiful solid case being built up out of [Darwin's] endless heroic *observations*' that Bishop describes in her letter to Stevenson is reminiscent of a museum cabinet. Careful observation, on the other hand, does not seek to cage and control, but allows its subjects to retain a sense of subjectivity and freedom. The theme of escape is also important here. As Bishop says in the Darwin letter, 'What one seems to want in art, in experiencing it, is the same thing necessary for its creation, a self-forgetful, perfectly useless concentration. (In this sense it is always "escape," don't you think?' (*Prose* 414). For Bishop, art can be an escape into a kind of dream world, albeit one that should still retain a connection with reality.

Bishop characterised her life in Brazil as a form of escapism. As her letters show, she was both giddy with the euphoria of her new-found Brazilian life, and sceptical of the illusions that accompany escape and exile. She writes to the Barkers in October 1952: 'My New England blood tells me no, it isn't true. Escape does not work; if you are really happy you should just naturally go to pieces and never write a line – but apparently that – and most psychological theories on the subject, too – is all wrong' (*One Art* 249). As 'Questions of Travel' demonstrates, Bishop's delight in her new surroundings was accompanied by a dogged questioning of its validity. The second stanza is almost entirely made up of questions. The initial delight at the beauty of the scenery in the first stanza slowly gives way to recognition of the absurdity present in a possessive desire for things and experiences. The traveller's wonder becomes an attempt to control, contain and cage. Bishop finds a visual metaphor for this in wooden clogs and birdcages, as the speaker muses:

> – Yes, a pity not to have pondered,
> blurr'dly and inconclusively,
> on what connection can exist for centuries
> between the crudest wooden footwear

and, careful and finicky,
the whittled fantasies of wooden cages.
– Never to have studied history in
the weak calligraphy of songbirds' cages. (*Poems* 92)

The lines meditate on wooden forms that cage and enclose, finding a parallel between clogs and cages, clogs being a kind of cage for the feet.

Like a letter, the poem's structure is conversational. Remarks like ' – Yes, a pity not to have pondered' seem to be directed at a particular other. The phrases are structured like fragments of a conversation, with the other half seemingly just out of earshot; or like the replies to elements of a previous letter the reader cannot access. The asymmetry of the poem also extends to its offbeat musicality, and a fascination with pairs that do not quite match. Like a lopsided conversation, the 'disparate wooden clogs' play 'a sad, two-noted, wooden tune'. The slant-rhymed pairing of 'blurr'dly and inconclusively' is repeated in 'careful and finicky', another pair of words whose 'f' sounds and falling rhythms are alike, although not exactly. The poem itself at this point becomes 'careful and finicky' – as if the poet is carving the elaborate façade of a baroque church or whittling a wooden cage, the words sound the repeated and concentrated motion of carving shapes in wood. Reading the poem aloud requires the kind of 'useless concentration' that Bishop says is necessary to the creation and experiencing of art, in order to say the right words.

As much as it reuses details from Darwin's account of his stay near Rio de Janeiro, 'Questions of Travel' also takes flight into an imaginary space that could be anywhere. The details of a 'bamboo church of Jesuit baroque' are only loosely sketched. And, like the 'disparate wooden clogs', some of these details do not quite fit together. The 'bamboo church' is a logical impossibility; a baroque church cannot be made of bamboo. It is more likely that Bishop is thinking here of an elaborate birdcage that she owned, which was shaped like a baroque church.[5] The impossible 'bamboo church' forms part of a fascination in the poem with the representations of things as much as with the things themselves, and with 'imagined places' as much as with the real places that Bishop visited on her travels. The 'bamboo church' is like the 'tiniest green hummingbird' in that both hinge on logical impossibilities. The birdcage-church represents the fantasy of a baroque church carved from wood. The 'tiniest green hummingbird' is, as in Dickinson's letter-poem, a representation of a bird rather than a real bird, and part of an imagined geography that connects the spaces of Brazil and Nova Scotia (or Amherst and Tunis). These carefully observed fantasies are part of Bishop's strategy of 'just [. . .] looking', and hinge on a paradoxical sense that exact observation might necessarily involve a form of looking that is blurred and inconclusive.

It is exactly these logical impossibilities, inaccuracies, mixed-up details and blurred lines between bird and letter, church and birdcage that contribute to the poem's fidelity to the multiple, various and somewhat ambivalent experiences of travel. The repetitions in the middle of the poem when the speaker ponders 'blurr'dly and inconclusively / on what connection can exist' between these various wooden elements are like careful checks and balances – 'careful and finicky' – as the poet carves her own elaborate birdcage in the form of a poem. The poem's conceits are reminiscent of Bishop's comment in her 1933 letter to Donald Stanford, in which she refers to 'The Baroque Style in Prose', and her attempts to emulate it in poetry, where 'an equally great "cumulative effect" might be built up by a series of irregularities' (*One Art* 11). The 'series of irregularities', in this case, could describe the clogs, bamboo church and birdcages. The carefully assembled images are a collection, analogous to Darwin's careful preservation of specimens.

Like the elements in the poem that are 'careful and finicky', Bishop often described her own need for accuracy in forms of observation as 'finicky'. In a letter to Anne Stevenson, she wrote: 'I am afraid you will think these many little corrections both finicky and egotistical' (*Prose* 442). This same, almost compulsive need to maintain accuracy and to tell the truth is found in Darwin's writing. The *Beagle Diary* strives always to be truthful, to express complex ideas simply, and deplores others' attempts to write about the journey in embellished prose. Referring to the Captain's own rival account of the voyage, Darwin writes in a letter: 'I looked over a few pages of Captain King's Journal: I was absolutely forced against all love of truth to tell the Captain that I supposed it was very good, but in honest reality no pudding for little school-boys ever was so heavy' (*Correspondence* II 80–1). Bishop called her own fidelity to truth her 'George Washington handicap' in a letter to Lowell in 1962: 'I can't tell a lie even for art, apparently; it takes an awful effort or a sudden jolt to make me alter facts' (*One Art* 408).

In the cases of Dickinson's 'A Route of Evanescence', Darwin's *Beagle Diary* and Bishop's 'Questions of Travel', fidelity to truth means capturing a sense of the original experience, if not always holding fast to exact details. The 'bamboo church of Jesuit baroque' is an alteration of facts, but one that adheres to what Croll calls in his essay on baroque style the 'imaginative truth' of experience (433). In her Brazil letters Bishop collected fragments to be reused and changed into poetry later. Descriptions in the letters, the image of the hummingbird from Dickinson's letter-poem and sections from Darwin's *Beagle Diary* found their way into the early Brazil poems, particularly 'Questions of Travel'. These hybrid prose-poetry elements are what Bishop used to lend her poems a sense of immediacy, and to create the impression of watching 'a mind thinking' and discovering form as it goes. In this way, Bishop's letters and letter-like poems conform to the key components of what Morris Croll termed, writing in 1929, the 'baroque style in prose' (427). However, in the context of 1950s Brazil, the baroque took on a new significance. 'Questions of Travel' contains a growing sense of the connection between intricate baroque forms, simulated energy and part-fantasy worlds and the impulses to cage and control that necessarily accompany them. Bishop's Brazil letters seek to collect and display a dazzling range of Brazilian images, and bring the correspondent into the partly imaginary space of correspondence with her. The poem 'Questions of Travel' is more ambivalent and questions the acquisitive gaze of the traveller. The lines at the end of the second stanza – 'Oh, must we dream our dreams / and have them, too?' – represent a turning point. In the poem this anxiety in relation to the dangers of viewing Brazil as a fantasy is more clearly tied to themes of mastery over animals and landscapes, and legacies of colonisation. Travel and tourism are presented as yet another acquisitive, possessive, even caging desire for objects, animals and experiences. The images of birdcages in the third stanza encapsulate (literally) this desire to control and contain things that were previously free. Careful observation, however, which paradoxically involves the accumulation of blurred and incomplete detail, goes some way to preserving a sense of freedom and vitality in letters and poems.

Notes

1. Brett Millier records that 'Questions of Travel' was 'published in 1956 [in *The New Yorker*] though begun much earlier' (273). Drafts of the poem held at Vassar College are dated 1955–1956 (*Bishop Papers* 57.8, 73.2).
2. Bishop notes in her review: 'Twenty-nine of the letters are included in the most recent edition of *Letters of Emily Dickinson*, edited by Mabel Loomis Todd' (*Prose* 263). This edition was published in 1951, and contains Dickinson's hummingbird poem sent as a letter to Todd in 1882 (368).
3. Francesco Rognoni has analysed Bishop's marked copies of *The Voyage of the Beagle* (1962) and *The Autobiography of Charles Darwin* (1958), pointing out that Bishop marked passages she liked and that may have influenced her poems (241). Jonathan Ellis argues that Bishop's appreciation of Darwin is based on his use of 'language and word association' rather than a detailed engagement with his scientific theories ('Reading Bishop' 190).
4. Millier writes, '[Bishop] complained often in early letters that she found herself unable to write about Brazil, but there she was, doing it, "working" in the best sense, to learn what she thought about the country, to discover what tone she would take when she did come to write formal prose and poetry' (259). Similarly, Biele observes that letters allowed Bishop to try out her writing voice, describing letters as a form of 'unconscious pre-writing' (93).
5. There is a picture of this birdcage, 'undated, painted wood and wire', in the exhibition catalogue *Objects and Apparitions* (2011), which shows objects and artwork from Bishop's collection (28).

Works Cited

Biele, Joelle, '"Like Working Without Really Doing It": Elizabeth Bishop's Brazil Letters and Poems', *The Antioch Review* 67.1 (2009): 90–8.

Bishop, Elizabeth, Drafts of 'Questions of Travel', Elizabeth Bishop Papers, Vassar College.

Bishop, Elizabeth, *Elizabeth Bishop: Objects and Apparitions*, ed. Joelle Biele, Dan Chiasson and Lloyd Schwartz (New York: Tibor de Nagy Gallery and James S. Jaffe Rare Books, 2011).

Bishop, Elizabeth, Notes for the E. Dickinson/Hopkins poem, Elizabeth Bishop Papers, Vassar College.

Bishop, Elizabeth, *One Art: The Selected Letters*, ed. Robert Giroux (London: Chatto & Windus, 1994).

Costello, Bonnie, 'The Mail from Tunis, Probably: A Hummingbird Fable of Proximity and Distance', *The Straddler* (Fall 2011), <http://www.thestraddler.com/20118/piece7.php> (last accessed 19 October 2018).

Croll, Morris W., 'The Baroque Style in Prose', in Kemp Malone and Martin Brown Ruud (eds), *Studies in English Philology: A Miscellany in Honour of Frederick Klaeber* (Minneapolis: University of Minnesota Press, 1929), pp. 427–56.

Darwin, Charles, *Charles Darwin's Beagle Diary*, ed. R. D. Keynes (Cambridge: Cambridge University Press, 1988).

Darwin, Charles, *The Correspondence of Charles Darwin, Vol. 2: 1837–1843*, ed. Frederick H. Burkhardt and Sydney Smith (Cambridge: Cambridge University Press, 1986).

Dickinson, Emily, *Letters of Emily Dickinson*, ed. Mabel Loomis Todd (London: Gollancz, 1951).

Dickinson, Emily, *The Letters of Emily Dickinson, Vol. II*, ed. Thomas H. Johnson and Theodora Ward (Cambridge, MA: Harvard University Press, 1958).

Ellis, Jonathan, *Art and Memory in the Work of Elizabeth Bishop* (Aldershot: Ashgate, 2006).

Ellis, Jonathan, 'Reading Bishop Reading Darwin', in John Holmes (ed.), *Science in Modern Poetry* (Liverpool: Liverpool University Press, 2012), pp. 181–93.

Haughton, Hugh, 'Just Letters: Corresponding Poets', in Jonathan Ellis (ed.), *Letter Writing Among Poets: From William Wordsworth to Elizabeth Bishop* (Edinburgh: Edinburgh University Press, 2015), pp. 57–78.

Millier, Brett C., *Elizabeth Bishop: Life and the Memory of It* (Berkeley: University of California Press, 1993).

Paulin, Tom, 'Writing to the Moment: Elizabeth Bishop', in *Writing to the Moment: Selected Critical Essays, 1980–1996* (London: Faber and Faber, 1996), pp. 215–39.

Phillips, Siobhan, 'Elizabeth Bishop and the Ethics of Correspondence', *Modernism/modernity* 19.2 (2012): 343–63.

Ravinthiran, Vidyan, *Elizabeth Bishop's Prosaic* (Lewisburg: Bucknell University Press, 2015).

Rognoni, Francesco, 'Reading Darwin: On Elizabeth Bishop's Marked Copies of *The Voyage of the Beagle* and *The Autobiography of Charles Darwin*', in Suzanne Ferguson (ed.) *Jarrell, Bishop, Lowell, & Co.* (Knoxville: University of Tennessee Press, 2003), pp. 239–48.

Treseler, Heather, 'Dreaming in Color: Bishop's Notebook Letter-Poems', in Angus Cleghorn, Bethany Hicok and Thomas Travisano (eds), *Elizabeth Bishop in the Twenty-First Century: Reading the New Editions* (Charlottesville: University of Virginia Press, 2012), pp. 88–103.

15

Patterns of Time and the Maternal in the Short Stories of Elizabeth Bishop and Katherine Mansfield

Laura Helyer

Empathy means realizing no trauma has discrete edges. Trauma bleeds. Out of wounds and across boundaries. Sadness becomes a seizure. Empathy demands another kind of porousness in response. (Jamison 6)

Elizabeth Bishop and Katherine Mansfield use poetic devices to structure, pattern and stress their prose. Both writers employ heightened language, fragmentation, symbolism and a close attention to rhythm and form to shape their stories. Mansfield sought an innovative form and technique, 'a kind of *special prose*' (*Journal* 94) which retained aspects of the poetic, for the writing of her autobiographical, elegiac and experimental short story 'The Aloe'. Like Bishop, she was interested in the prose poetry of Baudelaire. Bishop wrote stories as prose poems and fables, as well as demonstrating a critical interest in representations of time in experimental, modernist fiction in her undergraduate essays 'Dimensions for a Novel' and 'Time's Andromedas'. In this chapter I will focus on the poetic prose experiments of Bishop's 'In the Village' (1953) and Mansfield's manuscript 'The Aloe', which was subsequently revised and published as 'Prelude' (1917), to explore their shared modernist and existential aesthetic concerns, figured through representations of the childlike, the maternal, and mediated through depictions of time and nature. I'm concerned with how both writers engaged with lyricism in order to express personal loss in a narrative mode and with the significance of the mother-daughter relationship in their later development as artists and women.

Bishop was an admirer of Mansfield's work, as Joan Collingwood Disney affirms:

Elizabeth was familiar with everything to do with Katherine Mansfield, a favourite of hers – British writers that Mansfield was intimate with, the people around her, and the whole story of her life. (27)

The writers shared a love for Russian literature, particularly Chekhov. There are also many parallels between the contexts of the writing of these two key works and their nomadic, artistic lifestyles as women writers. Their autobiographical stories were in part motivated by loss, grief and nostalgia for the places and particular homes of their childhood. For Mansfield, living in London, this was New Zealand and the sudden

loss of her brother Leslie during the First World War. For Bishop, this was a reawak-
ened sense of her childhood in Nova Scotia and relationship with her troubled mother,
Gertrude Bulmer Bishop, from the perspective of her new life in Brazil. It was as if
the new context brought about a greater immediacy and awareness to memory. The
disorders of time and trauma were something Bishop alluded to in 'Dimensions for a
Novel':

> If I suffer a terrible loss and do not realize it till several years later among differ-
> ent surroundings, then the important fact is not the original loss so much as the
> circumstance of the new surroundings which succeeded in letting the loss through
> to my consciousness. (*Prose* 485)

For Bishop, then, the past is always a quality of the present which requires constant
reinterpretation: 'A constant process of adjustment is going on about the past – every
ingredient dropped into it from the present must affect the whole' (*Prose* 482).

I am concerned here with the sensibility with which both writers arrange their mate-
rial, adhering to a poetic design of fragments and moments, rather than according to
chronology or plot. At the same time, what kind of wholeness and separation from the
past is made possible by such formal experimentations? As Thom Gunn perceives, a
poet typically works with 'a very conscious arranging strength, keeping things in sche-
matic form'. This was particularly true of Bishop's artistic practice, in which she remained
committed to poetic form as a means of organising and controlling painful experience.
However, her innovations in prose were such that she moved beyond the containment
of poetic form, in order to explore what Leslie Jamison describes as the 'porousness' of
trauma, the way the past can haunt the present, and 'no trauma has discrete edges' (6).
For Bishop, this meant addressing the legacy of her childhood as an adult. The beginnings
of 'In the Village' can be traced to her only attempt at a novel, and it can be argued that
the expected and/or imposed linearity of characterisation and plot made greater demands
on the autobiographical than the more elliptical and controlled forms of her poetry. Prose
requires time and ordering – that of explaining the causation of events, or at least organ-
ising them in a logical, communicable manner that can make sense to a reader. This
represented a challenge to Bishop, both emotionally and artistically. As Bishop herself
understood: 'The crises of our lives do not come, I think, accurately dated; they crop up
unexpected and out of turn, and somehow or other arrange themselves according to a
calendar we cannot control' (*Prose* 485). Bishop instead pursued a lyric and elliptical
truth in prose rather than a dramatic one, in which, as Colm Tóibín observes of her story
'In the Village', 'the pain is in the tone' (*On Elizabeth Bishop* 111).

For Mansfield, there was a desire with 'The Aloe', which was also intended to be her
first full-length novel, to evoke the shared past with her younger brother. According to
Kirsty Gunn, she wanted 'to create a kind of memorial to the dead boy in her writing'
(13–14), and in her journal Mansfield writes: 'all must be told with a sense of mystery, a
radiance, and afterglow, because you, my little sun of it, are set' (*Journal* 94). However,
as Gerri Kimber understands, she was keen not to risk losing control of her material –
'that to arrive at more than personal nostalgia called for a "kind of special prose"' (xxi).
There was also a wider colonial context and literary ambition beyond the personal, as
Mansfield clearly states – 'Oh, I want for one moment to make our undiscovered coun-
try leap into the eyes of the Old World' (*Journal* 94). Both writers, in rendering their

motherlands in literary prose, were wrestling with a colonial context and class conflict. For Bishop, spending her early years in Nova Scotia, this was between her Canadian relations on her mother's side and those of her more affluent dead father's in the United States, as well as that of an emerging Canadian identity, which sought independence from the British Empire and the tensions surrounding this relationship during the First World War. Sandra Barry argues that this childhood 'mobility in the form of migration', both historical and personal, informed her later aesthetic (100). Mansfield in turn was keen to escape the frustrations of her bourgeois family in Wellington but felt herself to be marginal and an outsider in London: 'I am the little colonial walking in the London patch – allowed to look, perhaps, but not to linger' (*Notebooks* 166). According to Janet Wilson, this in turn uniquely shaped her relationship and perspective on avant-garde artistic movements in Europe.

'In the Village' was published within the context of a poetry collection and the story itself has been read by some critics as a prose poem, as Angus Cleghorn and Jonathan Ellis query:

> Is 'In the Village' actually a prose-poem? It is often described as such. Certainly, it is both a memoir *and* a story, a kind of half-remembered reverie like nearly all of Bishop's best work. [. . .] Bishop was always interested in blurring genre boundaries as her lifelong interest in the prose poem shows. (16)

Here, however, I analyse it as an evocative and successfully dramatic example of poetic prose, as Bishop might have conceived it, owing to her interest in the work of Baudelaire, who offers a helpful definition of poetic prose:

> Who among us has not, in his ambitious moments, dreamed of the miracle of a poetic prose, musical without meter or rhyme, supple enough and rugged enough to adapt itself to the lyrical impulses of the soul, the undulations of the psyche, the jolts of consciousness? (16)

Both verse and prose modes demand an attention to rhythm, 'verse with its rhythmical organization and prose with its rhythmical freedom' (Greene et al. 1507). However, the prosaic can also be found frequently in Bishop's poems through her privileging of the 'facts' of what happened, in particular the emphasis on description and accurate detail.

Vidyan Ravinthiran has considered the role of prosaic and prose rhythms in Bishop's verse and prose, as well as how her experimental literary prose complicates notions of the self and other (125–49). It is this latter aspect, and Bishop's engagement with surrealism, transitory states, thresholds of consciousness and dream as a narrative method, which is perhaps most relevant when comparing her narrative mode to Mansfield's. Bonnie Costello identifies these as the 'hypnagogic effects' of Bishop's style:

> As with Poe and Baudelaire, too, there are hypnagogic effects in Bishop's writing, moments when experience and dream converge and blur, sometimes through intoxication. [. . .] Bishop introduces antimimetic elements that disturb our sense of the real. Baudelaire's trademark synaesthesia adds to this dreamlike quality, as does a syntax that confuses the sense of transition from inner and outer worlds. (89–90)

Bishop's mother, Gertrude, is an inspiration for the 'she' in 'In the Village' and 'Easter' in the fragmentary 'Reminiscences of Great Village' (probably composed in the mid-1930s). In the latter, the mother is presented as a troubled figure and the child named Lucius is 'haunted by his mother's needs' (Millier 7). In the absence of a mother, the child is no longer able to remain a child. The mother is associated with dreams and hypnagogic states and becomes equated with moths, as Brett C. Millier illustrates, quoting Bishop:

> he dreams of the large moths that inhabit Nova Scotia in the summertime. They grow frightening and then in a linguistic turn – 'Easter came into it somehow' – become identified with 'mother.' 'I woke up, horrified with all the fluttering moths, and just as I woke, so that the feeling was neither a sleeping one nor a waking one, I became certain that the enemy was she.' (7)

Here, then, the mother is characterised as the opposite of the maternal; she has become a source of confusion and the 'enemy'. This portrait of crisis within the child and sense of disgust for the insect mother could be understood to give birth to Bishop's creativity and imaginative needs. The maternal body is associated with unexplained passions and scenes of metamorphoses. On another level, she possesses something of Baudelaire's 'jolts of consciousness' (16) in which the lost mother triggers a particular state of awareness. This aspect can also be traced to the influence of modernism on Bishop's prose, specifically her reflections on the felt experience of time and how to develop a prose style that sustained dramatic momentum, yet yielded to reflective lyric moments of stillness or strangeness, of a sudden encounter or recognition.

Similarly, William Boyd writes that 'there is another tone in Mansfield that seems exclusively her own and is very un-Chekhovian. It is almost a sense of controlled delirium: a combination of Joyce's idea of the epiphanic moment with something altogether more transcendental and passion-filled' (ix). 'The Aloe' and 'Prelude' in particular possess a heightened, timeless, dream-like quality. The shortened version, 'Prelude', is divided into twelve interludes and it is the quality of movement and rhythm between the characters, the adults and the children, with their differing yet associated perspectives and desires, that generates a similar 'hypnagogic effect' to that seen in Bishop's work. The intensity of the epiphanic, transformative moment is managed through a balancing of the mundane and the animistic. The poetic image or surreal, resonating symbol – the home they leave, and the wonder of the new house ('the soft white bulk of it lay stretched upon the green garden like a sleeping beast' (*The Aloe* 30)), the wallpaper, the garden, the birds, the aloe tree, for example – these are all available to the unsettled, sensitive mind, as the avoidant mother Linda observes in 'Prelude':

> She turned over to the wall and idly, with one finger, she traced a poppy on the wall-paper with a leaf and a stem and a fat bursting bud. In the quiet, and under her tracing finger, the poppy seemed to come alive. She could feel the sticky, silky petals, the stem, hairy like a gooseberry skin, the rough leaf and the tight glazed bud. Things had a habit of coming alive like that. (*Collected Stories* 27)

The private expansiveness of the imagination is captured here, as well as a sense of the otherness of quotidian experience. Linda's 'fantasies of escape' (Hankin 130) are achieved through entering further into the ordinary and overlooked which serve to unsettle a sense of a shared reality.

However, the epiphanic threshold is focused on the aloe plant in particular. It is the tree that mediates the relationship between the ambivalent mother figure and the curious child, between Linda and Kezia, and their respective innocence and experience. Indeed, C. A. Hankin argues that 'Kezia's sensibility is linked with that of her mother by the pattern of symbolism' (123). Kezia perceives the plant before her mother:

> 'Mother what is it?' asked Kezia. Linda looked up at the fat swelling plant with its cruel leaves its towering fleshy stem. High above them, as though becalmed in the air, and yet holding so fast to the earth it grew from it might have had claws and not roots. The curving leaves seemed to be hiding something; the big blind stem cut into the air as if no wind could ever shake it. 'That is an aloe, Kezia,' said Linda. 'Does it ever have any flowers?' 'Yes, my child' said her Mother and she smiled down at Kezia, half shutting her eyes, 'once every hundred years.' (*The Aloe* 54–5)

For Kezia, the aloe is an object of wonder, but her mother projects her fears, frustration, passivity and anger on to the plant. An undertone of aggression is conveyed by its 'claws' and 'cruel leaves', as well as a current of sexual domination. However, the aloe belongs to Linda. In the concluding passages of the story it metamorphoses into a ship for Linda with which she will escape – 'She particularly liked the long sharp thorns. Nobody would dare to come near her ship or to follow after' (*The Aloe* 79). As a symbol, it functions like the mother's scream in 'In the Village', colouring the rest of the narrative. For her nurturing and conventional mother, Mrs Fairfield, the aloe is going to blossom that year, but for Linda it means something radically different:

> As they stood on the steps the high grassy bank on which the aloe rested – rose up like a wave and the aloe seemed to ride upon it like a ship with the oars lifted – bright moonlight hung upon those lifted oars like water and on the green wave glittered the dew – 'Do you feel it too,' said Linda and she spoke, like her mother with the 'special' voice that women use at night to each other, as though they spoke in their sleep or from the bottom of a deep well – 'don't you feel that it is coming towards us?' And she dreamed that she and her mother were caught up on the cold water and into the ship with the lifted oars and the budding mast. And now the oars fell, striking quickly quickly and they rowed far away over the tops of the garden trees over the paddocks and the dark bush beyond. (*The Aloe* 78–9)

From Linda's perspective, then, the 'budding mast' and the flight enabled by the oars are both a magical fantasy and an expression of her desire for agency and change. Akin to the mother's resistance to the fitting of the dress in 'In the Village', Linda's resistance is one of visionary escape and transformation. Her dissociating perception cuts free of her body and immediate surroundings for survival.

Bruce Harding argues that 'The Aloe' is a more radical, feminist and political story than the shortened 'Prelude' in its 'examination of the neurasthenic woman as a valid, often necessary, existential form of female resistance to roles imposed by late Victorian society' (115). Furthermore, he persuasively emphasises 'the signal importance of garden and flower imagery in Mansfield's personal lexicon of liberation' (118). Nature also becomes a liberating presence for the maturing child in 'In the Village'. In 'The Aloe' in particular Harding proposes: 'the flowering of female selfhood is a recurrent textual concern in her adoption of a non-linear, spiral pattern of incremental construction held together by the logic of symbol and image' (118). This 'spiral pattern of incremental construction' resonates with the patterning evident in Bishop's prose in which rhythm and repetition serve to tell, to create, the story. I also prioritise Mansfield's earlier version because it represents a more empathic and inclusive depiction of its characters, in which the reader can witness the more untidy, emotional hinterland of their being-in-the-world. Harding suggests that with 'Prelude', Mansfield removed much that was 'psychically revelatory (by way of an ethically embracing confessional discourse), as well as much that was socially incisive' (120). The looser, open form of the notebook version of the story, 'The Aloe', is organised into four chapters and is perhaps more interesting for its uneasy fractured quality; as Kirsty Gunn asserts, it is 'a thing of fragments, held together as if by chance but never really whole' (7).

The novelist Colm Tóibín describes his process of writing prose in terms of patterning – 'images made to satisfy the pattern' and 'I knew I was patterning as I dramatized' (*All a Novelist Needs* 32–3). This 'impulse to pattern' (33) in a narrative art form offers a helpful framework with which to approach and appreciate Bishop's 'In the Village', for in many ways the story foregrounds pattern as both theme and structural device. It also privileges mood and atmosphere over plot. As with Mansfield's use of repeated symbols, the story is held together by pattern – by repetition, echo and reflective imagery. The types of poetic devices in evidence here include the use of paragraphing for rhythmic effect, the use of repeated colours, the presentation of dialogue as floating voices, chiasmus, synaesthesia and surrealistic effects.

'In the Village' and the unpublished fragments 'Reminiscences of Great Village', representing plans for Bishop's only attempted novel, act as an index to her feelings about her mother. They also hint at the retrospective formulations of her understandings of the maternal and feminine, that is, the way a child's consciousness processes the confusing language and behaviour of adults. This experimental story, published in *The New Yorker* (December 1953) and later in *Questions of Travel* (1965), is regarded as the 'masterpiece' (Giroux 29) amongst her collection of prose writings and stories, the latter of which are classified by Millier as 'fragmentary and slightly fictionalized autobiography' (253). I focus on it here because of its depiction of the mother figure and for its qualities as an extended traumatic dream or reverie, as indicated above. There are passages in 'In the Village' where the story resembles a prose poem according to David Lehman's definition – a prose poem may look like prose but it 'acts like a poem', rewarding close and repeated reading, despite the fact that 'it works in sentences rather than lines' (45). A poem requires a different quality of attention and listening. Ravinthiran makes this apparent in his study of Bishop's prosaic: 'In analyzing Bishop's letter prose, I had to argue the relevance of scansion – yet her literary prose often seems written by a poet who simply couldn't stop thinking about rhythm' (138). For Barry, the maternal influence on Bishop is also one of movement and rhythm and 'In the Village' is in itself 'a contemplation of motion' in which the 'mother embodies this mobility in the potent metaphor of tide' (101). She goes on to claim that this initiation into rhythm possessed a positive pedagogic and elemental aspect:

Gertrude was tide. Gertrude was time. Gertrude was voice. Bishop learned about ebb and flow, now and then, sound and silence from her mother. (109)

This is an attractive reading, albeit a slightly romanticised one. I also believe Gertrude was a muse of sorts for Bishop but one which arose from anxiety – that is, the disappointments or uncertainty of the maternal made possible a different quality of awareness, perception and anxious orientation in the world akin to Mansfield's development as a writer.

'In the Village' underwent a prolonged editorial process which is fully documented in Joelle Biele's edited collection of *The New Yorker* correspondence (2011). This correspondence offers an interesting insight into Bishop's artistic practice by providing evidence of the revisions she resisted and how she articulated her intentions for the piece. Her wider aesthetic values and stylistic priorities become apparent as a consequence. Some of the disagreements seemed to arise from its determined poetic qualities, as Katharine White's comments convey:

> Perhaps one difficulty that underlies all this is that because this story is written like a poem, you feel it will be read like a poem. But poems are not usually 26 pages long and though a reader is quite willing to read and reread a poem that is elusive and finally get to understand it, he is not so willing to reread a very long story. (101)

Bishop's notion of being 'caught in a skein of voices' (*Prose* 75), or repetitive, 'nervous voices' (*Elizabeth Bishop and The New Yorker* 98), was something she endeavoured to represent in her early drafts of the story and also resulted in criticism of the piece (*Elizabeth Bishop and The New Yorker* 95). Furthermore, she consciously shaped and arranged paragraphs for their poetic potential and rhythmic effect, revealing again the influence of poetic devices such as expressive timing, movement, pace and measure on her prose.

The sensitivity to 'timing' and 'tempo' in particular recalls her essays on Gerard Manley Hopkins and Gertrude Stein ('Gerard Manley Hopkins: Notes on Timing in His Poetry' and 'Time's Andromedas'). In 'Time's Andromedas', Bishop explores her ideas about time in the novel, following Stein's assertion that 'time in a composition is a thing that is very troublesome' (*Poems, Prose, and Letters* 653). The aspiration towards a mythic and uneasy timelessness in 'In the Village' is one of its major strengths. Bishop's own comments emphasise this focus:

> I'm not sure that I'll feel able to change as much as you may want changed – the paragraphing, for example, and the quotations. I worked over them for a long time to try to get a certain tempo that I *think* I've got. [. . .] I wanted to give the effect of nervous voices, exchanging often ambiguous remarks, floating in the air over the child's head. (*Elizabeth Bishop and The New Yorker* 98)

When the story was eventually published, it was critically received as a prose poem, as well as being appreciated as an experimental story in poetic prose.

Following Bishop's own approach and emphasis here, I have considered the bond between mother and daughter as a vocal, sonorous and therefore poetic one. Jean-Luc Nancy argues that

> To be listening is always to be on the edge of meaning, or in an edgy meaning of extremity, and as if the sound were precisely nothing else than this edge, this fringe, this margin — (7)

The focus and dramatic moment of 'In the Village' is centred on the mother's voice and the extremity, limit and meaning of her scream. It is a primal sound which governs the world of the village and reverberates throughout the story. The all-pervasiveness of the maternal scream is established and sustained through the use of repetition which creates a rhapsodic quality in key passages of the piece. With its carefully managed tonal variations, the story has the feel of a musical composition; the mother's scream is the central melody colouring and shaping it. At first, this scream is disembodied; it is only later that the reader understands it belongs to the suffering mother – 'Later, it was she who gave the scream' (*Prose* 62). The story opens with a distanced, omniscient perspective but under the terror and suspense of that scream:

> A scream, the echo of a scream, hangs over that Nova Scotian village. No one hears it; it hangs there forever, a slight stain in those pure blue skies [. . .] The scream hangs like that, unheard, in memory – in the past, in the present, and those years between. It was not even loud to begin with, perhaps. It just came there to live, forever – not loud, just alive forever. Its pitch would be the pitch of my village. (*Prose* 62)

Here the unnatural sound of the mother's cry is felt as polluting the peaceful, pastoral landscape of the village but, significantly, '[i]t was not even loud to begin with, perhaps' (*Prose* 62). This contributes to the fairy- or folk-tale atmosphere of the narrative which is established by the timeless, authorial tone of the opening paragraph, and particularly by the fantastical, miniaturising line 'Flick the lightning rod on top of the church steeple with your fingernail and you will hear it' (*Prose* 62). Here the reader is offered a strange, magical, god-like perspective on the village.

    As a sonorous haunting, the mother's voice resonates in the consciousness of the daughter, conveying the way in which the mother-daughter bond can be experienced as spectrality and possession, as a founding and mirroring relationship that cannot be escaped. However, it is also a preservation and an archiving of the mother's voice – and therefore also a recovery, as Barry suggests: 'Bishop needed Gertrude to be a mother, but when that was no longer possible, she claimed her for art. [. . .] Her scream is lost and found' (110). It is also how I read the significance of the image 'in the blacksmith's shop things hang up in the shadows and shadows hang up in the things' (*Prose* 63). The use of chiasmus here as a reflective 'crossing' has greater significance when appreciated in terms of a bond or relationship, one that is also an inescapable entanglement. Separation from the mother, for the daughter in particular, can be a difficult process and is governed by notions of self and other. As Mladen Dolar suggests, this represents an ethical struggle for self-definition, involving a sense of difference and empathic awareness of an other:

> And is not the mother's voice the first problematic connection to the other, the immaterial tie that comes to replace the umbilical cord, and shapes much of the fate of the earliest stages of life? (39)

This emphasis on the mother's voice as a way of thinking about the mother-child relationship, as the 'first problematic connection to the other', provides a helpful approach to reading 'In the Village'. Here, the character of the mother's scream and implied maternal body is all-pervasive and engulfing for the child, colouring her world and structuring perception and sensibility. In this sense, the child is overwhelmed by the presence of this particular other, that is the maternal. The widow depicted in 'In the Village' is seen as resisting the performance and visibility of society, and of time and change. This provokes the child's fear and ultimate dissociation which in turn provokes an existential relationship and sensitivity to the wider world.

The threat posed by the actual presence of the mother is maintained throughout by the use of subtle yet potentially disturbing poetic images. For example, there is the suggestion of violence and death in the following passage – 'The horseshoes sail through the dark like bloody little moons and follow each other like bloody little moons to drown in the black water, hissing, protesting' (*Prose* 63) – as well as of pain and being devoured: 'Outside, along the matted eaves, painstakingly, sweetly, wasps go over and over a honeysuckle vine' (63). The story in general trains the reader to attend to its soundscape. This privileging of aurality enables the reader to hear echoes of the maternal even in the word (and sound of) 'honeysuckle', thus also associating the breast with wasps and the threat of a sting or sudden pain. It recalls the painful knowledge and loss of innocence linked with the 'rocky breasts' (*Poems* 64) and images of the mouth and feeding in the poem 'At the Fishhouses'. The child's experience of the mother is also equated with or mirrored by the dressmaker's kitten:

> A gray kitten once lay on the treadle of her sewing machine, where she rocked it as she sewed, like a baby in a cradle, but it got hanged on the belt. Or did she make that up? (*Prose* 67)

The horror (and emotion) of this image is immediately diluted by the question that follows it, in order to diminish its expressive power. In this regard, the story often depends on understatement and poetic effects to communicate the domestic trauma behind its telling.

Similarly, there is ambiguity around the figure of the dressmaker, for it is understandably unclear to the child who or what is causing such distress to her mother. This is captured in the animated, creaturely image of the expensive purple material intended for the new dress which the mother is so keen to refuse. As such, the child, in sympathy with the mother, perceives something dangerous in the cloth itself:

> The purple stuff lies on a table; long white threads hang all about it. Oh, look away before it moves by itself, or makes a sound; before it echoes, echoes, what it has heard! (*Prose* 67)

Thus, the material itself absorbs and becomes the 'scream, the echo of a scream' (*Prose* 62). Perceiving the sinister in the commonplace is perhaps the child's inheritance from adapting to the chaotic presence and surviving the repeated unexplained disappearances of the mother. As such, the story is a negotiation with the memory of the mother as a 'sonorous envelope' (Silverman 72). For Adrienne Rich, 'the loss of the daughter to the mother, the mother to the daughter, is the essential female tragedy' (237). The mother, for the daughter, is the first mirror and model of being, the first world of the body. This narcissistic attachment or absence thereof can be read as a form of entrapment for the daughter, who is either overwhelmed or abandoned. In many ways 'In the Village' captures this quality of the mother and her voice as something both longed for and threatening, as 'uterine night', 'vocal continuum' and 'umbilical net' (Silverman 72).

The fear of abandonment is also a recurring one for the children and husband depicted in 'The Aloe' and 'Prelude'. In the opening scene of 'Prelude', when the women and children are leaving the old house and there is not enough room for them all in the buggy, Linda chooses her belongings over her two younger children, Lottie and Kezia. This sets up the tone and dramatic tension inherent in the story in much the same way as the scream does at the beginning of 'In the Village'. Furthermore, as Hankin argues, 'For all the understanding with which Linda Burnell's plight is depicted, the symbolism of "Prelude" unequivocally damns her for being an unloving mother' (131).

> Lottie and Kezia stood on the patch of lawn just inside the gate all ready [. . .] Hand in hand, they stared with round solemn eyes, first at the absolute necessities and then at their mother.
> 'We shall simply have to leave them. That is all. We shall simply have to cast them off,' said Linda Burnell. A strange little laugh flew from her lips; she leaned back against the buttoned leather cushions and shut her eyes, her lips trembling with laughter. (*Collected Stories* 11)

This subversive scene is effective for the way it quickly establishes a relationship with the reader and plays on defying their expectations of the maternal and feminine. The mother can be variously understood as cruel, amusing, mad or desperate, for example.

Bishop in turn feared inheriting her mother's 'madness', and whether read as prose or poetry, 'In the Village' captures the avoidant, tense and distanced nature of a mother-child relationship perhaps most powerfully and economically in these four lines:

> *Clang.*
> The pure note: pure and angelic.
> The dress was all wrong. She screamed.
> The child vanishes. (*Prose* 63)

Susan Lurie argues that the story 'traces the child Bishop's development in relation to domestic maternal and public "paternal" voices' and thus focuses 'on the construction of female subjectivity' (121). She proposes that the figure of the mother and of the horse are significantly juxtaposed so that the maternal cry is set against the blacksmith Nate's clang – human sounds pitted against the submissiveness of the domesticated animal (122). The child, who is witness again and again to the scream, is also forced into the passive position of listener according to Claire Kahane's analysis:

> As Kaja Silverman notes, the primal speaker is typically the mother; the primal listener, the child (1988, 80). The mother's voice is usually the first object to be isolated by the infant from its environs, the first object to be internalized. Recognized by the baby before the mother herself is perceived as an object, the maternal voice precedes the mirror stage in the constitution of the infant as a separate subject. Thus, Silverman points out, the female voice functions as a fetish, conveying a sense of presence that has been lost. (16)

The story, operating as a poem, fetishises this persistent cry of the mother; indeed, the mother is pictured as vulnerable and childlike herself: 'Now it is settling down, the scream' (*Prose* 64). As such, the story works to frame and therefore contain the expressive, lyric intensity of the mother's scream arising from personal crisis. It is an act of appropriation both of the mother's private distress and of poetry by prose. It is also an act of suppression, as Lurie again illustrates:

> the child's desire to eradicate both the mother's scream and the grandmother's sorrow turns out to have implications for her own self-expression [. . .] In response to the child's own 'shriek' of fright, we are told, her aunt 'almost shouts': 'Don't cry!' [. . .] 'Don't *cry*!' In exchange for the comfort of a mother-daughter bond that assuages the terrors of maternal rage, the child learns, she must censor her own expressions of anguish. (123)

Poetic form in prose might serve to act as a kind of censoring of uncontrollable expression. Bishop, as with Mansfield, is exploring the tensions around the myth of the 'good mother', and according to Lurie the ambivalence or diffusion at the end of the story results from Nate's clang 'repressing' the mother's cry (124). She argues that 'the initial gratitude for the disappearance of the scream coexists with a mourning for the "sickened and destroyed" voice of the resisting mother' (124).

As suggested above, the mother's voice is lost or judged against the nurturing 'skein of voices' (*Prose* 75) of other women in the household, as well as through the benevolent characters of other individuals in the village. The poet George Szirtes understands this to be a major strength of the story since it manages to situate the personal within a larger context and world of meaning. It represents an emotional development for the child:

> The village is introduced to us name by name, location by location. It is itemised much like the mother's belongings [. . .] The personal is not privileged. It is not presented as more important than the social, the natural, the temporal, and the incidental. But the scream hangs in a social world that is balanced between screams of horror and exclamations of delight [. . .] it is Nate at his anvil that keeps calling her back. Its *clang, clang* 'turns everything else to silence'. It is a man working. (57–8)

I read this through an appreciation of the modernist aesthetic which prevails throughout the story, governed by the child narrator's lyric epiphanies and 'moments of being' (Woolf 78). As Szirtes asserts here, the real literary achievement of the story resides in the way Bishop is able to conjoin this lyric sensibility of emerging selfhood and resonant being-in-the-world with the social, and the world of work – the sound of Nate's anvil, for example.

Her portrait of the child in the world resonates with my understanding of what Steven Earnshaw defines as a 'female Existentialist aesthetic' (11), an attitude which mediates alienation, anxiety and estrangement through a relationship and sense of wonder before the natural world. At the same time, the natural world is perceived in all its alien, indifferent otherness. The child is rightly afraid before it, because she recognises its opacity and thus realises, perhaps for the first time, her own 'glistening loneliness' (*Prose* 71).

> For a while I entertain the idea of not going home today at all, of staying safely here in the pasture all day, playing in the brook and climbing on the squishy, moss-covered hummocks in the swampy part. But an immense, sibilant, glistening loneliness suddenly faces me, and the cows are moving off to the shade of the fir trees, their bells chiming softly, individually. (*Prose* 71)

The existential anxiety and 'moment of being' (Woolf 78) depicted here once again shares a sensibility with the modernist experiments of Woolf and Mansfield. Earnshaw conceives this lyric intensity and heightened awareness in terms of excess, beyond the reach of prosaic language:

> The feeling of alienation mixed with an overwhelming wonder at the 'thisness' of the world and self is evident in Mansfield's stories. [. . .] In 'Bliss' there is the overflowing of a self that cannot be articulated in conventional language or behaviour. (11)

The child of 'In the Village' is immersed in her vision of 'an overwhelming wonder at the "thisness" of the world'. The predicament of the child abandoned by adults and/or coming to consciousness resonates with Mansfield's characterisation of the child Kezia in particular, and her fear of 'It' – 'Her old bogey, the dark, had overtaken her' (*The Aloe* 24). This moment of insecurity and fear is more expansively described in 'The Aloe' than in 'Prelude' and captures something of the existential crisis for the small child left alone in the house, yet at the same time captures the child's reasoning and rationalising of the fear – 'But Lottie was at the back door, too' (*The Aloe* 25).

> If she began to call Lottie *now* and went on calling her loudly all the while she flew downstairs and out of the house she might escape from *It* in time – *It* was round like the sun. *It* had a face. *It* smiled, but *It* had no eyes [. . .] *It* was at the top of the stair; *It* was at the bottom of the stairs, waiting in the little dark passage, guarding the back door – But Lottie was at the back door, too. (*The Aloe* 25)

Here Kezia's loneliness and vulnerability are lessened by the awareness of siblings, but the child in 'In the Village' is dependent entirely on distant adults and her own resources, such as curiosity and imagination. 'In the Village' is governed as much by this curiosity as by anxiety, and by registering places and moments of safety – the desire, for example, to stay 'safely here in the pasture all day' (*Prose* 71). Bishop's aesthetic and ethical vision as exemplified here suggests that it is not enough to remain in the solipsism of selfhood. Instead it is better to strive to formulate subjectivity in meaningful relationship with otherness. For the child here even perceives the cows as individuals, 'their bells chiming softly, individually' (*Prose* 71), and Nelly, the family cow, seems to possess a unique character, and perhaps a more nuanced personality than any of the humans depicted in the story. And yet this anthropomorphism is also held in check – 'At such close quarters my feelings for her are mixed' (*Prose* 71).

In their prose rendering of their childhoods, both Bishop and Mansfield resisted realism and the privileging of plot in favour of symbolism, pattern, a poetic prose and a sensitivity to finding a unique form and structure for their material. For Bishop, this was crucially a matter of finding the appropriate 'tempo' and 'time-pattern' (*Poems, Prose, and Letters* 642–3) for materialising and communicating the experience. Their aesthetic choices were governed by a desire for 'the truth of it [. . .] the ever-changing expression of it' (*Prose* 483). Mansfield's work and her engagement with Symbolist literature were a significant formative influence on Bishop's prose style and, in particular, the use of the aloe as expressive of the maternal and frustrated female voice. Victoria Harrison posits that '"In the Village" is about understanding and accepting not the mother, but the scream' (118). It is Bishop's acceptance of the symbol and the quality of this acceptance that matters most, as she strives to capture all the moments of its meaning:

> A symbol might remain the same for a lifetime, but surely its implications shift from one thing to another, come and go, always within relation to that particular tone of the present which called it forth. (*Prose* 483)

Works Cited

Barry, Sandra, 'In the Village: Bishop and Nova Scotia', in Angus Cleghorn and Jonathan Ellis (eds), *The Cambridge Companion to Elizabeth Bishop* (Cambridge: Cambridge University Press, 2014), pp. 97–110.

Baudelaire, Charles, *Great American Prose Poems*, ed. David Lehman (New York: Scribner Poetry, 2003).

Bishop, Elizabeth, *Elizabeth Bishop and The New Yorker: The Complete Correspondence*, ed. Joelle Biele (New York: Farrar, Straus and Giroux, 2011).

Bishop, Elizabeth, *Poems, Prose, and Letters*, ed. Robert Giroux and Lloyd Schwartz (New York: Library of America, 2008).

Boyd, William, 'Foreword', in Katherine Mansfield, *Prelude* (London: Hesperus, 2005), pp. vii–x.

Cleghorn, Angus, and Jonathan Ellis, 'Introduction: North *and* South', in Angus Cleghorn and Jonathan Ellis (eds), *The Cambridge Companion to Elizabeth Bishop* (Cambridge: Cambridge University Press, 2014), pp. 1–18.

Collingwood Disney, Joan, in Gary Fountain and Peter Brazeau (eds), *Remembering Elizabeth Bishop: An Oral Biography* (Amherst: University of Massachusetts Press, 1994).

Costello, Bonnie, 'Bishop and the Poetic Tradition', in Angus Cleghorn and Jonathan Ellis (eds), *The Cambridge Companion to Elizabeth Bishop* (Cambridge: Cambridge University Press, 2014), pp. 79–94.

Dolar, Mladen, *A Voice and Nothing More* (Cambridge, MA: MIT Press, 2006).

Earnshaw, Steven, *Existentialism: A Guide for the Perplexed* (London: Continuum, 2006).

Giroux, Robert, cited by Fiona Green, '"In the Village" in *The New Yorker*', *Critical Quarterly* 52.2 (2010): 29–46.

Greene, Roland, et al. (eds), *The Princeton Encyclopedia of Poetry and Poetics*, 4th edn (Princeton: Princeton University Press, 2012).

Gunn, Kirsty, 'Foreword', in Katherine Mansfield, *The Aloe*, ed. Vincent O'Sullivan (London: Capuchin Classics, 2010), pp. 7–15.

Gunn, Thom, 'The Art of Poetry', *Paris Review* 135 (Summer 1995), <http://www.theparis-review.org/interviews/1626/the-art-of-poetry-no-72-thom-gunn> (last accessed 19 October 2018).

Hankin, C. A., *Katherine Mansfield and her Confessional Stories* (London and Basingstoke: Macmillan, 1983).

Harding, Bruce, '"The Women in the Stor(y)": Disjunctive Vision in Katherine Mansfield's "The Aloe"', in Janet Wilson, Gerri Kimber and Susan Reid (eds), *Katherine Mansfield and Literary Modernism* (London: Bloomsbury, 2013), pp. 115–27.

Harrison, Victoria, *Elizabeth Bishop's Poetics of Intimacy* (New York: Cambridge University Press, 1993).

Jamison, Leslie, *The Empathy Exams* (London: Granta, 2014).

Kahane, Claire, *Passions of the Voice* (Baltimore and London: John Hopkins University Press, 1995).

Kimber, Gerri, 'Introduction', in Gerri Kimber and Vincent O'Sullivan (eds), *The Edinburgh Edition of the Collected Works of Katherine Mansfield, Vol. 1: The Collected Fiction of Katherine Mansfield 1898–1915* (Edinburgh: Edinburgh University Press, 2012), pp. xix–xxiii.

Lehman, David, 'The Prose Poem: An Alternative to Verse', *The American Poetry Review* 32.2 (March–April 2003): 45–9.

Lurie, Susan, *Unsettled Subjects: Restoring Feminist Politics to Poststructuralist Critique* (Durham, NC, and London: Duke University Press, 1997).

Mansfield, Katherine, *The Aloe*, ed. Vincent O'Sullivan (London: Capuchin Classics, 2010).

Mansfield, Katherine, *The Collected Stories* (London: Penguin Classics, 2007).

Mansfield, Katherine, *Journal of Katherine Mansfield*, ed. J. Middleton Murry (London: Constable, 1954).

Mansfield, Katherine, *The Katherine Mansfield Notebooks: Volume Two*, ed. Margaret Scott (Minneapolis: University of Minnesota Press, 2002).

Millier, Brett C., *Elizabeth Bishop: Life and the Memory of It* (Berkeley: University of California Press, 1993).

Nancy, Jean-Luc, *Listening* (New York: Fordham University Press, 2007).

Ravinthiran, Vidyan, *Elizabeth Bishop's Prosaic* (Lewisburg: Bucknell University Press, 2015).

Rich, Adrienne, *Of Woman Born: Motherhood as Experience and Institution* (New York: W. W. Norton & Company, 1986).

Silverman, Kaja, *The Acoustic Mirror: The Female Voice in Psychoanalysis and Cinema* (Bloomington and Indianapolis: Indiana University Press, 1988).

Szirtes, George, *Fortinbras at the Fishhouses* (Tarset: University of Newcastle and Bloodaxe Books, 2010).

Tóibín, Colm, *All a Novelist Needs* (Baltimore: Johns Hopkins University Press, 2010).

Tóibín, Colm, *On Elizabeth Bishop* (Princeton: Princeton University Press, 2015).

White, Katherine, letter to Elizabeth Bishop (20 January 1953), in Elizabeth Bishop, *Elizabeth Bishop and The New Yorker: The Complete Correspondence*, ed. Joelle Biele (New York: Farrar, Straus and Giroux, 2011), pp. 100–2.

Wilson, Janet M., 'Introduction', in Janet M. Wilson, Gerri Kimber and Delia da Sousa Correa (eds), *Katherine Mansfield and the (Post)colonial* (Edinburgh: Edinburgh University Press, 2013), pp. 1–11.

Woolf, Virginia, 'A Sketch of the Past', in *Moments of Being* (New York: Harcourt Brace, 1985), pp. 61–159.

16

'THINKING WITH ONE'S FEELINGS': ELIZABETH BISHOP'S LITERARY CRITICISM

Michael O'Neill

I

IN 'IT ALL DEPENDS', Bishop's response to a questionnaire, published in 1950 in *Mid-Century American Poets*, edited by John Ciardi, she offers a succinct statement of her view of 'theories' about poetry. Such theories, she thinks, are of limited value since they are unlikely to be in any poet's 'mind at the moment of writing a poem'; she expresses her dislike of 'making poetry monstrous or boring and proceeding to talk the very life out of it' through 'pretentious and deadly' analysis (*Poems, Prose, and Letters* 687). Yet her dislike of professional literary criticism should not obscure the fact that her scattered observations about poetry, chiefly in letters and brief prose-pieces, display an original and often brilliant critical intelligence about the local details of individual poems and poetic artistry, and the larger significance of poetic acts.

Such intelligence is evident in the way in which sticking up for 'the very life' of a poem does not prevent her from asserting, to use the title wording of another piece, that 'Writing poetry is an unnatural act . . .', albeit one that seeks a natural effect. If the 'act' is 'unnatural', the essay proceeds to affirm, with an appositional contrariness that recalls the opening of Yeats's 'A General Introduction for My Work', then 'It takes great skill to make it [poetry] seem natural'. 'Most of the poet's energies', 'Writing poetry is an unnatural act . . .' continues, 'are really directed towards this goal: to convince himself (perhaps, with luck, eventually some readers) that what he's up to and what's he saying is really an inevitable, *only* natural way of behaving under the circumstances' (*Prose* 327).

A lot is going on there, as 'up to', with knowing disingenuousness, separates itself from and joins itself to 'what he's saying', before the phrases merge into an account of a poem as a 'way of behaving'. The very emphasis taken by '*only*' suggests that this feeling of the 'inevitable' is an effect of the rhetoric of naturalness. Poetry shares in her maternal grandmother's ocular predicament, 'combining', as Bishop puts it in the same essay, 'the real with the decidedly un-real; the natural with the unnatural' (*Prose* 331). Bishop relishes contraries and inconsistencies in her thinking about poetry. She describes 'the curious effect that a poem produces of being as normal as *sight* and yet as synthetic, as artificial, as a *glass eye*'. If this 'artificial' quality has to do with the poetry's Herbert-like desire to 'aim and shoot at that which is on high' (*Prose* 331), it concedes, through the fact of its existence, that there is something in poetry that causes us disquiet, as, in their different ways, Czeslaw Milosz, Marianne Moore and, more recently, Ben Lerner (paraphrasing – the debt is acknowledged – Allen Grossman) have recognised.

Consideration of other poets' treatment of this issue helps sharpen a sense of what's at stake for Bishop in 'Writing poetry is an unnatural act . . .'. Milosz, in 'Ars Poetica?', defines the predicament of the modern poet in terms relevant to Bishop's negotiation in her poetry and literary criticism (formal and informal) of the relationship between 'the natural' and 'the unnatural'. His poem opens with a manifesto-like aspiration marked by a sense that it is probably unfulfillable: 'I have always aspired to a more spacious form / that would be free from the claims of poetry or prose'. Such a form, hinted at in the spacious movement of the poem's lines, expresses both the poet's flinching from the 'something indecent' which is discernible 'In the very essence of poetry' and the recognition that, inevitably, he is writing a poem and wishes to state a purpose (that the poet's function is to 'remind us / how difficult it is to remain just one person') and express a hope (that 'good spirits, not evil ones, choose us for their instrument'). This poem is in touch with Bishop's covertly ethical concern with poetry's seeming 'unnaturalness'; poetry's very reliance on rhetoric and art involves an ingrained crookedness at odds with the aim to 'shoot on high', to attempt a transcendental (with or without a capital T) purity of utterance. Something of this desire to aim high informs a notebook entry from 1937 in which Bishop likens prose to 'land transportation', music to 'sea transportation', and 'poetry' to 'air transportation' (*Edgar Allan Poe* 31).

If Milosz is an heir of Bishop's concerns, Moore is a forerunner. 'Poetry', published in multiple forms, appears in *Observations* (1924) as the apparent object of the poet's initial statement: 'I, too, dislike it; there are things that are important beyond all this fiddle' (24–5). The phrase 'all this fiddle' means something like 'all this fussing and fretting', but faintly recalls, if only as a distant association, the old phrase about 'Nero fiddling while Rome burns' and hints at the music involved in poetry through its mention of the 'fiddle' or violin. Like Milosz, like Bishop, Moore is aware she is playing an instrument, and it is an instrument played on by her artistic helpers and ministers, in the case of her poem, an exacting syllabic and stanzaic structure, alongside inflections that acknowledge the 'claims of poetry or prose'.

Crucially, in the midst of expressing her dislike of 'it' (probably poetry, or possibly all the associations that the timeworn word 'poetry' brings to mind), Moore feels compelled to observe that 'one discovers that there is in / it, after all, a place for the genuine'. It is a 'place' for the capturing of physical detail, 'phenomena' that in their very existence disrupt distinctions between animal behaviour and '"business documents and // school books"' and are 'important'; their importance, for Moore, subsists somewhere between being 'useful' and simply existing, inspiring observers like her, '"literalists of / the imagination"', as she writes, misquoting Yeats.[1]

That misquotation bears witness to the new life embodied in a poem's words. When poets are too natural or too artificial they make Bishop sigh with the exasperation that Lerner suggests is integral to our difficult relationship with poetry. 'Poetry', he writes,

> isn't hard, it's impossible. (Maybe this helps us understand Moore [in 'Poetry']: Our contempt for any particular poem must be perfect, be total because only a ruthless reading that allows us to measure the gap between the actual and the virtual will enable us to experience, if not a genuine poem – no such thing – a place for the genuine, whatever that might mean.) (Lerner 14–15)

Bishop herself can rise to grandly tempered censure, as in her objections to Robert Lowell's use of personal material in *The Dolphin* (quoting Elizabeth Hardwick's letters in poems). She admires the draft form of the volume, the so-called *Ur-Dolphin* (Lowell 1133, 1134), as 'magnificent poetry', adding that 'it's also honest poetry – *almost*'. In that '*almost*' lie the seeds of her 'one tremendous and awful BUT', the phrasing Dickinsonesque in its defiantly post-Puritan response to the spiritual challenge posed by Lowell's poetry. Even if permission were to be given and there were an avoidance of the 'mixing of fact and fiction in unknown proportions', a quotation from Hardy adduced in support of her position, there is, in what Lowell has done, a falling away from 'Hopkins' marvelous letter to Bridges about the idea of a "gentleman" being the highest thing ever conceived – higher than a "Christian" even, certainly than a poet'; '*art*', she bravely and revealingly asserts, '*just isn't worth that much*' (*Words in Air* 707, 708). If it isn't, one feels she is also saying, it's because art is so much more than '*art*' – where art is thought of in terms of effect, expressiveness and so on, and not, fundamentally, as a mode of comportment of the self and soul in the world. In 'One Art', the unity at which the title gestures, with whatever irony, involves life turning into art, art emerging from and taking on its own form of life.

Lowell's poetry moves with reckless virtuosity, its tread a coldly dynamic, bravely half-melodramatic wince of the nerves – 'I myself am hell, / nobody's here – // only skunks' as he has it in 'Skunk Hour' (quoted from Lowell 192), a poem in which he is indeed, as Maureen N. McLane puts it, 'wound tight and then unwound' (32). But it is also, in its own way, as vigilant as Bishop's is, in its way, Lowell's vigilance taking the form of scruples about scruples in spun-out, self-cancelling lines such as these from the close of 'Summer between Terms 2' in *The Dolphin*: 'I waste hours writing in and writing out a line, / as if listening to conscience were telling the truth' (658). Bishop keeps us in mind of an angelic apprehension, possibly ineffectual, always aware, an apprehension embodied in the bracketed close of 'Night City':

> (Still, there are creatures,
> careful ones, overhead.
> They set down their feet, they walk
> green, red; green, red.) (*Poems* 188)

Planes are honoured as 'careful ones', Eumenides guarding the hearth of the earth, momentarily and fictionally functioning like displaced angels on a higher if paren- thetical level as in Wim Wenders's 1998 film *Wings of Desire*. It is these 'careful ones' who, so to speak, have been unfairly banished (for Bishop) in Lowell's *The Dolphin*. Bishop's critique of Lowell in her letter is generous but absolute, and makes crystal clear that, for her, poetry is a form of ethical conduct, subject to the rules that we can- not but apply privately and publicly to forms of behaviour.

Lowell was certainly affected by her remonstrations, as is shown by various replies to Bishop and remarks about her letter. To Frank Bidart he wrote that her letter was 'a kind of masterpiece of criticism, though her extreme paranoia (for God's sake don't repeat this) about revelations gives it a wildness. Most people will feel something of her doubts' (Lowell 1133). To Bishop herself he wrote – wryly, at bay and self- deprecatingly – that 'I feel like Bridges getting one of Hopkins's letters, as disturbed as I am grateful' (*Words in Air* 714). Kalstone supports Lowell's sense that there are psychological problems with 'revelations' at the back of Bishop's principled objections to her fellow poet's practice, problems that centre on 'her deepest fears about the intersection of suffering and the written word' (Kalstone 244).

At the same time, Lowell openly acknowledges his own – to him – inexorable compulsion to print what he knows will hurt others: 'The problem of making the poem unwounding is impossible . . . Working my poem out is a must somehow' (*Words in Air* 715), a 'somehow' that may allude to Bishop's blurb for *Life Studies* (see below). In their letters about *The Dolphin*, these great poets address, with the desperately engaged, back-to-the-wall involvement of the creative practitioner, one of the major problems presented by post-1945 poetry: the role in it played by 'revelations'. Bishop's letter looks more and more like a major document of modern poetics; if that over- and often ill-used term means anything any more, it must mean the impassioned, deeply felt thinking about the limits of poetry she articulates.

The point about Hopkins's 'gentleman' was clearly closer to a sharp-tipped barb as far as Lowell was concerned, for all his sense that the central issue raised by her letter was 'oddly enough a technical problem as well as a gentleman's problem' (*Words in Air* 713). Bishop cites the Hopkins passage more fully in the penultimate paragraph of 'Efforts of Affection: A Memoir of Marianne Moore', where, after allowing for the embarrassment of the word and 'its feminine counterparts', Bishop doughtily and wittily expresses her assurance that 'Marianne would have "vehemently agreed" with Hopkins's strictures: to be a poet was not the be-all, end-all of existence' (*Prose* 139–40). The wit lies not only in the rejigged Shakespearean allusion to *Macbeth* 1.7 (the omission of 'and' after 'be-all' giving any such view of existence a particularly blinkered ring), but also in the quoted phrase which captures Moore's manner well – and implies that her concern for 'manners' is not at odds with vehemence or definiteness. The last paragraph of 'Efforts of Affection' has Bishop experiencing a 'sort of subliminal glimpse of the capital letter *M* multiplying', having an Alice-like sense of the words 'manners' and 'morals' blurring and entwining (*Prose* 140). The drollery throws the reader off-guard, and the final effect is one of 'affection' for Moore's idiosyncrasies and a concern to keep in play the connection between the alliterative twins 'morals' and 'manners'.

Kalstone was shrewd to position Bishop in relation to and even between Moore and Lowell, even when one allows for the fact that *Becoming a Poet* 'is neither the book its author first intended nor the one he might finally have written' (Kalstone xii). Throughout her companionable, intense poetic and personal friendship with Lowell, Bishop's critical guard rarely drops and often there is a teasing if indulgent and admiring suggestion that he figures all too easily as the masculine hero of his own rhetorical imagination. When Lowell remembered her as '"tall"' with '"long brown hair"' at their first meeting, she declines the role of remembered, iconised beloved or muse as she tartly comments that she 'was always 5 ft. 4 and ¼ inches – now shrunk to 4 inches' and that her hair was 'already somewhat grizzled when I met you'; 'so *please*', she adds at the end of the letter, 'don't put me in a beautiful poem tall with long brown hair!' (*Words in Air* 778, 779). It's a virtual parable – funny, poignant, tolerant and, ultimately, merciless – about the male poetic imagination. And one wonders whether it hints, on Bishop's part, at a serio-playful imagining of herself as what she must have known herself to be in Lowell's imagination: anima and counter-responsive poetic rival and shadow self.

II

Lowell challenged Bishop's own poetic values as well as in many ways reinforc-
ing them. Writing to him in 1957 about poems he had given her in typescript that
would appear two years later in *Life Studies*, she is admiring but cool-eyed, very
faintly underwhelmed for all her genuine affirmations and enthusiasm. She remarks
on the pleasure it gives the artist to have the command over subject matter that
she imagines him to have felt in writing the poems. Yet, in a blend of searching
empathy, even surrogacy and implicit confession of necessary distance, she writes
of that experience: 'It seems to me it's the whole purpose of art, to the artist (not
to the audience) – that rare feeling of control, illumination – life *is* all right, for the
time being. Anyway, when I read such an extended display of imagination as this, I
feel it *for* you' (*Words in Air* 246; emphasis in original). Momentarily she proposes
what it must have been like for Lowell to have written his deeply personal, if highly
fashioned poems and seeks to stake out a common ground: 'I feel it *for* you'. What
she evades stating fully, with the delicacy of reserved courtesy, is how she feels about
the subject matter and its treatment. This reserve means that when she does intimate
a response to the subject matter in her comment on 'Sailing Home from Rapallo',
'almost too awful to read, but a fine poem' (*Words in Air* 246), its effect is sharp,
like a glancingly pointed remark.

The glancingly pointed and the reservedly courteous are frequent co-presences in
Bishop's literary criticism. Watchfulness is her watchword as a critic. She is always
ready to be quickened into sympathy, but often unable to give total assent to a poet's
strategies. In the letter to Lowell she tells him that her favourite (or, rather, 'the one I
like best, I think') is 'My Last Afternoon with Uncle Devereux Winslow', though she
adds a rider: 'I think I'd like the title better without the "my" maybe' (*Words in Air*
246). And though she likes 'Practically all' of the poem, she's 'a bit confused about
why the maids shd. look like sunflowers or pumpkins. Fat, in yellow dresses?' (*Words
in Air* 246). This confusion and questioning may be the kind of affectionately 'finicky'
(*Words in Air* 246), to use her own word in the letter, slightly exasperated reading
that poets who are friends give one another's work, and Lowell appears not to have
changed any details as a consequence. But it is consistent with Bishop's self-described
tactic of liking this effect, hesitating over that one, swooping on a detail and doing
so with great acuteness, yet often in a way that tells us as much about her as about
the poem; an example might be her objection to the word 'My' in the title, which one
might surmise she found too egotistical and possessive.

In a 1965 (and positive) letter to Randall Jarrell about his volume *The Lost World*,
she says, characteristically, 'I am NOT an articulate critic, as you know – I don't really
try to be, since I read for my own pleasure and comfort and curiosity only – so I just
get intuitions here & there, and love this and am repelled by that, and let it go' (*One
Art* 434), possibly alluding to the last line of her own poem 'The Fish'. The sentence
serves as a mini-manifesto, as much in its manner as in its matter. The apparent mod-
esty of the opening quickly shows itself to be a gambit, since 'I don't really try to be'
casts cold water on the attempts of those who (perhaps like Jarrell himself) seek to
be 'an articulate critic'. In the concluding part of the sentence Bishop briskly sums
up what is valuable for her about literary criticism. The readiness to question effects
and tones is at work in her comments elsewhere on Jarrell's poetry, as when his poem

'Woman' elicits the response (in a letter to Robert Lowell) 'And Oh dear! Randall on the subject of women! Why didn't he think it over a little more!' (*Words in Air* 141).

Bishop's lifelong engagement with Lowell's poetry means that when one pieces together her scattered comments, various fascinating plots and sub-plots suggest themselves. One is the sense given by her 'Blurb for *Life Studies*' of generosity and respect overcoming reservations without any setting aside of critical intelligence. The blurb is a genre that encourages shoddy hyperbole. But, approaching her task as though writing her own prose poem, Bishop distils her depth of response to a contemporary volume of the highest significance. 'As a child I used to look at my grandfather's Bible', her blurb begins, 'under a powerful reading-glass', the image undergoing a sudden transference as it suggests how Lowell reads us and we should read him. The association of poetry with a kind of truth-telling and with intimations of childhood works like a 'powerful reading-glass' when attached to *Life Studies*, as does the connection with 'a volume of Henry James at its best'. The affecting final sentence, 'Somehow or other, by fair means or foul, and in the middle of our worst century so far, we have produced a magnificent poet' (*Prose* 326), almost mimics Lowellian eloquence, and the 'we' introduces a proudly American note, even as Bishop's inimitable sense of chaos and contingency finds expression in that opening 'Somehow or other'. And, as Lowell himself noted in his thank-you letter, there's an adroit control of tone involved in the way 'the burning glass, etc., softens one for the surprise of "in the middle of our worst century so far"' (*Words in Air* 290).

If criticism such as she articulates must, for her, be a record of 'intuitions', the criteria she develops in 'Writing poetry . . .' – '*Accuracy, Spontaneity, Mystery*' (*Prose* 328) – allow her to admire a wide range of poets, as her choice of touchstones reveals. This use of touchstones is a technique that is at once Arnoldian and Jarrellesque, and it works as a form of emblematic, suggestive demonstration. She quotes lines from Lowell's 'Salem' – 'Remember, seamen, Salem fishermen / Once hung their nimble fleets on the Great Banks' – and observes that '*hung* suggests the immensity, the depths of the cold stormy water and the tininess, the activity of the small "nimble" ships – and yet it's the simplest sort of natural verb to use – ' (*Prose* 330).

Bishop may be influenced by Wordsworth's virtuoso riff on the same verb in his 1815 Preface, as demonstrated in its use by Milton in lines about Satan – 'As when far off at Sea a Fleet descried / *Hangs*' – 'the full strength of the imagination' (Wordsworth 608–9).[2] Wordsworth goes on to write that the 'Fleet' is depicted by Milton as '*hanging in the clouds*, both for the gratification of the mind in contemplating the image itself, and in reference to the motion and appearance of the sublime object to which it is compared', drawing our attention to the aesthetic pleasure involved in imaginative uses of language that lead 'to the gratification of the mind' (Wordsworth 609).

Wordsworth's pleasure in such effects is deeply, even uncomfortably, self-gratifying, yet it derives from the imagination's ability to make us see newly, in a different way. Bishop's comment is itself 'nimble' and shows her hanging over the depths of the poem's 'cold stormy water', and displaying her kinship with the Romantic poet who would approve of her phrasing, 'the simplest sort of natural verb'. Bishop did, after all, describe herself as 'really a minor female Wordsworth. At least, I don't know anyone else who seems to be such a Nature Lover' (*Words in Air* 122). Admirers such as Susan Rosenbaum have tried to rescue her from the apparent self-deprecation in 'minor', suggesting that it might refer to 'a diminished musical key' and 'poses a challenge to and departure from Wordsworth's (major, male, Romantic) poetics'.[3] True, Bishop quickly asserts her originality ('I don't know anyone else'), yet the assertion coexists with an amused self-awareness (the capitals in 'Nature Lover') that is less anxiously modest than level-headed in its recognition of the unexpected ways in which tradition and the individual talent coalesce. Her next sentence, '*The New Yorker*, I'm delighted to say, is quibbling with me over an indelicacy in a poem', runs at a poker-faced tangent from the slightly sent-up notion of herself as a 'Nature Lover' (*Words in Air* 122), alerting us to the humour invariably at work in her literary-critical self-characterisations.

Bishop is capable of giving the essence of a poet or poem in a sentence or phrase: Hopkins's 'The Wreck of the Deutschland' with its 'mounting grandeur and partly self-instigated growth of feeling' (*Prose* 471), for instance, or Shelley as a 'bright, steadfast flame that by disillusionment and tragedy was strengthened and given deeper colors' (*Poems, Prose, and Letters* 639), or Marianne Moore as 'The World's Greatest Living Observer' as exemplified by the lines 'the blades of the oars / move together like the feet of water-spiders' (*Prose* 253, 254). This critical gift is accompanied by wry, witty self-awareness. In the Moore essay 'As We Like It', she deftly gives example after example of her subject's ability to observe, unobtrusively underscoring her own observant critical eye; it is she who effortlessly catalogues the stunning visual and descriptive effects to be found in Moore, something that demonstrates her inwardness with and feeling for the poetry. Moore is so important a poet for Bishop that Bishop's praise for Moore comes to seem like a swiftly sketched manifesto. Indeed, Shakespeare by comparison seems 'full of pre-conceived notions and over-sentimental' in *As You Like It*, where the quoted lines –

> The wretched animal heav'd forth such groans
> That their discharge did stretch his leathern coat
> Almost to bursting, and the big round tears
> Cours'd one another down his innocent nose
> In piteous chase . . .

– don't quite make Bishop's point since they surely exhibit Jacques's rather than Shakespeare's overblown sentimentality. The title of this essay-*hommage*, with quietly jaw-tilted adversarialness, plays Moore and Bishop, both writing 'As We Like It', against 'our greatest poet', author of *As You Like It*.[4] It is possible to trace a vein of understated canonical contestation here. But the desire to advance Moore's and by implication her own 'gift of being able to give herself up entirely to the object under contemplation, to feel in all sincerity how it is to be *it*' is impressively strong, running like an underground river below the cited examples before surfacing in the praise of Moore's ability, in creating a 'description or imitation', to be 'brief, or compact, and have at the least the effect of being spontaneous' (*Prose* 254, 254–5, 254, 255).

III

Suffering is a recurrent theme in Bishop's thinking about poetry, yet it causes her something close to embarrassment when it is overtly displayed in art. 'I don't like *heaviness* – in general, Germanic art. It seems often to amount', she asserts in her

letter of October 1964 to Anne Stevenson, a letter which is unusually intent on spell-
ing out her views, 'to complete self-absorption – like Mann & Wagner' she adds, in
case her 'Germanic' should seem unspecific' (*Prose* 417). She touches here on the
need to be *'grim without groaning'* and adds that 'It may amount to a kind of "good
manners"'; this 'amount to' is placed in the pan of the scales against that containing
'self-absorption' (*Prose* 417). The quotation marks around 'good manners' perform
a good-mannered grimace at falling back on so necessary and so bourgeois an idea:
they almost groan at their grim-faced solution to a problem posed by Dickinson –
'I still hate the oh-the-pain-of-it-all poems' (*Prose* 412) – and by Robert Lowell, as
we have seen.

     Yet manners preoccupy Bishop, as in her admiration for the mixture of 'morals'
and 'manners' in Moore. Her poem 'Manners' is written 'for a Child of 1918', a
dedication that reminds us of her comment that 'it is odd how often I feel myself to
be a late-late Post World War I generation-member, rather than a member of the Post
World War II generation'. In the same letter she adds, revealingly, that 'Cal (Lowell)
and I in our very different ways are both descendents from the Transcendentalists'
(*Prose* 396). Does one not sometimes sense in both poets expansive oversouls and
hard-boiled laconicism interacting?

     'Manners' is witty, touching, self-mocking:

> When automobiles went by,
> the dust hid the people's faces,
> but we shouted "Good day! Good day!
> Fine day!" at the top of our voices. (*Poems* 119)

Off-rhyme serves as the poem's latent recognition that there's always 'dust' hiding
'people's faces', however much we shout politely 'at the top of our voices'. Manners
over-protest their integrity here, as the eras of the horse-drawn 'wagon' and the com-
bustion engine collide. They curiously undo themselves – and maybe that is the point
for Bishop of manners: that they allow – and allow for – a sense of the limits of man-
ners in a way that the unmannerly does not.

     She writes to Lowell in September 1948: 'Sometimes I wish we could have a more
sensible conversation about this suffering business, anyway. I imagine we actually
agree fairly well. It is just that I guess I think it is so irresistible & unavoidable there's
no use talking about it, & that in itself it has no value, anyway' (*Words in Air* 59).[5]
That final shrug – 'in itself it has no value, anyway' – seems close to impatience with
a cultural, ultimately religious assumption: that suffering, if of no value in itself, is
potentially redemptive for the sufferer, spiritually good for the artist to confront.
Bishop suggests, by contrast, suffering's quotidian banality. Her wording delivers an
unnerving shock, as her poems do, because of its determination to see with a very
cold eye indeed.

     This is the poet who, according to Helen Vendler, in 'Brazil, January 1, 1502' admits
her 'complicity in social evil' (Vendler 293) when she depicts the 'Christians', conquis-
tadors, as 'hard as nails, / tiny as nails, and glinting / in creaking armor' (*Poems* 90).
One might wish to reply to Vendler, though, that the nails that enter the flesh of the
reader's mind are the 'tiny' jabs of post-colonial historical awareness. In her September
1948 letter to Lowell, Bishop goes on to express her objection to Auden's 'Musée des

Beaux Arts', not on the grounds of its 'attitude about suffering', but because 'it's just plain inaccurate in the last part. The ploughman & the people on the boat will rush to see the falling boy any minute, they always do, though maybe not to help.' She admits 'he's describing a painting' (*Words in Air* 60), but the impression is given that she feels Auden's wish to make a point has led him astray. Auden's emphasis on 'suffering' has led him to misunderstand how people respond to the tragedies of others; reticence, the implication might be, is more likely to offer a truer, more accurate picture of how suffering happens and occurs.

But she also admired Auden greatly; in 1966, to a friend 'seeking advice on love', Bishop replied, 'If you really are concerned about that subject' (beautifully laconic, that phrase), 'I'd suggest that you go and read Auden. If *he* doesn't know something about love, I just don't know who else does' (*Edgar Allan Poe* 268). The comment recalls, perhaps, that what Auden knew, at his most affecting about 'love', was that he needed to ask 'Tell me the truth about love' and that it caused a great deal of pain. Again, her note on his use of 'marvellous', for instance, equivo- cally defends his employment of one of the words she calls 'fashion-words, used ironically' (*Edgar Allan Poe* 268). One thinks of the famous close of 'The Bight': 'All the untidy activity continues, / awful but cheerful' (*Poems* 59). These last two lines remind us of her statement to Anne Stevenson that 'one can be cheerful AND profound!' (*Prose* 417); they also use 'fashion-words' ironically, with a kind of defensive, affectionate irony, as if to say that 'activity' cannot be fitted entirely into any sub- or post-Baudelairean system of 'correspondences', the 'Click. Click' (*Poems* 59) of artistic fitting.

With the poets who really mattered to her she responded with a mixture of love and exasperation. Stevens 'occasionally seems to make blank verse *moo*', though she likes *Owl's Clover* for its 'display of ideas at work – making poetry, the poetry making them, etc' (*One Art* 48). The making 'blank verse *moo*' may be less an objection to over-regular iambic rhythm (*Owl's Clover* modulates its syllable-count and rhythms expertly) than to Stevens's love of dolefully full-vowelled euphony, a quality evident in yet transcended by lines that Bishop praises for their suggestion 'of something new arising from the unhappiness' (*One Art* 48):

> as if the black of what she thought,
> Conflicting with the moving colors there
> Changed them, at last, to its triumphant hue (quoted as given in *One Art* 48)

It doesn't seem wholly accidental that this 'something new', with its darkly ambiva- lent 'triumphant hue', rhymes with the sound 'moo', nor that 'moving' joins in the dance of sound. Vidyan Ravinthiran suggests that the comment relates to Bish- op's sense of the 'cognitive quality of verse, and how difficult this is to keep up' (35). Jonathan Ellis argues that, though 'Bishop's meaning is a little obscure', it is when they 'stick to the same metrical beat' that Stevens's lines provoke her 'attack' (152). My counter-intuitive argument is that iambic 'mooing' is Bishop's hearing of a sound that can grate on her ear but is recognised by her, subliminally per- haps, as necessary for the poetry's conceptual discoveries. Richard Wilbur reports her admiration for Poe's 'Fairy-Land' and glosses this admiration in terms close to those I'm suggesting are relevant to Bishop's response to Stevens: 'its weeping trees

and multitudinous moons', writes Wilbur, 'are repeatedly and humorously chal-
lenged by the voice of common sense; out of which conflict the poem somehow
modulates, at the close, into a poignant yearning for transcendence' (Schwartz and
Estess 263). The Stevens she admires, with his 'display of ideas at work', is at one
with her deep conviction of the importance, as she puts the matter in her early
essay on Hopkins, in a quotation taken from M. W. Croll's article 'The Baroque
Style in Prose', of the writer portraying 'not a thought, but a mind thinking'
(*Prose* 473).

The phrase is effectively a ground or starting point for her literary criticism. The
result can be complexly ambivalent, as in her response to Frost: 'I hate his philosophy,
what I understand of it – I find it *mean* – while admiring his technique enormously'
(*Prose* 421). She goes on to say: 'Well – as Cal says frequently – "We're all flawed," –
and as far as poetry goes I think we have to be grateful for what we do get. They all
rise above their flaws, on occasion' (*Prose* 421). The diminuendo, there, suggests that
rising above meanness, as a critic, is not quite the same thing as overlooking technical
or emotional or moral 'flaws'.

IV

'They all rise above their flaws, on occasion'; the sentence wouldn't be out of place in
a Bishop poem, any homiletic wisdom proffered ironically and yet not only ironically.
Her prose, like her poetry, depends on pacing, interactions of sense and sound, shades
of meanings and tone, balances between stabs of insight and pauses for reflection. In
her 'Gerard Manley Hopkins: Notes on Timing in His Poetry', her emphasis moves
from prosody and sprung rhythm to the coexistence of the 'original emotion' and 'the
created, crystallized emotion' which gathers momentum as the poem unfolds. 'The
whole process', she writes memorably, 'is a continual flowing fullness kept moving
by its own weight'; she continues, 'Because of this constant fullness each part serves
as a check, a guide, and in a way a model, for each following part, and the whole is
weighed together. (This may explain why last lines in poetry are so often best lines;
and why, often too, they seem so concocted and over-drawn for the rest of the poem
[. . .])' (*Prose* 471).

As often, Bishop seems in proleptic dialogue with her poems. The whole of 'The
Moose' has a 'continual flowing fullness' as its six-line stanzas move between this and
that, the woman with 'two market bags' and 'Grandparents' voices' – across a stanza
break – 'uninterruptedly / talking, in Eternity', all resolved unsentimentally in the
poem's 'sweet / sensation of joy', which divides once again into animal and human, 'a
dim / smell of moose, an acrid / smell of gasoline'. The poem's 'flowing fullness' seems
key to its success, its immersion in yet withdrawal from 'a gentle, auditory, / slow hal-
lucination' (*Poems* 191, 193, 191). 'Immersion' takes a while – hence the experience
of succession, breaks, regathering, divagation, arrival at a way forward, as happens
elsewhere in Bishop's poems. 'North Haven', for example, itself is fated to follow
the fate of its subject, Robert Lowell: 'The words won't change again' (211). Bishop
could have revised the poem while alive, but the poem, as its final rhyme clicks into
place – 'you cannot change' playing against 'derange, or re-arrange' (211) – realises
surely that it is speaking, too, of death in relation to itself, or of the fixity which is
death's treacherous joke.

For her own enactment of what is meant by 'a continual flowing fullness', one might also cite the close of 'At the Fishhouses', lines in which, as John Hollander puts it in 'Elizabeth Bishop's Mappings of Life', 'images of place begin to be understood – almost to understand themselves – as images of the condition of consciousness itself' (Schwartz and Estess 247):

> It is like what we imagine knowledge to be:
> dark, salt, clear, moving, utterly free,
> drawn from the cold hard mouth
> of the world, derived from the rocky breasts
> forever, flowing and drawn, and since
> our knowledge is historical, flowing, and flown. (*Poems* 64)

'It is like' qualifies in the act of connecting, even as 'we imagine' has an Audenesque boldness (one might compare the use of 'we' in, say, 'In Praise of Limestone', published a few years earlier) that is not wholly typical of Bishop. And what we are persuaded to entertain is a vision of knowledge from which human subjectivity is almost wholly erased: it is a knowledge 'drawn' and 'derived' and what it is imagined as being 'free' from is, in part, the very impulse that compels imaginings of what knowledge might be – hence the irony lurking in the unobtrusive rhyme with which the passage begins. But it is 'our knowledge', and resides in what Hollander finely calls 'images of the condition of consciousness itself'.

If Bishop's lines are in accord with what the Hopkins essay calls 'continual flowing fullness', they are also in their subtle rhythmic retardations and syntactical modifications (that final 'since', for instance) able to retain a critical watchfulness about 'continual flowing fullness', to see such an oceanic image of consciousness as related to human desire. Bishop, too, aligns the 'flowing nature of knowledge' with the fact that it is always 'flown'. There is a built-in post-Keatsian sense that the vision is lost in the moment of articulating what it might be like to find it; the bird of paradise, knowledge, freedom, has 'flown'. The poem itself experiences 'knowledge' as 'historical'.

For Mark Strand, in 'Elizabeth Bishop Introduction', 'there is absolutely no self-pity in Elizabeth Bishop's writing. Instead, there is an unusual amount of common-sense: a kind of realism in which the poem is always responsible to the observable, factual world' (Schwartz and Estess 243). Her 'common-sense' is one reason why she can use the word 'we' as she derives a knowledge that is drawn from the senses we have in common. Yet in her thinking about poetry, and in the acts of literary criticism her poetry implicitly makes, one recalls Bishop's admiration for the close of 'The Circus Animals' Desertion' and the settling, there, on Yeats's part, for 'the foul rag and bone shop of the heart', itself a 'common' if individualised possession (see *One Art* 92). Yeats's poem about how poetry plots with and against life, how parts turn into larger designs, though often in tormented or conflicted ways, anticipates a theme explored by Bishop, herself (in 'Sonnet') a 'creature divided' (*Poems* 214) but able to imagine a poetry 'flying wherever / it feels like, gay!' (214).

Bishop's poems could be read as on the side of 'the observable, factual world' in their exact descriptions and ripples of design-undermining irreverence, but it is not an accident that her great villanelle is entitled 'One Art'. The poem's drafts (in *Edgar Allan Poe* 223–40) move from betrayal of feeling to attempted, laconic mastery. There is a Yeatsian refusal to break up her lines to weep that occurs after drafts 10 and 11. The conclusion in 10 reads: 'It's evident / the art of losing isn't hard to master / with one exception . . . (Say it.) [above and below deleted 'Write it!']. That's disaster' [or 'yes, disaster']. This'll turn into 'It's evident / the art of losing isn't hard to master / though it may look like (*Write* it!) like disaster' (*Poems* 198). Disaster is now part of the poem, a 'like' word, a written word, a word that tells not simply of experiential loss but of artistic longing, the ironised longing to master disaster.

In a letter of September 1955 to May Swenson, a phrase from which gives this chapter its title, Bishop, taking issue with her correspondent, says 'I am puzzled by what you mean by my poems not [. . .] appealing to the emotions'. She concedes or affirms that my 'best poems seem rather distant', but not before she slips in the Eliotic view (one thinks of intellects at the tips of the senses) that 'poetry is a way of thinking with one's feelings' (*Poems, Prose, and Letters* 809). Not, one notes, thinking about one's feelings, but thinking with them. She goes on to assert, and again Eliot comes to mind, that 'I don't think I'm very successful when I get personal – rather, sound personal – one always is, of course, one way or another' (*Poems, Prose, and Letters* 809–10).

What Bishop calls 'thinking with one's feelings' makes possible a poetic self-consciousness that forms an implicit and finely wrought literary criticism when it manifests itself in her own compositions, in her irresolute epiphanies, self-questioning, damped-down transmutations, as at the end of 'Questions of Travel', where the ability to question seems more than half to answer itself. Aware of limitations and self-division, the poem feels its way towards thinking, locating freedom in the italicised recognition that '*the choice is never wide and never free*'. This is not a statement, merely a felt thought imagined by a traveller after two hours of rain has fallen like 'unrelenting oratory'; that gives way to 'a sudden golden silence' (*Poems* 92). As a literary critic and poet, Bishop, like her sandpiper, experiences the world as 'a mist' and then as 'minute and vast and clear' (*Poems* 129), and it's her remarkable achievement to make us delight in her expressive enactments of doubt and clarity's mingled coexistence.

Notes

1. Moore alludes to Yeats's description of Blake (in 'William Blake and His Illustrations to *The Divine Comedy*' (1903)) as 'a too literal realist of imagination'; see note in Moore, *Observations*, p. 96.
2. This echo is noted in Ravinthiran, in the course of a fine discussion of the first paragraph of Bishop's 'In the Village', p. 139.
3. Susan Rosenbaum, cited and mildly qualified in Ravinthiran, pp. xiv–xv.
4. Bishop's poem (and title) 'Twelfth Morning; or What You Will' further revises Shakespeare. Her elegy for Lowell, 'North Haven', alludes to the song at the end of *Love's Labour's Lost*. See Lloyd Schwartz, 'Back to Boston: *Geography III* and Other Late Poems', in Angus Cleghorn and Jonathan Ellis (eds), *The Cambridge Companion to Elizabeth Bishop* (Cambridge: Cambridge University Press, 2014), p. 152.
5. *Words in Air*, among other differences, has the more dialogic 'we could' rather than 'I could' (the reading provided in *One Art*, p. 170).

Works Cited

Bishop, Elizabeth, *Edgar Allan Poe & the Juke-Box: Uncollected Poems, Drafts, and Fragments*, ed. Alice Quinn (Manchester: Carcanet, 2006).

Bishop, Elizabeth, *One Art: The Selected Letters*, ed. Robert Giroux (London: Chatto & Windus, 1994).

Bishop, Elizabeth, *Poems, Prose, and Letters*, ed. Robert Giroux and Lloyd Schwartz (New York: Library of America, 2008).

Bishop, Elizabeth, and Robert Lowell, *Words in Air: The Complete Correspondence between Elizabeth Bishop and Robert Lowell*, ed. Thomas Travisano with Saskia Hamilton (London: Faber and Faber, 2008).

Ellis, Jonathan, *Art and Memory in the Work of Elizabeth Bishop* (Aldershot: Ashgate, 2006).

Kalstone, David, *Becoming a Poet: Elizabeth Bishop with Marianne Moore and Robert Lowell* (Ann Arbor: University of Michigan Press, 2001).

Lerner, Ben, *The Hatred of Poetry* (London: Fitzcarraldo, 2016).

Lowell, Robert, *Collected Poems*, ed. Frank Bidart and David Gewanter (London: Faber and Faber, 2003).

McLane, Maureen N., *My Poets* (New York: Farrar, Straus and Giroux, 2012).

Milosz, Czeslaw, *Bells in Winter*, trans. the author and Lillian Vallee (Manchester: Carcanet, 1982).

Moore, Marianne, *Observations*, ed. Linda Levall (New York: Farrar, Straus and Giroux, 2016).

Ravinthiran, Vidyan, *Elizabeth Bishop's Prosaic* (Lewisburg: Bucknell University Press, 2015).

Schwartz, Lloyd, and Sybil P. Estess (eds), *Elizabeth Bishop and Her Art* (Ann Arbor: University of Michigan Press, 1983).

Vendler, Helen, *The Music of What Happens: Poems, Poets, Critics* (Cambridge, MA: Harvard University Press, 1988).

Wordsworth, William, *Selected Writings (21st-Century Oxford Authors)*, ed. Stephen Gill (Oxford: Oxford University Press, 2010).

PART V
OTHER PLACES, OTHER PEOPLE

17

'Private faces in public places': Bishop's Triptych of Cold War Washington

Heather Treseler

Private faces in public places
Are wiser and nicer
Than public faces in private places.

(W. H. Auden's dedication of *The Orators* to Stephen Spender)

In 1949, at the age of thirty-eight, Elizabeth Bishop began her first fully fledged job as Poetry Consultant to the Library of Congress, a position obtained through the political angling of her friend Robert Lowell (Millier 209). Bishop's scant work experience prior to assuming this national office included five days in 1943 at a Navy optics shop in Key West, grinding lenses for binoculars: a short-lived contribution to the war effort that aggravated her eczema. She also worked at a shady correspondence school in New York City in 1934, shortly after she graduated from Vassar College (Millier 171, 71). There, she wrote letters in the epistolary guise of an avuncular older man, Fred G. Margolies, offering mail-order subscribers instruction in 'Straight Reporting', 'Advertising' and 'True Confession', the very modes of writing she would parody in satiric poems over the next two decades (*Prose* 100, 105). Indeed, Bishop's work within a Navy optics shop and under an epistolary pseudonym at an illegal 'writing school' was strangely apt preparation for her year-long position in the nation's capital, where she responded to Cold War surveillance, jingoism and homophobia in a variety of poetic disguises.

Charmingly described in her story 'The U.S.A. School of Writing' (1966), Bishop's post-collegiate work for a correspondence school, later closed when her employer was indicted for mail fraud, featured her association – and dark fascination – with her colleague Rachel, an ardent Communist who tried to recruit Bishop to her cause. As Bishop relates, her disdain for her co-worker's politics grew as she discovered Rachel's proclivity for Walt Whitman and 'big books, with lots of ego and emotion in them', a bias that would also inform her uneasiness with Ezra Pound, her coeval in Washington during her tenure there (*Prose* 102). In his infamous radio broadcasts from Italy (1941–43), Pound had endorsed Mussolini, vilified Roosevelt, and delivered vitriolic anti-Semitic screeds. Extradited to the United States, he was found mentally unfit to be tried for treason in 1946 and committed to St Elizabeths Hospital (Norman 424). There, he was allowed to host visitors, play tennis, and give an occasional reading of Provençal poetry on hospital grounds (Norman 428, 438, 442). He was also awarded the Bollingen Prize for the *Pisan Cantos* in 1948, a decision that proved so controversial that Congress subsequently transferred the administration of the prize from the Library of Congress to Yale University (Roman 107).

But the federal indictment charge against Pound was not dismissed until 1958, and his twelve years in a psychiatric wing 'with catatonics and dementia praecox cases slithering about' was a cautionary tale for poets of Bishop's generation as they navigated their political allegiances (Weldon Kees quoted in Millier 221). Indeed, Bishop's office at the Library of Congress was a mere twenty minutes by taxi from the locked ward at St Elizabeths and, by 1949, the line between traitor and citizen, suspect and civilian, had thinned considerably (Norman 441). Pound's case made the stakes of political critique dramatically clear: had he been tried and found guilty of treason, he might have suffered death by electrocution, an ignominious fate for the once revered figurehead of Anglo-American modernism (Norman 422).

Given Bishop's retiring public persona and personal liabilities, her job could not have begun at a worse time: she succeeded Léonie Adams as Poetry Consultant while the Cold War underwent rapid acceleration. In her second week at the Library of Congress, the United States confirmed that Russia had recently tested its first nuclear weapon, a fact that shattered the 'atomic hegemony' thought to secure the United States' martial supremacy over its chief rival (Engelhardt 58). Less than a week later, Mao Zedong declared the triumph of Communist forces in China's civil war, establishing a new capital in Beijing (Engelhardt 58). In a now familiar inversion of logic, fears of Communism's spread abroad sparked a domestic persecution of difference within the United States. Picking up on George Kennan's description of the 'malignant parasite' of Communism in his 'Long Telegram' from Russia in 1946, politicians stressed moral hygiene and wholesome living as prophylactics against ideological disease (Davidson 271).

Suffering from asthma and alcoholic binges as well as bouts of flu and loneliness, Bishop was often absent from her federal post (Millier 223–5). But the capital's intensifying atmosphere of surveillance might have been as much a cause of her absenteeism as her physical woes. In 1950 the Senate Appropriations Committee, virtually next door to the Library of Congress, issued a report entitled 'On the Employment of Homosexuals and Other Perverts in Government Office' (Davidson 274). And Senator Kenneth Wherry, a gadfly in the Senate's investigation, declared that he was personally 'on a crusade to harry every last pervert from the Federal Government Services' (quoted in Faderman 143). Later that winter, Senator Joseph McCarthy began his witch-hunt for alleged Communists, and though his televised tribunals failed to result in a single conviction, by 1953, one out of every five Americans had been subject to a 'loyalty-security check' in an unprecedented policing of the populace (Engelhardt 122).

Thus, while Bishop's appointment signalled her national ascendancy, she was also a closeted lesbian in danger of losing her job. Staying for part of that year in a Georgetown boarding house ironically named Miss Looker's, she had difficulty maintaining her sobriety and living among strangers (Fountain and Brazeau 114–15). Indeed, in April of 1950, she moved to a residential hotel inauspiciously named Slaughter's, 'perhaps once again out of [alcoholic] embarrassment' (Millier 223).

Bishop's drinking bouts seem to have coincided, at times, with attempted liaisons. Maia Rodman, wife of the poet Selden Rodman, recounts meeting Bishop in Washington Square, New York, for 'lunch or dinner' in 1950 and receiving a phone call from

Bishop later that night in which Bishop propositioned her, asking Rodman to her hotel room and confessing to being 'in a horrible state of mind' (Fountain and Brazeau 118). Rodman noted, 'I thought that that scene in the hotel was one of many nights like that' (119). Steven Axelrod has also surmised that Bishop's taking prescribed amounts of adrenaline and ephedrine to control her asthma, aggravated by the city's climate, may have amplified her anxiety and unease, legible to many of her acquaintances that year (844). Joseph Frank, a biographer who befriended Bishop, noted her air of nervousness: 'Elizabeth certainly had lots of anxieties. I'm not so sure they were connected specifically with the job [...] Things would slip out in conversation [...] I always had the feeling that she didn't want to talk about anything personal' (Fountain and Brazeau 116).

As Poetry Consultant, Bishop was living the paradox of Cold War America in that civic privacy, the feature thought to distinguish American citizens from their Communist counterparts, was both fetishised and delimited, with sexuality as a prime target of investigation (Nelson 108). In *Odd Girls and Twilight Lovers*, Lillian Faderman notes that between 1947 and 1950, around 5,000 men and women were dismissed from government or military service after being accused of homosexuality, which was thought to make an employee vulnerable to blackmail and foreign espionage (140). In a letter to Robert Lowell in 1953, Bishop would bleakly refer to her stint as Poetry Consultant as 'that dismal year [...] when I thought my days were numbered' (*Words in Air* 143), and she noted on the first page of her journal from 1950 that it had been her 'worst' year, thus far (Vassar folder 77.4).

Yet Bishop's official duties as Poetry Consultant were not onerous. They entailed responding to research questions, organising readings, writing liner notes for recordings, hosting the occasional distinguished guest, and visiting Ezra Pound in his doorless room at St Elizabeths (Millier 220; Norman 436). Nevertheless, she demurred from giving any public readings and the prospect of attending a Board of Fellows meeting in January, the month in which she began drafting 'View of the Capitol from the Library of Congress', sparked a heavy two-day drinking spree (Fountain and Brazeau 115). Camille Roman reports that 'View of the Capitol from the Library of Congress' was, in fact, the only poem Bishop completed in those twelve tortured months (119). Later, while living in Brazil, she would conclude her collection *Questions of Travel* (1965) with two other poems, 'From Trollope's Journal' and 'Visits to St. Elizabeths', which triangulate her take on militarism, the domestic casualties of war, and the danger of conflating politics and poetics. In her literal 'View of the Capitol', Bishop was conscripted to witness an environment that, by all accounts, perturbed her and temporarily stymied her writing. Yet the three poems galvanised by her term in Washington collectively deliver one of the most affecting critiques of warfare's devastation by any poet of her generation.

Striking continuities among the Washington poems are probably related to the fact that Bishop assumed her government post shortly after intensive work with Dr Ruth Foster, a New York psychiatrist, on the nature of her creative process as well as the aetiology of her alcoholism and depression (Millier 194). Three letters Bishop addressed to Foster, from February of 1947, provide a portal into her suffering and the nature of her poetic response. In her first letter, Bishop notes that psychoanalysis has enabled her to stop viewing each poem as 'an isolated event' and to think, instead, of her poetry as 'really all one long poem anyway', a shift in perspective immediately evident in the circulation of images and tropes within *A Cold Spring* (1955) and *Questions of Travel* (Vassar folder 118.33). Indeed, Bishop's trio of poems about the US capital explores wartime hysteria, violations of privacy, and recuperative resistance in ways that evince the poet's aperçu that her new poems 'go on into each other or over lap [*sic*]' (Vassar folder 118.33).

Bishop's revealing letters to Foster also detail her amorous relationships with women; her mother's death and haunting presence in Bishop's life; the history of her drinking problem; and the sexual abuse by her uncle George Shepherdson, which began when she was eight years old and continued into her mid-adolescence. Tellingly, she refers to Shepherdson as a 'real storm trooper type', one of the 'real sadists' who 'gloats over violence' and whose 'streak of cruelty' was matched by 'his dreadful sentimentality' (Vassar folder 118.33). She recounts instances in which he hung her 'by the hair' over a second-storey balcony, fondled her in a bathtub, and threatened to beat her for 'answering back' (Vassar folder 118.33). Tellingly, the same traits Bishop attributes to her uncle in the Foster letters – lugubrious emotion, gratuitous displays of power, a militaristic temperament – reappear in her Washington 'triptych'. In these poems, she responds to another atmosphere of threat and incipient violence: she interprets the capital city in ways that resonate with her childhood memories of Great Village, Nova Scotia, and Worcester, Massachusetts.

The gross uncertainty of Bishop's early life in different households, the abuse she suffered from her uncle, and much of her traumatic history hinged on her status, after 1916, as a wartime orphan. As Sandra Barry's essay 'Elizabeth Bishop and World War I' sets forth, 'the private tragedy of Bishop's maternal family resonated with "the world tragedy of 1914"': in the year of the Great War's outbreak, Bishop's mother Gertrude Bulmer suffered an emotional breakdown for which she was hospitalised (96). By 1916, when Bulmer voluntarily admitted herself to the Nova Scotia Hospital, where she would remain for the rest of her life, the clinical file reports that Bulmer was convinced that she was 'going to die for her country' and was, in fact, 'the cause of the war' (97). Thus, Bishop's keen sensitivity to post-World War II triumphalism and Cold War rhetoric of psychological hygiene might have been linked to her mother's delusional conviction that she had triggered the Great War and would be martyred.

Diana Fuss situates Bulmer's wartime hysteria as part of a lengthy history of mental illness, including her suicide attempt a full decade before her marriage to William T. Bishop, the poet's father. But it was in 1914 that Bulmer jumped from a second-storey window at the Deaconess Hospital in Brookline, Massachusetts; and, prior to her third and final hospitalisation, she tried 'to strangle her mother and hang herself with a sheet' (Fuss). The Nova Scotia Hospital admittance form, completed by Bulmer's sister Grace in 1916, notes that Gertrude was suffering from hypochondria, thinking she had 'kidney, heart, and specific diseases'; paranoia, believing that she was being 'watched as a criminal'; and hysteria, fearing specifically that she would be 'hung, burnt as a witch or electrocuted' (Fuss).

As a child, Bishop probably witnessed some harrowing scenes. Her mother's descent into madness, marked by homicidal and suicidal impulses, is obliquely limned in 'In the Village', the prose story she suggestively positioned between the 'Brazil' and 'Elsewhere' sections of *Questions of Travel*, providing a context for her collection's motivating query, '*Should we have stayed at home / wherever that may be?*' (*Poems* 92). In one emblematic scene of 'In the Village', the child narrator studies her mother's postcard collection, which has arrived in Great Village – with her mother's other belongings – before her physical return from a hospital stay in Massachusetts.

Poignantly, the child regards the postcards as artefacts from her mother's shuttling journeys between home and asylum, sanity and madness. She notes that '[p]ostcards come from another world, the world of the grandparents who send things, the world of sad brown perfume, and morning' (*Prose* 65). The child, moreover, observes that some postcards feature glittery captions and 'have words written in their skies' that appear to be 'raining down' on the featured 'little people', much the way the mother's airborne scream of madness, with which the story begins and concludes, permeates village life 'in the past, in the present, and those years between' (65, 62).

Postcards' suggestive, secondary messages reappear as a trope in 'View of the Capitol from the Library of Congress', which Bishop stylised as a tourist's postcard about a military band's inability to sound, to deliver its intended message, to make a musical '*boom — boom*' indicative of its power (*Poems* 67). The postcards of 'In the Village' and Bishop's postcard-satire of Cold War Washington suggest, in their imagistic links, an association between patriotic displays and the maternal 'scream' of madness. Within 'View of the Capitol from the Library of Congress', the military music goes mute and, in that ' – queer – ' lacuna, the longitudinal reader of Bishop's oeuvre might hear the suppressed echo of Bulmer's scream: Bishop's mother's conviction that she had instigated the Great War (67). Indeed, the axial trope in Bishop's autobiographical story is 'A scream, the echo of a scream [that] hangs over that Nova Scotian village [. . .] alive forever', overwhelming in its sound, whereas in her poem, the 'Air Force Band' fails to sound at all. In a parody of bellicose pomp, the band's 'little flags', 'limpid stripes' and impotent music belie its 'hard and loud' attempts at persuasion, and in this way Bishop's poem can be read as a coded response to personal tragedy. A retort to martial display, Bishop's postcard-poem sends a missive back to 'the world of sad brown perfume, and morning', returning to the realm of her mother's wartime paranoia, where it symbolically turns off the music of madness. Among the 'war songs' Bishop reports resenting and feeling 'haunted' by in Worcester, Massachusetts, was one with the refrain 'Joan of Arc, they are ca-alllll-ing you' (*Prose* 95). Summonsed to serve, Joan answered 'the call' that Bulmer was also tragically convinced she heard: an imperative to die for her country.

Though Bishop has been categorised as a poet of 'political detachment', her shifting perspectives may have been too complex – or, in some instances, had too personal a register – to be reducible to 'causes', given that they were expressed within the constrictions of her immediate political context and the public suppression of her private history (Axelrod 848). Even in letters to close friends, Bishop often adopted a faux-naïf stance about her poetry's implications. In 1955, for example, she wrote to Joseph and U. T. Summers: 'I am so surprised that the "View of the Capitol" means something! Now I see it does. Please don't tell anyone this!' (*One Art* 307). Playfully disingenuous, Bishop probably knew full well the import of her satiric poem – though, in its subtlety, it has been chronically dismissed by critics as 'a wonderful bit of impressionism' (Millier 230) or as 'a slighter poem' (Cook 114).

Bishop waited until she had left Washington and settled at the Yaddo Writers' Colony in October of 1950 before she sent her poem to another set of friends, the painter Loren MacIver and the conscientious objector Lloyd Frankenberg. As Roman reports, Bishop had mailed the couple a string of pictorial postcards earlier that year (121). Though she sent her postcard-poem inside a traditional letter, 'View of the Capitol from the Library of Congress' apes a commercial postcard's descriptive caption. Moreover, Bishop described it to MacIver and Frankenberg as 'a little number I turned out the other day', as if it were a spontaneously composed song and not a politically edged poem, drafted in agonisingly staccato fashion, from as early as January 1950 (Roman 122).

'View of the Capitol from the Library of Congress' is a trenchant parody of patriotism that, if intercepted and properly understood, might have incurred political trouble. After Bishop left her post, William Carlos Williams's candidacy for the Poetry Consultant position was effectively derailed by Communist accusations from congressmen, the general public and publications such as *The Lyric* and *Counterattack: Facts to Combat Communism* (McGuire 151). Subsequently, he was subject to a federal 'loyalty investigation', and complications from these proceedings and ill health kept him from serving any portion of his appointed term (McGuire 151–61). Against the risk of such persecution, Bishop's coded poems explore the domestic implications of modern war, focusing on its conscription of the private citizen and the mentally infirm; victims of genocide; and the perennial suffering of animals and ecology. 'View of the Capitol from the Library of Congress' begins *in medias res* and immediately plays upon the politics of surveillance:

> Moving from left to left, the light
> is heavy on the Dome, and coarse.
> One small lunette turns it aside
> and blankly stares off to the side
> like a big white old wall-eyed horse. (*Poems* 67)

Bishop describes a 'heavy' and 'coarse' searchlight – or another focused beam – '[m]oving from left to left', across the Congressional dome's port side, or the 'left' associated with liberal and Communist sympathies. The dome itself, meanwhile, operates like an ineffective Orwellian eyeball: using a 'lunette' to refract the glare, it 'stares off to the side'. While Axelrod plausibly interprets the 'small lunette' to be one of the arch-shaped windows along the front of the Congressional dome, the word's alternative definitions as a double-flanked military fortification – or an equine blinker – suggest that Congress is unable to perceive anything outside of its defended, obstructed field of vision. In the 1950s, blinkered congressmen, scrutinising 'the left', were typically 'big white [and] old'; Bishop inscribes their physiognomy on the civic building, opting for a less risqué metaphor of the Congressional dome than the 'elaborate sugar-tit for a / nation / that likes sugar' which appears in earlier drafts (Vassar folder 77.4). Changing the gender, exchanging a surrogate breast for a blinkered horse, Bishop cloaked her critique of the Cold War's succour of American industries, turning a mammary image into an emblem of emasculated power (Roman 124).

In her story 'The Country Mouse' (1961), Bishop used remarkably similar imagery to describe her paternal grandfather, John W. Bishop, whose company built civic landmarks such as the Boston Public Library and the Museum of Fine Arts.[1]

(He [Grandfather Bishop] was walleyed. At least, one eye turned the wrong way, which made him endlessly interesting to me. The walleye only seemed right and natural, because my grandmother on the other side in Canada has a glass eye.) (*Prose* 86)

Bishop's depiction of the Capitol dome mimics her description of her conservative grandfather in their shared visual disability: 'wall-eyed' and 'walleyed', respectively, they are unable to see what is directly in front of them (*Prose* 87). And while Congress failed to grapple with the international scope of the Cold War, focusing narrowly on citizens' private lives, Bishop's grandparents failed to see the precocious traumatised child in their charge, whose intelligence and temperament outstripped her chronological age and the Victorian circumstances of their home. Indeed, 'The Country Mouse' recounts Bishop's formative nine months in Worcester, where she strongly resented the 'war songs', 'war cartoons', knitting projects and pledges of allegiance with which she was required to demonstrate her 'patriotism'. It was also in her grandparents' home that she began to suffer from the asthma and auto-immune disorders that would plague her for most of her life. Wheezing heavily in Washington, and suffering 'patriotic music' on buses and trolley cars, Bishop constructed a typology of the capital city – a manner of viewing and interpreting it – that hearkened back to childhood memories and her resistance, from an early age, to being rallied or 'forcibly soothed'.[2]

Mocking Congress's leftward astigmatism in the tone of a knowing child, Bishop inhabits the narrative sensibility with which she describes her Worcester environs in 'The Country Mouse': there 'the house was gloomy [. . .] and everyone seemed nervous and unsettled [. . .] something ominous, threatening, lowering in the air' (*Prose* 89). In Bishop's tale, the defining public concern is that 'The War was on', a circumstance that heightens the narrator's confusion about her Canadian or American allegiances and reinforces her antipathy toward the American songs at her Worcester school (95). Poignantly, she comments that the lyric '"*Between his loved home and the war's desolation*" made me think of my dead father, and conjured up strange pictures in my mind' (95). She also confesses to lying to a playmate about her mother's whereabouts. After telling her friend Emma that her mother is dead, the narrator notes with self-rebuke: 'I was aware of falsity and the great power of sentimentality [. . .] My mother was not dead. She was in a sanatorium, in another prolonged "nervous breakdown"' (98). Bishop's entwining of parental loss and patriotic activity – in school songs, pledges, marches, 'war cartoons', rationing and knitting for 'the soldier boys' – underpins the personal register of her critique of military machismo; in effect, she allows her typology of Worcester and Washington to 'go on into each other or over lap [*sic*]' (*Prose* 95, 92; Vassar folder 118.33).

Bishop's suspicion about what was 'in the air' reappears in the internal stanzas of 'View of the Capitol from the Library of Congress', in which she undermines the legitimating gestures of empire, particularly its 'force' of air. The second and third stanzas feature an 'Air Force Band', jaunty in their homogeneous 'uniforms of Air Force blue' (*Poems* 67). Standing on 'the east steps' and 'playing hard and loud', the band members cannot get their music to 'come through' (67). Bishop suggests that some acoustic *interruptus* has cancelled out its virile show of 'force', its 'hard and loud' effort (67). With the magical realism of a child's storybook, the narrator surmises that the large neighbouring trees 'must intervene' by 'catching the music in their leaves / like gold-dust, till each big leaf sags' and 'the band's efforts vanish there' (67). In essence, the natural landscape mutes the military band's peri-performative blare: the melody disappears before it can complete its affective circuitry, rousing the sentiments of a national audience. In a political context, Bishop's tableau might represent the US government's inability to rally support for the Korean War, which began during her summer in office and failed to garner more than 30 per cent of Americans' approval in its three-year duration (Donaldson 77).

Yet if the military cannot persuade the populace with music, it still has the capacity to obliterate the landscape. As Bishop's poem concludes, the tone is both playful and urgent:

> Great shades, edge over,
> give the music room.
> The gathered brasses want to go
> *boom — boom.* (67)

Jejune in its syllabic double-punch, the poem employs language alternately classical ('Great shades'), colloquial ('The gathered brasses') and outright cartoonish ('*boom — boom*'). With childlike logic, the speaker surmises that the 'Great shades' – of the arboreal landscape and of the venerable dead – have snuffed out the military's efforts. Yet the '*boom — boom*' in the last line also suggests that nuclear weaponry threatens, nonetheless, to annihilate all with its devastating power. Like the postcards in 'In the Village' with their ominous 'words written in their skies', the military music, in aping aerial bombardment, warns of murderous sound (*Prose* 65). Thus, while Bishop's poem playfully unplugs the 'Air Force Band', the last stanza reminds readers that the 'music' of bombs is poised to wreak destruction. Frequently misread as one of her minor poems, 'View of the Capitol from the Library of Congress' is as much an indictment of military machismo as the barnyard allegory 'Roosters'; the poem's conclusion, moreover, alludes to the unique threat of nuclear warfare, which does not require popular support to bring about mass annihilation.[3]

Two related poems, 'From Trollope's Journal' and 'Visits to St. Elizabeths', intensify Bishop's critique of triumphalism and the Cold War's insidious emphasis on psychological health. As George Kennan had stated in his 'Long Telegram' from Moscow in 1946, it was thought that 'World communism feeds only on diseased tissue' and thus 'Every courageous and incisive measure [. . .] to improve self-confidence, discipline, morale and community spirit [. . .] is a diplomatic victory over Moscow' (quoted in Davidson 271). Using the para-literary guises of a travelogue and a nursery rhyme, Bishop parodies Cold War anxiety about mental health and moral fortitude. In the two poems that conclude *Questions of Travel*, she takes the reader to Civil War Washington and into the psychiatric ward of St Elizabeths Hospital; in the latter, war veterans, war victims and a vituperative poet eke out a bleakly recursive existence, fixed actors in history's tragic play.

'From Trollope's Journal', which Bishop described to Lowell as her 'anti-Eisenhower poem', adopts the genial persona of the nineteenth-century British novelist and borrows directly from his published travelogue *North America* (1862), about his visit to the US capital in 1861 (*Words in Air* 594). A modified double sonnet, Bishop's poem begins conversationally:

> As far as statues go, so far there's not
> much choice: they're either Washingtons
> or Indians, a whitewashed, stubby lot,
> His country's Father or His foster sons.
> The White House in a sad, unhealthy spot (*Poems* 130)

Satirising the statues' depiction of patriarchal colonialism – with George Washington as the 'Father' and forcibly colonised Native Americans as his 'foster sons' – Bishop uses Trollope's description of Civil War Washington to undermine the Cold War's fetishising of heteronormative family life as the bastion of civic virtue. In Trollope's persona, Bishop asserts that colonial genocide has been 'whitewashed' in American mythology; thus, the statues depict Native Americans as parentless, a version of the 'orphan romance' she herself had suffered. '[F]oster' care, as Bishop knew, could entail benign neglect as well as abuse and violence; these lines, in connection with what the Dr Foster letters reveal about Bishop's childhood, acquire an oblique personal register.

Situating her Cold War critique in the Civil War experiences of a British novelist penning modified Shakespearean sonnets, Bishop plays with the masque and manufacture of national, literary and personal identities. Altogether, the poem is roughly divided into two sonnet-like sections of fourteen lines each. 'Americanising' the sonnet with casual phrasing, simple rhymes and homely imagery, Bishop's Trollope strolls down a muddy Pennsylvania Avenue, where he encounters bivouacked soldiers and 'hoof-pocked uncultivated [. . .] cattle' maintained to feed the army (130). Eight of the poem's twenty-eight lines are dedicated, in fact, to these 'starving' cattle, suggesting that they are part of the war's coextensive economy of suffering, one that blurs battlefield sacrifice with civilian and ecological privation (130). 'Their legs', Bishop's Trollope notes, 'were caked the color of dried blood; / their horns were wreathed with fog. Poor, starving, dumb / or lowing creatures' (130). Metonymically, the cattle stand in for the martial bodies that suffer the war's primary (but by no means exclusive) appetite for slaughter, which Bishop extends beyond the battlefield. Indeed, the ambient pestilence in Washington marks Trollope himself with an infectious souvenir: he must find a surgeon to lance an infection suggestively positioned on his forehead. Trollope moans, 'Th'effluvium / made that damned anthrax on my forehead throb. / I called a surgeon [. . .] he croaked out, "Sir, I do declare / everyone's sick! The soldiers poison the air"' (130). Innocent cattle, a British tourist and a surgeon 'with a sore throat himself' all suffer the somatic distress that Bishop links to the non-combatant experience of war (130).

Moreover, when the British novelist cites the cattle's 'effluvium' as the cause of his skin infection, Bishop uses a word that signifies a foul smell as well as the sickening aura of radiation, a linguistic hinge that embeds this seemingly historical travelogue in the contemporary Cold War moment. Inverting Containment policy's rhetoric of hygiene and Communist 'infection', she suggests that prolonged mobilisation itself is the source of disease: its pernicious atmosphere affects even the president, who has 'got / [. . .] fever in each backwoods limb' (130). Punning 'limb' and 'backwoods', Bishop connects a somaticised environment with the presidential physique, undoing the hierarchy of value in which human welfare is privileged over that of animals and landscape. Depicting war as a pervasive social disease, Bishop asserts that it draws civilians and cows, surgeons and soldiers, presidents and tourists alike into its thrall of threat and suffering.[4]

But it is the third poem of Bishop's Washington triptych, 'Visits to St. Elizabeths', which consolidates her critique of warfare in a trans-historical, deeply affecting context. Leading its reader, by way of a nursery rhyme, into Ezra Pound's psychiatric ward, Bishop portrays a gallery of lives derailed by the cataclysm of World War II. Unlike Robert Lowell's depictions of McLean Hospital near Boston, where he himself was periodically a patient, Bishop does not depict 'Mayflower / screwballs' with Brahmin airs and Ivy League pedigrees, 'figures of bravado ossified young', but rather persons whom history – and fortune – seems never to have favoured (*Life Studies* 82). In Bishop's 'house of Bedlam', readers encounter an addled sailor, obsessed with his wristwatch, moored within the claustrophobic 'years and the walls of the ward' where he sails a 'sea of board' (*Poems* 131). There is also a 'widowed Jew in the newspaper hat' who 'dances weeping down the ward', wearing the headlines, perhaps, of Hitler's genocide (132). Conducting his solitary waltz, a dance of German origin, he walks 'the plank of a coffin board', possibly choreographing his survival or the extremity of his grief (133). Indeed, the Jew's solitary dance is juxtaposed against the poem's disturbingly jaunty repetitions: things are not as they are being sung. This is 'a world of books gone flat', a world of ontological horror in which a young boy, another patient in St Elizabeths, neurotically 'pats the floor / to feel if the world is there and flat' (132).

Modelling her poem on the nursery rhyme 'This Is the House that Jack Built', Bishop catalogues the human devastation of total war, including its psychiatric victims. At the centre of this tableau is the unnamed figure of Ezra Pound, identifiable in Bishop's description of him as 'the poet, the man / that lies in the house of Bedlam' (132). Like Gertrude Bulmer, deluded about her culpability for the Great War and her sacrificial role in it, Pound's scurrilous radio broadcasts expounded irrational causes: he joined the Nazis to scapegoat European Jewry and the practice of so-called 'usura' for the putative downfall of Western civilisation. In the poem's twelve stanzas, Bishop offers several takes on Pound's character, portraying him as a figure worthy of revilement and pity: a poet whose derangement coincided, like her mother's, with political cataclysm. Thus, he is termed a 'tragic, talkative, honored, brave, cranky, cruel, busy, tedious, and wretched' man, descriptors suited to Pound's hateful broadcasts, dramatic extradition, and committal to 'the Bug House' for twelve long years (Norman 432–3).

As in the 'postcard' and 'travelogue' masques of 'View of the Capitol from the Library of Congress' and 'From Trollope's Journal', Bishop locates her elegy for the victims of world war in a nursery rhyme, disguising a sobering tribute. But Bishop may have also been connecting – and cathecting – her mother's madness and her childhood memories of wartime songs with Pound's incarceration. According to historian J. M. Winter, 'This Is the House that Jack Built', which dates from the sixteenth century, was reinvented during the Great War as a 'children's ditty' in which a child sang:

> This is the house that Jack built.
> This is the bomb that fell on the house that Jack built.
> This is the Hun who dropped the bomb that fell on the house that Jack built.
>
> This is the gun that killed the Hun who dropped the bomb that fell on the house that Jack built. (219)

According to Winter, a popular British cartoon featured this rhyme alongside a child carrying a gun, signifying the 'new mobilization of children in total war' (219). While it is unclear whether this version of the nursery rhyme circulated in Nova Scotia or reached Massachusetts, Bishop recalls in 'The Country Mouse' seeing 'war cartoons, several big books of them: German helmets and cut-off hands [that] haunted us'. So she may have been familiar with the 'mobilized' version of 'This Is the House that Jack Built' and its disturbing illustrations, which showcased children murdering 'the Hun' (219). This connection would be yet another ligature between her portrayal of Cold War Washington and her Great War experiences, her typology of the capital informed by her childhood memories. Depicting Pound as a psychiatric patient, one suffering from a wartime illness, Bishop revisits a primary trauma from her youth and – figuratively, belatedly – the psychiatric ward at Nova Scotia Hospital where Gertrude Bulmer lived for nearly two decades without a visit from her daughter. In the repetitions of a nursery rhyme, which play upon an auditor's sense of anticipation and surprise, Bishop haunts the reader with her own wartime song: an iterative score as poignant as any battlefield ballad. Never having visited her mother in the hospital, the poet may have written 'Visits to St. Elizabeths' with that irony in mind: she, an unsaintly Elizabeth, granted Pound the solicitude she could not give her mother. In cataloguing the residents of Pound's hospital ward, Bishop may have also explored her own perennial fear of losing her mind and joining the 'wretched' company of the mad. As she wrote to her physician, Anny Baumann, a few months after she left Washington about her drinking: 'I've been stalling along now for years [. . .] Dr. Foster said "Well, go ahead, then – ruin your life" – and I almost have, I also know I'll go insane if I keep it up' (quoted in Millier 228).

Using para-literary forms – a postcard, travelogue and nursery rhyme – Bishop conveyed the toxicity of total war with a disarmingly light touch: a strategy that allowed her to satirise military aggression, wartime mobilisation and patriotic hysteria while evading investigation or public rebuke. As in her first jobs, grinding binocular lenses and impersonating the instructor Fred G. Margolies, Bishop's triptych of Washington refocuses the glare of surveillance, comments knowingly in the voice of an older male figure, and subtly asserts principles contrary to the dominant political agenda. Altogether, Bishop's polyvalent poems critique the wars she suffered as a civilian, redressing both her miserable year as Poetry Consultant to the Library of Congress and her childhood traumas. Her trenchant perspective is sewn into her poems' codes: in the open secrets of a postcard; in a satire lodged within a travel diary; and in an elegy disguised as a nursery rhyme. Employing para-literary tropes, Bishop created a space within the lyric poem in which private faces might be worn in public places with some measure of impunity. Bishop's nimble masquerade, which lends these poems their trans-historical power, may have also served to safeguard her from being accused of Communism, denounced for homosexuality or sent, like the 'Great shades' of her mother and her poetic peer, to the unhappy house of Bedlam.

Notes

1. Bishop may have had her grandfather Bishop and his civic edifices in mind when she complained to a friend in 1949 that 'Washington doesn't seem quite real. All those piles of granite and marble, like an inflated copy of another capital city somewhere else' (*One Art* 194).

2. Bishop's childhood resentment of programmatic music, martial displays and declarative allegiances is tellingly mirrored in her complaint about the music played on public transportation in the capital to *New Yorker* editor Katharine White in January 1950, the month in which she began drafting 'View of the Capitol from the Library of Congress': 'thank you or your magazine for the campaign against radio broadcasting in the station – here we have it in trolley cars and busses and it is really pure torture. Every day I say to myself now you CAN read and forget it, if you try – but it's really impossible and I'm spending all my salary on taxicabs just to escape it [. . .] It is particularly painful here, I think – thousands of government workers being carted off to work every morning and being forcibly soothed all the way – as bad as "1984"' (*Elizabeth Bishop and The New Yorker* 47). Ruing the auditory invasion of music on public transport, Bishop describes it as an infringement on 'human rights' and on, perhaps, her private association of nationalism with loss.

3. Bishop also depicts an apocalyptic world in 'The moon burgled the house', a poem draft that appears in the '1951–1967' section of *Edgar Allan Poe & the Juke-Box*. The narrator describes a chillingly peaceful demise of the earth in a tone similar to the sangfroid of 'View of the Capitol from the Library of Congress'. The poem begins, 'The end of the world / proved to be nothing drastic // when everything was made of plastic', and it depicts the quiescence of the earth's human inhabitants, even after 'the pills gave out // and vast drops of the rivers ran / into the drying canyons of the sea' (110). Ecological devastation does not frighten those left, who sleep 'more and more', dream, stay at home 'holding hands', and abide as the world confronts 'its death / gently' (110). Bishop's poem depicts the end of the world with ironic calm, and she employs a similarly sardonic tone in 'View of the Capitol from the Library of Congress', where 'gathered brasses' want to unleash their violent music, their mimicry of war.

4. In Trollope's account, he notes: 'I was hardly out of the doctor's hands while I was there [Washington, DC], and he did not support my theory as to the goodness of the air. "It is poisoned by the soldiers," he said, "and everybody is ill." But then my doctor was perhaps a little tinged with southern proclivities' (319). In removing the Union and Confederate distinctions from Trollope's narrative in her own version, Bishop downplays the Civil War context, giving it greater allegorical force.

Works Cited

Auden, W. H., *The English Auden*, ed. Edward Mendelson (London: Faber and Faber, 1977).

Axelrod, Steven Gould, 'Elizabeth Bishop and Containment Policy', *American Literature* 75.4 (2003): 843–67.

Barry, Sandra, 'Elizabeth Bishop and World War I', *War, Literature, and the Arts* 11.1 (1999): 93–110.

Bishop, Elizabeth, *Edgar Allan Poe & the Juke-Box: Uncollected Poems, Drafts, and Fragments*, ed. Alice Quinn (New York: Farrar, Straus and Giroux, 2006).

Bishop, Elizabeth, *Elizabeth Bishop and The New Yorker: The Complete Correspondence*, ed. Joelle Biele (New York: Farrar, Straus and Giroux, 2011).

Bishop, Elizabeth, *One Art: Letters*, ed. Robert Giroux (New York: Farrar, Straus and Giroux, 1994).

Bishop, Elizabeth, Vassar College Libraries Special Collections, folders 77.4 and 118.33.

Bishop, Elizabeth, and Robert Lowell, *Words in Air: The Complete Correspondence between Elizabeth Bishop and Robert Lowell*, ed. Thomas Travisano with Saskia Hamilton (New York: Farrar, Straus and Giroux, 2008).

Cook, Eleanor, *Elizabeth Bishop at Work* (Cambridge, MA: Harvard University Press, 2016).

Davidson, Michael, 'From the Margin: Postwar Poetry and the Politics of Containment', *American Literary History* 10.2 (1998): 266–90.

Donaldson, Gary, *The Making of Modern America: The Nation from 1945 to the Present* (Lanham: Rowman and Littlefield, 2009).

Engelhardt, Tom, *The End of Victory Culture: Cold War and the Disillusionment of a Generation* (New York: Basic Books, 1995).

Faderman, Lillian, *Odd Girls and Twilight Lovers: A History of Lesbian Life in Twentieth-Century America* (New York: Penguin, 1991).

Fountain, Gary, and Peter Brazeau (eds), *Remembering Elizabeth Bishop: An Oral Biography* (Amherst: University of Massachusetts Press, 1994).

Fuss, Diana, 'How to Lose Things: Elizabeth Bishop's Child Mourning', <http://post45.research.yale.edu/2013/09/how-to-lose-things-elizabeth-bishops-child-mourning/> (last accessed 8 October 2018).

Gaddis, John Lewis, *Strategies of Containment: A Critical Appraisal of Postwar American National Security Policy* (New York: Oxford University Press, 1982).

Lowell, Robert, *Life Studies* (New York: Farrar, Straus and Cudahy, 1959).

McGuire, William, *Poetry's Catbird Seat* (Washington: Library of Congress, 1988).

Millier, Brett C., *Elizabeth Bishop: Life and the Memory of It* (Berkeley: University of California Press, 1993).

Nadel, Alan, *Containment Culture: American Narratives, Postmodernism and the Atomic Age* (Durham, NC: Duke University Press, 1995).

Nelson, Deborah, *Pursuing Privacy in Cold War America* (New York: Columbia University Press, 2002).

Norman, Charles, *Ezra Pound* (New York: Funk and Wagnalls, 1969).

Roman, Camille, *Elizabeth Bishop's World War II–Cold War View* (New York: Palgrave, 2001).

Trollope, Anthony, *North America* (New York: Alfred A. Knopf, 1951).

Vera, Dan, 'The Library and its Laureates: The Examples of Auslander, Williams, Dickey & Kumin', *Beltway Poetry Quarterly* 10.4 (2009), <http://washingtonart.com/beltway/four-laureates.html> (last accessed 22 October 2018).

Winter, J. M., 'Propaganda and the Mobilization of Consent', in Hugh Strachan (ed.), *The Oxford Illustrated History of the Great War* (Oxford: Oxford University Press, 2014), pp. 216–25.

18

ELIZABETH BISHOP'S POETICS OF ISLANDOLOGY

James McCorkle

DEFINED BY EDGES, ISLANDS are always undergoing reconfiguration by what surrounds and encompasses them. Islands are apparitional, appearing and disappearing on the horizon, eroding and accumulating by current, storm or human intervention. Tensed between a permeable edge mediating the sea and the seeming solidity of land, islands form geographical metaphors for the problematics of identity. Marc Shell's 2014 epistemological meditation on islands as a metaphor for modernity, *Islandology: Geography, Rhetoric, Politics*, explores associatively through philosophy, visual materials and literature the dynamic of ambivalency in geographical and political terms. Location, and thus definition, conforms to land and water as an ongoing process delineating truth, memory and national identity. 'All islands – and coasts – already have a floating, liminal aspect,' writes Shell. 'An island, which sailors often confound with a whale, is at the limit a sort of "swimming land," apparently self-moving like an animate being' (36). The metaphors of island and mainland are part of a geographic determinism Shell explores through the romantic visions, whether in the visual or literary arts, and imperial ambitions and identities of Germany and England: borders are mutable, changing, fluid, and confer power and significance through particularised locations.

While Shell draws upon Shakespeare, Defoe and Donne, and mentions in passing Kamau Brathwaite and Derek Walcott, Elizabeth Bishop, whose poetry and prose explore how memory and identity can be understood through the metaphorics of islands, is strangely absent. While Bishop's work can be discussed through the lens of islandology as a metaphor for imperial or national identity, islandology also unfolds a series of metaphoric constructions about the ambiguity of self and the making of poetry. In an early essay on Bishop's poetics, 'Shifting Islands: Elizabeth Bishop's Manuscripts', Barbara Page describes Bishop's compositional process like islands shifting about in successive drafts before she reaches a final, immutable version; in this we see in the composition of these poems 'the heroism of the artist who struggles with the recalcitrance of language – not to say all of the discouragements that flesh and spirit are heir to – toward the perfection of form' (59). As seen in her 'The Imaginary Iceberg', 'Late Air', 'Sandpiper' and 'Crusoe in England', islands, and shorelines, are hallucinatory, mirages appearing and vanishing, masses subject to erosion; thus the discussion of Bishop's islandological poetry embeds the question of visibility and invisibility, what Daniel Tiffany calls in *Toy Medium: Materialism and Modern Lyric* 'lyric substance'. It is through such metaphors that I wish to explore 'lyric substance' throughout Bishop's poetry.

The metaphorics of the island may imply travel, the touristic, the articulation and extension of imperialism as Mary Louise Pratt has explored, or has been discussed in regard to the mid- to late-twentieth-century poetry from the United States by such commentators as Robert von Hallberg and Jeffrey Gray. The issues of appropriation and hegemony, the imperial and the diminishment of others, unexamined racism and privilege, penetration and possession are often considered defining elements of the poetics, and reflective of the national ethos, of Bishop and many of her contemporaries. As Shell notes, the metaphor of the island poses deep political and national crises. At the heart of Shell's islandology is the acute listening to overlapping sounds, interpenetrating and permeable meanings, a shift from an insular reading to littoral and osmotic readings, or from a politics of containment to one of interconnection. Bishop and her island poetics encompass isolation and identity, containment and connectivity, and especially the permeability of the visible. Bishop constructs, as David Kalstone described in his 1977 study *Five Temperaments*, an imagined life, not quite autobiographical, but a 'compact with the self' (5). In her unpublished poem 'Apartment in Leme' (1963), 'Off to the left, those islands, named and re-named / so many times now everyone's forgotten / their names, are sleeping' (*Poems* 307), Bishop considers the making and re-visioning of constructs, whether of self, house, history, shoreline or poem.

It is the island, that Kantian metaphor, that Shell explores as the trope for understanding the boundaries and boundedness of knowledge and disciplines. Islandology, in the sense that I apply it to the poetics of Bishop, is a formation of interlocking and permeable spaces. Certainly, as Mark Ford has written, in Bishop's work 'coasts are often figured as the space where the contest between different systems of meaning can be most fully and rewardingly staged' (239). Ford, however, sets up – not incorrectly, but nonetheless reductively – various dualities, land and sea, north and south, cheerful and awful, freedom and constraint, that he argues Bishop's poetry inscribes. Rather than a traversal across space as in a linear narrative, the privileging of a specific line of gazing, or the convergence of lines of perspective, we should consider the metaphorics of islandology where the permeability of these lines is central. Ford locates Bishop's theatre of writing as the shoreline; however, instead of being a place of opposition, of antipodean forces, her poetics demonstrates the littoral processes, the site of overlap and interplay. The littoral becomes the place of writing into thought and thought into writing, where the lyric is made substantive.

Bishop's identity is bound to coastlines and islands, beginning with Nova Scotia, all but an island; her literal island sojourn continued with her nine-year residence on Key West, beginning in 1938. Subsequently she travelled to Haiti, Maine and Nova Scotia, before boarding the Norwegian freighter *SS Bowplate* for Brazil in 1951. For the next fifteen years she lived with Maria Carlota Costallat de Macedo Soares (Lota) in the house they built in the mountains, itself an island, above Petrópolis. Bishop's poetry, and her islandology, opens with 'The Map', which meditates on boundaries and horizons: 'Land lies in water; it is shadowed green. / Shadows, or are they shallows, at its edges / showing the line of long sea-weeded ledges / where weeds hang to the simple blue from green' (*Poems* 5). Bishop's mapping of the edges of knowing and the apparitional nature of knowledge – 'Shadows, or are they shallows' – echoes Kant's understanding of truth in *Critique of Pure Reason*: 'This domain of [possible truth] is an island by nature within unalterable limits' and that this island is 'the land of truth – enchanting name! – surrounded by a wide and stormy ocean, the native home of illusion, where many a fog bank and many a swiftly melting iceberg give the deceptive appearance of further shores, deluding the adventurous seafarer ever anew with empty hopes, and engaging him in enterprises which he can never abandon and yet is unable to bring to completion' (quoted in Shell 16, 254).While Kant sites truth as an island distinct from oceanic chaos and illusion counter to Bishop's littoral poetics, Kant's own interruption – 'enchanting name!' – parallels Bishop's interruptions and self-interrogations. Such moments could be seen as ruptures, but also discursive islands where one discourse surfaces amid a larger and distinctly different discourse. Excess – 'the printer here experiencing the same excitement / as when emotion too far exceeds its cause' – introduced here becomes, ironically, one of Bishop's aesthetic tropes: how can an island be excessive in its isolation?

Mapping the lyric, that is, making the lyric a place and substance, is a central and persisting concern. One of Bishop's last poems, 'North Haven' (1978), an elegy for Lowell yet also very much self-elegising, echoes the topographical reveries of 'The Map':

> The islands haven't shifted since last summer
> even if I like to pretend they have
> – drifting, in a dreamy sort of way
> a little north, a little south or sidewise,
> and that they're free within the blue frontiers of bay. (*Poems* 210)

Unanchored, shifting perspectives, resistant to fixity or definition, even immaterial – 'dreamy' – describe Bishop's topographies. Barbara Page notes that the poem's stanzas float from place to place in each version of the poem, either resisting coming to rest in some final form or tensed between fixity and the sense of being 'afloat in mystic blue' (Page 54–5). From her 1939 poem 'Pleasure Seas', Bishop describes the Florida Straits, where 'out among the keys',

> Where the water goes its own way, the shallow pleasure seas
> Drift this way and that mingling currents and tides
> In most of the colors that swarm around the sides
> Of soap-bubbles, poisonous and fabulous.
> & The keys float lightly like rolls of green dust. (*Poems* 279)

The view here is of the horizontal. We are essentially traversing the bay toward the Florida Keys that seem to float on the surface, and, as in Bishop's 'The Fish', the surface is an illusory rainbow of colours, deadly and 'fabulous'. Bishop tilts the perspective to what appears the vertical: 'From an airplane the water's heavy sheet / Of glass above a bas-relief: / Clay-yellow coral and purple dulces / And long, leaning, submerged green grass.' The view penetrates the travelled-across surface, to 'see' what would seem invisible, the 'long, leaning, submerged green grass', as certainly our sight would be deflected by the surface where two contrasting elements, fire and water, intersect: 'The water is a burning-glass / Turned to the sun' (279).

The visual splendour of Bishop's poem as it plays surface against depth while arraying across that surface a spectrum of colour recalls Ezra Pound's early 'The Sea of Glass':

> I looked and saw a sea
> > roofed over with rainbows,
> In the midst of each
> > two lovers met and departed;
> Then the sky was full of faces
> > with gold glories behind them. (131)

Pound's imagistic experiment prefigures Bishop's preoccupation with rainbows, sheltering the sea and the tenuousness of love. Pound conflates the sea's surface and the sky; the perspectives of looking both up and down on a single vertical parallels the shifting perspectives of Bishop's poem and the perpetuity of movement and travel. Pound creates an empty space between the two lovers who seem both arriving and departing, the space of meeting always and already vanishing. Whether or not Bishop read this particular poem (it was included in the 1917 edition from Knopf, *Lustra of Ezra Pound and Earlier Poems*, which contained some of Pound's most noted imagist poems as well as his versions from the Chinese), she was engaged throughout her writing life, beginning in Vassar, with contending with modernism and the modern. Bishop's celebrated visual acuity owes much to her understanding of twentieth-century visual arts. As her 22 February 1954 letter to Pearl Kazin suggests, Bishop was not simply a passive viewer but active in appreciative art collecting: 'Lota got two very nice Kokoschka lithographs, and I acquired another Joe Glasco drawing – I hadn't realized I liked them so much until I saw them again' (*Poems, Prose, and Letters* 799). Bishop's proclivity was, as she stated some ten years later to Anne Stevenson in the postscript to her letter of 20 January 1964, toward the instability of forms, 'that the "surrealism of everyday life" was always more successful, – or more amazing, than any they can think up' (*Prose* 417).

In contrast to the more serendipitous parallel to Pound's lyric, Bishop's poem draws explicitly upon Wallace Stevens, whom Bishop, in writing to Anne Stevenson in that same letter of January 1964, came to consider as 'an influence, I think. At college I knew "Harmonium" almost by heart. [. . .] But I got tired of him and now find him romantic and thin – but very cheering, because, in spite of his critical theories (very romantic), he did have such a wonderful time with all those odd words, and found a superior way of amusing himself' (*Prose* 415–16). The sense of cheer, not quite the comic, but a gesture toward levity and its proximal senses, distinguishes Bishop from many of her direct influences and contemporaries. This is probably most apparent in Stevens's 'Fabliau of Florida' and 'The Idea of Order at Key West', which complement Bishop's explorations. In the 1919 'Fabliau of Florida' from *Harmonium*, Stevens directs us away from immediacy:

> Move outward into heaven,
> Into the alabasters
> And night blues.
>
> Foam and cloud are one.
> Sultry moon-monsters
> Are dissolving. (23)

In a landscape where sea and sky merge, we are instructed to 'Move outward' from 'the palmy beach'. The poet, on a 'Barque of phosphor', seeks to possess 'white moonlight' much as a conquistador might, filling his 'black hull'. The ephemeral immateriality of moonlight is made tangible by the poet. The atmosphere itself is solidified, turned into 'alabasters', while the eroticised, as they appear as 'sultry moon-monsters', dissolve. The littoral zone becomes one of contrast, distillation and possession rather than permeability.

In Stevens's 1936 'The Idea of Order at Key West', the droning voice of the surf, suggesting the inchoate natural world, is reframed as sound given substance, an oceanic lyric substance, a dark matter filling the ocean:

> If it was only the dark voice of the sea
> That rose, or even colored by many waves;
> If it was only the outer voice of sky
> And cloud, of the sunken coral water-walled,
> However clear, it would have been deep air,
> The heaving speech of air, a summer sound
> Repeated in a summer without end
> And sound alone. (129)

Though the water's surface reflects the clouds, and implies depth, 'the sunken coral water-walled', these are spaces that are distinct, indeed, 'water-walled', and thus not overlapping, littoral, proximal and ambiguous zones. Stevens offers choices, 'The song and water were not medleyed sound', where 'medleyed', etymologically deriving from Old French for 'melee', implies a mixture, an assortment, but here, contrastive and contending. For Stevens, the poet imitates 'The maker's rage to order words of the sea', in contrast to Bishop, for whom, in 'The Map', for example, the mapmakers, her counterparts to the poet, transgress boundaries, allowing 'The names of seashore towns run out to sea' (*Poems* 5).

Within this intersection of perceptions in 'Pleasure Seas', Bishop interjects – embeds or islands – definitions: 'The sea is delight. The sea means *room*. / It is a dance-floor, a well-ventilated ball-room' (*Poems* 279). In fact, the whole poem is a series of openings, from the opening line, 'In the walled off swimming-pool the water is perfectly flat', where we enter a Seurat painting of bathers 'dipping themselves in and out', to the land/sea-scape of the Florida Keys, to the ballroom where 'from the deck of a ship / Pleasures strike off humming, skip / Over the glittering (tinsel?) surface' (279). As the poem tilts from the horizontal to the vertical, invoking the then-new technology and economics of air travel, it parallels the lines of Stevens's 'Farewell to Florida', where the perspective is that of the vertical or from a height: 'Key West sank downward under massive clouds / And silvers and greens spread over the sea. The moon / Is at the mast-head and the past is dead' (Stevens 117). The island melds into the sea's confused surface; its definition is lost, as is the past: nothing can be returned to. As Peggy Samuels writes in *Deep Skin: Elizabeth Bishop and the Visual Arts*, 'The consciousness of poet/observer has disappeared into the objects being described'; this movement is an 'interpermeation of mind, verse, and sea' (50); only at the end of the poem do we pull away to a distanced viewing: 'Lightly, lightly whitening in the air: / An acre of cold white spray is there' (*Poems* 281).

'Pleasure Seas' exemplifies how 'Bishop keeps multiplying the ways that surfaces can touch, move through, reflect, open to, or resist one another' (Samuels 45). Importantly, the mind of the observer enters and intervenes. 'Mermaid Milk' is 'a pure fantasy', writes Samuels, and 'a category applied to the color of the surface of the water. Yet it is also a human category derived from that encounter' (45). We see this in 'The Map', where thresholds are permeable and human intervention – naming and describing – are themselves at a threshold of apprehension: 'Are they assigned, or can the countries pick their colors? / – What suits the character or the native waters best' (*Poems* 5). Are there inherent conditions we perceive and, in response, name, or do we intervene, and by our actions 'assign' the colours and names to what we perceive? Yet our response is derived from that and previous encounters – 'Norway's hare runs south in agitation'. Islands pose questions of identity – certainly geographically and politically – as to what shapes or informs what: 'Mapped waters are more quiet than the land is, / lending the land their waves' own conformation' (*Poems* 5). Is land shaped by the action of waves or does land shape the water? How might land possess waves? Or how can the fluidity of water be contained, mapped? In these islandologies, what is known is put into question, as is the notion of insularity, isolation, or the disembodied self. It is not a far leap to ask whose bodies define whose bodies?

Stevens's 'Farewell to Florida', appearing alongside 'The Idea of Order at Key West', contrasts with Bishop's 'The Imaginary Iceberg'; Stevens's narrator melodramatically proclaims, 'To stand here on the deck in the dark and say / Farewell and to know that that land is forever gone / [. . .] / . . . Farewell. Go on, high ship', and again, in the closing line, 'To the cold, go on, high ship, go on, plunge on' (118). While Stevens sends his traveller further north and deeper into insularity, Bishop's traveller is caught between an ellipsis of desires. The apparitional 'The Imaginary Iceberg' echoes Darwin's own early island meditations on emergence and subsidence, on the creation of landmasses from the oceanic: 'The iceberg rises / and sinks again; its glassy pinnacles / correct elliptics in the sky.' Is the iceberg *there*; or as an imagined monument, apparitional, *there* only in its enunciation by the poet, and then, how long an inhabited enunciation for the poet? Daniel Tiffany, reflecting on Kant, notes that 'Poetry therefore apprehends sensuous nature by inventing it, by producing "illusions" or *impossible* pictures that exceed the qualities of intuitive experience or understanding'. Thus the poet, writes Tiffany, citing Kant, 'gives sensible expression in a way that goes beyond the limits of experience' (28). Bishop's choice is essentially between two islands. Selecting the iceberg implies the end of travel, yet remaining on board the ship binds one to the ship's destination. The poem could be read as electing the imaginary and solitary over the visible and social; however, as Bonnie Costello points out, the poem is far more ambivalent, complicating the apparent oppositional stances, as in the similes in its opening lines, the iceberg as a 'cloudy rock' or a 'breathing plain of snow' and the sea as 'moving marble'. 'Her beholder', Costello writes, 'identifies with the powerful object even while the sensible, contingent, and individual self is threatened by it' (94).

The imaginary is simultaneously real and apparitional, as Bishop's reference to the theatre in the interior stanza suggests:

> This is a scene where he who treads the boards
> is artlessly rhetorical. The curtain
> is light enough to rise on finest ropes

that airy twists of snow provide.
The wits of these white peaks
spar with the sun. Its weight the iceberg dares
upon a shifting stage and stands and stares. (*Poems* 6)

Bishop draws upon the metaphor of the theatre (itself likened to a ship and the cosmos) as real, with ropes, curtains, boards and stage, and also illusory (the source of the rhetoric of wit and lightness). Shakespeare, a dramatist of coastlines and littoral zones, seems appropriate, as Prospero implores at the end of *The Tempest*, 'With the help of your good hands: / Gentle breath of yours my sails / Must fill'. For the sailor/actor, 'art [is] to enchant [. . .] frees all faults [. . .] set[s] me free' (Epilogue 14–20). Compared to the natural magic of Caliban or the transformative magic of Ariel, Prospero's magic is artless rhetoric, word play, 'airy twists', or the slippage from 'finest ropes' to 'fine tropes'. The compounded 'is' at the centre of this interior stanza anaphorically underscores the presence of the imaginary – the question is not one or the other, but the simultaneous. Hence the line 'the snows / which so surprise us lying on the sea' embeds the imaginary within a travel narrative, putatively pragmatic and daily.

Donne's famous admonition in 'Meditation XVII', that 'No man is an island, entire of itself; every man is a piece of the continent, a part of the main', seems sedimented within Bishop's choice not to remain with the imaginary, but with the social: 'Good-bye, we say, good-bye, the ship steers off / where waves give in to one another's waves' (*Poems* 6). The compounding of waves, the gestural as well as the ocean's which shape and conform land and icebergs, suggests that language is that littoral zone where the slippage between soul and flesh, or the imaginary and the social, overlaps. The island becomes, within Bishop's islandology, the symbolic space of love. Certainly Bishop's late poem 'Crusoe in England' interrogates the vicissitudes of isolation and the need of the social and of love: 'Just when I thought I couldn't stand it / another minute longer, Friday came. / (Accounts of that have everything all wrong.)' (*Poems* 185). Love is both intimate and social, hidden and apparent, subject to reading and misreading, as might be the lyricism of poetry, or as in Donne's 'The Extasie', 'Loves mysteries in soules doe grow, / But yet the body is his booke', thus 'must pure lovers soules descend / T'affections, and to faculties, / Which sense may reach and apprehend' (57). One cannot exist without social, and physical, connections; yet the prohibitions against homosexuality essentially isolated Bishop.

The two poems 'Late Air' (in *North & South*, 1946) and the draft 'It is marvellous to wake up together' (circa 1941–46) are set in Key West. The intimacy of these poems contrasts with the unpublished but contemporaneous poem 'The Street by the Cemetery' (1941), also set in the Florida Keys, where neighbours sit 'hypnotized [. . .] on the verandahs / with nothing much to say / to the neighbors three feet away' (*Poems* 275). The neighbours, who sit 'on little verandahs in the moonlight / [. . .] / like passengers on ship-board', recall the passengers in 'Imaginary Iceberg', and the social world that retreats from the imaginary. Instead, within the house, which if 'caught in a bird-cage of lightning / Would be quite delightful rather than frightening', Bishop writes, 'It is marvellous to wake up together / At the same minute; marvellous to hear / The rain begin suddenly all over the roof' (*Poems* 283). The repetition of 'marvellous' implies the overlapping of the imaginary and that which may be possessed; or, as Stephen Greenblatt describes, a 'shift between the designation of a material object and the designation of a response to the object, between intense, almost phantasma-gorical inward states and thoroughly externalized objects that can, after the initial moments of astonishment have passed, be touched, cataloged, inventoried, possessed' (22). While the marvellous carries the sense of travel – Richard Halliburton's contem-poraneous *The Book of Marvels* (1937) was a popular mix of travelogue, history and the exotic – Bishop's use of the word interiorises those travels, and yet also shifts to an intimate plurality, 'And we imagine dreamily'. Through the doubling of 'marvellous', the compounded 'imagine dreamily', and the concluding lines with their own com-pounding, 'As the air changes or the lightning comes without our blinking, / Change as our kisses are changing without our thinking', the poem opens the space for the erotic without fixing or deadening it through naming.

Lorrie Goldensohn argues that, in contrast to Donne's 'The Extasie', Bishop's lov-ers remain imprisoned, that the cage – 'a bird-cage of lightning' – is a motif throughout her work, suggesting 'the delights of prison, in which we might be able to see a back-handed acceptance of the condition of flesh, a subterranean acceptance of gender, as well as a rather self-mocking, morose acceptance of the delights of guilt' (46). Yet in this lightning-charged house 'erotic love becomes a path', Goldensohn notes, 'in the mystical tradition, where through the union of self and Other we learn of the paral-lel junctions between flesh and spirit, heaven and earth, human and divine' (49). In this sense, we do in fact move closer to the release of the spirit, and the flesh, just as in Donne's poem; certainly 'Late Air' suggests the conjoining or overlapping of the spiritual and the physical:

> But on the Navy Yard aerial I find
> > better witnesses
> for love on summer nights.
> Five remote red lights
> > keep their nests there; Phoenixes
> burning quietly, where the dew cannot climb. (*Poems* 45)

Again Bishop finds herself and her expressions of intimacy outside social discourse. The radio-singers' love-song, an oblique and antithetical reference to Eliot's 'The Love Song of J. Alfred Prufrock' perhaps ('I have heard the mermaids singing, each to each. // I do not think that they will sing to me' (7)), with its littoral elements, is not, how-ever, adequate to Bishop's 'love on summer nights'. Here Bishop punningly invokes Ariel of *The Tempest*, who pursues her charms in order to be set free, and the mytho-logical phoenix, symbol of rebirth. Key West, like all islands, is not a desert island, but a place of indigenous forms, hybrids and arrivants. The 'radio-singers', with their commercially distributed love-songs, prove inadequate and inauthentic if not outright deceptive like a magician or fortune-teller. Instead, the remote and solitary red warn-ing lights on Key West's naval base's aerials, uncorrupted by dew, serve as better repre-sentatives and witnesses to 'love on summer nights'. With the complex and ambiguous associations of illicit sexuality, a Mars-like place in the night sky and warning signal to aviators, these lights suggest anything but domesticity.

'Late Air' compresses two spaces into one – it is set in Key West, and the red lights of the aerials penetrate the interior of the house to witness love. The movement from outside to inside, visually parallel to Bishop's undated watercolour 'Interior with Extension Cord', whose door opens to a landscape, describes the interpermeability of Bishop's work. Instead of being considered as a container, even one as open and mysterious as a Joseph Cornell construction, the house forms an island where space conforms or aligns itself to other spaces. Edwin Boomer's house, in the short story 'The Sea and Its Shore', which is contemporaneous with 'The Map' and 'Pleasure Seas', is first introduced, blandly, as 'very interesting':

> It was of wood, with a pitched roof, about 4 by 4 by 6 feet, set on pegs stuck in the sand. There was no window, no door set in the door-frame, and nothing at all inside. [. . .] As a house, it was more like an idea of a 'house,' than a real one. It could have stood at either end of a scale of ideas of houses. It could have been a child's perfect play-house, or an adult's ideal house – since everything that makes most houses nuisances had been done away with. (*Prose* 11)

From the unassuming beginning, Bishop travels into the interior as she does in 'The Fish', for example, where the unseen is exposed, the invisible is made, through the intervention of the poet's interrogative imagination, visible. Boomer, Crusoe-like, sorts and catalogues. From the papers he collects on the beach, he selects those that seem to be about himself, or others 'that caught his fancy', and still others that so 'bewildered him [. . .] he saved them to read' when he returned to his house. Boomer, situated at the edge of sea and land, becomes a version of the artist as a collagist or assemblagist that Bishop admired. Kurt Schwitters and Joseph Cornell are visual analogues to Bishop (and Boomer, whose name is homologous to Bulmer, Bishop's mother's maiden name). Peggy Samuels notes that Schwitters' collages are 'arranged sequences' which move from 'airiness to dense reality using transparent, semitransparent, and opaque papers [. . .] In organizing modulations from art to life and across representational levels, Schwitters provided Bishop with a model for imagining the poem as a site of assemblage or collage' (26). Art, then, like Boomer's house, is 'a shelter, but not for living in, for thinking in' (*Prose* 11). Boomer's methodical and selective *reading* of found texts reveals Bishop's own selective, often transparently self-corrective, process. That Bishop situates this dramatic scene on the littoral zone, the place where sea and land conform to each other, further emphasises the ambiguity of the process or the dynamics of conformation and permeability. As Samuels notes, Schwitters 'was interested in displaying not just the range of surfaces but also a surface's disintegration or dissolution and thereby "approach" to the other' (113).

If Schwitters does this visually – and we should note that Bishop purchased one of Schwitters' works ('I am also extremely fond of Schwitters – have one here that has to be watched for termites and mildew constantly'; letter to Anne Stevenson, 20 March 1963 (*Poems, Prose, and Letters* 844)) – Bishop accomplishes this tonally, as in the final stanza of 'Filling Station':

> Somebody embroidered the doily.
> Somebody waters the plant,
> or oils it, maybe. Somebody
> arranges the rows of cans
> so that they softly say:

ESSO – SO – SO – SO
to high-strung automobiles.
Somebody loves us all. (*Poems* 126)

The stanza creates affective spaces – that of an embroidered doily, the well-watered but 'extraneous' plant, the arranged cans of oil. The filling station's orderliness, conducted by unseen hands, parallels the overlaid elements of different densities and textualities in collages by Schwitters. Objects are placed into pictorial relationships, much as in a Morandi still life, but it is also the textual tactility found in Schwitters that informs this poem, and in this tactility there is an overlapping rather than a discreteness to these relations. 'Somebody' is not only an overlapping persona – poet? maternal figure? God? – but also a substrate of sound that connects these different sound-posts of doily, plant, cans, automobiles. The sibilant echoing 'SO-SO-SO' visually, or homologically, overlaps with the repeated 'somebody'.

The 'somebody' of 'Filling Station' is apparitional but also and always present. Bishop guides us toward a gendered reading with 'doily'; the presence of father and sons points to the mysterious absence of the mother, either as moniker or as allusion. Bishop then leaves us to question how we make identifications, and indeed establish presence: 'Why the extraneous plant? / Why the taboret? /Why, oh why, the doily?' (125). Like the repeated 'somebody', the repeated, interrogatory 'why' forms a sonic littoral zone connecting objects in this framed, housed ('Do they live in the station?') space. Though apparitional, or, in Daniel Tiffany's terms, invisible, these littoral zones are a version of what he describes as 'lyric substance'. Tiffany queries, 'But is poetry merely a "place" in which real things might appear? Or could it be that bodies possess, or are possessed by something called *lyric* substance, a consistent and perhaps even systematic doctrine of corporeality proper to the devices of lyric poetry?' (14–15). Examining Yeats's 'Sailing to Byzantium', Tiffany notes that lyric substance – or, as Yeats terms it, 'his soul' – 'is something the poet *makes*: the soul is an artifact' (Tiffany 19):

> Once out of nature I shall never take
> My bodily form from any natural thing,
> But such a form as Grecian goldsmiths make
> Of hammered gold and gold enameling
> To keep a drowsy Emperor awake;
> Or set upon a golden bough to sing
> To lords and ladies of Byzantium
> Of what is past, or passing, or to come. (194)

The poet refuses the body from nature, but assumes an eternal 'form' distinct from the sensual world yet very much imbricated within it, as it sings from its 'hammered gold and gold enameling'. As Tiffany notes, 'the mechanical bird comes to life when it sings and is transformed into a kind of living picture [which thus] illustrates the dual nature of lyrical substance' (19). Tiffany argues that 'Poetry therefore apprehends sensuous nature by inventing it [. . .] Hence the subtle body of lyric reflects the mind's independence from nature even as it evokes the sensuality of nature' (28–9). Language is not primarily that of communication, but rather a resistance to communication as its

primary expression; poetry dematerialises language, and, as Tiffany continues, draw-
ing on Lessing, Kant and Heidegger, 'the lyric artifact, the material opus, coincides
with, or indeed is identical to, an "open place" [. . .] The body of lyric appears to com-
prise a latent body – a form of *nothing*' (29–30). Lyric substance 'consists in "the nam-
ing power of the word"', and unlike the material dimensions of other art forms, the
materiality of the lyric is 'that its body possesses a kind of agency, like naming or light-
ing. Lyric substance, as Heidegger conceives it, therefore comprises what poetry brings
to light in a name' (30–1). Could we visualise that *open place* for Bishop as those
littoral zones or sites of overlapping substances? The sites where *somebody* moves,
arranges, loves? Sites that materialise without being contained? That may be named,
but not definitively communicated, as in the 'marvellous' or 'love on summer nights'?

Bishop's 'Sandpiper' evokes that *open place*, that latent *nothing*: 'The world is a
mist. And then the world is / minute and vast and clear. The tide / is higher or lower.
He couldn't tell you which' (*Poems* 129). With lines such as 'The beach hisses like
fat' and 'The millions of grains are black, white, tan, and gray, / mixed with quartz
grains, rose and amethyst' (129), the poem prefigures 'Crusoe in England', where tur-
tles are 'hissing like teakettles. / [. . .] / The folds of lava, running out to sea, / would
hiss [. . .] / [. . .] / The beaches were all lava, variegated, / black, red, and white, and
gray; / the marbled colors made a fine display' (*Poems* 183). The distracted sandpiper,
again much like the distracted and melancholy Crusoe, races along the shore, watch-
ing not his 'dark and brittle feet', but the 'spaces of sand between them, / where [. . .]
the Atlantic drains / rapidly backwards and downwards'. The sandpiper watches
time's littoral processes, echoing the concluding lines of Bishop's earlier poem 'At the
Fishhouses' (themselves a re-visioning of Yeats's lines from 'Sailing to Byzantium'),
'forever, flowing and drawn, and since / our knowledge is historical, flowing, and
flown' (*Poems* 64).

The sandpiper occupies a world of transience and process, and like the observer of
the iceberg, and perhaps all of us, is 'looking for something, something, something'.
Although the narrator claims the sandpiper is obsessed, the sandpiper is more akin to
Edwin Boomer searching for narratives that will make some order out of the flux he
is awash in. Yet this search is not finally that idealised Stevensian centred-ness, but
the sense of finding that 'something' within the waves' medleyed retreat. The thrice-
repeated 'something' is certainly the narrator's imitative tonal gesture of the sand-
piper's search as well as the bird's emotions, particularly of his frustrated particularity,
but the repetition also parallels the variety of colours of the grains of sand and the
sandpiper's perceptive reading of the beach's wash of wave and sand. The sandpiper is
as much 'looking for' as he is bringing to light and naming what he sees – the 'black,
white, tan, and gray'. The narrator, as she *reads* and *names* the sandpiper, drawing the
bird out of the overlapping conditions of mistiness, clarity, minuteness and vastness,
imitates the sandpiper's own agitated reading.

The sandpiper's agitated reading, like Crusoe's of his island, however, points to
something further. Tiffany's discussion of the work of the French surrealist Roger Cail-
lois, and Jacques Lacan's discussion of the compulsion to repeat and self-mimic, provide
a further consideration of the poem's repetition. The sandpiper acts as an automa-
ton, expressing the compulsion to repeat, and to mimic; 'Thus the human becomes an
automaton not so much by adopting [. . .] particular habits as by means of the body's
capacity to incorporate – even to the point of self-destruction – the *image* of another

creature' (Tiffany 84). For Caillois and Lacan, such automatic mimicry is not simply a form of adaptive survival, but, as Tiffany argues, citing Lacan's *Four Fundamental Concepts*, may relate to 'some formative power of the very organism' (83). The lyric, through repetition or the automata, is the realisation in the material world of affective elements of consciousness. Repetition is a materialisation of lyric substance – as in 'Crusoe in England', where the landscape is indeed a soundscape of echoes: was that 'why sometimes the whole place hissed?' (*Poems* 183) Crusoe wonders, the word 'hiss' repeating and hence not only animating the island in sound, but substantiating it in Crusoe's consciousness.

Bishop's littoral zone is a place of overlapping and seemingly insubstantial spaces, as in 'The Sandpiper', the clouded dreamscape of 'Sunday, 4 A.M.' ('An endless and flooded / dreamland, lying low' (*Poems* 127)), or the house of 'Song for the Rainy Season', which is 'Hidden, oh hidden / in the high fog' (*Poems* 99). The apparitional, that which shimmers between the material and invisibility, indicates the extreme limits of perception, a 'region', Tiffany writes, of 'phenomenological instability'; thus, Tiffany suggests, 'we could say that bodies radiate bodies in the turbulence of vision, or, with Yeats in mind, that images beget images' (204). In Bishop's translation of Octavio Paz's 'Objects & Apparitions', the apparitional is named:

> The apparitions are manifest,
> their bodies weigh less than light,
> lasting as long as this phrase lasts.
>
> Joseph Cornell: inside your boxes
> my words become visible for a moment. (*Poems* 202)

Bishop's translation, another form of overlapping discourses and permeability, fuses the materiality of light with language. For a moment lyric substance is made visible, but only through the apprehension of objects, not as communicative signifiers, but where 'things hurry away from their names' into a 'theatre of the spirits'. Cornell's constructions, like Paz's or Bishop's poetry, become 'The reflector of the inner eye', which sees that real bodies may be composed of non-visible, un-real substances; in other words, the lyric work becomes 'cages for infinity'.

The littoral zone, in its literal or environmental state as well as its place in the metaphorics of islandology, fuses the perceptual with the material. In 'Twelfth Morning; or What You Will', Bishop describes a scene on Cabo Frio, or Cold Key, a coastal resort town one hundred miles north and east of Rio de Janeiro:

> Like a first coat of whitewash when it's wet,
> the thin gray mist lets everything show through:
> the black boy Balthazár, a fence, a horse,
>   a foundered house
>
> – cement and rafters sticking from a dune. (*Poems* 108)

With the pictorial simile initiating the poem, we are reminded that language is itself a form of travelling or of carrying over; here we understand Tiffany's sense that from a space of nothing, poetry brings to light names. What is being likened to 'a first coat of whitewash when it's wet'? The landscape, we assume, but, like the 'somebody' of 'Filling Station' or the lovers of 'Late Air', for example, it is never named. From this 'thin gray mist', that which is perceived is named – 'the black boy Balthazár, a fence, a horse, / a foundered house'. With the puns on deception and revelation – 'whitewash' and 'show through' – Bishop further reflects the strangeness of poetics, where what seems to be described becomes only increasingly problematic, ambiguous and indeterminate. Boundaries are permeable and conformable: 'Don't ask the big white horse,' the narrator declares, '*Are you supposed / to be inside the fence or out?* He's still / asleep. Even awake, he probably / remains in doubt' (*Poems* 108). The discourse shifts boundaries here, moving from an address to the reader or perhaps a monologic moment, to addressing the horse, to finally a more generalised statement, 'He's still / asleep'. The horse, as object of address, is 'in doubt': is the horse caught between sleeping and waking in this foggy world, or is his very presence doubtful, apparitional? The horse, like the moose in Bishop's eponymously titled later poem, is likened to a house ('high as a church / homely as a house' (*Poems* 193)), though here the 'foundered house' may well be a '"Shipwreck" [. . .] [or] perhaps / this is a housewreck'. The end word 'perhaps' underscores the poem's reification of ambiguity.

Bishop's poetry addresses the substantiality of the real. Tiffany states that mathematics, which essentially informs scientific thought, 'guarantees only the authority of the real, not its intelligibility. The substance of lyric therefore remains an essential element in the fabrication of the real' (291). Crusoe, in his second solitude after losing Friday, laments,

> A new volcano has erupted,
> the papers say, and last week I was reading
> where some ship saw an island being born:
> at first a breath of steam, ten miles away;
> and then a black fleck – basalt, probably –
> rose in the mate's binoculars
> and caught on the horizon like a fly.
> They named it. But my poor old island's still
> un-rediscovered, un-renamable.
> None of the books has ever got it right. (*Poems* 182)

Bishop invokes the lyric's process of making the invisible or ephemeral into substance. The poem, as Bishop writes it, is the materialisation of the lyric as the littoral zone, that site of conformation of sea and land, of island and ocean. Here the formation of an island, from the provisional and undeterminable ('a breath of steam' or 'basalt, probably') and its informing metaphor of the island, becomes a substance, is the very image of a lyric materialising. Lyric substance provides coherence to the world. Such a formation is traumatic, as Crusoe explains, as there is no absolute stability. At best we have to make do with the marvellousness of love on a rainy summer's night or the arrival of Friday: 'Pretty to watch; he had a pretty body' (*Poems* 186). Like lightning, or light, lyric substance is transient and littoral, present but past, flowing and flown.

Works Cited

Bishop, Elizabeth, *Poems, Prose, and Letters*, ed. Robert Giroux and Lloyd Schwartz (New York: Library of America, 2008).

Costello, Bonnie, *Elizabeth Bishop: Questions of Mastery* (Cambridge, MA: Harvard University Press, 1991).

Donne, John, *John Donne: A Selection of his Poetry*, ed. John Haywood (Harmondsworth: Penguin, 1950).

Eliot, T. S., *The Complete Poems and Plays: 1909–1950* (New York: Harcourt, 1971).

Ford, Mark, 'Elizabeth Bishop at the Water's Edge', *Essays in Criticism* 53.3 (2003): 235–61.

Goldensohn, Lorrie, *Elizabeth Bishop: The Biography of a Poetry* (New York: Columbia University Press, 1992).

Gray, Jeffrey, *Mastery's End: Travel and Postwar American Poetry* (Athens: University of Georgia Press, 2005).

Greenblatt, Stephen, *Marvelous Possessions: The Wonder of the New World* (Chicago: University of Chicago Press, 1991).

Hallberg, Robert von, *American Poetry and Culture, 1945–1980* (Cambridge, MA: Harvard University Press, 1985).

Kalstone, David, *Five Temperaments: Elizabeth Bishop, Robert Lowell, James Merrill, Adrienne Rich, John Ashbery* (New York: Oxford University Press, 1977).

Page, Barbara, 'Shifting Islands: Elizabeth Bishop's Manuscripts', *Shenandoah* 33.1 (1981–82): 51–62.

Pound, Ezra, *Lustra of Ezra Pound and Earlier Poems* (New York: Knopf, 1917).

Pratt, Mary Louise, *Imperial Eyes: Travel Writing and Transculturation* (New York: Routledge, 1992).

Samuels, Peggy, *Deep Skin: Elizabeth Bishop and Visual Art* (Ithaca: Cornell University Press, 2010).

Shell, Marc, *Islandology: Geography, Rhetoric, Politics* (Stanford: Stanford University Press, 2014).

Stevens, Wallace, *The Collected Poems of Wallace Stevens* (New York: Knopf, 1980).

Tiffany, Daniel, *Toy Medium: Materialism and Modern Lyric* (Berkeley: University of California Press, 2000).

Yeats, William Butler, *The Poems of W. B. Yeats* (New York: Macmillan, 1983).

19

ELIZABETH BISHOP AND AUDRE LORDE: TWO VIEWS OF 'FLORIDA' IN THE GLOBAL SOUTH ATLANTIC

Marvin Campbell

ELIZABETH BISHOP AND AUDRE LORDE are almost never paired in readings of twentieth-century American poetry. Where Lorde brazenly and repeatedly declared her intersectional identities over the course of her career – 'I am a Black lesbian feminist warrior poet mother' (Lorde and Hall 146) – Bishop, ever circumspect, sidesteps such frank identifications with gender as well as sexuality, refusing women's anthologies and seeking out, in her often quoted remark, 'closets, closets, and more closets', as she told friend Richard Howard (Fountain and Brazeau 330), her poetry offering only the most coded engagements with these vectors of identity. Readers of Bishop such as Kirstin Hotelling Zona and Steven Axelrod have revealed the poet's unease with racial difference, and a poetic and personal discomfort with Gwendolyn Brooks, the first black woman to win the Pulitzer, that would not bode well for any rapprochement with Lorde's poetics of Black power and radicalism. And Lorde, disdainful of the white feminists her friend Adrienne Rich worked alongside, would have, one imagines, even less time for Bishop's political quietism, real or imagined. But in February 1969, Bishop interviewed Black Panther Kathleen Cleaver – wife of famed Party leader Eldridge Cleaver – with deep interest and obvious sympathy (Fountain and Brazeau 251–2). For all the discomfort with race exposed by Zona and Axelrod, she nonetheless put that hesitation to ample poetic use throughout her writing. Like Lorde, Bishop proved more than willing to explore this fraught terrain, whatever the cost, their shared interest converging in a literal space extending from the Southeastern United States to the world.

Bishop's investments in Nova Scotia, Florida and Brazil – long considered central to her poetics and increasingly mined by contemporary scholars for the historical and cultural contextualisation they provide for her work – reveal a transnational geography consistent with a commitment to interrogating how geographies have been drawn by cultural and state power. The organising figure of the map provides a through-line from *North & South* to *Geography III* that undermines the borders and boundaries of nation to collapse the space between 'home' and 'elsewhere'. From late 1936, when she began living in Key West for almost a decade, to the mid-1960s, when she reluctantly departed from a Brazil that had kept her fifteen years, some of which had been the happiest times in her life, Bishop forged the 'comprehensive island hemisphere' that Wallace Stevens – another habitué of poetic space operative from the Floridian shores of Key West – imagined in 'The Comedian as the Letter C' (Stevens 25–43) for his poetic manqué Crispin. Unlike Stevens's hapless poetaster, who embodied his creator's own germinal interest in a global perspective, Bishop traces a larger arc, if not an archipelago, that spans Great Village to Tierra del Fuego, Great Labrador to Port-au-Prince, Bermuda to the Galapagos, and Mexico City to Puerto Rico. For her, as the recent essay collection *Elizabeth Bishop in the Twenty-First Century* makes clear, 'geography is a prime determinant of knowledge' (Cleghorn et al. 4).

No less exploratory in her global peregrinations was Lorde, whose investments in Europe, the Caribbean, Mexico and Africa have begun to receive greater attention in recent years. As Stella Bolaki and Sabine Broeck observe in the introduction to their essay collection *Audre Lorde's Transnational Legacies*, Lorde 'never stopped crossing boundaries' geographically as well as conceptually, allowing the editors to 'situate her life and work within transatlantic and transnational perspectives' (1–2). Similarly, the 1995 documentary on Lorde – *A Litany for Survival* – situates the African-American poet firmly within her Caribbean heritage. During the opening montage, the film places Lorde against the backdrop of St Croix at the turn of the century, a voice-over layered over newsreel footage that depicts black figures disembarking from fishing boats. In a hushed, vatic voice, Lorde refers to an encounter undertaken at the 'point where the Atlantic meets the Caribbean', the tableau anticipating the consequent sequence in which she speaks of a childhood in Harlem framed by her parents' longing for the Grenada from where they had emigrated (Griffin and Parkerson).

Despite this increasing focus on the role of place in Bishop's and Lorde's work, however, little attention has been paid to the broader Global South these women mediate through such an expansive array of spaces – and none, to my knowledge, has shown how their project is a shared one. This is a mistake, for amidst a critical lexicon defined by terms such as 'homeless', 'alienated', 'outsider', 'periphery' and 'marginal', and a perspective dominated by racial and sexual tensions that emerge in precisely such spaces where the white observer becomes the outsider, Bishop's kinship with Lorde at once throws those explorations through difference into sharper relief and usefully extends them. Understanding this connection gives lie to the demure 'Miss Bishop' conceptualised even by admirers like Marianne Moore, Robert Lowell and Randall Jarrell, instead revealing a poet more radically preoccupied by place, history, race, gender and sexuality than any of her contemporaries writing in the aftermath of modernism. For Lorde, who forged transnational connections with the Caribbean and Latin America alongside African-American contemporaries such as Robert Hayden, Sonia Sanchez and June Jordan, among others, the pairing with Bishop aligns her with contemporaries outside Black feminist thought and the African-American literary tradition who sought, in concert, to remap the United States within the frame of the broader hemisphere.

What emerges from these American cross-currents which Bishop and Lorde undertook in parallel is – drawing on Paul Gilroy's influential and contested framework of the Black Atlantic – the Global South Atlantic. Proposed first as a conference panel at the American Comparative Literature Association that later informed an edited collection, the concept considers how 'individuals, governments or political movements, social imaginaries, texts or other cultural artifacts, and markets do (or do not) cross the oceanic space between Africa, Latin America, and surrounding "Southern" regions', with particular attention paid to how 'artists and intellectuals from [these regions] imagine the Atlantic' (Slaughter and Bystrom, 'CFP'), helping reshape our

understanding of twentieth-century American poetry and poetics. In concert with con-
temporaries like Lorde, and antecedents like Stevens, Bishop stretches the cartographic
limits of a space circumscribing Southern Africa and South America to encompass not
only the Caribbean but the United States and Canada. The Northern neighbour finds
itself imbricated in the same series of 'pathways, networks, transactions, and systems
of interchange and imagination' (Slaughter and Bystrom, 'Introduction') that define a
geographic region also shaped by the social politics of the Global South – countries,
across the surface of the earth, shaped by the multiple legacies of colonialism. These
crossings – drawn from the South Atlantic United States to Tierra del Fuego, and
westward, from West Africa to the Cape of Good Horn – destabilised national borders
and boundaries and allowed white poets like Bishop to explore race, often critically,
alongside the resistance that black peers like Lorde fomented.

The particular, if not peculiar, overlap in Bishop and Lorde took shape at the for-
mation's northern rim in Mexico and Florida. After settling in Key West permanently
in 1938, Bishop made one of her many intervening trips during the nearly ten years
she spent on the island, visiting Mexico over the spring and summer of 1942. She met
Pablo Neruda – the first of many cross-cultural connections she would forge with
poets in the southern hemisphere – and explored Mérida, Mexico City, Oaxaca and
Cuernavaca, among several other towns in the region, taking a particularly significant
interest in the indigenous cultures of the country. Key West, in many ways, anticipated
this interest in Mexico's otherness, if not ultimately encouraged it.

Bishop became, in the words of John Lowney, 'increasingly fascinated by [the
island's] racialized social difference' (88). In 'Jerónimo's House', for example,
Bishop rehabilitated the actual Afro-Caribbean district horrifically named 'Jungle
Town' (Fountain and Brazeau 72) by imagining a home that proves at once stable
and beautiful – the domicile's stability reproduced in the poem's columnar structure,
its beauty dispersed through fragile art-objects that have been gathered underneath
its roof. No less intimate than her address to the absent Jerónimo for whom Bishop
seeks to speak is her approach to the equally voiceless 'Cootchie' (*Poems* 46), a
member of the black servant class for whom the titular poem provides a parable of
Jim Crow. The subjugation suffered by the subject at the hands of her employer, Miss
Lula, survives her into death, with a grave where black and multicoloured 'marl'
and 'coral reef' contend against 'egg-white skies' and 'moonlight', but which also
elevates her beyond the earthly constraints where she was found 'eating her dinner
off the kitchen sink' – and insists her life mattered. The lighthouse 'discovers' only
her grave and 'dismiss[es]' the rest as trivial.

Indeed, as Lowney also notes, Bishop's 'interest in everyday African-American life
was more serious than fanciful comments she wrote to Moore [about the black popu-
lation on the island] suggest' (89). It is here where she first listened to Fats Waller,
Bessie Smith and 'Negro ballads', deeming them 'the best modern American [ones]'
(*One Art* 72), and where she found herself most stimulated by the sections of William
Carlos Williams's *In the American Grain* that addressed African-American life (*One
Art* 74). The 'Latin' character of the island was of no less curiosity. Enthralled by
'Rhumba nights' at Sloppy Joe's, a Key West dive Hemingway also favoured, she
described them in great detail in letters to Frani Blough (*One Art* 71). In Key West,
to use Barbara Page's formulation, 'Bishop found a place corresponding to her own
disposition for the margins' (197), the margin of racial and ethnic difference standing

squarely at the centre of the island's life. At least part of the reason she could imagine herself talking about Stevens's 'The Emperor of Ice Cream' with her students at Harvard 'for at least two hours' (*Words in Air* 686), as she wrote to Robert Lowell, was the poem's Cuban Key West donnée. Years later, one of those students, Dana Gioia, recalled that Bishop's exegesis of the poem was situated entirely within its historical context and geographical setting, because 'to Miss Bishop, Stevens' greatest subject was not poetry, the supreme fiction. It was Florida, the supreme landscape' (*Conversations* 146). As she also made certain to inform Gioia's class, Key West was closer to Cuba than Miami. That same landscape was supreme in her own imagination precisely because – as an American historian wrote hopefully in 1899 (Callahan 115) and a Cuban poet with deep grief in 1923 (Ragg 48) – Florida is a finger which points to Cuba and, by extension, the Caribbean and Latin American world of which it forms a part. Taking up residence there, as Thomas Travisano has observed, was a 'catalytic event' (19).

Bishop composed several of the poems from *North & South* (1946) on the peninsula and the corresponding keys, also travelling to Mexico and across the Yucatan peninsula. While 'most of these poems [from the volume] were written, or partly written, before 1942' – as Bishop herself noted in a note accompanying the volume – she worked on 'Cootchie' and 'Faustina', two of her Key West poems, in 1941 and 1943. In addition, the imprecision of 'mostly' leaves room for more having been written, revised or even conceptualised around 1942 – the inclusion of that year signalling its centrality in her mind. Whether or not any poems beyond these two received Bishop's close and careful revision – she published no poems in 1942 or 1943, after all (Millier 170) – her time in Mexico stimulated her imagination: the churches of Cholula, the Grutas caves, and 'the mixture of Catholicism and Indian mysticism and superstition' she noted in 'the details of decoration in the tiny churches' (Millier 167) all laid the groundwork for what she would come to find in Key West as well as Brazil. Bishop's remarks were often far from laudatory – Mexican art she despised; Neruda's poetry seemed expressive of a surrealism she disliked (*One Art* 107–9) – but for all her professed disdain of José Clemente Orozco and David Alfaro Siqueiros, major muralists of the Mexican Renaissance, she shared their abiding interest in folk culture, and later in life acknowledged her debt to Neruda, modelling 'Invitation to Miss Moore' on his elegy 'Alberto Rojas Jimenez Vienes Volando'.

Additionally, Bishop's often vocal antipathy for Mexican art and what she called a 'poverty stricken imagination' (quoted in Millier 167) – much like Stevens's own disdain for art from the region – may have been a reaction against 'the enormous vogue of things Mexican', to borrow the title of Helen Delpar's important study of cultural relations between the United States and Mexico in the wake of the Mexican Revolution. Throughout the 1920s and 1930s, American intellectuals and artists such as Hart Crane, Langston Hughes, Aaron Copland, John Dewey and Waldo Frank all found themselves, as James Oles argues, 'drawn by exoticism and motivated by revolutionary hope which led them to idealize Mexico as a pristine and revolutionary land' (Trillo 236). This extended even into the late 1940s.

Despite this pointed distance on Bishop's part from this wave of American enthusiasm, her regret at not producing more work during her time there (a perennial self-reproach for a poet with a notoriously spare oeuvre), and her failure to significantly improve her Spanish, there is no doubt her encounter with Mexico left a deep and lasting impression on her poetry. The strongest effect emerged in how Bishop saw *North & South*'s 'Florida' – one peninsula, quite simply, shaping another. It may have been in the eponymous poem of the 1965 volume *Questions of Travel* that Bishop famously wrote '*home / wherever that may be*', troubling the same distinctions between 'home' and 'elsewhere' the volume establishes and itself troubles, but almost twenty years earlier she had already performed a version of the same gesture. In *North & South*, the geographical boundary of the Southeast – like the political border of the Southwest – proves to be ultimately a mirage.

But before the New World could emerge fully into this hemispheric view shared with Mexico, Bishop had to deal properly with the Old. In 1937 – between her first visit to Florida with Louise Crane and January of 1938, when she moved there for almost a decade – she made a tour of Europe with Crane and Margaret Miller. Overwhelmed by the continent's pressures of history, she wrote 'Paris, 7 A.M.' (*Poems* 28). The poem, as Travisano has observed, 'presents a troubled observer trying to distinguish what is actual and what is imposed. Not even time seems to hold steady' (43). The sky imagined overhead, palimpsestic in its 'endless intersecting circles', is 'a dead one'.

From this funereal sky, Bishop escapes into Florida. Indulging in but ultimately moving beyond a 'Seascape' (*Poems* 41) that renders the state as a Botticelli tableau with 'white herons got up as angels', Bishop's ever-accurate eye can look beyond the conventionally named *Pascua Florida* ('flowering Easter') to prefer the harsh historical reality hidden underneath in 'brackish water / held together by mangrove roots'. In this 'Florida' (*Poems* 33–4), amongst the unstable foundations, Bishop decrypts the colonial legacy of 'the state with the prettiest name', reframing its Spanish derivation against the backdrop of violence and devastation. The opening line, as many have noted, provides an ironic acknowledgement of Florida's etymology, with a prettiness – almost always faint praise in the hands of poets who prefer the beautiful, if not the sublime – displaced to its appellation, and rendered ridiculous by the scene consequently described. She breaks from the European legacies of visual art and figurative constructions of the New World, abandoning the 'Gothic arches' of these same 'mangrove roots' that had been depicted in 'Seascape'.

Bishop offers a topo- and zoological view of its coastline that resonates with multiform historical pressures startling in their grotesqueness: 'white swamps with skeletons, / dotted as if bombarded, with green hummocks / like ancient cannon-balls sprouting grass' (*Poems* 33). These lines do not merely, or perhaps even primarily, refer to the once living, now skeletal oysters depicted in the poem. They also allegorise the dead US soldiers who forged the American iteration of Florida. During the Second Seminole War, according to historian John Mahon, 'cypress knees, mangrove roots, and sawgrass tortured the foot solider' (240) during swamp warfare against the indigenous tribes of the region. By acknowledging this natural fundament, Bishop also excavates the aboriginal presence that emerges later in the central figure of the Indian Princess. That act of historical recovery happens in two ways. The first is through the offices of etymology that Florida's naming shows is uppermost in the poet's mind, mangrove's Spanish-Portuguese origin in '*mangue*' arising from 'a Cariban or Arawakan language' (*OED*). The second is through the mangroves' importance to the Seminoles, who called them 'walking trees', a characterisation consistent with a poem invested in the human properties of fauna. Beyond refracting the state through the dual lenses of US expansionism and European colonialism, this reference to mangrove roots imbricates Florida in a broader geographical frame. Varieties are found through-out the Global South Atlantic, with Africa and the Americas containing almost half the world's mangroves.

Later in the poem, the human dimension of a death displaced to nature emerges in another avatar:

> Enormous turtles, helpless and mild,
> die and leave their barnacled shells on the beaches,
> their large white skulls with round eye-sockets,
> twice the size of a man's. (*Poems* 33)

Unlike the 'tanagers embarrassed by their flashiness' and 'pelicans whose delight it is to clown' who populate the intervening lines – New World alternatives to European songbirds – these turtles emerge as far more fraught symbols of personification. With references to human anatomy in addition to qualities of mind, they are more person than trope, revealing corpses that have been buried, but not deeply enough, beneath the flowers of paradise. Readers of Bishop have not stinted on exploring the signifi-cance of such imagery in the poem, but they have placed it under the aegis of a 'death-in-life' thematic (Doreski 113) that elides the political violence at its centre.

It is at the liminal shore where colonial violence becomes most evident, the victims of historical erasure most emergent:

> The tropical rain comes down
> to freshen the tide-looped strings of fading shells:
> Job's Tear, the Chinese Alphabet, the Scarce Junonia,
> parti-colored pectins and Ladies' Ears,
> arranged as on a gray rag of rotted calico,
> the buried Indian Princess's skirt. (*Poems* 33)

With the exception of the Indian Princess, these appear only to be shells placed at the centre of a peninsular ecosystem, the rain and tides that greet them generating a cycle of inexorable currents that alternate between 'fading' and 'freshen[ing]', thereby giv-ing us an orderly world governed by natural time as well as biology, the impressions of nature indelibly stamped in 'tide-looped strings'.

What Bishop adds, however, is a world scored by historical change. These objects she gathered along the shore during evening walks offered more than records of geo-logic time or artefacts for a naturalist to taxonomise, though they performed that function too. They stand as repositories of human culture. As Bethany Hicok has observed, 'Drawing on close observation and a visit she made to the naturalist E. Ross Allen [. . .] Bishop begins to read the landscape as a possible mirror of culture' (113). Jani Scandura, one of the few cultural geographers of Key West, is indispensable on the histories that the names of such shells might have indexed for a poet who memorised their names, a fact Bishop's oral history records (Fountain and Brazeau 71):

From the biblical 'Job's Tear' of native Arawak who were ravaged in the name of Christian conversion, to the Chinese alphabet of those indentured Caribbean labor-ers from Asia, to the mulatto parti-colored pectins of Bahamian immigrants and

Maroon, to the pioneer women's 'gray rug of rotted calico' and the 'buried Indian Princess's skirt,' Bishop resurrects the multiple forgotten histories of American nation building through found objects and skeletons, the material traces of those who were erased. (Scandura 100)

To extend Scandura's enormously helpful reading of the histories held in these shells, Bishop gives added force by dramatising the decimation in this allusion to Christian conversation. 'Job's Tear' implicates the watery cycle of ostensibly natural tides that has deposited this shell and its companions here in the first place, writing history into landscape. More specifically yet, Job's Tear also recalls the Trail of Tears, the forced migration of several Native American tribes from the Southeast to the prairie, in which the Seminoles played a central role. The pun on 'tear' captures the violence as well as the grief embedded in this historical event, acknowledging all native peoples who have been torn from the land no less than the shells from the sea, their bodies literally torn in the wars that Andrew Jackson and Christopher Columbus waged. And if 'Job's Tear' reflects the Christian empire that triumphed over these 'heathen' peoples, 'Junonia' identifies the corresponding paganism powerless to resist conversion enforced at the barrel of the gun, Juno the goddess of war who, despite having been inscripted, failed to protect her tribe.

Through such resonances, the shells map a wider and more precise world of Indian devastation than the Princess performs on her own, situating this paradigmatic avatar of North American experience in a global frame. The peoples that fall under the purview of such a narrative – Seminole, Maroon, Arawak, Bahamians – compass nearly every part of the Global South Atlantic. As Richard Price has shown, the reach of the maroons – fugitive slaves who built independent communities across the New World – extended across an immensity of space and time. For more than four centuries, runaways dotted the fringes of plantation America, from Brazil to the Southeastern United States, from Peru to the American Southwest (Price 1).

The resonances that such shells encode do not merely evoke a Latin American and Caribbean world where the distance between Mexico and Florida collapses; the landscape Bishop imagines also hearkens back to Mexico specifically. Notebooks from the period describe the Grutas caves and their 'arched ceilings as high and dark as if the heavens were made of stone'; the mountains of Oaxaca as 'beautiful dark blues and greens', with 'white clouds [that] drift around them', 'rainbows [that are] enormous bands of colors' and 'hills as they spread out on the valley [that] look quilted'; and Santa Maria Tonantzintla as one of 'the oddest looking churches', with 'all sorts of metallic paints, the most garish and incandescent possible' (Millier 167–8). The depth of description throughout Bishop's encounter with the cultural landscape rivals her engagement with Florida and Brazil, as does its earthly and spectral quality. References to 'shadow', 'smoke', blues and greens of the sea, greened over hills, 'thick & gray' clay and rocky valleys enact a dialectic of insubstantiality and solidity, grim death and evergreen beauty, that are equally operative in its United States analogue in Key West. For Bishop, as for Stevens, 'death is the mother of beauty' (Stevens 68) – and nowhere is that connection more manifest than here at the farthest reach of the Southeast. Each, too, remains steeped in a spatial grammar of verticality and horizontality, with Florida's vertiginous seascape resembling the perspectival shifts in Mexico that emerge from a gaze directed toward ceilings and mountains, hills and rainbows. Even the ambivalence Bishop experiences is a response both worlds provoke, with a

mixture of disgust and fascination, delight and revulsion. Beyond these stylistic affini-
ties, important though they may be, it is the figure of the Indian emerging gruesomely
at the end of the poem who stands most squarely at the centre of Bishop's interest
in Mexico and Florida. For the former, the Princess is the *genius loci*; for the latter,
Bishop excavates the detritus of her ghostly figure: the fragments of primitive pottery
at Mitla, the repainted interior of Santa Maria Tonantzintla.

Oaxaca – the region of Mexico Bishop liked most of all after Mérida – is the place
where Audre Lorde, over a decade later, found sustenance amidst the outcroppings of
dissipated white intellectuals still running on the fumes of the Mexican Revolution. To
borrow Lorde's own formulation, Mexico provided 'a haven for political and spiritual
refugees' (De Veaux 49) that comprised Hollywood figures exiled from McCarthyite
America, some of whom were lesbian or bisexual women. At twenty, Lorde arrived
as an even younger woman than Bishop, who was thirty at the time of her trip with
Marjorie Stevens. And like the elder poet, Lorde – as biographer Alexis De Veaux
notes – only came with 'the names of a few contacts, some savings, and a rudimentary
understanding of Spanish' (49). Although arriving in Mexico alone, she quickly fell in
love with Eudora Garrett, a 'lesbian journalist at least twenty-seven years older than
Audre and prone to alcoholic bouts' (52). The inverse of Bishop's own relationship
with the older Stevens, with Bishop the one who suffered from alcoholism, Lorde's
dalliance unlocked a great deal in the sexually naïve poet:

> It was Garrett who 'totally engaged' Audre in the erotic, psychic, and physical
> aspects of lesbian loving for the first time, embodying Audre's deepest desires for
> a sister-confidante-teacher-loving mother figure. Fluent in Spanish and in Mexican
> culture, Garrett showed Audre 'the way to Mexico' she'd 'come looking for, that
> nourishing land of light and color' where she found a sense of home. (De Veaux 52)

Lorde became alive to her sexual identity, as did, in some degree, Bishop – each having
their first serious female romantic partner – and worked through an equally 'fluid sense
of home' in poems as well as journals. Not only did her time there inspire two poems
about Oaxaca, but what she found there and in Mexico generally – the same folk culture
of indigenous peoples that fed into Bishop's Florida – had far-reaching implications for
her work. Studying Mexican history, ethnology and folk song at the Ciudad Universi-
taria helped forge later interests in African religion and history in her seminal volume
The Black Unicorn. That 'Oaxaca' was revised and republished in her 1976 volume
Coal (*Collected Poems* 166) – a mere two years before *The Black Unicorn* – only serves
to underscore this kinship, auguring a lineage worth further investigation. This reap-
pearance of the earlier poem, coincident with her first book-length foray into Yoruba
myth and Nigerian history, should not surprise: originally published in 1968, 'Oaxaca'
(*Collected Poems* 19) had been counted among, in her debut, the *First Cities*.

In Lorde's searching investigation, 'the land [here] moves slowly', developed under
the effort of 'the still-eyed men / who break the earth'. At once opaque myth and
historical reality, Oaxaca inspires a deep attention from Lorde on the material condi-
tions of the work that takes place from the very first line, and in the lived experience
of folk culture. 'Beneath the carving drag of wood' – an implement to till the land –
Lorde begins by revealing labourers who 'nurse their seed', engage in 'hard watching
through the dry season' and 'break the earth' – their folk culture hard, brutish, and

overlaid with fertility rituals evident in the personified earth ('brown earth / spread like a woman') and the quasi-personified natural spirits (thunder, lightning and storm).

These fugitive, if diffuse, energies of sexuality, myth, labour and folk culture Lorde carried onward, using them to render other spaces within the African diaspora and beyond in increasingly rich and sophisticated ways. They also led her to ask broader questions about how the Atlantic is shaped by entering the Caribbean. That inquiry occurred thirty years after the border-crossing into Mexico and ten years after Africa became the centre of her poetic investigations. In the 1986 volume *Our Dead Behind Us*, as Gloria Hull argues, Lorde finds herself 'living on the line' (150), 'fascinated by what happens as [the lines of identity] cross and recross, touch, and intersect with one another' (155). The line Lorde lives on – and blurs – contains a crucial geographical component. From poems like 'Diaspora' and 'Ethiopia' to 'Berlin Is Hard on Colored Girls' and 'This Urn Contains Earth from German Concentration Camps', Lorde wonders what happens when the borders and boundaries of nations operate in the same state of flux, shifting and commingling so that blackness stands to shape our perception of European history as well as African.

To draw such a variegated map of the Global South Atlantic, Lorde rejects the pencil that has excluded black subjectivity in favour of a 'colored pen [. . .] authorized to inscribe her [the black woman's] own law – an order that valorizes dreaming, speaking, and kissing the mother, and above all, does not seek to hide its hand in a transparently cloaked objectivity' (Hull 151). Thus, Lorde both valorises Bishop's map, in which 'more delicate than the historians are the mapmaker's colors', as well as adding, quite literally, more colour to it. She also adds the *life* of her black body, foregrounding the dispossession of a speaking subject that is neither simply a set of historical relics nor only a ventriloquised corpse. In doing so, Lorde imagines poetry as a viable replacement for history. As she asks rhetorically in 'On My Way Out I Passed Over You and the Verrazano Bridge': 'so where is true history written / except in the poems?' (*Collected Poems* 403). Lorde regarded 'On My Way Out' as so central to her preoccupations that the poem almost provided the title of the volume, making her way out of – and into – 'all the hot and troubled spots which engage her' (Hull 155) across Africa, Europe, the United States and the Caribbean.

Lorde's 'Florida' (*Collected Poems* 397–8) occupies pride of place in the volume, however, being one of the few poems in her entire corpus – 'Oaxaca', tellingly, is another – organised around a specific locale. Moreover, it is the only American state given this treatment. The only other American site centred by title is New York City. Set apart in this way, 'Florida' provides a central point in Lorde's geographic imaginary. It joins these American cities, and looks beyond to spaces in the African diaspora such as Harlem, Dahomey, Abomey, the Sahara and Ethiopia – all collectively framing the vast array of other sites that populate Lorde's poetry to inform her Global South Atlantic.

Within the context of *Our Dead Behind Us*, in particular, Florida offers an equally potent focal point, providing a kind of detail from the flight Lorde undertakes in 'On My Way Out I Passed Over You and the Verrazano Bridge'. Originally rendered as a journey to San Francisco in book form, 'On My Way Out' shifted into a poem of exodus from Staten Island, when Lorde reached the end of her seventeen-year relationship with Frances Clayton, to the sanctuary of St Croix, when she began a new relationship with sociologist Gloria Joseph and joined a broader community of black women in the Caribbean. Even when the trip imagined by Lorde in the poem was not predicated on this final break with the New York she had spent most of her life in, she was 'considering *leaving*' (Lorde and Hall 122). When the book was published, Lorde had indeed left to settle on an island where she would spend her last days while suffering from various forms of cancer, and still continued to forge transnational connections with writers, scholars and artists in Germany and South Africa. Like Bishop's, her mapping of this poetic region took place through literal forms of poetic exchange too.

As much as Lorde spent this period extending her investigations beyond the United States, she makes certain that it too is imbricated in the same Global South Atlantic. Hovering between an aerial view ('renting a biplane to stalk the full moon in Aquarius') and one closer to earth ('fire-damp sand between my toes'), Lorde pauses from the larger arc of her transnational journey to dissolve the same beauty of the Floridian landscape at which Bishop looked askance, destabilising with even deeper force the same horizon the earlier poem undercut and thereby challenging the integrity of its borders (Lorde 397). From the vantage point of her flight, Lorde juxtaposes the high culture of Europe that rendered Florida into a paradise shaped by desire and beauty ('Venus between propellers') with the low conditions of material black life such a tableau effaces ('feasting on frozen black beans Cubano from Grand Union / in the mangrove swamp'). Without a transition, logically or spatially, these two spheres converge, the poem brooking no separation.

In effect, Lorde returns to the same mangroves Bishop explored and yet pushes still deeper to an even more fraught historical foundation, roaming in the swamps where escaped slaves named 'maroons' once concealed themselves, isolated as small groups or larger communities. Although the *marronage* phenomenon was more extensive in the southern hemisphere, there was a significant presence of such individuals and communities in the United States – principally in the 'Great Dismal Swamp' that extended from southern Virginia to northeast North Carolina, and in the swamps of Florida, where many lived amongst the Seminoles, with whom they also allied. Literally above this submerged surface, Lorde finds a material trace of these Afro-Caribbean bodies in the 'frozen black beans Cubano', bodies which, in an ironic acknowledgement of multinational capitalism and its capacity for supporting national formation, remain in circulation as consumer goods. The source of these beans is 'Grand Union', short for Grand Union Supermarkets, a chain principally found in the northeast, but which also operated stores in the southeastern states and in the Caribbean. More than exhuming these bodies, Lorde 'feasts' on them. The gesture provides a form of playful, absent communion with her ancestors – not only in the abstract terms of the diaspora, but in the context of her own West Indian ancestry.

Appearing in the next stanza, Lorde's insect familiars reveal a black population pressed into a more provocative pose, having been isolated in another way. 'Huge arrogant cockroaches' – mainstays of the urban ghetto that draw on the space's role as a byword for the black underclass – are charged 'with white people's manners', revealing the racist stereotypes (e.g. 'uppity' and 'bestial') that Lorde roundly and indeed ironically undercuts by having them assimilate to white middle-class norms which may be what she slyly suggests is responsible for their size and arrogance. It is not only black bodies that are embedded in this natural world, however. Like Bishop, Lorde also encrypts the American soldiers who met their end in their war against the Seminoles through the 'elbow cypresses' that mark casualties transformed into landscape – corpses sunken even deeper into the Florida marshes than Bishop's.

Beyond the detritus of historical time these avatars offer, Lorde examines the 'black people' who remained only 'black specks' in Bishop's 'Florida'. Bookending the poem are scenes of African-American life made visible:

> Black people fishing the causeway
> full-skirted   bare brown to the bellyband
> atilt on the railing   near a concrete road
> where a crawler-transporter will move
> the space shuttle from hangar to gantry. (Lorde 397)

Here is a prototypical Caribbean scene of black figures fishing – the same kind of scene Lorde is situated against in *A Litany for Survival*. Depicting the gathered mass as 'full-skirted', as well as with the gender-neutral 'people', Lorde suggests women as well as men, evoking the archipelago in the aggregate. That aggregation also takes shape at the level of race, with the blackness Lorde savours through alliteration expanding to encompass a fuller colour spectrum, with brownness encompassed. Placed 'atilt on the railing', by a 'causeway' – i.e. a raised road bordering water – and 'near a concrete road', the fishing figures are revealed to be fundamentally liminal, poised between a history with its origins in the Middle Passage and a 'concrete' modernity where a 'space shuttle' is possible, if not at all for them.

Near the end of the poem, in place of the Indian Princess whom Bishop ventriloquises through an alligator who is buried alongside this *genius loci* in their shared, swampy grave, Lorde forges a community of black women:

> In Gainesville the last time there was only one
> sister present who said   'I'm gonna remember your name
> and the next time you come there'll be
> quite a few more of us, hear?'
> and there certainly was   a warm pool
> of dark women's faces
> in the sea of listening (Lorde 398)

From the sustenance of that 'warm pool' and 'sea of listening', Derek Walcott's 'sea [as] history' (364) has been returned to the body, appropriated by those for whom the body of water had only portended centuries of violence and enslavement. Lorde's own sated hunger underscores the rejuvenation these waters now provide:

> The first thing I did when I got home
> after kissing my honey
> was to wash my hair with small flowers
> and begin a five-day fast (Lorde 398)

On her return home, the encounter allows Lorde to embrace her desire, this intimacy with her partner reflected in a sweet unselfconsciousness coupled with a term of endearment ('honey'). In the same spirit, Lorde feels empowered to attend to her own body, purifying flesh both in part (i.e. 'wash my hair') and as a whole ('a five-day fast'). Perhaps most of all, Lorde imagines a Florida with the extensive array of flora that helped make the state so distinctive to the Spanish – e.g. the 'hibiscus', 'jacaranda' and 'palmetto' – and in which she has a meaningful part, self-crowned with 'small flowers' which at once bind her to the community of women and to the larger landscape, near and far, they all inhabit. The poem communally recasts the tender intimacies of the hair washing in Bishop's 'The Shampoo' (*Poems* 82), an office performed for her 'honey' Lota de Macedo Soares.

Given the rarity of place name poems in Lorde's corpus, particularly places in the United States; the centrality of 'Florida' in Bishop's early work, and her prominence in the postwar era; and the perspectival shifts and careful attention to the region's flora and fauna held in common, might not Lorde be actively engaging with the elder poet's model – a case of overt influence? There is no evidence that Lorde admired, or was even familiar with, Bishop's work, much less this poem in particular. But given Bishop's reputation, Lorde's extensive poetic education, and their mutual connection to Adrienne Rich, it is far from implausible that the later poem provides a direct reply. Irrespective of any direct lineage between the two, what engaged Bishop about the Florida peninsula and its keys engaged Lorde in turn, pushing the 'warrior poet' and the 'minor female Wordsworth' (*Words in Air* 122) alike to a world where they exercised their imaginative power to reshape the contours of history, geography, culture and identity, and thereby place the instability of each vector at the centre of their poetic region.

That legacy of decentring nation and continent in the Global South Atlantic has been taken up by major African-American poets in our contemporary moment to coruscating effect, with Rowan Ricardo Phillips and Claudia Rankine remapping not only the discursive spaces of lyric, the prose poem, and literary and cultural criticism, but, with no less staggering power, the world. Each was raised in New York with West Indian heritage (Antigua and Jamaica, the Bronx and Brooklyn, respectively); each is a pioneering figure seeking to reshape the transnational ferment of Lorde and Bishop from the ground up, refracting the energies of border-crossing and diaspora more squarely, and paradoxically, within the United States.

Phillips comfortably spans 'translator, poet, and literary and art critic' to remake forms, with 'made-over sonnets, pseudo-Spenserian stanzas, and unrhymed tercets loosely translated from the *Purgatorio*', traditions (placing Bob Marley in that same *Purgatorio*), and the very distinctions between sky and earth (Poetry Foundation). As Eric McHenry observed in a *New York Times* review of *The Ground* (2012), 'its title may suggest stability, but Phillips treads a middle ground – between spirit and flesh, heaven and earth, here and gone. His images are evanescent, twilit, and smoke-obscured' (Poetry Foundation). In 'Two Studies of Derek Walcott' (Phillips 54), he imagines 'a New Nation / Like New York, New London, maybe New Paltz', and elsewhere he contemplates a 'Map, Incomplete, 1665' (Phillips 13), where 'Africa, newly rivered, sits mysterious as the brain of his [the cartographer's] New World', and a 'Mappa Mundi' (Phillips 23) rendered through the lens of the Cross Bronx Freeway, where the focus shifts from the edifices of urban renewal constructed by Robert Moses to the green spaces that they are bordered by – that is, the margins to the centre.

In *Don't Let Me Be Lonely* and *Citizen*, each subtitled *An American Lyric*, Rankine straddles genres at once literary and visual to map the dislocations experienced within a contemporary landscape shaped by the multiform pressures of media as well as history, drawing on photography, art installations and YouTube videos. Even at the literary level, as Dan Chiasson observed in his review of *Citizen* for *The New Yorker*, the genre is committed to catholicity. The textual blocks that form the spine of the volume are at once indebted to 'the prose poem, the police log, the journal entry, and the confession board papered with anonymous note cards' (Chiasson). Like their antecedents, they plot the Global South Atlantic in concert to disrupt our understanding of an experimental, avant-garde poetics that is often seen as indifferent to race and isolated from the social reality of identity more broadly, and to reframe the urban geography of a New York in which blackness, and the black vernacular, blends and jostles with high European culture.

These deliberate confusions of genre and geography in contemporary African-American poetics emerge from the same cross-currents of identity and culture that distended the Florida horizon in Bishop and Lorde to reveal the material reality and global history seeding the soil of any place in the Global South Atlantic. Each female poet writing in the aftermath of modernism built on a legacy of poetics that operated from Key West and fanned outward to depict a world continually in flux, where 'knowledge' – to recollect the famous last line of 'At the Fishhouses' – 'is historical, flowing, and flown' (*Poems* 64).

Works Cited

Axelrod, Steven Gould, 'Bishop, History, and Politics', in Angus Cleghorn and Jonathan Ellis (eds), *The Cambridge Companion to Elizabeth Bishop* (Cambridge: Cambridge University Press, 2014), pp. 35–48.

Bishop, Elizabeth, *One Art: Letters*, ed. Robert Giroux (New York: Farrar, Straus and Giroux, 1994).

Bishop, Elizabeth, *Poems, Prose, and Letters*, ed. Robert Giroux and Lloyd Schwartz (New York: Library of America, 2008).

Bishop, Elizabeth, and Robert Lowell, *Words in Air: The Complete Correspondence between Elizabeth Bishop and Robert Lowell*, ed. Thomas Travisano with Saskia Hamilton (New York: Farrar, Straus and Giroux, 2008).

Bolaki, Stella, and Sabine Broeck (eds), *Audre Lorde's Transnational Legacies* (Boston: University of Massachusetts Press, 2015).

Callahan, James M., *Cuba and International Relations: A Historical Study in American Diplomacy* (Baltimore: Johns Hopkins University Press, 1899).

Chiasson, Dan, 'Color Codes', *The New Yorker*, 27 October 2014, <http://www.newyorker.com/magazine/2014/10/27/color-codes> (last accessed 24 October 2018).

Cleghorn, Angus, and Jonathan Ellis (eds), *The Cambridge Companion to Elizabeth Bishop* (Cambridge: Cambridge University Press, 2014).

Cleghorn, Angus, Bethany Hicok and Thomas J. Travisano (eds), *Elizabeth Bishop in the Twenty-First Century: Reading the New Editions* (Charlottesville: University of Virginia Press, 2012).

Delpar, Helen, *The Enormous Vogue of Things Mexican: Cultural Relations between the United States and Mexico, 1920–1935* (Tuscaloosa: University of Alabama Press, 1992).

De Veaux, Alexis, *Warrior Poet: A Biography of Audre Lorde* (New York: W. W. Norton & Company, 2004).

Doreski, Carole, *Elizabeth Bishop: The Restraints of Language* (New York: Oxford University Press, 1993).

Fountain, Gary, and Peter Brazeau (eds), *Remembering Elizabeth Bishop: An Oral Biography* (Amherst: University of Massachusetts Press, 1994).

Griffin, Ada G., and Michelle Parkerson, *A Litany for Survival: The Life and Work of Audre Lorde* (New York: Third World Newsreel, 1996).

Hicok, Bethany, 'Becoming a Poet: From North to South', in Angus Cleghorn and Jonathan Ellis (eds), *The Cambridge Companion to Elizabeth Bishop* (Cambridge: Cambridge University Press, 2014), pp. 111–23.

Hull, Gloria T., 'Living on the Line: Audre Lorde and *Our Dead Behind Us*', in Cheryl A. Wall (ed.), *Changing Our Own Words: Essays on Criticism, Theory, and Writing by Black Women* (New Brunswick, NJ: Rutgers University Press, 1989), pp. 150–72.

Lorde, Audre, *The Collected Poems of Audre Lorde* (New York: W. W. Norton & Company, 1997).

Lorde, Audre, and Joan W. Hall, *Conversations with Audre Lorde* (Jackson: University Press of Mississippi, 2004).

Lowney, John, *History, Memory, and the Literary Left: Modern American Poetry, 1935–1968* (Iowa City: University of Iowa Press, 2006).

Mahon, John K., *History of the Second Seminole War, 1835–1842* (Tallahassee: University Press of Florida, 2010).

Millier, Brett C., *Elizabeth Bishop: Life and the Memory of It* (Berkeley: University of California Press, 1993).

Monteiro, George (ed.), *Conversations with Elizabeth Bishop* (Jackson: University Press of Mississippi, 1996).

Page, Barbara, 'Off-Beat Claves, Oblique Realities: The Key West Notebooks of Elizabeth Bishop', in Marilyn May Lombardi (ed.), *Elizabeth Bishop: The Geography of Gender* (Charlottesville: University Press of Virginia, 1993), pp. 196–211.

Phillips, Rowan R., *The Ground: Poems* (New York: Farrar, Straus and Giroux, 2012).

Poetry Foundation, 'Rowan Ricardo Phillips', <https://www.poetryfoundation.org/poets/rowan-ricardo-phillips> (last accessed 24 October 2018).

Price, Richard, *Maroon Societies: Rebel Slave Communities in the Americas* (Baltimore: Johns Hopkins University Press, 1996).

Ragg, Edward, *Wallace Stevens and the Aesthetics of Abstraction* (Cambridge: Cambridge University Press, 2010).

Rankine, Claudia, *Citizen: An American Lyric* (Minneapolis: Graywolf Press, 2014).

Rankine, Claudia, *Don't Let Me Be Lonely: An American Lyric* (Minneapolis: Graywolf Press, 2004).

Scandura, Jani, *Down in the Dumps: Place, Modernity, American Depression* (Durham, NC: Duke University Press, 2008).

Slaughter, Joseph, and Kerry Bystrom (eds), 'CFP: The Global South Atlantic (Deadline: September 30)', Doreen B. Townsend Center for the Humanities, <http://townsendgroups.berkeley.edu/blog/cfp-global-south-atlantic-deadline-september-30> (last accessed 24 October 2018).

Slaughter, Joseph, and Kerry Bystrom, 'Introduction to The Global South Atlantic', <http://www.academia.edu/28317302/Introduction_to_The_Global_South_Atlantic> (last accessed 24 October 2018).

Stevens, Wallace, *The Collected Poems of Wallace Stevens* (New York: Knopf, 2000).

Travisano, Thomas, *Elizabeth Bishop: Her Artistic Development* (Charlottesville: University Press of Virginia, 1988).

Trillo, Mauricio Tenorio, 'The Cosmopolitan Mexican Summer, 1920–1949', *Latin American Research Review* 32.3 (1997): 224–42.

Walcott, Derek, *Collected Poems, 1948–1984* (New York: Farrar, Straus and Giroux, 1986).

Zona, Kirstin Hotelling, 'Bishop: Race, Class, and Gender', in Angus Cleghorn and Jonathan Ellis (eds), *The Cambridge Companion to Elizabeth Bishop* (Cambridge: Cambridge University Press, 2014), pp. 49–61.

20

INNOCENTS ABROAD? ELIZABETH BISHOP AND JAMES MERRILL OVERSEAS

Ben Leubner

> He loves
> that sense of constant re-adjustment.
>
> (Elizabeth Bishop, 'The Gentleman of Shalott')

On 10 November 1959, Elizabeth Bishop posted a letter from Brazil to her friend, the American poet May Swenson, thanking her for a gift she had sent Bishop: a pair of binoculars. Bishop was ecstatic: 'You have FLOORED me,' she begins (*One Art* 377). 'But of course I am perfectly delighted. It is the nicest and most overwhelming present I've received for years and years.'

It had been sixteen years since Bishop had lasted just five days at a job in what she called an 'Optical Shop' on a Navy base in Key West, 'taking binoculars apart and putting them together again' (*One Art* 115). Over that intervening decade and a half, she tells Swenson, she'd 'forgotten about binoculars, or put the science [of them] out of my mind' (377). But her descriptions of binoculars in 1943 anticipate the descriptions of 1959. In a letter to Marianne Moore, she described the instruments she worked on in the shop as 'magnificent', 'delicate' and 'maddening' (115), a range of adjectives comparable to 'nice', 'delightful' and 'overwhelming'. These are also adjectives that can profitably be used to describe poems – compare 'magnificent', 'delicate' and 'maddening', for instance, with '*Accuracy, Spontaneity, Mystery*', the three qualities Bishop claimed she admired most in poems (*Poems, Prose, and Letters* 703). Binoculars, then, are not entirely unlike poems in the range of reactions they can provoke from those who handle them. Bishop the 'Industrial Worker' (*One Art* 115) of 1943 had to quit her job so soon because of the eyestrain it caused her; she describes for Moore the tasks she had to perform in the shop: 'the work was so finicky and tedious that it was getting to be a torture to me' (115). Bishop made variations of this remark about her poems as well. Poems, too, had, or were, lenses. As Bishop wrote to Robert Lowell in 1962, 'If after I read a poem, the world looks like that poem for 24 hours or so, I'm sure it's a good one' (409).

Five days at the Optical Shop, then, might have provided invaluable training for a lifetime of writing poetry. When the work proved too finicky and torturous for Bishop, she became exasperated. She wrote to Moore, 'The foreman, who was perfectly happy spending *five* days adjusting one lens, or *four* hours on one screw the size of a pin, would look at me very mildly and say, "Don't let it get you kiddo"' (*One Art* 116). 'Kiddo' famously went on to become a poet who would spend years, even decades, meticulously working on the lens of a poem before finally considering it finished.

Bishop enjoyed the presence of her 'heavily tattooed' co-workers in the shop, most of whom were sailors; the only thing that upset her about them was their 'lack of imagination', which became 'more and more depressing' with each passing day (*One Art* 115–16). 'Not one of them had any idea of the *theory* of the thing,' she lamented to Moore, 'why the prisms go this way or that way, or what "collimate" and "optical center" really mean' (116). She might just as well have complained to Moore in 1966 about some of her poetry students at the University of Washington, lamenting, perhaps, that they didn't know what 'enjambment' and 'chiasmus' meant. She did lament to James Merrill that year, 'The problem all along has been iambic pentameter [. . .] tomorrow I'll see if their 10 lines of iambic pentameter scan at last' (445). This is Bishop the industrial worker still at it, herself the 'foreman' now, trying to adjust and repair the poems of her students. Only this time the eyestrain wasn't so bad that she had to quit after five days; she got through the entire quarter.

As Barbara Page and Carmen Oliveira note, there is a 'disturbing ethics of distanced observation' at work throughout Elizabeth Bishop's poetry (118), a disturbing ethics of which Bishop herself was aware. Much of the famous observational precision and visual detail of her poems can be characterised in terms of what Bethany Hicok calls 'forms of surveillance' (146). Bishop's poetics of 'distanced observation' has many components, from the metaphysical and the epistemological to the social and political, where the overlap between components makes the entire viewing mechanism a complex instrument indeed, difficult to take apart and put back together again. The political facet of Bishop's poetry constitutes one particular 'screw the size of a pin' that scholars have been fidgeting with and adjusting for years now, somewhat maddened by its delicateness. 'Although not overtly political,' writes Steven Gould Axelrod, '[Bishop's] poems are indirectly so. Even if one does not know fully what to make of the political implications, one feels their presence and wrestles with them' (36). Acquiring a theory of the thing is no easy matter when all one can do is 'feel [its] presence'. But this is no more the case for the reader of Bishop's poetry than it was for Bishop herself, who was always constantly adjusting her lenses, as it were, trying to make sense of her position as an American abroad in the mid-twentieth century. As such, she recognised all too clearly the 'connection between tourism and imperialism', in Robert von Hallberg's words (79), even as she indulged in the one while she resisted the other. Here was an implication to wrestle with indeed: the 'possibility', according to James Longenbach, of 'complicity in the continuing imposition of [colonial] values' even as one critiqued them (30). And one could put oneself in such a difficult bind so easily, merely by picking up a pair of binoculars – or by writing a poem.

The binoculars that Swenson sent to Bishop subsequently appeared in two of her poems, 'The Burglar of Babylon' and 'The End of March'. 'The Burglar of Babylon' (*Poems* 110–15) was first published in the 21 November 1964 edition of *The New Yorker* before appearing a year later in *Questions of Travel*. According to Robert Lowell, Marianne Moore (bizarrely, appropriately) thought it Bishop's 'finest poem', while Lowell himself called it another of Bishop's 'peculiar triumphs' (*Words in Air* 560). Lowell's praise of the poem reassured Bishop, who said she couldn't 'make up [her] mind about [it]' (561–2); Moore's favouring it, though, made her 'a bit uneasy!' (563). 'I think she likes the message: "Crime does not pay" too well,' she said, where what made Bishop uneasy in this regard was precisely the fact that that wasn't the poem's message at all. The long ballad about the police pursuit of a criminal through the *favelas* of Rio de Janeiro features at its optical centre the poet herself, where one clue to her identity lies in the poem's inclusion of Swenson's gift. A little more than halfway through the ballad we're told, 'Rich people in apartments / Watched through binoculars / As long as the daylight lasted' (*Poems* 113). It is easy to peg Bishop, in her top-floor Copacabana apartment, as one of these 'Rich people', tracking the hunt of the burglar Micuçu. Bishop, it seems, made a habit of tracking – or scanning – the goings-on of Rio from her position of privileged distance; in September of 1961 she wrote to Lowell about the political turmoil then engulfing Rio: 'The Navy steamed up and down right in front of our apartment here and I watched through binoculars' (*Words in Air* 376). And when 'The Burglar of Babylon' was published as a small, stand-alone book in 1968, Bishop admitted, in an introduction, that she was indeed one of the people who attempted to track the hunt 'through binoculars, although really we could see very little of it' (quoted in Monteiro 61).

Bishop said of the binoculars that Swenson sent her, 'They seem *fearfully* powerful to me' (*One Art* 377), powerful, perhaps, not only in terms of orders of magnitude but also insofar as they had the capacity to put oneself in power, or at the very least in a position of privilege from which one might safely espy a multitude of things, maybe even a murder. One might think of Alfred Hitchcock's 1954 thriller *Rear Window* here, as George Monteiro notes (61). In both Bishop's ballad and the film, the binoculars, or the telephoto lens, accord one both the power to see and the pleasure that comes with it, while at the same time rendering one complicit in what one sees. What makes the powerful lens so '*fearfully* powerful', then, is that it has the capacity to simultaneously render one both powerful and powerless. Bishop, that is, in her indulgence of surveillance, becomes partially, helplessly and indirectly responsible for the plight of Micuçu. The two, after all, reside on opposite ends of the class spectrum in Rio, where the concentration of wealth among the rich ensconced in their beachside apartments leaves much of the rest of the city's population trying to survive in the *favelas*, with a large gap between them, the bridging of which requires binoculars.

'The Burglar of Babylon' both opens and closes with a lament for the 'fearful stain' that grows on the city's many 'fair green hills': 'The poor who come to Rio / And can't go home again' (*Poems* 110, 115). One might criticise Bishop for these lines, but to do so would be to ignore the complexity of the poem's voice, its decentred nature, for it is not solely Bishop's voice, by any stretch, even though she does later place herself, albeit obliquely, within the poem. Much of the ballad's language, in fact, came from subsequent newspaper accounts of the incident (Monteiro 61). The result, in the poem, is a three-way tension between the folk stylings of the ballad, the rhetoric of local journalism, and the poet's own perspective. True, these last two occupy a similar socio-economic space, at least in terms of their relation to the *favelas*. Still, the poem's overall tone fairly demands that we read not only these opening and closing lines but the entire poem as consisting of a good deal of irony; the newspapers might have insisted that 'crime does not pay', but the poet is conflicted on this matter. Perhaps it didn't pay for Micuçu, but if it was a crime to indulge oneself in tracking via binoculars the downfall of a desperate outlaw from one's own secure penthouse in a foreign country, then crime most certainly did pay: 'The Burglar of Babylon' is Bishop's longest poem, and *The New Yorker* paid poets by the line. The real stain on the city is, quite possibly, not the *favelas* of its hillsides but the string of hotels and apartments that makes up Copacabana itself, where the poet makes her own abode, and the interests of whose inhabitants the local newspapers, as well as international magazines, both represent and serve.

Elizabeth Bishop *was* binocular. She was a binocular poet; she saw everything, including herself, both ways.[1] That Bishop couldn't make up her mind about 'The Burglar of Babylon' should come as no surprise. She was herself something of a dual enigma about whom *we* might have difficulty making up our minds: a poet of privilege and – or but – a poet of poverty. After having forgotten about binoculars for sixteen years, Bishop suddenly realised, she told Swenson, how 'very much [she'd] been need-ing [them], living in the mountains *and* on the ocean' (*One Art* 378). And, we might add, in the city. She called it a 'pleasure' to be able to 'read the titles on the pocket books at the other end of the airport' with her new binoculars, where there also seems to be something potentially intrusive in the act, maybe even something unethical (377). But for Bishop it's simply as if the binoculars were merely very powerful – or '*fearfully*' so – reading glasses.

Eleven years after the appearance of 'The Burglar of Babylon' in *The New Yorker*, 'The End of March' (*Poems* 199–200) was published in the same magazine, in, appro-priately, the 24 March edition of 1975, at which time it was over thirty years since Bishop's five-day stint at the Optical Shop, and over fifteen years since she had opened Swenson's present. But she still has her binoculars, and she is still employing them in a complex matrix of reading, surveillance and observation.

Whereas in the ballad Bishop seems to live vicariously through Micuçu as she fol-lows him through the *favelas*, in this later poem she daydreams about living in her *own* shack, a 'crooked box / set up on pilings'. In both cases she indulges some sort of fantasy of poverty. In the first poem, her binoculars enable the fantasy; in the second, they are part of it, as she muses on the idea of a rustic, solitary retirement. Gone is the warm, overcrowded, southern beach of Copacabana, replaced by a cold, deserted, northern stretch of Duxbury sand, where the poet says she would like to retire and 'do *nothing*, / or nothing much, forever, in two bare rooms: / look through binoculars, read boring books'.

What else? 'Talk to myself', 'watch the droplets slipping' on the windowpanes on foggy days, and, 'At night, a *grog à l'américaine*. / I'd blaze it with a kitchen match'. 'Many things about this place', the speaker remarks parenthetically, 'are dubious.' So, we might say, is the speaker herself. Talking to oneself, for instance, might be innocent, but it might also indicate a significant degree of instability. And the spectre of alcohol-ism lurks as surely in that '*grog*' as it does in Crusoe's home-brew (*Poems* 182–6). Is the radical isolation that the speaker of 'The End of March' desires the result of a too-strong predilection for 'distanced observation', a natural consequence of practis-ing for too long a disturbing ethics? 'The End of March' intriguingly recalls two of Bishop's earliest short stories, both of which feature protagonists who favour solitude, but whose motives for doing so are obscure. There is the 1938 fantasy of isolation, seclusion and, it would seem, guilt, 'In Prison', in which the narrator dreams of being given only 'one very dull book to read, the duller the better' (*Poems, Prose, and Let-ters* 587). And just a year before it came 'The Sea and Its Shore', whose only character, Edwin Boomer (note both the initials and the resemblance of 'Boomer' to 'Bulmer', Bishop's mother's maiden name), lives in a remote tumbledown shack on a deserted

beach and occupies himself with drunkenly 'blazing' things indeed, not his own alco-
holic beverages, but scraps of paper with writing on them that he picks up off the
beach, scraps of literature, scraps, perhaps, *of* 'boring books'. Brett C. Miller says that
Bishop finally resolved the conflict at the heart of these stories, a conflict having to do
with the disturbing 'daydream of solitary confinement', in 'The End of March', written
almost forty years later (134). But in optics, resolution is the act, process or capability
of distinguishing between two separate but adjacent objects or sources of light, and
not foreclosing on one at the expense of the other. Bishop thus resolves the conflict at
the heart of these early stories precisely by continuing to perpetuate it forty years later;
her closure comes from being at home with a lack of closure. The speaker of 'The End
of March' might finally conclude 'impossible' in regard to her fantasy of literal retire-
ment, but the point was never so much to bring about these conditions as to imagine
them in the first place. Bishop's 'proto-dream-house', her 'crypto-dream-house', exists
only in the confines of the poem's binocular resolution; it is in this removed locale that
she truly dwells.

In order for binoculars to work, you have to be far away, 'withdrawn as far as
possible, / indrawn', leaving yourself in a potentially ethically compromised position
for the sake of an ideal resolution. One can observe this dynamic at work throughout
Bishop's poetry, from 'Cirque d'Hiver' to 'The Bight' to 'The End of March'. The last
poem's dedication, not unlike 'The Bight's' 'On my birthday', is telling in this regard,
insofar as it informs us that although the poem's 'we' consists of three people (the
couple John Malcolm Brinnin and Bill Read, and the poet herself), the poet, despite her
company, remains intensely preoccupied and no less isolated than the younger, solitary
speaker of 'The Bight', who perhaps *should* be with others on her birthday.

Laurie Colwin's 1975 short story 'Travel', a story that would then appear in
Colwin's 1981 collection *The Lone Pilgrim*, shares one of its pages in the 24 March
1975 edition of *The New Yorker* with 'The End of March', a poem that itself might
have been titled 'The Lone Pilgrim'. Meanwhile, on the facing page is an Edward
Koren cartoon that features a lone man walking into a crowded bar and asking
the bartender, 'Excuse me, but what's the nature of this bar? Political, literary, or
singles?' The 'singles' and 'literary' components of 'The End of March' are fairly
obvious, but it has its own political component as well. The very fact of the poem's
publication in *The New Yorker* is politically significant. The poem is both at home
and not at home in the magazine's pages, surrounded by Colwin's story and Koren's
cartoon. All three share similar concerns, dealing as they do with human relation-
ships and human isolation, but the story is about a husband and wife, and the man
walking into the bar doesn't inquire as to whether or not it might be a gay bar. In
order for Bishop's poem to fit in among this crowd, then, no mention can be made of
the fact that the two men to whom it is dedicated are a couple.

Additionally, in a letter to Robert Lowell, Bishop referred to the poem's 'artichoke
of a house' as an 'ugly little green shack' that 'John B' was appalled by: 'he doesn't
share my taste for the awful, I'm afraid' (*Elizabeth Bishop and The New Yorker*
xlix). Was Bishop's fascination with the *favelas* of Rio, consisting as they did mainly
of 'ugly little shacks', an additional instance of her 'taste for the awful'? And how
are we supposed to read the word 'awful' here – as indicating unpleasantness or as
inspiring wonder? Certainly, the word carries a good deal of binocular weight in
Bishop's poetry due to its appearance in 'The Bight' alongside the word 'cheerful',

another word Bishop used frequently in her descriptions of Brazil and Brazilians, with similarly dubious implications.

The New Yorker rejected 'The Shampoo' on the grounds of its subtle lesbian content (*Elizabeth Bishop and The New Yorker* xxiv–xxv). While in that particular instance Bishop was the victim of a lack of vision, it might be argued that with 'The Burglar of Babylon's' own initial publication in the magazine she was its perpetrator. When Howard Moss suggested several changes to the poem, Bishop agreed to them all except for those pertaining to 'questions of "style,"' where the poem's style 'was, of course, repetitious & a bit clumsy on purpose' (264), a claim that hints at a potentially damning marriage of form and content. Fittingly, the poem's forty-seven 'clumsy', shack-like stanzas were too much for a single page in *The New Yorker*, so the last nine sprawl on to the bottom of the facing page, three-quarters of which is taken up by another cartoon, this one by Whitney Darrow Jr: a stern businessman walking into a boardroom where seven subordinates greet him in chirping unison: 'Good morning to you! Good morning to you! / We're all in our places, with bright, shining faces . . .'. All the untidy activity continues indeed (*Poems* 59).

In a 2000 study of H.D., Bishop and Sylvia Plath, Renée Curry argues, controversially, that Bishop writes 'a polite whiteness into her poetry' that isn't present in her letters (77). In this regard Bishop and James Merrill surely have something to commiserate over together, as Merrill is pretty much the poster boy for 'polite whiteness' in the world of poetry criticism. While Bishop is a relatively new target for this kind of criticism, as early appraisals of her work, both during her life and shortly after her death, tended to focus more on its objective, aesthetic qualities than on its political components, Merrill was accustomed to these kinds of charges from very early on in his career, and they have yet to abate. In her introduction to the 2011 *Penguin Anthology of Twentieth-Century American Poetry*, Rita Dove, who edited the volume and included only one Merrill poem in it ('The Victor Dog', written for Bishop), all but singles Merrill out as the CEO of 'a largely whitewashed poetry establishment' (xlvii) we would presumably do better to neglect than to indulge. Helen Vendler, who openly attacked Dove over the contents of her anthology, had remarked a decade earlier upon how Merrill had proceeded, all his life, so 'intrepidly through [such] accusations of snobbery, affectation, preciousness, artifice, perversity, and elitism' (*The Ocean, the Bird, and the Scholar* 200) as Dove's remark epitomises. Merrill thus would not have been surprised by Curry's kind of criticism had it been made of him (though he would have found it dismaying), as he encountered the likes of it throughout his career, mainly as a result of the circumstances of his birth.[2] The sort of criticism that has only accrued to Bishop from the 1990s onwards thus plagued Merrill from the very beginning. And, as is the case with Bishop, some of the criticism has to do with his modes of habitation in and attitudes towards some of the places he called home. For Bishop, it was Brazil; for Merrill, Greece and, to a lesser extent, Key West.

Some of the criticism, of course, is warranted. Curry, certainly, and Dove, too, have pertinent points to make, even if they could be made more aptly. But when Merrill's 'neo-formalism' is made to seem tantamount to neo-Nazism, as it is in a 1990 essay by Ira Sadoff, it is no longer a case of criticism but instead one of personal attack, usually grounded, as is the case here, in ignorance. The entire premise of Sadoff's reading of the late poem 'Clearing the Title' lies in the assumption that the poem is 'inherent[ly] racis[t]' because Merrill 'uses poor blacks as a backdrop for condominiums', one of which he and his 'lover' have just bought in Key West. This will do for an example of 'criticism' of Merrill that stems merely from his wealth and not from a reading of his poetry. Not once in the poem's nineteen octaves is the house David Jackson bought for himself and Merrill referred to as a 'condominium', and certainly not one among several. Langdon Hammer describes the actual house as a 'small, modest home' that was located in a neighbourhood that housed families whose members 'had once worked at the naval yard' nearby, the same naval yard where Bishop had once been employed for five days (623). The house itself, amusingly, to Merrill, was on Elizabeth Street, and Alison Lurie described it as 'a dark filthy ruin' (quoted in Hammer 624). Hammer's and Lurie's descriptions actually match the description of the house found in the poem: termite-infested, featuring floors with 'muddy varnish', and possessing a 'bare', 'ravenous' interior. Hardly a posh condominium. Nor are there any 'poor blacks' in the poem, only a single African-American girl who sways in the face of a sunset that several people, including the poet and his partner, are watching from a wharf.

'Anything worth having's had both ways', though, as Merrill writes in the second book of his *Sandover* trilogy (*The Changing Light at Sandover* 174), and this must presumably include responses to one's poetry. Regarding the question of how seriously even he took the material of his epic poem, Merrill insisted to Vendler in 1979 that the point was 'to be always of two minds' (*Recitative* 51), neither 'merely skeptical nor merely credulous', as he put it in response to another interviewer at around the same time (53). Merrill, too, then, was a binocular poet. And before the house in Key West, the poet who made a point of being always of two minds was, during the two decades of his peak years as a poet, also of two homes: one in Stonington, Connecticut, the other in Athens, Greece, a city Merrill had first visited and fell in love with as a young man in 1950, and where he first made a home in 1964. Merrill's years in Greece, then, overlap with Bishop's in Brazil, where Merrill's own *Questions of Travel*, his Greece-book to Bishop's Brazil-book, is 1969's *The Fire Screen*, published four years after Bishop's book, which Merrill had taught extensively during a brief stint at the University of Wisconsin in 1967. Merrill's volume doesn't feature the same kind of structure as Bishop's, but it could: with some slight rearrangement of the poems, one could divide it into two sections, 'Greece' and 'Elsewhere', where most of the poems would fall under 'Greece', though its longest poem by far, 'The Summer People' – which Merrill might have titled 'In the Village' – would lie in 'Elsewhere'.[3]

The question about Merrill in Greece, as about Bishop in Brazil, is to what extent does exposure *to* constitute a form of exploitation *of*? Merrill had discovered a new life in Greece, and a new self. At first, he said, he went there 'very much in the spirit of one who embarks upon a double life [. . .] I felt for the first time that I was doing exactly as I pleased' (Hammer 305). Greece acted on Merrill, freeing him from many of the restrictions of his life in America, but Merrill also acted on Greece, and took advantage of it in more ways than one. Greece, for Merrill, was, among other things, a kind of sexual playground where he felt free to roam and indulge himself in ways that were considerably less feasible at home. 'Eros in Greece', Vendler notes, 'gave permission for love still illegal in the United States' (*The Ocean, the Bird, and the Scholar* 369). Merrill thus became a different person overseas, to borrow the title of his late memoir, in which he writes, 'Freedom to be oneself is all very well; the greater freedom is not to be oneself' (*A Different Person* 129). Hammer refers to Merrill's early life in Greece as a 'carefully circumscribed diversion, like Algernon's weekends with Bunbury in *The Importance of Being Earnest*' (305). But Merrill *was* earnest, only, as in the case of Bishop, being earnest did not suffice to ensure that his own personal agenda was not at least partially complicit in forces at work in his adopted country (pollution, commercialisation, overcrowdedness) that he decried. It's not as though Merrill was living a life of irresponsible luxury and total decadence, however; the house in Athens he bought with David Jackson was as modest as the one in Key West, nestled between two neighbourhoods, one highly 'fashionable', the other more 'ordinary'; it was a house that 'did not announce its owner's wealth' (352), and one that many of Merrill's friends, as was the case with Lurie in Florida, found sub-standard.

Still, Merrill lived in a Greece that was undergoing as much political turmoil at the time as Bishop's Brazil, where the very facts of his wealth and nationality placed him in part on that end of the political spectrum opposite to many of his own convictions and beliefs. He knew, as Hammer writes, 'that he was a rich American at a moment when it was unpopular and possibly even dangerous to be one' (388). He wasn't quite as involved in Grecian politics as Bishop was in Brazilian politics, but he wasn't uninvolved either. As his politically active Greek friend Vassili Vassilikos put it, 'It wasn't [that] Jimmy was *un*political. He was deeply political' (388). But the latter could easily look like the former, a fact that has fuelled criticism of both Merrill and his poetry for half a century now, for his poems, too, are often more 'deeply political' than unpolitical, or, to use Axelrod's words regarding Bishop's poems, more 'indirectly' political than 'overtly' so.

Justin Quinn says of Merrill's overseas life, 'It is as though Merrill began his sojourns in Europe intent solely on the pageant going on in his skull only to be interrupted by voices [. . .] that simply could not be pushed aside' (116). In this way self-centredness gave way to self-marginalisation, self-importance to the importance of others. One might assume that the forceful voices Quinn speaks of are those intruding voices from the other world that would eventually come to make up so much of the *Sandover* trilogy. But they aren't. They are the voices from the other world of Greece, voices that begin to suffuse Merrill's poetry in the mid-1960s, a decade before the appearance of Ephraim, himself a Greek, in *Divine Comedies*. One of these voices is the voice that speaks in 'Kostas Tympakianakis' (*Collected Poems* 238–9), a dramatic monologue that, like Bishop's 'Manuelzinho', is spoken by a foreign 'friend of the writer'.

Tympakianakis was a young Cretan to whom Merrill was introduced in 1966 and with whom he had a brief affair in the midst of his more prolonged relationships with David Jackson and Strato Mouflouzélis. He had served in the special forces of the Greek Navy, specialising in underwater demolition, and had lost a brother in the Greek Civil War (Hammer 425–6). The dramatic monologue begins thus:

> Sit, friend. We'll be drinking and I'll tell you why.
> Today I went to Customs to identify
> My brother – it was him, all right, in spite of both
> Feet missing from beneath his Army overcoat.
>
> He was a handsome devil twice the size of me.
> We're all good-looking in my family.
> If you saw that brother, or what's left of him,
> You'd understand at once the kind of man he'd been.

Vendler herself dismisses this poem and another one like it, the later 'Manos Karoste-fanís', curiously, as 'Greek poems that fail', and fail 'notably', where what constitutes their failure is the manner in which they are 'phrased in an uneasy demotic' (*The Ocean, the Bird, and the Scholar* 369–70), 'demotic' here evoking vulgarity and coarseness more than a simple voice 'of the people'. The poems, then, are presumably built less on empathy than on exploitation. Rachel Hadas, however, says that at the heart of many of Merrill's Greece poems lies what might be called 'reduction', where she means reduction not in the sense of a belittling or making small, as Vendler seems to think is happening in these dramatic monologues, but in the culinary sense of a thickening and intensification (12). We could also call a poem like 'Kostas Tympakianakis', she says, a 'distillation', a poem the style of which is 'elemental'. Hadas, who knew Merrill in Greece and is fluent in Greek herself, says that Merrill's poems spoken *by* Greeks 'achieve the remarkable effect of being at once in Merrill's fluent and elegant English and in demotic Greek' (15), where the word 'demotic' now has no pejorative strings attached to it. This blending of voices, according to Hadas, is neither an accident nor a flaw but a deliberate choice and accomplishment, the result of which perhaps *should* make us uneasy, just as the house Merrill chose to buy in Athens 'dismayed' some of his friends there in large part because of its somewhat dubious location (Hammer 352). The voice of 'Kostas Tympakianakis' is similarly located on the border between two neighbourhoods, the one highly fashionable, Merrill's 'elegant' English, and the other more ordinary and working class, Tympakiana-kis's own demotic Greek. The latter is permitted to speak through the former – or perhaps demands to, just as Ephraim, with his more demonic than demotic speech, will similarly speak through JM (the poet's persona in *Sandover*) a decade later. If it seems that there is condescension present here, and the use of one person by another, it is because there is. But for Merrill 'use' and 'love' were by no means mutually exclusive. And it is unclear, to me, anyway, just who is using whom in the poem – the condescension works 'both ways'. Tympakianakis, says Quinn, 'is more than just a quaint native who[m] Merrill employs for local color' (116). Indeed, it is the Greek who, at the end of the poem, employs, or at least enjoins, Merrill:

> Take me with you when you sail next week,
> You'll see a different cosmos through the eyes of a Greek.
>
> Or write my story down for people. Use my name.
> And may it bring you all the wealth and fame
> It hasn't brought its bearer. Here, let's drink our wine!
> Who could have imagined such a life as mine?

'Take me with you' – is this a plea or a command? Kostas bargains; there is something to be gained for the poet from a continued interaction with him: 'You'll see a different cosmos through the eyes of a Greek.' Merrill no doubt did see quite the different cosmos indeed through the eyes of Ephraim, but no more so than through the eyes of Kostas; both were part of the process whereby Merrill was accorded the 'greater freedom' to *not* be himself. But if Merrill can't take Kostas with him, as Kostas seems to guess is likely, there remains another gesture Merrill could make, and one that, perhaps, is even owed Kostas: 'write my story down for people. Use my name.' In fact, 'Take me with you' and 'write my story down' might amount to the same thing. Kostas's pleas phrased as commands position him in a stance of both subservience and power, therefore leaving his partner equally in both positions. Merrill is both the silent friend who says nothing in reply and the poet who says all.

After having initially pledged to, in fact, bring Kostas with him back to the US, Merrill ultimately reneged on his promise. But he adhered to Kostas's second suggestion; he wrote down Kostas's own story in the poem we're reading, where the dynamic here evokes Dante as much as it does Shakespeare. In the spirit of Shakespeare's sonnets, Merrill has bestowed upon his beloved the favour of immortality through the enshrinement of the beloved's name and story in verse. In the spirit of Dante, though, it is Kostas who has enjoined Merrill to ensure his, Kostas's, own immortality; the task is one Merrill *must* perform, it is a duty to be discharged: tell my story, refresh or create the fame of my name, be the one who ensures that I endure. 'The Greek', writes Quinn, 'is fully aware that he will probably be "used" as material' (116) – as, in fact, we can gather he already has been. One form of use comes on the heels of another; you've used my body, now 'use my name'. But 'rather than hide this transaction', says Quinn, 'Merrill is out in the open about his appropriations'. About *these* appropriations, I would say, Merrill's *and* Kostas's, for Kostas is using Merrill, too; the transaction is no less his. If Tympakianakis in this poem is not unlike a shade waylaying Dante on the course of his journey and enjoining him to perform a favour, the question remains as to whether he is one of the damned or one of the saved. And, unlike the case of Dante, we have to ask this question of the poet, too.

'We don't know what to do with other worlds,' says a character in Andrei Tarkovsky's 1972 science fiction film *Solaris*. The idea is that we are less interested in discovering other worlds than we are in extending our own world to the very ends of the cosmos. 'We substitute something of our own' in the place of the unknown. But rather than drape the world of Greece in American threads from what Merrill called the costume box of his own imagination, he instead incorporated Greek threads into that costume box (*Recitative* 68). Was he still a poet-tourist in this regard, appropriating the foreign even as he embraced it? Undoubtedly, but the 'poet' part of the poet-tourist eliminated much of what is usually most disagreeable about the 'tourist' part, mainly by way of awareness, observation, even surveillance, a watching over that, in this case, was as embedded in care as it was in a desire for power. And for Merrill, the important thing was to keep *oneself* under surveillance as well, constantly monitoring one's own complicity in events as they unfolded. Asked in 1982 by J. D. McClatchy about the first things that attracted him to Greece, Merrill responded, 'Things that have mostly disappeared, I'm afraid. The dazzling air, the drowsy waterfronts [. . .] In those days foreign tourists were both rare and welcome' (*Recitative* 62). What he missed, of course, were things that disappeared largely as a result of forces that Merrill knew all too well that he himself represented.

In a poem that itself first appeared in 1982, Merrill reflected on a favourite bar in Athens, the bar where he'd first met Strato Mouflouzélis in 1964 and where the two of them had spent many subsequent evenings together and with friends:

> One level below street, an airless tank –
> We'd go there, evenings, watch through glass the world
> Eddy by, winking, casting up
> Such gorgeous flotsam that hearts leapt, or sank.

Written on the other side of the Stonewall riots from Bishop's 'The Shampoo', Merrill's
'The "Métro"' (*Collected Poems* 435) was first published in the 10 May 1982 edition
of *The New Yorker*. In the first of its three quatrains it cleverly establishes the bar itself
as a kind of aquarium, or 'tank', before inverting this metaphor by turning the world
outside of the bar into a subaqueous realm that 'Edd[ies] by [. . .] casting up / Such
gorgeous flotsam' in the form of men 'on their way', according to Hammer, 'in or out
of the train station in the city center' (347). The bar itself was 'an orange- and yellow-
tiled dive' in Omonia Square. According to Donald Richie, it was pretty exclusively for
'hustlers and johns', an Athenian Stonewall, as it were. The colour of the tile matched
other items of décor in the establishment, most notably, 'Over the bar, in polychrome
relief, / A jungle idyll: tiger, water hole, / Mate lolling on her branch.' The painting,
Merrill makes clear, was also a mirror, reflecting the watering hole of the bar itself
where 'we also lolled and drank',

> Joking with scarface Kosta, destitute
> Sotíri, Plato in his new striped suit . . .
> Those tigers are no more now. The bar's gone,
> and in its place, O memory! a bank.

The crushing irony of a bank replacing his favourite bar in Athens was obviously not
lost on the son of Charles Merrill. The name 'Merrill', after all, to this day evokes
for most people not a gay poet but a financial institution. The son may have eventu-
ally supplanted the father, but the father's bank, as it were, supplanted the son's bar,
making the son himself complicit in the act by virtue of his inheritance. After all,
the money that bought Strato that first drink in 1964 was probably money made by
Charles Merrill. But even as James acknowledges the irony of this transformation, he
forestalls, at least in part, the transformation itself, by safely depositing and preserv-
ing in the memory bank of his own poetry the bar as it once was. The exclamation
'O memory!' is both a pang and an affirmation. The 'cloud banks' that the young pilot
Charles Merrill forsook for Wall Street were more to his son's liking than their terres-
trial counterparts (*Collected Poems* 197).

   Poet, tourist, burglar, banker, inmate, spy – the choice is never wide and never
free.

Notes

1. Stephanie Burt uses the adjective 'binocular' to describe the vision of the poet Paul Mul-
    doon in a 1994 article the focus of which is the way that, 'again and again, Muldoon's
    personae embrace the aesthetic after being cheated by the wider social world' (97). Burt
    then posits that Muldoon 'has perhaps learned from the perspectival variation that Bonnie
    Costello describes in the early Elizabeth Bishop, which ended in the discovery of "per-
    spectives that discovered or acknowledged their own inadequacy"' (101). The quotation
    employed by Burt is from Costello's *Elizabeth Bishop: Questions of Mastery*, p. 42. The
    manner in which Burt uses 'binocular', then, is not dissimilar from the way in which I
    am using it. Helen Vendler also uses the adjective in *Last Looks, Last Books* to describe
    the style adopted by several poets in their late writings: 'my topic is the strange binocular
    style they must invent to render the reality contemplated in that last look [before death]'

(1). Though Bishop is indeed one of the five poets on whom Vendler focuses, her usage of 'binocular' is distinct from and more specific than Burt's and my own. I owe a debt of gratitude to Jonathan Ellis for bringing these texts to my attention.

2. In 1959 James Dickey, who would later become Merrill's friend, said that to read Merrill was to 'enter a realm of connoisseurish aesthetic contemplation' that was 'enough to drive you mad over the needless artificiality, prim finickiness, and determined inconsequence of it all' (Hammer 273). In 1973, despite the fact that Merrill's poetic voice had changed considerably in the intervening fourteen years, similar criticisms persisted, as Richard Pevear wrote of *Braving the Elements* that it was the work of 'a specifically middle-class' poetics in which there was 'no responsibility'; 'there is nothing happening in the world that he portrays' (Hammer 531). And in 1980 Denis Donoghue derisively suggested a passage from Ronald Firbank as an epigraph to *Scripts for the Pageant*: 'Help me, heaven, to be decorative and to do right!' (Hammer 634) – a suggestion that Merrill probably would have liked, or even loved. Amid such accusations of primness, politeness and decorativeness, of course, were numerous more insightful appraisals from poets and critics of varying tastes and backgrounds.

3. 'The Summer People', in fact, was modelled in part on 'The Burglar of Babylon'; it is a ballad of equally loose, equally dexterous metre, but one that more than triples Bishop's in length: 156 quatrains. Howard Moss rejected it at *The New Yorker* somewhat ironically on the grounds of its being too slight. On the one hand, the poem was anything but slight, at least in terms of length; on the other hand, if the poem *was* slight in its attitude, it was so intentionally, and was indebted in this regard to a poem that Moss had accepted just a few years earlier.

Works Cited

Axelrod, Stephen Gould, 'Bishop, History, and Politics', in Angus Cleghorn and Jonathan Ellis (eds), *The Cambridge Companion to Elizabeth Bishop* (Cambridge: Cambridge University Press, 2014), pp. 35–48.

Bishop, Elizabeth, *Elizabeth Bishop and The New Yorker: The Complete Correspondence*, ed. Joelle Biele (New York: Farrar, Straus and Giroux, 2011).

Bishop, Elizabeth, *One Art: Letters*, ed. Robert Giroux (New York: Farrar, Straus and Giroux, 1994).

Bishop, Elizabeth, *Poems, Prose, and Letters*, ed. Robert Giroux and Lloyd Schwartz (New York: Library of America, 2008).

Bishop, Elizabeth, and Robert Lowell, *Words in Air: The Complete Correspondence between Elizabeth Bishop and Robert Lowell*, ed. Thomas Travisano with Saskia Hamilton (New York: Farrar, Straus and Giroux, 2008).

Burt, Stephanie, 'Paul Muldoon's Binocular Vision', *Harvard Review* 7 (Fall 1994): 95–107.

Cleghorn, Angus, and Jonathan Ellis (eds), *The Cambridge Companion to Elizabeth Bishop* (Cambridge: Cambridge University Press, 2014).

Cleghorn, Angus, Bethany Hicok and Thomas Travisano (eds), *Elizabeth Bishop in the Twenty-First Century: Reading the New Editions* (Charlottesville: University of Virginia Press, 2012).

Costello, Bonnie, *Elizabeth Bishop: Questions of Mastery* (Cambridge, MA: Harvard University Press, 1991).

Curry, Renée R., *White Women Writing White: H.D., Elizabeth Bishop, Sylvia Plath, and Whiteness* (London: Greenwood Press, 2000).

Darrow, Whitney, Jr, cartoon, *The New Yorker*, 25 November 1964, p. 57.

Dove, Rita (ed.), *The Penguin Anthology of Twentieth-Century American Poetry* (New York: Penguin Books, 2011).

Hadas, Rachel, 'From Stage Set to Heirloom: Greece in the Work of James Merrill', *Arion* 6.3 (Winter 1999): 1–19.

Hammer, Langdon, *James Merrill: Life and Art* (New York: Knopf, 2015).

Hicok, Bethany, 'Bishop's Brazilian Politics', in Angus Cleghorn, Bethany Hicok and Thomas Travisano (eds), *Elizabeth Bishop in the Twenty-First Century: Reading the New Editions* (Charlottesville: University of Virginia Press, 2012), pp. 133–50.

Koren, Edward, cartoon, *The New Yorker*, 24 March 1975, p. 41.

Longenbach, James, *Modern Poetry After Modernism* (Oxford: Oxford University Press, 1997).

Merrill, James, *The Changing Light at Sandover: A Poem* (New York: Knopf, 2003).

Merrill, James, *Collected Poems*, ed. J. D. McClatchy and Stephen Yenser (New York: Knopf, 2001).

Merrill, James, *A Different Person* (New York: Knopf, 1993).

Merrill, James, *Recitative*, ed. J. D. McClatchy (San Francisco: North Point Press, 1986).

Millier, Brett C., *Elizabeth Bishop: Life and the Memory of It* (Berkeley: University of California Press, 1993).

Monteiro, George, *Elizabeth Bishop in Brazil and After: A Poetic Career Transformed* (Jefferson, NC: McFarland, 2012).

Page, Barbara, and Carmen L. Oliveira, 'Foreign-Domestic: Elizabeth Bishop at Home/Not at Home in Brazil', in Angus Cleghorn, Bethany Hicok and Thomas Travisano (eds), *Elizabeth Bishop in the Twenty-First Century: Reading the New Editions* (Charlottesville: University of Virginia Press, 2012), pp. 117–32.

Quinn, Justin, 'Europe in the Work of Anthony Hecht and James Merrill', *Irish Journal of American Studies* 5 (1996): 107–18.

Rear Window, dir. Alfred Hitchcock (Paramount Pictures, 1954).

Sadoff, Ira, 'Neo-Formalism: A Dangerous Nostalgia', *The American Poetry Review* (January/February 1990), <http://www.writing.upenn.edu/~afilreis/88/sadoff.html> (last accessed 24 October 2018).

Solaris, dir. Andrei Tarkovsky (Creative Unit of Writers and Cinema Workers, 1972).

Vendler, Helen, *Last Looks, Last Books: Stevens, Plath, Lowell, Bishop, Merrill* (Princeton: Princeton University Press, 2010).

Vendler, Helen, *The Ocean, the Bird, and the Scholar: Essays on Poets and Poetry* (Cambridge, MA: Harvard University Press, 2015).

Von Hallberg, Robert, *American Poetry and Culture, 1945–1980* (Cambridge, MA: Harvard University Press, 1985).

21

ELIZABETH BISHOP IN IRELAND: FROM SEAMUS HEANEY TO COLM TÓIBÍN

Jonathan Ellis

IRISH AUTHORS, NORTH AND SOUTH, love Elizabeth Bishop. They also love writing about her: in essays, interviews and reviews. Sometimes, she even makes a guest appearance in their novels and poems. Other poetic communities have taken Bishop's writing to heart over the years – a by no means exhaustive list might include New York School poets John Ashbery and James Schuyler, pioneers of queer poetry May Swenson and Adrienne Rich, members of the so-called Martian School of poetry James Fenton and Craig Raine, and New Formalists like Dana Gioia – but none of these groups have responded with as much collective enthusiasm and unequivocal gratitude as in Ireland. When did this love story begin? Who were its first members? And why does the Irish literary community continue to claim Bishop as, if not one of their own, at least an honorary member?

Tom Paulin, in an essay for *The Irish Times*, perceptively noted Bishop's influence on 'many writers, especially in Ireland, where the formal authority and the subtlety of the poetry of Seamus Heaney, Derek Mahon and Paul Muldoon often carries an invisible tribute to a poet who is often described as a poet's poet. [. . .] Her poetry, like theirs, teaches us to value the local, but not to be sucked into it – her cosmopolitanism speaks to those writers who like the Russian Acmeists discovered "a nostalgia for world culture"' ('The Poet's Poet'). Bishop's influence on Irish poetry is not as 'invisible' as Paulin would have us believe, even when writing this column in 2004 – hardly a year goes by without one or frequently more Irish poets writing about her – but he does pinpoint her particular attraction for writers like Heaney and Muldoon: the local detail, landscape or story seen not from the perspective of somebody who has lived there all their life, though this may be the case, but from that of somebody who is passing by or through but has the wherewithal to notice its beautiful strangeness, what Bishop in a famous letter to Anne Stevenson calls 'the always-more-successful surrealism of everyday life' (*Prose* 414). Paulin calls this 'her homeless, orphaned imagination' ('The Poet's Poet'); one could equally say that she was not homeless at all so much as at home wherever she travelled, that travel for her was not a journey away from or in search of home but a means of understanding home more deeply. By this, I include the possibility, one Bishop always leaves open, that home may be little more than a figment of the imagination, a questionable memory, or perhaps, worst of all, just a figure of speech. As she concludes the poem 'Questions of Travel':

> Continent, city, country, society:
> the choice is never wide and never free.
> And here, or there . . . No. Should we have stayed at home,
> wherever that may be? (*Poems* 92)

To conclude on a question is often seen as a sign of weakness yet Bishop does so in numerous poems: explicitly, as here, with a question mark; implicitly, as in 'The Bight' ('All the untidy activity continues, / awful but cheerful'), by leaving two options open. With such concluding lines in mind, it is easy to see why Bishop's hybrid, hyphenated, self-consciously untidy poetry appealed to writers living on an island frequently divided, like her first book, *North & South*, into historically charged regions that experience and of course poetry often challenged and side-stepped. She might not have been an Irish poet (though she did once describe her ancestry as 'Scots-Irish' (*Prose* 425), a biographical fact Paulin states it is 'important to know'), but she certainly behaved like one.

Bishop knew Nova Scotia, the Atlantic region of Canada she left permanently at primary-school age even though she returned there later, not by being there but by remembering it from elsewhere. Like so many Irish authors, she was a poet in exile from this, her first real homeland, even if her exile was relatively short-lived and, later in life, self-imposed. In the poem 'Sandpiper' that critics have frequently called 'a kind of self-portrait' (McCabe 219), the (male) bird is distracted by watching 'the spaces of sand' between his toes, 'where (no detail too small) the Atlantic drains / rapidly backwards and downwards' (*Poems* 129). Bishop's details are often in flux as here. Nothing ever seems to stay still for long as if not just the scene but also the spectator watching it were in motion. Note how the miniature space of a bird's toes that cannot be more than a couple of centimetres apart becomes a place to reflect on an entire ocean's unfathomable gravity. It is not the beach's grains that drain rapidly but the whole Atlantic. The horizontal, visible pull of the water becomes the vertical and mostly unseen 'backwards and downwards' motion of the tide. By isolating the detail at the end of the line, the Atlantic becomes curiously both a human-sized drain, something like a bathtub, and a roaring force we can only imagine. (Bishop's words frequently hover between noun and verb as here, perhaps reflecting her distrust in any object, particularly language, to lie still.) Where does all that water go, we often ask as children at bath-time, but forget to ask as adults when we visit the sea? If this is autobiography, it is autobiography not by the back door, but in bird form. We find it, and other Nova Scotia-set writing, in the 'Elsewhere' section of Bishop's third book, *Questions of Travel* (1965). 'Elsewhere', like 'disaster' from her most iconic poem 'One Art', is one of those words Bishop practically trademarks. For a generation of Irish poets who, like Bishop, also spent much of their adulthood outside the country of their birth, her life and poetry testify to the paradoxical importance and irrelevance of roots. Bishop wrote best about Nova Scotia from Brazil, just as her best poems about Brazil (I am thinking of the late poems 'Pink Dog' and 'Santarém') were written in Boston. She didn't have to be there to be there. Similarly, her most intimate self-portrait might very well be 'Sandpiper'.

Bishop travelled to Ireland as a young woman in 1937. It is one of the few places she travelled to (England being another) that she didn't write a poem or story about.[1] In a letter to Marianne Moore on 9 August 1937, written from Paris in the aftermath of a car accident in which one of her best friends was thrown from the car and had to have part of her arm amputated, Bishop followed an account of this accident by drawing a line on the page and then sharing with Moore her memories of visiting Dublin Zoo:

> I think you will like the pictures from Dublin Zoo. It's the nicest, most informal zoo I have ever seen. Did you know that they raised lions there? Sometime I want to tell you about Merrion Square, the wonderful flowers, the beautiful things we saw at Trinity College and in the museum. (*One Art* 61)

Although Bishop and Moore famously met for the first time at the New York Public Library, the entrance to which takes one past a pair of (I'm citing Bishop's own description in the poem 'Invitation to Miss Marianne Moore') 'agreeable lions' (*Poems* 81), their follow-up meeting the following Saturday was to the local circus where, Bishop remembers, Moore stole three or four greyish hairs from one of the baby elephants. It's difficult not to think of her remembering these stone lions in Manhattan when she wrote to Moore from Paris about having seen real ones in Ireland. It is the sort of private in-joke between friends that many of us share in letters.

My point here is that Ireland, unlike France, which she did write about in several published poems from the same period, did not register much on Bishop's imagination as a young writer, apart from reminding her of absent friends. She was able to make an impression on Irish poets later on in her career not because she knew much about living in Ireland as a place but because she knew what writing about Ireland might be like as a poet. There are, for example, numerous references to W. B. Yeats throughout her correspondence, including the admission that she had borrowed a detail from Yeats's poem 'The Dawn' when writing 'Manuelzinho' (*Words in Air* 171). Her most lengthy discussion of Yeats comes in a 1955 letter to Robert Lowell in which she shares her thoughts on his work after reading Allan Wate's edition of the letters: 'He is so Olympian always, so calm, so really unrevealing, and yet I was fascinated. Imagine being able to say you'd always finished everything you'd started, from the age of 17. And he is much more kind, and more right about everything than I'd ever thought – right, until the age of 65, say' (160). In 1974 she described 'The End of March' as 'my version of The Lake Isle of Innisfree' (*Elizabeth Bishop and The New Yorker* 360). And when Mildred Nash helped Bishop organise her library in late 1978, the year before Bishop's death, Nash was gifted a 'well-worn' duplicate copy of Yeats's *Complete Poems*, suggesting that Bishop had several copies of Yeats's poetry and that she must have read him frequently throughout her life (Nash 138). In Bishop's archive there are even drafts of an unpublished poem called 'Leda and the/a Duck'.

The first Irish poet to read Bishop as thoroughly as Bishop read Yeats was almost certainly Seamus Heaney, who was Bishop's replacement at Harvard when she was compulsorily retired following her sixty-sixth birthday in 1977.[2] Heaney knew Bishop socially in the last year of her life, but had read her work and actually taught it as a lecturer at Queen's University Belfast years earlier. In *Stepping Stones*, his book-length interview with Dennis O'Driscoll, he recalled reading Bishop in the old *Selected Poems* that Chatto & Windus had first published in 1967 and placing 'The Map' on a hand-out 'for a group that included on that particular day, I remember, Ciaran Carson; so Medbh McGuckian and Paul Muldoon may have been there as well – unless, of course, it was a day when they were cutting class' (279). It's tempting to see this as the day Elizabeth Bishop entered the consciousness of Irish poets.

What did Heaney tell Carson, McGuckian and Muldoon about 'The Map'? And what did he talk to Bishop about when they met for the first time at Harvard? There are relatively few comments by Bishop about Heaney. To her friend Dorothee Bowie, she described him as 'nice and *very* Irish' (*One Art* 630). Heaney had helped celebrate what turned out to be Bishop's last birthday in February 1979. A few months later, in a letter to her editor Robert Giroux, she praised his poetry and his readings from it. 'I avoid readings wherever I can,' she admitted, 'but I did like Heaney's reading' (632). During the summer, when Bishop was in Maine, Heaney sent her a poem called 'A Hank of Wool'[3] which he described as 'a *billet-doux*': 'I've an idea that some day

I might do a collection called "Giveaways" and these poems, or some of them, would be included. Each one would be dedicated to, and have some integral connection with what they used to call in Berkeley "a real human being"' (Vassar College, Series 1, 'Correspondence'). Bishop replied to him 'saying she liked this and that in the poems, and telling how her grandmother in Nova Scotia had taught her how to knit during the First World War' (O'Driscoll 278),[4] an anecdote Heaney would cite and work into the poem when he published it in *The Times Literary Supplement*, with the sub-heading 'i.m. Elizabeth Bishop', the year after.

   Here are the first two sections of the poem as it was published for the first and only time in 1980. Heaney thought it 'was OK as a personal salute' but that it lacked 'proper purchase' (O'Driscoll 278):

   i

   'Hank?' I hear you say,
   all tact and masquerade.
   'Sounds like a name for a cowboy.'

   But didn't you hold the wool –
   shop wool, ticketed bought wool –
   until your shoulders ached?

   I used to sit like a hermit
   with my two arms held out
   to stretch the hank between them.

   ii

   To unwind it, Elizabeth,
   come back in a cardigan
   knitted grey or brown

   so that we can imagine
   the click and flash of needles,
   see them like fireflies

   in our tranquil recollection
   of those supple mysteries,
   knit one, drop one, slip one . . . (Heaney 261)

Heaney's '*billet-doux*', a love letter in three parts, is worth more than his apologetic comments to O'Driscoll thirty years after its only publication suggest. Its tripartite structure is itself Bishopesque. Bishop loved using the triplet form. Two of her most well-known poems, 'Roosters' and 'Pink Dog', both deploy that rhyme scheme, as do, in less easy-to-see-on-the-page variations, her sestinas and villanelles which also conclude or turn on multiples of three. Bishop drew attention to this, as she often did in her titles, by calling her last collection *Geography III*.

Heaney's poem captures Bishop's poetic voice in other ways. He quite literally cites her voice in the quotation that begins the poem – '"Hank?" I hear you say, / all tact and masquerade. / "Sounds like a name for a cowboy."' The word 'hank', meaning a coil of yarn or thread, is more commonly known as a 'skein' in North America. When Heaney says 'hank', Bishop at first hears cowboy, but what he is really talking about, as becomes clear in the rest of the poem, is an experience that was very close to home for her once it had been translated. The act of knitting is tied to Bishop's memories, not just of her childhood home in Great Village, Nova Scotia, but to the specific memories of her mother's mourning (Bishop's father died before she was one) and her relatives' attempts to shake her out of that state by dressing her in a new outfit. Readers of Bishop will recognise these details from her 1953 short story 'In the Village', published in *The New Yorker* and in her third book of poems, *Questions of Travel*. The mother in the story rejects being fitted into a new dress; her habitual response to the dress-maker's arrival is a scream. Visiting the dressmaker's house, the young girl remembers hearing stories of a kitten getting caught in the sewing machine. On another night, the child wakes, unaware of who is crying, her grandmother, her aunts, or her mother:

But now I am caught in a skein of voices, my aunts' and my grandmother's, saying the same things, over and over, sometimes loudly, sometimes in whispers:
   'Hurry. For heaven's sake, *shut the door!*'
   'Sh!'
   'Oh, we can't go on like this, we . . .'
   'Sh! Don't let her . . .' (*Prose* 75)

Did Heaney realise any of this when he presented the poem as a gift? If he only knew Bishop's poetry from the 1967 Chatto & Windus *Selected Poems* he had probably never read 'In the Village', in which case he would not have known of the very real connection he was making. Other words and phrases cite and recall Bishop's poetry more consciously: the 'Click. Click' of 'The Bight', the fireflies from the end of 'A Cold Spring', 'the map-makers' colors' from, of course, 'The Map'. Heaney's phrase 'so that we can imagine' evokes another conclusion to a poem, in this case 'At the Fishhouses', whose last long line begins 'It is like what we imagine knowledge to be'. The first line of section three, 'Goodbye to Maine', looks to the list of farewells in Bishop's recently published 'The Moose': 'Goodbye to the elms, / to the farm, to the dog.'

In one small poem, Heaney crams a lifetime of Bishop's writing. It is a generous and heartfelt tribute. We see what he admires in her poetry – her 'tact and masquerade' – and how he knits her skein into his own hank of wool. 'Bishop is an artful stylist,' he said to an interviewer, 'a maker if ever there was one, a text-weaver, a very self-conscious writer, but in the old orality/textuality debate, she can be cited by both sides' (O'Driscoll 281). That doubleness again.

In the 1980s and 1990s, Heaney was not the only Irish poet to single out Bishop for praise, though he did so memorably in both the T. S. Eliot lectures, published as *The Government of the Tongue*, and the Oxford lectures, published as *The Redress of Poetry*, public statements of admiration for Bishop's importance as a writer that certainly contributed to her rising reputation as a major American poet in Britain and Ireland. Eavan Boland and Tom Paulin both published important essays on Bishop's work around the same time, Boland on her link to the Romantic tradition, Paulin a seminal and still widely cited reflection on her letter writing.[5] Paul Muldoon, who, you might remember, may or may not have attended Heaney's class on Bishop in the late 1960s, dedicated one of his Oxford lectures to Bishop's prose poem '12 O'Clock News',[6] and has also published an essay on her teasing, testing correspondence with Robert Lowell, making the case for their letters as a form of gentle and not-so-gentle disagreement about poetry as public speech. 'I'll be thinking', he writes, 'about the extent to which it is appropriate for either the reader or the writer to draw on material from "private" letters in making literature, an issue on which Lowell and Bishop disagreed' ('Fire Balloons' 217).

It is at this point that I would like to drop in, I hope tactfully, some of my own recent feelings about Bishop's poetry. A few years ago my father died in his sleep. We buried him on what would have been his sixty-eighth birthday, the same age as Elizabeth Bishop when she died in 1979. For a long time I was not sure whether to include these facts in a chapter of a book. To me, of course, they are more than facts. They represent the violent intrusion of life, or should that be death, into the mundane passing of time I had taken for granted. Bishop's poem 'A Short, Slow Life', from the mid- to late-1950s, personifies Time in precisely these terms, his nails scratching 'the shingled roof. / Roughly his hand reached in, / and tumbled us out' (*Poems* 235).

As Heaney's poem reminds us, Bishop always believed in tact. What elsewhere she called 'closets' (Fountain and Brazeau 330). In her postscript to the famous 'Darwin letter' to Anne Stevenson, she elaborated on this via a scathing attack on Orson Welles's 1962 film adaptation of *The Trial*:

> All the way through the film I kept thinking that any of Buster Keaton's films give one the sense of the tragedy of the human situation, the weirdness of it all, the pathos of man's trying to do the right thing – all in a twinkling, besides being *fun* – all the very things poor Orson Welles was trying desperately to illustrate by laying it on with a trowel. I don't like *heaviness* – in general, Germanic art. It seems often to amount to complete self-absorption – like Mann & Wagner. I think one can be cheerful AND profound! – *or, how to be grim without groaning* –
>
> Hopkins' 'terrible' sonnets are terrible – but he kept them short, and in form.
>
> It may amount to a kind of 'good manners', I'm not sure. The good artist assumes a certain amount of sensitivity in his audience and doesn't attempt to flay himself to get sympathy or understanding. (The same way I feel the 'Christians' I know suffer from bad manners – they refuse to assume that other people can be good, too, and so constantly condescend without realizing it. And – now that I come to think of it – so do communists! I've had far-left acquaintances come here and point out the slums to me, ask if I'd seen them – after 12 years – how can I bear to live here, etc. . . .)
>
> (*Prose* 417)

I've not elided Bishop's conclusion. This is where she ends the postscript, with at least three forms of moving to a close without getting there: a comma, an etcetera, an ellipsis, before finally closing the parenthesis. It is as if she doesn't want to make a final statement, doesn't want to be caught out saying anything *too* definitive. In the final paragraph of the letter before the postscript, we find her saying just this: 'It would take me months to answer your letter properly so I shall send this jumble along. [. . .] Just please don't quote me exactly, however, without telling me? – because I think I've put things rather badly' (*Prose* 417).

Bishop protests too much here. At least two generations of readers, and certainly two generations of critics, have been grateful she did send 'this jumble along'. It is difficult to be 'cheerful AND profound'. Is this what Bishop manages in her best work? To give one 'the sense of the tragedy of the human situation' while at the same time being and having '*fun*'? A few years on from my own family 'tragedy', her advice feels even more difficult to follow than before, her achievement in the fact of her own many losses even more remarkable.

I am not about to turn to Bishop for life advice, however. I am embarrassingly and painfully aware that I am writing about me, not her, writing about my experiences in England, not hers in Brazil. This feels like a departure for me, an almost confessional turn. I'm allowing Bishop to read me, rather than read her.[7] Gillian White, in her important book *Lyric Shame*, discusses the lyric tradition itself as potentially shameful. She explores how for critics like Marjorie Perloff Bishop's poetry epitomises a rush to cohere and conclude that avant-garde poetics has spent at least the last half-century opposing. Might Bishop be representative of what White calls 'a shame-inducing brand' of conservative poetics (47)? Do we find ourselves, as White does, in a 'shame situation' with Bishop (46)? This is not necessarily the cul-de-sac it sounds. What White finds 'appealing about her poems is what they teach about how entangled with acts of projection and identification we become when interacting with art, and people, in moments of interpretation' (46). This is precisely what happens in Heaney's poem 'A Hank of Wool', in which a skein of shared experiences and words entangles the two poets across time.

I am going to stay with this idea of entanglement in my analysis of Colm Tóibín's 2015 biography of Bishop, the culmination of a lifetime of writing about her in various essays and reviews, most for the *London Review of Books*, though she also has a starring role in his justly acclaimed 2001 book *Love in a Dark Time: Gay Lives from Wilde to Almodóvar*. (I am entangled, too, in both Tóibín's critical reading of Bishop and his Bishop-inspired fiction.) *On Elizabeth Bishop* is as much an autobiography of Tóibín's own life as a life of Bishop. Certainly there are no biographical surprises here, nothing one could not find out about Bishop elsewhere. Yet if it is an autobiography, it is an autobiography almost by accident. We learn as much about Tóibín's reading life as his non-reading life, about the books that matter to him rather than the people, perhaps even that books matter to him more than people.

Tóibín's book is part of Princeton's Writers on Writers series. We should therefore not be surprised to find so much *on* writing. According to Boland, like Heaney and Tóibín a lifelong admirer and occasional essayist on Bishop's poetry, Tóibín is not just the most 'accurate' of Bishop's critics writing in the last thirty years but one of the few to understand her 'radicalism':

> Oddly enough, although Bishop has attracted passionate readers, she has not always had accurate critics. David Kalstone's early studies, *Becoming a Poet* and *Five Temperaments*, remain important. And there have been other careful readers. There is, for instance, a fine oral history. But too often the critique has seemed to portray her as a miniaturist, an artist on ivory. Too often the great poet of *Geography III* has been diminished by the conversation. ('Review')

This says more about Boland's ignorance of Bishop scholarship than Tóibín, who is generous in both his acknowledgements and bibliography to cite at least some Bishop critics. Much of what Boland implies is new and original in the book is not. That is not to say Tóibín does not say it well. My copy of the book is full of underlining based not on what Tóibín is arguing but on how it is phrased. A few months ago I photocopied two pages of the opening chapter as an example of nonfiction writing for my final-year undergraduates. Here is an example from the first paragraph of the book:

> She began with the idea that little is known and much is puzzling. The effort, then, to make a true statement in poetry – to claim that something *is* something, or *does* something – required a hushed, solitary concentration. A true statement for her carried with it, buried in its rhythm, considerable degrees of irony because it was oddly futile; it was either too simple or too loaded to mean a great deal. (1)

Lavinia Greenlaw, another poet keen to acknowledge her indebtedness to Bishop, calls Tóibín 'an exceptionally musical writer [. . .] The point of formulation is, for him, one of orchestration as it is for the poet. Bishop's music is plain, resistant and takes some getting used to. It attracts those in danger of loving the music of language too much' ('Colm Tóibín on Elizabeth Bishop'). Greenlaw calls this approach 'neither criticism nor biography'. Boland asks rhetorically whether it is 'an exercise in subjectivity'. 'Not at all,' she replies. 'This is critical method. And critical method at its best. This is what was pioneered in William Hazlitt, admired in TS Eliot; this is what makes John Berryman's essay on Dylan Thomas great and Adrienne Rich's on Emily Dickinson essential. This is what sorts out the true difference: the competent critic of poetry analyses; the great critic of poetry testifies' ('Review').

Analysis and testimony. Is the former what most of us do, the latter what 'great critic[s]' like Hazlitt, Eliot, Berryman, Rich and Tóibín perform? Boland does describe the methodology of the book well: 'Instead of beginning with a poem and listing the elements that might transform the reader, he begins at the end: with the transformation itself. The transformation, that is, of his life by her language. He holds the mirror of one up to the other [. . .] Therefore Bishop is not just critiqued in this book: she is translated' ('Review').

Having loved Bishop and Tóibín equally for many years, I am probably the book's ideal reader. That is not to say I think it is flawless. In many respects, it goes over familiar ground. I am sure there are new things to say about Bishop and Moore and Bishop and Lowell but they are not said here. Tóibín could afford to be more comprehensive in his citation of other critics. It might intrude on the intimate tone of his reading of Bishop's work but it would also correct the false impression that nobody has ever felt or thought similarly to him about these poems. The book's overall thesis – that omissions of every kind are significant – is a clever one but perhaps over-repeated. I disagree, as happens with any criticism, with individual line readings. I disagree, as is perhaps less common, with his dismissal or at least downgrading of Bishop's letters in favour of her poetry. This is Tóibín explaining what cannot be mentioned in 'One Art' but is expressed in a letter to Robert Lowell four years after the poem's publication:

> In this letter, she suddenly moved, almost, it seems, without knowing, almost unwittingly, into creating the missing lines from her own poem 'One Art' when she wrote

for once, in private, what she could not bring herself to write in public, in an aston-
ishing line with five beats like gasps or cries: 'I lost my mother, and Lota, and others,
too.' These are the figures whom she survives; they are left out of the poetry.

This is not to suggest that the poem 'One Art' was damaged by what was
excluded, and not to suggest either that it would have been a better poem had she
mentioned what she put in the letter. In that case, 'One Art' would not have been
a poem at all, because the tone of the poem depended on the tension between
jokiness and self-pity, and on what was withheld, rather than on anything as
banal as honesty. If honesty, full disclosure, were what was at stake, then the
poem would not be one of the most memorable poems Bishop wrote, merely as
ephemeral as a letter. Bishop, perhaps more than any other poet of her genera-
tion, especially more than Robert Lowell, knew the difference between a poem
and a letter. (122–3)

I do not see why letters and poems cannot both be 'memorable'. I do not agree that
letters are 'ephemeral', particularly not Bishop's letters. (As an aside here, might the
'ephemeral' be a category Bishop actually valued? Not just in letters but in her paint-
ings as well. Perhaps this explains her love of notebooks, scraps and fragments. Like
Emily Dickinson she took care to preserve all of her writings, her will giving other
people the responsibility to destroy or publish them.) Although, as Tóibín argues,
there is a difference 'between a poem and a letter', I do not think the difference is
as stark as he implies. Was Bishop really that successful at keeping them apart? Isn't
epistolary intimacy, or the illusion of intimacy, the sort of writing relationship that
Bishop's poetry often copies?

Greenlaw, remembering Ashbery's description of Bishop as 'the writer's writer's
writer', calls Tóibín 'the reader's reader's reader' ('Colm Tóibín on Elizabeth Bishop').
Stephanie Burt, in her blurb for Tóibín's book, speaks about it in similar terms. This is
'an almost ideal introduction to the poetry of Elizabeth Bishop,' she writes. 'This could
become the introduction to Bishop for people who intend to read her for pleasure.'
One of the most pleasurable chapters is the final one, titled 'North Atlantic Light', in
which Tóibín reflects on his memories of a place, in his case a house close to the sea
in Ballyconnigar Upper, and how these memories are modified and transformed by
the purchase of a painting that depicts the scene he remembers. In the process, as is
clear from this summary, Tóibín is also remembering and partially rewriting Bishop's
poem about a similar experience, a poem she called (not modestly) 'Poem'. Thomas
Travisano calls it an 'eloquent coda', 'almost a prose poem' ('Conversations'). Here is
the conclusion:

Tom O'Malley saw it in 1952, and I saw it some years later. Both of us looked at it;
he must have studied it closely to get it as exact as he did. It must have mattered to
him to make a painting from precise looking and rendering, or finding shapes and
colors that would approximate what he saw, but capture it, envision it, re-create it.
I never looked at it like that. It was part of what was normal, what was there. But I
remember it. I believed perhaps that it would always be there. I must have taken it
in on the same summer days, or days like them, days a few years after the painting
was done. In any case, we both were there. 'Our visions coincided,' as Elizabeth
Bishop wrote in 'Poem,' on seeing a painting from a childhood scene, and then

she tempered that with '"visions" is / too serious a word – our looks, two looks: / art "copying from life" and life itself, / life and the memory of it so compressed / they've turned into each other.' This feeling that we know somewhere, or we knew it, and it is 'live' and 'touching in detail,' is, as Bishop says, 'the little that we get for free / the little of our earthly trust. Not much.'

Not much perhaps, but enough to be going on with. Or perhaps not. (198–9)

Bishop had a problem with narrative, as David Kalstone points out in *Becoming a Poet* (252). But it also inspired her thinking about poetics, as Vidyan Ravinthiran's brilliant book *Elizabeth Bishop's Prosaic* proves. This is what Tóibín says about it: 'As a poet, Bishop stole a great deal from the sound of prose, as a painter might steal from photography' (47). I wonder if Tóibín is not doing the same in reverse. As a novelist, he steals a great deal from the sound of poetry, or rather from the sound of poets like Bishop that also favoured silence. As he writes earlier in the book: 'In certain societies, including rural Nova Scotia where Bishop spent much of her childhood, and in the southeast of Ireland where I am from, language was also a way to restrain experience, take it down to a level where it might stay' (2).

As Lloyd Schwartz points out: 'In some essential and large way, Irish novelist Colm Tóibín gets Elizabeth Bishop right [. . .] What makes Tóibín's book unique in the Bishop bibliography is the centrality of his identification with Bishop, and the parallels he sees between their two lives' ('Review'). We are back in the realm of identification again, what White calls 'entanglement'. How do lives become entangled? How and to what extent do we identify with others? These are some of the questions (of travel and of identity) Bishop asks of herself and her readers. For all Tóibín's identification with Bishop, he also acknowledges her difference, a difference from every other human being that she is relatively unique in expressing: 'The sense that we are only ourselves and that other people feel the same way – that they too are only themselves – is a curious thought. It is so obviously true that it is barely worth mentioning. Most people seem happier constructing other ideas that mask this basic one' (9).

Tóibín credits Bishop with a similar insight about animals. This is what he has to say about her famous moose:

It would be easy to say that the moose, since this is a poem, must stand for something – the eternal, say, or the disruptive in nature, or the mystery of things – other than being a mere moose. But it resists the idea that it stands for something. Rather, it *is something*. It is another part of the specific night in question, and haunting, among other reasons, because of the precise way it stayed in the memory. In other words, it is not an easy metaphor; it is hardly a metaphor at all. (Or a symbol, for that matter.) Emphatically, it is a moose before it is a metaphor, and indeed for a good while afterward. (22)

Tóibín works just as hard not to let his moose become a metaphor or a symbol, at least for a time. I can think of few better examples of this than the following description of his own childhood loss, analogous in many ways to Bishop's:

I came from a house where Time's hand had also reached in. Toward the end of 1963, when I was eight, in the town of Enniscorthy in the southeast of Ireland,

I arrived home from school one day to find both of my parents standing still, look-
ing into a mirror. My father, my mother said, would have to have an operation. She
spoke, I remember, both to myself and to the mirror, and, of course, to my father,
who was looking at her in the mirror as she spoke, as I was. Between then and
sometime later – four, maybe five, months – myself and my brother, who was four,
were looked after by an aunt a good distance away, and we did not see our parents
or hear anything about them [. . .] In July 1967 my father died. There was a funeral
and the house was full of people, but there was silence again soon afterward. My
other siblings went away, back to what they were doing. My younger brother and
I stayed there with my mother. We thought about my father, or we did sometimes,
but we did not talk about him. (30, 32)

Just as Bishop must have thought frequently about her mother even if she did not dote
or make a fuss about it, so Tóibín has kept writing about this period of his life, most
movingly in his most autobiographical novel, *Nora Webster*. After my own father's
funeral, I too wished for silence, when I could think about Dad but not talk about
him. When I thought of that future time, I hoped I would feel a little like Tóibín's Nora
Webster, the character based on his own mother, who cherishes the silent house after
her sons are asleep.

The house was silent now.
    She thought of the book she had bought in Dublin. She could not remember
what had made her buy it. She went out to the kitchen and searched for it in her
bag. As soon as she opened the book she put it down again. She closed her eyes. In
future, she hoped, fewer people would call. In future, once the boys went to bed,
she might have the house to herself more often. She would learn how to spend
these hours. In the peace of these winter evenings, she would work out how she
was going to live. (28)

Which book did Nora pick up in Dublin in 1967? Might it have been the new 1967
Chatto & Windus copy of Bishop's *Selected Poems* that Heaney bought around that
time, the one Tóibín himself recalls buying in London in 1975?
    In *On Elizabeth Bishop*, Tóibín remembers the fact his mother 'had some poetry
books and anthologies. She had written and published poems before her marriage.
The Penguin Book of Contemporary Verse was in her house, and through this
I found poems by W. H. Auden, Louis MacNeice, William Empson, Thom Gunn,
Sylvia Plath' (32). In a speculative mood, I like to imagine his fictional mother, Nora,
buying a copy of Bishop's *Selected Poems* or perhaps even *Questions of Travel*, pub-
lished two years earlier in 1965. Tóibín certainly has 'In the Village' in mind when
remembering the effect of death on a busy household, especially the silence, but also
working out how to live. This is what Bishop, in a different register, calls '*how to be
grim without groaning*'.
    The Elizabeth Bishop we find in Irish writing is a touching, deeply personal figure,
and not just for those Irish authors like Heaney who knew her. In Heaney's published
but sadly not collected poem, she is an aunt-like presence 'in a cardigan / knitted
grey or brown' who has never knitted with wool since childhood but who became a
'text-weaver' with words. In the second section of the poem, Heaney imagines himself

and Bishop unwinding time 'in our tranquil recollection / of those supple mysteries', the line echoing in phrase and sentiment William Wordsworth's poetic tributes to his female muse and sister Dorothy Wordsworth. We are accustomed to thinking about Heaney's close relationship with Ted Hughes. Perhaps he felt equally close to Bishop, if only through reading her poetry. Tóibín's Bishop is less approachable than Heaney's, but her poetry is no less important to him for that. On the contrary, he appears to find in her 'great modesty' a 'restrained but serious ambition' (3), the same qualities that Bishop admired in Yeats. For Tóibín it mattered that Bishop often wrote about 'northern light, northern weather. Ireland and Nova Scotia have their inhospitable seasons and their barren hinterlands; they are places where the light is often scarce and the memory of poverty is close; they are places in which the spirit is wary and the past comes haunting and much is unresolved. Mist, wind, clouds, short days, the proximity of the sea, the quickly changing weather, all suggest a world in which little can be taken for granted' (60).

'A world in which little can be taken for granted.' Perhaps that's ultimately Bishop's motto, or certainly the motto many Irish authors take from reading her. In Bishop's own words, 'the little that we get for free, / the little of our earthly trust' (*Poems* 197) turns out to be not that little at all.

Notes

1. The obvious exception to this is 'Crusoe in England', though here there is very little reference to England given that the poem mostly focuses on Crusoe's memories of island life with, and poignantly without, Friday. Lloyd Schwartz isn't alone in seeing the poem's title as misleading: 'Wasn't Cambridge, Massachusetts, this Crusoe's England, just as her lover in Brazil, Lota de Macedo Soares, had been her lifelong Friday?' ('Back to Boston' 144). Tom Paulin is one of the few critics to interpret the poem as in any significant way about Englishness. In a review of *One Art*, he objects to the omission of a 1964 letter to Robert Lowell in which Bishop attacks the London literary scene. For him the letter articulates the inspiration behind 'Crusoe in England' in which 'Bishop lovingly but critically recreates [Philip] Larkin as Crusoe' ('Writing to the Moment' 236). I do not find this reading especially convincing.
2. I am extremely grateful to Christopher Laverty for sharing with me a chapter on Heaney and Bishop from his forthcoming thesis, 'Heaney and the American Tradition' (unpublished PhD thesis, Queen's University Belfast). In his introduction to the chapter 'Heaney and Bishop: The Harvard Years', Laverty correctly notes that the relationship between Heaney and Bishop has been more or less ignored by Bishop and Heaney critics and that 'aside from a 1992 PhD dissertation exploring the use of animal imagery in Heaney and Bishop's poetry the attention given to the connection has been limited to the citation of Heaney's approval of Bishop rather than comparative readings of their poetry or consideration of the specific terms in which Heaney endorses Bishop'. Laverty's scholarship corrects these oversights, offering a compelling and original look at Heaney's Bishop-inflected poetics of the 1980s and 1990s.
3. Sincere thanks to Philip McGowan for helping me find this poem.
4. According to Heaney, he only received one letter from Bishop (Bartlett 6).
5. See Boland, 'An Un-Romantic American', and Paulin, 'Writing to the Moment: Elizabeth Bishop'.
6. See Muldoon, '*12 O'Clock News* by Elizabeth Bishop'.

7. Maureen McLane's book of experimental prose, *My Poets* (2012), includes a dazzling chapter on Bishop and Stein that describes this process of identity confusion. 'I do not know thoroughly how she made me,' she admits (34). 'I do not know what I know about Bishop but what I came to through Bishop,' she concludes (52).

Works Cited

Bartlett, Brian, '"As If You Might Be Here": Poems Addressing Elizabeth Bishop', *Elizabeth Bishop Society of Nova Scotia Newsletter* 7.1 (Spring 2000): 2–10.

Bishop, Elizabeth, *Elizabeth Bishop and The New Yorker: The Complete Correspondence*, ed. Joelle Biele (New York: Farrar, Straus and Giroux, 2011).

Bishop, Elizabeth, *One Art: The Selected Letters*, ed. Robert Giroux (London: Chatto & Windus, 1994).

Bishop, Elizabeth, and Robert Lowell, *Words in Air: The Complete Correspondence between Elizabeth Bishop and Robert Lowell*, ed. Thomas Travisano with Saskia Hamilton (London: Faber and Faber, 2008).

Boland, Eavan, 'Review of *On Elizabeth Bishop* by Colm Tóibín', *The Irish Times*, 21 March 2015, <https://www.irishtimes.com/culture/books/eavan-boland-reviews-on-elizabeth-bishop-by-colm-t%C3%B3ib%C3%ADn-1.2146004> (last accessed 24 October 2018).

Boland, Eavan, 'An Un-Romantic American', *Parnassus* 14.2 (1988): 73–92.

Fountain, Gary, and Peter Brazeau (eds), *Remembering Elizabeth Bishop: An Oral Biography* (Amherst: University of Massachusetts Press, 1994).

Greenlaw, Lavinia, 'Colm Tóibín on Elizabeth Bishop: "Closets, closets and more closets"', *The Daily Telegraph*, 11 April 2015, <https://www.telegraph.co.uk/culture/books/bookreviews/11524638/Colm-Toibin-on-Elizabeth-Bishop.html> (last accessed 24 October 2018).

Heaney, Seamus, 'A Hank of Wool', *The Times Literary Supplement*, 7 March 1980, p. 261.

Kalstone, David, *Becoming a Poet: Elizabeth Bishop with Marianne Moore and Robert Lowell* (London: Hogarth Press, 1989).

McCabe, Susan, *Elizabeth Bishop: Her Poetics of Loss* (University Park: Pennsylvania State University Press, 1994).

McLane, Maureen N., *My Poets* (New York: Farrar, Straus and Giroux, 2012).

Muldoon, Paul, '*12 O'Clock News* by Elizabeth Bishop', in *The End of the Poem* (London: Faber and Faber, 2006), pp. 82–113.

Muldoon, Paul, 'Fire Balloons: The Letters of Robert Lowell and Elizabeth Bishop', in Jonathan Ellis (ed.), *Letter Writing Among Poets: From William Wordsworth to Elizabeth Bishop* (Edinburgh: Edinburgh University Press, 2015), pp. 216–30.

Nash, Mildred, 'Elizabeth Bishop's Library: A Reminiscence', in George Monteiro (ed.), *Conversations with Elizabeth Bishop* (Jackson: University Press of Mississippi, 1996), pp. 133–8.

O'Driscoll, Dennis, *Stepping Stones: Interviews with Seamus Heaney* (London: Faber and Faber, 2008).

Paulin, Tom, 'The Poet's Poet', *The Irish Times*, 11 September 2004, <https://www.irishtimes.com/news/the-poet-s-poet-1.1157220> (last accessed 24 October 2018).

Paulin, Tom, 'Writing to the Moment: Elizabeth Bishop', in *Writing to the Moment* (London: Faber and Faber, 1996), pp. 215–39.

Schwartz, Lloyd, 'Back to Boston: *Geography III* and Other Late Poems', in Angus Cleghorn and Jonathan Ellis (eds), *The Cambridge Companion to Elizabeth Bishop* (Cambridge: Cambridge University Press, 2014), pp. 141–54.

Schwartz, Lloyd, 'Review of *On Elizabeth Bishop* by Colm Tóibín', *The Arts Fuse*, 5 March 2015, <http://artsfuse.org/123735/fuse-book-review-colm-toibin-on-elizabeth-bishop/> (last accessed 24 October 2018).

Tóibín, Colm, *Nora Webster* (London: Penguin, 2014).

Tóibín, Colm, *On Elizabeth Bishop* (Princeton: Princeton University Press, 2015).

Travisano, Thomas, 'Conversations in the Village', *The Smart Set*, 4 June 2015, <https://thesmartset.com/conversations-in-the-village/> (last accessed 24 October 2018).

White, Gillian, *Lyric Shame: The 'Lyric' Subject of Contemporary American Poetry* (Cambridge, MA: Harvard University Press, 2014).

22

ELIZABETH BISHOP AT THE END OF THE RAINBOW

Stephanie Burt

'B ISHOP'S POETRY IS A CONCERN of the present and the recent past, rather than of the future.' That's not anything anyone has said, verbatim, about Bishop; it's T. S. Eliot, writing in 1931, with 'Donne' in place of 'Bishop', and I begin with this altered quotation because it articulates a suspicion that some of us who love Bishop, or who study Bishop, have probably had (5). I want to explain how that suspicion arose (at least for me), and then to show why it no longer troubles me much, and why I think Bishop is still a concern, indeed an available influence, for the English-language poetry of the near future. In between I'm going to talk about rainbows.

You can make Bishop look like Donne if you try hard: she is intellectually reward-ing, sometimes intellectually demanding, intricately involved with doubt and disbelief, and with code or indirection about sexuality. It's easier today, though, to make her reception look like Eliot's: she is, as he is, the author of a relatively small body of published verse whose highlights are clear, and which many poets have already imi-tated; a poet who might be taken to encapsulate her culture's concerns; a poet whose major poems are surrounded by an expanding body of prose, much of it hard to find for decades after its first appearance, some of it still in the archive, where it serves a continuing scholarly industry. Among the twentieth-century anglophone poets around whom you might plausibly organise an international conference, just a few (Eliot, Hart Crane, William Empson, possibly Christopher Okigbo) have smaller bodies of published verse. One way to read the explosion of attention to the work that Bishop left unpublished or unfinished is to say how hard it feels (as with Eliot) for a young scholar to say something new about the published poems.

But there are other reasons Bishop's receptions can seem to resemble Eliot's, other reasons why her work might seem – for twenty-first-century poets – to belong to the twentieth century, to the recent past. It's dangerous to call a poet or a critic 'conserva-tive' these days unless you mean that she votes Tory, but it is undeniable that Bishop has been embraced, defended, admired by critics and poets whose interests are liter-ally conservative – they would like to conserve, to protect, to keep from change or difference (the 'difference that kills / or intimidates, much / of all our small shadowy life') those ways of reading and writing that they take Bishop's published poetry to embody (83).[1]

These are the critics who call Bishop's published works 'perfect' (Adam Kirsch, for example) and a version of that thesis is intuitively correct (96). Bishop did work to perfect the poems that she published, they do envision continuity between pre-modern and twentieth-century forms, they imagine single speakers (rather than dissolving into multiple discourses), and they have closure: Bishop's published poems do not usually end with a bang, but neither do they leave off unexpectedly, mid-sentence or mid-idea. They adhere to prose conventions and prose sense, and they have recognisable roots (however far they ascend) in possible, and paraphrasable, claims about perceptions and actions in a visible world.

In all these respects Bishop's poems can look (I use the word in scare quotes) 'conservative'. That does not make them any worse, of course, but it may seem to make them untimely, or to make their use as models obsolete, especially when young poets are told, within the British university system, to read as much Jeremy Prynne as they can understand, or outside it, to catch up with Sam Riviere; when they feel, within American MFA programs, that the modern world began with Ashbery, Spicer or Stein, and that our moment is the moment of C. A. Conrad and Ariana Reines, or (worse) the moment of Conceptualism vs Flarf. Vernon Shetley, in his study of American poetry circa 1992, cast Bishop as the ideal-typical model for MFA-holding mainstream poets focused on 'craft, decorum and attentive description' (58): not a cool model, perhaps, twenty-five years on.

To model oneself on Bishop in this climate, to consider Bishop your contemporary, is to experience what Gillian White – who began by writing about Bishop – identifies as 'lyric shame', the embarrassment of feeling attached, emotionally and intellectually, to props or models or ideas that the most powerful or influential people around you have already given up, and in particular to the idea of a unitary speaker's 'expressive privacy' (6). To attach oneself to, to model one's poems on, the kinds of poems that Bishop wrote (much less on individual poems by Bishop) is not quite like being publicly Republican, but it might be like coming to high school with a security blanket, or believing in phlogiston, or wearing last decade's couture: it shows that you are immature, insufficiently aware of what time it is, or unable to act your age. Or, if you prefer, it is to be too mature, like a grown-up in a room full of teens: it is to value the carefully, patiently made and the potentially permanent over what's new, probably temporary, unsettled and insistently present-tense.

Nathan Hamilton's terrific 2013 anthology *Dear World & Everyone in It* says that young poets 'choose between [. . .] two general modes in UK & US poetry: "Product" and "Process"' and that 'the product-focused aesthetic' involves 'self-contained, more or less complete thoughts', 'a concern for descriptive accuracy' and 'an expressive selfhood, readable as an individual poet or as a character in a novel' (17). That's Bishop – or it's where Bishop begins, even if she reaches towards, acknowledges, performs its antithesis, Process, 'a way of speaking about the world that simultaneously presents the difficulties of doing so', 'a textual performance' in time rather than an object that stands for another object in space (Hamilton 18).

Hamilton goes on to reject this divide as an effect of 'business and corporate language and ideology': 'dismiss them from your mind entirely' (18). But it is not so easily dismissed, or rather (as with the bear and the mountain) we can't get around it: we have to go over the top. If we want to see how and why Bishop – how and why the ways of writing, of knowing when a poem is a poem and when a poem is finished, that Bishop represents – remains available, we can look at a few poets who still seem close to those ways of writing, one English and famous, one American and not yet well known. When we do that we can see an important contradiction that Bishop's legacy, probably more than the legacy of any other poet, bequeaths for our time.

First, though, let's look at rainbows. Bishop published six works that use the word 'rainbow' (so you can find out from Anne Merrill Greenhalgh's *Concordance to Elizabeth Bishop's Poetry*, laboriously completed in 1985). The first and by far the most famous was 'The Fish', which uses the word four times: first 'oil had spread a rainbow / around the rusted engine' of 'the little rented boat', where the refracted and changeable colours in oil on water sum up the names of the colours given, most of them earlier, one by one: brown, white, green, 'dramatic reds and blacks', pink and finally orange. Then, of course, 'everything / was rainbow, rainbow, rainbow!'

Most of us have read undergraduate papers – some of us have probably read plagiarised undergraduate papers – where that rainbow is a Joycean epiphany, a sceptic's substitute for religious vision, a surprising communion with non-human nature, or a reminder that God 'promised Noah not to flood again' (I quote the end of Empson's 1928 poem 'Dissatisfaction with Metaphysics', which may be a source for Bishop). But the rainbows in 'The Fish' are not really rainbows: the first consists of iridescence in oil, and the last either of oil again, or of many droplets in air very close to the poet. And an actual rainbow, an arc in the sky (Spanish *arcoiris*, Portuguese *arco-íris*, like the fish's 'irises'), is itself an illusion: you can't catch or catch up to or stand under or touch one, and you certainly can't find out where it ends.

Bishop's rainbows are always like that: if you follow the rainbows – and no serious poet has envisioned more rainbows per unit of work – you will see an unbroken queue of objects that are not solid, or are not objects, or are never what they appear to be. You will see occasions for what used to be called deconstruction, what's now called attention to process or open-endedness: moments where Bishop undoes what she does, unsees what she sees, discovers with us that what looks like closure or assurance or definition is in fact a fleeting, potentially protean series of observer effects.

At this point such discoveries might not surprise you: they occur in Bonnie Costello's wonderful early study of Bishop's poetry, with its insistence that Bishop 'dismantles the transcendent gaze' and 'projects into the fixed objects of perception a knowledge of their transience' (6–7). Peggy Samuels has noticed how the many poems in which Bishop looks at 'glassy water' show how the poet's subject risked becoming 'scattered by its multiple and shifting sensations'; Bishop could save herself from that kind of chaos, Samuels argues, through complex analogies from modern art (25, 43). Jonathan Ellis suggests not only that Bishop's poems found themselves on 'uncertainty' (*Art and Memory* 16) but that her epistemological unsettlement within the poems, the way that they 'never really conclude', helps explain some decisions she made about the poems, about what to publish, what counted as a draft, what counted as complete or finished: 'perhaps Bishop was always saving drafts for later, never-to-be-finished volumes' ('Alice in Wonderland' 13). When the poems do sound certain about something, half the time it's Bishop's knowledge that no truth is certain, that experience is at best a 'watery, dazzling dialectic' (175), that 'our knowledge is historical, flowing, and flown' (52).

Those claims, I think, are where Bishop's rainbows begin. Rainbows gave Bishop uniquely powerful reminders that what we see is not just what we see: it is also produced, and reproduced, by what we expect, by our angles, by what we know – and yet it seems single, closed and distinct to us when we perceive it nonetheless. It seems to have borders and ends, keeps on seeming that way, even when we know that 'really', physically, geographically, it does not: you can't get to the end of the rainbow, nor can you isolate a border in the sky, independent of any perceiver, and call that zero-width border the rainbow's curved edge.

'From Aristotle on it was known that the rainbow involved subjectivity in a unique way,' writes Philip Fisher; 'we each see the same sun' but 'two viewers see two different rainbows [. . .] Each person's rainbow, like his or her reflection in a pool of water, is uniquely determined by the point where he or she stands' (36). 'Without human observers', Fisher continues, 'there are no rainbows' (37). Immanuel Kant, as Bishop would probably have known, used the distinction between rainbows and raindrops (which *seem* real in ways that rainbows do not) as an example in the *Critique of Pure Reason*. Bishop's rainbows, or her hints of rainbows – long after 'The Fish', and in more self-sceptical, or ironic, or even flirtatious ways – now look like fit symbols both for her inconclusiveness about what's out there, what's distinct as an object, what's real, and for the drive toward unique shapes and formal closure that nonetheless sets apart her poems. Those rainbows help show us why she has a future, why not only the interest but the influence her work exerts seems unlikely to end.

Where are the rest of those rainbows? You might expect one, or the image of one, in 'Rainy Season; Sub-Tropics' and Bishop comes close. 'The rain has stopped. The waterfall makes such a noise!' muses her giant snail, who leaves 'a lovely opalescent ribbon' on its genderless way to a home-like crack in a rock: 'In that steady pulsing I can rest. All night I shall be like a sleeping ear' (135). Such a snail might live under the actual house in Petrópolis in Bishop's most underrated poem, her most fully realised poem about domestic and amorous satisfaction, 'Song for the Rainy Season', with its 'house and rock / in a private cloud' (82). The Petrópolis house and its careful ten-line dimeter stanzas ought to support a rainbow, but we see that rainbow only once it's gone:

> Without water
>
> the great rock will stare
> unmagnetized, bare,
> no longer wearing
> rainbows or rain,
> the forgiving air
> and the high fog gone. (83)

The paired rhymes land (almost every line-terminal word has a rhyme or half-rhyme) but 'the owls will move on'.

The promise of the rainbow here is the promise of Eurydice coming up from the underworld: you can get what you want, or you can know what you see, but you can't do both. There is, of course, nothing at the end of this rainbow; by the end of the poem there is nothing underneath it either, just rocks in dry sun. Clarity is the enemy of the 'magnetism' that is erotic affection; time may be the enemy of love. To remain in love not only do you have to live in the present; you have to live in a fog.

Like the glassy water that Samuels traced, the rainbows in Bishop start early: the teen-aged Bishop wrote a riddle in tercets ('I am neither here nor there') whose answer appears to be 'rainbow' (207). Those glassy waters, spectroscopic or mirrorlike shores and wet sands also start early, in 1929, with 'a gold-leaf film of sea / re-brushed, re-grained by random cloud' (*Edgar Allan Poe* 11). 'Random': no special providence in the fall of a sparrow here. Bishop also finds her iridescence and opalescence in oils – not oil paints but oil puddles, oil slicks, the 'black translucency' of 'Filling Station' (123) or the oil 'like bits of mirror – no, more blue than that' in 'Under the Window: Ouro Prêto' (145).

Other poets use rainbows as gestures towards exactly the promise of coherence, of continuity, the guarantee that all beginnings have ends, which Bishop's own rainbows almost always abjure. 'The Lord survives the rainbow of his will,' concluded Robert Lowell in 'The Quaker Graveyard in Nantucket', the anchor poem in *Lord Weary's Castle* (1946), published after 'The Fish' but before Bishop came to Brazil, and a poem whose prominence during the 1950s it would be hard to overstate (*Selected Poems* 10). Lowell's book concluded with 'Where the Rainbow Ends', in which 'the dove of Jesus' brings 'wisdom' to sinful Boston after a wintry flood (*Selected Poems* 31). Hopkins's writings include three rainbows, and as you'd expect they stand up for God's promise to Earth: a short triolet-like poem considers, and tries to solve, the paradox of where the rainbow *is*:

> It was a hard thing to undo this knot.
> The rainbow shines, but only in the thought.
> Of him that looks. Yet not in that alone,
> For who makes rainbows by invention?
> [. . .]
> The sun on falling waters writes the text
> Which yet is in the eye or in the thought.
> It was a hard thing to undo this knot. (29)

Like the balanced rainbow of Noah's promise, Hopkins's pentameters end where they begin; the rainbow exists both outside and inside us, guaranteed by the divine presence that 'invented' everything in the perceptual world. Another short poem or fragment of Hopkins's places one end of 'The Rainbow' in Havering, Essex, 'with his other foot three miles beyond' (35). (Bishop's much-discussed undergraduate essay on Hopkins argued that he did not push too hard for intelligibility, that he stopped his poems 'at the point in their development where they are still incomplete' (665). She did not discuss his rainbows there; she may well have had in mind, though, the third rainbow in Hopkins's completed poems, which I'll reach shortly.)

In 1950 – after 'The Fish', after *Lord Weary's Castle*, but before Brazil – Bishop translated, and published in *Poetry*, Max Jacob's 'Rainbow', a poem about Christ on the cross, where 'the poet stretched out his arms toward the Savior / and everything vanished: the somber night and the beasts. / The poet followed God for his happiness' (268). It is not an outcome we find in Bishop's own work. There is not even a rainbow in Bishop's 'Squatter's Children', though we might feel that there ought to be, since the children are trying and failing to build a 'little, soluble, / unwarrantable ark' (76): no covenant, no law divine or human, can protect them.

What Eliot in his essay on Donne called 'our own more conscious awareness of the apparent irrelevance and unrelatedness of things' (8) becomes for Bishop, from the start of her writing life all the way to the end, a temporal awareness that things will not keep any order we find for them: rainbows literally illuminate that awareness. When Bishop lists rainbow colours, she emphasises perceptual or cognitive inconclusion: we can find only a temporary order in the glittering variety of 'black, white, tan, and gray [. . .] rose and amethyst' (126). That poem, 'Sandpiper', returns to her 1933 ballad 'The Flood', where 'two sand-pipers' are the only survivors in a steeple-drowning apocalypse (191). On the 1960 river journey that produced the draft that Alice Quinn entitles 'On the Amazon', the glassy river 'reflects, reflects – nothing' and 'the world, all pink, / has dissolved at last / and is going somewhere / under a rainbow, too' (*Edgar Allan Poe* 125, 124). This 'gentle acquiescent world' is yet one more revision of Noah's flood, where everything that survives is in boats or 'on stilts' (125), like Jerónimo's house in the poem of that name (26). So much for that promise not to flood us again.

The rainbows in Bishop testify to perceptual fullness – even to what Fisher calls 'wonder' – but they are always also broken promises, either promises that cannot last (as in 'Song for the Rainy Season') or promises that nobody ever fulfilled (as in the absent rainbow of 'Squatter's Children', or the absent explanation for the proliferating colours on the sandpiper's beach). Then there is the rainbow of Bishop's unpublished – perhaps unfinished, perhaps merely unsatisfactory (to Bishop) – 'Suicide of a Moderate Dictator', which ends on yet one more prismatic beach:

> This is a day that's beautiful as well,
> and warm and clear. At seven o'clock I saw
> the dogs being walked along the famous beach
> as usual, in a shiny gray-green dawn,
> leaving their paw prints draining in the wet.
> The line of breakers was steady and the pinkish
> segmented rainbow steadily hung above it.
> At eight two little boys were flying kites. (236)

Bishop can let the rainbow be (rather than telling us that it will disappear, or showing us only its partial reflection somewhere) because the whole scene serves as an ironic contrast to her earlier insight that civil order can disappear, that the true foundations of government are both shaky and unknowable: 'truths will out, *perhaps*' (236; emphasis mine). The real kites flown by real boys (real within the world of the poem) match the imagined kites, the 'kite string but no kite' (168) in 'The End of March', whose reuse of 'Suicide' Joelle Biele has described (131–2):

> For just a minute, set in their bezels of sand,
> the drab, damp, scattered stones
> were multi-colored,
> and all those high enough threw out long shadows,
> individual shadows, then pulled them in again.

These aurally varied ('out', then 'in') lines trace what Zachariah Pickard calls Bishop's 'ongoing interest in the work of knowing', in how to get the visible world just right (85). Thanks to her verbal labour, we think we see what she says she has seen. If we then try to interpret it, we get symbols for what we can't know, and for what cannot last. This polychromatic transience, which characterises the rocks, not the skies above them, is exactly not a contract or a promise or a correspondence between the sky and the earth, or the sky and the sea, or the present and the future: Bishop does not envision those kinds of promises, or when she does, they never get kept.

These broken promises can make the final rainbow in Bishop's work joyful by contrast: impermanence, lack of fixity, and an inability to be permanently represented, understood, 'mirrored', become in 'Sonnet' a source of delight. Drafts, as Victoria Harrison notes, have 'rainbow' before they have 'rainbow-bird'; the same drafts refer to Marianne Moore's optimistic poem 'The Mind Is an Enchanting Thing', where iridescence in animals ('the dove- / neck animated by / sun', for instance) allows Moore to celebrate 'change' (209–10). If you've taught 'Sonnet' you've probably been asked about the word 'gay', which had changed its dominant public meaning considerably since 'A Cold Spring' (where 'the calf got up promptly / and seemed inclined to feel gay' (43). Both Steven Axelrod and Lloyd Schwartz are certain that 'gay' means 'gay' (48; 153). The Rainbow Pride flag first appeared in June 1978, in a San Francisco parade; Bishop, the poet of 'and more closets', might not have cared for it, but would probably have seen it by that autumn, when she finished the poem (Fountain and Brazeau 293).

She had certainly seen the rainbow in Hopkins's strongest, longest poem to use the word, 'The Caged Skylark'. In the octave of that sonnet 'man's mounting spirit' is stuck in the cage of its body, and wants to fly free. The sestet remembers that not every body, nor every kind of material embodiment, feels like a cage or a curse: 'Man's spirit will be flesh-bound, when found at best, / But úncúmberèd: meadow-dówn is nót distressed / For a raínbow foóting it nor hé for his bónes rísen' (133). For Hopkins the end of the rainbow is liberation, not so much *from*, but *in*, the flesh: the Resurrection will confirm God's promise to humanity that our bodies will someday suit us. For the Bishop of 'Sonnet', no such promise holds.

George Monteiro, in his study of Bishop's debts to Brazil and Brazilian Portuguese, believes that the 'rainbow bird is assuredly Brazilian', like the toucan that Bishop named Uncle Sam (178). Brazilians also held superstitions about rainbows, as James Merrill recalled: when he visited her at Ouro Preto,

a taxi was jouncing through sparkling red-and-green country, downhill, uphill, then, suddenly, *under* a rainbow! Elizabeth said some words in Portuguese, the driver began to shake with laughter. 'In the north of Brazil,' she explained, 'they have this superstition, if you pass underneath a rainbow you change sex.' (We were to pass more than once under this one.) ('Elizabeth Bishop')

Bishop may or may not have had identifiable species of bird, or rainbow flags, or reversals of gender, in mind when she wrote this broken-open sonnet; she was, characteristically, coy if she did. But this last rainbow poem, this poem (in Lloyd Schwartz's phrase) 'virtually intended to seem posthumous' (153), is certainly coy in another sense: it uses its endless rainbow, its anti-rainbow, its bird that flies 'wherever' and never comes back to earth, as a way to imagine evading fixed representation. The rainbow bird, the spirit or soul, leaves an 'empty mirror' – it's gone.

But rainbows themselves (like the soul) do not return to earth: they do not complete themselves, nor do they return to us. Nor do they have, as toucans and fish and boats and sand grains have, persistence in time, or solidity in space, or an independent existence, or a stable location, beyond the viewer. *But they look like they do*: the rainbow appears in

Bishop as the conscious illusion of closure, the suspension of disbelief, that protects our imagination and our emotions from the flux and open-endedness, the unpredictability, the chaos, or – if you prefer – the freedom, that both the social and the physical worlds in fact present.

And that means that even a poem about freedom, for Bishop, requires that there be something, a set of echoes, a set of expectations, a method of representation (a mirror, or a realist mode) from which the soul-bird-rainbow can break free. 'The sense of freedom' in 'Sonnet', as Costello put it, 'depends on the prior constraint of form' (242). More generally: the feeling of freedom, the sense of unboundedness, depends in Bishop on the presence of something from which to break free.

Put more crudely: you can't come out of the closet without a closet; you can't run away without something to run from. And you can't depict – that is, Bishop could not depict in a way that gave her aesthetic satisfaction, a way that produced a completed poem – the uncertainties, the precariousness, the mutability, the resistance to closure, that we seek now, and that our climate tells us to seek, and that we sometimes call liberation, unless she could maintain, as a matter of tone and form, some sense of the expectations about closure, about perception, about recognition, about a real world and its people, that the substance of the poem denies. The rainbows in Bishop's work are symbols of momentary and merely formal closure: symbols of perceptual certainty, symbols of reward, symbols of a promise (like God's to Noah), and as you might expect they are almost always notional, or partial, or illusory, or ironised, or at best temporary. But we see them. Sometimes we go out of our way to see them: we are so made as to want them, most of the time, and sometimes we get them, but we should not trust that they can last.

Those rainbows – which are, strictly speaking, optical illusions, even when they occur in the sky and not as fragments in mirrors or oil or puddles – may stand not for closure in the standard sense of the word used by literary critics, the sense that Barbara Herrnstein Smith anatomised in her book about how poems end and that Lyn Hejinian rejected in her essay 'The Rejection of Closure'. They also stand for 'closure' in the sense used by gestalt psychologists such as Wolfgang Köhler in the 1930s and later by comics theorists like Scott McCloud, who defines it concisely as 'observing the parts but perceiving the whole', 'mentally completing that which is incomplete based on past experience' (63). When you see the front surface of a banana, you assume a banana is there; when you see a suspended arc whose ends are obscured, you assume it continues until it has somewhere to land, and when you see a lot of tiny glittery objects (as in a painting by Georges Seurat) they can make one big object in your brain (that's what, surprisingly, does *not* happen in 'Sandpiper'). All those effects take place when we see, or 'see', what we call a rainbow. But closure (as McCloud, and David Hume, point out) also works over time: we infer that adjacent events are connected, and that observed correlations recur.

Without closure (in Köhler's and McCloud's sense of 'closure') we could not plan – we could barely experience – our lives. But the assumptions that it gives us, as Bishop's poems point out, do not always fit the facts. Bishop is great because – among other reasons – she depicts both the reasons we expect closure and resolution, and also the reasons why we so often can't have them. The rainbows scattered through her poetry – the contracts with God that God never made or kept, the most famous of all optical illusions, the one a child can see (and see through) – become reminders of that dual vision. The Bishop who once feared becoming a 'minor female Wordsworth' adopted Wordsworth's rainbow – or rather bits and parts of Wordsworth's rainbow, the one that made his heart leap up – as a symbol for that insight (772).

Bishop's rainbow vision, her sense of illusion, her knowledge that we expect a consistency where we know there is none, also speaks to what social critics call our moment of economic precarity. I do not mean, in particular, that she speaks to the Global South (though she certainly addressed it in some of her writings about Brazil). Rather, I mean that she speaks to an uncertainty felt also in the relatively secure precincts of the so-called First World; her poems anticipate our dual awareness, first, that we could all lose everything we have (a sense that the poets of the Cold War shared, though they feared nuclear war more than climate change), and second, that any sense of security we may have about our professional lives, our physical safety, our families, our housing, our food supply and so on is more a fact about our current social position than it is a fact about the world. Part of what's unsatisfying about 'Squatter's Children', or about 'Twelfth Morning' (another poem with polychromatic mists), is the way the poet's authoritative voice speaks to, or over, its impoverished actors: she knows what's up. Part of the beauty in 'Song for the Rainy Season', as in 'Filling Station', is the ultimate vulnerability in that voice: she knows that everything could fall down. The former pair of poems sound dated, 1950s-ish; the latter, equally Bishopesque, and alive.

They also sound more like the best poets who resemble, sometimes consciously, Bishop now. One such poet is Lavinia Greenlaw. When Greenlaw reviewed Bishop's *Poems* for the *The Telegraph* in 2011 she let us know she, too, had seen the Bay of Fundy:

> The scale of the Bay of Fundy is hard to describe. It cuts so far inland that you forget it is the actual sea. Even so it is a definite edge where as the tide roars in and retreats, things fall into place only to be washed away again. I might be describing a Bishop poem or her life, or any life. As she put it in 'The Sandpiper': 'The world is a mist. And then the world is / minute and vast and clear.' This movement between the contingent and the absolute is something she understood and articulated better than anyone else. ('Elizabeth Bishop and Nova Scotia')

'Or any life.' 'Better than anyone else.' For this poet Bishop got life right: Greenlaw's problem in her own poems has not been how to make Bishop relevant (she does not suffer from White's 'lyric shame') but how to avoid mere transposition, or imitation. She called her most recent collection *The Casual Perfect*, a jarring – or boasting – quotation from Lowell's poem on Bishop. 'Mine was the world of the close-up,' Greenlaw writes of her teenage self, 'of corners and cracks, tight frames and vivid abstraction' (*Importance of Music* 142). She might have come straight from Bishop's prose.

At her most original, Greenlaw takes that Bishopesque frame, that attraction to corners and cracks, and applies it to subjects that Bishop would never have tackled: punk rock, for example, and liking boys, or men, and suburban Englishness, and digital capitalism. When Greenlaw writes 'I live in the world too fast, too far, / virtual, residual', she could be quoting Bishop's giant toad. Instead she is describing a fatigue specific to suburban England, where important events are always taking place just a few miles away, just a few years ago: 'This island of sky / is filled with signs and arrows', pointing elsewhere (*The Casual Perfect* 22). Greenlaw calls that poem 'English Lullaby'.

It seems almost circular to say that Bishop seems relevant now because some poets model their work on hers; if you think that Bishop is passé you will probably think the same of Greenlaw. Yet Greenlaw helps make my larger point about Bishop's rainbows: that while she is a poet of closure and well-made poems and an external world, she is also a poet who took a consistent interest in the opposites of those things, in objects that are not objects, in closures that do not close, or do not represent the world as closed, in perception represented in such a way that you cannot say what is real, or what will come next. That dual interest, signalled by her rainbows, is what makes her such an interesting model, and analogue, for contemporary poets.

This doubled quality of persistent uncertainty, represented by those approximate, or refracted, or ironised, rainbows, makes her a poet of process, if you want process, and a poet of precariousness about who is speaking and where she is coming from, not only in terms of cognition but also in terms of national canons (is she Canadian?) and sexuality (when is she lesbian?) and even age. And those qualities make her a poet for our time, a poet whose salient interests and moves reappear in writers who are not obviously, outwardly, influenced by her, among them – perhaps surprisingly – the American poet Lorna Dee Cervantes, best known for her early poems about Latina and Chicana identity. Cervantes's 2006 collection *Drive* includes erasures and collages from Bishop's poems, among them 'For Love, Sept. 11', derived from 'The Fish' ('they didn't fight. / They hadn't fought at all') (8, 26, 30).

You can find more such writers, younger ones, in Hamilton's anthology. Emily Berry's poem 'Manners', with its awkward grief, might put you in mind not of Bishop's 'Manners' but of 'First Death in Nova Scotia': 'My mother is dead – it's classic. / It means I'm both precocious and heartbroken, / but that's no excuse for bad manners' (Hamilton 113). Berry – apparently a much younger Berry – gave her psychiatrist a handmade comic book. In her poem, she speaks to him:

> In my one memory of my mother I am filling
> her belly-button with shingle on a beach in Brighton.
> When I told the Doctor this he mused: 'A dog bites
> the hand it knows,' and 'The fruit will swallow the tree.'
> He's recording me on tape so he can sell my story
> to a documentary-maker when I'm famous. Today
> he's making me list everything my parents ever gave me,
> like 1) A rabbit 2) Medicine 3) An interior feeling
> of shipwreckedness. While I list he reads my comic,
> chuckling. He doesn't notice that the last page is torn off. (Hamilton 113)

We are in the world of 'In the Waiting Room', with an overlay of millennial satire; we are also in the world of Bishop's rainbows, where you never find the foundation or get to the end.

What about economic precarity? What about the social critique that advanced young poets demand? Here is a poem that Michael Kindellan entitles 'The Flight to Quality', constructed almost entirely from the jargon and doublespeak of the financial pages, until we get to the end:

> It was within the reach of an all-time
> low that the jump in oil prices turmoil
> as confidence that slides back to fade
> the economies desire. The yellow
> metal, the red chest threaded by paper
> into harder assets. Coins are running
> at a super pace: nothing pecks faster
> than the datastream, fumbling for stones. (Hamilton 213)

If you want to evoke the fragility, the consensus-dependence, the potential for bubbles, in the post-crash markets that determine, invisibly, so much about our lives, maybe you should look to Bishop for that; here are silver and gold and yellow and red and the pecks of her sandpiper, seeking patterns that aren't there.

I ought to make clear here that I am not saying that Berry or Kindellan or anyone else under thirty in Britain learned to write poetry by reading Bishop's own verse; Berry said (via Twitter) in 2015 that she had 'hardly read her'. Rather, I am making a claim about attitude, about a frame of mind; Berry, and not only Berry, through her poems' sometimes astonishing overlap with Bishop's attitudes and even her characters and settings ('In the Waiting Room' and 'Manners' so resemble Berry's 'Manners'), makes Bishop's attitudes towards her poems seem available, contemporary, useful, for readers and writers of poetry being written now. The rainbows in Bishop's poems, as they point both to her lack of closure and to our desire for closure, signal that availability.

If you want conscious, direct allusions to Bishop in a celebrated poet who is just starting out, a poet whose style also owes much to the indirections and evasions that Bishop's direct imitators have failed to capture, you can find that poet too, albeit in America: Margaret Ross is a former student of Jorie Graham, and an Iowa Writers Workshop graduate, whose first book, *A Timeshare*, came out in 2015. It contains a poem entitled 'The Unbeliever', whose opening lines riff on Bishop's work: 'Sea beaten to Lucite: retaining little / nicks the wind chiseled, kelp lashes / and shade, distant specks of fish / the size of flies' (55). Ross's sceptic sees the same hard sea that Bishop's eponymous sceptic had observed.

As in Bishop, the people in Ross's poems are always looking, but they are rarely sure what they have seen: Ross entitles another poem 'Are Our Eyes Our Own' (49). Her sceptical vision incorporates not just Bishop's refusals of closures but Bishop's reflective, wet beaches, Bishop's maps that suddenly become territory, as in the opening of Ross's 'Parts Unknown': 'Then any sense of where we were / gone [. . .] Foam on the water / laced maps whose every route // unraveled' (18). Ross's collection begins with an aerial view (as in '12 O'Clock News', as in 'The Bight') of a glowing space that might almost be another map, but is also a city seen from the air, one that looks (in turn) like a sinister research lab, or an asylum, with its 'starched whitecoats': 'All along the river flickering pills / if they would just align / could be taken to mean *Tear Here*' (17).

I want to conclude by introducing a poet who isn't a millennial like Hamilton or Ross, but who does track shimmery, uncertain perceptual feedback, who even likes glassy water, a poet who is (like Bishop) a painter, and who (like Bishop) paints Florida, and who (like Bishop) looks both at non-human nature and at the rickety homes that humans build, a poet who belongs to our time, not to hers, and a poet that people who like Bishop should like. That poet is Allan Peterson, and I'm going to give you some parts of his work; I hope you'll see why I like them so much, as well as why I think they evidence Bishop's continued importance, and how they show where her rainbows can lead.

Peterson earned his living as a painter and teacher of painting, becoming chair of the art department at Pensacola Junior College, from which he retired in 2005. Many of his poems describe scenes, or sets of scenes; some of the rest are meta-description, art theory, thinking about what it means to get a scene right. One poem from Peterson's first book begins with what sounds like an offhand reference to 'Arrival at Santos': 'you can go anywhere using one guidebook, experience. / It gets you through the first chapter, awe' (*Anonymous Or* 36).

Peterson's later book *Fragile Acts* returns to 'the anomalies of vision', the way that we half-create the things we see: 'In one of the anomalies of vision, I stare at the wharf pilings / till they turn to flashlights, / white shafts shooting up from the gull perches' (*Fragile Acts* 8). Here we are in the world of 'The Bight', where synaesthesia steps in, but never overtakes the desire to get the seen world right. To look at the wharf and see the posts glow, Peterson says, 'fills the moment like someone in 1610 receiving a copy / of Galileo's Starry Messenger, / *Sidereus Nuncius*, with pictures of the moon in raking light' (*Fragile Acts* 8). In a poem called 'Lost and Found', we watch a river: 'An east wind sends shadows on the ruffled surface / flicking like the dock on fire. / It looks the same as hair braiding with glass from a sunset window' (*Fragile Acts* 68). Again, reflective surfaces in water let the poet think about the welcome and some-times necessary illusions of perceptual closure, about how we can't hold on to the thing we perceive: 'reality is both created and displayed', its 'take-back-and-give / like the pass-it-on notes in school' (*Fragile Acts* 77).

Just as Bishop used to get depicted, or dismissed, as a miniaturist, a poet of pure description, Peterson can get dismissed, or pigeonholed, as a poet of purely visual or epistemological inquiry. He is curious, and he is an observer, and he does try to make his complex sentences – whose clauses slip and slide across one another in ways that make them easy to read clumsily – reflect the process of observation. But Peterson is also a love poet, a poet of domesticity, apology, intimacy, apprehension and grati-tude: you can draw a line from 'Song for the Rainy Season' right to Peterson's poems addressed to his wife, Frances, an environmental activist whose work to save estuaries and watersheds enters his poems. Peterson's 2014 volume *Precarious* concentrates on domestic space: here is the start of 'I Speak to the House about Water':

> It tells me rock scissors roof
> that seepage has patterns
> we cannot anticipate
> that leaves clogging gutters
> fall by abscission and clouds
> are the ghosts of moisture (35)

'Rock scissors roof' is a game, like rock-paper-scissors, with arbitrary and inconstant outcomes: this house is, like Bishop's house in 'Song for the Rainy Season', at once a form of cosy domesticity (it almost seems to whisper to the poet) and a sign that gutters clog, clouds gain water weight, and nothing lasts.

Bishop's rainbows and glassy waters tend to represent the frangibility and the unsteadiness of human perception – they show how we make what we see, or make it make sense. Peterson keeps on seeking new, tentative, comic symbols for that same phenomenon. The opening page of *Precarious* gives us a skeleton, or rather a Hallow-een costume that looks like a skeleton:

> how we look lovingly seeing a body
> that does not clatter apart, that articulates
> without ligaments, that presents in October
> poignant reminders begging at our doors. (11)

The ligaments, for this skeleton, come from social convention, from people who greet it with sweets: its life is a trick of the eye, as well as a treat. Another example is the international date line; another is weather radar:

> How does the dateline work   How far west of recovery
> does the arbitrary start   How thin the appearances we trust
>
> We think we can stand in the present and reconstruct the past
> from leftovers but look what is happening to Phoenix
>
> on weather radar how braid and ribbon come together
> like bees and wind at the entrance of a flower (*Precarious* 49)

Peterson's choice of Phoenix, Arizona, is not arbitrary: our sense of the world (like the sandpiper's) keeps breaking apart and coming back together, collapsing in flames and then resurrecting itself, as the data get rearranged. And in Peterson, as in Bishop, the precariousness of what we know is not just an intellectual problem, but a symbol for the disturbing fragility of houses, families, promises, human relations. A poem called 'Fear of Fire', set at a dock, is Peterson's 'One Art':

> Cloud smoke layers at the edge
> of the shadow of the fear of everything in sight catching
> and each diesel leaving the slips in this early light is a fireboat.
> I see yesterday burns up and today is burning down,
> that everyday fear runs from the actual, each morning a fire drill,
> each boat a rescue. Each piston escaping hoofbeats on a bridge. (*Precarious* 59)

The 'is' in 'is a fireboat' refers not to what the boat's pilots believe the boats are, but to what Peterson imagines or half-expects them to be.

Peterson incorporates into his own more expository language something of Bishop's dry humour, something of her way of savouring letdowns, and a great deal of her punctiliousness: he knows that we never get everything right, that there may be nothing lasting out there to 'get'. Another one of Peterson's new poems promises to avoid

> the forcing of facts into a philosophy
> someone is paying to maintain. The moment the sugar
> crystals surrender to syrup out of sheer curiosity
> they start to rebuild against drying to a small city on the knife. (*Precarious* 27)

The patterns won't stay with us, but the patterns are real, and the promise that we can describe them is sweet. We live in a radically variable, potentially dangerous world, one in which no promise is divinely guaranteed, no rainbow ends, everything can succumb to difference, to mould, to fire, get lost. And yet we seek, and recognise, promises; crystals dry on the knife.

I'll end with a caveat. One thing we don't get from the world of Peterson's poems, nor of Ross's, however careful their observations, is the sense I mentioned earlier, the sense that we get from Bishop's published volumes – though, importantly, not from much unpublished work – that each poem has been a perfect, unique construction, not just a thing with a form, but a thing with its own, *unrepeatable*, potentially permanent, achieved form. Bishop's recently discovered letters to Dr Ruth Foster confirm (even as they record misgivings about) just that aesthetic goal, making 'each poem an isolated event' (quoted in Marshall 81). This idea that each poem has to be unique not just in its details but in its use of form, in its kind of closure (even if it knows that closure is an illusion), the idea that the poet must not repeat herself, is another idea that you get from reading the completed works of Elizabeth Bishop, an idea we should not lose as we keep delving into the work she chose not to publish, and it is an idea relatively rare even among poets most of us agree are major: it would have been foreign, as an idea, to the Wordsworths.

To read the completed works of Elizabeth Bishop is to find a poet who both pursues and acknowledges the illusion of closure, which her rainbows represent. It is also to read a poet who really seems to do something new each time. The bafflement in 'North Haven' about a poet, Robert Lowell, willing to '*repeat, repeat, repeat*' (as in his sonnets) and to '*revise, revise, revise*' (even after publication, repeatedly) is the bafflement of a poet who really wanted to make her poems not just formally finished (which is to say over and done with) but also formally unique. And that kind of aesthetic goal has been sacrificed – it is tempting to say not just in Peterson, or in Hamilton's anthology, but in much of the strongest poetry of our time. The formal completions we get now, instead, seem more fleeting, and take place at the level of the sentence – the poem sounds like something that nobody else could have written, but it may look like many other poems. The poems of a poet much more prolific, or more process-oriented, than Bishop are new as rainbows are new: they might still be the same kind of thing. They are not, necessarily, objects of *unique* construction, much less of the perfection they reject as an explicit goal. And yet, as Peterson says, 'The opposite of clockwork is not chaos' (*Precarious* 91); it is the unstable order that Bishop's forms, as well as her tones, and his tones (which are not hers), along with her rainbows, subtend. That order is what we find at the end of Bishop's rainbows, what later poets will continue to find, and it will continue to let our hearts leap up.

Note

1. Except where otherwise indicated, page numbers following quotations from Elizabeth Bishop refer to *Poems, Prose, and Letters*, ed. Robert Giroux and Lloyd Schwartz.

Works Cited

Axelrod, Steven Gould, 'Bishop, History and Politics', in Angus Cleghorn and Jonathan Ellis (eds), *The Cambridge Companion to Elizabeth Bishop* (Cambridge: Cambridge University Press, 2014), pp. 35–48.

Berry, Emily, 'Seems offensive to mention this in the context of an Elizabeth Bishop conference, but I have hardly read her' (Twitter), <https://twitter.com/no1_emily/status/616515730041929728> (last accessed 24 October 2018).

Biele, Joelle, 'Revise, Revise', in Laura Jehn Menides and Angela G. Dorenkamp (eds), 'In Worcester, Massachusetts': Essays on Elizabeth Bishop (New York: Peter Lang, 1999), pp. 129–38.

Bishop, Elizabeth, Edgar Allan Poe & the Juke-Box: Uncollected Poems, Drafts, and Fragments, ed. Alice Quinn (New York: Farrar, Straus and Giroux, 2006).

Bishop, Elizabeth, Poems, Prose, and Letters, ed. Robert Giroux and Lloyd Schwartz (New York: Library of America, 2008).

Cervantes, Lorna Dee, Drive (San Antonio: Wings Press, 2006).

Costello, Bonnie, Elizabeth Bishop: Questions of Mastery (Cambridge, MA: Harvard University Press, 1991).

Eliot, T. S., 'Donne in Our Time', in Theodore Spencer (ed.), A Garland for John Donne (Cambridge, MA: Harvard University Press, 1931), pp. 3–19.

Ellis, Jonathan, 'Alice in Wonderland', in Angus Cleghorn, Bethany Hicok and Thomas Travisano (eds), Elizabeth Bishop in the Twenty-First Century: Reading the New Editions (Charlottesville: University of Virginia Press, 2012), pp. 11–25.

Ellis, Jonathan, Art and Memory in the Work of Elizabeth Bishop (Aldershot: Ashgate, 2006).

Fisher, Philip, Wonder, the Rainbow, and the Aesthetics of Rare Experiences (Cambridge, MA: Harvard University Press, 1998).

Fountain, Gary, and Peter Brazeau (eds), Remembering Elizabeth Bishop: An Oral Biography (Amherst: University of Massachusetts Press, 1994).

Greenhalgh, Anne Merrill, A Concordance to Elizabeth Bishop's Poetry (New York: Garland Publishing, 1985).

Greenlaw, Lavinia, The Casual Perfect (London: Faber and Faber, 2011).

Greenlaw, Lavinia, 'Elizabeth Bishop and Nova Scotia', The Telegraph, 4 February 2011, <http://www.telegraph.co.uk/culture/books/bookreviews/8300772/Elizabeth-Bishop-and-Nova-Scotia.html> (last accessed 24 October 2018).

Greenlaw, Lavinia, The Importance of Music to Girls (New York: Farrar, Straus and Giroux, 2007).

Hamilton, Nathan (ed.), Dear World & Everyone in It (Newcastle upon Tyne: Bloodaxe Books, 2013).

Harrison, Victoria, Elizabeth Bishop's Poetics of Intimacy (Cambridge: Cambridge University Press, 1993).

Hopkins, Gerard Manley, The Major Works, ed. Catherine Phillips, 2nd edn (Oxford: Oxford University Press, 2006).

Kirsch, Adam, The Wounded Surgeon: Confessions and Transformations in Six American Poets (New York: W. W. Norton & Company, 2005).

Lowell, Robert, Selected Poems (New York: Farrar, Straus and Giroux, 2006).

McCloud, Scott, Understanding Comics (New York: William Morrow, 1993).

Marshall, Megan, Elizabeth Bishop: A Miracle for Breakfast (New York: Houghton Mifflin Harcourt, 2017).

Merrill, James, 'Elizabeth Bishop (1911–1979)', New York Review of Books, 6 December 1979, <http://www.nybooks.com/articles/1979/12/06/elizabeth-bishop-19111979/> (last accessed 24 October 2018).

Monteiro, George, Elizabeth Bishop in Brazil and After: A Poetic Career Transformed (Jefferson, NC: McFarland, 2012).

Peterson, Allan, Anonymous Or (Fort Montgomery, NY: Defined Providence, 2002).

Peterson, Allan, Fragile Acts (San Francisco: McSweeney's, 2012).

Peterson, Allan, Precarious (Tallahassee: 42 Miles, 2015).

Pickard, Zachariah, *Elizabeth Bishop's Poetics of Description* (Montreal: McGill-Queen's University Press, 2009).

Ross, Margaret, *A Timeshare* (Richmond, CA: Omnidawn, 2015).

Samuels, Peggy, *Deep Skin: Elizabeth Bishop and Visual Art* (Ithaca: Cornell University Press, 2010).

Schwartz, Lloyd, 'Back to Boston: *Geography III* and Other Late Poems', in Angus Cleghorn and Jonathan Ellis (eds), *The Cambridge Companion to Elizabeth Bishop* (Cambridge: Cambridge University Press, 2014), pp. 141–54.

Shetley, Vernon, *After the Death of Poetry* (Durham, NC: Duke University Press, 1994).

White, Gillian C., *Lyric Shame: The 'Lyric' Subject of Contemporary American Poetry* (Cambridge, MA: Harvard University Press, 2014).

INDEX

Breton, André, 179, 186, 188, 188n
Bridges, Robert, 168, 239
Brinnin, John Malcolm, 298
Broeck, Sabine, 281
Bromwich, David, 38
Brooks, Gwendolyn, 280
Brown, Ashley, 168
Browne, Thomas, 209, 216–17
Bulmer, Elizabeth, 259
Burt, E. S., 91, 91n, 96
Burt, Jonathan, 197
Burt, Stephanie, 297n, 315, 321–36
Burton, Richard, 210
Butler, Judith, 19, 85, 159

Cabo Frio, Brazil, 277–8
Cagney, James, 195
Caillois, Roger, 276–7
Calder, Alexander, 10, 177, 181, 188n
Cambridge, MA, xxiv, 141–2, 144, 148, 151
Cameron, Agnes Dean, 203
Camões, Luís Vaz de, 172
Camp, Cynthia, 187
Campbell, Marvin, 280–93
Campion, Thomas, 49–50
Campos, Augusto de, 178
Campos, Haroldo de, 178
Carlyle, Jane, 211
Carlyle, Thomas, 211
Carroll, Lewis, 7, 48, 240
Carson, Ciaron, 309
Caruth, Cathy, 23, 137
Caselli, Daniela, 157n
Cather, Willa, 55
Cendrars, Blaise, 179
Cervantes, Lorna Dee, 330
Chai, Eleanor, 10
Chaplin, Charlie, 195
Chateaubriand, François-René de, 93
Chaucer, Geoffrey, 187, 187n
Chekhov, Anton, 223, 225
Cheng, Anne Anlin, 159
Chiasson, Dan, 291–2
Cholula, Mexico, 283
Ciardi, John, 149, 237
Clark, Kenneth and Mamie, 22
Clayton, Frances, 288
Cleaver, Eldridge, 280
Cleaver, Kathleen, 280
Cleghorn, Angus, 9, 13, 164, 197, 225
Clooney, George, 202
Cold War, 3, 11, 253–65
Coleridge, Samuel Taylor, 150

Collingwood Disney, Joan, 223
Columbus, Christopher, 286
Colwell, Anne, 3
Colwin, Laurie, 298
Comins, Barbara, 78–9
Condon, William, 121
Conrad, C. A., 322
Cook, Eleanor, 11–12, 49, 91n, 96, 164n, 167, 179n, 257
Copacabana Beach, Rio de Janeiro, 296–7
Copland, Aaron, 283
Corelle, Laurel Snow, 11
Corn, Alfred, 95, 98n
Cornell, Joseph, 65, 172–5, 177, 274, 277
Costello, Bonnie, 2–5, 11, 25, 60, 78, 85, 93–4, 96, 98, 118, 156n, 194, 195, 214, 225, 271, 297n, 323, 328
Cotton, Jess, 149–63
Crane, Hart, 283, 321
Crane, Louise, 284
Crewe, Jonathan, 48n
Croll, Maurice, 125, 167n, 209–10, 216–17, 220, 246
Cuba, 214, 283
Cucinella, Catherine, 3, 82, 185n
Culler, Jonathan, 135
Cummings, E. E., 78, 178–80, 179n, 183–4, 188–9, 188n
Curry, Renée, 3, 11, 299

Dante, 303
Darrow Jr., Whitney, 299
Darwin, Charles, 94, 112–13, 125, 210, 216–20, 216n, 271, 312
Davidson, Michael, 186n
De Man, Paul, 155
De Sousa, Decio, 188n
De Veaux, Alexis, 287
Deaconess Hospital, Brookline, 256
Dear World & Everyone in It (2013), 322, 330
Defoe, Daniel, 266
Degas, Edgar, 23–4, 28
Deleuze, Gilles, 120n
Delpar, Helen, 283
Dennis, Helen, 182, 184n
Derrida, Jacques, 202
Dewey, Jane, 45, 53, 95
Dewey, John, 283
Dickey, James, 299n
Dickie, Margaret, 3
Dickinson, Emily, 19–20, 188n, 211, 213–17, 214n, 219–20, 239, 244, 314, 315
Diehl, Joanne Feit, 3, 52–3

EU Authorised Representative:

Easy Access System Europe Mustamäe tee 50, 10621 Tallinn, Estonia

gpsr.requests@easproject.com

Printed and bound by CPI Group (UK) Ltd, Croydon, CR0 4YY

04/06/2025

01892475-0007